INTERNATIONAL MARKETING

European Edition

International Marketing

EUROPEAN EDITION

Philip R. Cateora and Pervez N. Ghauri

McGraw-Hill Publishing Company

London · Burr Ridge, IL · New York · St Louis · San Francisco · Auckland · Bogotá
Caracas · Lisbon · Madrid · Mexico · Milan · Montreal · New Delhi · Panama · Paris
San Juan · São Paulo · Singapore · Sydney · Tokyo · Toronto

Published by
McGraw-Hill Publishing Company
Shoppenhangers Road, Maidenhead, Berkshire, SL6 2QL, England
Telephone 01628 502500
Facsimile 01628 770224

British Library Cataloguing in Publication Data
A CIP catalogue record for this book is available from the British Library

Further information on this title is to be found at http://www.mcgraw-hill.co.uk/textbooks/ghauri

Publisher: Dominic Recaldin
Desk Editor: Alastair Lindsay
Editorial Assistant: Caroline Howell
Cover design by Octopus Design

Created for McGraw-Hill by the independent production company
Steven Gardiner Ltd TEL +44 (0)1223 364868 FAX +44 (0)1223 364875

ISBN 0256-23654-2

McGraw-Hill

A Division of The McGraw-Hill Companies

2 3 4 5 IP 3 2 1 0

Printed and bound by Interprint, Malta

Contents

Contents

PART IV   Developing International Marketing Strategies

Contents

Preface

As the drive for efficiency, productivity and open, unregulated markets sweeps the world, a global economic boom is under way. Whether or not a company wants to participate directly in international business, it cannot escape ever-increasing competition from international firms. We are coming to a situation where hardly any company can claim that it is a domestic one. The globalization of the marketplace is already a reality.

This globalization has led us to some misunderstandings. The concept of the global market, or global marketing, thus needs some clarification. Generally, the concept views the world as one market and is based on identifying and targeting cross-cultural similarities. In our opinion, the international marketing concept is based on the premise of cultural differences and is guided by the belief that each foreign market requires its own culturally adapted marketing strategies. Although consumers dining at McDonald's in New Delhi, Moscow and Beijing is a reality, the idea of marketing a standardized product with a uniform marketing plan remains 'purely theoretical.'

The global marketing strategy is thus different from the globalization of the market. One has to do with efficiency of operations, competitiveness and orientation, the other with homogeneity of demand across cultures. In this book we consider it important to make this distinction and to see how it affects international marketing strategies.

There is no better illustration of the changes that have occurred in the competition for global markets in the last quarter century than that experienced by General Electric Lighting (GEL). Begun in 1887, GEL dominated the US lighting market until its traditional rival Westinghouse sold its lamp operations to Philips Electronics of Holland in 1983. 'Suddenly', reflected GEL's chief, 'we have bigger, stronger competition. They're coming to our market, but we're not in theirs. So we're on the defensive.' Not long after, GEL acquired Tungsram, a Hungarian lighting company, and Thorn EMI in Britain, and then moved into Asia via a joint venture with Hitachi. As recently as 1988, GEL got less than 20 per cent of its sales from outside the United States; in 1997, more than half came from abroad. What happened at GEL has occurred over and over again to multinational corporations in the United States, Europe and Asia. In Europe, where home markets are smaller, companies like Philips, Unilever, Ericsson, Nokia, Akzo Nobel and Marks and Spencer are deriving up to 80 per cent of their revenues from abroad. The companies that succeed in the 21st century will be those capable of adapting to constant change and adjusting to new challenges.

The economic, political and social changes that have occurred over the last decade have dramatically altered the landscape of global business. Consider the present and future impact of:

- The European Monetary Union and the switch from local country currencies to one monetary unit for Europe.
- Emerging markets in Eastern Europe, Asia, and Latin America, where in spite of the economic and political crisis, more than 75 per cent of the growth in world trade over the next 20 years is expected to occur.
- The reunification of Hong Kong, Macao and China, which finally puts all of Asia under the control of Asians for the first time in over a century.
- The rapid move away from traditional distribution structures in Japan, Europe and many emerging markets.

- The growth of middle-income households the world over.
- The continued strengthening and creation of regional market groups such as the European Union (EU), the North American Free Trade Area (NAFTA), ASEAN Free Trade Area (AFTA), the Free Trade Area of the Americas (FTAA), the Southern Cone Free Trade Area (Mercosur), and the Asian–Pacific Economic Cooperation (APEC).
- The creation of the World Trade Organization (WTO).
- The transformation of the Internet from a toy for 'cybernerds' to a major international business tool for research, advertising, communications, exporting and marketing.

As global economic growth occurs, understanding marketing in all cultures is increasingly important. This book addresses global issues and describes concepts relevant to all international marketers, regardless of the extent of their international involvement. Emphasis is on the strategic implications of competition in the markets of different countries. An environmental/cultural approach to international marketing permits a truly global orientation. The reader's horizons are not limited to any specific nation or to the particular ways of doing business in a single country. Instead, we provide an approach and framework for identifying and analysing the important cultural and environmental uniqueness of any country or global region. Thus, when surveying the tasks of marketing in a foreign milieu, the reader will not overlook the impact of crucial cultural issues.

The text is designed to stimulate curiosity about management practices of companies, large and small, seeking market opportunities outside their home country and to raise the reader's consciousness about the importance of viewing the international marketing management strategies from a global perspective.

Although this revised edition is infused throughout with a global orientation, export marketing and operations of smaller companies are not overlooked. Issues specific to exporting are discussed where strategies applicable to exporting arise and examples of marketing practices of smaller companies are examined.

NEW AND EXPANDED TOPICS IN THIS EDITION

The new and expanded topics in this edition reflect issues in competition, changing marketing structures, ethics and social responsibility, negotiations and the development of the manager for the 21st century. Competition is raising the global standards for quality, increasing the demand for advanced technology and innovation, and increasing the value of customer satisfaction. The global market is swiftly changing from a seller's market to a buyer's market. This is a period of profound social, economic and political change. To remain competitive globally, companies must be aware of all aspects of the emerging global economic order.

Additionally, the evolution of global communications and its known and unknown impact on how international business is conducted cannot be minimized. In the third millennium, people in the 'global village' will grow closer than ever, and will hear and see each other as a matter of course. An executive in Germany will be able to routinely pick up his or her videophone to hear and see his or her counterpart in an Australian company or anywhere else in the world. In many respects, distance is becoming irrelevant. Telecommunications, videophones, facsimile machines, the Internet and satellites are helping companies optimize their planning, production and procurement processes. Information—and, in its wake, the flow of goods—is moving around the globe at lightning speed. Increasingly powerful global networks spanning the globe enable the delivery of services that reach far beyond national and continental boundaries, fuelling and fostering international trade. The connections of global communications bring people all around the world together in new and better forms of dialogue and understanding.

This dynamic nature of the international marketplace is reflected in the number of new and expanded topics in this edition, including:

- The European Union and the impact of euro.
- The Internet and its expanding role in international marketing.
- Big emerging markets (BEMs).
- Evolving global middle-income households.
- World Trade Organization.
- Multicultural research.
- Qualitative and quantitative research.
- Trends in channel structures in Europe, Japan, the United States and developing countries.
- Negotiations with customers, partners and regulators.
- Ethics and socially responsible decisions.
- Green marketing.
- Changing profiles of global managers.
- Financial and organizational issues in international marketing.

STRUCTURE OF THE TEXT

The text is divided into six parts. In Part I, An Overview, the four chapters introduce the reader to international marketing and to three international marketing management concepts: the domestic market expansion concept, the multidomestic market concept and the global marketing concept. As companies restructure for the global competitive rigours of the 21st century, so too must tomorrow's managers. The successful manager must be globally aware and have a frame of reference that goes beyond a country, or even a region, and encompasses the world. What global awareness means and how it is acquired is discussed early in the text; it is the foundation of global marketing.

Chapter 2 focuses on the dynamic environment of international trade and the competitive challenges and opportunities confronting today's international marketer. The importance of the Uruguay Round of the General Agreement on Tariffs and Trade (GATT) and the creation of the World Trade Organization (WTO), the successor to GATT, are fully explored .

The political climate in a country is a critical concern for the international marketer. In Chapter 3, we take a closer look at the political environment. We discuss the stability of government policies, the political risks confronting a company, and the assessment and reduction of political vulnerability of products.

Chapter 4 focuses on the international legal environment. Legal problems common to most international marketing transactions, that must be given special attention when operating abroad, are discussed.

The three chapters in Part II deal with the impact of culture on international marketing. A global orientation requires the recognition of cultural differences and the critical decision of whether or not it is necessary to accommodate them.

Geography and history (Chapter 5) are included as important dimensions in understanding cultural and market differences among countries. Not to be overlooked is concern for the deterioration of the global ecological environment and the multinational company's critical responsibility to protect it.

Chapter 6 presents a broad review of culture and its impact on human behaviour as it relates to international marketing. Specific attention is paid to Geert Hofstede's study of cultural value and behaviour.

Chapter 7 focuses on business customs and practices. A knowledge of the business culture, management attitudes and business methods existing in a country and a willingness to accommodate the differences are important to success in an international market. Ethics and social responsibility are presented in the context of the dilemma that often confronts the international manager; that is, balancing corporate profits against the social and ethical consequences of their decisions.

Chapters 8, 9 and 10 in Part III are concerned with assessing global market opportunities. As markets expand, segments grow within markets, and as market segments across country markets evolve marketers are forced to understand market behaviour within and across different cultural contexts. Multicultural research and qualitative and quantitative research are discussed in Chapter 8.

Chapters 9 and 10 explore the impact of the three important trends in global marketing: (1) the growth and expansion of the world's big emerging markets; (2) the rapid growth of middle-income market segments; (3) the steady creation of regional market groups that include the European Union (EU), the North American Free Trade Agreement (NAFTA), the Southern Cone Free Trade Area (Mercosur), ASEAN Free Trade Area (AFTA) and the Asian–Pacific Economic Cooperation (APEC).

The strategic implications of the dissolution of the USSR, the emergence of new independent republics, the shift from socialist-based to market-based economies in Eastern Europe, and the return of South Africa to international commerce are examined. Attention is also given to the efforts of the governments of India and many Latin American countries to reduce or eliminate barriers to trade, open their countries to foreign investment and privatize state-owned enterprises.

These political, social and economic changes that are sweeping the world are creating new markets and opportunities, making some markets more accessible while creating the potential for greater protectionism in others.

In Part IV, Developing International Marketing Strategies, planning and organizing for international marketing are discussed in Chapter 11. The discussion of collaborative relationships, including strategic alliances, recognizes the importance of relational collaborations among firms, suppliers and customers in the success of the global marketer. Many multinational companies realize that to fully capitalize on opportunities offered by global markets, they must have strengths that often exceed their capabilities. Collaborative relationships can provide technology, innovations, productivity, capital and market access that strengthen a company's competitive position.

In Chapter 12, the special issues involved in moving a product from one country market to another, and the accompanying mechanics of exporting, are addressed.

Chapters 13 and 14 focus on product management, reflecting the differences in strategies between consumer and industrial products and the growing importance in world markets for business services. Additionally, the discussion on the development of global products stresses the importance of approaching the adaptation issue from the viewpoint of building a standardized product platform that can be adapted to reflect cultural differences. The competitive importance in today's global market for quality, innovation and technology as the keys to marketing success is explored.

Chapter 15 takes the reader through the distribution process, from home country to the consumer, in the target country market. The structural impediments to market entry imposed by a country's distribution system are examined in the framework of a detailed presentation of the American and European distribution structure. In addition, the rapid changes in channel structure that are occurring in Japan and in other countries and the emergence of the World Wide Web as a distribution channel are presented.

Chapter 16 covers advertising and addresses the promotional element of the international marketing mix. Included in the discussion of global market segmentation are recognition of the rapid growth of market segments across country markets and the importance of market segmentation as a strategic competitive tool in creating an effective promotional message.

Chapter 17 discusses personal selling and sales management and the critical nature of training, evaluating and controlling sales representatives. Here we also pay attention to negotiating with customers, partners and other actors in our networks. We discuss the factors influencing business negotiations, and varying negotiation styles.

Price escalations and ways in which it can be lessened, countertrade practices and price strategies under varying currency conditions are concepts presented in Chapter 18.

In Part V, Financing and Managing International Marketing Operations, Chapter 19 deals with the financial aspect of marketing internationally. We look into the capital needs for international marketing, the available sources of funding and the management of financial risk.

Organizing international marketing activities is the subject of Chapter 20. The efficient management of international operations is becoming increasingly important. Here we also discuss how to recruit, train and motivate the staff that is to be sent abroad for managing these operations.

PEDAGOGICAL FEATURES OF THE TEXT

The text portion of the book provides a thorough coverage of its subject, with specific emphasis on the planning and strategic problems confronting companies that market across cultural boundaries.

Current, pithy, sometimes humorous, and always relevant, examples are used to stimulate interest and increase understanding of the ideas, concepts and strategies presented emphasizing the importance of understanding the cultural uniqueness and relevant business practices and strategies.

The boxed 'Going Internationals', an innovation of the first edition of *International Marketing*, have always been popular with students. This edition includes many new incidents that provide insightful examples of cultural differences, while illustrating concepts presented in the text. They reflect contemporary issues in international marketing and can be used to illustrate real-life situations and as the basis for class discussion. They are selected to be unique, humorous and of general interest to the reader.

Besides the special section of colour maps in Part I, there are numerous maps that reflect changes important to the chapter and that help the reader observe features of countries and regions discussed in the text.

New photographs of current and relevant international marketing events are found as three special photo essays. One on Emerging Markets: Challenges and Opportunities, one on Globalization and Competition and the third on Advertising: Standardization vs Adaptation.

'The Country Notebook—A Guide for Developing a Marketing Plan', found in Part VI, Supplementary Material, is a detailed outline that provides both a format for a complete cultural and economic analysis of a country and guidelines for a marketing plan.

CASES

In addition to 'The Country Notebook', Part VI comprises a selection of short and long cases. The short cases focus on a single problem, serving as the basis for discussion of a specific concept or issue. The longer, more integrated cases are broader in scope and focus on more than one marketing management problem. More than two-thirds of the cases are new or revised. New cases focus on health-care marketing, negotiations, services and industrial marketing and marketing research. The cases can be analysed by using the information provided. They also lend themselves to more in-depth analysis, requiring the student to engage in additional research and data collection.

SUPPLEMENTS

We have taken great care to offer new features and improvements to every part of the teaching aid package. Below is a list of specific features:

Instructor's Manual

The Instructor's Manual, prepared by the authors, contains lecture notes and/or teaching suggestions for each chapter. A case correlation grid at the beginning of the case notes offers alternative uses for the cases.

PowerPoint Slides

The PowerPoint presentation that accompanies *International Marketing* contains approximately 150 exhibits from the text and other sources. Fourteen maps from the text are included as well.

ACKNOWLEDGMENTS

The success of a text depends on the contributions of many people, especially those who take the time to share their thoughtful criticisms and suggestions to improve the text.

We would especially like to thank the reviewers who gave us valuable insights into this revision:

Dr Joan Buckley, Management and Marketing Department, University College Cork, Ireland

Dr Ruud T. Frambach, University of Tilburg, The Netherlands

Paul T.J. James, Department of Marketing, HES ISER, The Netherlands

I.C.M. van Kooten, Department of Marketing, Free University of Amsterdam, The Netherlands

Dr Deon Nel, Aston Business School, Aston University, UK

Nathalie Prime, Department of Marketing, ESCP, France

Graham Spickett-Jones, Department of International Marketing and Languages, Hull Business School, Humberside University, UK

Professor Ronald Tuninga, Open University, The Netherlands

Walther de Vries, Marketing Department, Free University of Amsterdam, The Netherlands
Jeryl Whitelock, NW Centre for European Studies, University of Salford, UK

In addition, over 200 instructors, unfortunately too many to list here, responded to surveys that helped shape the content and structure of this edition, as well as provided impetus for some very positive changes in the supplement package.

Other than these we also would like to thank a team of colleagues who helped us in typing, editing and preparing the manuscript. Our special thanks in this regard to Rieks Bos, Jeannette Scheidema and Babette Gaus.

We appreciate the help of all the many students and professors who have shared their opinions of past editions, and we welcome their comments and suggestions on this and future editions of *International Marketing*.

A very special thanks to Alfred Waller and Alastair Lindsay at McGraw-Hill, London.

Philip Cateora and Pervez Ghauri

PART

I

An Overview

Part Outline

CHAPTER

1

The Scope and Challenge of International Marketing

Chapter Learning Objectives

What you should learn from Chapter 1

- What is meant by international marketing.
- The scope of the international marketing task.
- The importance of the self-reference criterion (SRC) in international marketing.
- The importance of environmental adjustments.
- The progression of becoming an international marketer.
- International marketing concepts.
- The increasing importance of global awareness.

The modern world is organized on the theory that each nation state is sovereign and independent from other countries. In reality, however, no country can completely isolate its internal affairs from external forces. Even the most inward-looking regimes have realized the limitations of their own resources as well as the benefits of opening up their borders. This major change in the orientation of most regimes has led to an enormous amount of activity in the international marketplace.

A global economic boom, unprecedented in modern economic history, is under way as the drive for efficiency, productivity and open, unregulated markets sweep the world.[1] Never before in world history have businesses been so deeply involved in and affected by international global developments. Powerful economic, technological, industrial, political and demographic forces are converging to build the foundation of a new global economic order on which the structure of a world economic and market system will be built.[2]

Whether or not a company wants to participate directly in international business, it cannot escape the effect of the ever-increasing number of domestic firms exporting, importing, and/or manufacturing abroad; the number of foreign-based firms operating in most markets; the growth of regional trade areas; the rapid growth of world markets; and the increasing number of competitors for global markets.

Of all the trends affecting global business today, five stand out as the most dynamic and as the ones that are influencing the shape of international business:

1. The interdependence of the world economies.
2. The rapid growth of regional free trade areas such as EU, NAFTA, ASEAN and APEC.
3. The increase in wealth and growth in most parts of the world, causing enhanced purchasing power.
4. The evolution of large emerging markets such as Argentina, China, India, Indonesia, Malaysia, Russia, Hungary and Poland.
5. Availability of advanced methods of communication and transportation due to developments in information technology.

Today most business activities are global in scope. Finance, technology, research, capital and investment flows, production facilities, purchasing and marketing and distribution networks all have global dimensions. Every business must be prepared to compete in an increasingly interdependent global economic environment, and all business people must be aware of the effects of these trends when managing a multinational conglomerate or a domestic company that exports. As one international expert noted, 'every company is international, at least to the extent that its business performance is conditioned in part by events that occur abroad.'[3] Even companies that do not operate in the international arena are affected to some degree by the success of the European Union, the Asian crisis, the revitalized Mexican economy and the economic changes taking place in China and India.

As competition for world markets intensifies, the number of companies operating solely in domestic markets will decrease. Or, to put it another way, it is increasingly true that the business of any business is international business. The challenge of international marketing is to develop strategic plans that are competitive in the intensifying global markets. These and other issues affecting the world economy, trade, markets and competition will be discussed throughout this text.

THE INTERNATIONALIZATION OF BUSINESS

Current interest in international marketing can be explained by the changing competitive structures coupled with shifts in demand characteristics in markets throughout the world.

GOING INTERNATIONAL 1.1

WORLD WITHOUT BORDERS: GOODBYE WIDGET, HELLO NIKE

For decades the widget has served as the paradigm for business texts: a basic, uncomplicated manufacture. But in the postnational economy we live in today, even the simplest products—a pair of shoes—are based on a complex and international manufacturing process. We know that things like cars and computers are complicated products, parts of which are produced in different countries and by different companies. But when a tourist from Japan buys a pair of Nike in Amsterdam, does he or she have any idea about the process behind that pair?

Nike does not own any manufacturing facility. However, factories such as Yue Yuen in an industrial estate in Dongguan, China, is geared towards Nike standards and reflects Nike needs. The chart illustrates that a particular Nike shoe, Air Max Penny, is made up of 52 different components, coming from five different countries, excluding nonmaterial inputs such as design, transportation and marketing. Air Max Penny will be touched by at least 120 pairs of hands during production. The new production system is a network of logistics, not only all the materials have to come together, they have to come together at the right time. Moreover, constant upgrading of materials and of process and workers is required. The designs and models are changed every week.

What does this mean for the business world? For one thing, it suggests the futility of trying to apply borders to today's business. Nike, for example, is an American firm that started in Japan, and though our statesmen and trade negotiators haggle over local content, how would they classify Nike from the Dongguan factory? The leather comes from South Korea. Those putting it together are mainland Chinese. The factory is owned by a Taiwanese, some components come from Japan and Indonesia, and the design and marketing come from America. And if this is the case for a simple pair of shoes, imagine what it must be for a computer or a car.

The New Nike Economy
WORLD WITHOUT BORDERS

Brave New Widget

Nike's Air Max Penny basketball shoe boasts a complicated, international pedigree

Upper

- Designed in Oregon and Tennessee
- Developed jointly by U.S., and Asian technicians in Oregon, Taiwan and South Korea

Dynamic-Fit™ Tongue

- Produced by factories in South Korea (men's sizes) and Indonesia (boy's sizes)
- 52 different components from five different countries (U.S., Taiwan, South Korea, Indonesia and Japan)

Sockliner

- A single pair of Nike shoes is touched by more than 120 pairs of hands during production

Midsole

Heel Air-Sole® Unit

Forefoot Zoom Air™ Unit

Carbon Fiber Composite Plate

Outsole

Source: Nike

Source: Abstracted from *Far Eastern Economic Review*, 29 August 1996, p. 5.

Table 1.1   European Takeovers in the United States

	Number of Takeovers	Total Value of Takeovers in Billion € ($)
UK	939	69.1 (76.5)
Germany	233	27.5 (30.5)
The Netherlands	225	21.1 (23.4)
France	216	11.9 (13.2)
Denmark	74	0.5 (0.6)
Ireland	71	4.3 (4.8)
Sweden	61	4.5 (5.0)
Italy	56	2.7 (3.0)
Belgium	35	4.8 (5.3)
Finland	26	1.0 (1.1)

Source: Based on 'Bedrijfsleven Houdt Grenzenloze Herverkaveling', *Volkskrant*, 23 May 1998, p. 2.

With the increasing globalization of markets, companies find they are unavoidably enmeshed with foreign customers, competitors and suppliers, even within their own borders. They face competition on all fronts—from domestic firms and from foreign firms. A significant portion of all televisions, tape players, video recorders, clothes and tableware sold in Western Europe is foreign made. Sony, Panasonic, Mitsubishi, Samsung, Fujitsu, Toyota and Nissan are familiar brands in Europe and North America, and for Western industry, they are formidable opponents in a competitive struggle for European and world markets.

Many familiar domestic companies are now foreign controlled. When you shop for groceries at Aldi, A&P supermarkets or buy Alka-Seltzer, you are buying indirectly from a German company. Some well-known brands no longer owned by US companies are Carnation (Swiss), Brooks Brothers clothing (Canada) and the all-American Smith and Wesson handgun, which is now owned by a British firm. Travelodge, Saks Fifth Avenue and many more US companies are currently owned or controlled by European multinational businesses (see Table 1.1). In fact, foreign investment in Western countries by other industrialized countries is quite common. This is illustrated by Table 1.2. We can see that companies from Germany, Japan, the United States and the United Kingdom lead the group of investors, with companies from Switzerland, The Netherlands and France following in that order.

Companies with only domestic markets have found it increasingly difficult to sustain customary rates of growth, and many are seeking foreign markets to absorb surplus productive capacity. Companies with foreign operations find foreign earnings make an important overall contribution to total corporate profits. Companies that never ventured abroad until recently are now seeking foreign markets. Companies with existing foreign operations realize they must be more competitive to succeed against foreign multinationals. They have found it necessary to spend more money and time improving their marketing positions abroad because competition for these growing markets is intensifying. For the firm venturing into international marketing for the first time, and for those already experienced, the requirement is generally the same—a thorough and complete commitment to foreign markets and, for many, new ways of operating.

Table 1.2   Direct Investment Flows Around Europe, the United States and Japan, 1995

Countries	Inflow (million $)	Outflow (million $)	Net Outflow (million $)
Germany	9 012	34 890	25 878
Japan	33	22 262	22 229
US	74 701	96 897	22 196
UK	29 910	37 839	7 929
Switzerland	2 947	10 554*	7 607
The Netherlands	5 889	7 929	2 040
Norway	1 363	2 446	1 083
Finland	917	1 517	600
Austria	530	1 050	520
Portugal	533	606	73
Czech Republic	862	116*	−746
Italy	4 347	3 210	−1 137
Denmark	4 179	3 018	−1 161
France	12 156	9 582	−2 574
Hungary	4 570	1 480	−3 090
Sweden	13 672	10 367	−3 305
Spain	6 936	3 532	−3 404
Belgium and Luxembourg	8 899	2 492*	−6 407

*1994 figures.
Source: Based on *The European*, 12–25 September 1996, p. 28.

INTERNATIONAL MARKETING DEFINED

International marketing is the performance of business activities that direct the flow of a company's goods and services to consumers or users in more than one nation for a profit. The only difference in the definitions of domestic marketing and international marketing is that the marketing activities take place in more than one country. This apparently minor difference accounts for the complexity and diversity found in international marketing operations. Marketing concepts, processes and principles are to a great extent universally applicable, and the marketer's task is the same whether doing business in Amsterdam, London or Kuala Lumpur. The goal of a business is to make a profit by promoting, pricing and distributing products for which there is a market. If this is the case, what is the difference between domestic and international marketing?

The answer lies not with different concepts of marketing, but with the environment within which marketing plans must be implemented. The uniqueness of foreign marketing comes from the range of unfamiliar problems and the variety of strategies necessary to cope with different levels of uncertainty encountered in foreign markets.

Competition, legal restraints, government controls, weather, fickle consumers and any number of other uncontrollable elements can, and frequently do, affect the profitable outcome of good, sound marketing plans. Generally speaking, the marketer cannot control or influence these uncontrollable elements, but instead must adjust or adapt to them in a manner consistent with a successful outcome. What makes marketing interesting is the challenge of moulding the controllable elements of marketing decisions (product, price, promotion and distribution) within the framework of the uncontrollable elements of the marketplace (competition, politics, laws, consumer behaviour, level of technology and so forth) in such a way that marketing objectives are achieved. Even though marketing principles and concepts are universally applicable, the environment within which the marketer must implement marketing plans can change dramatically from country to country. The difficulties created by different environments are the international marketer's primary concern.

THE INTERNATIONAL MARKETING TASK

The international marketer's task is more complicated than that of the domestic marketer because the international marketer must deal with at least two levels of uncontrollable uncertainty instead of one. Uncertainty is created by the uncontrollable elements of all business environments, but each foreign country in which a company operates adds its own unique set of uncontrollables. Figure 1.1 illustrates the total environment of an international marketer. The inner circle depicts the controllable elements that constitute a marketer's decision area, the second circle encompasses those environmental elements at home that have some effect on foreign-operation decisions and the outer circles represent the elements of the foreign environment for each foreign market within which the marketer operates. As the outer circles illustrate, each foreign market in which the company does business can (and usually does) present separate problems involving some or all of the uncontrollable elements. Thus, the more foreign markets in which a company operates, the greater the possible variety of foreign environmental uncontrollables with which to contend. Frequently, a solution to a problem in country market A is not applicable to a problem in country market B.

Marketing Controllables

The successful manager constructs a marketing programme designed for optimal adjustment to the uncertainty of the business climate. The inner circle in Figure 1.1 represents the area under the control of the marketing manager. Assuming the necessary overall corporate resources, the marketing manager blends price, product, promotion and channels-of-distribution activities to capitalize on anticipated demand. The controllable elements can be altered in the long run and, usually, in the short run, to adjust to changing market conditions or corporate objectives.

The outer circles surrounding the market controllables represent the levels of uncertainty that are created by the domestic and foreign environments. Although the marketer can blend a marketing mix from the controllable elements, the uncontrollables are precisely that and there must be active adaptation. That effort, the adaptation of the marketing mix to the uncontrollables, determines the ultimate outcome of the marketing enterprise.

Domestic Uncontrollables

The second circle, representing the domestic environment in Figure 1.1, includes home-country elements that can have a direct effect on the success of a foreign venture: political forces, legal structure and economic climate.

A political decision involving domestic foreign policy can have a direct effect on a firm's international marketing success. For example, most Western governments imposed restrictions on trade with South Africa to protest about apartheid, and placed a total ban on trade

Figure 1.1   The International Marketing Task

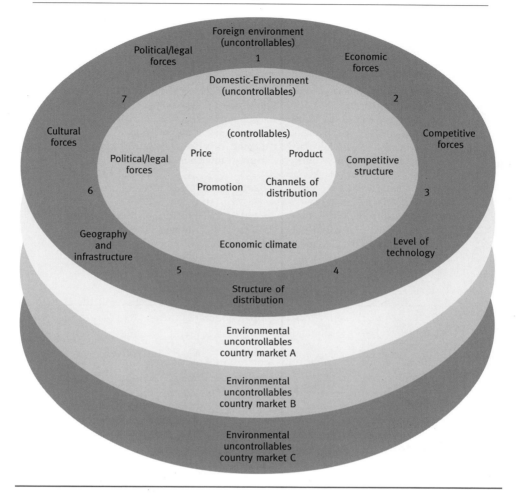

with Iraq, whose actions constituted a threat to the national security of their allies. In each case the international marketing programmes of such companies as Shell, IBM and British Petroleum (BP) were restricted by domestic uncontrollables. Conversely, positive effects occur when there are changes in foreign policy and countries are given favoured treatment. Such were the cases when South Africa abolished apartheid and the embargo was lifted, and when the US government decided to uncouple human rights issues from foreign trade policy and granted most-favoured nation status (MFN) to China.[4] In both cases, opportunities were created for international companies.

The domestic economic climate is another important home-based uncontrollable variable with far-reaching effects on a company's competitive position in foreign markets. The capacity to invest in plants and facilities either in domestic or foreign markets is to a large extent a function of domestic economic vitality. It is generally true that capital tends to flow towards optimum use; however, capital must be generated before it can have mobility. Furthermore,

GOING INTERNATIONAL 1.2

IS A CHEETO A CHEETO IF IT DOESN'T TASTE LIKE CHEESE?

PepsiCo, the maker of Cheetos, announced a $1 million (€0.9 million)[5] joint venture to produce the little crispy-tasting cheese puffs in Guangdong province. The estimated market for Western snack foods in Guangdong province is $40 million (€36 million) to $70 million (€63 million). The province, with 70 million consumers, represents a market that is one-third the size of the United States. Between-meal snacking is rising rapidly along with disposable income as the Chinese economy gains momentum and work hours increase.

This is the first time a major snack-food brand will be produced in China for Chinese tastes. In adapting Cheetos to the Chinese market, a new flavour had to be found. Cheese is not a mainstay in the Chinese diet and, in focus groups, the cheese-ish taste of American Cheetos did not test well. More than 600 flavours, ranging from Roasted Cuttlefish to Sweet Caramel were tested before settling on Savoury American Cream (a buttered popcorn flavour) and Zesty Japanese Steak (a teriyake-type taste).

But, is it a Cheeto if it doesn't taste like cheese? 'It's still crispy, it has a Cheeto shape, and it's fun to eat, so it's a Cheeto', says the general manager of PepsiCo Foods International.

The introduction of Cheetos was backed by television, print advertising, and promotions based on Chester Cheetah, the brand's feline symbol, riding a Harley-Davidson motorcycle. The packages will carry the Cheeto logo in English along with the Chinese characters *qi duo*, which translates to *new surprise*.

Source: Adapted from Glenn Collins, 'Chinese to Get a Taste of Cheese-less Cheetos', *The New York Times*, 2 September 1994, p. C4.

if internal economic conditions deteriorate, restrictions against foreign investment and purchasing may be imposed to strengthen the domestic economy.

Inextricably entwined with the effects of the domestic environment are the constraints imposed by the environment of each foreign country.

Foreign Uncontrollables

In addition to uncontrollable domestic elements, a significant source of uncertainty is the number of uncontrollable foreign business environments (depicted in Figure 1.1 by the outer circles). A business operating in its home country undoubtedly feels comfortable in forecasting the business climate and adjusting business decisions to these elements. The process of evaluating the uncontrollable elements in an international marketing programme, however, often involves substantial doses of cultural, political and economic shock.

A business operating in a number of foreign countries might find polar extremes in political stability, class structure and economic climate—critical elements in business decisions. The dynamic upheavals in some countries further illustrate the problems of dramatic change in cultural, political and economic climates over relatively short periods of time. A case in point is the Soviet Union—a single market that divided into 15 independent republics, 11 of which re-formed in a matter of days as the Commonwealth of Independent States (CIS), leaving investors uncertain about the future. They found themselves asking whether contracts and agreements with the Soviet government were valid in individual independent states. Was the Republic of Russia empowered to represent the CIS, would the rouble survive as the currency of the CIS and who had the authority to negotiate the sale of property or the purchase of equipment? In a very short period, the foreign investors' enthusiasm for investment in the former USSR and its republics turned to caution in the face

Table 1.3   Rouble Exchange Rate against the Dollar

1989	0.6	1994 (Dec)	3 800.0
1990	1.7	1995 (Jan)	4 500.0
1991 (Jan)	37.6	1995 (Dec)	4 523.0
1991 (Dec)	60.0	1996 (Jan)	4 999.0
1992 (Jan)	110.0	1996 (Dec)	5 499.0
1992 (Dec)	398.0	1997 (Jan)	5 585.0
1993 (Jan)	417.0	1997 (Dec)	5 963.0
1993 (Dec)	1 100.0	1998 (Jan)	5.9980
1994 (Jan)	1 400.0	1998 July 31	6.2800

Sources: Peter Buckley and Pervez Ghauri, *The Economics of Change in Eastern Europe*, 1994, p. 25; *The Economist*, 21 January 1995, p. 32; Business Central Europe, The Economist Group, June 1996, and July 1997, and Custom House Currency Exchange, http://www.oanda.com/converter/classic.

of drastic changes as it transformed itself into a market economy.[6] Ever since its liberalization, Russia, the biggest market among the CIS, has had an inflation of 15 per cent per month. This has caused enormous exchange variation as illustrated by Table 1.3. Such are the uncertainties of the uncontrollable political factors of international business.

The more significant elements in the uncontrollable international environment, shown in the outer circles of Figure 1.1, include (1) political/legal forces, (2) economic forces, (3) competitive forces, (4) level of technology, (5) structure of distribution, (6) geography and infrastructure and (7) cultural forces. They constitute the principal elements of uncertainty an international marketer must cope with in designing a marketing programme. Each is discussed in some detail in subsequent chapters.

Also a problem for some marketers attuned to one environment is the inability to easily recognize the potential impact of certain uncontrollable elements within another environment, one to which they have not been culturally acclimatized. Road signs of danger and indicators of potential in a foreign market may not always be read or interpreted accurately. The level of technology is an uncontrollable element that can often be misread because of the vast differences that may exist between developed and developing countries. For example, a marketer cannot assume that the understanding of the concept of preventive maintenance for machinery and equipment is the same in other countries as it is in the home country. Thus, in a developing country where the general population does not have the same level of technical knowledge that exists in a developed country, a marketer will have to take extra steps to ensure that routine maintenance procedures and their importance are understood.

The problem of foreign uncertainty is further complicated by a frequently imposed 'alien status' that increases the difficulty of properly assessing and forecasting the dynamic international business climate. There are two dimensions to the alien status of a foreign business: alien in that the business is controlled by foreigners and alien in that the culture of the host country is alien to the foreign company. The alien status of a business results in greater emphasis being placed on many of the uncontrollable elements than would be found with relation to those same elements in the domestic market.

The political environment offers the best example of the alien status. Domestic marketers must consider the political ramifications of their decisions although the consequences of this environmental element are generally minor. Even a noticeable change in government attitudes towards domestic business with a change of political parties is seldom serious; such is not the case in a foreign country. The political environment can be extremely critical, and shifts in governments often mean sudden changes in attitudes that can result in expropriation, expulsion or major restrictions on operations. The fact is that the foreign company is foreign and thus always subject to the political whims of the government to a greater degree than a domestic firm.

The uncertainty of different foreign business environments creates the need for a close study of the operating environment within each new country. Different solutions to fundamentally identical marketing tasks are often in order and are generally the result of changes in the environment of the market. Thus, a strategy successful in one country can be rendered ineffective in another by differences in political climate, stages of economic development, level of technology or other cultural variation.

ENVIRONMENTAL ADJUSTMENT NEEDED

To adjust and adapt a marketing programme to foreign markets, marketers must be able to interpret effectively the influence and impact of each of the uncontrollable environmental elements on the marketing plan for each foreign market in which they hope to do business. In a broad sense, the uncontrollable elements constitute the culture; the difficulty facing the marketer in adjusting to the culture (i.e. uncontrollable elements of the marketplace) lies in recognizing their impact. In a domestic market, the reaction to much of the uncontrollables' (cultural) impact on the marketer's activities is automatic; the various cultural influences that fill our lives are simply a part of our history. We react in a manner acceptable to our society without thinking about it because we are culturally responsive to our environment. The experiences we have gained throughout life have become second nature and serve as the basis for our behaviour.

The task of cultural adjustment is perhaps the most challenging and important one confronting international marketers; they must adjust their marketing efforts to cultures to which they are not attuned. In dealing with unfamiliar markets, marketers must be aware of the frames of reference they are using in making their decisions or evaluating the potential of a market because judgements are derived from experience that is the result of the enculturative process. Once a frame of reference is established, it becomes an important factor in determining or modifying a marketer's reaction to situations—social and even non-social—especially if experience or knowledge of accustomed behaviour is lacking.

When a marketer operates in other cultures, marketing attempts may fail because of unconscious responses based on frames of reference acceptable in one's own culture but unacceptable in different surroundings. Unless special efforts are made to determine local cultural meanings for every market, the marketer is likely to overlook the significance of certain behaviours or activities and proceed with plans that result in a negative or unwanted response.

For example, a Westerner must learn that white is a symbol of mourning in parts of Asia, quite different from Western culture's white for bridal gowns. Also, time-conscious Westerners are not culturally prepared to understand the meaning of time to Latin Americans. These differences must be learned to avoid misunderstandings that can lead to marketing failures. Such a failure actually occurred in the one situation when ignorance led to ineffective advertising on the part of a Western firm; and a second misunderstanding resulted in lost sales when a 'long waiting period' in the outer office of an emerging market customer was misinterpreted by a Western sales executive.

To avoid such errors, the foreign marketer should be aware of the principle of *marketing relativism*, that is, marketing strategies and judgements are based on experience, and experience

GOING INTERNATIONAL 1.3	**SO, JOSE GOMEZ-MEADE—ARE YOU SEÑOR GOMEZ OR SEÑOR MEADE?**

In most Western countries, we try to get on a first-name basis quickly. In some countries, however, to do so makes you appear brash, if not rude. The best policy is to use the last name with a proper and respectful title until specifically invited to do otherwise. But the problem doesn't end there because the 'proper' last name can vary among cultures.

In China, the first name is the surname. Hence Chairman Mao Zedong was Chairman Mao, not Chairman Zedong. The problem in China is further complicated by the few surnames that exist. There are only 438 Chinese surnames, the most common being Wang, Zhang and Li; 10 per cent of the total population (over 100 million) is named Zhang; 60 per cent have only 19 surnames; 90 per cent have only 100 surnames. The Chinese themselves generally address each other by the family name and an appropriate title, or by both the family name and full given name together, with the family name first. The obvious reason for this custom is that it helps distinguish all the Wangs, Zhangs and Lis from one another.

In Brazil and Portugal, people are addressed by their Christian names, along with the proper title or simply, Mr, so that Manuel Santos is Señor Manuel. In Spain and Spanish-heritage South America, it is not unusual to use a double surname—from the maternal and paternal family names. The last name is the main one, so that Jose Garcia-Alvarez is Señor Alvarez.

Sources: Adapted from Lennie Copeland and Lewis Griggs, *Going International* (New York: Random House, 1985), p. 158, and Boye Lafayette De Mente, *Chinese Etiquette & Ethics in Business* (Lincolnwood, Illinois: NTC Business Books, 1994), pp. 14–15.

is interpreted by each marketer in terms of his or her own culture and experience. We take into the marketplace, at home or in a foreign country, frames of reference developed from past experiences that determine or modify our reactions to the situations we face.

Cultural conditioning is like an iceberg—we are not aware of nine-tenths of it. In any study of the market systems of different peoples, their political and economic structures, religions and other elements of culture, foreign marketers must constantly guard against measuring and assessing the markets against the fixed values and assumptions of their own cultures. They must take specific steps to make themselves aware of the home cultural reference in their analyses and decision making.

SELF-REFERENCE CRITERION: AN OBSTACLE

The key to successful international marketing is adaptation to the environmental differences from one market to another. Adaptation is a conscious effort on the part of the international marketer to anticipate the influences of both the foreign and domestic uncontrollable environments on a marketing mix, and then to adjust the marketing mix to minimize the effects.

The primary obstacle to success in international marketing is a person's *self-reference criterion* (*SRC*) in making decisions, that is, an unconscious reference to one's own cultural values, experiences, and knowledge as a basis for decisions. The SRC impedes the ability to assess a foreign market in its true light.

When confronted with a set of facts, we react spontaneously on the basis of knowledge assimilated over a lifetime; knowledge that is a product of the history of our culture. We seldom stop to think about a reaction, we react. Thus, when faced with a problem in another culture, the tendency is to react instinctively and refer to our SRC for a solution. Our

Figure 1.2   Four Circles of Intimacy

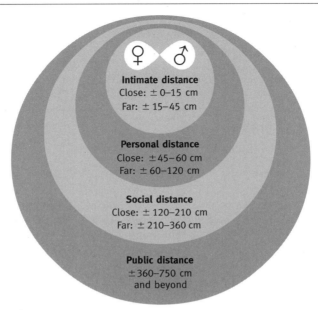

Intimate distance
Close: ± 0–15 cm
Far: ± 15–45 cm

Personal distance
Close: ± 45–60 cm
Far: ± 60–120 cm

Social distance
Close: ± 120–210 cm
Far: ± 210–360 cm

Public distance
± 360–750 cm
and beyond

Source: Based on Raymond Lesikar and John Pettit, *Business Communication: Theory and Practice* (Homewood, IL: Irwin, 1989).

reaction, however, is based on meanings, values, symbols and behaviour relevant to our own culture and usually different from those of the foreign culture. Such decisions are often not valid.

To illustrate the impact of the SRC, consider misunderstandings that can occur about personal space between people of different cultures. In the West, unrelated individuals keep a certain physical distance between themselves and others when talking to each other or in groups. We do not consciously think about that distance; we just know what feels right without thinking. When someone is too close or too far away, we feel uncomfortable and either move further away or get closer to correct the distance—we are relying on our SRC (see Figure 1.2). In some cultures, the acceptable distance between individuals is substantially less than that comfortable to Westerners. When they, unaware of another culture's acceptable distance, are approached too closely by someone from another culture, they unconsciously react by backing away to restore the proper distance (i.e. proper by their own standards) and confusion results for both parties. Westerners assume foreigners are pushy, while foreigners assume Westerners are unfriendly and stand-offish. Both react to the values of their own SRCs, making them all victims of a cultural misunderstanding.

Your SRC can prevent you from being aware that there are cultural differences or from recognizing the importance of those differences. Thus, you fail to recognize the need to take action, discount the cultural differences that exist among countries or react to a situation in a way offensive to your hosts. A common mistake made by Westerners is to refuse food or drink when offered. In Europe, a polite refusal is certainly acceptable, but in many countries in Asia and the Middle East, a host is offended if you refuse hospitality. While you do not

GOING INTERNATIONAL 1.4

YOU'RE SICK? IS IT THE HEART, A VIRUS OR LIVER? IT DEPENDS WHERE YOU ARE FROM

Pharmaceutical companies have commissioned concurrent studies to help them package and market their products throughout Europe simultaneously, rather than country by country. This is because they know there are deep-rooted national differences in how people think about health, disease and medicine. In the United Kingdom and the Netherlands, people prefer tablets when taking medicine. In France, suppositories are preferred, while in Germany an injection will do.

In different countries, different organs are believed to be the cause of illness. Germans are almost obsessive about the heart and circulation—they are Europe's largest consumers of heart medicine. Southern Europeans assign almost mystical qualities to the liver. In the United Kingdom, doctors tend to look for external agents attacking the body and they prescribe antibiotics. In the central European countries, people turn first to herbal treatments and hot and cold baths, relying on antibiotics only as remedies of last resort. If you say you are tired, the Germans would say that it was cardiac insufficiency. In England they would consider you depressed.

Source: Abstracted from Lynn Payer, *Medicine and Culture* (New York: Henry Holt, 1988), p. 265.

have to eat or drink much, you do have to accept the offering of hospitality. Understanding and dealing with the self-reference criterion are two of the more important facets in international marketing.

The SRC can influence an evaluation of the appropriateness of a domestically designed marketing mix for a foreign market. If the Western marketers are not aware, they may evaluate a marketing mix on Western experiences (i.e. their SRC) without fully appreciating the cultural differences requiring adaptation. Esso, the brand name of a petrol, was a successful name in the United States and would seem harmless enough for foreign countries; however, in Japan, the name phonetically means 'stalled car', an undesirable image for petrol. Another example is 'Pet' in Pet Milk. The name has been used for decades; yet in France, the word *pet* means, among other things, flatulence—again, not the desired image for canned milk. Both of these examples of real mistakes made by major companies stem from relying on SRC in making a decision. In international marketing, relying on one's SRC can produce an inadequately adapted marketing programme that ends in failure.

The most effective way to control the influence of the SRC is to recognize its existence in our behaviour. Although it is almost impossible for someone to learn every culture in depth and to be aware of every important difference, an awareness of the need to be sensitive to differences and to ask questions when doing business in another culture can avoid many of the mistakes possible in international marketing. Asking the appropriate question helped the Vicks Company avoid making a mistake in Germany. It discovered that, in German, 'Vicks' sounds like the crudest slang equivalent of intercourse, so they changed the name to 'Wicks' before introducing the product.[7]

Also be aware that not every activity within a marketing programme is different from one country to another: there probably are more similarities than differences. Such similarities may lull the marketer into a false sense of apparent sameness. This apparent sameness, coupled with our SRC, is often the cause of international marketing problems. Undetected similarities do not cause problems; however, the one difference that goes undetected can create a marketing failure.

BECOMING INTERNATIONAL

Once a company has decided to go international, it has to decide the way it will enter a foreign market and the degree of marketing involvement and commitment it is prepared to make. These decisions should reflect considerable study and analysis of market potential and company capabilities, a process not always followed. Many companies appear to grow into international marketing through a series of phased developments. They gradually change strategy and tactics as they become more involved. Others enter international marketing after much research, with long-range plans fully developed.[8]

Phases of International Marketing Involvement

Regardless of the means employed to gain entry into a foreign market, a company may, from a marketing viewpoint, make no market investment, that is, its marketing involvement may be limited to selling a product with little or no thought given to development of market control. Or a company may become totally involved and invest large sums of money and effort to capture and maintain a permanent, specific share of the market. In general, a business can be placed in at least one of five distinct but overlapping phases of international marketing involvement.

No Direct Foreign Marketing.   In this phase, there is no active cultivation of customers outside national boundaries; however, this company's products may reach foreign markets. Sales may be made to trading companies and other foreign customers who come directly to the firm. Or products reach foreign markets via domestic wholesalers or distributors who sell abroad on their own without explicit encouragement or even knowledge of the producer. An unsolicited order from a foreign buyer is often what piques the interest of a company to seek additional international sales.

Infrequent Foreign Marketing.   Temporary surpluses caused by variations in production levels or demand may result in infrequent marketing overseas. The surpluses are characterized by their temporary nature; therefore, sales to foreign markets are made as goods are available, with little or no intention of maintaining continuous market representation. As domestic demand increases and absorbs surpluses, foreign sales activity is withdrawn. In this phase, there is little or no change in company organization or product lines.

Regular Foreign Marketing.   At this level, the firm has permanent productive capacity devoted to the production of goods to be marketed on a continuing basis in foreign markets. A firm may employ foreign or domestic overseas middlemen or it may have its own salesforce or sales subsidiaries in important foreign markets. The primary focus for products presently being produced is to meet domestic market needs. Investments in marketing and management effort and in overseas manufacturing and/or assembly are generally begun in this phase. Further, some products may become specialized to meet the needs of individual foreign markets, pricing and profit policies tend to become equal with domestic business, and the company begins to become dependent on foreign profits.

International Marketing.   Companies in this phase are fully committed and involved in international marketing activities. Such companies seek markets throughout the world and sell products that are a result of planned production for markets in various countries. This generally entails not only the marketing, but also the production of goods throughout the world. At this point, a company becomes an international or multinational marketing firm dependent on foreign revenues.

Global Marketing.   At the global marketing level, companies treat the world, including their home market, as their market. This is one step further than the multinational or international company that views the world as a series of country markets (including their home market) with unique sets of market characteristics for which products and marketing strategies must be developed. A global company develops an overall strategy to reflect the existing commonalities of market needs among many countries to maximize returns through some global standardization of its business activities— as much as it is culturally possible to achieve efficiencies.

Changes in International Orientation

Experience shows that a significant change in the international orientation of a firm occurs when that company relies on foreign markets to absorb permanent production surpluses and comes to depend on foreign profits. Businesses usually move through the phases of international marketing involvement one at a time, but it is not unusual for a company to skip one or more phases. As a firm moves from one phase to another, the complexity and sophistication of international marketing activity tends to increase and the degree of internationalization to which management is philosophically committed tends to change. Such commitment affects the specific international strategies and decisions of the firm.

International operations of businesses reflect the changing competitiveness brought about by the globalization of markets, interdependence of the world's economies, and the growing number of competing firms from developed and developing countries vying for the world's markets. *Global companies* and *global marketing* are terms frequently used to describe the scope of operations and marketing management orientation of these companies. Global markets are evolving for some products but do not exist yet for most products. In many countries, there are still consumers for many products, reflecting the differences in needs and wants, and there are different ways of satisfying these needs and wants based on cultural influences.[9]

INTERNATIONAL MARKETING CONCEPTS

Although not articulated as such in current literature, it appears that the differences in the international orientation and approach to international markets that guide the international business activities of companies can be described by one of three orientations to international marketing management:

1. Domestic market extension concept.
2. Multidomestic market concept.
3. Global marketing concept.

It is to be expected that differences in the complexity and sophistication of a company's marketing activity depend on which of these orientations guides its operations. The ideas expressed in each concept reflect the philosophical orientation that also can be associated with successive stages in the evolution of the international operations in a company.

Among the approaches describing the different orientations that evolve in a company as it moves through different phases of international marketing involvement—from casual exporting to global marketing—is the often-quoted EPRG schema. The authors of this schema suggest that firms can be classified as having an ethnocentric, polycentric, regiocentric or geocentric orientation (EPRG) depending on the international commitment of the firm. Further, the authors state that 'a key assumption underlying the EPRG framework is that the degree of internationalization to which management is committed or willing to move towards affects the specific international strategies and decision rules of the firm'.[10] The EPRG schema is incorporated into the discussion of the three concepts that follows in that the philosophical orientations described by the EPRG schema help explain management's view when guided by one of the concepts.

The Domestic Market Extension Concept

This orientation to international marketing is illustrated by the domestic company seeking sales extension of its domestic products into foreign markets. It views its international operations as secondary to and an extension of its domestic operations; the primary motive is to dispose of excess domestic production. Domestic business is its priority and foreign sales are seen as a profitable extension of domestic operations. Even though foreign markets may be vigorously pursued, the firm's orientation remains basically domestic. Its attitude towards international sales is typified by the belief that if it sells in Manchester it will sell anywhere else in the world. Minimal, if any, efforts are made to adapt the marketing mix to foreign markets; the firm's orientation is to market to foreign customers in the same manner the company markets to domestic customers. It seeks markets where demand is similar to the home market and its domestic product will be acceptable. This domestic market extension strategy can be very profitable; large and small exporting companies approach international marketing from this perspective. Sporadic export of cheese to Germany and Belgium by some Dutch dairy producers is an example of this concept. Firms with this marketing approach are classified as *ethnocentric* in the EPRG schema.

Multidomestic Market Concept

Once a company recognizes the importance of differences in overseas markets and the importance of offshore business to the organization, its orientation towards international business may shift to a multidomestic market strategy. A company guided by this concept has a strong sense that country markets are vastly different (and they may be, depending on the product) and that market success requires an almost independent programme for each country. Firms with this orientation market on a country-by-country basis, with separate marketing strategies for each country.

Subsidiaries operate independently of one another in establishing marketing objectives and plans, and the domestic market and each of the country markets have separate marketing mixes with little interaction among them. Products are adapted for each market without coordination with other country markets; advertising campaigns are localized as are the pricing and distribution decisions.

A company with this concept does not look for similarity among elements of the marketing mix that might respond to standardization; rather it aims for adaptation to local country markets. Control is typically decentralized to reflect the belief that the uniqueness of each market requires local marketing input and control. Production and sale of detergents and soaps by Unilever, all over the world, is a typical example of this concept. Firms with this orientation would be classified in the EPRG schema as *polycentric*.

INTERNATIONAL BRANDS IN ASIA

Asia has become the fastest-growing market for most of the West's top brands. Not only Tokyo, Hong Kong and Singapore, but also Jakarta, Bangkok and Kuala Lumpur host Gucci, Louis Vuitton, Gianni Versace, Calvin Klein, Lacoste, Dior, Rolex and Cartier. Those in the luxury goods and fashion businesses are now getting more than one-third of their sales from Asia. According to Comité Colbert, an association of France's top 75 luxury-goods producers, their sales in Asia rose from 20 per cent (1984) to 35 per cent (1995). It is predicted that, within a decade, Asia will make up half of the world's luxury-goods market. By that time, Asian retailers will no longer be content merely with the franchise to sell Western brands, but by that time they might own most of the brands they sell. More and more Asian groups are thus buying stocks in foreign brands not only for their own markets but for the region.

For example, Mr Ong Beng Seng of Singapore, together with his wife, has gathered more than 40 top European and American brands, not only in Asia but also in Australia and the United Kingdom. Last year they acquired a controlling interest in DKNY, a fashion brand founded by Donna Karan, a New York designer. His companies also own 10 per cent of Planet Hollywood, a restaurant chain founded by Arnold Schwarzenegger, Sylvester Stallone, Bruce Willis and Demi Moore, and 50 per cent of the main franchise holder for Asia–Pacific, the Middle East and South Africa. Mr Ong is also partner in Singapore and Hong Kong for Hard Rock Café and Häagen-Dazs ice cream.

Another Singaporean company, The Hour Glass, recently bought controlling status in two of Switzerland's most exclusive watch makers: Daniel Roth and Gerald Genta. These companies produce watches in the price range of $3000 (€2700) to $2 million (€1.8 million). Hong Kong's Joyce Ma, one of the world's largest buyers of designer clothing, is opening stores and restaurants throughout South-east Asia. Dickson Poon, another Hong Kong businessman, bought his first brand, ST Dupont (France), in 1987. Recently he bought Seibu, a Hong Kong department store, and Shenzhen in China from their Japanese owners and then Harvey Nichols, a posh British department store which was listed on the London Stock Exchange in April 1996. As a result of all this, Calvin Klein's underwear is sold through aggressive advertising through Pan-Asian satellite TV and DKNY appears on everything from coffee cups to inflatable swimming rings.

Source: Abstracted from *The Economist*, 10 August 1996, pp. 49–50.

Global Marketing Concept

A company guided by this orientation or philosophy is generally referred to as a *global company*, its marketing activity is global, and its market coverage is the world. A company employing a global marketing strategy strives for efficiencies of scale by developing a product, to be sold at a reasonable price to a global market, that is, somewhat the same country market set throughout the world. Important to the global marketing concept is the premise that world markets are being 'driven towards a converging commonality',[11] seeking in much the same ways to satisfy their needs and desires. Thus, they constitute significant market segments with similar demands for the same basic product the world over. With this orientation a company attempts to standardize as much of the company effort as is practical on a worldwide basis.

Some decisions are viewed as applicable worldwide, while others require consideration of local influences. The world as a whole is viewed as the market and the firm develops a global marketing strategy, although pricing, advertising or distribution channels may differ in different markets. The development and marketing of the Sony Walkman is a good example of a global marketing concept. The global marketing company would fit the *regiocentric* or *geocentric* classifications of the EPRG schema.

The global marketing concept views an entire set of country markets (whether the home market and only one other, or the home market and 100 other countries) as a unit, identifying groups of prospective buyers with similar needs as a global market segment and developing a marketing plan that strives for some level of standardization wherever it is cost and culturally effective. This might mean a company's global marketing plan has a standardized product but country-specific advertising, or has a standardized theme in all countries with country- or cultural-specific appeals to a unique market characteristic, a standardized brand or image but adapted products to meet specific country needs, and so on. In other words, the marketing planning and marketing mix are approached from a global perspective and, where feasible in the marketing mix, efficiencies of standardization are sought. Wherever cultural uniqueness dictates the need for adaptation of the product, its image and so on, it is accommodated.

As the competitive environment facing today's businesses becomes more internationalized, the most effective orientation for all firms involved in marketing into another country will be a multidomestic or a global orientation. This means operating as if all the country markets in a company's scope of operations (including the domestic market) are approachable standardizing the overall marketing strategy and adopting the marketing mix as much as possible according to cultural and other uncontrollable factors.

Although the world has not become a homogeneous market, there is strong evidence of identifiable groups of consumers (segments) across country borders with similar purchasing power, needs and behaviour patterns. However, the same product might need a different marketing mix in different countries. Sometimes, it is forced by environments, such as government regulations and income levels, sometimes it is influenced by the fact that the product is in different stages of the product life cycle in different markets. Regardless of the degree to which global markets exist, a company can benefit from a global orientation. The issue of whether marketing programmes should be standardized or localized is not as critical as the recognition that marketing planning processes need to be coordinated across markets.

GLOBAL MARKETS

Theodore Levitt's article, 'The Globalization of Markets', has spawned a host of new references to marketing activities: global marketing, global business, global advertising and global brands, as well as serious discussions of the processes of international marketing.[12] Professor Levitt's premise is that world markets are being driven 'towards a converging commonality.' Almost everyone everywhere wants all the things they have heard about, seen or experienced via the new technologies. He sees substantial market segments with common needs, that is, a high-quality, reasonably priced, standardized product. The 'global corporation sells the same thing in the same way everywhere'. Professor Levitt argues that segmenting international markets on political boundaries and customizing products and marketing strategies for country markets or on national or regional preferences are not cost effective. The company of the future, according to Levitt, will be a global company that views the world as one market to which it sells a global product.[13]

As with all new ideas, interpretations abound and discussions and debates flow. Professor Levitt's article has provoked many companies and marketing scholars to reexamine a fundamental idea that has prevailed for decades; that is, products and strategies must be adapted to the cultural needs of each country when marketing internationally. This approach is contrasted with a global orientation suggesting a commonality in marketing needs and thus a standardized product for all the world. While the need for cultural adaptation exists in most markets and for most products, the influence of mass communications in the world today and its influence on consumer wants and needs cannot be denied.[14]

Certainly, the homogenizing effect of mass communications in the European Union has eliminated many of the regional differences that once existed. Based on these experiences, it seems reasonable to believe that to some extent people in other cultures exposed to the same influences will react similarly and that there is a converging commonality of the world's needs and desires.

Does this mean markets are now global? The answer is yes, to some extent; there are market segments in most countries with similar demands for the same product. Levi Strauss, Revlon, Toyota, Ford, Philips, Sony, McDonald's and Coca-Cola are companies that sell a relatively standardized product throughout the world to market segments seeking the same products to satisfy their needs and desires. Does this mean there is no need to be concerned with cultural differences when marketing in different countries? The answer is no, in most of the cases; for some products adaptation is not necessary, but for other products adaptation is still necessary. The issue of modification versus standardization of marketing effort is, however, more complicated. Even an apparently standardized product such as McDonald's hamburgers needs a different marketing effort and mix. For example, for a McDonald's restaurant in Manhattan, New York, the target customers are working people coming for breakfast or lunch. In Maastricht, the target customers are families with children, here the restaurant has a big playground with swings and slides attached to it. The restaurant is thus almost empty during the evenings. In Jakarta, the target market is more well-to-do youngsters and yuppies. In this case, the restaurant is placed beside Hard Rock Café and is open 24 hours a day and, in fact, does more business in the night than during the day. The astute marketer always strives to present products that fulfil the perceived needs and wants of the consumer. An apparently standardized product is also modified according to the tastes and wants of the customers in different markets. McDonald's, for example, has recently opened restaurants in India, but it serves non-beef beefburgers.

Marketing internationally should entail looking for market segments with similar demands that can be satisfied with the same product, standardizing the components of the marketing mix that can be standardized and, where there are significant cultural differences that require parts of the marketing mix to be culturally adapted, adapting. Throughout the text, the question of adaptation versus standardization of products and marketing effort will be discussed.

DEVELOPING A GLOBAL AWARENESS

Opportunities in global business abound for those prepared to confront the myriad obstacles with optimism and a willingness to continue learning new ways. The successful business-person in the 21st century will be globally aware and have a frame of reference that goes beyond a region or even a country and encompasses the world. To be globally aware is to have:

- Objectivity.
- Tolerance towards cultural differences.[15]
- Knowledge of:
    cultures
    history
    world market potential
    global economic, social and political trends.

To be globally aware is to be *objective*. Objectivity is important in assessing opportunities, evaluating potential and responding to problems. Millions of dollars were lost by companies that blindly entered the Chinese market in the belief that there were untold opportunities, when, in reality, opportunities were in very select areas and generally for those with the resources to sustain a long-term commitment. Many were caught up in the euphoria of envisioning one billion consumers; they made uninformed and not very objective decisions.

To be globally aware is to have *tolerance towards cultural differences*. Tolerance is understanding cultural differences and accepting and working with others whose behaviour may be different from yours. You do not have to accept, as your own, the cultural ways of another but you must allow others to be different and equal. The fact that punctuality is less important in some cultures does not make them less productive, only different. The tolerant person understands the differences that may exist between cultures and uses that knowledge to relate effectively.

A globally aware person is *knowledgeable* about cultures, history, world market potentials and global economic and social trends. Knowledge of cultures is important in understanding behaviour in the marketplace or in the boardroom. Knowledge of history is important because the way people think and act is influenced by their history. An Asian's reluctance about foreign investment, Chinese reluctance to open completely to the outsider, or the many in Britain who were hesitant about the tunnel between France and England, can all be understood better if you have a historical perspective.

Over the next few decades there will be enormous changes in market potential in almost every region of the world. A globally aware person will continuously monitor the markets of the world. Finally, a globally aware person will keep abreast of the social and economic trends because a country's prospects can change as social and economic trends shift direction or accelerate. Not only the former republics of the USSR, but also Eastern Europe, China and other Asian emerging countries are undergoing social and economic changes that have already altered the course of trade and defined new economic powers. The knowledgeable marketer will identify opportunity long before it becomes evident to others. It is our goal in this text to guide the reader towards acquiring a global awareness.

ORIENTATION OF INTERNATIONAL MARKETING

Most problems encountered by the foreign marketer result from the unfamiliar environment within which marketing programmes must be implemented. Success hinges, in part, on the ability to assess and adjust properly to the impact of a strange environment.[16] The successful international marketer possesses the best qualities of the sociologist, psychologist, diplomat, lawyer and businessperson.

In light of all the variables involved, with what should a text in international marketing be concerned? In our opinion, a study of foreign-marketing environments and their influences on the total marketing process is of primary concern and is the most effective approach to a meaningful presentation.

Consequently, the orientation of this text can best be described as an environmental approach to international strategic marketing. By no means is it intended to present principles of marketing; rather it is intended to demonstrate the unique problems of international marketing. It attempts to relate the foreign environment to the marketing process and to illustrate the many ways in which the environment can influence the marketing task. Although marketing principles are universally applicable, the environment within which the marketer must implement marketing plans can change dramatically from country to country.

It is with the difficulties created by different environments that this text is primarily concerned.

Further, the text is concerned with any company marketing in or into any other country or groups of countries, however slight the involvement or the method of involvement. Hence, this discussion of international marketing ranges from the marketing and business practices of small exporters such as a Groningen-based company that generates more than 50 per cent of its $40 000 (€36 000) annual sales of fish-egg sorters in Canada, Germany and Australia to the practices of global companies such as Philips, Ericsson, ABB and Sony that generate more than 70 per cent of their annual profits from the sales of multiple products to multiple country-market segments all over the world.

SUMMARY

The first section of *International Marketing* offers an overview of international marketing and a discussion of the global business, political and legal environments confronting the marketer. This section deals exclusively with the uncontrollable elements of the environment and their assessment. The next section offers chapters on assessing international market opportunities. Then, management issues in developing global marketing strategies are discussed. In each chapter the impact of the environment on the marketing process is illustrated. Space prohibits an encyclopaedic approach to all the issues, nevertheless, the authors have tried to present sufficient detail so readers appreciate the real need to make a thorough analysis whenever the challenge arises. The text provides a framework for this task.

QUESTIONS

1. 'The marketer's task is the same whether applied in Amsterdam, London or Kuala Lumpur.' Discuss.
2. How can the increased interest in international marketing on the part of the European firms be explained?
3. Discuss the four phases of international marketing involvement.
4. Discuss the conditions that have led to the development of global markets.
5. Differentiate between a global company and a multinational company.
6. Differentiate among the three international marketing concepts.
7. Relate the three international marketing concepts to the EPRG schema.
8. Discuss the three factors necessary to achieve global awareness.
9. What is meant by global markets? How does this influence the adaptation of products and marketing strategies?

REFERENCES

1. Louis S. Richman, 'Global Growth Is on a Tear', *Fortune*, 20 March 1995, pp. 108–114.
2. Dan Biers, 'Now in First World, Asia's Tigers Act Like It', *The Wall Street Journal*, 28 February 1995, p. A-15.
3. 'Borderless Management: Companies Strive to Become Truly Stateless', *Business Week*, 23 May 1994, pp. 24–26.
4. 'Ron Brown's "Lovefest" in Beijing', *Business Week*, 12 September 1994, p. 54.
5. Here, and in the rest of the book, the euro (€) to dollar ($) exchange rate is that of Friday, 31 July 1998, as given by the Custom House Currency Exchange currency converter (http://www.oanda.com/converter/classic): US$1 = €0.9026; €1 = US$1.1079.
6. Gina Gianzero, 'Order from Chaos: Who's Who in the Republics', *Europe*, February 1994, pp. 16–19.
7. David A. Ricks, *Blunders in International Business* (Cambridge, Mass.: Blackwell Publishers, 1993), p. 43.
8. For a report on research that examines the internationalization of a firm, see Peter Buckley and Pervez Ghauri (eds), *The Internationalization of the Firm: A Reader* (London: Dryden Press, 1994).
9. Regina Fazio Maruca, 'The Right Way to Go Global: An Interview with Whirlpool CEO David Whitwam', *Harvard Business Review*, March–April 1994, pp. 135–145.
10. Yoram Wind, Susan P. Douglas and Howard V. Perlmutter, 'Guidelines for Developing International Marketing Strategy', *Journal of Marketing*, April 1973, pp. 14–23.
11. Theodore Levitt, 'The Globalization of Markets', *Harvard Business Review*, May–June 1983, pp. 92–102.
12. Levitt, 'Globalization', p. 92.
13. For an opposing view, see Richard A. Kustin, 'Marketing Globalization: A Didactic Examination of Corporate Strategy', *International Executive*, January–February 1994, pp. 79–93.
14. Juliana Kordnteng, 'MTV: Targeting Europe Market-by-Market', *Advertising Age*, 20 March 1995, p. I-13.
15. The Webster unabridged dictionary defines tolerance as a fair and objective attitude towards those whose opinions, practices, race, religion, nationality, etc., differ from one's own: freedom from bigotry. It is with this meaning that the authors are using tolerance.
16. Pascale Quester and Jodie Conduit, 'Standardization, Centralism and Marketing in Multi-National companies', *International Business Review*, vol. 5, no. 4, 1996.

Chapter Outline

Chapter Learning Objectives

What you should learn from Chapter 2

- The basis for the reestablishment of world trade following World War II.
- The emergence of MNCs and its impact on international marketing.
- The importance of balance-of-payment figures to a country's economy.
- The effects of protectionism on world trade.
- The seven types of trade barriers.
- The importance of GATT and the emergence of the World Trade Organization.
- The role of the International Monetary Fund.

Yesterday's competitive market battles were fought in Western Europe, Japan and the United States; tomorrow's competitive battles will extend to Eastern Europe, Russia, China, Asia, Latin America and Africa as these emerging markets become more actively involved in international business. More of the world's people, from the richest to the poorest, will participate in the world's wealth through global trade. The emerging global economy in which we live brings us into worldwide competition with significant advantages for both marketers and consumers.[1] Marketers benefit from new markets opening and smaller markets growing large enough to become viable business opportunities. Consumers benefit by being able to select the lowest priced and widest range of goods produced anywhere in the world. Bound together by satellite communications and global companies, consumers in every corner of the world are demanding an ever-expanding variety of goods.

As Table 2.1 illustrates, world trade is an important economic activity. Because of this importance, the inclination is for countries to control international trade to their own advantage. As competition intensifies, the tendency towards protectionism gains momentum. If the benefits of the social, political and economic changes now taking place are to be fully realized, free trade must prevail throughout the global marketplace. The Uruguay Round of the General Agreement on Tariffs and Trade (GATT), completed in 1994, was one of the biggest victories for free trade in decades.

THE TWENTIETH CENTURY

At no time in modern economic history have countries been more economically interdependent, have greater opportunities for international trade existed, or has the potential for increased demand existed than during the last decade of the 20th century. In the preceding 90 years, world economic development has been erratic.

The first half of the century was marred by a major worldwide economic depression that occurred between the two world wars and that all but destroyed most of the industrialized world. The last half of the century, while free of a world war, was marred by struggles between countries espousing the Marxist–socialist approach and those following a democratic, capitalist approach to economic development. As a result of this ideological split, traditional trade patterns were disrupted.

After World War II, as a means to dampen the spread of communism, the United States set out to infuse the ideal of capitalism throughout as much of the world as possible. The Marshall Plan to assist in rebuilding Europe, financial and industrial development assistance to rebuild Japan and funds channelled through the Agency for International Development and other groups designed to foster economic growth in the underdeveloped world were used to help create a strong world economy. The dissolution of colonial powers created scores of new countries in Asia and Africa. With the striving of these countries to gain economic independence and the financial assistance offered by the Western countries, most of the developing world's economies grew and new markets were created.

The benefits from the foreign economic assistance given by the West flowed both ways. For every dollar the West invested in the economic development and rebuilding of other countries, hundreds of dollars more returned in the form of purchases of Western agricultural products, manufactured goods and services. During this period of economic growth in the rest of the world, the West experienced a major economic boom and an increased standard of living. Certainly a part of Western economic prosperity can be attributed to Western industry supplying the world demand created by economic growth.

In addition to Western economic assistance, a move towards international cooperation

Table 2.1   Leading World Exporters (1996)

	Biggest Export Markets	Percentage of Total Exports
US	Canada	21.3
Germany	EU	56.4
Japan	US	27.5
France	EU	62.6
Britain	EU	52.7
Italy	EU	55.4
Netherlands	EU	78.1
Canada	US	82.3
Belgium–Luxembourg	EU	70.4
China	Hong Kong	21.8
South Korea	US	16.7
Singapore	US	18.4
Taiwan	Hong Kong	39.6
Spain	EU	79.0

Source: IMF, *The Economist*, 15 November 1997, p. 89.

among trading nations was manifest in the negotiation of the General Agreement on Tariffs and Trade (GATT). International trade had ground to a halt following World War I when nations followed the example set by the US enactment of the Smoot–Hawley Law (1930) that raised average US tariffs to levels in excess of 60 per cent. In retaliation, other countries erected high tariff walls and international trade was stalled, along with most economies. GATT therefore provided a forum for member countries to negotiate a reduction of tariffs and other barriers to trade, and the forum proved successful in reaching those objectives. With the ratification of the Uruguay Round agreements, the GATT was replaced by the World Trade Organization (WTO) and its 117 members moved into a new era of free trade.[2]

World Trade and Emergence of Multinational Corporations

The rapid growth of war-torn economies and previously underdeveloped countries, coupled with large-scale economic cooperation and assistance, led to new global marketing opportunities. Rising standards of living and broad-based consumer and industrial markets in Europe and elsewhere created opportunities for US companies to expand exports and investment worldwide.

The worldwide economic growth and rebuilding after World War II was beginning to surface in competition that challenged the supremacy of US industry. Competition arose on all fronts; Japan, Germany, most of the industrialized world and many developing countries were competing for demand in their own countries and were looking for world markets as well. Countries once classified as less developed were reclassified as newly industrialized countries (NICs). The NICs, such as South Korea, Taiwan, Singapore and Hong Kong, experienced rapid industrialization in selected industries and became aggressive world competitors in steel, shipbuilding, consumer electronics, automobiles, light aircraft, shoes, textiles, clothing and so forth. In addition to the NICs, a number of developing countries have been reclassified as emerging markets. Some of these countries are China, India, Indonesia, Thailand, Malaysia, Brazil, Mexico and Vietnam. A number of countries from the

Table 2.2   The Nationality of the World's 100 Largest Industrial Corporations (by Country of Origin)

	1963	1979	1984	1990	1993	1997
US	67	47	47	33	32	32
Germany	13	13	8	12	14	13
Britain	7	7	5	6	4	2
France	4	11	5	10	6	13
Japan	3	7	12	18	23	26
Italy	2	3	3	4	4	3
The Netherlands–UK	2	2	2	2	2	2
The Netherlands	1	3	1	1	1	3
Switzerland	1	1	2	3	3	3
Argentina	–	–	1	–	–	–
Belgium	–	1	1	1	–	–
Brazil	–	1	–	1	1	–
Canada	–	2	3	–	–	–
India	–	–	1	–	–	–
Kuwait	–	–	1	–	–	–
Mexico	–	1	1	1	1	–
Venezuela	–	1	1	1	1	1
South Korea	–	–	4	2	4	2
Sweden	–	–	1	2	1	–
South Africa	–	–	1	1	–	–
Spain	–	–	–	2	2	–
Turkey	–	–	–	–	1	–

Source: Adapted from 'The World's 500 Largest Industrial Corporations', *Fortune*, 25 July 1994, pp. 137–144. And 'The Fortune Global 500: The World's Largest Corporations', *Fortune*, 3 August 1998, pp. F-1, F-2.

former Eastern bloc such as Poland, Hungary and the Czech Republic are also included in the list.

In short, economic power and potential became more evenly distributed among countries than was the case when Servan-Schreiber warned Europe about US multinational domination. Instead, the US position in world trade is now shared with multinational corporations (MNCs) from other countries. Table 2.2 shows the dramatic change between 1963 and 1997. In 1963, the United States had 67 of the world's largest industrial corporations; by 1997, that number had dropped to 32 while Japan moved from having three of the largest to 26 and South Korea from none to two.

Although European markets are quite diverse and constantly changing, Europe, and more so the European Union (EU), present a highly interdependent group of economies in which consumer segments can show a great deal of similarity as well as dissimilarity. Careful thought and analysis is required to plan marketing strategies in Europe. Different industrial sectors, such as capital goods manufacturers, financial services, telecommunication, retail chains and branded goods, show different trends and structures. The restructuring of most industries at European level is posing new challenges for companies within as well as outside Europe.

This heightened competition for European businesses is raising questions such as how to maintain the competitive strength of European business, to avoid the domination of European markets by foreign multinationals. Among the more important questions raised have been those concerning the ability of European firms to compete in foreign markets and the fairness of international trade policies of some countries. The EU, a strong advocate of free trade, is now confronted with the dilemma of how to encourage trading partners to reciprocate with open access to their markets without provoking increased protectionism. Equalizing trade imbalance without resorting to increased protectionism is a challenge.

The Decade of the Nineties and Beyond

Trends already under way in the last decade of the 20th century are destined to change the patterns of trade for decades to come. The economies of the industrialized world have begun to mature and rates of growth will be more modest in the future than they have been for the past 20 years. Conversely, the economies of the developing world will grow at unprecedented rates. As a consequence, there will be a definite shift in economic power and influence away from industrialized countries—Japan, the United States and the European Union—to countries in Asia, Latin America, Eastern Europe and Africa. According to recent calculations a number of Asian countries will join Western economies as the world's largest economies. This is illustrated in Figure 2.1.

Exports and investments are on a steadily accelerating growth curve in emerging markets where the greatest opportunities for growth will be. China, for example, is projected by the World Bank to have the world's largest economy by the year 2010. As much as 50 per cent of the expected increase in global exports, from approximately €3.6 trillion ($4 trillion) in 1993 to €6.3 trillion ($7 trillion) in 2005, will come from developing countries.[3]

It is estimated that between 1995 and 2000, the number of households with annual incomes approaching $18 000 (€16 300) in Pacific Rim countries will increase from 32.5 million to over 73 million.[4] Demand in Asia for motor vehicles is expected to more than

---

Figure 2.1   Buying Boom for Asia, 1995–2000

Millions of households approaching $18 000 per year buying power
Indexed to Singapore prices

	1991	1995	2000
	14.4	32.5	73.3

What the added middle class will buy In millions	Between 1993 and 1995	2000
Bedrooms	32	116
Living rooms	16	58
Kitchens	16	58
Bathrooms	32	116
Living space (m²)	1200	4350
Large appliances	16	58
Televisions	24	87
Telephones	24	87
Cars	16	58

Source: Bill Saporito, 'Where the Global Action Is', *Fortune*, Autumn–Winter 1993, p. 64.

Figure 2.2   The 21st Century Economy—Rapid Innovation and Surging Trade Will Pave the Way for Growth

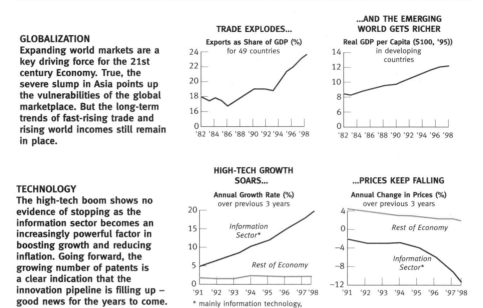

GLOBALIZATION
Expanding world markets are a key driving force for the 21st century Economy. True, the severe slump in Asia points up the vulnerabilities of the global marketplace. But the long-term trends of fast-rising trade and rising world incomes still remain in place.

TRADE EXPLODES...
Exports as Share of GDP (%)
for 49 countries

...AND THE EMERGING WORLD GETS RICHER
Real GDP per Capita ($100, '95))
in developing countries

TECHNOLOGY
The high-tech boom shows no evidence of stopping as the information sector becomes an increasingly powerful factor in boosting growth and reducing inflation. Going forward, the growing number of patents is a clear indication that the innovation pipeline is filling up – good news for the years to come.

HIGH-TECH GROWTH SOARS...
Annual Growth Rate (%)
over previous 3 years
Information Sector*
Rest of Economy
* mainly information technology, hardware and household telephone

...PRICES KEEP FALLING
Annual Change in Prices (%)
over previous 3 years
Rest of Economy
Information Sector*

Source: *Business Week*, 31 August 1998, pp. 32–33.

triple, from 16 to 58 million in less than a decade. China is a good example of what is happening in Asia that will make such a prediction reality. The Chinese government has announced a consolidation of its motor vehicle production into a few large manufacturing plants to produce an affordable compact sedan for the masses.[5] Production is expected to double to 3 million units over the next five years.[6] Such increases in consumer demand are not limited to motor vehicles; the shopping lists of the hundreds of millions of households that will enter or approach the middle class over the next decade will include washing machines, televisions and all the other trappings of affluence (see Figure 2.1). Similar changes are expected to occur in Latin America and Eastern Europe as well.

This does not mean that markets in Europe, Japan and the United States will cease to be important; those economies will continue to produce large, lucrative markets and the companies established in those markets will benefit. It does mean that for a company to be a major player in the next century, now is the time to begin laying the groundwork.

How will these changes that are taking place in the global marketplace impact on international business? For one thing, the level and intensity of competition will change as companies focus on gaining entry into or maintaining their position in emerging markets, regional trade areas, and the established markets in Europe, Japan and the United States (see Figure 2.2).

Companies are looking for ways to become more efficient, improve productivity and expand their global reach while maintaining an ability to respond quickly to deliver a product the market demands. For example, large multinational companies, such as Matsushita of

GOING INTERNATIONAL 2.1

IT'S TIME TO TALK FOR SWATCH

Swatch, the Swiss watch maker and Olympic Games timekeeper, is joining forces with Siemens of Germany to research and develop a wristwatch by turning it into an indispensable vehicle for data smart cards, pagers and portable phones.

Swatch chief executive Nicolas Hayek, attending the Centennial Olympic Games in Atlanta, had other things on his mind and would not confirm Siemens' involvement. But a spokesman for Siemens UK in London said: 'A 50–50 joint venture company has been established in Switzerland to look at the development of small telecoms items. Products will appear under the Swatch name.'

Sweltering in the 90-degree heat at the Swatch pavilion in Atlanta, Hayek said: 'The first watch phones are now being tested. They should be available in 1999 at the earliest.'

Siemens unveiled a design study of a watch-phone three weeks ago, at an innovation exhibition outside Milan. The key feature is a receiver which slots out from behind the watch and hooks to the user's ear.

Siemens' chief telephone designer, Rabold Lutz, said the phone was 'part of a joint venture with Swatch'.

It is designed to operate within a range of 500 metres from a base station sited at home or in a car.

Swatch now makes between 35 and 40 million watches each year, and total production reached 200 million in July.

The 67-year-old Hayek, mercurial and demanding, sees innovative technology as the key to the next generation of watch products. 'I don't make business decisions', he growled. 'I'm in the creativity business.'

Swatch is also moving into the car market in a joint venture with Mercedes-Benz. Microcompact cars are to be built at a factory in Lorraine, France, with a production target of 99 000 cars in the first year.

Hayek is famous for rescuing the Swiss watch industry from near-oblivion as a result of competition from cheap quartz watches made by the Japanese, especially Citizen and Seiko.

Swatch, which is the only European company among the elite group of Olympic suppliers and sponsors, is determined to exploit the Games to strengthen its world-brand status. The Swiss SMH group, of which Swatch is the largest single company, could do with a boost; last year SMH sales fell one per cent to Sfr2.63 billion ($2.2 billion), and net profits fell sharply by 20 per cent to Sfr232 million.

At the Atlanta Olympics, each of the 10 500 competitors was given a Swatch. By the 2000 games in Sydney, winners may be able to phone their families on their wristwatches as they stand on the medal podium.

Source: *The European*, 28 March–3 April 1996.

Japan, continue to expand their global reach.[7] Nestlé is consolidating its dominance in global consumer markets by acquiring and vigorously marketing local-country major brands;[8] Samsung of South Korea is investing (€450 million/$500 million) in Mexico to secure access to markets in the North American Free Trade Area;[9] and Whirlpool, the US appliance manufacturer, which secured first place in the global appliance business by acquiring the European appliance maker NV Philips, immediately began restructuring itself into its version of a global company.[10] These are a few examples of changes that are sweeping multinational companies as they gear up for the next century.

BALANCE OF PAYMENTS

When countries trade, financial transactions among businesses or consumers of different nations occur. Products and services are exported and imported, monetary gifts are exchanged, investments are made, cash payments are made and cash receipts received and vacation and foreign travel occurs. In short, over a period of time, there is a constant flow of money into and out of a country. The system of accounts that records a nation's international financial transactions is called its *balance of payments*.

A nation's balance-of-payments statement records all financial transactions between its residents and those of the rest of the world during a given period of time—usually one year. Because the balance-of-payments record is maintained on a double-entry bookkeeping system, it must always be in balance. As on an individual's financial statement, the assets and liabilities or the credits and debits must offset each other. And, like an individual's statement, the fact that they balance does not mean a nation is in particularly good or poor financial condition. A balance of payments is a record of condition, not a determinant of condition. Each of the nation's financial transactions with other countries is reflected in its balance of payments.

A nation's balance of payments presents an overall view of its international economic position and is an important economic measure used by treasuries, central banks and other government agencies whose responsibility it is to maintain external and internal economic stability. A balance of payments represents the difference between receipts from foreign countries on one side and payments to them on the other. On the plus side are export sales, money spent by foreign tourists, payments to the country for insurance, transportation and similar services, payments of dividends and interest on investments abroad, return on capital invested abroad, new foreign investments in the country and foreign government payments to the country.

On the minus side are costs of goods imported, spending by tourists overseas, new overseas investments and the cost of foreign military and economic aid. A deficit results when international payments are greater than receipts. It can be reduced or eliminated by increasing a country's international receipts (i.e. gain more exports to other countries or more tourists from other countries) and/or reducing expenditures in other countries.

A balance-of-payments statement includes three accounts: the current account—a record of all merchandise exports, imports and services plus unilateral transfers of funds; the capital account—a record of direct investment portfolio investment, and short-term capital movements to and from countries; and the official reserves account—a record of exports and imports of gold, increases or decreases in foreign exchange and increases or decreases in liabilities to foreign central banks. Of the three, the current account is of primary interest to international business.

Current Account

The *current account* is important because it includes all international trade and service accounts. These are the accounts for the value of all merchandise and services imported and exported and all receipts and payments from investments. (See Table 2.3.)

Balance of Trade

The relationship between merchandise imports and exports is referred to as the *balance of merchandise trade* or *trade balance*. If a country exports more goods than it imports, it has a favourable balance of trade; if it imports more goods than it exports, it has an unfavourable balance of trade. Usually a country that has a negative balance of trade also has a negative

Table 2.3   Trade and Current Account Balance

	Trade balance* (billion dollar)			Current account (billion dollar)	
	Latest month		Latest 12 months	Latest 12 months	
Australia	+0.05	(Apr)	−0.3	−14.3	(Q1**)
Austria	n.a.	(Dec)	−9.5	−7.9	(Mar)
Belgium	−0.13	(Mar)	+10.6	+15.4	(Dec)
Britain	−1.08	(Mar)	−16.7	+0.1	(Q4)
Canada	+2.27	(Mar)	+25.4	+1.6	(Q1)
Denmark	+0.34	(Mar)	+5.0	+1.6	(Q1)
France	+1.72	(Mar**)	+20.0	+22.5	(Feb)
Germany	+7.37	(Mar)	+67.1	−18.5	(Mar)
Italy	+2.49	(Mar)	+43.7	+42.1	(Dec)
Japan	+8.08	(Apr)	+81.2	+66.8	(Apr)
The Netherlands	+2.08	(Dec***)	+16.8	+21.1	(Q3)
Spain	−1.00	(Mar)	−18.3	+9.7	(Mar)
Sweden	+1.59	(Apr)	+17.4	+5.3	(Mar)
Switzerland	+0.23	(Mar)	+1.2	+19.7	(Q1)
USA	−15.06	(Mar)	−195.3	−165.1	(Q4)

*Australia, Britain, France, Canada, Japan and USA imports fob, exports fob. All others cif/fob.
**New series.
***Not seasonally adjusted.
Source: Based on *The Economist*, 14 June 1997, p. 127.

balance of payments. Both the balance of trade and the balance of payments do not have to be negative; at times a country may have a favourable balance of trade and a negative balance of payments or vice versa.

PROTECTIONISM

International business must face the reality that this is a world of tariffs, quotas and nontariff barriers designed to protect a country's markets from intrusion by foreign companies. Although the General Agreement on Tariffs and Trade has been effective in reducing tariffs, countries still resort to protectionist measures. Countries utilize legal barriers, exchange barriers and psychological barriers to restrain entry of unwanted goods. Businesses work together to establish private market barriers while the market structure itself may provide formidable barriers to imported goods. The complex distribution system in Japan is a good example of a market structure creating a barrier to trade. However, as effective as it is in keeping some products out of the market, in a legal sense it cannot be viewed as a trade barrier. Figure 2.3 illustrates some transatlantic tariffs.

Protection Logic and Illogic

Countless reasons are espoused by protectionists to maintain government restrictions on trade, but essentially all arguments can be classified as follows: (1) protection of an infant industry; (2) protection of the home market; (3) need to keep money at home; (4) encouragement of capital accumulation; (5) maintenance of the standard of living and real wages;

Figure 2.3   Transatlantic Trade Tiffs

Bananas	The EU discriminates against bananas from US-owned plantations in Central and Latin America, according to the World Trade Organization.
Beef and Corn	The EU excludes US beef amid fears of growth hormones used in US cattle production. France has also blocked imports of genetically altered corn from the US.
US sanctions	Congress refuses to lift US sanctions on countries that do business with Cuba, Libya and Iran. The EU threatens to take the US to the WTO over the matter.
Subsidies	The EU has filed a WTO complaint against US tax breaks for exporters, and the US has a dispute with Europe over subsidies to Airbus and to European farm products.

Source: *Business Week*, 27 July 1998, p. 39.

(6) conservation of natural resources; (7) industrialization of a low-wage nation; (8) maintenance of employment and reduction of unemployment; (9) national defence; (10) increase of business size; (11) retaliation and bargaining. Economists in general recognize as valid only the arguments for infant industry, national defence, and industrialization of developing countries. The resource conservation argument becomes increasingly valid in an era of environmental consciousness and worldwide shortages of raw materials and agricultural commodities.

There might be a case for temporary protection of markets with excess productive capacity or excess labour when such protection could facilitate an orderly transition. Unfortunately such protection becomes long term and contributes to industrial inefficiency while detracting from a country's realistic adjustment to its world situation.

Most protectionists argue the need for tariffs on one of the three premises recognized by economists whether or not they are relevant to their products. Proponents are also likely to call on the maintenance-of-employment argument because it has substantial political appeal. When arguing for protection, the basic economic advantages of international trade are ignored. The fact that the consumer ultimately bears the cost of tariffs and other protective measures is conveniently overlooked. Agriculture and textiles are good examples of protected industries in a number of European countries that cannot be justified by any of the three arguments. Local prices are artificially held higher than world prices for no sound economic reason. (See Table 2.4.)

Trade Barriers

To encourage the development of domestic industry and protect existing industry, governments may establish such barriers to trade as tariffs, quotas, boycotts, monetary barriers, non-tariff barriers and market barriers. Barriers are imposed against imports and against foreign businesses. While the inspiration for such barriers may be economic or political, they are encouraged by local industry. Whether or not the barriers are economically logical, the fact is that they exist.

Tariffs.   A tariff, simply defined, is a tax imposed by a government on goods entering at its borders. Tariffs may be used as a revenue-generating tax or to discourage the importation of

FOR SALE, BUT NOT FOR FOREIGNERS

In spite of all the drivers of globalizations, some European governments are not fully convinced. Look at the following examples of three companies, about to be disposed of in Europe:

1. France is seeking a buyer for Thomson, a huge consumer and defence electronics group. The CEO, Alain Gomez, who believed it made sense to merge it with its British counterpart GEC, was sacked for this treasonable thought.
2. Germany's government is planning to sell one of the subsidiaries of Bremer Vulkan, a shipbuilding conglomerate. The subsidiary, STN Atlas, makes fire control systems for Germany's Leopard tanks and torpedoes. The government has received 30 bids of which some 30 per cent come from abroad. But the defence industry has advised the German government that for reasons of national security the firm should stay in German hands.
3. The Austrian government has spent five years trying to sell a 49 per cent stake in Credietanstallt, the country's best-known bank, but has failed to attract a buyer. In 1994, the most interesting party, Switzerland's CS Holding, withdrew its bid as it was made known that politicians from both main parties were against letting the national assets go into foreign hands. The share prices, rising because of the Swiss takeover, declined considerably and the government was unable to privatize. As a result, the bank lost money and confidence of the stock market as it slowed down the restructuring of Austria's over-crowded banking sector.

Source: Abstracted from *The Economist*, 'Business Europe: Game with Frontiers', 21 September 1996, p. 69.

Table 2.4   The Price of Protectionism

Industry	Total Costs to Consumers (million $)	Number of Jobs Saved	Cost per Job Saved ($)
Textiles and apparel	27 000	640 000	42 000
Carbon steel	6 800	9 000	750 000
Autos	5 800	55 000	105 000
Dairy products	5 500	25 000	220 000
Shipping	3 000	11 000	270 000
Meat	1 800	11 000	160 000

Source: Michael McFadden, 'Protectionism Can't Protect Jobs', *Fortune*, 11 May 1987, p. 125.

goods, or for both reasons. In general, tariffs:

- Increase:
    inflationary pressures
    special interests' privileges
    government control and political considerations in economic matters
    the number of tariffs (they beget other tariffs).
- Weaken:
    balance-of-payments positions
    supply-and-demand patterns
    international understanding (they can start trade wars).

Figure 2.4 Types of Nontariff Barriers

Specific Limitations on Trade:
  Quotas
  Import licensing requirements
  Proportion restrictions of foreign to domestic goods (local content requirements)
  Minimum import price limits
  Embargoes

Customs and Administrative Entry Procedures:
  Valuation systems
  Antidumping practices
  Tariff classifications
  Documentation requirements
  Fees

Standards:
  Standards disparities
  Intergovernmental acceptances of testing methods and standards
  Packaging, labelling, marking standards

Governmental Participation in Trade:
  Government procurement policies
  Export subsidies
  Countervailing duties
  Domestic assistance programmes

Charges on Imports:
  Prior import deposit requirements
  Administrative fees
  Special supplementary duties
  Import credit discriminations
  Variable levies
  Border taxes

Others:
  Voluntary export restraints
  Orderly marketing agreements

Source: A.D. Cao, 'Non Tariff Barriers to US Manufactured Exports', *The Columbia Journal of World Business*, Summer 1980, p. 94.

■ Restrict:
    manufacturers' supply sources
    choices available to consumers
    competition.

In addition, tariffs are arbitrary, discriminatory and require constant administration and supervision. They often are used as reprisals against protectionist moves of trading partners. In a dispute with the European Community over pasta export subsidies, the United States ordered a 40 per cent increase in tariffs on European spaghetti and fancy pasta. The EC retaliated against US walnuts and lemons. The pasta war raged on as Europe increased tariffs on US fertilizer, paper products and beef tallow, and the United States responded in kind. The war ended when the Europeans finally dropped pasta export subsidies.

Imports are restricted in a variety of ways other than tariffs. These nontariff barriers

GOING INTERNATIONAL 2.3

THE JAPANESE MARKET IS OPEN—IF YOU CAN SURVIVE THE TEST

Japanese set tough standards that products must pass before they can be imported. Porta-bote International of California attempted to sell their boat in Japan and encountered the following:

The president of the company knew he had a perfect product for Japan. Because storage space is at a premium in Japanese homes, he reasoned that the Japanese who loved fishing needed his boat—an $895 motorized or sailing craft that folds to four inches flat and can be carried on top of a car.

He turned to a Japanese distributor willing to test market his boat. Like most imported consumer products, the boat first had to clear Japanese safety tests. The president describes the test as 'a veiled attempt to reject Porta-bote' and to protect domestic manufacturers. The Japanese Coast Guard filled one of the boats with 600 pounds of concrete and dropped it 20 feet into the water. The boat was examined for structural damage and then, to the amazement of the distributor who was snapping pictures, it was subjected to the same test twice more. The polypropylene boat held together and—ironically the distributor used the photo to convince retailers of its strength and durability. The test was a success and the boat was allowed to enter the Japanese market.

Source: Reprinted by permission, *Nation's Business*, October 1986. Copyright 1986, US Chamber of Commerce.

include quality standards on imported products, sanitary and health standards, quotas, embargoes and boycotts. Figure 2.4 provides a list of nontariff barriers.

Quotas.   A quota is a specific unit or dollar limit applied to a particular type of good. There is a limit on imported television sets in the United Kingdom, and there are German quotas on Japanese ball bearings, Italian restrictions on Japanese cars and motorcycles, and US quotas on sugar, textiles and peanuts. Quotas put an absolute restriction on the quantity of a specific item that can be imported. Like tariffs, quotas tend to increase prices. In Europe, quotas on textiles are estimated to add 50 to 100 per cent to the wholesale price of clothing.

Voluntary Export Restraints.   Similar to quotas are the voluntary export restraints (VER). Common in textiles, clothing, steel, agriculture and motor vehicles, the VER is an agreement between the importing country and the exporting country for a restriction on the volume of exports. Japan has a VER on vehicles to France, Italy and the United States; that is, Japan has agreed to export a fixed number of these annually. A VER is called voluntary in that the exporting country sets the limits; however, it is generally imposed under the threat of stiffer quotas and tariffs being set by the importing country if a VER is not established.

Boycott.   A government boycott is an absolute restriction against the purchase and importation of certain goods from other countries. A public boycott can be either formal or informal and may be government sponsored or sponsored by an industry. It is not unusual for the citizens of a country to boycott goods of other countries at the urging of their government or civic groups. Nestlé products were boycotted by a citizens group that considered that the way Nestlé promoted baby milk formula to Third World mothers was misleading and harmful to their babies.[11]

Monetary Barriers.   A government can effectively regulate its international trade position by various forms of exchange-control restrictions. A government may enact such restrictions to preserve its balance-of-payments position or specifically for the advantage or encouragement of particular industries. There are three barriers to consider: blocked currency, differential exchange rates and government approval requirements for securing foreign exchange.

Blocked currency is used as a political weapon or as a response to difficult balance-of-payments situations. In effect, blockage cuts off all importing or all importing above a certain level. Blockage is accomplished by refusing to allow importers to exchange national currency for the sellers' currency.

The *differential exchange* rate is a particularly ingenious method of controlling imports. It encourages the importation of goods the government deems desirable and discourages importation of goods the government does not want. The essential mechanism requires the importer to pay varying amounts of domestic currency for foreign exchange with which to purchase products in different categories. For example, the exchange rate for a desirable category of goods might be one unit of domestic money for one unit of a specific foreign currency. For a less desirable product, the rate might be two domestic currency units for one foreign unit. For an undesirable product, the rate might be three domestic units for one foreign unit. An importer of an undesirable product has to pay three times as much for the foreign exchange as the importer of a desired product.

Government approval to secure foreign exchange is often used by countries experiencing severe shortages of foreign exchange. At one time or another, most Latin American and East European and some Asian countries have required all foreign exchange transactions to be approved by a central minister or bank. Thus, importers who want to buy a foreign good must apply for an exchange permit, that is, permission to exchange an amount of local currency for foreign currency.

The exchange permit may also stipulate the rate of exchange, which can be an unfavourable rate depending on the desires of the government. In addition, the exchange permit may stipulate that the amount to be exchanged must be deposited in a local bank for a set period prior to the transfer of goods. For example, Brazil has at times required funds to be deposited 360 days prior to the import date. This is extremely restrictive because funds are out of circulation and subject to the ravages of inflation. Such policies cause major cash-flow problems for the importer and greatly increase the price of imports. Needless to say, these currency-exchange barriers constitute a major deterrent to trade.[12]

Standards.   Nontariff barriers of this category include standards to protect health, safety and product quality. The standards are sometimes used in an unduly stringent or discriminating way to restrict trade, but the sheer volume of regulations in this category is a problem in itself. Fruit content regulations for jam vary so much from country to country that one agricultural specialist says, 'A jam exporter needs a computer to avoid one or another country's regulations'. Differing standards is one of the major disagreements between the United States and Japan. The size of knotholes in plywood shipped to Japan can determine whether or not the shipment is accepted; if a knothole is too large, the shipment is rejected because quality standards are not met.

The United States, France, Italy and other countries require some products (motor vehicles in particular) to contain a percentage of 'local content' to gain admission to their markets. The North American Free Trade Agreement (NAFTA) stipulates that all vehicles coming from member countries must have at least 62.5 per cent North American content to deter foreign manufacturers from using one member nation as the back door to another.[13]

While countries create barriers to trade, they appreciate the growing interdependence of the world's economies and thus strive to lower barriers in a controlled and equitable manner.

GOING INTERNATIONAL 2.4

A WORD FOR OPEN MARKETS

Bastiat's century-old farcical letter to the French Chamber of Deputies points up the ultimate folly of tariffs and the advantages of utilizing the superior production advantage of others.

To the Chamber of Deputies:
We are subjected to the intolerable competition of a foreign rival, who enjoys such superior facilities for the production of light that he can inundate our national market at reduced price. This rival is no other than the sun. Our petition is to pass a law shutting up all windows, openings and fissures through which the light of the sun is used to penetrate our dwellings, to the prejudice of the profitable manufacture we have been enabled to bestow on the country.

Signed: Candlestick Makers,
F. Bastiat

The World Trade Organization (WTO) is one attempt by countries to work together to promote free trade.

EASING TRADE RESTRICTIONS

As the global marketplace evolves, trading countries have focused attention on ways of eliminating tariffs, quotas and other barriers to trade. Two ongoing activities to make international trade easier are (1) GATT/WTO and (2) the International Monetary Fund (IMF).

General Agreement on Tariffs and Trade

Historically, trade treaties were negotiated on a bilateral (between two nations) basis, with little attention given to relationships with other countries. Further, there was a tendency to raise barriers rather than extend markets and restore world trade. In total, 23 countries signed the *General Agreement on Tariffs and Trade* (*GATT*) shortly after World War II. Although not all countries participated, this agreement paved the way for the first effective worldwide tariff agreement. The original agreement provided a process to reduce tariffs and created an agency to serve as watchdog over world trade. GATT's agency director and staff offer countries a forum for negotiating trade and related issues. Member countries (117 in 1994) seek to resolve their trade disputes bilaterally; if that fails, special GATT panels are set up to recommend action. The panels are only advisory and have no enforcement powers.

The GATT treaty and subsequent meetings have produced agreements significantly reducing tariffs on a wide range of goods. Periodically, member nations meet to reevaluate trade barriers and establish international codes designed to foster trade among members. In general, the agreement covers three basic elements: (1) trade shall be conducted on a non-discriminatory basis; (2) protection shall be afforded domestic industries through customs tariffs, not through such commercial measures as import quotas; (3) consultation shall be the primary method used to solve global trade problems.

Since GATT's inception there have been eight 'rounds' of intergovernmental tariff negotiations. The most recently completed was the Uruguay Round, which built on the successes of the Tokyo Round—the most comprehensive and far-reaching round undertaken by GATT up to that time. The Tokyo Round resulted in tariff cuts and set out new international rules for subsidies and countervailing measures, antidumping, government procurement, technical barriers to trade (standards), customs valuation and import licensing.

While the Tokyo Round addressed nontariff barriers, there were some areas not covered which continued to impede free trade. In addition to market access, there were issues of trade in services, agriculture and textiles, intellectual property rights and investment and capital flows. Based on these concerns, the eighth set of negotiations (the Uruguay Round) was begun in 1986 at a GATT Trade Minister's meeting in Punta del Este, Uruguay, and finally concluded in 1994. By 1995, 80 GATT members including the United States, the European Union (and its member states), Japan, a number of Asian countries and Canada had accepted the agreement.[14]

The market access segment (tariff and nontariff measures) was initially considered to be of secondary importance in the negotiations, but the final outcome went well beyond the initial Uruguay Round goal of a one-third reduction in tariffs. Instead, virtually all tariffs in 10 vital industrial sectors[15] with key trading partners were eliminated.[16] This resulted in deep cuts (ranging from 50–100 per cent) on electronic items and scientific equipment, and the harmonization of tariffs in the chemical sector at very low rates (5.5–0 per cent).[17] Exporters of paper products in the United States serve as a good example of the opportunities that will be opened as a result of these changes. Currently, US companies competing for a share of the paper products market in the EU have to pay tariffs as high as 9 per cent while European competitors enjoy duty-free access within the EU. Once the results of the Uruguay Round market-access package are implemented, these high tariffs will be eliminated. Another example is Korean tariffs as high as 20 per cent on scientific equipment that will be reduced to an average of 7 per cent, permitting European and US exporters to be more competitive in that market.

An important objective of the Uruguay Round was to reduce or eliminate barriers to international trade in services. While there is still much progress to be made before free trade in services will exist throughout the world, the *General Agreement on Trade in Services* (*GATS*) is the first multilateral, legally enforceable agreement covering trade and investment in the services sector. It provides a legal basis for future negotiations aimed at eliminating barriers that discriminate against foreign services and deny them market access. For the first time, comprehensive multilateral disciplines and procedures covering trade and investment in services have been established. Specific market-opening concessions from a wide range of individual countries were achieved, and provision was made for continued negotiations to further liberalize telecommunications and financial services.[18]

Equally significant were the results of negotiations in the investment sector. *Trade-Related Investment Measures* (*TRIMs*) established the basic principle that investment restrictions can be major trade barriers and are therefore included, for the first time, under GATT procedures. An initial set of prohibited practices included local content requirements specifying that some amount of the value of the investor's production must be purchased from local sources or produced locally, trade balancing requirements specifying that an investor must export an amount equivalent to some proportion of imports or condition the amount of imports permitted on export levels and foreign exchange balancing requirements limiting the importation of products used in local production by restricting its access to foreign exchange to an amount related to its exchange inflow. As a result of TRIMs, restrictions in Indonesia, which prohibit foreign firms from opening their own wholesale or retail distribution channels,

GOING INTERNATIONAL 2.5

ROUND AND ROUND: A GATT/WTO CHRONOLOGY

1947	Birth of the GATT, signed by 23 countries on 30 October at the Palais des Nations in Geneva.
1948	The GATT comes into force. First meeting of its members in Havana, Cuba.
1949	Second round of talks in Annecy, France. Some 5000 tariff cuts agreed to; 10 new countries admitted.
1950–51	Third Round in Torquay, England. Members exchange 8700 trade concessions and welcome four new countries.
1956	Fourth round in Geneva. Tariff cuts worth $1.3 trillion (€1.17 trillion) at today's prices.
1960–62	The Dillon Round, named after US Under-Secretary of State Douglas Dillon, who proposed the talks. A further 4400 tariff cuts.
1964–67	The Kennedy Round. Many industrial tariffs halved. Signed by 50 countries. Code on dumping agreed to separately.
1973–79	The Tokyo Round, involving 99 countries. First of serious discussion of nontariff trade barriers, such as subsidies and licensing requirements. Average tariff on manufactured goods in the nine biggest markets cut from 7–4.7 per cent.
1986–93	The Uruguay Round. Further cuts in industrial tariffs, export subsidies, licensing and customs valuation. First agreements on trade in services and intellectual property.
1995	Formation of World Trade Organization with power to settle disputes between members.
1997	Agreements concluded on telecommunication services, information technology and financial services.
1998	Today the WTO has 132 members. More than 30 others are waiting to join.

Source: *The Economist*, 16 May 1998, p. 20.

can be challenged. And so can investment restrictions in Brazil that require foreign-owned manufacturers to buy most of their components from high-cost local suppliers and that require affiliates of foreign multinationals to maintain a trade surplus in Brazil's favour by exporting more than they sell within.[19]

Another objective of the EU for the Uruguay Round was achieved by an agreement on *Trade Related Aspects of Intellectual Property Rights* (*TRIPs*). The TRIPs agreement establishes substantially higher standards of protection for a full range of intellectual property rights (patents, copyrights, trademarks, trade secrets, industrial designs and semiconductor chip mask works) than are embodied in current international agreements, and it provides for the effective enforcement of those standards both internally and at the border.[20]

The Uruguay Round also provides for a better integration of the agricultural and textiles areas into the overall trading system. The reduction of export subsidies, internal supports and actual import barriers for agricultural products are included in the agreement. The Uruguay Round also includes another set of improvements in rules covering antidumping, standards, safeguards, customs valuation, rules of origin and import licensing. In each case, rules and procedures were made more open, equitable and predictable, thus leading to a more level playing field for trade. Perhaps the most notable achievement of the Uruguay Round was the creation of a new institution as a successor to the GATT—the World Trade Organization.[21]

World Trade Organization

At the signing of the Uruguay Round trade agreement in Marrakech, Morocco, in April 1994, representatives pushed for an enormous expansion of the definition of trade issues.[22] The

Figure 2.5   Joining the Club—Increasing Number of GATT/WTO Members

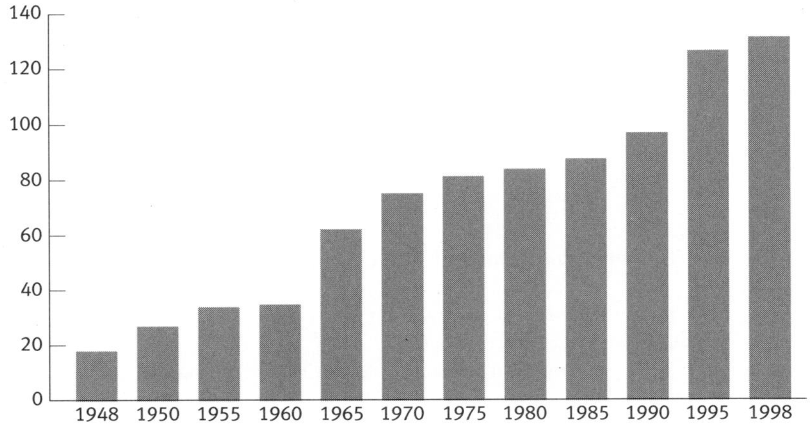

Source: The WTO in *The Economist*, 3 October 1998, World Trade Survey, p. 5.

result was the creation of the *World Trade Organization* which encompassed the GATT structure and extended it to new areas not adequately covered in the past. The WTO is an institution, not an agreement as was GATT. It sets the rules governing trade between its members, provides a panel of experts to hear and rule on trade disputes between members, and, unlike GATT, issues binding decisions. It requires, for the first time, the full participation of all members in all aspects of the current GATT and the Uruguay Round agreements, and, through its enhanced stature and scope, provides a permanent, comprehensive forum to address the trade issues of the 21st century global market.

The membership of the GATT rose from 92 in 1986 to 132 in 1998 (see Figure 2.5), and another 30 countries, including China and Russia, want to join. The world trade has also been booming, it grew by 8 per cent in 1995, four times the rate of growth of world GDP. Foreign Direct investment, another measure of international economy integration, also soared, in 1995 cross-border investment flows rose by 40 per cent. Finally, the spread of regional trading agreement, from the EU, NAFTA to APEC, is gaining ground. Almost every member of the WTO is also a member of such a group. According to WTO records, there have been 76 free trade areas or customs unions set up since 1948. Of these, more than 50 per cent have come in the 1990s.[23]

All member countries have equal representation in the WTO's ministerial conference which meets at least every two years to vote for a director-general who appoints other officials. Trade disputes are heard by a panel of experts selected by the WTO from a list of trade experts provided by member countries. The panel hears both sides and issues a decision; the winning side is authorized to retaliate with trade sanctions if the losing country does not change its practices. While the WTO has no actual means of enforcement, international pressure to comply with WTO decisions from other member countries is expected to force compliance. The WTO ensures that member countries agree to the obligations of all the agreements, not just those they like. For the first time, member countries, including developing countries (the fastest-growing markets of the world), will undertake obligations to open their markets and to be bound by the rules of the multilateral trading system. (See Figure 2.6.)

Figure 2.6   What WTO Will Mean to Different Industries

Gainers

1. Banks would be allowed to compete freely in South Korea and other places where they are now restricted.
2. Insurance companies would be able to sell policies in India, one of the world's most tightly closed markets.
3. Movies would have better protection from Thai film counterfeiters.
4. Pharmaceuticals would have better protection from Argentine imitators.
5. Computer software makers would have better protection from Brazilians who rip off copyrighted programs.

Losers

1. Glassware tariffs as high as 30 per cent on inexpensive drinking glasses would be reduced, threatening some 40 000 jobs.
2. Textiles would gradually lose quotas and tariffs that protect 1.1 million US workers—and add 50 per cent to wholesale prices of clothing.
3. Peanuts would lose quotas that limit imports to a handful and that protect 19 000 American farmers.
4. Dairy imports of foreign cheese, now limited to 110 000 tons a year, would go up, hurting 240 000 US farmers.
5. Sugar import ceilings, now 25 per cent of the 9 million tons the United States uses each year, would go, threatening 11 000 sugar beet and cane growers.

Source: Adapted from 'What Tree Trade Will Mean to Different Industries', *Fortune*, 26 August 1991, p. 92.

There was some resistance to the WTO provision of the Uruguay Round before it was finally ratified by the three superpowers, Japan, the EU and the United States.[24] A legal wrangle between EU countries centred on whether the EU's founding treaty gives the European Commission the sole right to negotiate for its members in all areas covered by the WTO.

In the United States, ratification was challenged because of concern for the possible loss of sovereignty over its trade laws to WTO, the lack of veto power (the United States could have a decision imposed on it by a majority of the WTO's members) and the role the United States would assume when a conflict arises over an individual state's laws that might be challenged by a WTO member.[25] The GATT agreement was ratified by the US Congress, and soon after the EU, Japan and more than 60 other countries followed. It is expected that all 117 members of the former GATT will support the Uruguay agreement. Had the Uruguay Round not been ratified by the major trading nations, there was concern countries would lose confidence in global free trade and begin to retreat to regional trade arrangements risking fragmentation of the world into rival trade blocs. Almost immediately after its inception on 1 January 1995, the WTO's agenda has been full of issues ranging from threats of boycotts and sanctions and the membership of China to who will be selected to be the director general of the organization (see Figure 2.7).[26] In spite of all this, the number of WTO members is increasing every year.

International Monetary Fund

Inadequate monetary reserves and unstable currencies are particularly vexing problems in world trade. So long as these conditions exist, world markets cannot develop and function as

Figure 2.7   Trade-off—WTO Trade Disputes (Consultations, Panels and Appeals, Estimates)

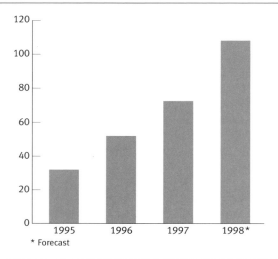

* Forecast

Source: Based on WTO and *The Economist*, World Trade Survey, 3 October 1998.

effectively as they should. To overcome these particular market barriers, which plagued international trading before World War II, the *International Monetary Fund* (*IMF*) was formed. Among its objectives was the stabilization of foreign exchange rates and the establishment of freely convertible currencies. Later, the European Payments Union was formed to facilitate multinational payments. While the IMF has some severe critics, most agree that it has performed a valuable service and at least partially achieved many of its objectives.

To cope with universally floating exchange rates, the IMF developed *special drawing rights* (*SDRs*), one of its more useful inventions. Because both gold and the US dollar have lost their utility as the basic medium of financial exchange, most monetary statistics relate to SDRs rather than dollars. The SDR is, in effect, 'paper gold' and represents an average base of value derived from the value of a group of major currencies. Rather than being denominated in the currency of any given country, trade contracts are frequently written in SDRs because they are much less susceptible to exchange rate fluctuations. Even floating rates do not necessarily accurately reflect exchange relationships. Some countries permit their currencies to float cleanly without manipulation (clean float) while other nations systematically manipulate the value of their currency (dirty float), thus modifying the accuracy of the monetary marketplace. Although much has changed in the world's monetary system since the IMF was first established, it still plays an important role in providing short-term financing to governments struggling to pay current-account debts, and it will be instrumental in helping to establish free markets in Eastern Europe.

SUMMARY

Regardless of the theoretical approach used in defence of international trade, it is clear that the benefits from absolute or comparative advantage can accrue to any country. Heightened competitors from around the world have created increased pressure for protectionism from every region of the globe at a time when open markets are needed if world resources are to be developed and utilized in the most beneficial manner. It is true there are circumstances when market protection may be needed and may be beneficial to national defence or the encouragement of infant industries in developing countries, but the consumer seldom benefits from such protection.

Free international markets help developing countries become self-sufficient, and because open markets provide new customers most industrialized nations have, since World War II, cooperated in working towards freer trade. Such trade will always be partially threatened by various governmental and market barriers that exist or are created for the protection of local businesses. However, the trend has been towards freer trade. The changing economic and political realities are producing unique business structures that continue to protect certain major industries. The future of open global markets lies with the controlled and equitable reduction of trade barriers.

QUESTIONS

1. Discuss the globalization of the European economy.
2. Differentiate among the current account, balance of trade and balance of payments.
3. 'Theoretically, the market is an automatic, competitive, self-regulating mechanism that provides for the maximum consumer welfare and that best regulates the use of the factors of production.' Explain.
4. Why does the balance of payments always balance even though the balance of trade does not?
5. Enumerate the ways in which a country can overcome an unfavourable balance of trade.
6. France exports about 18 per cent of its gross domestic product, while neighbouring Belgium exports 46 per cent. What areas of economic policy are likely to be affected by such variations in exports?
7. Does widespread unemployment change the economic logic of protectionism?
8. The Tokyo Round of GATT emphasized the reduction of nontariff barriers. How does the Uruguay Round differ?
9. Discuss the evolution of world trade that has led to the formation of the WTO.
10. What are the major differences between GATT and WTO?

REFERENCES

1. Paul Krugman, 'Does Third World Growth Hurt First World Prosperity?' *Harvard Business Review*, July 1994, pp. 113–121.
2. Richard Harmsen, 'The Uruguay Round: A Boon for the World Economy', *Finance & Development*, March 1995, pp. 24–26.
3. Bill Saporito, 'Where the Global Action Is', *Fortune*, Autumn–Winter 1993, p. 64.
4. Edward M. Mervosh, 'Winning With the Trade Agreement', *International Business*, January 1994, p. 17.
5. Joseph Kahn, 'China to Give Special Support to 4 Car Makers', *The Wall Street Journal*, 11 September 1994, p. A-10.
6. Patrick E. Tyler, 'Motoring Masses: China Is Planning the People's Car', *The New York Times*, 22 September 1994, p. A-1.
7. Brenton R. Schlender, 'Matsushita Shows How to Go Global', *Fortune*, 11 July 1994, pp. 159–166.
8. Carla Rapoport, 'Nestlé's Brand Building Machine', *Fortune*, 19 September 1994, pp. 147–166.
9. 'Samsung Putting $500 Million in Mexico', Associated Press, 27 September 1994.
10. Regina Fazio Maruca, 'The Right Way to Go Global: An Interview with Whirlpool CEO David Whitwam', *Harvard Business Review*, March–April 1994, pp. 135–145.
11. For a comprehensive review, see Thomas V. Greer, 'International Infant Formula Marketing: The Debate Continues', *Advances in International Marketing,* vol. 4, 1990, pp. 207–225.
12. See, for example, 'Guide to Exchange Controls', *Business Latin America*, 27 June 1994, pp. 4–6, and 'Foreign Trade Regulations', *Business Latin America*, 14 August 1995, pp. 4–5.
13. Anne M. Driscoll, 'Embracing Change, Enhancing Competitiveness: NAFTA's Key Provisions', *Business America*, 18 October 1993, pp. 14–25.
14. Jim Sanford, 'World Trade Organization Opens Global Markets, Protects US Rights', *Business America*, January 1995, p. 4.
15. Construction, agriculture, medical equipment, steel, beer, brown distilled spirits, pharmaceuticals, paper, pulp and printed matter, furniture and toys.
16. European Union, Japan, Austria, Switzerland, Sweden, Finland, Norway, New Zealand, Korea, Hong Kong and Singapore.
17. Sarah E. Shackelton, 'Market Access', *Business America*, January 1994, pp. 7–8.
18. For a complete review of the Uruguay Round of the GATT, see Louis J. Murphy, 'Successful Uruguay Round Launches Revitalized World Trading System', *Business America*, January 1994, pp. 4–27.
19. Louis S. Richman, 'What's Next after GATT's Victory?' *Fortune*, 10 January 1994, pp. 66–71.
20. 'The Uruguay Round Will Fuel More US Export Success Stories', *Business America*, June 1994, pp. 4–5.
21. Hideo Sato, 'The Intelligent Agreement', *Look Japan*, May 1994, pp. 12–13.
22. George Melloan, 'Even before Birth, the WTO Is a Troublemaker', *The Wall Street Journal*, 8 August 1994, p. A-11.
23. *The Economist*, 'All free traders now?' 7 December 1996 pp. 23–25.
24. 'Wrangle May Tie Up Trade Group', *The Wall Street Journal*, 27 June 1994, p. A-10.
25. Ralph Nader, 'WTO Means Rule by Unaccountable Tribunals', *The Wall Street Journal*, 17 August 1994, p. A-4.
26. 'No End of Woe at the WTO?' *The Economist*, 4 February 1995, p. 59.

The Political Environment

Chapter Outline

Chapter Learning Objectives

What you should learn from Chapter 3

- The political environment for foreign investment and the factors that affect stability.

- The importance of the political system to international marketing and its effect on foreign investors.

- What is political risk?

- The risks and controls associated with investments in foreign markets.

- How political vulnerability can be assessed and reduced.

- The means of protecting an investment in a foreign market.

- Alternatives to loss of markets through political instability.

- How to manage external affairs.

One of the most undeniable and crucial realities of doing business in a foreign country is that both the host and home governments are partners. Every country has the recognized right to grant or withhold permission to do business within its political boundaries and to control where its citizens conduct business. A government controls and restricts a company's activities by encouraging and offering support or by discouraging and banning its activities—depending on the pleasure of the government. A country's overall goals for its economic, political and social systems form the base for the political environment. Thus, the political climate in a country is a critical concern for the international marketer.[1]

A government reacts to its environment by initiating and pursuing policies deemed necessary to solve the problems created by its particular environment. National environments differ widely. Some countries are economically developed, some underdeveloped; some countries have an abundance of resources, others few or none; some countries are content with the *status quo*, others seek drastic changes to improve their relative positions in the world community.[2] Reflected in its policies and attitudes towards business are a government's ideas of how best to promote the national interest, considering its own resources and political philosophy. The government is an integral part of every foreign and domestic business activity—a silent partner with nearly total control. Thus, a multinational firm is affected by the political environment of the home country as well as the host country.

The ideal political climate for a multinational firm is a stable and friendly government. Unfortunately, governments are not always friendly and stable, nor do friendly, stable governments remain so; changes in attitudes and goals can cause a stable and friendly situation to become risky. Changes are brought about by any number of events: a radical shift in the government when a political party with a philosophy different from the one it replaces ascends to power, government response to pressure from nationalist and self-interest groups, weakened economic conditions that cause a government to recant trade commitments or an increasing bias against foreign investment. Since foreign businesses are judged by standards as variable as there are countries, the friendliness and stability of the government in each one must be assessed as an ongoing business practice. In so doing, a manager is better able to anticipate and plan for change and to know the boundaries within which the company can successfully operate. This chapter explores some of the more salient political considerations in assessing world markets.

STABILITY OF GOVERNMENT POLICIES

At the top of the list of political conditions that concern foreign businesses is the stability or instability of prevailing government policies. Governments might change or new political parties might be elected, but the concern of the multinational corporation (MNC) is the continuity of the set of rules or code of behaviour—regardless of which government is in power. A change in government, whether by elections or coups, does not always mean a change in the level of political risk. In Italy, for example, there have been more than 50 different governments formed since the end of World War II.[3] While the political turmoil in Italy continues, business goes on as usual.

Conversely, radical changes in policies towards foreign business can occur in the most stable governments. In Mexico, the same political party, the Institutional Revolutionary Party (PRI), has been in control for almost 70 years, yet during that period political risk for foreign investors has ranged from expropriation to Mexico's membership in the North American Free Trade Agreement (NAFTA) and an open door for foreign investment and trade.[4]

If there is potential for profit and if permitted to operate within a country, companies can function under any type of government as long as there is some long-run predictability and stability. PepsiCo operated profitably in the Soviet Union under one of the most extreme political systems. Years before the era of *glasnost* and *perestroika* in the 1980s and the disintegration of the Communist Party, PepsiCo established a very profitable business with the USSR by exchanging Pepsi syrup for Russian vodka. Socioeconomic and political environments invariably change, as they did in the USSR, both within the home and host countries. These changes are often brought about or reflected in changes in political philosophy and/or a surge in feelings of nationalistic pride.

Political Parties

Particularly important to the marketer is knowledge of the philosophies of all major political parties within the country, because any one of them might come into power and alter prevailing attitudes. In those countries where there are two strong political parties that typically succeed one another in control of the government, it is important to know the direction each party is likely to take. In the United Kingdom, for example, the Labour Party has traditionally tended to be more restrictive on foreign trade than the Conservative Party. The Labour Party, when in control, has limited imports, while the Conservative Party has tended to liberalize foreign trade when it is in power. However, New Labour, after winning the elections in 1997, has behaved differently.

Unpredictable and drastic shifts in government policies deter investments, whatever the cause of the shift. As a result of the Chinese government's hard-line response to the student rebellion in 1989 at Tiananmen Square in Beijing, questions of stability caused many firms to postpone future investments and put those already under way on hold. The government was not overthrown and, when stability was reestablished, businesses resumed investments.[5] Although there are business opportunities in the former republics of the USSR, the uncertainty of the direction of some of them makes political knowledge a crucial aspect of market analysis. In short, an assessment of political philosophy and attitudes is important in gauging the stability and attractiveness of a government in terms of market potential.

Nationalism

Economic nationalism, which exists to some degree within all countries, is another factor leading to an unfavourable business climate. *Nationalism* can best be described as an intense feeling of national pride and unity, an awakening of a nation's people to pride in their country. Public opinion often tends to become anti-foreign business, and many minor harassments and controls of foreign investment are supported, if not applauded. Economic nationalism has, as one of its central aims, the preservation of national economic autonomy in that residents identify their interests with the preservation of the sovereignty of the state in which they reside. In other words, national interest and security are more important than international consideration.

These feelings of nationalism can be manifest in a variety of ways including 'buy our country's products only', restrictions on imports, restrictive tariffs and other barriers to trade. They may also lead to control over foreign investment which is often regarded with suspicion and may be the object of intense scrutiny and control.[6] Generally speaking, the more a country feels threatened by some outside force, the more nationalistic it becomes in protecting itself against the intrusion.[7]

During the period after World War II when many new countries were founded and many others were seeking economic independence, manifestations of militant nationalism were rampant. Expropriation of foreign companies, restrictive investment policies and nationalization of industries were common practices in some parts of the world. This was the period when India imposed such restrictive practices on foreign investments that companies such as Coca-Cola, IBM and many others chose to leave rather than face the uncertainty of a hostile economic climate.[8] In many Latin American countries, similar attitudes prevailed and led to expropriations and even confiscation of foreign investment.

The World Bank reported that between 1960 and 1980 a total of 1535 firms from 22 different capital-exporting countries had been expropriated in 511 separate actions by 76 nations. By the late 1980s, that level of militant nationalism had subsided and, today, the foreign investor, once feared as a dominant tyrant that threatened economic development, is often sought after as a source of needed capital investment. Nationalism comes and goes as conditions and attitudes change, and foreign companies welcome today may be harassed tomorrow and vice versa.[9]

While militant economic nationalism has subsided, nationalistic feelings can be found even in the most economically prosperous countries. Nationalism became an issue when Norwegian people said 'NO' to the membership of the European Union in a referendum. The United Kingdom has been reluctant to adopt the single European currency (the euro) for the same reasons.

It is important to appreciate that no nation-state, however secure, will tolerate penetration by a foreign company into its market and economy if it perceives a social, cultural or economic threat to its well-being.[10]

POLITICAL RISKS

The kinds of political risks confronting a company range from confiscation through many lesser but still significant government activities such as exchange controls, import restrictions and price controls. The most severe political risk is confiscation—seizing a company's assets without payment. The most notable expropriation occurred when the Shah of Iran was overthrown and all Western investments were taken over by the new government. Less drastic, but still severe, is expropriation, requiring some reimbursement for the government-seized investment. A third type of risk is domestication, when host countries take steps to transfer foreign investments to national control and ownership through a series of government decrees. Governments seek to domesticate foreign-held assets by mandating:

- A transfer of ownership in part or totally to nationals.
- The promotion of a large number of nationals to higher levels of management.
- Greater decision-making powers resting with nationals. For example, a number of countries demand that the foreign companies can enter their market only through minority joint ventures.
- A greater number of component products locally produced. For example, a number of countries demand that a product must contain 60 per cent of its content to be produced in the country to be classified as a local product and to avoid taxes or quotas.
- Specific export regulations designed to dictate participation in world markets. For example, a number of countries, such as China, demand that foreign firms investing in China must export a certain proportion of its production.

A combination or all of these mandates are issued over a period of time and eventually control is shifted to nationals. The ultimate goal of domestication is to force foreign investors

GOING INTERNATIONAL 3.1

BENEFITS OF PRIVATIZATION

After having privatized, and selling off its mobile telephone operations (TIM), Telecom Italia ended the financial year 1995 with a turnover of L.30 088 billion. A gross operating margin of L.16 070 billion and a net profit of L.1745 billion (up 23 per cent from 1994). Its turnover, profits and dividends are expected to be running even stronger for 1996. The first quarter turnover L.7200 billion indicated this upward trend. The winning strategy was based on supplying innovative services and on a watchful pricing policy. The reduction of a number of international rates and tariffs led to a 14 per cent increase in traffic. TIM, the new wireless communication company that has taken over the mobile telephone operations previously run by Telecom, has shown a net profit of L.350 billion on a turnover of L.2800 billion for the first five months. The turnover for 1995 amounted to L.5290 billion (up 43 per cent from 1994). The subscribers grew from 2.2 million to 3.9 million in 1995 (up 73 per cent). TIM claims to be the largest cellphone operator in Europe and third largest in the world. In June 1996, it has approximately 4.5 million subscribers and quotes one of the highest annual growth rates in the world.

Source: Samuel Huntington, *The Clash of Civilizations and the Remaking of the World Order* (New York: Simon & Schuster, 1996).

to share more of the ownership and management with nationals than was the case before domestication.

A change in government attitudes, policies, economic plans and/or philosophy towards the role of foreign investment in national economic and social goals is behind the decision to confiscate, expropriate or domesticate existing foreign assets. Risks of confiscation and expropriation have lessened over the last decade because experience has shown that few of the desired benefits materialized after government takeover. Rather than a quick answer to economic development, expropriation and nationalization often led to nationalized businesses that were inefficient, technologically weak and noncompetitive in world markets. Today, countries that are concerned that foreign investments may not be in harmony with social and economic goals often require prospective investors to agree to share ownership, local content, labour and management agreements and participation in export sales as a condition of entry.

As the world has become more economically interdependent and it has become obvious that much of the economic success of countries such as South Korea, Singapore and Taiwan are tied to foreign investments, countries are viewing foreign investment as a means of economic growth. Countries throughout the world that only a few years ago restricted or forbade foreign investments are now courting them as a much-needed source of capital and technology. Additionally, they have begun to privatize telecommunications, broadcasting, airlines, banks and other nationally owned companies.

The benefits of privatizing are many. In Sweden, for example, privatization of the national telephone company resulted in almost immediate benefits when the government received hundreds of millions of dollars of much-needed capital from the sale. In addition, the market was open for competition which brought a lot of benefits for consumers. A similar scenario is being played out in The Netherlands, Brazil, Argentina, India and many Eastern European countries. Ironically, many of the businesses that were expropriated and nationalized earlier are now being privatized.

Political risk is still an important issue despite a more positive attitude towards MNCs and foreign investment. The transformation of China, the Commonwealth of Independent States

Figure 3.1   Factors Influencing the Risk Reduction Process in International Marketing

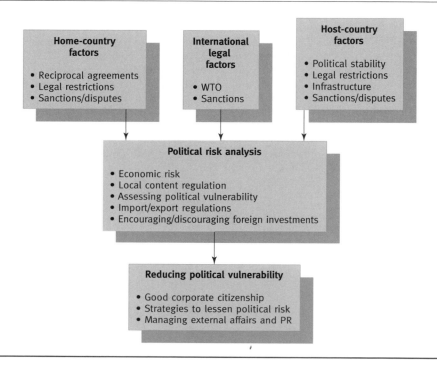

(CIS), and Eastern Europe from Marxist–socialist economies to free market economies is a reality. However, during the transition, companies are facing political and economic uncertainty, currency conversion restrictions, unresponsive bureaucrats and other kinds of political risks. (See Figure 3.1.)

Economic Risks

Even though expropriation and confiscation are waning in importance as a risk of doing business abroad, international companies are still confronted with a variety of economic risks often imposed with little warning. Restraints on business activity may be imposed under the banner of national security, to protect an infant industry, to conserve scarce foreign exchange, to raise revenue, to retaliate against unfair trade practices and a score of other real or imagined reasons. These economic risks are an important and recurring part of the political environment that few international companies can avoid.

Exchange Controls.   Exchange controls stem from shortages of foreign exchange held by a country. When a nation faces shortages of foreign exchange, controls may be levied over all movements of capital or, selectively, against the most politically vulnerable companies to conserve the supply of foreign exchange for the most essential uses. A recurrent problem for the foreign investor is getting profits and investments into the currency of the home country.

Exchange controls are also extended to products by applying a system of multiple exchange rates to regulate trade in specific commodities classified as necessities or luxuries. Necessary products are placed in the most favourable (low) exchange categories, while luxuries are heavily penalized with high foreign-exchange rates. Venezuela, for example, once had a three-tiered exchange rate system to protect scarce foreign reserves. Depending on the transaction, the bolivar had a value in US dollars of 6.5 cents for essential goods, 3.4 cents for nonessential goods, and 0.01 cent for unapproved transactions. A number of Eastern European countries have had multiple exchanges rates. South Africa has also until recently had this type of exchange rate for its rand.

Currency convertibility is a continuing problem because most countries maintain regulations for control of currency, and in the event an economy should suffer an economic setback or foreign exchange reserves suffer severely the controls on convertibility are imposed quickly. At the time when the Eastern bloc, countries of the former Soviet Union and Eastern Europe, opened their economies most foreign firms were reluctant to do business in these markets due to the nonconvertibility of their currencies.

Local-Content Laws.   In addition to restricting imports of essential supplies to force local purchase, countries often require a portion of any product sold within the country to have local content, that is, to contain locally made parts. This is often imposed on foreign companies that assemble products from foreign-made components. Local-content requirements are not restricted to developing countries. The European Union has had a local-content requirement as high as 45–60 per cent for 'screwdriver operations', a name often given to foreign-owned assemblers such as Japanese motor vehicle assembly plants in the United Kingdom.

Import Restrictions.   Selective restrictions on the import of raw materials, machines and spare parts are fairly common strategies to force foreign industry to purchase more supplies within the host country and thereby create markets for local industry. Although this is done in an attempt to support the development of domestic industry, the result is often to hamstring and sometimes interrupt the operations of established industries. The problem then becomes critical when there are no adequately developed sources of supply within the country.

Tax Controls.   Taxes must be classified as a political risk when used as a means of controlling foreign investments. In such cases, they are raised without warning and in violation of formal agreements. A squeeze on profits results from taxes being raised significantly as a business becomes established. In those developing countries where the economy is constantly threatened with a shortage of funds, unreasonable taxation of successful foreign investments appeals to some governments as the handiest and quickest means of finding operating funds.

Price Controls.   Essential products that command considerable public interest, such as pharmaceuticals, food, petrol and cars, are often subjected to price controls. Such controls applied during inflationary periods can be used by a government to control the cost of living. They may also be used to force foreign companies to sell equity to local interests. A side-effect to the local economy can be to slow or even stop capital investment.

Labour Problems.   In many countries, labour unions have strong government support that they use effectively in obtaining special concessions from business. Layoffs may be forbidden, profits may have to be shared and an extraordinary number of services may have to be provided. In fact, in many countries, foreign firms are considered fair game for the demands of the domestic labour supply. In some countries, the belief in full employment is almost religious in fervour; layoffs of any size, especially by foreign-owned companies, are regarded as national crises.

Political Sanctions

In addition to economic risks, companies may be caught in the crossfire of political disputes between countries or between political factions within a country and become unwitting victims of political reprisals. For political reasons, one country may boycott another, thereby stopping all trade between them. The United Nations imposed sanctions on Iraq after the Gulf War and forbade all countries to trade with Iraq. Social issues may also be a basis for restricting trade to a country as was the case in South Africa when several countries boycotted it to force it to eliminate apartheid. Once apartheid was renounced, boycotts were lifted and business resumed, but during the years the boycott was in force MNCs were denied operating in that market.[11]

ENCOURAGING FOREIGN INVESTMENT

Governments also encourage foreign investment. In fact, within the same country, some foreign businesses fall prey to politically induced harassment while others may be placed under a government umbrella of protection and preferential treatment. The difference lies in the evaluation of a company's contribution to the national interest.

Foreign Governments

The most important reason to encourage foreign investment is to accelerate the development of an economy. An increasing number of countries are encouraging foreign investment with specific guidelines aimed towards economic goals. Multinational corporations may be expected to create local employment, transfer technology, generate export sales, stimulate growth and development of local industry and/or conserve foreign exchange as a requirement for market concessions.[12] Recent investments in China, India and the former republics of the USSR include provisions stipulating specific contributions to economic goals of the country that must be made by foreign investors.[13]

The most recent trend in India, however, has been towards dropping preconditions for entry and liberalizing requirements in order to encourage further investment. In just the few years between the time Pepsi-Cola was given permission to enter the Indian market and the Coca-Cola Company reentered, requirements were eased considerably.[14]

Pepsi was restricted to a minority position (40 per cent) in a joint venture. In addition, Pepsi was required to develop an agricultural research centre to produce high-yielding seed varieties, construct and operate a snack-food processing plant and a vegetable processing plant, and, among other foreign exchange requirements, guarantee that export revenues would be five times greater than money spent on imports. Pepsi agreed to these conditions and by 1994 had captured 26 per cent of the Indian soft drink market. In contrast, when Coke reentered the Indian market a few years later, requirements for entry were minimal. Unlike Pepsi, Coca-Cola was able to have 100 per cent ownership of its subsidiary.[15]

Along with direct encouragement from a host country, a Western company may receive

COKE'S BACK AND STILL HAS THE SECRET

For 91 years, the formula for making Coca-Cola has been a closely guarded secret. Then the government of India ordered Coca-Cola to disclose it or cease operations in that country. A secret ingredient called 7-X supposedly gives Coke its distinctive flavour. The government's minister for industry told the Indian parliament that Coca-Cola's Indian branch would have to transfer 60 per cent of its equity shares to Indians and hand over its know-how by April 1978 or shut down. Indian sales accounted for less than 1 per cent of Coca-Cola's worldwide sales. The potential market in India, a country of 800 million, is tremendous.

The government refused to let the branch import the necessary ingredients, and Coke—once as abundant as bottled drinking water and sold in almost every Indian town of more than 50 000—packed up their bags and left the country. The minister for industry said that Coca-Cola activities in India ' . . . furnish a classic example of how multinational corporations operating in a low-priority, high-profit area in a developing country attain run-away growth and . . . trifle with the weaker indigenous industry'. Coke said they wouldn't give up the formula and India said they had to leave.

Sixteen years later, India's attitudes towards foreign investment changed and Coke reentered the market without having to divulge its formula. During Coke's 16-year exile, however, Pepsi Cola came to India and captured a 26 per cent market share. Not to worry, there is plenty of market for both considering India's per capita consumption is just three eight-ounce bottles a year, versus about 12 for Pakistan and 731 in the United States.

Sources: 'Indian Government Rejects Coke's Bid to Sell Soft Drinks', *The Wall Street Journal*, 16 March 1990, p. B-5; and 'Coke Adds Fizz to India', *Fortune*, 10 January 1994, pp. 14–15.

assistance from its home government. The intent is to encourage investment by helping to minimize and shift some of the risks encountered in some foreign markets. A number of other facilities are often also available such as export credit guarantee.

In addition to governments sponsoring political risk insurance, private sources such as Lloyd's of London will issue insurance against political risk but at a substantially higher cost. Also, a number of companies specialize in export credit guarantees and consultancy services.

ASSESSING POLITICAL VULNERABILITY

Some products appear to be more politically vulnerable than others, in that they receive special government attention. This special attention may result in positive actions towards the company or in negative attention, depending on the desirability of the product. It is not unusual for countries seeking investments in high-priority industries to excuse companies from taxes, customs duties, quotas, exchange controls and other impediments to investment.

Conversely, firms marketing products not considered high priority or that fall from favour often face unpredictable government restrictions. Continental Can Company's joint venture to manufacture cans for the Chinese market faced a barrage of restrictions when the Chinese economy weakened. China decreed that canned beverages were wasteful and must be banned from all state functions and banquets. Tariffs on aluminium and other materials imported for producing cans were doubled and a new tax was imposed on canned drink consumption. An investment that had the potential for profit after a few years was rendered profitless by a change in the attitude of the Chinese government.

Politically Sensitive Products

There are at least as many reasons for a product's political vulnerability as there are political philosophies, economic variations and cultural differences. Unfortunately, there are no absolute guidelines a marketer can follow to determine whether or not a product will be subject to political attention. But, by answering the following questions a marketer may detect clues to a product's vulnerability.

1. Is the availability of supply of the product ever subject to important political debates (sugar, salt, petrol, public utilities, medicines, food stuffs)?
2. Do other industries depend on the production of the product (cement, power machine tools, construction machinery, steel)?
3. Is the product considered socially or economically essential (key drugs, laboratory equipment, medicines)?
4. Is the product essential to agricultural industries (farm tools and machinery, crops, fertilizers, seed)?
5. Does the product affect national defence capabilities (transportation, industry, communications)?
6. Does the product include important components that would be available from local sources and that otherwise would not be used as effectively (labour, skills, materials)?
7. Is there local competition or potential local competition from manufacturers in the near future (small, low-investment manufacturing)?
8. Does the product relate to channels of mass communication (newsprint, radio equipment)?
9. Is the product primarily a service?
10. Does the use of the product, or its design, rest on some legal requirements?
11. Is the product potentially dangerous to the user (explosives, drugs)?
12. Does the product induce a net drain on scarce foreign exchange?[16]

Depending on the answers and the particular philosophy of those in power at the time, a company might expect to receive favourable political attention if it contributed to the achievement of national goals or, conversely, unfavourable attention if it were nonessential in view of current national needs. For products judged nonessential, the risk would be great, but for those thought to be making an important contribution, encouragement and special considerations could be available.

Forecasting Political Risk

In addition to qualitative measures of political vulnerability, a number of firms are employing systematic methods of measuring political risk.[17] Political risk assessment is an attempt to forecast political instability to help management identify and evaluate political events and their potential influence on current and future international business decisions. Political risk assessment can:

- Help managers decide if risk insurance is necessary.
- Devise an intelligence network and an early warning system.
- Help managers develop contingency plans for unfavourable future political events.
- Build a database of past political events for use by corporate management.

- Interpret the data gathered by its intelligence network to advise and forewarn corporate decision makers about political and economic situations.

Risk assessment is used not only to determine whether to make an investment in a country, but also to determine the amount of risk a company is prepared to accept. In the Commonwealth of Independent States (CIS) and China the risk may be too high for some companies, but stronger and better financed companies can make long-term investments that will be profitable in the future. Early risk is accepted in exchange for being in the country when the economy begins to grow and risk subsides.

During the chaos that arose in 1991 after the political and economic changes in the USSR, the newly formed republics were anxious to make deals with foreign investors, yet the problems and uncertainty made many investors take a wait-and-see attitude. Certainly the many companies that are investing in the CIS or China do not expect big returns immediately; they are betting on the future. The unfortunate situation is with the company that does not assess the risk properly. After making a sizeable initial investment they realize they are not financially able to bear all the future risks and costs while waiting for more prosperous times, so they lose their capital. Better political risk analysis might have helped them make the decision not to go into the market, but to make an investment in a country with more predictability and less risk (see Figure 3.2).

There are a variety of methods used to measure political risk. They range from in-house political analysts to external sources that specialize in analysing political risk. Presently, all methods are far from being perfected; however, the very fact a company attempts to systematically examine the problem is significant.

For a marketer doing business in a foreign country, a necessary part of any market analysis is an assessment of the probable political consequences of a marketing plan—some marketing activities are more susceptible to political considerations than others. Basically, it boils down to evaluating the essential nature of the immediate activity. The following section explores ways businesses can reduce political vulnerability.

REDUCING POLITICAL VULNERABILITY

Even though a company cannot directly control or alter the political environment of the country within which it operates, there are measures that can lessen the degree of susceptibility of a specific business venture to politically induced risks. Foreign investors are frequently accused of exploiting a country's wealth at the expense of the national population and for the sole benefit of the foreign investor.

These charges are not wholly unsupported by past experiences, but today's enlightened investor is seeking a return on investment commensurate with the risk involved. To achieve such a return, hostile and generally unfounded fears must be overcome. Countries, especially the less developed ones, fear foreign investment for many reasons. They fear the multinationals' interest is only to exploit their labour, markets or raw materials and to leave nothing behind except the wealthy who become wealthier.

Good Corporate Citizenship

As long as such fears persist, the political climate for foreign investors will continue to be hostile. Are there ways of allaying these fears? A list of suggestions made years ago is still appropriate for a company that intends to be a good corporate citizen and thereby minimize its political vulnerability. A company is advised to remember:

Figure 3.2   Political Risk Ratings

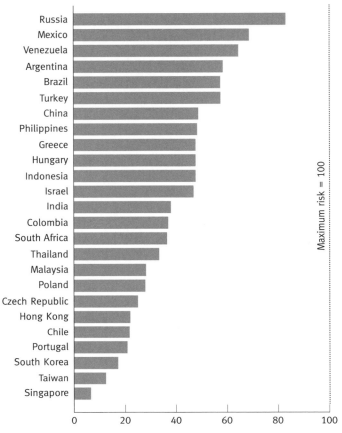

Note: The chart shows the risk ratings based on economic and political factors. Although Russia is shown as the riskiest country, we believe it has become much safer in 1997. Same goes for Indonesia, where the political situation has improved after the general elections.

Source: 'EIU Country Risk Service', *The Economist*, 7 December 1996, p. 120.

1. It is a guest in the country and should act accordingly.
2. The profits of an enterprise are not solely any company's; the local national employees and the economy of the country should also benefit.
3. It is not wise to try to win over new customers by completely Westernizing them.
4. Although English is an accepted language overseas, a fluency in the local language goes far in making sales and cementing good public relations.
5. It should try to contribute to the country's economy and culture with worthwhile public projects.
6. It should train its executives and their families to act appropriately in the foreign environment.
7. It is best not to conduct business from the home office, but to staff foreign offices with competent nationals and supervise the operation from the head office.

Table 3.1 The MNCs Publics and Issues

Publics	Issues*
Church	Nationalism
Labour	Industrial democracy
Suppliers	Environment protection
Customers	Energy and raw materials
Competitors	Taxes
Pressure groups	Incentives and restrictions
Shareholders	Investment approvals and permits
Academia	Personnel relations
General public	Attracting personnel
Minority groups	Mergers and acquisitions
Public media	Money and credit
Governments and agencies	Legitimacy
Conservationists	Prices and profits
Financial community	Image (company and product)
	Consumerism
	Women's liberation
	Union relations
	Equal opportunities

*The issues do not correspond with the publics listed.
Source: Adapted from 'How Embattled MNCs Can Devise Strategies for External Affairs', *Business International*, 12 December 1975, p. 394.

Many companies survive even the most hostile environments; through their operating methods, they have been able to minimize their political vulnerability. There is certainly much to be said for attempting to become more closely identified with the ideals and desires of the host country. To do so might render a marketer's activities and products less politically vulnerable; and, although it would not eliminate all the risks of the political environment, it might reduce the likelihood and frequency of some politically motivated risks. In addition to being good citizens, responsive to various publics (see Table 3.1), there are other approaches that help minimize the effects of hostile political environments.[18]

Strategies to Lessen Political Risk

In addition to corporate activities focused on the social and economic goals of the host country and good corporate citizenship, MNCs can use other strategies to minimize political vulnerability and risk.

Joint Ventures. Typically less susceptible to political harassment, joint ventures can be with either locals or other third-country multinational companies; in both cases, a company's financial exposure is limited. A joint venture with locals helps minimize anti-MNC feelings, and a joint venture with another MNC adds the additional bargaining power of a third country.

It is also a preferred entry strategy in countries with relatively higher political risk. This has been the main reason that most foreign firms are entering former Eastern bloc markets through joint ventures, as illustrated by Table 3.2.

Table 3.2   Registered Joint Ventures in Selected Eastern European Countries

Country	Registered Joint Ventures		
	1989	1992	1994
Bulgaria	35	239	2 185
Czech & Slovak Republics	50	3 000	10 700
Hungary	600	11 000	15 205
Poland	400	5 286	17 577
Romania	9 327	9 327	30 441
Russia (CIS)	1 000	2 600	30 187
Former Yugoslavia	1 100	2 669	n.a.
Total	12 512	34 121	106 295

Source: Based on Van Berendonk, Oosterveer and Associates, 1992, ECE, East-Western Joint Ventures, No. 31989, and ECE, *East-Western Investment News*, No. 3/4/4, 1994.

Expanding the Investment Base.   Including several investors and banks in financing an investment in the host country is another strategy. This has the advantage of engaging the power of the banks whenever any kind of government takeover or harassment is threatened. This strategy becomes especially powerful if the banks have made loans to the host country; if the government threatens expropriation or other types of takeover, the financing bank has substantial power with the government.

Marketing and Distribution.   Controlling distribution in world markets can be used effectively if an investment should be expropriated; the expropriating country would lose access to world markets. This has proved especially useful for MNCs in the extractive industries where world markets for iron ore, copper and so forth are crucial to the success of the investment. Peru found that when Marcona Mining Company was expropriated, the country lost access to iron-ore markets around the world and ultimately had to deal with Marcona on a much more favourable basis than first thought possible.

Licensing.   A strategy some firms find that eliminates almost all risks is to license technology for a fee. It can be effective in situations where the technology is unique and the risk is high. Of course, there is some risk assumed because the licensee can refuse to pay the required fees while continuing to use the technology.

Planned Domestication.   The strategies just discussed can be effective in forestalling or minimizing the effect of a total takeover. However, in those cases where an investment is being domesticated by the host country, the most effective long-range solution is planned phasing out, that is, *planned domestication*. This is not the preferred business practice, but the alternative of government-initiated domestication can be as disastrous as confiscation. As a reasonable response to the potential of domestication, planned domestication can be profitable and operationally expedient for the foreign investor. Planned domestication is, in essence, a gradual process of participating with nationals in all phases of company operations.

Initial investment planning provides for eventual sale of a significant interest (perhaps even controlling interest) to nationals and incorporation of national economic needs and national managerial talent into the business as quickly as possible. Such a policy is more likely to result in reasonable control remaining with the parent company even though nationals would hold

GOING INTERNATIONAL 3.3

LICENSING DESIGNS ON FIVE CONTINENTS

V&A Enterprises, the commercial arm of Victoria & Albert Museum, launched its licensing initiative—Inspiring Design—in November 1994. Under this drive it can license 'William Morris' prints on fabrics and wallpapers designed in 1870, for desks and covers for note pads and other stationery items. These and other designs from the museum's decorative art archives, which consist of more than 50 million objects, are now being licensed all over the world. According to Ken Mannering, head of licensing at V&A, 'What we are doing is exporting a brand. Over the past few years we have realized that we are much more than a picture library and that there is a great deal of marketing potential.' By mid 1995 V&A had given 78 licences in 12 countries which accounted for a worldwide sales of licensed products of £30 million.

The licensing operations represent 35 per cent of the turnover of commercial operations which is expected to double in a couple of years. The profits earned are ploughed back into the museum. Under the agreement the licensees are charged a royalty of between 3 and 10 per cent on every product. V&A is planning to establish links with companies in which a long-term relationship is possible. V&A is proactive in looking for overseas agents in Japan and the USA where the company has opened its own offices. It is currently looking for an agent in South-east Asia, a market seen as having great potential. The company has its own research team and does research into looks and designs, invites licensees to see the original objects and to get their input. The same design is offered only to one company and there is a strict approval process for the selection of licensees. For example, Royal Selanger International, the Malaysian pewter manufacturer, has signed to produce tableware and jewellery collections to be sold under the V&A brand name. Under the licensing agreement it will make a range of products using the museum's designs. Royal Selanger's business is rooted in Malaysia, Australia, UK, Hong Kong, Singapore, Canada and the USA.

Source: 'FT Exporter', *Financial Times*, Autumn 1995, p. 19.

important positions in management and ownership. Company-trained nationals would be more likely to have a strong corporate point of view than a national perspective.

Local suppliers developed over a period of time could ultimately handle a significant portion of total needs, thus meeting government demands for local content. Further, a sound, sensible plan to sell ownership over a number of years would ensure a fair and equitable return on investment in addition to encouraging ownership throughout the populace. Finally, if government concessions and incentives essential in early stages of investment were rendered economically unnecessary, the company's political vulnerability would be lessened considerably.

Today, the climate for foreign investment is more positive than a decade ago, so planned domestication may not be necessary. Many countries, open to foreign investment, impose requirements similar to those discussed in planned domestication as a precondition for entry.

Political Payoffs

One approach to dealing with political vulnerability is the *political payoff*—an attempt to lessen political risks by paying those in power to intervene on behalf of the multinational company. Political payoffs or bribery have been used to lessen the negative effects of a variety of problems. Paying heads of state to avoid confiscatory taxes or expulsion, paying fees to agents to ensure the acceptance of sales contracts, and providing monetary encouragement to an assortment of people whose actions can affect the effectiveness of a company's programmes are decisions that frequently confront multinational managers and raise ethical questions.

THE LOSER WINS WHEN MAH-JONGG AND BRIBERY MEET

A fashionable way of disguising bribes, payoffs or gifts in both business and political circles in Japan is to purposely lose when playing Mah-Jongg or golf. If you can lose skilfully, your services may be in demand. Losing at Mah-Jongg and golf are classic examples of indirect but preferred ways the Japanese use when it comes to greasing palms.

Mah-Jongg is a Chinese table game played with ivory tiles, having rules similar to gin rummy. Gambling is a minor crime in Japan, whereas bribery is a major one. To skirt the law, Japanese business people invite officials or others to a discreet high-class restaurant or club that provides a salon for private Mah-Jongg games. Executives of the host company bring along young employees noted for their abilities to deftly lead their opponent to a successful win at a substantial loss for themselves. If your guests prefer golf to Mah-Jongg, no problem. They can have a golf game with the company's 'reverse pro', that is, a duffer who specializes in hooking and slicing his way to sure defeat.

Source: Adapted from 'Those Who Lose Really Win in Japan; The Fine Art of Mah-Jongg as Bribery', *The Wall Street Journal*, 20 January 1984, p. 28. Reprinted by permission of The Wall Street Journal, $CG 1984 Dow Jones & Company, Inc. All Rights Reserved Worldwide.

Bribery poses problems for the marketer at home and abroad. It is illegal to pay a bribe even if it is a common practice in the host country. Further, in most countries, once exposed, those involved are punished.[19] There may be short-run benefits to political payoffs, but, in the long run, the risks are high and bribery should be avoided.

MANAGING EXTERNAL AFFAIRS

Companies manage external affairs in foreign markets to ensure that the host government and the public are aware of their contributions to the economic, social or human development of the country.

Government–MNC relations are generally positive if the investment (1) improves the balance of payments by increasing exports or reducing imports through import substitution, (2) uses locally produced resources, (3) transfers capital, technology and/or skills, (4) creates jobs and/or (5) makes tax contributions.

An external affairs programme, however well designed and executed, is never better than the behaviour of the company. Regardless of how well multinational companies lessen political vulnerability through investment and business decisions, a task they all face is maintaining a positive public image where they do business. Faced with growing anti-Japanese sentiment in the 1980s and early 1990s, Japanese companies with US subsidiaries, such as Honda and Toyota, mounted an extensive advertising campaign to promote an all-American image for their US operations.

Most companies today strive to become good corporate citizens in their host countries, but because of overheated feelings of nationalism, or political parties seeking publicity or scapegoats for their own failures, the negative aspects of MNCs, whether true or false, are the ones that frequently reach the public. The only effective defence for the multinational company is to actively tell its own story. As one authority states: 'Passivity is passé. It is high time for a high profile'.

SUMMARY

Vital to every marketer's assessment of a foreign market is an appreciation for the political environment of the country within which he or she plans to operate. Government involvement in business activities, especially foreign-controlled business, is generally much greater than business is accustomed to in the West. The foreign firm must strive to make its activities politically acceptable or it may be subjected to a variety of politically condoned harassment.

In addition to the harassment that can be imposed by a government, the foreign marketer frequently faces the problem of uncertainty of continuity in government policy. As governments change political philosophies, a marketing firm accepted under one administration may find its activities completely undesirable under another. The EU may aid European business in its foreign operations, and if a company is considered vital to achieving national economic goals, the host country often provides an umbrella of protection not extended to others. An unfamiliar or hostile political environment does not necessarily preclude success for a foreign marketer if the marketer's plans are such that the company becomes a local economic asset.

QUESTIONS

1. Why would a country rather domesticate than expropriate?
2. How can government-initiated domestication be the same as confiscation?
3. 'A crucial fact when doing business in a foreign country is that permission to conduct business is controlled by the government of the host country.' Comment.
4. What are the main factors to consider in assessing the dominant political climate within a country?
5. Why is a working knowledge of political party philosophy so important in a political assessment of a market? Discuss.
6. Discuss how governmental instability can affect marketing.
7. What are the most frequently encountered political risks in foreign business? Discuss.
8. How do exchange controls impede foreign business? Discuss.
9. What are the factors that influence the risk reduction process in international marketing?
10. Discuss measures a company might take to lessen its political vulnerability.
11. Select a country and analyse it politically from a marketing viewpoint.
12. There is evidence that expropriation and confiscation are less frequently encountered today than just a few years ago. Why? What other types of political risks have replaced expropriation and confiscation in importance?

REFERENCES

1. For an account of political change and potential effect on economic growth, see 'China: Is Prosperity Creating a Freer Society?' *Business Week*, 6 June 1994, pp. 94–99.

2. Jean J. Boddewyn and Thomas L. Brewer, 'International-Business Political Behavior: New Theoretical Directions', *Academy of Management Review*, vol. 19, no. 1, 1994, pp. 119–143.

3. Niccolo d'Aguino, 'Italy's Political Future', *Europe*, June 1994, pp. 4–8.

4. Lorenzo Meyer, 'A New Chapter in Mexican Politics', *World Press Review*, January 1994, pp. 14–15.

5. 'China Fever Strikes Again', *Business Week*, 29 March 1993, pp. 46–47; and John J. Curran, 'China's Investment Boom', *Fortune*, 7 March 1994, pp. 116–121.

6. Mike Millard, 'Indonesia: Economic Nationalism Still Blocking Badly Needed Foreign Capital', *Tokyo Business Today*, May 1994, pp. 26–29.

7. 'Indonesia: A Risky Turn to the Left? Economic Nationalism May Discourage Foreign Investors', *Fortune*, 3 May 1993, pp. 13–14.

8. Amitaz Ghosh, 'The Mask of Nationalism', *Business India*, 1993 Anniversary Issue, pp. 47–50.

9. Peter J. Buckley and Pervez N. Ghauri (eds), *Multinationals and Emerging Markets: Managing the Increasing Inter-dependence* (Oxford: Pergamon, 1999).

10. Marina V.N.K. Whitman, 'The State of Business: Global Competitiveness and Economic Nationalism', *Harvard International Review*, Summer 1993, pp. 4–7.

11. 'South Africa: Mandela's Early Decisions Will Be Key to Luring Outside Investment', *Business Week*, 16 May 1994, pp. 52–54.

12. Lars Oxeleheim (ed.), *The Global Race for Foreign Direct Investment: Prospects for Future* (Berlin: Springer-Verlag, 1993).

13. Peter J. Buckley and Pervez N. Ghauri (eds), *Multinationals and Emerging Markets* (Oxford: Pergamon, 1999).

14. Sandeep Tyagi, 'The Giant Awakens: An Interview with Professor Jagdish Bhagwatti on Economic Reform in India', *Columbia Journal of World Business*, Spring 1994, pp. 14–23.

15. Rahul Jacob, 'Coke Adds Fizz to India', *Fortune*, 10 January 1994, pp. 14–15.

16. Richard D. Robinson, 'The Challenge of the Underdeveloped National Market', *Journal of Marketing*, October 1961, pp. 24–25. Reprinted from *Journal of Marketing*, published by the American Marketing Association.

17. For a comprehensive review of political risk analysis, see Frederick Stapenhurst, 'Political Risk Analysis in North American Multinationals: An Empirical Review and Assessment', *The International Executive*, March–April 1995, pp. 127–145.

18. For a discussion of problems associated with hostile publics and infrastructure projects, see Amjad Hadjikhani, 'International Businesses and Political Crisis: Swedish MNCs in a Turbulent Market', *Acta Universitatis Uppsaliances*, series Studia Oeconomiae Negotiorum, no. 40, Uppsala, 1996

19. Masayoshi Kanabayashi, 'Scandal Widens at GE Medical Venture in Japan: Four More Arrested as Firm Apologizes for Bribing Officials at University', *The Wall Street Journal*, 1 March 1991, p. A-10.

Chapter Outline

Chapter Learning Objectives

What you should learn from Chapter 4

- The four heritages of today's legal systems.

- The important factors in jurisdiction of international legal disputes.

- The problems of protecting intellectual property rights.

- The legal differences between countries that affect international marketing plans.

- The importance of 'green marketing'.

- The complications for marketers in adhering to European Union laws while marketing internationally.

The legal systems of the world are so disparate and complex it is beyond the scope of this text to explore the laws of each country individually. There are, however, legal problems common to most international marketing transactions that must be given special attention when operating abroad.

Laws governing business activities within and between countries are an integral part of the legal environment of international business. A Japanese company doing business with France has to contend with two jurisdictions (Japan and France), two tax systems, two legal systems and a third supranational set of European Union laws and regulations that may override French commercial law. Because no single, uniform international commercial law governing foreign business transactions exists, the international marketer must pay particular attention to the legal environment of each country within which it operates.

This chapter provides a broad view of the international legal environment with the hope that the reader will appreciate the need for knowledge of all legal systems likely to be encountered and the necessity of securing expert legal advice when doing business in another country.

BASES FOR LEGAL SYSTEMS

Four common heritages form the bases for the majority of the legal systems of the world—Islamic law, derived from the interpretation of the Koran and found in Iran, Saudi Arabia and some other Islamic states; socialist law, derived from the Marxist–socialist system and found in some of the Newly Independent States (NIS) of the former Soviet Union and in China and other Marxist–socialist states; common law, derived from English law and found in England, Australia, the United States, Canada[1] and other countries once under English influence; and civil or code law, derived from Roman law and found in Germany, Japan, France and the remaining non-Islamic and non-Marxist countries. The differences among these four systems are of more than theoretical importance because due process of law may vary considerably among and within these legal systems. Even though a country's laws may be based on one of the four legal systems, its individual interpretation may vary significantly—from a fundamentalist interpretation of Islamic law as found in Iran to a combination of several legal systems found in the United States, where both common and code law are reflected in their laws.

Islamic and Socialist Law.   The basis for the Shari'ah (Islamic law) is the interpretation of the Koran. It encompasses religious duties and obligations as well as the secular aspect of law regulating human acts. Broadly speaking, Islamic law defines a complete system that prescribes specific patterns of social and economic behaviour for all individuals. It includes issues such as property rights, economic decision making and types of economic freedom. The overriding objective of the Islamic system is social justice.

Among the unique aspects of Islamic law is the prohibition against the payment of interest. The Islamic law of contracts states that any given transaction should be devoid of *riba*, defined as the unlawful advantage by way of excess of deferment; that is, interest or usury. Prohibition against the payment of interest impacts on banking practices severely; however, a method for payment for the use of money has been developed by some Islamic banks through an ingenious compromise.[2] Instead of an interest-bearing loan, banks finance trade by buying some of the borrower's stock, which it then sells back to the company at a higher price. The size of the markup is determined by the amount and maturity of the loan and the creditworthiness of the borrower—all traditional yardsticks for determining interest rates. This practice is frowned on by strict fundamentalists, but it is practised and is an example of the way the Islamic law can be reconciled with the laws of non-Islamic legal systems.[3]

Socialist laws, based on the fundamental tenets of the Marxist–socialist state, cluster around the core concept of economic, political and social policies of the state. Marxist–socialist countries are, or were, generally those that formerly had laws derived from the Roman or code-law system. Some of the characteristics of Roman law have been preserved within their legal systems. Although much of the terminology and other similarities of code law have been retained in socialist law, the basic premise on which socialist law is based is that 'law, according to Marxist–socialist tenets, is strictly subordinate to prevailing economic conditions'.[4] Thus, the words property, contract and arbitration denote different realities because of the collectivization of the means of production and state planning.

As socialist countries become more directly involved in trade with non-Marxist countries, laws governing ownership, contracts and other business realities have been developed to reconcile the differences between socialist law and the common or code law that prevails in most of the industrialized world.[5] China, for example, has had to pass laws covering the protection of intellectual property rights, clarifying ownership rights in joint ventures, and other pieces of commercial legislation necessary for international business. Even within existing laws, the interpretation is influenced by the basic tenets of the Marxist–socialist state.

Common and Code Law.   The basis for *common law* is tradition, past practices and legal precedents set by the courts through interpretations of statutes, legal legislation and past rulings. Common law seeks 'interpretation through the past decisions of higher courts which interpret the same statutes or apply established and customary principles of law to a similar set of facts'.

Code law is based on an all-inclusive system of written rules (codes) of law. Under code law, the legal system is generally divided into three separate codes: commercial, civil and criminal. Common law is recognized as not being all-inclusive, while code law is considered complete as a result of catchall provisions found in most code-law systems. For example, under the commercial code in a code-law country, the law governing contracts is made inclusive with the statement that 'a person performing a contract shall do so in conformity with good faith as determined by custom and good morals'. Although code law is considered all-inclusive, it is apparent from the foregoing statement that some broad interpretations are possible in order to include everything under the existing code.

As we discuss later in the section on protection of intellectual property rights, laws governing intellectual property offer the most striking differences between common-law and code-law systems.[6] Under common law, ownership is established by use; under code law, ownership is determined by registration.

Although every country has elements of both common and code law, the differences in interpretation between common- and code-law systems regarding contracts, sales agreements and other legal issues are significant enough that an international marketer familiar with only one system must enlist the aid of legal counsel for the most basic legal questions.

An illustration of where fundamental differences in the two systems can cause difficulty is in the performance of a contract. Under common law in the United States, it is fairly clear that impossibility of performance does not necessarily excuse compliance with the provisions of a contract unless it is impossible to comply for reasons of an act of God, such as some extra-ordinary happening of nature not reasonably anticipated by either party to a contract. Hence, floods, lightning, earthquakes and similar occurrences are generally considered acts of God. Under code law, acts of God are not limited solely to acts of nature but are extended to include

ČESKÉ BUDĚJOVICE, PRIVATIZATION, TRADEMARKS — WHAT DO THEY HAVE IN COMMON WITH ANHEUSER–BUSCH?

Budweiser, that's what!

Anheuser–Busch has launched a massive public relations programme in the small Czech town of České Budějovice where a local brewery produces Budweiser Budvar—no relation to Anheuser–Busch. Their goal is to win support for a minority stake in the Czech state-owned brewery, Budějovic Budvar NP, when the government privatizes it. Trees are being planted along main avenues, a new cultural centre was recently opened offering free English courses to citizens and management advice to budding entrepreneurs, and newspaper ads tout the possibilities of future cooperation.

So why the interest in a brewery whose annual production of 500 000 barrels is the equivalent of two days' output for Anheuser–Busch? Part-ownership is critically important to Anheuser–Busch for two reasons. They are in search of new markets and Europe is their target, and they want to be able to market the Budweiser brand in Europe to achieve a presence there. So what's the connection? They don't have the rights to use the Budweiser brand name in Europe since it is owned by Budějovic Budvar NP, a local brewery in České Budějovice.

Anheuser–Busch established the name Budweiser in the United States when German immigrants founded their St Louis family brewery in the latter part of last century. The Czechs claim they have been using the name since before Columbus discovered the New World, even though they did not legally register it until the 1920s. The Anheuser–Busch Company markets Budweiser brand beer in North America, but in Europe it markets Busch brand beer because the Czechs have the rights to the use of the name Budweiser. The Czech government has given Anheuser–Busch the right to negotiate for a minority stake in Budvar as part of the privatization of the brewery, which claims to have its roots when beer making was licensed by the Bohemian king Otakar II in 1256. If all goes well and Anheuser–Busch is allowed to buy a one-third interest in Budvar, then it will be able to settle the trademark battle over the Czech Budweiser brand.

Sources: Adapted from 'Anheuser–Busch Says Skoal, Salud, Prosit', *Business Week*, 20 September 1993, pp. 76–77; and 'This Bud's for Whom?', *Reuters News Service*, 1 July 1994.

'unavoidable interferences with performance, whether resulting from forces of nature or unforeseeable human acts', including such things as labour strikes and riots.

Consider the following situations: a contract was entered into to deliver a specific quantity of cloth. In one case, before delivery could be made by the seller, an earthquake caused the destruction of the cloth and compliance was then impossible. In a second case, pipes in the sprinkler system where the material was stored froze and broke, spilling water on the cloth and destroying it. In each case, loss of the merchandise was sustained and delivery could not be made. Were the parties in these cases absolved of their obligations under the contract because of the impossibility of delivery? The answer depends on the system of law invoked.

In the first situation, the earthquake would be considered an act of God under both common and code law and impossibility of performance would excuse compliance under the contract. In the second situation, courts in common-law countries would probably rule that the bursting of the water pipes did not constitute an act of God if it happened in a climate where freezing could be expected. Therefore, impossibility of delivery would not necessarily excuse compliance with the provisions of the contract. In code-law countries where the scope of impossibility of performance is extended considerably, the destruction might very well be ruled an act of God, and thus release from compliance with the contract could be obtained.

The international marketer must be concerned with the differences among Islamic, socialist, common-law and code-law systems when operating between countries using different systems; the rights of the principals of a contract or some other legal document under one law may be significantly different from the rights under the other. It should be kept in mind that there can also be differences between the laws of two countries whose laws are based on the same legal system. Thus, the problem of the marketer is one of anticipating the different laws regulating business, regardless of the legal system of the country.

JURISDICTION IN INTERNATIONAL LEGAL DISPUTES

Determining whose legal system has jurisdiction when a commercial dispute arises is another problem of international marketing. A frequent error is to assume that disputes between citizens of different nations are adjudicated under some supranational system of laws. Unfortunately, no judicial body exists to deal with legal commercial problems arising between citizens of different countries. Confusion probably stems from the existence of international courts, such as the World Court in The Hague and the International Court of Justice, the principal judicial organ of the United Nations. These courts are operative in international disputes between sovereign nations of the world rather than between private citizens.

Legal disputes can arise in three situations: (1) between governments; (2) between a company and a government; and (3) between two companies. Disputes between governments can be adjudicated by the World Court, whereas the other two situations must be handled in the courts of the country of one of the parties involved or through arbitration. Unless a commercial dispute involves a national issue between states, it is not handled by the International Court of Justice or any similar world court. Because there is no 'international commercial law', the foreign marketer must look to the legal system of each country involved—the laws of the home country, and/or the laws of the countries within which business is conducted.

When international commercial disputes must be settled under the laws of one of the countries concerned, the paramount question in a dispute is: Which law governs? Jurisdiction is generally determined in one of three ways: (1) on the basis of jurisdictional clauses included in contracts; (2) on the basis of where a contract was entered into; or (3) on the basis of where the provisions of the contract were performed.

The most clear-cut decision can be made when the contracts or legal documents supporting a business transaction include a jurisdictional clause. A clause similar to the following establishes jurisdiction in the event of disagreements:

> That the parties hereby agree that the agreement is made in London, UK, and that
> any question regarding this agreement shall be governed by the law of the United
> Kingdom.

This clause establishes that the UK laws would be invoked should a dispute arise. If the complaint were brought in the court of another country, it is probable that the same law would govern the decision. Cooperation and a definite desire to be judicious in foreign legal problems have led to the practice of foreign courts judging disputes on the basis of the law of another country or state whenever applicable. Thus, if an injured party from the United Kingdom brings suit in the courts of India against an Indian party over a contract that included the preceding clause, it would not be unusual for the Indian courts to decide on the basis of UK law.

LEGAL RECOURSE IN RESOLVING INTERNATIONAL DISPUTES

Should the settlement of a dispute on a private basis become impossible, the foreign marketer must resort to more resolute action. Such action can take the form of conciliation, arbitration or, as a last resort, litigation. Most international business people prefer a settlement through arbitration rather than by suing a foreign company.

Conciliation

Although arbitration is recommended as the best means of settling international disputes, conciliation can be an important first step for resolving commercial disputes. *Conciliation* is a nonbinding agreement between parties to resolve disputes by asking a third party to mediate the differences.

Conciliation is considered to be especially effective when resolving disputes with Chinese business partners because they are less threatened by conciliation than arbitration. The Chinese believe that when a dispute occurs, friendly negotiation should be used first to solve the problem; if that fails, conciliation should be tried. In fact, some Chinese companies may avoid doing business with companies that resort first to arbitration.

Conciliation can be either formal or informal. Informal conciliation can be established by both sides agreeing on a third party to mediate. Formal conciliation is conducted under the auspices of the Beijing Conciliation Centre that assigns one or two conciliators to mediate. If agreement is reached, a conciliation statement based on the signed agreement is recorded. Although conciliation may be the friendly route to resolving disputes in China, it is not legally binding so an arbitration clause should be included in all conciliation agreements.

Arbitration

International commercial disputes are often resolved by *arbitration* rather than litigation. The usual arbitration procedure is for the parties involved to select a disinterested and informed party or parties as referee(s) to determine the merits of the case and make a judgement that both parties agree to honour.

Tribunals for Arbitration.   Although the preceding informal method of arbitration is workable, most arbitration is conducted under the auspices of one of the more formal domestic and international arbitration groups organized specifically to facilitate the mediation of commercial disputes. These groups have experienced arbitrators available and formal rules for the process of arbitration. In most countries, decisions reached in formal mediation are enforceable under the law.

Among the formal arbitration organizations are:

1. The International Chamber of Commerce.
2. The London Court of Arbitration. Decisions are enforceable under English law and in English courts.
3. The American Arbitration Association.

International Chamber of Commerce.   The procedures used by formal arbitration organizations are similar. Arbitration under the rules of the International Chamber of Commerce (ICC) affords an excellent example of how most organizations operate. When an initial request for arbitration is received, the chamber first attempts a conciliation between the disputants. If this fails, the process of arbitration is started. The plaintiff and the defendant select one person each from among acceptable arbitrators to defend their case, and the ICC Court of Arbitration appoints a third member, generally chosen from a list of distinguished lawyers, jurists and/or professors.

The history of ICC effectiveness in arbitration has been spectacular. An example of a case that involved arbitration by the ICC concerned a contract between an English business and a Japanese manufacturer. The English business agreed to buy 100 000 plastic dolls for 80 cents each. On the strength of the contract, the English business sold the entire lot at $1.40 per doll. Before the dolls were delivered, the Japanese manufacturer had a strike; the settlement of the strike increased costs and the English business was informed that the delivery price of the dolls had increased from 80 cents to $1.50 each. The English business maintained that the Japanese firm had committed to make delivery at 80 cents and should deliver at that price. Each side was convinced that it was right. The Japanese, accustomed to code law, felt that the strike was beyond control, was an act of God, and thus compliance with the original provisions of the contract was excused. The English, accustomed to common law, did not accept the Japanese reasons for not complying because they considered a strike the normal course of doing business and not an act of God. The dispute could not be settled except through arbitration or litigation. They chose arbitration; the ICC appointed an arbitrator who heard both sides and ruled that the two parties would share proportionately in the loss. Both parties were satisfied with the arbitration decision and costly litigation was avoided. Most arbitration is successful, but success depends on the willingness of both parties to accept the arbitrator's rulings.

Arbitration Clauses.   Contracts and other legal documents should include clauses specifying the use of arbitration to settle disputes. Unless a provision for arbitration of any dispute is incorporated as part of a contract, the likelihood of securing agreement for arbitration after a dispute arises is reduced. An arbitration clause suggested by the International Chamber of Commerce is:

> All disputes arising in connection with the present contract shall be finally settled under the rules of conciliation and arbitration of the International Chamber of Commerce by one or more arbitrators appointed in accordance with the said rules.

Enforcement of Arbitration Clauses.   Arbitration clauses require agreement on two counts: (1) the parties agree to arbitrate in a case of a dispute according to the rules and procedures of some arbitration tribunal; and (2) they agree to abide by the awards resulting from the arbitration. Difficulty arises when the parties to a contract fail to honour the agreements. Companies may refuse to name arbitrators, refuse to arbitrate, or after arbitration awards are made, they may refuse to honour the award. In most countries, arbitration clauses are recognized by the courts and are enforceable by law within those countries.

Litigation

Lawsuits in public courts are avoided for many reasons. Most observers of litigation between citizens of different countries believe that almost all victories are spurious because the cost, frustrating delays and extended aggravation that these cases produce are more oppressive by far than any matter of comparable size. The best advice is to seek a settlement, if possible, rather than sue. Other deterrents to litigation are:

1. Fear of creating a poor image and damaging public relations.
2. Fear of unfair treatment in a foreign court. (Although not intentional, there is

COUNTERFEIT, PIRATED OR THE ORIGINAL: TAKE YOUR CHOICE

Intellectual properties—trademarks, brand names, designs, manufacturing processes, formulas—are valuable company assets that US officials estimate are knocked off to the tune of $800 million (€720 million) a year due to counterfeiting and/or pirating. Some examples from China:

- Design Rip-Offs. Beijing Jeep Corporation, a Chrysler Corporation joint venture, found more than 2000 four-wheel-drive vehicles designed to look nearly identical to its popular Cherokee model.
- Product Rip-Offs. Exact copies of products made by Procter & Gamble, Colgate Palmolive, Reebok and Nike are common throughout southern China. Exact copies of any Madonna album are available for as little as $1, as are CDs and movies. One executive says, 'They'll actually hire workers away from the real factories'.
- Brand Name Rip-Offs. Bausch & Lomb's Ray Ban sunglasses become Ran Bans. Colgate in the familiar bright red becomes Cologate. The familiar Red Rooster on Kellogg's Corn Flakes appears on Kongalu Corn Strips packages that state 'the trustworthy sign of quality which is famous around the world'.
- Book Rip-Offs. Even the rich and powerful fall prey to pirating. Soon after *My Father, Deng Xiaoping*, a biography written by Deng Rong, daughter of Deng Xiaoping, was published thousands of illegal copies flooded the market.
- Original versions of the products mentioned above are also sold in China by the true owners.

Sources: Adapted from Marcus W. Brauchli, 'Chinese Flagrantly Copy Trademarks of Foreigners', *The Wall Street Journal*, 26 June 1994, p. B-1; and Bob Davis, 'US Plans to Probe Piracy in China, Raising Possibility of Trade Sanctions', *The Wall Street Journal*, 28 June 1994, p. A-2.

justifiable fear that a lawsuit could result in unfair treatment because the decision could be made by either a jury or judge not well versed in trade problems and the intricacies of international business transactions.)

3. Difficulty in collecting a judgement that may otherwise have been collected in a mutually agreed settlement through arbitration.
4. The relatively high cost and time required when bringing legal action.
5. Loss of confidentiality.

One authority suggests that the settlement of every dispute should follow three steps: first, try to placate the injured party; if this does not work, conciliate, arbitrate; and, finally, litigate. The final step is typically taken only when all other methods fail. Actually, this advice is probably wise whether one is involved in an international dispute or a domestic one.

PROTECTION OF INTELLECTUAL PROPERTY RIGHTS—A SPECIAL PROBLEM

Companies spend millions of dollars establishing brand names or trademarks to symbolize quality and a host of other product features designed to entice customers to buy their brands to the exclusion of all others. Millions more are spent on research to develop products, processes, designs and formulas that provide companies with advantages over their competitors. Such intellectual or industrial properties are among the more valuable assets a company may possess. Names such as Philips, Sony, Swatch, Kodak, Coca-Cola and Gucci, and rights to processes such as xerography and rights to computer software are invaluable.

Table 4.1   What Piracy Costs US Business

Product	Loss 1995 (million $)	
Motion pictures	124	
Books	125	
Records and music	527	(1994)
Business software	400	
Entertainment software	1300	
Total	*2476*	

Source: *Business Week*, 8 April 1996, p. 16.

One financial group estimated that the Marlboro brand had a value of €29.8 billion ($33 billion), Kellogg's €8.1 billion ($9 billion), Microsoft a value of €8.9 billion ($9.8 billion), and €4.5 billion ($5 billion) for Levi's. All these have experienced infringement of their intellectual property rights.[7]

Estimates are that more than 10 million fake Swiss timepieces carrying famous brand names such as Cartier and Rolex are sold every year netting illegal profits of at least €450 million ($500 million). Although difficult to pinpoint, lost sales from the unauthorized use of Western patents, trademarks and copyrights amount to more than €90 billion ($100 billion) annually. That translates into more than a million lost jobs. Software is an especially attractive target for pirates because it is costly to develop but cheap to reproduce. Unauthorized US software that sells for €450 ($500) in the United States can be purchased for less than €9 ($10) in the Far East. Table 4.1 illustrates the costs of this problem.

A major provision of the Uruguay Round of GATT establishes substantially higher standards of protection for a full range of intellectual property rights (IPR) than are embodied in current international agreements, and provides for the effective enforcement of those standards both internally and at the border. Counterfeit and pirated goods come from a wide range of industries—clothing, automotive parts, agricultural chemicals, pharmaceuticals, books, records, films and computer software, to name a few.

Inadequate Protection

The failure to protect intellectual or industrial property rights adequately in the world marketplace can lead to the legal loss of these rights in potentially profitable markets. Because patents, processes, trademarks and copyrights are valuable in all countries, some companies have found their assets appropriated and profitably exploited in foreign countries without a licence or reimbursement. Further, they often learn not only that other firms are producing and selling their products or using their trademarks, but that the foreign companies are the rightful owners in the countries where they are operating.

There have been many cases where companies have legally lost the rights to trademarks and have had to buy back these rights or pay royalties for their use. The problems of inadequate protective measures taken by the owners of valuable assets stem from a variety of causes. One of the more frequent errors is assuming that because the company has established rights in the home country, they will be protected around the world, or that rightful ownership can be established should the need arise. Such was the case with McDonald's in Japan. Its 'Golden Arches' trademark was registered by an enterprising Japanese company. Only after a lengthy and costly legal action with a trip to the Japanese supreme court was McDonald's able to

ASPIRIN IN RUSSIA, BAYER IN THE WEST—IT'S ENOUGH TO GIVE YOU A HEADACHE

Russia's patent office awarded the German chemical company, Bayer AG, the registered trademark to the word 'aspirin'. If the trademark award holds, Bayer will have the exclusive right to market pain relievers under the brand name Aspirin in Russia. The word and labelling 'aspirin' fell out of use in Russia in the 1970s, when the chemical name acetylsalicylic acid, the main ingredient, came into use. Bayer AG believes its trademark rights will be upheld and they will be the only company able to sell acetylsalicylic acid as Aspirin; the Russian patent office agrees. There are several reasons for granting Bayer the trademark: aspirin had fallen out of popular use in Russia, Bayer was the world's first manufacturer of aspirin and marketed acetylsalicylic acid under the brand name Aspirin a century ago, Bayer holds trademark rights to Aspirin in many countries and they registered the name first.

In the United States it's a different story. Bayer AG lost the exclusive right to Aspirin when US courts declared aspirin as the generic term for acetylsalicylic acid. Later, Bayer AG lost the right to the name Bayer as well. Bayer AG does not sell the famous Bayer aspirin in the United States, where the Bayer trademark is owned by Sterling Winthrop, Inc. The US government confiscated the domestic assets of Bayer AG after World War I, and in 1919 sold them along with the rights to the Bayer name. While Sterling Winthrop has the exclusive use of the name Bayer, it does not have the exclusive use of the term 'aspirin' since US courts ruled aspirin to be a generic term.

Ownership changes rapidly in international business. Bayer of Germany bought Sterling Winthrop, the US owner of the Bayer brand, from the Kodak Company in 1994, and now Bayer of Germany once again owns the brand Bayer worldwide. The change in ownership in the United States, however, does not affect the trademark dispute over the brand name Aspirin discussed above.

Moral to the story? Patent and trademark protection is a complicated issue for international companies.

Sources: Adapted from Marya Fogel, 'Bayer Trademarks the Word "Aspirin" in Russia, Leaving Rivals Apoplectic', *The Wall Street Journal*, 29 October 1993, p. A-9; and 'SmithKline to Sell Some Sterling Assets to Bayer for $1 billion', *The Wall Street Journal*, 13 September 1994, p. A-3.

regain the exclusive right to use the trademark in Japan. After having to 'buy' its trademark for an undisclosed amount, McDonald's maintains a very active programme to protect its trademarks. Many businesses fail to understand that most countries do not follow the common-law principle that ownership is established by prior use or that registration and legal ownership in one country does not necessarily mean ownership in another.

Prior Use versus Registration

In many code-law countries, ownership is established by registration rather than by prior use—the first to register a trademark or other property right is considered the rightful owner. In the United States, a common-law country, ownership of intellectual property rights is established by prior use—whoever can establish first use is typically considered the rightful owner. In Jordan a trademark belongs to whomever registers it first in Jordan. Thus, you can find 'McDonald's' restaurant, 'Microsoft' software and 'Safeway' groceries all legally belonging to a Jordanian.[8] A company that believes it can always establish ownership in another country by proving it used the trademark or brand name first is wrong and risks the loss of these assets. It is best to protect intellectual property rights through registration. Several international conventions provide for simultaneous registration in member countries.

GOING INTERNATIONAL 4.4

BRAND-NAME PIRATES PLUNDER OPEN BORDERS

In the heart of Istanbul's covered bazaar the stalls are piled high with Benetton, Lacoste T-shirts, Nike and Reebok Sweatshirts and Levi's Jeans. The T-shirts sell for \$2–3 (€1.8–2.7) and a pair of Levi's for \$15 (€13.5). All are counterfeit copies produced in hundreds of small factories in the city. Turkey is not the only producer of counterfeit products: China, Thailand, Italy and Cambodia are other big players.

According to a 1994 survey by the Service de Statistique Industries, 60 per cent of the world's counterfeit goods end up for sale in the EU, with France receiving 25 per cent. It is estimated that financial losses caused by counterfeiting account to 7 per cent of world trade, or \$250 to \$350 billion (€225–315 billion). And it is a fast-growing business: while world trade grew 47 per cent between 1990 and 1995 trade in counterfeit grew by 150 per cent.

A study of international fraud within the EU by Deloitte and Touche warned that counterfeit distorts competition, affects investment levels, reduces the level of legitimate employment and taxation revenues, creates safety risks and affects relations between member states. Any well-known product that can be sold to mass market is vulnerable to counterfeit. Companies such as Nike, Levi's, Gucci, Louis Vuitton, software and music CDs are on the top of this list. The International Federation for Phonography Industry (IFPI) believes that IFPI industry alone lost \$2 billion (€1.8 billion) in 1996 which is about 5 per cent of the legitimate sales. In software this ratio is about 35 per cent and in audio-video together 25 per cent.

What is attractive to counterfeit is a product where the cost of the physical material is a small part of the overall price. Pharmaceuticals, CDs and clothing are thus most vulnerable. A major proportion of these counterfeits enter EU countries and move freely within Europe. With pressures from the EU, countries like China and Turkey are passing new laws and are trying to control these practices. The EU commission announced a plan in May 1997 to fight economic fraud especially counterfeiting.

Source: Abstracted from Sandra Smith's 'Brand-Name Pirates plunder Open Borders', *The European*, 19–25 June 1997, p. 4.

International Conventions

Many countries participate in international conventions designed for mutual recognition and protection of intellectual property rights. There are three major international conventions.

1. The Paris Convention for the Protection of Industrial Property, commonly referred to as the Paris Convention, is a group of 100 nations that have agreed to recognize the rights of all members in the protection of trademarks, patents and other property rights. Registration in one of the member countries ensures the same protection afforded by the home country in all the member countries.

2. The Madrid Arrangement established the Bureau for International Registration of Trademarks. There are some 26 member countries in Europe that have agreed to automatic trademark protection for all members. Even though the United States is not a participant of the Madrid Arrangement, if a subsidiary of a US company is located in one of the member countries, the subsidiary could file through the membership of its host country and thereby provide protection in all 26 countries for the US company.

3. The Inter-American Convention includes most of the Latin American nations and the United States. It provides protection similar to that afforded by the Paris Convention.

With these three agreements, two multicountry patent arrangements have streamlined patent procedures in Europe. The Patent Cooperation Treaty (PCT) facilitates the application of patents among its member countries. It provides comprehensive coverage in supplying the interested party with an international search report on other patents to help evaluate whether or not to seek protection in each of the countries cooperating under the PCT.

The European Patent Convention (EPC) establishes a regional patent system allowing any nationality to file a single international application for a European patent. Once the patent is approved, the patent has the same effect as a national patent in each individual country designated on the application.

In addition, the European Union (EU) has approved its Trademark Regulation which will provide intellectual property protection throughout all member states. Companies have a choice between relying on national systems, when they want to protect a trademark in just a few member countries, or the European system, when protection is sought throughout the EU. Trademark protection is valid for 10 years and is renewable. However, if the mark is not used for five years, protection is forfeited.[9]

Individual countries expect companies to actively police their intellectual property by bringing violators to court. Policing can be a difficult task, with success depending in large measure on the cooperation of the country within which the infringement or piracy takes place. A lack of cooperation in some countries may stem from cultural differences of how intellectual property is viewed. In Western countries, the goal of protection of intellectual property is to encourage invention and to protect and reward innovative businesses. In Korea, the attitude is that the thoughts of one person should benefit all. In Japan, the intent is to share technology rather than protect it; an invention should serve a larger, national goal with the rapid spread of technology among competitors in a manner that promotes cooperation. In the light of such attitudes, the lack of enthusiasm towards protecting intellectual property is better understood.[10]

COMMERCIAL LAW WITHIN COUNTRIES

When doing business in more than one country, a marketer must remain alert to the different legal systems. This problem is especially troublesome for the marketer who formulates a common marketing plan to be implemented in several countries. Although differences in languages and customs may be negated, legal differences between countries may still prevent a standardized marketing programme.

Marketing Laws

All countries have laws regulating marketing activities in promotion, product development, labelling, pricing and channels of distribution. In some, there may be only a few laws, with lax enforcement; in others, there may be detailed, complicated rules to follow that are stringently enforced. There often are vast differences in enforcement and interpretation among countries having laws covering the same activities. Laws governing sales promotions in the EU offer good examples of such diversity.

In Austria, premium offers to consumers come under the discount law that prohibits any cash reductions that give preferential treatment to different groups of customers. Because most premium offers would result in discriminatory treatment of buyers, they normally are not allowed. Premium offers in Finland are allowed with considerable scope as long as the word 'free' is not used and consumers are not coerced into buying products. France also regulates premium offers, which are, for all practical purposes, illegal because it is illegal to sell for less than cost price or to offer a customer a gift or premium conditional on the purchase of another product. Furthermore, a manufacturer or retailer cannot offer products different from the kind regularly offered (i.e. a detergent manufacturer cannot offer clothing or kitchen utensils). German law covering promotion in general is about as stringent as can be found. Building on an 80-year-old statute against 'unfair competition', the German courts currently prevent businesses from offering all sorts of incentives to lure customers. Most incentives that target particular groups of customers are illegal, as are most offers of gifts.[11]

The various laws concerning product comparison, a natural and effective means of expression, are another major stumbling block. In Germany, comparisons in advertisements are always subject to the competitor's right to go to the courts and ask for proof of any implied or stated superiority. In a recent decision, the European Court ruled that a French cosmetics company could sell its wares by mail in Germany by advertising them at a markdown from their original prices, a direct violation of German law.

Green Marketing Legislation

Multinational corporations are facing a growing variety of legislation designed to address environmental issues. Global concern for the environment extends beyond industrial pollution, hazardous waste disposal and rampant deforestation to include issues that focus directly on consumer products. Green marketing laws focus on product packaging and its effect on solid waste management and environmentally friendly products.

Germany has passed the most stringent green marketing laws that regulate the management and recycling of packaging waste. The new packaging law was introduced in three phases. The first phase requires all transport packaging such as crates, drums, pallets and Styrofoam containers to be accepted back by the manufacturers and distributors for recycling. The second phase requires manufacturers, distributors and retailers to accept all returned secondary packaging, including corrugated boxes, blister packs, all packaging designed to prevent theft, packaging for vending machine applications and packaging for promotional purposes. The third phase requires all retailers, distributors and manufacturers to accept returned sales packaging including cans, plastic containers for dairy products, foil wrapping, Styrofoam packages and folding cartons such as cereal boxes. The requirement for retailers to take back sales packaging has been suspended as long as the voluntary green dot programme remains a viable substitute.[12]

The green dot programme mandates that the manufacturer must ensure a regular collection of used packaging materials directly from the consumer's home or from designated local collection points. A green dot on a package will identify those manufacturers participating in this programme. France, Belgium, Denmark and Austria have similar regulations to deal with solid waste disposal.[13]

Alarmed at the diversity of 'green' laws that were evolving and the difficulty of harmonizing them across the EU, the European Commission issued a global packaging directive that is considered more reasonable than the German law. The main differences from the German law were a longer period for attaining full recovery of packaging waste (10 years versus 5) and allowing incineration of 30 per cent of the recyclables. The EU programme left rules on collection of packaging up to the individual countries.

In addition to laws that restrict the amount of solid waste that can be generated, many European countries, including Germany and France, have devised schemes to identify products that comply with certain criteria that make them more environmentally friendly than similar products. Products that meet these criteria will be awarded an 'eco-label' that the manufacturer can display on packaging as a signal to customers of an environmentally friendly product.

GOING INTERNATIONAL 4.5

WHATEVER YOU CALL IT—IT'S STILL A BRIBE

English expressions such as bribe or payoff all sound a little stiff and cold. In some countries, the terms for the same activities have a little more character.*

Country	Term	Translation
Japan	Kuroi kiri	Black mist
Germany	Schmiergeld	Grease money
Latin America	El soborno	Payoff
Mexico	La mordida	The bite
Middle East	Baksheesh	Tip, gratuity
France	Pot-de-vin	Jug of wine
East Africa	Chai	Tea
Italy	Bustarella	Little envelope

*Other terms are wairo (Japan) and backhander (India).

Antitrust—An Evolving Issue

With the exception of the United States and some European countries, antitrust laws have been either nonexistent or unenforced in most of the world's countries for the better part of the 20th century. However, the European Union has begun to actively enforce its antitrust laws. Antimonopoly, price discrimination, supply restrictions and full-line forcing are areas in which the European Court of Justice has dealt severe penalties. For example, before Procter & Gamble Company was allowed to buy VP-Schickedanz AG, a German hygiene products company, it had to agree to sell off one of the German company's divisions that produced Camelia, a brand of sanitary napkins. P&G already marketed a brand in Europe, and the Commission was concerned that allowing them to keep Camelia would give them a controlling 60 per cent of the German sanitary products market and 81 per cent of Spain's.[14] In another instance, Michelin was fined €630 000 ($700 000) for operating a system of discriminatory rebates to Dutch tyre dealers. Similar penalties have been assessed against such companies as United Brands for price discrimination and F. Hoffmann-LaRoche for noncost-justified fidelity discounts to its dealers.

LEGAL ENVIRONMENT OF THE EUROPEAN UNION

The concept of free competition is a fundamental element in the Rome Treaty, which embodies the premise that any restriction on free competition is intrinsically reprehensible. There are in practice some exceptions, but the principle itself is that of positive general condemnation of any limits on competition. Article 85(1) of the Treaty declares:

> The following shall be prohibited as incompatible with the Common Market: all agreements between undertakings, decisions by associations of undertakings and concerted practices which may affect trade between member states and which had as their object or effect the prevention, restriction or distortion of competition within the Common Market.

GOING INTERNATIONAL 4.6

THE ESTABLISHMENT OF THE EUROPEAN UNION

The European Community functions in accordance with constitution based on services of basic treaties that define powers of main institutions and their relationships with member states. These treaties include:

- European Coal and Steel Community (ECSC), signed in 1951.
- Two separate Treaties of Rome, signed in March 1957, establishing European Atomic Energy Community (EURATOM) and European Economic Community (EEC). Here it was agreed to establish a single Assembly, Court of Justice and Economic Social Committee for all three communities.
- A Treaty signed in Brussels in April 1965, to create a single council of the European Communities, replacing ECSC, EEC and EURATOM. A single audit board was created for all three communities.
- The Treaty of Brussels of 1972, which brought about the employment of the community. Also stipulating the Single European Act of 1987 allowing qualified majority voting (QMV).
- The Maastricht Treaty 1991, adding powers of the European Parliament and European Court. This Treaty, also known as the Treaty on European Union, reconfirmed political and economic union. It was considered as a historical turning point for Europe. The Maastricht Treaty also included the establishment of European Monetary Union (EMU), Security and Home Affairs and Justice.

Source: Abstracted from: Keith Perry, *Business and the European Community* (Oxford: Butterworth-Heinemann, 1994).

Article 85 deals with agreements, between two or more parties, that constitute restrictive practices. Article 86 is concerned with the abuse by individual organizations of a dominant trading position enjoyed in the Union, that is to say monopolies. Article 86 of the Rome Treaty declares:

> Any abuse by one or more undertakings of a dominant position within the Common Market or in a substantial part of it shall be prohibited.

An illustrative list is given of the types of abuses that will be prohibited: directly or indirectly imposing unfair purchase or selling prices or other unfair trading conditions, limiting production, markets or technical development to the prejudice of consumers, applying dissimilar conditions to equivalent transactions with different trading partners, or imposing contracts with supplementary obligations on trading partners that have no real connection with the subject of such contracts. Article 86 is concerned essentially with the abuse of a dominant position in a particular market, but there is no condemnation of a large share of the market as such.

The Decision-Making Process

One practice that has developed has been that of giving publicity to any Commission decision in an attempt to influence and educate the market as a whole. Indeed, to the annoyance of a number of firms, commissioners responsible for the competition rules have often called press conferences to inform the public of decisions actually made, the state of investigations in progress and, indeed, those about to begin.

When an investigation is launched, the Commission is not required to ask for the cooperation of the company concerned. It can be brusque, enter premises of the company to examine books and other business records, take copies of extracts from these documents and ask for oral explanations on the spot. This is known as 'the dawn raid'.

State Aids.   State aids can result in an artificially low export price, and the consequences to industry in the country where such goods are sold are the same as those caused by dumped goods. Like products may become uncompetitive and the industry suffers injury.

The 1979 Union regulation deals with state aids in a similar way to the way it deals with dumping. When a complaint is received, the Commission will investigate, and if it finds that goods have been subsidized, a countervailing duty may be imposed. Various practices are deemed to constitute indirect subsidies in a list that is illustrative, not exhaustive: currency retention schemes which give a bonus on exports, government-sponsored schemes for cheaper freight charges for exports, reduced taxes levied on exports, some export credit guarantee systems and special low interest credit schemes sponsored by governments for exports.

In practice, all countries give aid to their export industries, and the Commission must be aware that it cannot succeed in stamping out such practices. All it can do is to attempt to reduce the more blatant forms of state aid. The Commission is particularly vigilant in trying to remove state aid from interstate trade in the Common Market, because such an aim is a fundamental part of the Rome Treaty. Article 92 of the Treaty lays down that

> any aid granted by a member state or through state resources in any form whatsoever which distorts or threatens to distort competition by favouring certain undertakings or the production of certain goods shall, in so far as it affects trade between member states, be incompatible with the Common Market.

Mergers.   The years after 1985 saw a wave of mergers in the European Union. However, such mergers could threaten the existence of competition in important markets by giving the newly merged company a dominant position. It was clear that national legislation was inadequate for the control of many of the new mergers, because they were often transfrontier, whereas national legislation was confined to the territory of the individual member state.

The new Commission regulation applied to Unionwide mergers, which were defined by three criteria:

1. A threshold of combined worldwide turnover for the companies concerned of at least €5 billion. A turnover on this scale would reflect the financial and economic power of the participants.
2. A threshold of Unionwide turnover of at least €250 million for at least two of the firms merging. Thus only companies with a definite Union presence would be governed by the regulation.
3. A transnationality criterion. If each of the parties concerned derived two-thirds of their Union business in one and the same member state, the merger would not be subject to Union control. This criterion was designed to exclude from Union control predominantly national mergers, which would be subject to national merger control.

Companies considering merging were obliged to give the Commission prior notification, after which the Commission was to operate under strict time limits. It had one month after notification in which to decide whether to initiate proceedings, so that where it saw no objection, the parties would receive the green light to go ahead promptly. If an investigation into the proposed merger was mounted, the Commission had four months in which either to approve or block the merger. During the investigation period companies concerned could propose changes in the merger arrangements that would make the merger more acceptable to

BONN AND BRUSSELS IN DEAL OVER AID FOR VW

A compromise has been reached over state aid payments for Volkswagen, averting a full-scale confrontation between Bonn and the European Commission. Under the deal, the German government will freeze funds it was due to pay Volkswagen equivalent to the disputed DM90.7m ($61.20m) already paid to VW by Saxony state authorities.

The European competition commissioner said the deal would 'neutralize' the effect of the aid, and the Commission had dropped plans to seek a court injunction against Bonn to freeze the payment. He warned, however, that the Commission reserved the right to 'return and take action should the commitment not be fulfilled'. The Commission has been at loggerheads with Bonn since July, when Saxony paid Volkswagen DM90.7 million as part of a DM240 million aid package blocked by the Commission in June 1996.

The deal, however, is unlikely to end the dispute. It fails to settle the issue at the centre of the row and one of the most sensitive areas in relations between Germany and the European Commission—the extent to which the federal government can subsidize the east. Volkswagen and the German government yesterday insisted that the deal was temporary and did not affect the company's legal claims to the money. Volkswagen threatened to reclaim the frozen subsidy before the end of the year.

The Bonn government was due to give VW about DM120 million in tax credits as part of an aid package already cleared by the Commission. It is part of this package that Bonn has offered to freeze. Volkswagen said it would go ahead with two projects in eastern Germany—the extension of existing car plants in Mosel and Zwickau. It had threatened to pull its investment out of Saxony if it failed to get the full aid package.

The German economics minister said the agreement 'gives us time to arrive at a rational solution'. However, the Commission would press ahead with a case in the European Court of Justice against legality of the payment. 'The treaty article under which the money was paid is not applicable. This is a route which we cannot go down'. Germany claims that state support for eastern Germany is exempt from EU competition rules.

Source: Abstracted from *Financial Times*, 5 September 1996, p. 12.

the Commission. Given the small numbers in the Competition Directorate's executive staff, such stringent time limits appeared to be a heavy additional burden on already overstretched officials, but longer time limits could lead to unreasonable delays for companies attempting to develop appropriate strategies for the single market or facing strong competitors from Japan or the United States.

Problems of Competition Policy

Competition policy has three established objectives. As the Commission has stated, it aims to keep the Common Market 'open and unified', i.e. to create a single market for the benefit of industry and consumers. Second, it must 'ensure that at all stages of the Common Market's development, there exists the right amount of competition'. By ensuring some degree of commercial rivalry, the Union can help European industry to be competitive in world markets, as the competition will encourage firms to rationalize and change. The third objective is to ensure that competition is subject to 'the principles of fairness in the market place', by which the Commission means 'equality of opportunity for all operators in the Common Market'. In practice, this means preventing companies from setting up restrictive agreements and cartels or from abusing a dominant position.

The sheer complexity of the cases imposes a formidable strain on the Commission, as the

Continental Can decision demonstrated. The Continental Can Company, an American packaging firm, acquired, via its Belgian subsidiary, control of the largest German producer of packaging and metal boxes—Schalbach–Lubeca–Werke AG of Brunswick. It later acquired a majority holding in a Dutch company, Thomassen and Drijver–Verblifa NV of Deventer, which was the leading manufacturer of packaging material in the Benelux countries. The Commission felt that these mergers produced such a dominant position for Continental Can that it constituted an abuse, a violation of Article 86. Continental Can, however, appealed against the Commission decision to the European Court. The Court agreed with the Commission's legal reasoning, but found in favour of the company on the grounds that the Commission had got the facts of the case wrong.

Competition Policy in Action after 1985

The European Union competition policy depends for much of its effectiveness on the beliefs, political skills and determination of the Commissioner in charge of the Competition Directorate. The Commissioner in charge of competition policy from 1989 to 1992 was Leon Brittan. The basis of his political belief was a commitment to the benefits of the free-market system. As he expressed it, 'effective competition not only ensures the most efficient allocation of resources, but provides the stimulus for efficiency, innovation and, most important of all, the widest possible choice for consumers'. In his view the establishment of rules within which competition could flourish was vital if the single market was to work properly.

In a number of cases Brittan showed real determination. The capacity of the Commission to fine heavily was amply demonstrated in the Tetra-Pak case. In July 1991, this Swedish–Swiss-based packaging company was fined ECU 75 million for abusing its dominant position in breach of Article 86. Following a complaint from Elepak, one of Tetra-Pak's main competitors, the Commission concluded that Tetra-Pak had carried out a deliberate policy of eliminating actual or potential competitors in the aseptic and nonaseptic markets in machinery and cartons. Tetra-Pak's restrictive use of contracts enabled it to segment the European market and therefore charge prices that differed between state members by up to about 300 per cent for machines and up to about 50 per cent for cartons. Evidence gathered during the Commission's inquiry also showed that, at least in Italy and the United Kingdom, Tetra-Pak sold its 'Rex' nonaseptic products at a loss for a long time in order to eliminate competitors.[15]

SUMMARY

Business faces a multitude of problems in its efforts to develop a successful marketing programme. Not the least of these problems are the varying legal systems of the world and their effect on business transactions. Just as political climate, cultural differences, local geography, different business customs and the stage of economic development must be taken into account, so must such legal questions as jurisdictional and legal recourse in disputes, protection of industrial property rights, extended law enforcement and enforcement of antitrust legislation by foreign governments. A primary marketing task is to develop a plan that will be enhanced, or at least not adversely affected, by these and other environmental elements. The myriad questions created by different laws and different legal systems indicate that the prudent path to follow at all stages of foreign marketing operations is one leading to competent counsel well versed in the intricacies of the international legal environment.

QUESTIONS

1. How does the international marketer determine which legal system will have jurisdiction when legal disputes arise?
2. Discuss the limitations of jurisdictional clauses in contracts.
3. Discuss some of the reasons why it is probably best to seek an out-of-court settlement in international commercial legal disputes rather than to sue.
4. Illustrate the procedure generally followed in international commercial disputes when settled under the auspices of a formal arbitration tribunal.
5. What are intellectual property rights? Why should a company in international marketing take special steps to protect them?
6. In many code-law countries, ownership of intellectual property rights is established by registration rather than prior use. Comment.
7. Discuss the advantages to the international marketer arising from the existence of the various international conventions on trademarks, patents and copyrights.
8. 'The legal environment of the foreign marketer takes on an added dimension of importance because there is no single uniform international commercial law that governs foreign business transactions.' Comment.
9. Differentiate between the European Patent Convention (EPC) and the Patent Cooperation Treaty (PCT) in their effectiveness in protecting industrial property rights.
10. Discuss the German 'green marketing' law. How does the 'green dot' programme affect recycling?
11. Why is conciliation a better way to resolve a commercial dispute than arbitration?
12. Differentiate between conciliation and arbitration.

REFERENCES

1. All of the provinces of Canada have a common law system with the exception of Quebec, which is a code law province.
2. See, for example, Mokhtar M. Metwally, 'Interest Free (Islamic) Banking: A New Concept in Finance', *Journal of Banking and Finance Law and Practice*, June 1994, pp. 119–128.
3. An interesting report on doing business in Islamic Countries can be found in 'Fundamental Facts', *Business Traveler*, February 1994, pp. 8–10.
4. Rene David and John E.C. Brierley, *Major Legal Systems in the World Today* (London: The Free Press, 1968), p. 18.
5. Eastern European countries are rapidly revising their legal structures to create a positive investment climate. A comprehensive review of the Czech Republic and Slovakia's efforts to enact a Commercial Code is found in Sarah Andrus, 'The Czech Republic and Slovakia: Foreign Participation in Changing Economies', *Hastings International and Comparative Law Review*, Spring 1994, pp. 611–632.
6. Industrial property rights and intellectual property rights are used interchangeably. The more common term used today is intellectual property rights to refer to patents, copyrights, trademarks and so forth.
7. The valuations are based on branded products' worldwide sales, profitability and growth potential minus costs such as plants, equipment, and taxes. Keith J. Kelly, 'Coca-Cola Shows that Top-Brand Fizz', *Advertising Age*, 11 July 1994, p. 3.
8. 'If It's Fake, This Must Be Jordan', *Reuters News Service*, 27 February 1994.
9. 'EU Trademark Regulation', *Business Europe*, 10–16 January 1994, p. 6.
10. See 'Modern Day Pirates a Threat Worldwide', *Advertising Age*, 20 March 1995, pp. 1–3.
11. 'Consumer Protection Swaddled', *The Economist*, 24 July 1993, p. 67.
12. 'German Waste Law Changes', *Business Europe*, 7–13 February 1994, p. 4.
13. 'European Rubbish: Tied Up in Knots', *The Economist*, 28 January 1995, p. 62.
14. 'P&G Will Drop Brand to Gain EU Takeover Clearance', *Reuters News Service*, 17 June 1994.
15. Keith Perry, *Business and the European Community* (Oxford: Made Simple, Butterworth-Heinemann , 1994), pp. 82–97.

The Impact of Culture on International Marketing

Part Outline

CHAPTER 5

Geography and History: The Foundations of Cultural Understanding

Chapter Learning Objectives

What you should learn from Chapter 5

- The importance of geography and history in the understanding of international markets.

- The effects of topography and climate on products, population centres, transportation and economic growth.

- The growing problem and importance of environmental damage to world trade.

- The social and moral responsibility each citizen has to protect the environment.

- The importance of nonrenewable resources.

- The effects on the world economy of population increases and shifts, and of the level of employment.

- The importance of the history of each culture in understanding its response to international marketing.

Knowledge of a country's geography and history is essential if a marketer is to interpret a society's behaviour and fundamental attitudes. Culture can be defined as a society's programme for survival, the accepted basis for responding to external and internal events. Without understanding the geographical characteristics to which a culture has had to adapt and to which it must continuously respond, it cannot be completely understood. Nor can one fully appreciate the fundamental attitudes or behaviour of a society without knowledge of the historical events that have shaped its cultural evolution.[1]

Marketers can observe the nuances of a culture, but without an appreciation for the role geography and history play in moulding that culture, they cannot expect to understand fully why it responds as it does. This chapter discusses how geography and history affect behaviour and why they should be taken into account when examining the environmental aspects of marketing in another country.

GEOGRAPHY AND INTERNATIONAL MARKETS

Geography, the study of the earth's surface, climate, continents, countries, peoples, industries and resources is an element of the uncontrollable environment that confronts every marketer but which receives inadequate attention. There is a tendency to study climate, topography and available resources as isolated entities rather than as important causal agents in the marketing environment. The physical character of a nation is perhaps the principal and broadest determinant of both the characteristics of a society and the means by which that society undertakes to supply its needs. Thus, the study of geography is important for the student of marketing when evaluating marketing and its environment.

The purpose of this section is to provide a greater awareness of the world, its complexities, and its diversities—an awareness that can mean the difference between success and failure in marketing ventures. Climate and topography are examined as facets of the broader and more important elements of geography. A brief look at the earth's resources and population—the building blocks of world markets—and world trade routes completes the presentation on geography and global markets.

Climate and Topography

As elements of geography, the physical terrain and climate of a country are important environmental considerations when appraising a market. The effect of these geographical features on marketing ranges from the obvious influences on product adaptation to more profound influences on the development of marketing systems.

Altitude, humidity and temperature extremes are climatic features that affect the uses and functions of products and equipment. Products that perform well in temperate zones may deteriorate rapidly or require special cooling or lubrication to function adequately in tropical zones. Manufacturers found that construction equipment used in northern Europe required extensive modifications to cope with the intense heat and dust of the Sahara Desert. Within even a single national market, climate can be sufficiently diverse to require major adjustments. In Ghana, a product adaptable to the entire market must operate effectively in extreme desert heat and low humidity and in tropical rainforests with consistently high humidity.

South America represents an extreme but well-defined example of the importance of geography in marketing considerations. The economic and social systems there can be explained, in part, in terms of the geographical characteristics of the area. It is a continent 7242 km (4500 mls) long and 4800 km (3000 mls) wide at its broadest point. Two-thirds of it is comparable to Africa in its climate, 48 per cent of its total area is made up of forest and jungle, and only 5 per cent is arable. Mountain ranges cover South America's west coast for 7242 km (4500 mls), with an average height of 4000 m (13 000 ft) and a width of 480–650 km (300–400 mls). This is a natural, formidable barrier that has precluded the establishment of commercial routes between the Pacific and Atlantic coasts.

Once the Andes are surmounted, the Amazon basin of 2.5 million km² (2 million mls²) lies ahead. It is the world's greatest rainforest, almost uninhabitable and impenetrable. Through it runs the Amazon, the world's second longest river which, with its tributaries, has almost 65 000 km (40 000 mls) of navigable water. On the east coast is another mountain range covering almost the entire coast of Brazil, with an average height of 1200 m (4000 ft).

There are many other regions of the world that have extreme topographic and climatic variations as well. China, the former Soviet Union, India, Pakistan and Canada each have formidable physical and/or climatic conditions within their trading regions.

Rolls-Royce found that fully armour-plated cars from England required extensive body work and renovations after a short time in Canada. It was not the cold that damaged the cars but the salted sand spread to keep the streets passable throughout the four or five months of virtually continuous snow. The bumpers and side panels corroded and rusted and the oil system leaked. This problem illustrates the harshness of a climate and why it needs to be considered in all facets of product development.

Geographic hurdles must be recognized as having a direct effect on marketing and the related activities of communications and distribution. Furthermore, there may be indirect effects from the geographical ramifications on society and culture that are ultimately reflected in marketing activities. Many of the peculiarities of a country (i.e. peculiar to the foreigner) would be better understood and anticipated if its geography were studied more closely.

The effect of natural barriers on market development is also important. Because of the ease of distribution, coastal cities or cities situated on navigable waterways are more likely to be trading centres than are landlocked cities. Cities not near natural physical transportation routes generally are isolated from one another, even within the same country. Consequently, natural barriers rather than actual distance may dictate distribution points.

In discussing distribution in Africa, one marketer pointed out that a shipment from Mombassa on the Kenya east coast to Freetown on the bulge of West Africa could require more time than a shipment from New York or London to Kenya over established freight routes.

Road conditions in Ecuador are such that it is almost impossible to drive a car from the port of Guayaquil to the capital of Quito only 320 km (200 mls) away. Contrast this to more economically advanced countries where formidable mountain barriers have been overcome. A case in point is the 11.6 km (7.2 mls) tunnel that cuts through the base of Mont Blanc in the Alps. This highway tunnel brings Rome and Paris 200 km (125 mls) closer and provides a year-round route between Geneva and Turin of only 270 km (170 mls). Before the tunnel opened, it was a trip of nearly 800 km (500 mls) when snow closed the highway over the Alps.

Some countries have preserved physical barriers as protection and have viewed them as political as well as economic statements. Increasing globalization, however, has brought about changes in attitudes. The recent decision made by Sweden and Denmark to build a bridge and tunnel across the Baltic Strait to continental Europe reflects these changes. The project will make it possible to drive from Lapland in northernmost Scandinavia to Calabria in southern Italy. It will end millennia of geographic isolation for these Nordic nations. Politically the agreement is seen as a powerful, tangible symbol that they are ending their political isolation from the rest of Europe and are linking themselves economically to the continent's future and membership in the European Union.

After more than 200 years of speculation, a tunnel under the English Channel between Britain and France was officially opened in 1994.[2] Historically, the British have resisted a tunnel; they did not trust the French or any other European country and saw the English Channel as protection. When they became members of the EC, economic reality meant that a tunnel had to be built. The Chunnel, as it is called, carried more than 17 million tonnes of freight and over 30 million people the first year it was opened.[3]

GEOGRAPHY, NATURE AND ECONOMIC GROWTH

As countries prosper and expand their economies, natural barriers are overcome. Tunnels are dug, bridges and dams built and sound environmental practices implemented to control or adapt to climate, topography and the recurring extremes of nature. Man has been reasonably successful in overcoming or minimizing the effects of geographical barriers and natural disasters except in the developing countries of the world.

Always on the slim margin between subsistence and disaster, some developing countries suffer disproportionately from natural and human-assisted catastrophes. Climate and topography coupled with civil wars, poor environmental policies and natural disasters push these countries further into economic ruin. Without irrigation and water management, they are afflicted by droughts, floods, soil erosion and creeping deserts, which reduce the long-term fertility of the land. Population increases, deforestation and overgrazing intensify the impact of drought and lead to malnutrition and ill health, further undermining the countries' ability to solve their problems. Experts expect mass famine to have killed between 20 million and 30 million Africans in the 1990s. Cyclones cannot be prevented, nor inadequate rainfall, but there are means to control their effects. Unfortunately, each disaster seems to push these countries further away from effective solutions. Countries that suffer the most from major calamities are among the poorest in the world. Many have neither the capital nor the technical ability to minimize the effects of natural phenomena; they are at the mercy of nature.

Industrialized nations have the capital and technical ability to control the harshness of nature, but in striving for more and greater economic wealth, they court other disasters of their own making. Poor hazardous waste management and the increase of industrial pollution are environmental problems for which the industrialized world and those reaching for economic development must assume responsibility. The problems are mostly by-products of processes that have contributed significantly to economic development in many countries and to the life-styles they seek.[4]

Social Responsibility and Environmental Management

The 1990s have been called the 'Decade of the Environment', in that nations, companies and people are reaching a consensus: environmental protection is not an optional extra, 'it is an essential part of the complex process of doing business.'[5] The self-styled Green activists, and governments, media and businesses are focusing on ways to stem the tide of pollution and to clean up their decades of neglect. Many view the problem as a global issue rather than a national issue and one that poses common threats to humankind and thus cannot be addressed by nations in isolation.[6]

Companies looking to build manufacturing plants in countries with more liberal pollution regulations than they have at home are finding that regulations everywhere are becoming stricter. Many Asian governments are drafting new regulations and strictly enforcing existing ones. A strong motivator for Asia and the rest of the world is the realization that pollution is

---

GOING INTERNATIONAL 5.1

CLIMATE AND SUCCESS

A major food processing company had production problems after it built a pineapple cannery at the delta of a river in Mexico. It built the pineapple plantation upstream and planned to barge the ripe fruit downstream for canning, load them directly on ocean liners, and ship them to the company's various markets. When the pineapples were ripe, however, the company found itself in trouble: crop maturity coincided with the flood stage of the river. The current in the river during this period was far too strong to permit the backhauling of barges upstream; the plan for transporting the fruit on barges could not be implemented. With no alternative means of transport, the company was forced to close the operation. The new equipment was sold for 5 per cent of original cost to a Mexican group which immediately relocated the cannery. A seemingly simple, harmless oversight of weather and navigation conditions was the primary cause for major losses to the company.

Source: David A. Ricks, *Blunders in International Business* (Cambridge, MA: Blackwell Publishers, 1993), p. 16.

---

on the verge of getting completely out of control. An examination of China's rivers, lakes and reservoirs revealed that 21 per cent were polluted by toxic substances and that 16 per cent of the rivers were seriously polluted with excrement.

One of the revelations after Eastern Europe became independent was the seriousness of pollution in those countries. Eastern Europe has a long, hard road to bring their environment under control. Most factories are antiquated, use the cheapest and most polluting fuels and have few laws to control pollution. The list of environmental problems is overwhelming: Bulgaria's drinking water is contaminated by nitrates and the Black Sea is polluted by sewage, oil and industrial waste. In Hungary, the Danube River runs black with industrial and municipal wastes, and drinking water in the south is seriously contaminated with arsenic. In East Germany, now part of unified Germany, urban pollution is so serious that much of the water in lakes is undrinkable and many rivers are biologically dead because of toxic waste from chemical plants. It is estimated that over seven million Eastern Germans currently consume drinking water which is polluted beyond European Union maximum allowable guidelines for levels of iron, manganese, nitrates, odour, turbidity and microbiologic agents.[7]

Neither Western Europe nor the rest of the industrialized world is free of environmental damage. Rivers are polluted and the atmosphere in many major urban areas is far from clean (e.g. Athens, Los Angeles, Rome and Mexico City to mention a few). The very process of controlling industrial wastes leads to another and perhaps equally critical issue, the disposal of hazardous waste, a by-product of pollution control. Estimates of hazardous wastes collected annually exceed 300 million tonnes; the critical question is disposal that does not move the problem elsewhere.

The export of hazardous wastes by developed countries to developing nations has ethical implications and environmental consequences. Countries finding it more difficult to dispose of wastes at home are seeking countries willing to assume the burden of disposal. Some waste disposal in developing countries is illegal and some is perfectly legal because of governments that are directly involved in the business of hazardous waste. Illegal dumping is the most reprehensible act since it is done clandestinely and often without proper protection for those who unknowingly come in contact with the poisons.

91

Governments, organizations and businesses are becoming increasingly concerned with the social responsibility and ethical issues surrounding the problem of generating and disposing of wastes. The Organization for Economic Cooperation and Development (OECD), the United Nations, the European Union and international activist groups are undertaking programmes to strengthen environmental policies. Their influence and leadership are reflected in a broader awareness of pollution problems by businesses and people in general. Responsibility for cleaning up the environment does not rest solely with governments, businesses or activist groups; each citizen has a social and moral responsibility to include environmental protection among his or her highest goals.

Resources

The availability of minerals and the ability to generate energy are the foundations of modern technology. The location of the earth's resources, as well as the available sources of energy, are geographical accidents, and the world's nations are not equally endowed; nor does a nation's demand for a particular mineral or energy source necessarily coincide with domestic supply.

Energy is necessary to power the machinery of modern production and to extract and process the resources necessary to produce the goods of economic prosperity. In much of the underdeveloped world, human labour provides the preponderance of energy. The principal supplements to human energy are animals, wood, fossil fuel, nuclear power, and, to a lesser and more experimental extent, the ocean's tides, geothermal power and the sun. Of all the energy sources, petroleum usage is increasing most rapidly because of its versatility and the ease with which it is stored and transported.

As an environmental consideration in world marketing, the location, quality and availability of resources will affect the pattern of world economic development and trade for at least the remainder of the century. This factor must be weighed carefully by astute international marketers in making worldwide international investment decisions. In addition to the raw materials of industrialization, there must be an available and economically feasible energy supply to successfully transform resources into usable products.

Because of the great disparity in the location of the earth's resources, there is world trade between those who do not have all they need and those who have more than they need and are willing to sell. Importers of most of the resources are industrial nations with insufficient domestic supplies. Oil is a good example; the Middle East accounts for over 65 per cent of the world's reserves, while Western countries consume most of it. Figure 5.1 shows the oil reserves in the world.

Aside from the geographical unevenness in which most resources occur, there is no immediate cause for concern about the availability of supply of most resources. Figure 5.1 illustrates the approximate time when known oil reserves will be depleted. These estimates of reserves are based on current rates of consumption and will change as new reserves are discovered, as greater proportions are obtained by recycling, as substitutes are introduced, and as rates of consumption increase or abate. Substitutions are already being used to replace many of the minerals. The replacement of steel with fibreglass and plastic in automobile manufacturing is but one example.

One possible source of scarce minerals still untapped can be found in the ocean floors. Undersea mining may provide the world with new reserves of scarce minerals. Nodules of nickel, copper, cobalt and magnesium at the bottom of the Pacific have been estimated to total 10 billion tonnes of rich ore, with 10 million new tonnes formed every year. Similar fields of ore-rich nodules exist in all the world's oceans and seas.

This undersea wealth of minerals will not be easy to exploit because of the cost of under-

Figure 5.1   The World's Oil Reserves and Years to Depletion

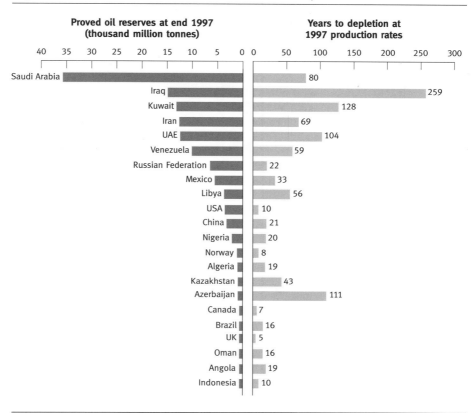

Source: Based on *BP Statistical Review of World Energy 1998*, The British Petroleum Company, http://www.bp.com/bpstats.

sea mining (higher than traditional mining), disputes over ownership of minerals outside territorial waters and the potential for upsetting the sensitive ocean ecosystem. Yet, like other natural barriers, these, too, eventually will be overcome as world demand increases and current reserves dwindle.

World Population Trends

While not the only determinant, the existence of sheer numbers of people is significant in appraising potential consumer demand. Current population, rates of growth, age levels and rural/urban population distribution are closely related to today's demand for various categories of goods. Changes in the composition and distribution of population among the world's countries during the next 40 years will profoundly affect future demand.

Recent estimates claim there are over 5.2 billion people in the world. Table 5.1 presents the population by major areas and the change expected between 1995 and 2150. At present growth rates, world population could leap to 9.3 billion by 2010, from 5.7 billion in 1995.[8] The majority of the people will reside in less developed countries least able to support such population increases. Kenya is a good example of what is happening in many developing

Table 5.1   World Population Projections by Major Areas, Based on a Medium Fertility Scenario,* 1950–2150

	1950 (millions)	1995 (millions)	2010 (millions)	2100 (millions)	2150 (millions)
World	2 524	5 687	9 364	10 414	10 806
Africa	224	719	2 046	2 646	2 770
Asia (including China and India)	1 402	3 438	5 443	5 851	6 059
China	555	1 220	1 517	1 535	1 596
India	358	929	1 533	1 617	1 669
Europe	547	728	638	579	595
Latin America	166	477	810	889	916
Northern America	172	297	384	401	414
Oceania	13	28	46	49	51

*The medium-fertility scenario assumes that the total fertility rates will ultimately stabilize by the year 2055 at replacement levels, which are slightly above two children per woman. If fertility rates would stay constant at 1990–1995 levels, the world population projection is 14 941 million in 2050; 57 182 million in 2100; and 296 333 million in 2150.
Source: World Population Projections to 2150 (New York: United Nations, Department of Economic and Social Affairs, Population Division, 1998.

countries. The average number of children born to a woman in Kenya is now 5.4, a rate that, combined with a declining infant mortality rate, could double the country's population almost overnight, increasing it from 27 million in 1993 to 45 million in 2010. Kenya's present economic growth rate will not support the demands created by such growth. By the year 2025, the World Bank predicts over four-fifths of the world's population will be concentrated in developing countries. Most governments are trying to control the explosive birthrates by encouraging birth control. China has the strictest policy; only one child is allowed per couple except in rural areas where, if the first child is female, a second child is permitted.

Rural/Urban Shifts.   A relatively recent phenomenon is a pronounced shift of the world's population from rural to urban areas. In the early 1800s, less than 3.5 per cent of the world's people were living in cities of 20 000 or more and less than 2 per cent in cities of 100 000 or more. Today, more than 40 per cent of the world's people are urbanites and the trend is accelerating (see Figure 5.2).

By 2020, it is estimated that more than 60 per cent of the world's population will live in urban areas, and at least 26 cities will have populations of 10 million or more, 13 of which will be in Asia.[9] Tokyo has already overtaken Mexico City as the largest city on Earth with a population of 26 million,[10] a jump of almost 8 million since 1990.[11] Migration from rural to urban areas is largely a result of a desire for greater access to sources of education, health care and improved job opportunities. Once in the city, perhaps three out of four migrants make economic gains. Family income of a manual worker in urban Brazil is almost five times that of a farm labourer in a rural area.

Although migrants experience some relative improvement in their living standards, intense urban growth without commensurate investment in services eventually leads to profound problems. Slums populated with unskilled workers living hand to mouth puts excessive pressure on sanitation systems, water supplies and other social services. At some point, the disadvantages of unregulated urban growth begin to outweigh the advantages for all concerned.

HOW MANY SLAVES WORK FOR YOU?

GOING INTERNATIONAL 5.2

A healthy, hard-working person can produce just enough energy to keep a 100-watt bulb burning. This may seem unimportant, but it is a humbling reminder that muscle power is really very puny.

Supplementary energy now exceeds muscle energy in every part of our lives from food production to recreation. It is like a gang of silent slaves who labour continually and uncomplainingly to feed, clothe and maintain us. The energy comes, of course, from mineral resources such as coal, oil and uranium, not from real slaves, but everyone on the earth now has 'energy slaves'. . . . In India the total supplementary energy produced is equivalent to the work of 15 slaves, each working an eight-hour day, for every man, woman and child. In South America everyone has approximately 30 'energy slaves'; in Japan, 75; Russia, 120; Europe, 150; and in the United States and Canada, a huge 300. The concept of 'energy slaves' demonstrates how utterly dependent the world has become on mineral resources. If the 'slaves' were to strike (which means if the supplies ran out), the world's peoples could not keep themselves alive and healthy. Reverting to muscle power alone would bring starvation, famine and pestilence. Nature would quickly reduce the population.

Source: Brian J. Skinner, *Earth Resources*, 2nd edn, 1976, pp. 3–4. Reprinted by permission of Prentice-Hall, Inc., Englewood Cliffs, NJ.

Figure 5.2   Urban Populations: per cent of Total, 1995

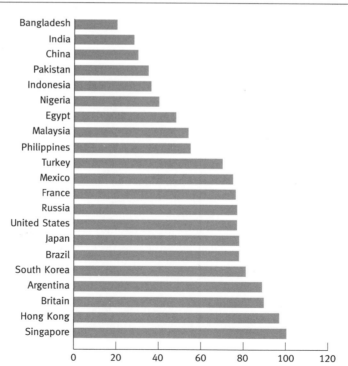

Source: Based on United Nations Population Division, and *The Economist*, 22 November 1997, p. 140.

HOW MANY COUNTRIES ARE THERE ANYWAY?

Just how many countries are there in the world? Seems like there should be an exact count in this era of modern technology, but there is some disagreement. The United Nations has 184 member states, but 185 countries are part of the international postal union. Not all countries have telephones, which explains why there are only 182 'country codes' for international calls. The International Olympic Committee lists 186 members, while the British *Statesman's Yearbook* lists 194 countries. The correct answer has to be 195—that's the number of countries where Coca-Cola claims it sells Coke, and they claim Coca-Cola is sold all over the world.

Source: Adapted from 'Counting Countries', *World Press Review*, March 1994, p. 4.

Many fear that, as we approach the year 2000, the bulging cities will become fertile fields for social unrest unless conditions in urban areas are improved. Prospects for improvement are not encouraging because most of the growth will take place in developing countries already economically strained. Further, there is little progress in controlling birthrates.

Increasing Unemployment.   Rapid population increases without commensurate economic development create other difficulties. Among the most pressing are the number of new jobs needed to accommodate the flood of people entering the labour pool. In the 1970s, 200 million people entered the labour market in the Third World; by the turn of the century, an additional 700 million will be of working age. The International Labour Organization (ILO) estimated that 1 billion jobs must be created worldwide by the end of the century.

The mismatch between population growth and economic growth is another major problem to be faced in the next century. Most of the population increases are occurring in the developing world while most of the jobs are being created in the developed world. The vast majority of new workers—500–700 million—will be found in developing countries[12] while the majority of jobs will be found in the industrialized world. While it is true that cheap labour costs, brought on in part by vast labour pools in less developed countries, attract labour-intensive manufacturers from higher cost industrialized countries, the number of new jobs created will not be sufficient to absorb the projected population growth. The ability to create enough jobs to keep pace with population growth is one problem of uncontrolled growth; another is providing enough to eat.

World Food Production.   Having enough food to eat depends on a country's ability to produce sufficient quantities, the ability to buy food from other sources when not self-sufficient, and the physical ability to distribute food when the need arises. The world produces enough food to provide adequate diets for all its estimated 5 billion people, yet famine exists, most notably in Africa. Long-term drought, economic weakness, inefficient distribution and civil unrest have created conditions that have led to tens of thousands of people starving.

GOING INTERNATIONAL 5.4

WHERE HAVE ALL THE WOMEN GONE?

Three converging issues in China have the potential of causing a serious gender imbalance by the year 2000: Issue 1—China, the world's most populous country, has a strict one-child policy to curb population growth; Issue 2—Traditional values dictate male superiority and a definite parental preference for boys; and Issue 3—Prenatal scanning allows women to discover the sex of their foetuses and thereby abort unwanted female foetuses.

As a consequence, Chinese statisticians have begun to forecast a big marriage gap for the generation born in the late 1980s and early 1990s. In 1990, China recorded 113.8 male births for every 100 female births, far higher than the natural ratio of 106 to 100. In rural areas, where parental preference for boys is especially strong, newborn boys outnumber girls by an average of 144.6 to 100. In one rural township, the ratio was reported to be 163.8 to 100.

Not only will there be a gender mismatch after the year 2000, but there may also be a social mismatch because most of the men will be peasants with little education, while most of the women will live in cities and more likely have high school or college degrees. In China, men who do physical labour are least attractive as mates, while women who labour with their minds are least popular.

Communist party members, cadres and civil servants were warned that using prenatal scanning for sex determination would result in loss of their posts and membership.

Sources: Adapted from 'Sex Determination before Birth', *Reuters News Service*, 3 May 1994, and 'Seven Times as Many Men', *AP News Service*, 31 March 1994.

Controlling Population Growth.   Faced with the ominous consequences of the population explosion, it would seem logical for countries to take appropriate steps to reduce growth to manageable rates, but procreation is one of the most culturally sensitive uncontrollables. Economics, self-esteem, religion, politics and education all play a critical role in attitudes about family size.

The prerequisites to population control are adequate incomes, higher literacy levels, education for women, better hygiene, universal access to health care, improved nutrition and, perhaps most important, a change in basic cultural beliefs toward the importance of large families. Unfortunately, progress in providing improved conditions and changing beliefs is hampered by the increasingly heavy demand placed on institutions responsible for change and improvement.

In many cultures, the prestige of a man, whether alive or dead, depends on the number of his progeny, and a family's only wealth is its children. Many religions discourage or ban family planning and thus serve as a deterrent to control. Nigeria has a strong Muslim tradition in the north and a strong Roman Catholic tradition in the east, and both faiths favour large families. Most traditional religions in Africa encourage large families; in fact, the principal deity for many is the goddess of land and fertility.

Population control is often a political issue. Overpopulation and the resulting problems have been labelled by some as an imperialist myth to support a devious plot by rich countries to keep developing world population down and maintain the developed world's dominance of the globe. Instead of seeking ways to reduce population growth, some politicians encourage growth as the most vital asset of poor countries. As long as such attitudes prevail, it will be extremely difficult, if not impossible, to control population.

Developed-World Population Decline.   While the developing world faces a rapidly growing population, it is estimated that the industrialized world's population will decline.

Birthrates in Western Europe and Japan have been decreasing since the early or mid-1960s; more women are choosing careers instead of children, and many working couples are electing to remain childless. As a result of these and other contemporary factors, population growth in many countries has dropped below the rate necessary to maintain present levels. The populations of France, Sweden, Switzerland and Belgium are all expected to drop within a few years. Austria, Denmark, Germany, Japan and several other nations are now at about zero population growth and probably will slip to the minus side in another decade. Recent reports by the Japanese government indicate that Japan's birthrate has dropped to 1.46 births per female, which is below the 2.08 presumed necessary to maintain a nation's population.[13] Japan's rural areas have steadily lost young people to the cities and, to counteract the trend, governments in rural prefectures are giving mothers 'Congratulatory Birth Money', up to 3 million yen ($30 400), to have a seventh child.[14]

The economic fallout of a declining population has many ramifications. Businesses find their domestic market shrinking for items such as maternity and infant goods, school equipment and selected durables. This leads to reduced production and worker layoffs that affect living standards. Europe, Japan and the United States have special problems because of the increasing percentage of elderly people who must be supported by shrinking numbers of active workers. The elderly require higher government outlays for health care and hospitals, special housing and nursing homes, and pension and welfare assistance, but the workforce that supports these costs is dwindling. In addition, a shortage of skilled workers is anticipated in these countries because of the decreasing population. The trends of increasing population in the developing world with substantial shifts from rural to urban areas, and declining birthrates in the industrialized world, will have profound effects on the state of world business and world economic conditions well beyond 2000. And, while world population is increasing, multinational firms could see world markets decreasing on a relative basis because the monied world is losing numbers and poor nations are gaining numbers. Population size is important in marketing, but people must have a means to buy for there to be an effective market.

WORLD TRADE ROUTES

Major world trade routes have developed among the most industrialized countries of the world—Europe, North America and Japan. It might be said that trade routes bind the world together, minimizing distance, natural barriers, lack of resources and the fundamental differences between peoples and economies. Early trade routes were, of course, overland; later came sea routes and, finally, air routes to connect countries. Trade routes represent the attempts of countries to overcome economic and social imbalances created in part by the influence of geography.

A careful comparison among world population figures in Table 5.1, Triad trade figures in Figure 5.3 and world trade figures in Table 5.2 illustrate how small a percentage of the world's land mass and population account for the majority of trade. It is no surprise that the major sea lanes and the most developed highway and rail systems link these major trade areas. The more economically developed a country, the better developed the surface transportation infrastructure is to support trade.

Although air freight is not extremely important as a percentage of total freight transportation, an interesting comparison between surface routes and air routes is air service to the world's less industrialized countries. Although air routes are the heaviest between points in the major industrial centres, they are also heavy to points in less developed countries. The

Table 5.2   Leading Exporters and Importers in World Merchandise Trade and World Trade in Commercial Services, 1995 ($ millions)

Country*	Exports	Imports	Total
United States	$772.1	$902.9	$1 675
Germany	577.3	562.4	1 139.7
Japan	507	457.6	964.6
France	381.3	350.9	732.2
United Kingdom	308.5	320.6	629.1
Italy	301.4	273	574.4
Netherlands	241.8	220.5	462.3
Hong Kong	211.5	217.1	428.6
Canada	213.9	197.7	411.6
Belgium/Luxembourg	204.4	189.1	393.5
China	165**	147.8**	312.8**
Korea	150.2	162.6	312.8
Singapore	146.4	137.4**	283.8**
Spain	131.2	136.4	267.6
Chinese Taipei	127.3	127.4	254.7

*Order determined by total dollar value of exports and imports.
**In 1994.
Source: World Trade Organization, *Annual Report 1996*, Volume I and II.

Figure 5.3   The Triad: Trade between the US and Canada, the EU and Japan, 1995 ($ billions)

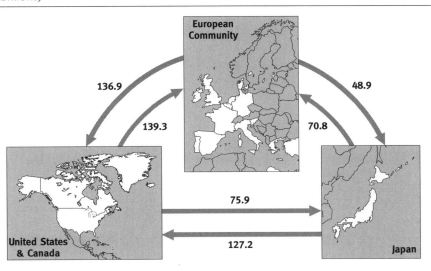

For additional trade figures see 'Indicators of Market Size for 115 Countries, Part I', *Crossborder Monitor*, 27 August 1997, pp. 4–8.

obvious reason is that for areas not located on navigable waters or where the investment in railways and effective roads is not yet feasible, air service is often the best answer. Air communications have made otherwise isolated parts of the world reasonably accessible.

EXPORTING ICE TO INDIA

A mainstay of New England's 19th-century commerce was the ice trade between New England and the world. In 1806, before the invention of mechanical ice making, a demand for ice in the tropics led a New England resident, Frederic Tudor, to pioneer the transportation of ice to the tropics. His first shipment to Martinique, 130 tons, was harvested from a family pond in New England. The venture was not at first a financial success. Tudor had to solve problems with inefficiency in harvesting, keeping the ice from melting and developing a market. He demonstrated how ice could be used to make ice cream; he promoted the use of iceboxes for keeping food fresh; he fostered the medical application of ice in reducing fever and he sold his ice cheaply to encourage customers and to build his market. The ice was stored in insulated ice houses where preservation was improved by the simple innovation of packing sawdust between the ice blocks.

By 1833 his ice-exporting business was a financial success. It was at this time that he began exporting ice to Calcutta. His ice exporting was such a success in India that three ice houses were built to store the ice once it arrived by ship. An ice house at Madras still stands today. And so went one of the first global marketing ventures.

Source: Reprinted by permission of *American Heritage* magazine, a division of Forbes, Inc., $CG 1991 Forbes, Inc.

HISTORICAL PERSPECTIVE IN GLOBAL BUSINESS

To understand, explain and appreciate a people's image of itself and the fundamental attitudes and unconscious fears that are often reflected in its view of foreign cultures, it is necessary to study the culture as it is now as well as to understand the culture as it was, that is, a country's history. An awareness of the history of a country is particularly effective for understanding attitudes about the role of government and business, the relations between managers and the managed, the sources of management authority, and attitudes towards foreign multinational corporations. History helps define a nation's 'mission', how it perceives its neighbours, and how it sees its place in the world.

History and Contemporary Behaviour

Unless you have a historical sense of the many changes that have buffeted Japan, the isolation before the coming of Admiral Perry in 1853, the threat of domination by colonial powers, the rise of new social classes, Western influences, the humiliation of World War II and involvement in the international community, it is difficult to fully understand its contemporary behaviour. Why do the Japanese have such strong loyalty towards their companies? Why is the loyalty found among participants in the Japanese distribution systems so difficult for an outsider to develop? Why are decisions made by consensus? Answers to such questions can be explained in part by some sense of Japanese history.[15]

History Is Subjective

History is important in understanding why a country behaves as it does, but history from whose viewpoint? Historical events are always viewed from one's own biases, and thus what is recorded by one historian may not be what another records, especially if the historians are from different cultures. Historians are traditionally objective, but few can help filtering events through their own cultural biases. Not only is history sometimes subjective, but there are other subtle influences to our perspective. Maps of the world sold in the United States generally show the United States as the centre, as maps in Britain show Britain at the centre, while maps in Australia look totally different.

SUMMARY

One British authority admonishes foreign marketers to study the world until 'the mere mention of a town, country or river enables it to be picked out immediately on the map'. Although it may not be necessary for the student of international marketing to memorize the world map to that extent, a prospective international marketer should be reasonably familiar with the world, its climate and topographic differences. Otherwise, the important marketing characteristics of geography could be completely overlooked when marketing in another country. The need for geographical and historical knowledge goes deeper than being able to locate continents and their countries. For someone who has never been in a tropical rainforest with an annual rainfall of at least one and a half metres and sometimes more than five metres, it is difficult to anticipate the need for protection against high humidity, or to anticipate the difficult problems caused by dehydration in constant 38 °C or more heat in the Sahara region. Without a historical understanding of a culture, the attitudes within the marketplace may not be understood.

Aside from the simpler and more obvious ramifications of climate and topography, there are complex geographical and historical influences on the development of the general economy and society of a country. In this case, the need for studying geography and history is to provide the marketer with an understanding of why a country has developed as it has rather than as a guide for adapting marketing plans. Geography and history are two of the environments of foreign marketing that should be understood and that must be included in foreign marketing plans to a degree commensurate with their influence on marketing effort.

QUESTIONS

1. Study the data in Figure 5.1 and briefly discuss the long-term prospects for industrialization of an underdeveloped country with a high population growth and minimum resources.
2. Why study geography in international marketing? Discuss.
3. Pick a country and show how employment and topography affect marketing within the country.
4. Discuss the bases of world trade. Give examples illustrating the different bases.
5. The marketer 'should also examine the more complex effect of geography on general market characteristics, distribution systems, and the state of the economy'. Comment.
6. The world population pattern trend is shifting from rural to urban areas. Discuss the marketing ramifications.
7. Select a country with a stable population and one with a rapidly growing population. Contrast the marketing implications of these two situations.
8. 'The basis of world trade can be simply stated as the result of equalizing an imbalance in the needs and wants of society on one hand and its supply of goods on the other.' Explain.
9. How do differences in people constitute a basis for trade?
10. 'World trade routes bind the world together'. Discuss.
11. Why are the 1990s called the 'Decade of the Environment'? Explain.
12. Some say the global environment is a global issue rather than a national one. What does this mean? Discuss.

REFERENCES

1. For an interesting book on the effects of geography, technology, and capitalism on an economy, see Dean M. Hanik, *The International Economy: A Geographical Perspective* (New York: Wiley, 1994).
2. 'Chunnel Vision', *Europe*, May 1994, p. 43.
3. 'Assessing the Channel Tunnel's Benefits', *Business Europe*, 10–16 January 1994, p. 2.
4. World Bank, *World Development Indicators*, CD-rom, 1998.
5. 'A Survey on Development and the Environment', *The Economist*, 21 March 1998.
6. Yoshihide Soeya, 'Balance and Growth', *Look Japan*, January 1994, p. 19.
7. Marlise Simons, 'East Europe Still Choking On Air of the Past', *The New York Times*, 3 November 1994, p. A-1.
8. United Nations, *World Population Projections to 2150*, Department of Economic and Social Affairs, Population Division (New York: United Nations, 1998).
9. 'The Battle of the Bulge: Population', *The Economist*, 3 September 1994, pp. 23–26.
10. This figure represents Tokyo's core suburbs, and exurbs. The core city has 8 million people.
11. 'Tokyo: Top Metropolis: Japanese Capital Overtakes Mexico City as the Largest City on Earth', *The Futurist*, September–October 1993, pp. 54–56.
12. United Nations, *World Population Projections to 2150*, Department of Economic and Social Affairs, Population Division (New York: United Nations, 1998).
13. Yukie Sasaki, '1.46', *Look Japan*, October 1994, p. 38.
14. 'Local Governments', *The Wall Street Journal*, 7 July 1994, p. A-1.
15. For insights to some of these questions, see Boye Lafayette DeMente, *Japanese Etiquette and Ethics in Business*, 6th edn (Lincolnwood, IL: NTC Business Books, 1994).

Cultural Dynamics in International Marketing

Chapter Outline

Chapter Learning Objectives

What you should learn from Chapter 6

- The importance of culture to an international marketer.
- The effects of the self-reference criterion (SRC) on marketing objectives.
- The elements of culture.
- The impact of cultural borrowing.
- The strategy of planned change and its consequences.

Humans are born creatures of need; as they mature, want is added to need. Economic needs are spontaneous and, in their crudest sense, limited. Humans, like all living things, need a minimum of nourishment and, like a few other living things they need shelter. Unlike any other being, they also need essential clothing. Economic wants, however, are for nonessentials and, hence, are limitless. Unlike basic needs, wants are not spontaneous and not characteristic of the lower animals. They arise not from an inner desire for preservation of self or species, but from a desire for satisfaction above absolute necessity. To satisfy their material needs and wants, humans consume.

The manner in which people consume, the priority of needs and the wants they attempt to satisfy, and the manner in which they satisfy them are functions of their culture that temper, mould and dictate their style of living. *Culture* is the human-made part of human environment—the sum total of knowledge, beliefs, art, morals, laws, customs and any other capabilities and habits acquired by humans as members of society. Culture is 'everything that people have, think and do as members of their society'.[1]

Culture is often defined as 'inherited ethical habit', consisting of values and ideas. Ethical systems create moral communities because their shared languages of good and evil give their members a common moral life.[2]

According to Hofstede,[3]

> culture (two) is always a collective phenomenon, because it is at least partially shared with people who live or lived within the same environment, which is where it was learned. It is the collective programming of the mind which distinguishes the members of one group or category of people from another.

Some authors claim that the world is moving towards a 'civilizational clash' in which primary identification of people will not be ideological but cultural.[4] Accordingly the world is divided into major cultures such as: Western, Islamic, Confucian, Japanese, Hindu and so on. In our opinion, however, firstly it is somewhat of an oversimplification as among 'Western' we have several cultures such as American, Nordic, Southern Europe and so on. And among Islamic, there are huge cultural differences between the Middle East and the Far East. Moreover, that cultural differences will necessarily be the source of conflict is highly speculative.

Hofstede's seminal work on culture contains more than 11 600 questionnaires in more than 50 countries. He derived four main conceptual dimensions on which national cultures exhibit significant differences. The dimensions are named *individualism/collectivism, power distance, masculinity/femininity* and *uncertainty avoidance*. For example, in collective countries there is a close-knit social structure, while in individualistic countries people are basically supposed to care for themselves. Power distance refers to the extent to which a society and its individuals tolerate an unequal distribution of power. A society is masculine when it favours assertiveness, earning money, showing off possessions and caring little for others, while feminine societies are the opposite. Uncertainty avoidance refers to the degree to which a society feels threatened by uncertain, ambiguous or undefined situations. In high uncertainty avoidance society people look for stable careers and follow rules and procedures. Table 6.1 shows the values of these dimensions for 52 different countries/regions.[5]

Because culture deals with a group's design for living, it is pertinent to the study of marketing, especially international marketing. If you consider for a moment the scope of the marketing concept—the satisfaction of consumer needs and wants at a profit—it becomes apparent that the successful marketer must be a student of culture. What a marketer is constantly dealing with is the culture of the people (the market). When a promotional message is written, symbols recognizable and meaningful to the market (the culture) must be used. When designing a product, the style, uses and other related marketing activities

Table 6.1   Values of Hofstede's Cultural Dimensions for 52 Countries or Regions

| Country/region | Dimensions | | | |
	Power Distance	Uncertainty Avoidance	Individualism	Masculinity
Arabic countries (ARA)	80	68	38	53
Argentina (ARG)	49	86	46	56
Australia (AUL)	36	51	90	61
Austria (AUS)	11	70	55	79
Belgium (BEL)	65	94	75	54
Brazil (BRA)	69	76	38	49
Canada (CAN)	39	48	80	52
Chile (CHI)	63	86	23	28
Colombia (COL)	67	80	13	64
Costa Rica (COS)	35	86	15	21
Denmark (DEN)	18	23	74	16
East African region (EA)	64	52	27	41
Ecuador (ECUA)	78	67	8	63
Finland (FIN)	33	59	63	26
France (FRA)	68	86	71	43
Great Britain (GB)	35	35	89	66
Greece (GRE)	60	112	35	57
Guatemala (GUA)	96	101	6	37
Hong Kong (HON)	68	29	25	57
India (IND)	77	40	48	56
Indonesia (INDO)	78	48	14	46
Iran (IRA)	58	59	41	43
Ireland (IRE)	28	35	70	68
Israel (ISR)	13	81	54	47
Italy (ITA)	50	75	76	70
Jamaica (JAM)	45	13	39	68
Japan (JAP)	54	92	46	95
Malaysia (MAL)	104	36	26	50
Mexico (MEX)	81	82	30	69
Netherlands (NETH)	38	53	80	14
New Zealand (NZ)	22	49	79	58
Norway (NOR)	31	50	69	8
Pakistan (PAK)	55	70	14	50
Panama (PAN)	95	86	11	44
Peru (PER)	64	87	16	42
Philippines (PHI)	94	44	32	64
Portugal (POR)	63	104	27	31
Salvador (SAL)	66	94	19	40
Singapore (SIN)	74	8	20	48
South Africa (SA)	49	49	65	63
South Korea (KOR)	60	85	18	39
Spain (SPA)	57	86	51	42
Sweden (SWE)	31	29	71	5
Switzerland (SWI)	34	58	68	70
Taiwan (TAI)	58	69	17	45
Thailand (THA)	64	64	20	34
Turkey (TUR)	66	85	37	45
United States (USA)	40	46	91	62
Uruguay (URU)	61	100	36	38
Venezuela (VEN)	81	76	12	73
West African region (WA)	77	54	20	46
West Germany (WG)	35	65	67	66
Overall mean	*57*	*65*	*43*	*49*
Standard deviation	*22*	*24*	*25*	*18*

Source: Cited from J.C. Usunier, *Marketing Across Cultures*, 2nd edn, 1996 (Hemel Hempstead: Prentice-Hall, pp. 78–79).

'QUESTION AUTHORITY' vs. 'RESPECT AUTHORITY'

A car commercial shown on American television portrays a young girl sitting in an oppressive classroom, being told by a stern teacher in a monotonous voice over and over to 'draw between the lines'. The scene suddenly cuts to the same girl as a young woman—shown now in colour rather than black and white—driving her own car with the top down and the wind ruffling her hair. She not only fails to stay within the lines on the highway but is shown having the time of her life driving off-road across an open field. Though the makers of the commercial did not include this detail, her car might well have sported a bumper sticker reading 'Question Authority'. The same commercial, were it produced in Asia, would likely portray a sympathetic teacher showing the girl how to draw carefully between the lines. The girl, after patient practice, would do so with the utmost precision. Only then would she be rewarded with a new car, whose bumper sticker would read 'Respect Authority'. In both cases the moral lessons are conveyed not rationally but through images, habits, and social opinions.

Source: Francis Fukuyama, *Trust: The Social Virtues and the Creation of Prosperity* (London, Penguin, 1996), p. 35.

must be made culturally acceptable (i.e. acceptable to the present society) if they are to be operative and meaningful. In fact, culture is pervasive in all marketing activities—in pricing, promotion, channels of distribution, product, packaging and styling—and the marketer's efforts actually become a part of the fabric of culture. The marketer's efforts are judged in a cultural context for acceptance, resistance or rejection. How such efforts interact with a culture determines the degree of success or failure of the marketing effort.

The marketer's frame of reference must be that markets are not, they become; they are not static but change, expand and contract in response to marketing effort, economic conditions and other cultural influences. Markets and market behaviour are part of a country's culture. One cannot truly understand how markets evolve or how they react to a marketer's effort without appreciating that markets are a result of culture. Markets are dynamic living phenomena, expanding and contracting not only in response to economic change, but also in response to changes in other aspects of the culture. Markets are the result of the three-way interaction of a marketer's efforts, economic conditions and all other elements of the culture. Marketers are constantly adjusting their efforts to cultural demands of the market, but they are also acting as agents of change whenever the product or idea being marketed is innovative. Whatever the degree of acceptance in whatever level of culture, the use of something new is the beginning of cultural change and the marketer becomes a change agent.

This chapter's purpose is to heighten the reader's sensitivity to the dynamics of culture. It is not a treatise on cultural information about a particular country; rather, it is designed to emphasize the need for study of each country's culture and to point up some relevant aspects on which to focus. This chapter explores briefly the concept of culture related to international marketing. Subsequent chapters explore particular features of each of the cultural elements as they affect the marketing process.

CULTURAL KNOWLEDGE

There are two kinds of knowledge about cultures. One is *factual knowledge* about a culture; it is usually obvious and must be learned. Different meanings of colour, different tastes and

'TEETH ARE EXTRACTED BY THE LATEST METHODISTS'

So reads a sign by a Hong Kong dentist. Translating a message and getting the right meaning is a problem for all cultures. The following examples illustrate:

A Polish menu: 'Beef rashers beaten up in the country people's fashion.'

An Acapulco hotel gives new meaning to quality control: 'The manager has personally passed all the water served here.'

In an Austrian hotel catering to skiers: 'Not to perambulate the corridors in the hours of repose in the boots of ascension.'

A Bangkok dry cleaner: 'Drop your trousers here for best results.'

A Zurich hotel: 'Because of the impropriety of entertaining guests of the opposite sex in the bedroom, it is suggested that the lobby be used for this purpose.'

A sign posted in Germany's Black Forest: 'It is strictly forbidden on our Black Forest camping site that people of different sex, for instance, men and women, to live together in one tent unless they are married with each other for that purpose.'

A Swiss restaurant menu: 'Our wines leave you nothing to hope for.'

A Tokyo car-rental firm's driving manual: 'When passengers of foot heave in sight, tootle the horn, trumpet him melodiously at first, if he still obstacles your passings, then tootle him with vigour.'

And finally, truth in advertising in a Copenhagen airline ticket office: 'We take your bags and send them in all directions.'

Sources: From the author and Charles Goldsmith, 'Look See! Anyone Do Read This and It Will Make You Laughable', *The Wall Street Journal*, 19 November 1992, p. B-1, and 'Cook's Travellers' Tales', *World Press Review*, June 1994, p. 26.

other traits indigenous to a culture are facts that a marketer can anticipate, study and absorb. The other is *interpretive knowledge*—an ability to understand and to appreciate fully the nuances of different cultural traits and patterns. For example, the meaning of time, attitudes towards other people and certain objects, the understanding of one's role in society, and the meanings of life can differ considerably from one culture to another and may require more than factual knowledge to be fully appreciated.

Factual Knowledge

Frequently, factual knowledge has meaning as a straightforward fact about a culture, but assumes additional significance when interpreted within the context of the culture. For example, that Mexico is 98 per cent Roman Catholic is an important bit of factual knowledge. But equally important is what it means to be a Catholic within Mexican culture versus being Catholic in Spain or Italy. Each culture practises Catholicism in slightly different ways. For example, All Soul's Day is an important celebration among some Catholic countries; in Mexico, however, the celebration receives special emphasis. The Mexican observance is a unique combination of pagan (mostly Indian influence) and Catholic tradition. On the Day of the Dead, as All Soul's Day is called by many in Mexico, it is believed that the dead return to feast. Hence, many Mexicans visit the graves of their departed, taking the dead's favourite foods to place on the graves for them to enjoy. Prior to All Soul's Day, bakeries pile their shelves with bread shaped like bones and coffins, and candy stores sell sugar skulls and other special treats to commemorate the day. As the souls feast on the food, so do the living

MORE EQUAL THAN OTHERS

In a peaceful revolution—the last revolution in Swedish history—the nobles of Sweden in 1809 deposed King Gustav IV whom they considered incompetent, and surprisingly invited Jean Baptiste Bernadotte, a French general who served under their enemy Napoleon, to become King of Sweden. Bernadotte accepted and he became King Charles XIV; his descendants occupy the Swedish throne to this day. When the new king was installed he addressed the Swedish parliament in their language. His broken Swedish amused the Swedes and they roared with laughter. The Frenchman who had become King was so upset he never tried to speak Swedish again. In this incident Bernadotte was a victim of culture shock: never in his French upbringing and military career had he experienced subordinates who laughed at the mistakes of their superior. Historians tell us he had more problems adapting to the egalitarian Swedish and Norwegian mentality (he later became King of Norway as well) and to his subordinates' constitutional rights. He was a good learner, however (except for language), and he ruled the country as a highly respected constitutional monarch until 1844.

One of the aspects in which Sweden differs from France is the way its society handles *inequality*. There is inequality in any society. Even in the most simple huntergatherer band, some people are bigger, stronger or smarter than others. The next thing is that some people have more power than others: they are more able to determine the behaviour of others than vice versa. Some people are given more status and respect than others.

Source: Geert Hofstede, *Cultures and Organizations: Software of the Mind* (London: McGraw-Hill, 1991), p. 23.

celebrants. Although the prayers, candles and the idea of the soul are Catholic, the idea of the dead feasting is very pre-Christian Mexican. Thus, a Catholic in Mexico observes All Soul's Day quite differently from a Catholic in Spain. This interpretive, as well as factual, knowledge about a religion in Mexico is necessary to fully understand Mexican culture.[6]

Interpretive Knowledge

Interpretive knowledge requires a degree of insight that may best be described as a feeling. It is the kind of knowledge most dependent on past experience for interpretation and most frequently prone to misinterpretation if relying on one's self-reference criterion (SRC).

Ideally, the foreign marketer should possess both kinds of knowledge about a market. Most facts about a particular culture can be learned by researching published material about that culture. This effort can also transmit a small degree of empathy, but to appreciate the culture fully, it is necessary to live with the people for some time. Because this ideal solution is not practical for a marketer, other solutions are sought. Consultation and cooperation with bilingual nationals with marketing backgrounds is the most effective answer to the problem. This has the further advantage of helping the marketer acquire an increasing degree of empathy through association with people who understand the culture best—the locals.

Cultural Sensitivity and Tolerance

Successful foreign marketing begins with *cultural sensitivity*—being attuned to the nuances of culture so that a new culture can be viewed objectively, evaluated and appreciated. Cultural empathy must be carefully cultivated. Perhaps the most important step is the recognition that cultures are not right or wrong, better or worse; they are simply different. For every amusing, annoying, peculiar or repulsive cultural trait we find in a country, there is a similarly amusing, annoying or repulsive trait others see in our culture. We find it peculiar that the Chinese eat dog, while they find it peculiar that we buy packaged, processed dog food in supermarkets and keep dogs as pets.

Just because a culture is different does not make it wrong. Marketers must understand how their own culture influences their assumptions about another culture. The more exotic the situation, the more sensitive, tolerant and flexible one needs to be. Being more culturally sensitive will reduce conflict, improve communications and thereby increase success in collaborative relationships.

It is necessary for a marketer to investigate the assumptions on which judgements are based, especially when the frames of reference are strictly from his or her own culture. As products of our own culture we instinctively evaluate foreign cultural patterns from a personal perspective.

CULTURE AND ITS ELEMENTS

The student of international marketing should approach an understanding of culture from the viewpoint of the anthropologist. Every group of people or society has a culture because culture is the entire social heritage of the human race: 'the totality of the knowledge and practices, both intellectual and material of society . . . [it] embraces everything from food to dress, from household techniques to industrial techniques, from forms of politeness to mass media, from work rhythms to the learning of familiar rules.'[7] Culture exists in New York, London and Moscow just as it does among the Gypsies, the South Sea islanders or the Aborigines of Australia.

Elements of Culture

The anthropologist studying culture as a science must investigate every aspect of a culture if an accurate, total picture is to emerge. To implement this goal, there has evolved a cultural scheme that defines the parts of culture. For the marketer, the same thoroughness is necessary if the marketing consequences of cultural differences within a foreign market are to be accurately assessed.

Culture includes every part of life. The scope of the term *culture* to the anthropologist is illustrated by the elements included within the meaning of the term. They are:

1. Material culture
   Technology
   Economics
2. Social institutions
   Social organization
   Political structures
3. Education
   Literacy rate
   Role and levels
4. Belief systems
   Religion
   Superstitions
   Power structure

Figure 6.1   Elements of Culture

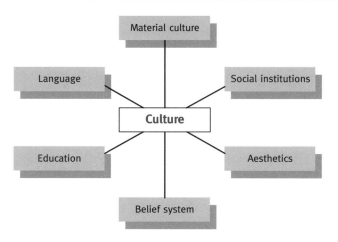

5. Aesthetics
   Graphic and plastic arts
   Folklore
   Music, drama, and dance
6. Language[8]
   Usage of foreign languages
   Spoken versus written language

In the study of humanity's way of life, the anthropologist finds these six dimensions useful because they encompass all the activities of social heritage that constitute culture (Figure 6.1). Foreign marketers may find such a cultural scheme a useful framework in evaluating a marketing plan or in studying the potential of foreign markets. All the elements are instrumental to some extent in the success or failure of a marketing effort because they constitute the environment within which the marketer operates. Furthermore, because we automatically react to many of these factors in our native culture, we must purposely learn them in another. Finally, these are the elements with which marketing efforts interact and so are critical to understanding the character of the marketing system of any society. It is necessary to study the various implications of the differences of each of these factors in any analysis of a specific foreign market.

Material Culture.   Material culture is divided into two parts, technology and economics. Technology includes the techniques used in the creation of material goods; it is the technical know-how possessed by the people of a society. For example, the vast majority of Western citizens understand the simple concepts involved in reading gauges, but in many countries of the world, this seemingly simple concept is not part of their common culture and is therefore a major technical limitation.

A culture's level of technology is manifest in many ways. Such concepts as preventive maintenance are foreign in many low-technology cultures. In Germany, the United States, Japan or other countries with high levels of technology, the general population has a broad level of technical understanding that allows them to adapt and learn new technology more easily than populations with lower levels of technology. Simple repairs, preventive maintenance and a general understanding of how things work all constitute a high level of technology. In China, one of the burdens of that country's economic growth is providing the general working population with a modest level of mechanical skill, that is, a level of technology.

Economics is the manner in which people employ their capabilities and the resulting benefits. Included in the subject of economics are the production of goods and services, their distribution, consumption, means of exchange and the income derived from the creation of utilities.

Material culture affects the level of demand, the quality and types of products demanded and their functional features, as well as the means of production of these goods and their distribution. The marketing implications of the material culture of a country are many; electrical appliances sell in England or France, but have few buyers in countries where less than 1 per cent of the homes have electricity. Even with electrification, economic characteristics represented by the level and distribution of income may limit the desirability of products. Electric can openers and electric juicers are acceptable in the United States, but, in less affluent countries, not only are they unattainable and probably unwanted, they would be a spectacular waste because disposable income could be spent more meaningfully on better houses, clothing or food.

Social Institutions.   Social organization and political structures are concerned with the ways in which people relate to one another, organize their activities to live in harmony with one another and govern themselves. The positions of men and women in society, the family, social classes, group behaviour and age groups are interpreted differently within every culture (see Figure 6.2). Each institution has an effect on marketing because each influences behaviour, values and the overall patterns of life. In cultures where the social organizations result in close-knit family units, for example, it is more effective to aim a promotion campaign at the family unit than at individual family members. Travel advertising in culturally divided Canada pictures a wife alone for the English audience, but a man and wife together for the French segments of the population because the French are traditionally more closely bound by family ties. The roles and status positions found within a society are influenced by the dictates of social organizations.

Education.   In each society, we teach our generation what is acceptable or not acceptable, right or wrong and other ways of behaviour. The literacy rate in each society is an important aspect and influences the behaviour of people. For a marketer it is important to know the role and level of education in a particular market. It would influence the marketing strategy and techniques used. Which type of advertising and communication is used, depends highly on the level of education.

Belief System.   Within this category are religion, superstitions and their related power structures. The impact of religion on the value systems of a society and the effect of value systems on marketing must not be underestimated. Religion impacts people's habits, their outlook on life, the products they buy, the way they buy them, even the newspapers they read. Acceptance of certain types of food, clothing and behaviour are frequently affected by religion, and such influence can extend to the acceptance or rejection of promotional messages as well. In some countries, too much attention to bodily functions featured in advertisements would be judged immoral or improper and the products would be rejected. What might seem innocent and acceptable in one culture could be considered too personal or vulgar in another. Such was the case when Saudi Arabian customs officials impounded

---

Figure 6.2   Concepts of Self and Others

Basic problem/cultural orientations	*Contrasts across cultures*
How should we treat unknown people?	
(a) Is human nature basically good or bad?	Unknown people are considered favourably and shown confidence or, conversely, they are treated with suspicion when met for the first time
Appraising others	

(b) When appraising others, emphasis placed on:
    (i) age
   (ii) sex
   (iii) social class
	Who are the persons to be considered trustworthy and reliable, with whom it is possible to do business?
	    (i) Older (younger) people are seen more favourably
	   (ii) Trustworthiness is based on sex or not
	   (iii) Social class plays a significant role (or not) in concepts of the self and others

Appraising oneself	

(c) Emphasis placed on the self-concept perceived as culturally appropriate:
    (i) self-esteem: low/high
   (ii) perceived potency: low/high
   (iii) level of activity: low/high
	
	    (i) Shyly and modestly vs. extrovert or even arrogant
	   (ii) Power should be shown vs. hidden
	   (iii) Busy people are the good ones vs. unoccupied/ idle people are well considered

Relating to the group (d) Individualism vs. collectivism	The individual is seen as the basic resource and therefore individual-related values are strongly emphasized (personal freedom, human rights, equality between men and women); versus the group is seen as the basic resource and therefore group values favoured (loyalty, sense of belonging, sense of personal sacrifice for the community, etc.)

Source: J.C. Usunier, *Marketing Across Cultures*, 2nd edn (Hemel Hempstead: Prentice-Hall, 1996), p. 66.

---

a shipment of French perfume because the bottle stopper was in the shape of a nude female.[9]

Religion is one of the most sensitive elements of a culture. When the marketer has little or no understanding of a religion, it is easy to offend, albeit unintentionally. Like all cultural elements, one's own religion is often not a reliable guide of another's beliefs. Many do not understand religions other than their own, and what is 'known' about other religions is often incorrect. The Islamic religion is a good example of the need for a basic understanding. There are more than 1 billion in the world who embrace Islam, yet major multinational companies often offend Muslims. A recent incident (1994) involved the French fashion house of Chanel which unwittingly desecrated the Koran by embroidering verses from the sacred book of Islam on several dresses shown in its summer collections. The designer said he took the design, which was aesthetically pleasing to him, from a book on India's Taj Mahal palace and that he was unaware of its meaning. To placate a Muslim group that felt the use of the verses desecrated the Koran, Chanel had to destroy the dresses with the offending designs along

GOING INTERNATIONAL 6.4

GAINING CULTURAL AWARENESS IN 17TH- AND 18TH-CENTURY ENGLAND—THE GRAND TOUR

Gaining cultural awareness has been a centuries-old need for anyone involved in international relations. The term *Grand Tour*, first applied over three hundred years ago in England, was, by 1706, firmly established as the ideal preparation for soldiers, diplomats and civil servants. It was seen as the best means of imparting to young men of fortune a modicum of taste and a knowledge of other countries. By the summer of 1785, there were an estimated 40 000 English on the Continent.

The Grand Tourist was expected to conduct a systematic survey of each country's language, history, geography, clothes, food, customs, politics and laws. In particular, he was to study its most important buildings with their valuable contents, and he was encouraged to collect prints, paintings, drawings and sculpture. All this could not be achieved in a few weeks, and several years were to lapse before some tourists saw England's shores again. Vast sums of money were spent. At times, touring was not the relatively secure affair of today. If the Grand Tourist managed to avoid the pirates of Dunkirk, he then had to run a gauntlet of highwaymen on Dutch roads, thieves in Italy and France, marauding packs of disbanded soldiery everywhere and the Inquisition in Spain, to say nothing of ravenous wolves and dogs.

He had to be self-contained; he carried with him not only the obligatory sword and pistols but also a box of medicines and other spices and condiments, a means of securing hotel rooms at night and an overall to protect his clothes while in bed. At the end of these Grand Tours, many returned with as many as eight or nine hundred pieces of baggage. These collections of art, sculpture and writings can be seen today in many of the mansions throughout the British Isles.

Source: Nigel Sale, *Historic Houses and Gardens of East Anglia* (Norwich, England: Jarrold Colour Publications, 1976), p. 1.

with negatives of the photos made of the garments. Chanel certainly had no intention of offending Muslims because some of their most important customers are of that religion. This example shows how easy it is to offend if the marketer, in this case the designer, has not familiarized him- or herself with other religions.[10]

Superstition plays a much larger role in a society's belief system in some parts of the world than it does in the Western culture. What might be considered by Westerners as mere superstition can be a critical aspect of a belief system in another culture. For example, in parts of Asia, ghosts, fortune-telling, palmistry, head-bump reading, phases of the moon, demons and soothsayers are all integral parts of certain cultures. Astrologers are routinely called on in India and Thailand to determine the best location for a structure. The Thai insist that all wood in a new building must come from the same forest to prevent the boards from quarrelling with each other. Houses should have an odd number of rooms for luck, and they should be one storey because it is unlucky to have another's foot over your head.

An incident reported in Malaysia involved mass hysteria from fear of evil spirits. Most of a factory's labourers were involved, and production ground to a halt until a 'bomoh' was called, a goat sacrificed and its blood sprinkled on the factory floor; the goat was then roasted and eaten. The next day the hysteria was over and everyone was back at work.[11]

It can be an expensive mistake to make light of superstitions in other cultures when doing business there. To make a fuss about being born in the right year under the right phase of the moon and to rely heavily on handwriting and palm-reading experts, as in Japan, can be worrisome to a Westerner who seldom sees a 13th floor in a building, refuses to walk under a ladder or worries about the next seven years after breaking a mirror.[12]

Aesthetics.   Closely interwoven with the effect of people and the universe on a culture are its aesthetics; that is, the arts, folklore, music, drama and dance. Aesthetics are of particular interest to the marketer because of their role in interpreting the symbolic meanings of various methods of artistic expression, colour and standards of beauty in each culture. The uniqueness of a culture can be spotted quickly in symbols having distinct meanings.

Without a culturally correct interpretation of a country's aesthetic values, a whole host of marketing problems can arise. Product styling must be aesthetically pleasing to be successful, as must advertisements and package designs. Insensitivity to aesthetic values can offend, create a negative impression and, in general, render marketing efforts ineffective. Strong symbolic meanings may be overlooked if one is not familiar with a culture's aesthetic values. The Japanese, for example, revere the crane as being very lucky for it is said to live a thousand years; however, the use of the number four should be completely avoided since the word for four, *shi*, is also the Japanese word for death.

Language.   The importance of understanding the language of a country cannot be overestimated. The successful marketer must achieve expert communication; this requires a thorough understanding of the language as well as the ability to speak it. Advertising copywriters should be concerned less with obvious differences between languages and more with the idiomatic meanings expressed.

A dictionary translation is not the same as an idiomatic interpretation, and seldom will the dictionary translation suffice. Quite often there is a difference between spoken and written language. A national food processor's familiar 'Jolly Green Giant' translated into Arabic as 'Intimidating Green Ogre'. One airline's advertising campaign designed to promote its plush leather seats urged customers to 'fly on leather'; when translated for its Hispanic and Latin American customers, it told passengers to 'fly naked'. Pepsi's familiar 'Come Alive with Pepsi', when translated into German, conveyed the idea of coming alive from the grave. Schweppes was not pleased with its tonic water translation into Italian: 'Il Water' idiomatically means the bathroom. Electrolux's advertisement for its vacuum cleaner with the slogan 'Nothing Sucks Better than Electrolux', in Ireland was not particularly appreciated. Carelessly translated advertising statements not only lose their intended meaning, but can suggest something very different, obscene, offensive or just plain ridiculous. One authority suggests, as a cultural translator, a person who translates not only among languages, but also among different ways of thinking and among different cultures.[13]

Many believe that to appreciate the true meaning of a language it is necessary to live with the language for years. Whether or not this is the case, foreign marketers should never take it for granted that they are effectively communicating in another language. Until a marketer can master the vernacular, the aid of a national within the foreign country should be enlisted; even then, the problem of effective communications may still exist. For example, in French-speaking countries, the trademark toothpaste brand name, 'Cue,' was a crude slang expression for derrière. The intent of a major fountain pen company advertising in Latin America suffered in translation when the new pen was promoted to 'help prevent unwanted pregnancies'. The poster of an engineering company at a Russian trade show did not mean to promise that its oil well completion equipment was dandy for 'improving a person's sex life'.[14]

Analysis of Elements

Each cultural element must be evaluated in light of how it could affect a proposed marketing programme; some may have only indirect impact, others may be totally involved. Generally, it could be said that the more complete the marketing involvement or the more unique the

IT'S NOT THE GIFT THAT COUNTS, BUT HOW YOU PRESENT IT

Giving a gift in another country requires careful attention if it is to be done properly. Here are a few suggestions:

Japan

Do not open a gift in front of a Japanese counterpart unless asked and do not expect the Japanese to open your gift.

Avoid ribbons and bows as part of gift wrapping. Bows as we know them are considered unattractive and ribbon colours can have different meanings.

Do not offer a gift depicting a fox or badger. The fox is the symbol of fertility, the badger, cunning.

Europe

Avoid red roses and white flowers, even numbers, and the number 13. Unwrap flowers before presenting.

Do not risk the impression of bribery by spending too much on a gift.

Arab World

Do not give a gift when you first meet someone. It may be interpreted as a bribe.

Do not let it appear that you contrived to present the gift when the recipient is alone. It looks bad unless you know the person well. Give the gift in front of others in less personal relationships.

Latin America

Do not give a gift until after a somewhat personal relationship has developed unless it is given to express appreciation for hospitality.

Gifts should be given during social encounters, not in the course of business.

Avoid the colours black and purple; both are associated with the Catholic lenten season.

China

Never make an issue of a gift presentation—publicly or privately.

Gifts should be presented privately, with the exception of collective ceremonial gifts at banquets.

Source: Adapted from 'International Business Gift-Giving Customs', available from The Parker Pen Company, nd.

product, the more need for thorough study of each cultural element. If a company is simply marketing an existing product in an already developed market, studying the total culture is certainly less crucial than for the marketer involved in total marketing—from product development, through promotion, to the final selling.

While analysis of each cultural element *vis-à-vis* a marketing programme could ensure that each facet of a culture is included, it should not be forgotten that culture is a total picture, not a group of unrelated elements. Culture cannot be separated into parts and be fully understood. Every facet of culture is intricately intertwined and cannot be viewed singly; each must be considered for its synergistic effects. The ultimate personal motives and interests of people are determined by all the interwoven facets of the culture rather than by the individual parts. While some specific cultural elements have a direct influence on individual marketing efforts and must be viewed individually in terms of their potential or real effect on marketing strategy, the whole of cultural elements is manifested in a broader sense on the basic cultural patterns. In a market, basic consumption patterns, that is, who buys, what they buy, frequency of purchases, sizes purchased and so on, are established by cultural values of right and wrong, acceptable and unacceptable. The basic motives for consumption that help define fundamental needs and different forms of decision making have strong cultural underpinnings that are critical knowledge for the marketer.

WHY DON'T MONKEYS GO BANANAS

A number of behavioural scientists concluded an experiment where 10 monkeys were held in a room. A ladder was standing in the middle of the room and on top of the ladder some bananas were placed. It did not take long before one of the monkeys discovered the bananas and tried to reach them. As soon as the monkey climbed the ladder the whole group of monkeys were hosed down with pressured water by the scientists.

The drill was repeated until not one of the monkeys dared to reach the bananas. Now one monkey was replaced by a new monkey. Of course the new monkey discovered the bananas. On his attempt to reach the bananas, the other monkeys attacked him because they knew what was going to happen to them if this new monkey tried to reach the bananas.

The scientists kept replacing the monkeys who experienced the hosing until all of them were replaced by new monkeys. Eventually none of the monkeys in the community had experienced the hosing, yet as soon as a new monkey tried to reach for the bananas the other monkeys would pull him down from the ladder and attacked him. The monkeys thus declined to get the bananas.

Source: Translated from T. Pauka and R. Zunderdorp, *De Banaan Wordt Bespreekbaar. Cultuurverandering in Ambtelijk en Politiek* (Amsterdam: Groningen, 1988).

Culture is dynamic in nature; culture is not static but a living process. That change is constant seems paradoxical in that another important attribute of culture is that it is conservative and resists change. The dynamic character of culture is significant in assessing new markets even though changes occur in the face of resistance. In fact, any change in the currently accepted way of life meets with more initial resistance than acceptance.[15]

CULTURAL CHANGE

One view of culture sees it as the accumulation of a series of the best solutions to problems faced in common by members of a given society. In other words, culture is the means used in adjusting to the biological, environmental, psychological and historical components of human existence.

There are a variety of ways a society solves the problems created by its existence. Accident has provided solutions to some of them; invention has solved many others. More commonly, however, societies have found answers by looking to other cultures from which they can borrow ideas. Cultural borrowing is common to all cultures. Although each society has a few truly unique situations facing it, most problems confronting all societies are similar in nature, with alterations for each particular environment and culture.[16]

Cultural Borrowing

Cultural borrowing is a responsible effort to borrow those cultural ways seen as helpful in the quest for better solutions to a society's particular problems. If what it does adopt is adapted to local needs, once the adaptation becomes commonplace, it is passed on as cultural heritage. Thus, cultures unique in their own right are the result, in part, of borrowing from others. Consider, for example, American culture (United States) and the typical US citizen who

> . . . begins breakfast with an orange from the eastern Mediterranean, a cantaloupe from Egypt, or perhaps a piece of African watermelon. . . . After his fruit and Colombian

coffee he goes on to waffles, cakes made by a Scandinavian technique from wheat domesticated in Asia Minor. Over these he pours maple syrup, invented by the Indians of the Eastern US woodlands. As a side dish he may have the eggs of a species of bird domesticated in Indo-China, or thin strips of the flesh of an animal domesticated in Eastern Asia which have been salted and smoked by a process developed in northern Europe. . . .

While smoking, he reads the news of the day, imprinted in characters invented by the ancient Semites upon a material invented in China by a process invented in Germany. As he absorbs the accounts of foreign troubles he will, if he is a good conservative citizen, thank a Hebrew deity in an Indo-European language that he is 100 per cent American.[17]

Actually, this citizen is correct to assume that he or she is 100 per cent American because each of the borrowed cultural facets has been adapted to fit his or her needs, moulded into uniquely American habits, foods and customs. Americans behave as they do because of the dictates of their culture. Regardless of how or where solutions are found, once a particular pattern of action is judged acceptable by society, it becomes the approved way and is passed on and taught as part of the group's cultural heritage. Cultural heritage is one of the fundamental differences between humans and other animals. Culture is learned; societies pass on to succeeding generations solutions to problems, constantly building on and expanding the culture so that a wide range of behaviour is possible. The point is, of course, that although much behaviour is borrowed from other cultures, it is combined in a unique manner which becomes typical for a particular society. To the foreign marketer, this similar-but-different feature of cultures has important meaning in gaining cultural empathy.

Similarities: An Illusion

For the inexperienced marketer, the similar-but-different aspect of culture creates illusions of similarity that usually do not exist. Several nationalities can speak the same language or have similar race and heritage, but it does not follow that similarities exist in other respects—that a product acceptable to one culture will be readily acceptable to the other, or that a promotional message that succeeds in one country will succeed in the other. Even though a people start with a common idea or approach, as is the case among English-speaking Australians, Americans and the British, cultural borrowing and assimilation to meet individual needs translate over time into quite distinct cultures. A common language does not guarantee a similar interpretation of even a word or phrase. Both the British and the Americans speak English, but their cultures are sufficiently different so that a single phrase has different meanings to each and can even be completely misunderstood. In England, one asks for a lift instead of an elevator, and an American, when speaking of a bathroom, generally refers to a toilet, while in England a bathroom is a place to take a tub bath. Also, the English 'hoover' a carpet whereas Americans vacuum clean it.

Differences run much deeper than language differences, however. The approach to life, values and concepts of acceptable and unacceptable behaviour may all have a common heritage and may appear superficially to be the same. In reality, profound differences do exist. Among the Spanish-speaking Latin American countries, the problem becomes even more difficult because the idiom is unique to each country, and national pride tends to cause a mute rejection of any 'foreign-Spanish' language. In some cases, an acceptable phrase or word in one country is not only unacceptable in another, it can very well be indecent or vulgar. In

Spanish, *coger* is the verb 'to catch', but in some countries it is used as a euphemism with a baser meaning.

Asians are frequently grouped together as if there were no cultural distinctions among Japanese, Koreans and Chinese, to name but a few of the many ethnic groups in the Pacific region. Asia cannot be viewed as a homogeneous entity and the marketer must understand the subtle and not-so-subtle differences among Asian cultures. Each country (culture) has its own unique national character.

There is also the tendency to speak of the 'European consumer' as a result of growing integration of Europe. Many of the obstacles to doing business in Europe have been or will be eliminated as the EU takes shape, but marketers, anxious to enter the market, must not jump to the conclusion that a unified Europe means a common set of consumer wants and needs. Cultural differences among the members of the EU are the product of centuries of history that will take centuries to erase.

Even the United States has many subcultures that today, with mass communications and rapid travel, defy complete homogenization. It would be folly to suggest that the South is in all respects culturally the same as the Northeastern or Midwestern parts of the United States. It also would be folly to assume that the unification of Germany has erased cultural differences that have arisen from over 40 years of political and social separation.[18]

A single geopolitical boundary does not necessarily mean a single culture: Canada is divided culturally between its French and English heritages although it is politically one country. A successful marketing strategy among the French Canadians may be a certain failure among remaining Canadians. Within most cultures there are many subcultures that can have marketing significance.

India is another example, people from the South speak different languages and do not even understand Hindi or other languages of the north, west or east. There are more than 100 languages spoken in India, 25 of which are official languages. In fact, the only language that unites India is English.

Resistance to Change

A characteristic of human culture is that change occurs.[19] That people's habits, tastes, styles, behaviour and values are not constant but are continually changing can be verified by reading 20-year-old magazines. This gradual cultural growth does not occur without some resistance. New methods, ideas and products are held to be suspect before they are accepted, if ever, as right.

The degree of resistance to new patterns varies; in some situations new elements are accepted completely and rapidly, and in others, resistance is so strong that acceptance is never forthcoming. Studies show that the most important factor in determining what kind and how much of an innovation will be accepted is the degree of interest in the particular subject, as well as how drastically the new will change the old, that is, how disruptive the innovation will be to presently acceptable values and patterns of behaviour. Observations indicate that those innovations most readily accepted are those holding the greatest interest within the society and those least disruptive. For example, rapid industrialization in parts of Europe has changed many long-honoured attitudes involving time and working women. Today, there is an interest in ways to save time and make life more productive; the leisurely continental life is rapidly disappearing. With this time-consciousness has come the very rapid acceptance of many innovations that might have been resisted by most just a few years ago. Instant foods, mobile telephones, McDonald's and other fast-food establishments, all supportive of a changing attitude towards work and time, are rapidly gaining acceptance.

GOING INTERNATIONAL 6.7

OPENING A MEDICAL OFFICE IN SAUDI ARABIA

Dr Tom McDivern, a physician from New York City, was offered a two-year assignment to practise medicine in a growing urban centre in Saudi Arabia. Many of the residents he was assigned to were recent immigrants of the much smaller outlying rural areas. Because Western medicine was relatively unknown to many of these people, one of Tom's main responsibilities was to introduce himself and his services to those in the community. A meeting at a local school was organized for that specific purpose. Many people turned out. Tom's presentation went well. Some local residents also presented their experiences with Western medicine so others could hear the value of using his service. Some of Tom's office staff were also present to make appointments for those interested in seeing him when his doors opened one week later. The meeting was an obvious success. His opening day was booked solid.

When that day finally arrived, Tom was anxious to greet his first patients. Thirty minutes had passed, however, and neither of his first two patients had arrived. He was beginning to worry about the future of his practice while wondering where his patients were.

What's the major cause of Tom's worries?

1. Although in Tom's mind and by his standards his presentation was a success, people actually only made appointments so as not to hurt his feelings. They really had no intention of using his services as modern medicine is so foreign to their past experiences.
2. Given the time lag between sign up and the actual day of appointment, people had time to rethink their decision. They had just changed their minds.
3. Units of time differ between Arabs and Americans. Whereas to Tom his patients were very late, the Arab patient could still arrive and be on time.
4. Tom's patients were seeing their own traditional healers from their own culture; after that, they could go on to see this new doctor, Tom.

Source: Richard Brisling *et al.*, *Intercultural Interactions, A Practical Guide* (Newbury Park, CA: Sage, 1986), pp. 160–161.

Although a variety of innovations are completely and quickly accepted, others meet with firm resistance. India has been engaged in intensive population-control programmes for over 20 years, but the process has not worked well and India's population remains among the highest in the world; it is forecasted to exceed 1.1 billion by the year 2000. Why has birth control not been accepted? Most attribute the failure to the nature of Indian culture. Among the influences that help to sustain the high birthrate are early marriage, the Hindu societies emphasis on bearing sons, dependence on children for security in old age and a low level of education among the rural masses. All are important cultural patterns at variance with the concept of birth control. Acceptance of birth control would mean rejection of too many fundamental cultural concepts. For the Indian people, it is easier and more familiar to reject the new idea.

Most cultures tend to be *ethnocentric*; that is, they have intense identification with the known and the familiar of their culture and tend to devalue the foreign and unknown of other cultures. Ethnocentrism complicates the process of cultural assimilation by producing feelings of superiority about one's own culture and, in varying degrees, generates attitudes that other cultures are inferior, barbaric or at least peculiar. Ethnocentric feelings generally give way if a new idea is considered necessary or particularly appealing.

Although cultures meet most newness with some resistance or rejection, that resistance can be overcome. Cultures are dynamic and change occurs when resistance slowly yields to acceptance so the basis for resistance becomes unimportant or forgotten. Gradually there comes an awareness of the need for change, ideas once too complex become less so because of cultural gains in understanding, or an idea is restructured in a less complex way, and so on.

PLANNED CULTURAL CHANGE

The first step in bringing about planned change in a society is to determine which cultural factors conflict with an innovation, thus creating resistance to its acceptance. The next step is an effort to change those factors from obstacles to acceptance into stimulants for change. The same deliberate approaches used by the social planner to gain acceptance for hybrid grains, better sanitation methods, improved farming techniques, or protein-rich diets among the peoples of underdeveloped societies can be adopted by marketers to achieve marketing goals.[20]

Marketers have two options when introducing an innovation to a culture. They can wait, or they can cause change. The former requires hopeful waiting for eventual cultural changes that prove their innovations of value to the culture; the latter involves introducing an idea or product and deliberately setting about to overcome resistance and to cause change that accelerates the rate of acceptance.

An innovation that has advantages, but requires a culture to learn new ways to benefit from these advantages, establishes the basis for eventual cultural change. Both a strategy of unplanned change and a strategy of planned change produce cultural change. The fundamental difference is that unplanned change proceeds at its own pace whereas in planned change, the process of change is accelerated by the change agent. While culturally congruent strategy, strategy of unplanned change and strategy of planned change are not clearly articulated in international business literature, the third situation occurs. The marketer's efforts become part of the fabric of culture, planned or unplanned.

Take, for example, the change in diet in Japan since the introduction of milk and bread soon after World War II. Most Japanese, who are predominantly fish and rice eaters, have increased their intake of animal fat and protein to the point at which fat and protein now exceed vegetable intake. As many McDonald's hamburgers are apt to be eaten in Japan as the traditional rice ball wrapped in edible seaweed. A Westernized diet has caused many Japanese to become overweight. To counter this, the Japanese are buying low-calorie, low-fat foods to help shed excess weight and are flocking to health studios. All this began when US occupation forces introduced bread, milk and steak to Japanese culture. The effect on the Japanese was unintentional; nevertheless, change occurred. Had the intent been to introduce a new diet—that is, a strategy of planned change—specific steps could have been taken to identify resistance to dietary change and then to overcome these resistances, thus accelerating the process of change.

CONSEQUENCES OF AN INNOVATION

When product diffusion (acceptance) occurs, a process of social change may also occur. One issue frequently addressed concerns the consequences of the changes that happen within a social system as a result of acceptance of an innovation. The marketer seeking product diffusion and adoption may inadvertently bring about change which affects the very fabric of a social system. Consequences of diffusion of an innovation may be functional or dysfunctional, depending on whether the effects on the social system are desirable or undesirable. In

GOING INTERNATIONAL 6.8

ICI ON PARLE FRANÇAIS

Frequently there is a conflict between a desire to borrow from another culture and the natural inclination not to pollute one's own culture by borrowing from others. France offers a good example of this conflict. On the one hand, the French accept such US culture as the Oprah Winfrey show on television, award Sylvester 'Rambo' Stallone the Order of Arts and Letters, listen to Bruce Springsteen, and dine on all-American gastronomic delights such as the Big Mac and Kentucky Fried Chicken. At the same time, there is an uneasy feeling that accepting so much from America will somehow dilute the true French culture. Thus, in an attempt to somehow control cultural pollution, France is embarking on a campaign to expunge examples of 'franglais' from all walks of life, including television, billboards and business contracts. If the culture ministry has its way, violators will be fined. A list of correct translations include *heures de grande écoute* for 'prime time', *coussin gonflable de protection* for 'airbag', *sablé américain* for 'cookie', and some 3500 other offensive expressions. While the demand for hamburger and US television shows cannot be stemmed, perhaps the language can be saved.

With a tongue-in-cheek response, an English lawmaker said that he would introduce a bill in Parliament to ban the use of French words in public. Order an 'aperitif' in a British bar or demand an 'encore' at the end of an opera and you might be in trouble—and so goes the 'language wars'.

Postscript. The use of foreign words in media and advertising got a last-minute reprieve when France's highest constitutional authority struck down the most controversial parts of the law, saying it only applies to public services and not to private citizens.

Sources: Adapted from Maarten Huygen, 'The Invasion of the American Way', *World Press Review*, November 1992, pp. 28–29; 'La Guerre Franglaise', *Fortune*, 13 June 1994, p. 14; and 'Briton Escalates French Word-War', Reuters, 21 June 1994.

most instances, the marketer's concern is with perceived functional consequences—the positive benefits of product use. Indeed, in most situations, innovative products for which the marketer purposely sets out to gain cultural acceptance have minimal, if any, dysfunctional consequences, but that cannot be taken for granted.

On the surface, it would appear that the introduction of a processed feeding formula into the diet of babies in developing countries where protein deficiency is a health problem would have all the functional consequences of better nutrition and health, stronger and faster growth, and so forth.[21] There is evidence, however, that in at least one situation, the dysfunctional consequences far exceeded the benefits. In India, as the result of the introduction of the formula, a significant number of babies annually were changed from breast feeding to bottle feeding before the age of six months. In Western countries, with appropriate refrigeration and sanitation standards, a similar pattern exists with no apparent negative consequences. In India, however, where sanitation methods are inadequate, a substantial increase in dysentery and diarrhoea and a higher infant mortality rate have resulted. A change from breast feeding to bottle feeding at an early age without the users' complete understanding of purification has caused dysfunctional consequences. This was the result of two factors: the impurity of the water used with the milk and the loss of the natural immunity to childhood disease a mother's milk provides.

SUMMARY

A complete and thorough appreciation of the dimensions of culture may well be the single most important gain to a foreign marketer in the preparation of marketing plans and strategies. Marketers can control the product offered to a market—its promotion, price and eventual distribution methods—but they have only limited control over the cultural environment within which these plans must be implemented. Because they cannot control all the influences on their marketing plans, they must attempt to anticipate the eventual effect of the uncontrollable elements and plan in such a way that these elements do not preclude the achievement of marketing objectives. They can also set about to effect changes that lead to quicker acceptance of their products or marketing programmes. Planning marketing strategy in terms of the uncontrollable elements of a market is necessary in a domestic market as well, but when a company is operating internationally, each new environment influenced by elements unfamiliar and sometimes unrecognizable to the marketer complicates the task. For these reasons, special effort and study are needed to absorb enough understanding of the foreign culture to cope with the uncontrollable features. Perhaps it is safe to generalize that of all the tools the foreign marketer must have, those that help generate empathy for another culture are the most valuable. Each of the cultural elements is explored in depth in subsequent chapters. Specific attention is given to business customs, political culture and legal culture in the following chapters.

QUESTIONS

1. Which role does the marketer play as a change agent?
2. Discuss the three cultural change strategies a foreign marketer can pursue.
3. 'Culture is pervasive in all marketing activities.' Discuss.
4. What is the importance of cultural empathy to foreign marketers? How do they acquire cultural empathy?
5. Why should a foreign marketer be concerned with the study of culture?
6. What is the popular definition of culture? What is the viewpoint of cultural anthropologists? What is the importance of the difference?
7. It is stated that members of a society borrow from other cultures to solve problems which they face in common. What does this mean? What is the significance to marketing?
8. 'For the inexperienced marketer, the "similar-but-different" aspect of culture creates an illusion of similarity that usually does not exist.' Discuss and give examples.
9. Outline the elements of culture as seen by an anthropologist. How can a marketer use this 'cultural scheme'?
10. What is material culture? What are its implications for marketing? Give examples.
11. What are some particularly troublesome problems caused by language in foreign marketing? Discuss.
12. Suppose you were requested to prepare a cultural analysis for a potential market. What would you do? Outline the steps and comment briefly on each.
13. Cultures are dynamic. How do they change? Are there cases where changes are not resisted but actually preferred? Explain. What is the relevance to marketing?
14. How can resistance to cultural change influence product introduction? Are there any similarities in domestic marketing? Explain, giving examples.
15. Defend the proposition that a multinational corporation has no responsibility for the consequences of an innovation beyond the direct effects of the innovation such as the product's safety, performance and so forth.
16. Find a product whose introduction into a foreign culture may cause dysfunctional consequences and describe how the consequences might be eliminated and the product still profitably introduced.

World Maps

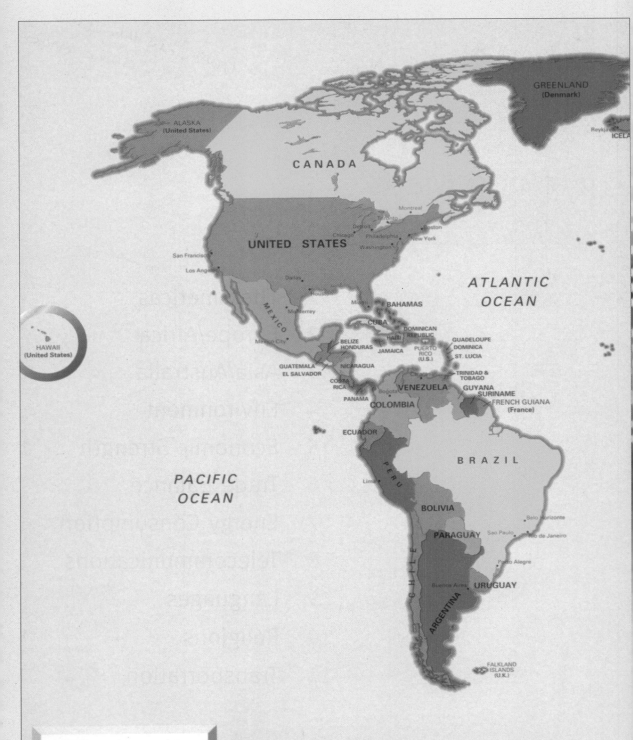

1 The Americas

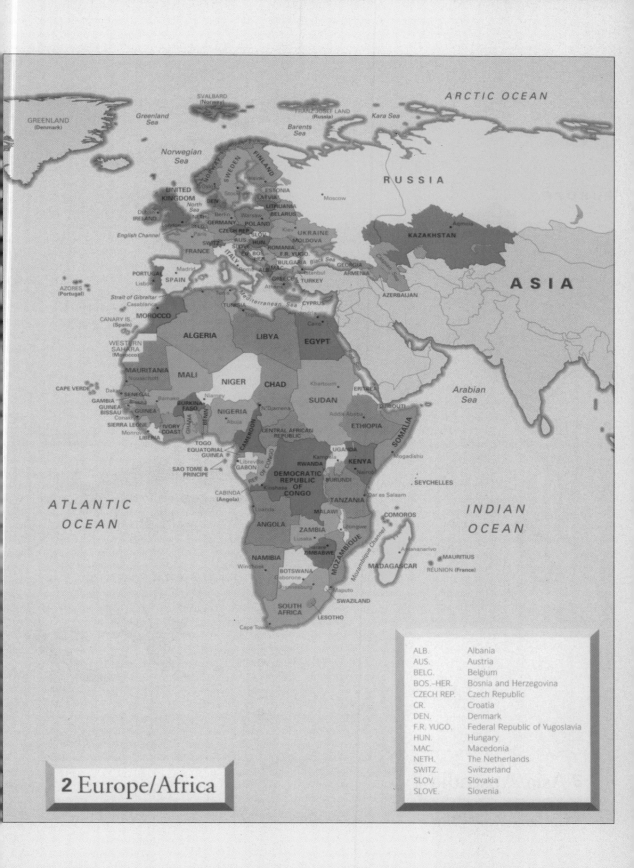

ARCTIC OCEAN

GREENLAND
(Denmark)

Greenland
Sea

SVALBARD
(Norway)

FRANZ JOSEF LAND
(Russia)

Kara Sea

Barents
Sea

Norwegian
Sea

RUSSIA

NORWAY

SWEDEN

FINLAND

Helsinki

Stockholm

ESTONIA

LATVIA

LITUANIA

Moscow

KAZAKHSTAN

Aqmia

ASIA

UNITED
KINGDOM

DEN.

North
Sea

Dublin
IRELAND

Berlin

Warsaw

BELARUS

Kiev

UKRAINE

NETH.

GERMANY

POLAND

English Channel

BELG.

CZECH REP.

SLOV.

Paris

FRANCE

SWITZ.

AUS.

HUN.

SLOVE.

CR.

ROMANIA

MOLDOVA

ITALY

BOS.-
HER.

F.R. YUGO.

BULGARIA

Black Sea

Istanbul

GEORGIA

ARMENIA

PORTUGAL

Madrid

Rome

MAC.

ALB.

GREECE

TURKEY

Lisbon

SPAIN

AZERBAIJAN

AZORES
(Portugal)

Strait of Gibraltar

Casablanca

CYPRUS

Mediterranean Sea

Alexandria

CANARY IS.
(Spain)

MOROCCO

TUNISIA

Tripoli

Arabian
Sea

WESTERN
SAHARA
(Morocco)

ALGERIA

LIBYA

EGYPT

Cairo

CAPE VERDE

MAURITANIA

Nouakchott

MALI

NIGER

CHAD

Khartoum

ERITREA

DJIBOUTI

Dakar

SENEGAL

Bamako

Niamey

SUDAN

Addis Ababa

GAMBIA

BURKINA
FASO

N'Djamena

GUINEA
BISSAU

Conakry

GUINEA

NIGERIA

Abuja

ETHIOPIA

SOMALIA

SIERRA LEONE

Monrovia

IVORY
COAST

GHANA

BENIN

CENTRAL AFRICAN
REPUBLIC

LIBERIA

TOGO

CAMEROON

Mogadishu

EQUATORIAL
GUINEA

UGANDA

Kampala

KENYA

SAO TOME &
PRINCIPE

Libreville

GABON

REP. OF CONGO

RWANDA

Nairobi

SEYCHELLES

CABINDA
(Angola)

Kinshasa

DEMOCRATIC
REPUBLIC
OF
CONGO

BURUNDI

Luanda

TANZANIA

Dar es Salaam

ATLANTIC
OCEAN

ANGOLA

MALAWI

COMOROS

INDIAN
OCEAN

ZAMBIA

Lilongwe

Lusaka

MOZAMBIQUE

Antananarivo

MAURITIUS

NAMIBIA

ZIMBABWE

MADAGASCAR

RÉUNION (France)

Windhoek

BOTSWANA

Mozambique Channel

Gaborone

Johannesburg

Maputo

SOUTH
AFRICA

SWAZILAND

Cape Town

LESOTHO

ALB.	Albania
AUS.	Austria
BELG.	Belgium
BOS.-HER.	Bosnia and Herzegovina
CZECH REP.	Czech Republic
CR.	Croatia
DEN.	Denmark
F.R. YUGO.	Federal Republic of Yugoslavia
HUN.	Hungary
MAC.	Macedonia
NETH.	The Netherlands
SWITZ.	Switzerland
SLOV.	Slovakia
SLOVE.	Slovenia

2 Europe/Africa

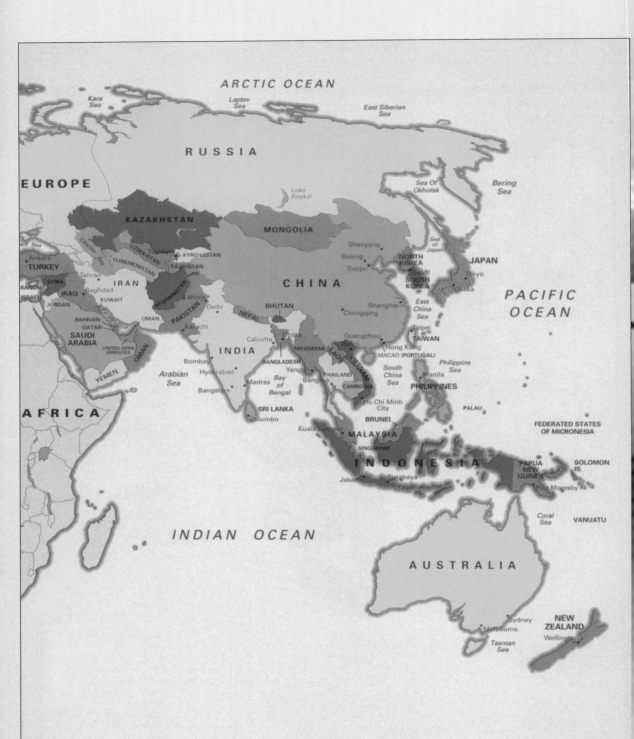

ARCTIC OCEAN

Kara
Sea

Laptev
Sea

East Siberian
Sea

RUSSIA

EUROPE

Lake
Baykal

KAZAKHSTAN

MONGOLIA

Shenyang

Sea Of
Okhotsk

Bering
Sea

Beijing

NORTH
KOREA

JAPAN

Sea
of
Japan

Tashkent
UZBEKISTAN
KYRGYZSTAN
TURKMENISTAN
TAJIKISTAN

Ankara

TURKEY

Tehran

IRAN

Baghdad

SYRIA
IRAQ

LEB.

ISRAEL
JORDAN

KUWAIT

BAHRAIN
QATAR

SAUDI
ARABIA

UNITED ARAB
EMIRATES

YEMEN

OMAN

OMAN

Caspian Sea

AFGHANISTAN

Lahore

PAKISTAN

Karachi

Delhi

NEPAL

BHUTAN

CHINA

Tianjin

SOUTH
KOREA

Seoul

Osaka

Tokyo

PACIFIC
OCEAN

Shanghai

Chongqing

East
China
Sea

Taipei

TAIWAN

Guangzhou

Hong Kong
MACAO (PORTUGAL)

Hanoi

Calcutta

Dhaka

INDIA

BANGLADESH

MYANMAR

LAOS

VIETNAM

Philippine
Sea

Bombay

Hyderabad

Arabian
Sea

Yangon

Madras

Bay
of
Bengal

Bangalore

THAILAND

Bangkok

CAMBODIA

South
China
Sea

Manila

PHILIPPINES

PALAU

Ho Chi Minh
City

SRI LANKA

Colombo

BRUNEI

Kuala Lumpur

MALAYSIA

SINGAPORE

FEDERATED STATES
OF MICRONESIA

SOLOMON
IS.

I N D O N E S I A

PAPUA
NEW
GUINEA

Jakarta

Surabaya

Port Moresby

AFRICA

INDIAN OCEAN

Coral
Sea

VANUATU

AUSTRALIA

Sydney

Melbourne

Tasman
Sea

NEW
ZEALAND

Wellington

3 Asia/Australia

4 Environment

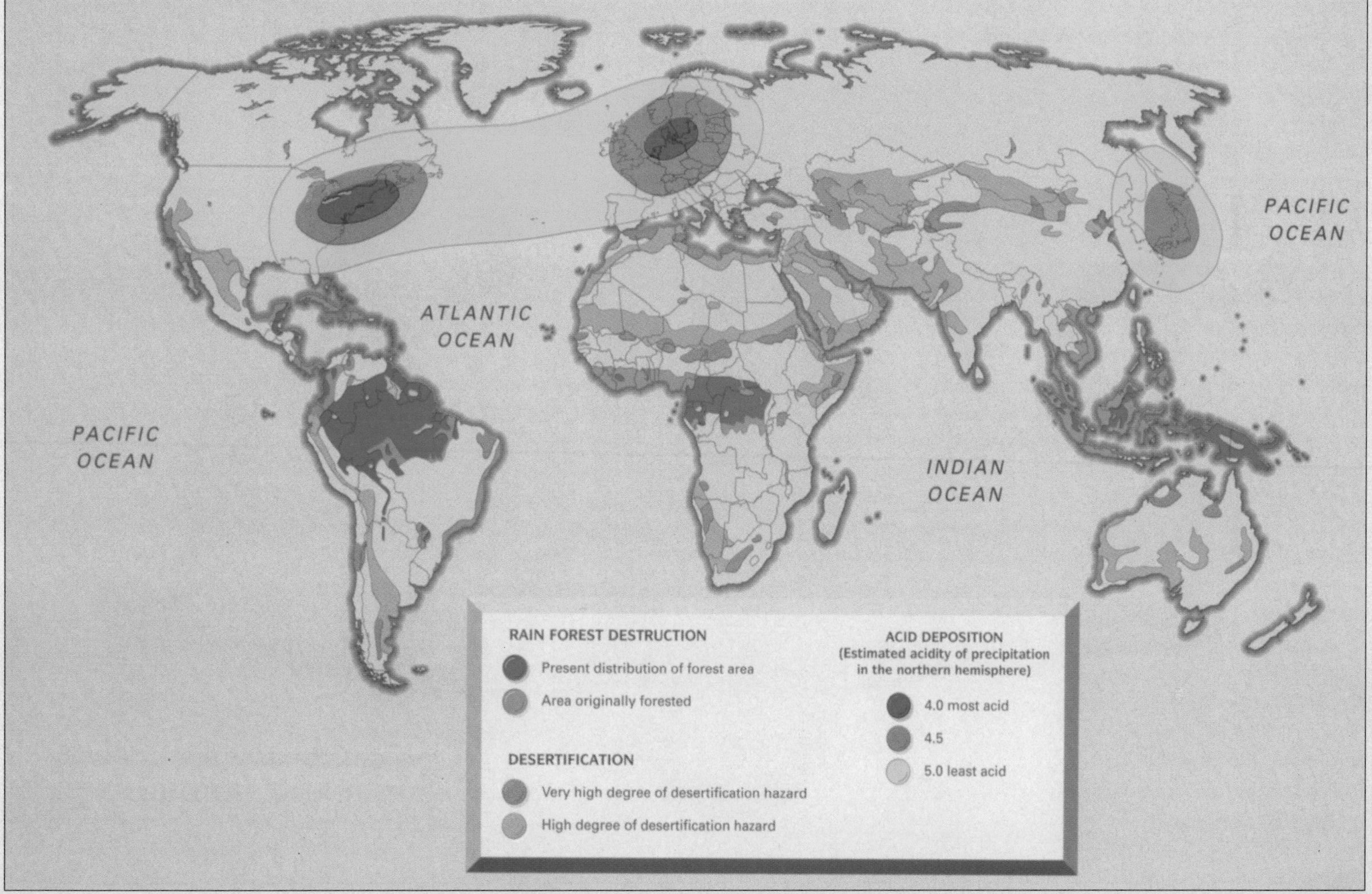

RAIN FOREST DESTRUCTION

Present distribution of forest area

Area originally forested

DESERTIFICATION

Very high degree of desertification hazard

High degree of desertification hazard

ACID DEPOSITION
(Estimated acidity of precipitation
in the northern hemisphere)

4.0 most acid

4.5

5.0 least acid

PACIFIC OCEAN

PACIFIC OCEAN

ATLANTIC OCEAN

INDIAN OCEAN

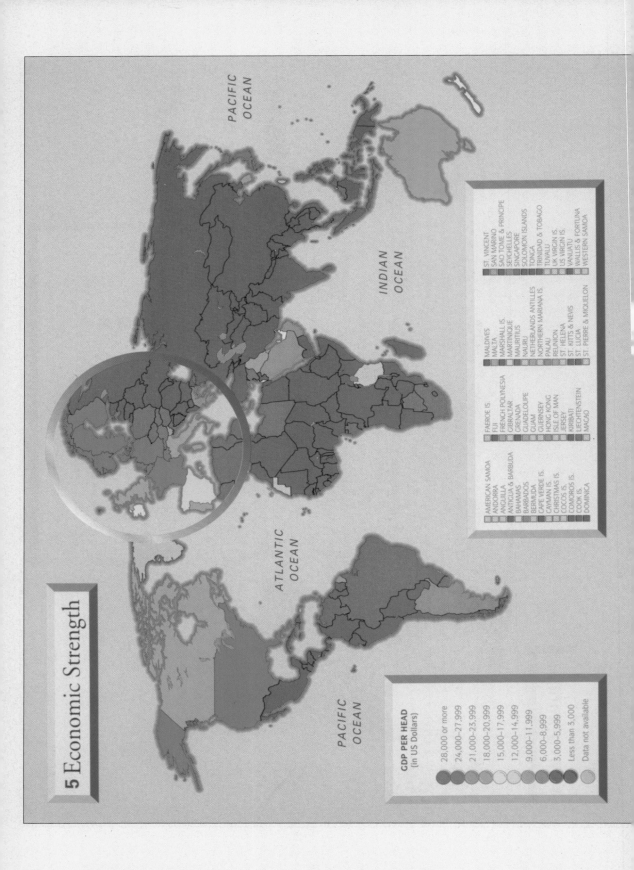

5 Economic Strength

GDP PER HEAD
(in US Dollars)

- 28,000 or more
- 24,000–27,999
- 21,000–23,999
- 18,000–20,999
- 15,000–17,999
- 12,000–14,999
- 9,000–11,999
- 6,000–8,999
- 3,000–5,999
- Less than 3,000
- Data not available

PACIFIC OCEAN

ATLANTIC OCEAN

PACIFIC OCEAN

INDIAN OCEAN

AMERICAN SAMOA
ANDORRA
ANGUILLA
ANTIGUA & BARBUDA
BAHAMAS
BARBADOS
BERMUDA
CAPE VERDE IS.
CAYMAN IS.
CHRISTMAS IS.
COCOS IS.
COMOROS IS.
COOK IS.
DOMINICA

FAEROE IS.
FIJI
FRENCH POLYNESIA
GIBRALTAR
GRENADA
GUADELOUPE
GUAM
GUERNSEY
HONG KONG
ISLE OF MAN
JERSEY
KIRIBATI
LIECHTENSTEIN
MACAO

MALDIVES
MALTA
MARSHALL IS.
MARTINIQUE
MAURITIUS
NAURU
NETHERLANDS ANTILLES
NORTHERN MARIANA IS.
PALAU
REUNION
ST. HELENA
ST. KITTS & NEVIS
ST. LUCIA
ST. PIERRE & MIQUELON

ST. VINCENT
SAN MARINO
SAO TOME & PRINCIPE
SEYCHELLES
SINGAPORE
SOLOMON ISLANDS
TONGA
TRINIDAD & TOBAGO
TUVALU
UK VIRGIN IS.
US VIRGIN IS.
VANUATU
WALLIS & FORTUNA
WESTERN SAMOA

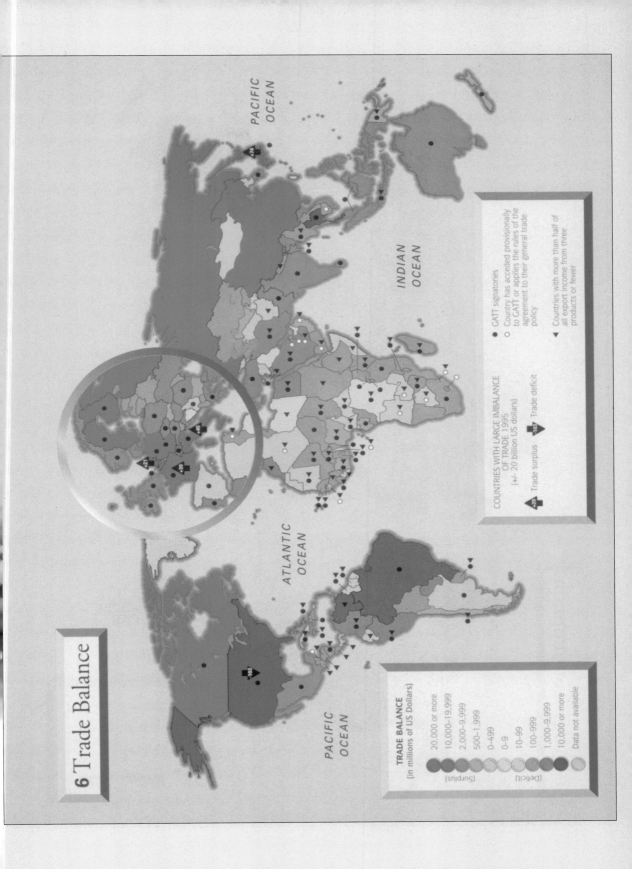

6 Trade Balance

PACIFIC OCEAN

ATLANTIC OCEAN

INDIAN OCEAN

PACIFIC OCEAN

TRADE BALANCE
(in millions of US Dollars)

20,000 or more
10,000–19,999
2,000–9,999
500–1,999
0–499
(Surplus)

0–9
10–99
100–999
1,000–9,999
10,000 or more
(Deficit)

Data not available

**COUNTRIES WITH LARGE IMBALANCE
OF TRADE 1995**
(+/- 20 billion US dollars)

Trade surplus   Trade deficit

● GATT signatories

○ Country has acceded provisionally
to GATT or applies the rules of the
agreement to their general trade
policy

▼ Countries with more than half of
all export income from three
products or fewer

7 Energy Consumption

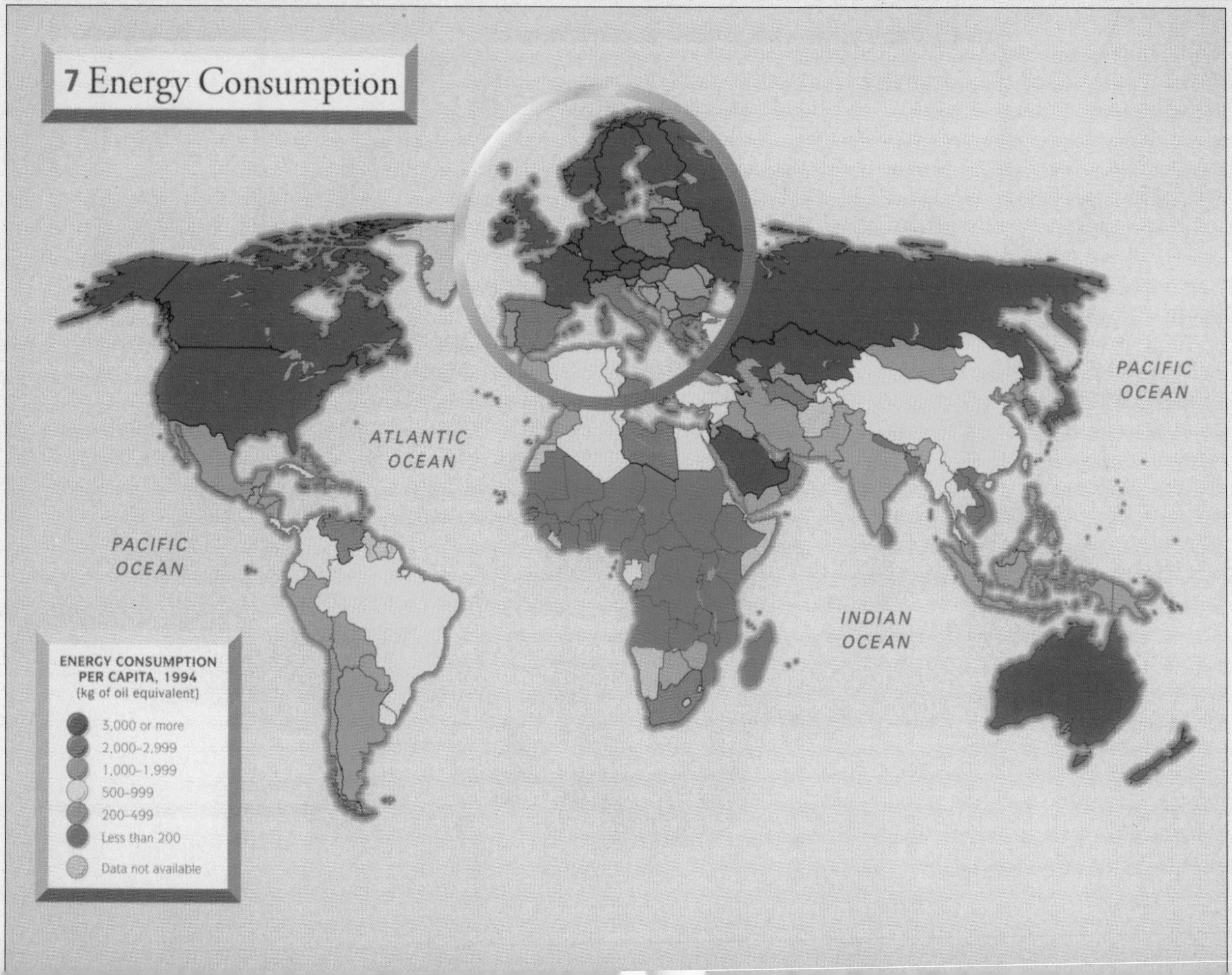

PACIFIC
OCEAN

INDIAN
OCEAN

ATLANTIC
OCEAN

PACIFIC
OCEAN

**ENERGY CONSUMPTION
PER CAPITA, 1994**
(kg of oil equivalent)

3,000 or more

2,000–2,999

1,000–1,999

500–999

200–499

Less than 200

Data not available

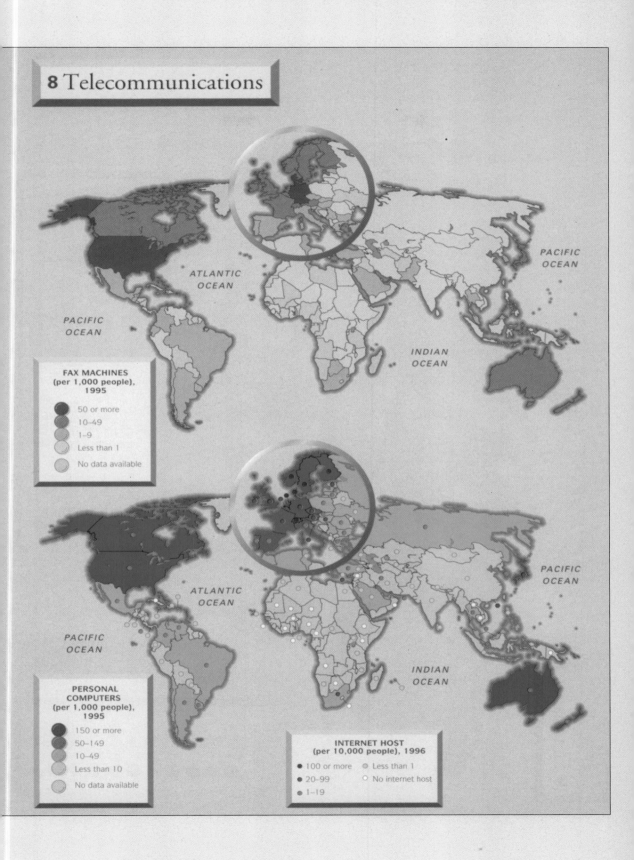

8 Telecommunications

FAX MACHINES
(per 1,000 people),
1995

- 50 or more
- 10–49
- 1–9
- Less than 1
- No data available

ATLANTIC
OCEAN

PACIFIC
OCEAN

PACIFIC
OCEAN

INDIAN
OCEAN

PERSONAL
COMPUTERS
(per 1,000 people),
1995

- 150 or more
- 50–149
- 10–49
- Less than 10
- No data available

INTERNET HOST
(per 10,000 people), 1996

- 100 or more
- 20–99
- 1–19
- Less than 1
- No internet host

ATLANTIC
OCEAN

PACIFIC
OCEAN

PACIFIC
OCEAN

INDIAN
OCEAN

9 Languages

PACIFIC OCEAN

PACIFIC OCEAN

ATLANTIC OCEAN

ATLANTIC OCEAN

INDIAN OCEAN

LANGUAGES
- Arabic
- English
- French
- German
- Hindi
- Japanese
- Mandarin
- Portuguese
- Russian
- Spanish
- Other

AMERICAN SAMOA
ANDORRA
ANGUILLA
BAHAMAS
BARBADOS
BERMUDA
CAPE VERDE IS.
CAYMAN IS.
CHRISTMAS IS.
COCOS IS.
COMOROS IS.
COOK IS.
DOMINICA
FAEROE IS.

FIJI
FRENCH POLYNESIA
GIBRALTAR
GRENADA
GUADELOUPE
GUAM
GUERNSEY
HONG KONG
ISLE OF MAN
JERSEY
KIRIBATI
LIECHTENSTEIN
MACAO
MALDIVES

MALTA
MAURITIUS
MAYOTTE
MONTSERRAT
NAURU
NETHERLANDS ANTILLES
NIUE
NORFOLK IS.
REUNION
ST. HELENA
ST. KITTS & NEVIS
ST. LUCIA
ST. PIERRE & MIQUELON
ST. VINCENT

SAN MARINO
SAO TOME & PRINCIPE
SEYCHELLES
SINGAPORE
TONGA
TRINIDAD & TOBAGO
TURKS & CAICOS IS.
TUVALU
UK VIRGIN IS.
US VIRGIN IS.
VANUATU
WALLIS & FORTUNA
WESTERN SAMOA

10 Religions

PACIFIC
OCEAN

PACIFIC
OCEAN

ATLANTIC
OCEAN

INDIAN
OCEAN

RELIGIONS

- Atheism (and Communism)
- Buddhism
- Hindu
- Muslim
- Traditional/Tribal
- Others
- Christian (Orthodox)
- Christian (no major sect)
- Christian (Protestant)
- Christian (Roman Catholic)

- Christian (no major sect), Muslim, Hindu
- Christian (no major sect), Traditional, Buddhism
- Christian (no major sect), Traditional, Hindu, Muslim
- Christian (no major sect), Christian (Roman Catholic), Hindu, Muslim, Others
- Christian (Roman Catholic), Buddhism, Others

- Christian (Roman Catholic), Muslim, Traditional
- Christian (no major sect), Muslim, Traditional
- Christian (Orthodox), Muslim, Atheism
- Christian (Roman Catholic), Muslim, Others

11 Transportation

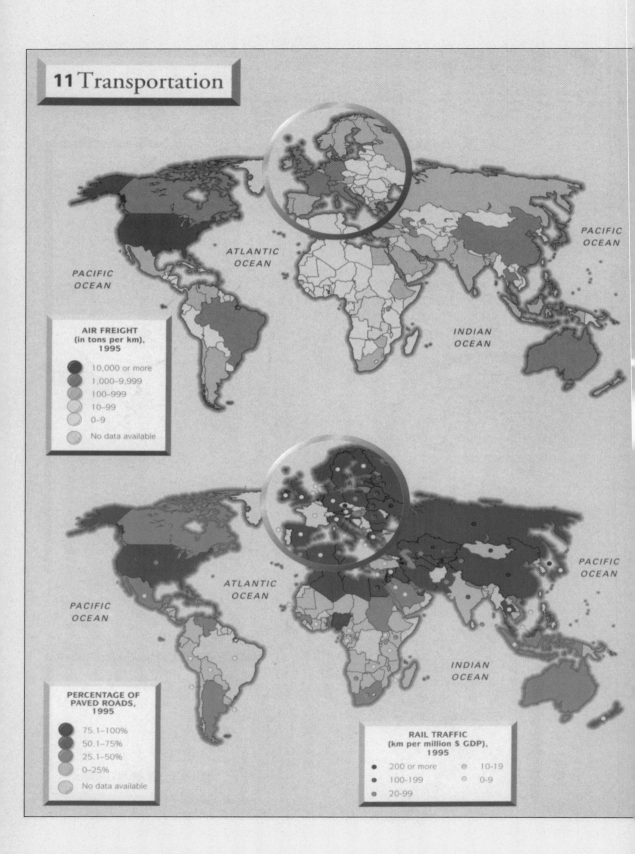

AIR FREIGHT
(in tons per km),
1995

- 10,000 or more
- 1,000–9,999
- 100–999
- 10–99
- 0–9
- No data available

**PERCENTAGE OF
PAVED ROADS,
1995**

- 75.1–100%
- 50.1–75%
- 25.1–50%
- 0–25%
- No data available

**RAIL TRAFFIC
(km per million $ GDP),
1995**

- 200 or more
- 100–199
- 20–99
- 10–19
- 0–9

PACIFIC OCEAN

ATLANTIC OCEAN

PACIFIC OCEAN

INDIAN OCEAN

PACIFIC OCEAN

PACIFIC OCEAN

ATLANTIC OCEAN

PACIFIC OCEAN

INDIAN OCEAN

PACIFIC OCEAN

REFERENCES

1. Gary P. Ferraro, *The Culture Dimension of International Business*, 2nd edn (Englewood Cliffs, NJ: Prentice-Hall, 1994), p. 17.

2. Francis Fukuyama, *Trust: The Social Virtues and the Creation of Prosperity* (London: Penguin, 1996).

3. Geert Hofstede, *Cultures and Organizations: Software of the Mind* (London: McGraw-Hill, 1991), p. 5; see also other publications by Hofstede, e.g. *Culture's Consequences: International Differences in Work-Related Values* (Beverly Hills, CA: Sage, 1984).

4. Samuel Huntington, *The Clash of Civilizations and the Remaking of the World Order* (New York: Simon & Schuster, 1996).

5. Cited in: Jean-Claude Usunier, *Marketing Across Cultures*, 2nd edn (Hemel Hempstead: Prentice-Hall, 1996), pp. 78–79.

6. Lawrence Rout, 'To Understand Life in Mexico, Consider the Day of the Dead', *The Wall Street Journal*, 4 November 1981, p. 1; and John Rice, 'In Mexico, Death Takes A Holiday', *Associated Press*, 20 October 1994.

7. Colette Guillaumin, 'Culture and Cultures', *Cultures*, vol. 6, no. 1, 1979, p. 1.

8. Melvin Herskovits, *Man and His Works* (New York: Knopf, 1952), p. 634.

9. 'Arabian Slights', *International Business*, June 1993, p. 98.

10. 'Designer Apologizes to Muslims', *The Wall Street Journal*, 21 January 1994, p. A-8.

11. For an interesting article on folklore in Malaysia, see M.S. Hood, 'Man, Forest and Spirits: Images and Survival Among Forest-Dwellers of Malaysia', *Tonan Ajia Kenkyu*, March 1993, p. 444.

12. See, for example, R.W. Scribner, 'Magic, Witchcraft and Superstition', *The Historical Journal*, March 1994, p. 219.

13. For a comprehensive business guide to cultures and customs in Europe, see John Mole, *When in Rome* (New York: Amacom, 1991).

14. For other examples of mistakes, see David A. Ricks, *Blunders in International Business* (Cambridge, MA: Blackwell, 1994).

15. Elizabeth K. Briody, 'On Trade and Cultures,' *Trade & Culture*, March–April 1995, pp. 5–6.

16. For an interesting article on cultural change, see Norihiko Shimizu, 'Today's Taboos May Be Gone Tomorrow', *Tokyo Business Today*, January 1995, pp. 29–51.

17. R. Linton, *The Study of Man* (New York: Appleton-Century-Crofts, 1936), p. 327.

18. See, for example, Denise M. Johnson and Scott D. Johnson, 'One Germany . . . But Is There a Common German Consumer? East–West Differences for Marketers to Consider', *The International Executive*, May–June 1993, pp. 221–228.

19. The diversity in tastes and customs of the member countries of the EU and their resistance to change is discussed in Katharine Whitehorn, 'In the United Europe, "Vive les Différences" ', *World Press Review*, March 1992, p. 28.

20. For an interesting text on change agents, see Gerald Zaltman and Robert Duncan, *Strategies for Planned Change* (New York: Wiley, 1979).

21. For a comprehensive look at this issue, see S. Prakash Sethi, *Multinational Corporations and the Impact of Public Advocacy on Corporate Strategy: Nestlé and the Infant Formula Controversy* (Boston, MA: Kluwer Academic, 1994).

CHAPTER

7

Business Customs and Practices in International Marketing

Chapter Learning Objectives

What you should learn from Chapter 7

- The obstacles to business transactions in international marketing.

- The influences of a culture on the modes of doing business.

- The effect of high-context, low-context cultures on business practices.

- The effects of disparate business ethics on international marketing.

- The importance of negotiations in international marketing.

Business customs are as much a cultural element of a society as is the language. Culture not only establishes the criteria for day-to-day business behaviour but also forms general patterns of attitude and motivation. Executives are to some extent captives of their cultural heritages and cannot totally escape language, heritage, political and family ties or religious backgrounds. One report notes that Japanese culture, permeated by Shinto precepts, is not something apart from business but determines its very essence. Thus, the many business and trade problems between Japan and the West reflect the widespread ignorance of Japanese culture by European and American business people.[1] Although international business managers may take on the trappings and appearances of the business behaviour of another country, their basic frame of references is most likely to be that of their own people.

In the United States, for example, the historical perspective of individualism and 'winning the West' seem to be manifest in individual wealth or corporate profit being dominant measures of success. Japan's lack of frontiers and natural resources and its dependence on trade have focused individual and corporate success criteria on uniformity, subordination to the group and society's ability to maintain high levels of employment. The feudal background of Southern Europe tends to emphasize maintenance of both individual and corporate power and authority while blending those feudal traits with paternalistic concern for minimal welfare for workers and other members of society. Various studies identify North Americans as individualists, Japanese as consensus-oriented and committed to their group and Central and Southern Europeans as elitists and rank conscious. While these descriptions are stereotypical, they illustrate cultural differences that are often manifest in business behaviour and practices.[2]

A knowledge of the business culture, management attitudes and business methods existing in a country and a willingness to accommodate the differences are important to success in an international market.[3] Unless marketers remain flexible in their own attitudes by accepting differences in basic patterns of thinking, local business tempo, religious practices, political structure and family loyalty, they are hampered, if not prevented, from reaching satisfactory conclusions to business transactions.

This chapter focuses on matters specifically related to the business environment. Besides an analysis of the need for adaptation, it will review the structural elements, attitudes and behaviour of international business processes.

REQUIRED ADAPTATION

Adaptation is a key concept in international marketing and willingness to adapt is a crucial attitude. Adaptation, or at least accommodation, is required on small matters as well as large ones. In fact, the small, seemingly insignificant situations are often the most crucial. More than tolerance of an alien culture is required. There is a need for affirmative acceptance, that is, open tolerance of the concept 'different but equal'. Through such affirmative acceptance, adaptation becomes easier because empathy for another's point of view naturally leads to ideas for meeting cultural differences.

As a guide to adaptation, there are 10 basic criteria that all who wish to deal with individuals, firms or authorities in foreign countries should be able to meet. They are (1) open tolerance, (2) flexibility, (3) humility, (4) justice/fairness, (5) adjustability to varying tempos, (6) curiosity/interest, (7) knowledge of the country, (8) liking for others, (9) ability to command respect and (10) ability to integrate oneself into the environment. In short, add the quality of adaptability to the qualities of a good executive for a composite of the perfect international marketer.

Degree of Adaptation

Adaptation does not require business executives to forsake their ways and change to conform with local customs; rather, executives must be aware of local customs and be willing to accommodate those differences that can cause misunderstanding. Essential to effective adaptation is awareness of one's own culture and the recognition that differences in others can cause anxiety, frustration and misunderstanding of the host's intentions. Also, the differences the host sees in the business executive can create the same potential for misunderstanding. The self-reference criterion (SRC) is especially operative in business customs. If we do not understand our foreign counterpart's customs, we are more likely to evaluate that person's behaviour in terms of what is acceptable to us.

The key to adaptation is to remain yourself but to develop an understanding and willingness to accommodate differences that exist. A successful marketer knows that in Asia it is important to make points without winning arguments; criticism, even if asked for, can cause a host to 'lose face'. In Germany and the Netherlands it is considered discourteous to use first names unless specifically invited to do so; always address a person as Herr, Frau or Fraulein and Meneer or Mevrouw with the last name. In Brazil and in Indonesia do not be offended by the Brazilian or Indonesian inclination towards touching during conversation. Such a custom is not a violation of your personal space but the way of greeting, emphasizing a point or as a gesture of goodwill and friendship.

A Chinese, Indian or Brazilian does not expect you to act like one of them. After all, you are not Chinese, Indian or Brazilian, but a Westerner, and it would be foolish for a Westerner to give up the ways that have contributed so notably to Western success. It would be equally foolish for others to give up their ways. When different cultures meet, open tolerance and a willingness to accommodate each other's differences are necessary. Once a marketer is aware of the possibility of cultural differences and the probable consequences of failure to adapt or accommodate, the seemingly endless variety of customs must be assessed. Where does one begin? Which customs should be adhered to absolutely, which others can be ignored? Fortunately, among the many obvious differences that exist between cultures, only a few are troubling.

Imperatives, Adiaphora and Exclusives

Business customs can be grouped into imperatives—customs that must be recognized and accommodated, adiaphora—customs to which adaptation is optional and exclusives—customs in which an outsider must not participate. An international marketer must appreciate the nuances of cultural imperative, cultural adiaphora and cultural exclusives.

Cultural imperative refers to the business customs and expectations that must be met and conformed to if relationships are to be successful. Successful business people know the Chinese word *guan-xi*, the Japanese *ningen kankei*, or the Latin American *compadre*. All refer to friendship, human relations or attaining a level of trust. They also know there is no substitute for establishing friendship in some cultures before effective business relationships can begin.

Informal discussions, entertaining, mutual friends, contacts, and just spending time with others are ways *guan-xi*, *ningen kankei*, *compadre* and other trusting relationships are developed. In those cultures where friendships are a key to success, the businessperson should not slight the time required for their development. Friendship motivates local agents to make more sales and friendship helps establish the right relationship with end users, leading to more

COLOURS, THINGS, NUMBERS AND EVEN SMELLS HAVE SYMBOLIC MEANINGS . . . OFTEN NOT THE ONES YOU THINK!

Green, America's favourite colour for suggesting freshness and good health is often associated with disease in countries with dense green jungles; it is a favourite colour among Arabs but forbidden in portions of Indonesia. In Japan green is a good high-tech colour, but Americans would shy away from green electronic equipment. Black is not universal for mourning: in many Asian countries it is white; in Brazil it is purple, yellow in Mexico and dark red in the Ivory Coast. Americans think of blue as the most masculine colour, but red is more manly in the United Kingdom or France. While pink is the most feminine colour in America, yellow is more feminine in most of the world. Red suggests good fortune in China but death in Turkey. In America a candy wrapped in blue or green is probably a mint; in Africa the same candy would be wrapped in red, our colour of cinnamon . . . in every culture, things, numbers and even smells have meanings. Lemon scent in the United States suggests freshness; in the Philippines lemon scent is associated with illness. In Japan the number 4 is like our 13; and 7 is unlucky in Ghana, Kenya and Singapore. The owl in India is bad luck, like our black cat. In Japan a fox is associated with witches. In China a green hat is like a dunce cap; specifically it marks a man with an unfaithful wife. The stork symbolizes maternal death in Singapore, not the kind of message you want to send to a new mother.

Source: from Lennie Copeland and Lewis Griggs, *Going International* (New York: Plume, 1986), p. 63.

sales over a longer period.[4] Naturally, after-sales service, price and the product must be competitive, but the marketer who has established *guan-xi*, *ningen kankei* or *compadre* has the edge. Establishing friendship is an important Asian and Latin American custom. It is imperative that establishing friendship be observed or one risks not earning trust and acceptance, the basic cultural prerequisites for developing and retaining effective business relationships.

Cultural adiaphora relates to areas of behaviour or to customs that cultural aliens may wish to conform to or participate in but that are not required. It is not particularly important, but it is permissible to follow the custom in question; the majority of customs fit into this category. One need not adhere to local dress, greet another man with a kiss (a custom in some countries) or eat foods that disagree with the digestive system (so long as the refusal is gracious). On the other hand, a symbolic attempt to participate in adiaphora is not only acceptable, but may also help to establish rapport. It demonstrates that the marketer has studied the culture. A Japanese does not expect a Westerner to bow and to understand the ritual of bowing among Japanese; yet, a symbolic bow indicates interest and some sensitivity to their culture which is acknowledged as a gesture of goodwill. It may well pave the way to a strong, trusting relationship. At the same time, cultural adiaphora are the most visibly different customs and thus more tempting for the foreigner to try to adapt to when, in fact, adaptation is unnecessary and, if overdone, unwelcome.

Most jokes, even though well intended, don't translate well. Sometimes a translator can help you out. One speaker, in describing his experience, said, 'I began my speech with a joke that took me about two minutes to tell. Then my interpreter translated my story. About thirty seconds later the Japanese audience laughed loudly. I continued with my talk which seemed well received', he said, 'but at the end, just to make sure, I asked the interpreter, "How did you translate my joke so quickly?" The interpreter replied, "Oh I didn't translate your story at all. I didn't understand it. I simply said our foreign speaker has just told a joke so would you all please laugh." '

Some international managers and marketers argue that interpreters aren't necessary because English is the language of international business. This view is obviously not appreciated in most countries. The Japanese have a joke that goes, 'What do you call a person that can speak two languages? Bilingual. What do you call a person that can speak three languages? Trilingual. What do you call a person that can speak one language? An Englishman.' This may be funny to the Japanese, but is it to English people?[5]

Cultural exclusives are those customs or behaviour patterns reserved exclusively for the local people and from which the foreigner is excluded. For example, a foreigner criticizing a country's politics, mores and peculiarities (that is, peculiar to the foreigner) is offensive even though locals may, among themselves, criticize such issues. There is truth in the old adage, 'I'll curse my brother, but if you curse him, you'll have a fight.' There are few cultural traits reserved exclusively for locals, but a foreigner must refrain from participating in those that are reserved. Religion, politics, treatment of women and minorities are some of the examples of such traits.

DIFFERENT BUSINESS PRACTICES

Because of the diverse structures, management attitudes and behaviours encountered in international business, there is considerable latitude in methods of doing business. No matter how thoroughly prepared a marketer may be when approaching a foreign market, there is a certain amount of cultural shock when the uninitiated trader encounters actual business situations. In business transactions, the international marketer becomes aware of the differences in contact level, communications emphasis, tempo and formality of foreign businesses. Ethical standards are likely to differ, as will the negotiation emphasis. In most countries, the foreign trader is also likely to encounter a fairly high degree of government involvement.

Sources and Level of Authority

Business size, ownership and public accountability combine to influence the authority structure of business. The international businessperson is confronted with a variety of authority patterns but most are a variation of three typical patterns: top-level management decisions, decentralized decisions and committee or group decisions.

Top-level management decision making is generally found in those situations where family or close ownership gives absolute control to owners and where businesses are small enough to make such centralized decision making possible. In many European businesses, decision-making authority is guarded jealously by a few at the top who exercise tight control. In many developing countries with a semifeudal, land-equals-power heritage, decision-making participation by middle management tends to be de-emphasized; decisions are made by dominant family members.

In Middle Eastern countries, the top man makes all decisions and prefers to deal only with other executives with decision-making powers. There, one always does business with an individual per se rather than an office or title.

As businesses grow and professional management develops, there is a shift towards decentralized management decision making. Decentralized decision making allows executives, at various levels of management, authority over their own functions. This mode is typical of

MEISHI—PRESENTING A BUSINESS CARD IN JAPAN

In Japan the business card, or *Meishi*, is the executive's trademark. It is both a mini résumé and a friendly deity that draws people together. No matter how many times you have talked with a businessperson by phone before you actually meet, business cannot really begin until you formally exchange cards.

The value of a *Meishi* cannot be overemphasized; up to 12 million are exchanged daily and a staggering 4.4 billion annually. For a businessperson to make a call or receive a visitor without a card is like a Samurai going off to battle without his sword.

There are a variety of ways to present a card, depending on the giver's personality and style:

Crab style—held out between the index and middle fingers.
Pincer—clamped between the thumb and index finger.
Pointer—offered with the index finger pressed along the edge.
Upside down—the name is facing away from the recipient.
Platter fashion—served in the palm of the hand.

Not only is there a way to present a card, there is also a way of receiving a card. It makes a good impression to receive a card in both hands, especially when the other party is senior in age or status.

The card should be presented during the earliest stages of introduction, so the Japanese recipient will be able to determine your position and rank and know how to respond to you. The normal procedure is for the Japanese to hand you their name card and accept yours at the same time. They read your card and then formally greet you either by bowing or shaking hands or both.

Sources: Adapted from: 'Meishi', *Sumitomo Quarterly*, Autumn 1986, p. 3; and Boye Lafayette DeMente, *Japanese Etiquette and Ethics in Business*, 6th edn (Lincolnwood, IL: NTC Business Books, 1994), p. 24.

large-scale businesses with highly developed management systems such as those found in the United States. A trader in the United States is likely to be dealing with middle management, and title or position generally takes precedence over the individual holding the job.

Committee decision making is by group or consensus. Committees may operate on a centralized or decentralized basis, but the concept of committee management implies something quite different from the individualized functioning of top management and decentralized decision-making arrangements just discussed. Because Asian cultures and religions tend to emphasize harmony, it is not surprising that group decision making predominates there. Despite the emphasis on rank and hierarchy in Japanese social structure, business emphasizes group participation, group harmony and group decision making—but at top management level.

The demands of these three types of authority systems on a marketer's ingenuity and adaptability are evident. In the case of the authoritative and delegated societies, the chief problem would be to identify the individual with authority. In the committee decision setup, it is necessary that every committee member be convinced of the merits of the proposition or product in question. The marketing approach to each of these situations differs.

Management Objectives and Aspirations

The training and background (i.e. cultural environment) of managers significantly affect their personal and business outlooks. Society as a whole establishes the social rank or status of

BUSINESS PROTOCOL IN A UNIFIED EUROPE

Now that 1992 has come and gone and the European Union is now a single market, does it mean that all differences have been wiped away? For some of the legal differences, Yes! For cultural differences, No!

There is always the issue of language and meaning even when you both speak English. Then there is the matter of humour. The anecdote you open a meeting with may fly well with your own audience. However, the French will smile, the Belgians laugh, the Dutch will be puzzled and the Germans will take you literally. Humour is strongly influenced by culture and thus doesn't travel well.

And then there are the French, who are very attentive to hierarchy and ceremony. When first meeting with a French-speaking businessperson, stick with *monsieur, madame* or *mademoiselle*; the use of first names is disrespectful to the French. If you don't speak French fluently, apologize. Such apology shows general respect for the language and dismisses any stigma of arrogance.

The formality of dress can vary with each country also. The Brit, the Swede and the Dutchman will take off their jackets and literally roll up their sleeves; they mean to get down to business. The Spaniard will loosen his tie, while the German disapproves. He thinks they look sloppy and unbusinesslike. He keeps his coat on throughout the meeting. So does the Italian, but that was because he dressed especially for the look of the meeting.

With all that, did the meeting decide anything? It was, after all, a first meeting. The Brits were just exploring the terrain, checking out the broad perimeters and all that. The French were assessing the other players' strengths and weaknesses and deciding what position to take at the next meeting. The Italians also won't have taken it too seriously. For them it was a meeting to arrange the meeting agenda for the real meeting. Only the Germans will have assumed it was what it seemed and be surprised when the next meeting starts open-ended.

Sources: Adapted from Barry Day, 'The Art of Conducting International Business', *Advertising Age*, 8 October 1990, p. 46, and Brad Ketchum Jr., 'Faux Pas Go with the Territory', *Inc.*, May 1994, pp. 4–5.

management, and cultural background dictates patterns of aspirations and objectives among business people. These cultural influences affect the attitude of managers towards innovation, new products and conducting business with foreigners. To fully understand another's management style, one must appreciate an individual's objectives and aspirations which are usually reflected in the goals of the business organization and in the practices that prevail within the company. In dealing with foreign business, a marketer must be particularly aware of the varying objectives and aspirations of management.

Personal Goals.   Some cultures emphasize profit or high wages while in other countries security, good personal life, acceptance, status, advancement or power may be emphasized. Individual goals are highly personal in any country, so one cannot generalize to the extent of saying that managers in any one country always have a specific orientation.

Security and Mobility.   Personal security and job mobility relate directly to basic human motivation and therefore have widespread economic and social implications. The word security is somewhat ambiguous and this very ambiguity provides some clues to managerial variation. To some, security means good wages and the training and ability required for moving from company to company within the business hierarchy; for others, it means the security of lifetime positions with their companies; to still others, it means adequate retirement plans and other welfare benefits. In European companies, particularly in the countries late in industrializing such as Spain and Italy, there is a strong paternalistic orientation, and it is assumed that individuals will work for one company for the majority of their lives.

Personal Life.   For many individuals, a good personal life takes priority over profit, security or any other goal. In his worldwide study of individual aspirations, David McClelland discovered that the culture of some countries stressed the virtue of a good personal life as being far more important than profit or achievement. The hedonistic outlook of ancient Greece explicitly included work as an undesirable factor that got in the way of the search for pleasure or a good personal life. Perhaps at least part of the standard of living that we enjoy in the Western world today can be attributed to the hard-working ethic from which we derive much of our business heritage.[6]

Social Acceptance.   In some countries, acceptance by neighbours and fellow workers appears to be a predominant goal within business. The Asian outlook is reflected in the group decision making so important in Japan, and the Japanese place high importance on fitting in with their group. Group identification is so strong in Japan and some other Asian countries that when a worker is asked what he does for a living, he generally answers by telling you he works for Sumitomo or Mitsubishi or Matsushita, rather than that he is a chauffeur, an engineer or a chemist.

Power.   Although there is some power seeking by business managers throughout the world, power seems to be a more important motivating force in the Middle East and South American countries. In these countries, many business leaders are not only profit-oriented, but also use their business positions to become social and political leaders.

Communications Emphasis

Probably no language readily translates into another because the meanings of words differ widely among languages. Even though it is the basic communication tool of marketers trading in foreign lands, managers, particularly from the United States and the United Kingdom, often fail to develop even a basic understanding of a foreign language, much less master the linguistic nuances that reveal unspoken attitudes and information. One writer comments that 'even a good interpreter doesn't solve the language problem'. Seemingly similar business terms in English and Japanese often have different meanings. In fact, the Japanese language is so inherently vague that even the well-educated have difficulty communicating clearly among themselves. A communications authority on the Japanese language estimates that the Japanese are able to fully understand each other only about 85 per cent of the time. The Japanese prefer English-language contracts where words have specific meanings.[7]

The translation and interpretation of clearly worded statements and common usage is difficult enough, but when slang is added, the task is almost impossible. In an exchange between an American and a Chinese official, the American answered affirmatively to a Chinese proposal with, 'It's a great idea, Mr Li, but who's going to put wheels on it?' The interpreter, not wanting to lose face but not understanding, turned to the Chinese official and said, 'And now the American has made a proposal regarding the automobile industry'; the entire conversation was disrupted by a misunderstanding of a slang expression.

The best policy when dealing in other languages, even with a skilled interpreter, is to stick to formal language patterns. The use of slang phrases puts the interpreter in the

YOU DON'T HAVE TO BE A HOLLYWOOD STAR TO WEAR DARK GLASSES

Arabs may watch the pupils of your eyes to judge your responses to different topics.

A psychologist at the University of Chicago discovered that the pupil is a very sensitive indicator of how people respond to a situation. When you are interested in something, your pupils dilate; if I say something you don't like, they tend to contract. But the Arabs have known about the pupil response for hundreds if not thousands of years. Because people can't control the response of their eyes, which is a dead giveaway, many Arabs wear dark glasses, even indoors.

These are people reading the personal interaction on a second-to-second basis. By watching the pupils, they can respond rapidly to mood changes. That's one of the reasons why they use a closer conversational distance than Westerners do. At about one metre, the normal distance between two Westerners who are talking, we have a hard time following eye movement. But if you use an Arab distance, which would be about half that distance, you can watch the pupil of the eye.

Direct eye contact for a Westerner is difficult to achieve because we are taught in the West not to stare, not to look at the eyes that carefully. If you stare at someone, it is too intense, too sexy or too hostile. It also may mean that we are not totally tuned into the situation. Maybe we should all wear dark glasses.

uncomfortable position of guessing at meanings. Foreign language skills are critical in all negotiations, so it is imperative to seek the best possible personnel. Even then, especially in translations involving Asian languages, misunderstandings occur.[8]

Linguistic communication, no matter how imprecise, is explicit, but much business communication depends on implicit messages that are not verbalized. E.T. Hall, professor of anthropology and for decades consultant to business and government on intercultural relations, says, 'In some cultures, messages are explicit; the words carry most of the information. In other cultures . . . less information is contained in the verbal part of the message since more is in the context'.[9] Hall divides cultures into high-context and low-context cultures. Communication in a high-context culture depends heavily on the context or non-verbal aspects of communication, whereas the low-context culture depends more on explicit, verbally expressed communications (see Figure 7.1). Managers in general probably function best at a low-context level because they are accustomed to reports, contracts and other written communications.

In a low-context culture, one gets down to business quickly. In a high-context culture it takes considerably longer to conduct business because of the need to know more about a businessperson before a relationship develops. They simply do not know how to handle a low-context relationship with other people. Hall suggests that, 'in the Middle East, if you aren't willing to take the time to sit down and have coffee with people, you have a problem. You must learn to wait and not be too eager to talk business. You can ask about the family or ask, "how are you feeling?" but avoid too many personal questions about wives because people are apt to get suspicious. Learn to make what we call chit-chat. If you don't, you can't go to the next step. It's a little bit like a courtship'—the preliminaries establish a firm foundation for a relationship.[10]

Even in low-context cultures, our communication is heavily dependent on our cultural context. Most of us are not aware of how dependent we are on the context, and, as Hall suggests, 'since much of our culture operates outside our awareness, frequently we don't even know what we know.'

Figure 7.1   Contextual Background of Various Countries

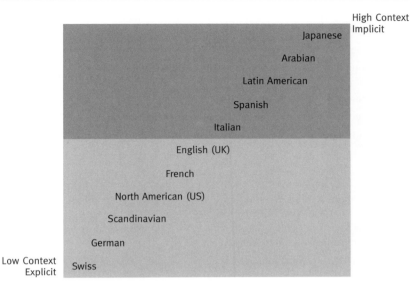

Source: Patterned after E.T. Hall.

Probably every businessperson from the West or other relatively low-context countries who has had dealings with counterparts in high-context countries can tell stories about the confusion on both sides because of the different perceptual frameworks of the communication process. Communication mastery is not only the mastery of a language, but also a mastery of customs and culture. Such mastery develops only through long association.[11]

Formality and Tempo

The breezy informality and haste that seem to characterize the American business relationship appear to be American exclusives that business people from other countries not only fail to share, but also fail to appreciate. This apparent informality, however, does not indicate a lack of commitment to the job. Comparing British and American business managers, an English executive commented about the American manager's compelling involvement in business, 'At a cocktail party or a dinner, the American is still on duty'.

Even though Northern Europeans seem to have picked up some American attitudes in recent years, do not count on them being 'Americanized'. As one writer says, 'While using first names in business encounters is regarded as an American vice in many countries, nowhere is it found more offensive than in Germany and France', where formality still reigns. Those who work side by side for years still address one another with formal pronouns.[12]

Marketers who expect maximum success have to deal with foreign executives in ways that are acceptable to the foreigner. Latin Americans depend greatly on friendships but establish these friendships only in the South American way: slowly, over a considerable period of time. A typical Latin American is highly formal until a genuine relationship of respect and friendship is established. Even then the Latin American is slow to get down to business and will not

YOU SAY YOU SPEAK ENGLISH?

The English speak English, North Americans speak English, but can we communicate? It is difficult unless you understand that in England:

Newspapers are sold at book stalls.

The ground floor is the main floor, while the first floor is what we call the second, and so on up the building.

An apartment house is a block of flats.

You will be putting your clothes not in a closet, but in a cupboard.

A closet usually refers to the WC or water closet, which is the toilet.

When one of your British friends says she is going to 'spend a penny,' she is going to the ladies' room.

A bathing dress or bathing costume is what the British call a bathing suit, and for those who want to go shopping, it is essential to know that a tunic is a blouse; a stud is a collar button, nothing more; and garters are suspenders. Suspenders are braces.

If you want to buy a sweater, you should ask for a jumper or a jersey as the recognizable item will be marked in British clothing stores.

A ladder is not used for climbing but refers to a run in a stocking.

If you called up someone, it means to your British friend that you have drafted the person—probably for military service.

To ring someone up is to telephone them.

You put your packages in the boot of your car, not the trunk.

When you table something, you mean you want to discuss it, not postpone it as in the United States.

Any reference by you to an MD will probably not bring a doctor. The term means mental deficient or Managing Director in Britain.

When the desk clerk asks what time you want to be knocked up in the morning, he is only referring to your wake-up call.

Sources: Adapted from Margaret Zellers, 'How to Speak English', *Denver Post*, date unknown; and Lennie Copeland and Lewis Griggs, *Going International* (New York: Plume, 1986), pp. 101–102.

be pushed. In keeping with the culture, *mañana* is good enough. How people perceive time helps to explain some of the differences between Western managers and those from other cultures.

P-Time versus M-Time

Westerners are a more time-bound culture than Asian and Latin cultures. Our stereotype of those cultures is 'They are always late', and their view of us is 'You are always prompt'. Neither statement is completely true though both contain some truth. What is true, however, is that we are a very time-oriented society—time is money to us—whereas, in other cultures, time is to be savoured, not spent. For Westerners the time is running (going), for Asians the time comes. Thus they take it easy and when asked, respond they will do a certain thing when the time comes.

GOING INTERNATIONAL 7.6

TIME—A MANY CULTURED THING

Time is cultural, subjective and variable. One of the most serious causes of frustration and friction in cross-cultural business dealings occurs when counterparts are out of sync with each other.

Differences often appear with respect to the pace of time, its perceived nature, and its function. Insights into a culture's view of time may be found in their sayings and proverbs. For example:

'Time is money.' United States
'Those who rush arrive first at the grave.' Spain
'The clock did not invent man.' Nigeria
'If you wait long enough, even an egg will walk.' Ethiopia
'Before the time, it is not yet the time; after the time, it's too late.' France

Sources: Adapted from Edward T. Hall and Mildred Reed Hall, *Understanding Cultural Differences* (Yarmouth, ME: Intercultural Press, 1990), p. 196; and Gart M. Wederspahn, 'On Trade and Cultures', *Trade and Culture*, Winter 1993–94, pp. 4–6.

Edward Hall defines two time systems in the world—monochronic and polychronic time. *M-time* (monochronic) typifies most North Americans, Dutch, Swiss, Germans and Scandinavians. These Western cultures tend to concentrate on one thing at a time. They divide time into small units and are concerned with promptness. M-time is used in a linear way and it is experienced as being almost tangible in that we save time, waste time, bide time, spend time and lose time. Most low-context cultures operate on M-time.

P-time, or polychronic time, is more dominant in high-context cultures where the completion of a human transaction is emphasized more than holding to schedules. P-time is characterized by the simultaneous occurrence of many things and by 'a great involvement with people'. P-time allows for relationships to build and context to be absorbed as parts of high-context cultures.

The Westerner's desire to get straight to the point, to get down to business and other indications of directness are all manifestations of M-time cultures. The P-time system gives rise to looser time schedules, deeper involvement with individuals and a wait-and-see-what-develops attitude. For example, two Latins conversing would probably opt to be late for their next appointments rather than abruptly terminate the conversation before it came to a natural conclusion.

P-time is characterized by a much looser notion of on time or late. Interruptions are routine; delays to be expected. It is not so much putting things off until *mañana* but the concept that human activities are not expected to proceed like clockwork.

Most cultures offer a mix of P-time and M-time behaviour, but have a tendency to be either more P-time or M-time in regard to the role time plays. Some are similar to Japan where appointments are adhered to with the greatest M-time precision, but P-time is followed once a meeting begins. The Japanese see Western business people as too time-bound and driven by schedules and deadlines which thwart the easy development of friendships. The differences between M-time and P-time are reflected in a variety of ways throughout a culture.

When business people from M-time and P-time meet, adjustments need to be made for a harmonious relationship. Often clarity can be gained by specifying tactfully, for example,

WHEN YES MEANS NO, OR MAYBE, OR I DON'T KNOW, OR?

Once my youngest child asked if we could go to the circus and my reply was 'maybe'. My older child asked the younger sibling, 'What did he say?' The prompt reply, 'He said NO!'

All cultures have ways to avoid saying 'no' when they really mean 'no'. After all, arguments can be avoided, hurt feelings postponed and so on. In some cultures, saying 'no' is to be avoided at all costs—to say no is rude, offensive and disrupts harmony. When the maintenance of long-lasting, stable personal relationships is of utmost importance, as in Japan, to say 'no' is to be avoided because of the possible damage to a relationship. As a result, the Japanese have developed numerous euphemisms and paralinguistic behaviour to express negation. To the unknowing American, who has been taught not to take 'no' for an answer, the unwillingness to say 'no' is often misinterpreted to mean that there is hope—the right argument or more forceful persuasion is all that is needed to get a 'yes'. But don't be misled—the Japanese listen politely and, when the American is finished, respond with 'hai'. Literally it means 'yes', but usually it only means, 'I hear you'. When a Japanese avoids saying yes or no clearly, it most likely means that he or she wishes to say no. One example at the highest levels of government occurred in negotiations between the Prime Minister of Japan and the President of the United States. The Prime Minister responded with 'we'll deal with it' to a request by the President. It was only later that the US side discovered that such a response generally means 'no'—to the frustration of all concerned. Other euphemistic, 'decorative' no's sometimes used by Japanese: 'It's very difficult.' 'We will think about it.' 'I'm not sure.' 'We'll give this some more thought.' Or they leave the room with an apology.

Westerners generally respond directly with a yes or no and then give you their reasons why. The Japanese tend to embark on long explanations first, and then leave the conclusion extremely ambiguous. Etiquette dictates that a Japanese may tell you what you want to hear, not respond at all or be evasive. This ambiguity often leads to misunderstanding and cultural friction.

Sources: Adapted from Mark Zimmerman, *How to Do Business with the Japanese* (New York: Random House, 1985), pp. 105–110; and Osamu Katayame, 'Speaking in Tongues', *Look Japan*, March 1993, pp. 18–19.

whether a meeting is to be on Middle Eastern time or Western time. A Westerner who has been working successfully with the Saudis for many years says he has learned to take plenty of things to do when he travels. Others schedule appointments in their offices so they can work until their P-time friend arrives. The important thing for the Western manager to learn is adjustment to P-time in order to avoid the anxiety and frustration that comes from being out of synchronization with local time. As global markets expand, more business people from P-time cultures are adapting to M-time.

Negotiations Emphasis

All the just-discussed differences in business customs and culture come into play more frequently and are more obvious in the negotiating process than in any other aspect of business. The basic elements of business negotiations are the same in any country; they relate to the product, its price and terms, services associated with the product and, finally, friendship between vendors and customers. But it is important to remember that the negotiating process is complicated and the risk of misunderstanding increases when negotiating with someone from another culture.[13]

Attitudes brought to the negotiating table by each individual are affected by many cultural factors and customs often unknown to the other individuals and perhaps unrecognized by the individuals themselves. Each negotiator's understanding and interpretation of what transpires in negotiating sessions is conditioned by his or her cultural background.[14] The possibility of offending one another or misinterpreting each other's motives is especially high when one's SRC is the basis for assessing a situation. One standard rule in negotiating is 'know thyself' first and, second, 'know your opponent'. The SRCs of both parties can come into play here if care is not taken.[15]

Gender Bias in International Business

The gender bias towards women managers that exists in many countries creates a hesitancy among Western multinational companies to offer women international assignments. Questions such as 'Are there opportunities for women in international business?' and 'Should women represent Western firms abroad?' frequently arise as Western companies become more international. As women move up in domestic management ranks and seek career-related international assignments, companies need to examine their positions on women managers in international business.[16]

In many cultures—Asian, Arab, Latin American and even some European ones—women are not typically found in upper levels of management. Traditional roles in male-dominated societies are often translated into minimal business opportunities for women. This cultural bias raises questions about the effectiveness of women in establishing successful relationships with host-country associates. An often-asked question is whether it is appropriate to send a woman to conduct business with foreign customers. To some it appears logical that if women are not accepted in managerial roles within their own cultures, a foreign woman would not be any more acceptable. This is but one of the myths used to support decisions to exclude women from foreign assignments.[17]

It is a fact that men and women are treated very differently in some cultures. In Saudi Arabia, for example, women are segregated, expected to wear veils and forbidden even to drive, while in Kuwait a large number of women are working in managerial positions and they drive and wear Western clothes. Evidence suggests, however, that prejudice towards foreign women executives may be exaggerated and that the treatment local women receive in their own cultures is not necessarily an indicator of how a foreign businesswoman is treated.

When a company gives management responsibility and authority to someone, a large measure of the respect initially shown that person is the result of respect for the firm. When a woman manager receives the strong backing of her firm, she usually receives the respect commensurate with the position she holds and the firm she represents. Thus, resistance to her as a female either does not materialize or is less severe than anticipated. Even in those cultures where a female would not ordinarily be a manager, foreign female executives benefit, at least initially, from the status, respect and importance attributed to the firms they represent. In Japan, where Japanese women rarely achieve even lower-level management positions, representatives of Western firms, for example, are seen first as Germans, second as representatives of firms and then as males or females. Once business negotiations begin, the willingness of a business host to engage in business transactions and the respect shown to a foreign businessperson grows or diminishes depending on the business skills he or she demonstrates, regardless of gender.[18]

BUSINESS ETHICS

The moral question of what is right and/or appropriate poses many dilemmas for domestic marketers. Even within a country, ethical standards are frequently not defined or always clear.

The problem of business ethics is infinitely more complex in the international marketplace because value judgements differ widely among culturally diverse groups. What is commonly accepted as right in one country may be completely unacceptable in another. Giving business gifts of high value, for example, is generally condemned in the Western countries, but in many countries of the world, gifts are not only accepted but expected.

Bribery—Variations on a Theme

Bribery must be defined because of the limitless variations. The difference between bribery and extortion must be established: voluntarily offered payments by someone seeking unlawful advantage is *bribery*; payments extracted under duress by someone in authority from a person seeking only what they are lawfully entitled to is *extortion*. An example of extortion would be a finance minister of a country demanding heavy payments under the threat that millions of dollars of investment would be confiscated.

Another variation of bribery is the difference between lubrication and subornation. *Lubrication* involves a relatively small sum of cash, a gift, or a service made to a low-ranking official in a country where such offerings are not prohibited by law; the purpose of such a gift is to facilitate or expedite the normal, lawful performance of a duty by that official (a practice common in many countries of the world). *Subornation*, on the other hand, generally involves large sums of money, frequently not properly accounted for, designed to entice an official to commit an illegal act on behalf of the one paying the bribe. Lubrication payments accompany requests for a person to do a job more rapidly or more efficiently; subornation is a request for officials to turn their heads, to not do their jobs or to break the law.

A third type of payment that can appear to be a bribe, but may not be, is an agent's fee. When a businessperson is uncertain of a country's rules and regulations, an agent may be hired to represent the company in that country. This would be similar to hiring an agent in the home country; for example, an attorney to file an appeal for a variance in a building code on the basis that the attorney will do a more efficient and thorough job than someone unfamiliar with such procedures. Similar services may be requested of an agent in a foreign country when problems occur. However, if a part of that agent's fees is used to pay bribes, the intermediary's fees are being used unlawfully.

The answer to the question of bribery is not an unqualified one. It is easy to generalize about the ethics of political payoffs and other types of payments; it is much more difficult to make the decision to withhold payment of money when the consequences of not making the payment may affect the company's ability to do business profitably or at all. With the variety of ethical standards and levels of morality that exist in different cultures, the dilemma of ethics and pragmatism that faces international business cannot be resolved until more countries decide to deal effectively with the issue.[19]

Ethical and Socially Responsible Decisions

To behave in an ethically and socially responsible way should be the hallmark of every businessperson's behaviour, domestic or international. It requires little thought for most of us to know the socially responsible or ethically correct response to questions about knowingly breaking the law, harming the environment, denying someone his or her rights, taking unfair advantage or behaving in a manner that would bring bodily harm or damage. Unfortunately, the difficult issues are not the obvious and simple 'right' or 'wrong' ones. In many countries, the international marketer faces the dilemma of responding to sundry situations where there is no local law, where local practices appear to condone a certain behaviour, or where the company willing to 'do what is necessary' is favoured over the company that refuses to engage in certain practices. In short, being socially responsible and ethically correct is not a simple task for the international marketer operating in countries whose cultural and social values, and/or economic needs are different from those of the marketer.

In normal business operations there are five broad areas where difficulties arise in making decisions, establishing policies, and engaging in business operations: (1) employment practices and policies; (2) consumer protection; (3) environmental protection; (4) political payments and involvement in political affairs of the country; and (5) basic human rights and fundamental freedoms. In many countries, the law may help define the borders of minimum ethical or social responsibility, but the law is only the floor above which one's social and personal morality is tested. 'Ethical business conduct should normally exist at a level well above the minimum required by law.'[20] In fact, laws are the markers of past behaviour that society has deemed unethical or socially irresponsible.[21]

SUMMARY

Business customs and practices in different world markets vary so much that it is difficult to make valid generalizations about them; it is even difficult to classify the different kinds of business behaviour that are encountered from country to country. The only safe generalizations are that businesspersons working in another country must be sensitive to the business environment and must be willing to adapt when necessary. Unfortunately, it is not always easy to know when such adaptation is necessary; in some instances adaptation is optional and, in others, it is actually undesirable. Understanding the culture you are entering is the only sound basis for planning.

Business behaviour is derived in large part from the basic cultural environment in which the business operates, and, as such, is subject to the extreme diversity encountered among various cultures and subcultures. Environmental considerations significantly affect the attitudes, behaviour, and outlook of foreign business people. Motivational patterns of such business people depend in part on their personal backgrounds, their business positions, sources of authority and their own personalities.

Varying motivational patterns inevitably affect methods of doing business in different countries. Marketers in some countries thrive on competition, while in others they do everything possible to eliminate it. The authoritarian, centralized decision-making orientation in some countries contrasts sharply with democratic decentralization in others. International variation characterizes contact level, ethical orientation, negotiation outlook, and nearly every part of doing business. The foreign marketer can take no phase of business behaviour for granted.

The new breed of international businessperson who has emerged in recent years appears to have a heightened sensitivity to cultural variations. Sensitivity, however, is not enough; the international trader must be constantly alert and prepared to adapt when necessary. One must always realize that, no matter how long the outsider is in a country, that person is not a native; in many countries he or she may always be treated as an outsider. Finally, one must avoid the critical mistake of assuming that a knowledge of one culture will provide acceptability in another.

QUESTIONS

1. 'More than tolerance of an alien culture is required; there is a need for affirmative acceptance of the concept "different but equal".' Elaborate.

2. 'We should also bear in mind that in today's business-oriented world economy, the cultures themselves are being significantly affected by business activities and business practices.' Comment.

3. 'In dealing with foreign businesses, the marketer must be particularly aware of the varying objectives and aspirations of management.' Explain.

4. Suggest ways in which persons might prepare themselves to handle unique business customs that may be encountered during a trip abroad.

5. Business customs and national customs are closely interrelated. In which ways would one expect the two areas to coincide and in which ways would they show differences? How could such areas of similarity and difference be identified?

6. Identify both local and foreign examples of cultural imperatives, adiaphora and exclusives. Be prepared to explain why each example fits into the category you have selected.

7. Contrast the authority roles of top management in different societies. How do the different views of authority affect marketing activities?

8. What effects on business customs might be anticipated from the recent rapid integration of Europe?

9. Interview some foreign students to determine the types of cultural shock they encountered when they first came to your country.

10. In which ways does the size of a customer's business affect business behaviour?

11. Compare three decision-making authority patterns in international business.

12. Explore the various ways in which business customs can affect the structure of competition.

13. Why is it important that the business executive be alert to the significance of business customs?

14. Suggest some cautions that an individual from a high-context culture should bear in mind when dealing with someone from a low-context culture. Do the same for facing low- to high-context situations.

15. Political payoffs are a problem. How would you react if you faced the prospect of paying a bribe? If you knew that by not paying you would not be able to complete a $10-million contract?

16. Distinguish between P-time and M-time.

17. Discuss how a P-time person reacts differently from an M-time person in keeping an appointment.

REFERENCES

1. Yim Yu Wong, 'The Impact of Cultural Differences on the Growing Tensions between Japan and the United States', *SAM Advanced Management Journal*, Winter 1994, pp. 40–48.

2. Edward T. Hall and Mildred Reed Hall, *Understanding Cultural Differences* (Yarmouth, ME: Intercultural Press, 1990), p. 196.

3. Geert Hofstede, 'The Business of International Business Is Culture', in Peter J. Buckley and Pervez N. Ghauri (eds), *The Internationalization of the Firm* (London: International Thompson Business Press, 1999), pp. 381–393.

4. Farid Elashmawi, 'China: The Many Faces of Chinese Business Culture', *Trade & Culture*, March–April 1995, pp. 30–32.

5. Haruyasu Ohsumi, 'Cultural Differences and Japan–US Economic Frictions', *Tokyo Business Today*, February 1995, pp. 49–52.

6. For an interesting report on how Japan may be changing, see Ted Holden and Neil Gross, 'Japan Just May Be Ready to Change Its Ways', *Business Week*, 27 January 1992, p. 30.

7. For a discussion of the problems of interpretation of Japanese to English, see Osamu Katayama, 'Speaking in Tongues', *Look Japan*, March 1993, pp. 18–19.

8. Ronald E. Dulek, John S. Fielden and John Hill, 'International Communication: An Executive Primer', *Business Horizons*, January–February 1991, pp. 20–25.

9. Edward T. Hall, 'Learning the Arabs' Silent Language', *Psychology Today*, August 1979, pp. 45–53. Hall has several books that should be read by everyone involved in international business: *Beyond Culture* (New York: Anchor Press-Doubleday, 1976); *The Hidden Dimension* (New York: Doubleday, 1966); and *The Silent Language* (New York: Doubleday, 1959).

10. For a detailed presentation of the differences in high- and low-context cultures, see Edward T. Hall and Mildred Reed Hall, *Hidden Differences: Doing Business with the Japanese* (New York: Doubleday Anchor Books, 1990), p. 172.

11. Robert Moran, 'Watch My Lips', *International Management*, September 1990, p. 77.

12. 'Tradition Plays an Important Role in the Business Culture of France', *Business America*, 6 May 1991, pp. 22–23.

13. See, for example, Stephen E. Weiss, 'Negotiating with "Romans"—Part 1', *Sloan Management Review*, Winter 1994, pp. 51–62.

14. David Tong, 'Negotiating: Two to Tango', *Business Asia*, 17 January 1994, p. 8.

15. Min Chen, 'Understanding Chinese and Japanese Negotiating Styles', *The International Executive*, March–April 1993, pp. 147–159.

16. Nancy J. Adler, 'Women Managers in a Global Economy,' Training and Development, April 1994, pp. 31–36.

17. Nancy J. Adler, 'Going Global: Women Managers in a Global Economy', *HR Magazine*, September 1993, pp. 52–55.

18. Dafna Izraeli and Yoram Zeira, 'Woman Managers in International Business: A Research Review and Appraisal', *Business and the Contemporary World*, Summer 1993, p. 35.

19. For a detailed discussion and guidelines for international business negotiations and ethics, see Pervez Ghauri and Jean-Claude Usunier, *International Business Negotiations* (Oxford: Pergamon Press, 1996).

20. 'A Code of Worldwide Business Conduct and Operating Principles', published by Caterpillar Inc., nd, p. 4.

21. For a discussion of guiding principles of ethical and socially responsible behaviour, see Joel Makower and Business for Social Responsibility, *Beyond the Bottom Line: Putting Social Responsibility to Work for Your Business and the World* (New York: Simon and Schuster, 1994).

PART

Assessing International
Market Opportunities

Part Outline

CHAPTER

8

Researching International Markets

Chapter Learning Objectives

What you should learn from Chapter 8

- Additional marketing factors involved in international market research.
- The problems of availability and use of secondary data.
- How to handle the international marketing research process.
- Quantitative and qualitative research.
- Multicultural sampling and its problems in less-developed countries.
- How to estimate market demand.
- Analysing and using research information.
- The function of multinational marketing information systems.
- Sources of available secondary data.

Information is the key component in developing successful marketing strategies. Information needs range from the general data required to assess market opportunities to specific market information for decisions about product, promotion, distribution and price. A study of international marketing blunders leads to one conclusion—the majority of mistakes cited could have been avoided if the decision maker had better knowledge of the market.[1] The quality of information available varies from uninformed opinion, i.e. the marketer's self-reference criterion (SRC), to thoroughly researched fact. As an enterprise broadens its scope of operations to include international markets, the need for current, accurate information is magnified. A marketer must find the most accurate and reliable data possible within the limits imposed by time, cost and the present state of the art.[2]

Marketing research is the systematic gathering, recording and analysing of data to provide information useful in marketing decision making. When operating in foreign markets, the need for thorough information as a substitute for uninformed opinion is at least as important as it is in domestic marketing.

Generally, the tools and techniques for research remain the same for foreign and domestic marketing, but the environments within which they are applied are different. Rather than acquire new and exotic methods of research, the international marketing researcher must develop the ability for imaginative and deft application of tried and tested techniques in sometimes totally strange milieux. The mechanical problems of implementing foreign marketing research might vary from country to country, but the overall objectives for foreign and domestic marketing research are basically the same. Within a foreign environment, the frequently differing emphasis on the kinds of information needed, the often limited variety of appropriate tools and techniques available and the difficulty of implementing the research process constitute the challenges facing most international marketing researchers.[3]

This chapter deals with the operational problems encountered in gathering information in foreign countries for use by international marketers. Emphasis is on those elements of data generation that usually prove troublesome in conducting research in an environment other than the home market. The section 'Multinational Marketing Information Systems' is followed by a summary of secondary sources available through public and private agencies.

BREADTH AND SCOPE OF INTERNATIONAL MARKETING RESEARCH

A basic difference between domestic and international market research is the broader scope needed for foreign research. Research can be divided into three types based on information needs: (1) general information about the country, area and/or market; (2) information necessary to forecast future marketing requirements by anticipating social, economic and consumer trends within specific markets or countries; and (3) specific market information used to make product, promotion, distribution and price decisions and to develop marketing plans. In domestic operations, most emphasis is placed on the third type, gathering specific market information because the other data are often available from secondary sources.

A country's political stability, cultural attributes and geographical characteristics are some of the kinds of information not ordinarily gathered by domestic company marketing research departments but which are required for a sound assessment of a foreign country market. This broader scope of international marketing research entails collecting and assessing information that includes:

1. *Economic*: General data on growth of the economy, inflation, business cycle trends and the like, profitability analysis for the division's products, specific industry

ONE QUESTION MAY HAVE MADE THE DIFFERENCE

Marketing research means asking the right questions. This is where culture gets in the way—the most obvious questions are often the ones not asked. Such seems to be the case in the following example.

Kids "R" Us, the fast-expanding clothing subsidiary of toy retailer Toys "R" Us, has seen its invasion of Puerto Rico wilt in the tropical sun. The children's clothier has opened three stores on the island since 1992, next to Toys "R" Us outlets. But an uncharacteristically ill-conceived marketing effort led to poor sales, so the three outlets will be closed, and plans for five more are shelved.

Puerto Rico looked like a paradise for the Paramus (NJ) company's clothing stores. Although the island trails even the poorest US state in per capita income, retailers such as Kmart and J.C. Penney prosper there. Puerto Ricans spend 55 per cent of disposable income in retail stores versus 43 per cent on the mainland.

But analysts say the chain banked on back-to-school sales, not understanding that Puerto Rican kids all wear uniforms to school. Plus, a lot of the togs were too heavy for the climate. Jeff Handler, the company's marketing director, says its centrally run operations missed on market tastes in Puerto Rico.

What happened? A failure to understand local custom and the effect of climate on the product.

Source: Adapted from 'Mismarketing in Puerto Rico, Kids "R" Us', *Business Week*, 28 February 1994, p. 8.

economic studies analysis of overseas economies and key economic indicators for the home country and major foreign countries.

2. *Sociological and political climate*: A general noneconomic review of conditions affecting the division's business. In addition to the more obvious subjects, it also covers ecology, safety, leisure time and their potential impact on the division's business.

3. *Overview of market conditions*: A detailed analysis of market conditions the division faces, by market segment, including international.

4. *Summary of the technological environment*: A summary of the state-of-the-art technology as it relates to the division's business, carefully broken down by product segments.

5. A review of competitors' market shares, methods of market segmentation, products and apparent strategies on an international scope.[4]

For the domestic marketer, most information such as this has been acquired after years of experience with a single market; but in foreign markets this information must be gathered for each new market.

There is a basic difference between information ideally needed and that which is collectible and/or used. Many firms engaged in foreign marketing do not make decisions with the benefit of the information listed. Some firms have neither the appreciation for information nor adequate time or money for implementation of research. As a firm becomes more committed to international marketing and the cost of possible failure increases, greater emphasis is placed on research. Consequently, a global firm is or should be engaged in the most sophisticated and exhaustive kinds of research activities.

THE RESEARCH PROCESS

A marketing research study is always a compromise dictated by limits of time, cost and the present state of the art. The researcher must strive for the most accurate and reliable information within existing constraints. A key to successful research is a systematic and orderly approach to the collection and analysis of data. Whether a research programme is conducted in London or Jakarta, the research process should follow these steps:

1. Define the research problem and establish research objectives.
2. Develop a research plan.
3. Gather the relevant data from secondary and/or primary sources.
4. Analyse and interpret the collected data.
5. Summarize findings and present the results.

Although the steps in a research programme are similar for all countries, variations and problems in implementation occur because of differences in cultural and economic conditions. While the problems of research in England or Canada may be similar to those in the United States, research in Germany, South Africa or Mexico may offer a multitude of very different and difficult distinctions. These distinctions become apparent with the first step in the research process—formulation of the problem. Figure 8.1 illustrates the marketing research process and some international dimensions.

Defining the Problem and Establishing Research Objectives

The research process should begin with a definition of the research problem and the establishment of specific research objectives. The major difficulty here is converting a series of business problems into tightly drawn and achievable research objectives.[5] In this initial stage, researchers often embark on the research process with only a vague grasp of the total problem.

This first step in research is more critical in foreign markets since an unfamiliar environment tends to cloud problem definition. Researchers either fail to anticipate the influence of the local culture on the problem or fail to identify the self-reference criterion (SRC) and so treat the problem definition as if it were in the researcher's home environment. In assessing some foreign business failures it is apparent that research was conducted, but the questions asked were more appropriate for the home market than for the foreign one. For example, Unilever introduced a super concentrated detergent to the Japanese market only to find out that a premeasured package on which they were trying to differentiate their product was unacceptable to the market because it didn't dissolve in the wash, the product was not designed to work in a new, popular low-agitation washing machine and the 'fresh smell' positioning of the detergent was not relevant in Japan since most consumers hang their wash outside to dry in the fresh air.[6] Did the company conduct research? Yes, but were appropriate questions asked?

Other difficulties in foreign research stem from a failure to establish problem limits broad enough to include all relevant variables. Information on a far greater range of factors is necessary to offset the unfamiliar cultural background of the foreign market. Consider proposed research about consumption patterns and attitudes towards hot milk-based drinks. In the United Kingdom, hot milk-based drinks are considered to have sleep-inducing, restful and relaxing properties and are traditionally consumed prior to bedtime. People in Thailand, however, drink the same hot milk-based drinks in the morning on the way to work and see them as being invigorating, energy-giving and stimulating. If one's only experience is the

Figure 8.1   The Marketing Research Process and the International Dimension

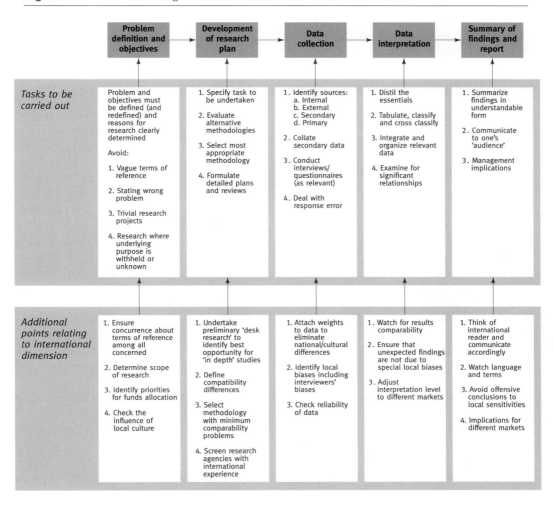

	Problem definition and objectives	Development of research plan	Data collection	Data interpretation	Summary of findings and report

Tasks to be carried out	Problem and objectives must be defined (and redefined) and reasons for research clearly determined
	
	Avoid:
	
	1. Vague terms of reference
	
	2. Stating wrong problem
	
	3. Trivial research projects
	
	4. Research where underlying purpose is withheld or unknown
		1. Specify task to be undertaken
		
		2. Evaluate alternative methodologies
		
		3. Select most appropriate methodology
		
		4. Formulate detailed plans and reviews
			1. Identify sources:
			   a. Internal
			   b. External
			   c. Secondary
			   d. Primary
			
			2. Collate secondary data
			
			3. Conduct interviews/ questionnaires (as relevant)
			
			4. Deal with response error
				1. Distil the essentials
				
				2. Tabulate, classify and cross classify
				
				3. Integrate and organize relevant data
				
				4. Examine for significant relationships
					1. Summarize findings in understandable form
					
					2. Communicate to one's 'audience'
					
					3. Management implications

Additional points relating to international dimension	1. Ensure concurrence about terms of reference among all concerned 2. Determine scope of research 3. Identify priorities for funds allocation 4. Check the influence of local culture	1. Undertake preliminary 'desk research' to identify best opportunity for 'in depth' studies 2. Define compatibility differences 3. Select methodology with minimum comparability problems 4. Screen research agencies with international experience	1. Attach weights to data to eliminate national/cultural differences 2. Identify local biases including interviewers' biases 3. Check reliability of data	1. Watch for results comparability 2. Ensure that unexpected findings are not due to special local biases 3. Adjust interpretation level to different markets	1. Think of international reader and communicate accordingly 2. Watch language and terms 3. Avoid offensive conclusions to local sensitivities 4. Implications for different markets

Source: Based on Simon Majaro, *International Marketing* (London: Routledge, 1993), p. 64.

United States, the picture is further clouded since hot milk-based drinks are frequently associated with cold weather, either in the morning or the evening, and for different reasons each time of day. The market researcher must be certain the problem definition is sufficiently defined to cover the relevant range of response possibilities and not be clouded by his or her SRC.

Developing a Research Plan

Once a research problem is clear and its objectives have been defined, it is important to plan the research process. This should be done irrespective of whether the company will undertake the work with its own resources or use outside agencies. The tasks to be undertaken should be specified and alternative methodologies should be evaluated. In this process an appropriate methodology should be selected. For example, which type of research, quantitative or qualitative, should be done. What are the theories/models we can use to find answers to research questions, are also to be identified here. While selecting these methodologies, the comparability of research findings and their usefulness must be kept in mind.

Quantitative and Qualitative Research

Marketing research methods can be grouped into two basic types, quantitative and qualitative research. In both methods, the marketer is interested in gaining knowledge about the market.

In *quantitative research*, the respondent is asked to reply either verbally or in writing to structured questions using a specific response format such as 'yes' or 'no', or to select a response from a set of choices. Questions are designed to get a specific response to aspects of the respondent's behaviour, intentions, attitudes, motives and demographic characteristics. Quantitative or survey research provides the marketer with responses that can be presented with precise estimations. The structured responses received in a survey can be summarized in percentages, averages or other statistics. For example, 76 per cent of the respondents prefer product A over product B and so on. Survey research is generally associated with quantitative research, and the typical instrument used is the questionnaire administered by personal interview, mail or telephone.

Qualitative research, on the other hand, is open-ended, in-depth and seeks unstructured responses that reflect the person's thoughts and feelings on the subject. Qualitative research interprets what the ' . . . people in the sample are like, their outlooks, their feelings, the dynamic interplay of their feelings and ideas, their attitudes and opinions, and their resulting actions'.[7] The most often used forms of qualitative questioning are the focus group, interviews and case studies.

Qualitative research is also used in international marketing research to formulate and define a problem more clearly and to determine relevant questions to be examined in subsequent research. It is used where interest is centred on gaining an understanding of a market, rather than quantifying relevant aspects.

When a British children's wear subsidiary of Sears was planning to enter the Spanish market, there was concern about the differences in attitudes and buying patterns of the Spanish from those in the United Kingdom and about market differences that might possibly exist among Spain's five major trading areas, Barcelona, Madrid, Seville, Bilbao and Valencia. Because the types of retail outlets in Spain were substantially different from those in the United Kingdom, 'accompanied shopping interviews'[8] were used to explore shoppers' attitudes about different types of stores. In the interviews, respondents were accompanied on visits to different outlets selling children's wear. During the visit to each shop, the respondent talked the interviewer through what she was seeing and feeling. This enabled the interviewer to see the outlet through the eyes of the shopper and to determine the criteria with which she evaluated the shopping environment and the products available. Information gathered in these studies and other focus group studies helped the company develop a successful entry strategy into Spain.

Qualitative research is also helpful in revealing the impact of sociocultural factors on behaviour patterns and to develop research hypotheses that can be tested in subsequent studies designed to quantify the concepts and relevant relationships uncovered in qualitative data collection. Research conducted by Procter & Gamble in Egypt is an example of how qualitative research leads to specific points that can later be measured by using survey or quantitative research.

For years Procter & Gamble had marketed Ariel Low Suds brand laundry detergent to the 5 per cent of homes in the Egyptian market that had automatic washing machines. They planned to expand their presence in the Egyptian market, and commissioned a study to: (1) identify the most lucrative opportunities in the Egyptian laundry market and (2) develop the right concept, product, price, brand name, package and advertising copy once the decision was made to pursue a segment of the laundry market.

The 'Habits and Practices' study, P&G's name for this phase, consisted of home visits and discussion groups (qualitative research) to understand how the Egyptian housewife did her laundry. They wanted to know her likes, dislikes and habits (the company's knowledge of laundry practices in Egypt had been limited to automatic washing machines). From this study, it was determined that the Egyptian consumer goes through a very laborious washing process to achieve the desired results. Among the 95 per cent of homes that washed in a non-automatic washing machine or by hand, the process consisted of soaking, boiling, bleaching and washing each load several times. Several products were used in the process; bar soaps or flakes were added to the main wash, along with liquid bleach and bluing to enhance the cleaning performance of the poor quality of locally produced powders. These findings highlighted the potential for a high-performing detergent that would accomplish everything that currently required several products. The decision was made to proceed with the development and introduction of a superior-performing high-suds granular detergent.

Once the basic product concept (i.e. one product instead of several to do laundry) was decided on, the company needed to determine the best components for a marketing mix to introduce the new product. The company went back to focus groups to assess reactions to different brand names (they were considering Ariel, already in the market as a low-suds detergent for automatic washers, and Tide, which had been marketed in Egypt in the 1960s and 1970s) to get ideas about the appeal and relevant wording for promotions and to test various price ranges, package design and size. Information derived from focus group encounters helped the company eliminate ideas with low consumer appeal and to focus on those that triggered the most interest. Further, the groups helped refine advertising and promotion wording to ensure clarity of communication through the use of everyday consumer language.

At the end of this stage, the company had well-defined ideas garnered from several focus groups, but did not have a 'feel' for the rest of those in the target market. Would they respond the same way the focus groups had? To answer this question, the company proceeded to the next step, a research programme to validate the relative appeal of the concepts generated from focus groups with a survey (quantitative research) of a large sample from the target market. Additionally, brand name, price, size and the product's intended benefits were tested in large sample surveys. Information gathered in the final surveys provided the company with the specific information used to develop a marketing programme that led to a successful product introduction and brand recognition for Ariel throughout Egypt.[9]

Qualitative and quantitative research are not always coupled as in the example of Procter & Gamble's research on Ariel. Qualitative research is also used alone where a small sample of carefully selected consumers is sufficient. For example, it is often difficult for respondents to know whether a product, flavour, concept or some other new idea is appealing if they have no experience with the issue being studied. To simply ask in a direct way may result in no response or, worse, a response that does not reflect how respondents would react if they had more experience.

In another case, Cadbury's, a UK firm, was looking for a way to give its chocolate cream liqueur a unique flavour. One idea was to add a hint of hazelnut flavouring. Yet when the company verbally suggested that the liqueur should be changed in this way consumers reacted negatively because they were unfamiliar with the mix of the two flavours. However, when taste tests were done without revealing what the extra flavours were, consumers loved the result.[10]

Gathering Secondary Data

The breadth of many foreign marketing research studies and the marketer's lack of familiarity with a country's basic socioeconomic and cultural data result in considerable demand for information generally available from secondary sources in the Western countries. Unfortunately, such data are not as available in foreign markets. Most Western governments provide comprehensive statistics for their home markets; periodic censuses of population, housing, business, and agriculture are conducted and, in some cases, have been taken for over 100 years. Commercial sources, trade associations, management groups and state and local governments also provide the researcher with additional sources of detailed market information.

While data collection has only recently begun in many countries, it is improving substantially through the efforts of organizations such as the United Nations and the Organization for Economic Cooperation and Development (OECD). As a country becomes more important as a market, a greater interest in basic data and better collection methods develop. The problems of availability, reliability, comparability of data and validating secondary data are described below.

With the emergence of Eastern European countries as potentially viable markets, a number of private and public groups are funding the collection of information to offset a lack of comprehensive market data. Several Japanese consumer goods manufacturers are coordinating market research on a corporate level and have funded 47 research centres throughout Eastern Europe. As market activity continues in Eastern Europe and elsewhere, market information will improve in quantity and quality. To build a database on Russian consumers, one Western firm used a novel approach to conduct a survey. It ran a questionnaire in Moscow's *Komsomolskaya Pravda* newspaper asking for replies to be sent to the company. The 350 000 replies received (3000 by registered mail) attested to the willingness of Russian consumers to respond to market enquiries.

Availability of Data.   A critical shortcoming of secondary data on foreign markets is the paucity of detailed data for many market areas. Much of the secondary data a Western marketer is accustomed to having about Western markets is just not available for many countries. Detailed data on the numbers of wholesalers, retailers, manufacturers and facilitating services, for example, are unavailable for many parts of the world, as are data on population and income. Most countries simply do not have governmental agencies that collect, on a regular basis, the kinds of secondary data readily available in the United States, the Netherlands, Germany and the Scandinavian countries. If such information is important, the marketer must initiate the research or rely on private sources of data. One research firm in Israel claims it can provide clients with information on everything from the types of women's undergarments that sell best to the most popular brand of cheese at the local supermarket.[11]

Reliability of Data.   Available data may not have the level of reliability necessary for confident decision making for many reasons. Official statistics are sometimes too optimistic, reflecting national pride rather than practical reality, while tax structures and fear of the tax collector often adversely affect data.

China's National Statistics Enforcement Office recently acknowledged that it had uncovered about 60 000 instances of false statistical reports since beginning a crackdown on false data reporting several months earlier.[12] Seeking advantages or hiding failures, local officials, factory managers, rural enterprises and others filed fake numbers on everything from production levels to birth rates. For example, a petrochemical plant reported one year's output to be $20 million (€18 million), 50 per cent higher than its actual output of $13.4 million (€12.1 million).[13] An American survey team verified that 60 million frozen chickens had been imported into Saudi Arabia in one year, even though official figures reported only 10 million. A Japanese company found that 40 000 air conditioners had actually been imported, but official figures were underestimated by 30 000 units. Whether errors of such magnitude are intentional or simply the result of sloppy record keeping is not always clear.

The European Union (EU) tax policies can affect the accuracy of reported data also. Production statistics are frequently inaccurate because the countries in the EU collect taxes on domestic sales. Thus, some companies shave their production statistics a bit to match the sales reported to tax authorities. Conversely, foreign trade statistics may be blown up slightly because many countries in the EU grant some form of export subsidy. Knowledge of such 'adjusted reporting' is critical for a marketer who relies on secondary data for forecasting or estimating market demand.

Comparability of Data.   Comparability and currency of available data is the third short-coming faced by international marketers. In most Western countries, current sources of reliable and valid estimates of socioeconomic factors and business indicators are readily available. In other countries, especially those less developed, data can be many years out of date as well as having been collected on an infrequent and unpredictable schedule. Further, even though many countries are now gathering reliable data, there are generally no historical series with which to compare the current information.

A related problem is the manner in which data are collected and reported. Too frequently, data are reported in different categories or in categories much too broad to be of specific value. The term 'supermarket', for example, has a variety of meanings around the world. In Japan a supermarket is quite different from its UK counterpart. Japanese supermarkets usually occupy two- or three-storey structures; they sell foodstuffs, daily necessities and clothing on respective floors. Some even sell furniture, electrical home appliances, stationery and sporting goods and have a restaurant. General merchandise stores, shopping centres and department stores are different from stores of the same name in the United Kingdom or Germany. Furthermore, data from different countries are often not comparable. One report on the problems of comparing European cross-border retail store audit data states: 'Some define the market one way, others another; some define price categories one way, and others another. Even within the same research agency, auditing periods are defined differently in different countries.'[14] As a result, audit data are largely incomparable.

Validating Secondary Data.   The shortcomings discussed here should be considered when using any source of information. Many Western countries have the same high standards of collection and preparation of data, but secondary data from any source, including the Western countries, must be checked and interpreted carefully. As a practical matter, the following questions should be asked to judge the reliability of data sources effectively:

1. Who collected the data? Would there be any reason for purposely misrepresenting the facts?

GOING INTERNATIONAL 8.2

INTERNATIONAL DATA: CAVEAT EMPTOR

The statistics used . . . are subject to more than the usual number of caveats and qualifications concerning comparability that are usually attached to economic data. Statistics on income and consumption were drawn from national-accounts data published regularly by the United Nations (UN) and the Organization for Economic Cooperation and Development (OECD). These data, designed to provide a 'comprehensive statistical statement about the economic activity of a country', are compiled from surveys sent to each of the participating countries (118 nations were surveyed by the UN). However, despite efforts by the UN and the OECD to present the data on a comparable basis, differences among countries concerning definitions, accounting practices and recording methods persist. In Germany, for instance, consumer expenditures are estimated largely on the basis of the turnover tax, while in the United Kingdom, tax-receipt data are frequently supplemented by household surveys and production data.

Even if data-gathering techniques in each country were standardized, definitional differences would still remain. These differences are relatively minor except in a few cases; for example, Germany classifies the purchase of a television set as an expenditure for 'recreation and entertainment', while the same expenditure falls into the 'furniture, furnishings and household equipment' classification in the United States.

While income and consumption expenditures consist primarily of cash transactions, there are several important exceptions. Both income and expenditures include the monetary value of food, clothing and shelter received in lieu of wages. Also included are imputed rents on owner-occupied dwellings, in addition to actual rents paid by tenants. Wages and salaries, which make up the largest share of consumer income, include employer contributions to social security systems, private pension plans, life and casualty insurance plans and family allowance programmes. Consumer expenditures include medical services even though the recipient may make only partial payment; if, however, the same services are subsidized wholly by public funds, the transaction is listed as a government rather than a consumer expenditure.

Expenditures, as defined by both the UN and the OECD, include consumption outlays by households (including individuals living alone) and private nonprofit organizations. The latter include churches, schools, hospitals, foundations, fraternal organizations, trade unions and other groups which furnish services to households free of charge or at prices that do not cover costs.

Source: David Bauer, 'The Dimensions of Consumer Markets Abroad', *The Conference Board Record*, reprinted with permission.

---

2. For what purpose were the data collected?
3. How were the data collected (methodology)?
4. Are the data internally consistent and logical in light of known data sources or market factors?

Checking the consistency of one set of secondary data with other data of known validity is an effective and often-used way of judging validity. For example, check the validity of the sale of baby products with the number of women of childbearing age and with birthrates, or the number of patient beds in hospitals with the sale of related hospital equipment. Such correlations can also be useful in estimating demand and forecasting sales.

In general, the availability and accuracy of recorded secondary data increase as the level of economic development increases. There are many exceptions: India is at a lower level of economic development than many countries but has accurate and complete development of government-collected data.

Figure 8.2   Problems with Gathering Primary Data

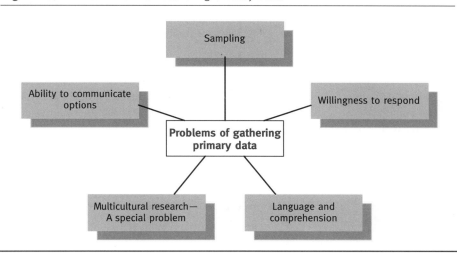

Gathering Primary Data

If, after seeking all reasonable secondary data sources, research questions are still not adequately answered, the market researcher must collect primary data. The researcher may question the firm's salesforce, distributors, middlemen and/or customers to get appropriate market information. In most primary data collection, the researcher questions respondents to determine what they think about some topic or how they might behave under certain conditions.

The problems of collecting primary data in foreign countries are different only in degree from those encountered at home. Assuming the research problems are well defined and objectives are properly formulated, the success of primary research hinges on the ability of the researcher to get correct and truthful information that addresses the research objectives. Most problems in collecting primary data in international marketing research stem from cultural differences among countries, and range from the inability of respondents to communicate their opinions to inadequacies in questionnaire translation. (See Figure 8.2.)

Ability to Communicate Opinions.   The ability to express attitudes and opinions about a product or concept depends on the respondent's ability to recognize the usefulness and value of such a product or concept. It is difficult for a person to formulate needs, attitudes and opinions about goods whose use may not be understood, that are not in common use within the community or that have never been available. For example, it may be impossible for someone who has never had the benefits of some type of air conditioning in the home to express accurate feelings or provide any reasonable information about purchase intentions, or likes and dislikes concerning electric air conditioning. The more complex the concept, the more difficult it is to design research that will help the respondent communicate meaningful opinions and reactions. Under these circumstances, the creative capabilities of the foreign marketing researcher are challenged.

Willingness to Respond.   Cultural differences offer the best explanation for the unwillingness or the inability of many to respond to research surveys. The role of the male, the suitability of personal gender-based enquiries, and other gender-related issues can affect willingness to respond. In some countries, the husband not only earns the money, but also dictates exactly how it is to be spent. Because the husband controls the spending, it is he, not the wife, who should be questioned to determine preferences and demand for many consumer goods.

In some cultures, women would never consent to be interviewed by a male or a stranger. A French Canadian woman does not like to be questioned and is likely to be reticent in her responses. In some societies, a man would certainly consider it beneath his dignity to discuss shaving habits or brand preference in personal clothing with anyone and, most emphatically, not with a female interviewer.

Anyone asking questions about any topic from which tax assessment could be inferred is immediately suspected of being a tax agent. Citizens of many Western countries do not feel the same legal and moral obligations to pay their taxes. So, tax evasion is an accepted practice for many and a source of pride for the more adept. Where such an attitude exists, taxes are arbitrarily assessed by the government, which results in much incomplete or misleading information being reported. One of the problems revealed by the government of India in a recent population census was the underreporting of tenants by landlords trying to hide the actual number of people living in houses and flats. The landlords had been subletting accommodations illegally and were concealing their activities from the tax department.

In many European countries, such information is seldom if ever released and then most reluctantly. Attempts to enlist the cooperation of retailers in setting up a store sample for shelf inventory and sales information ran into strong resistance because of suspicions and a tradition of competitive secrecy. The resistance was overcome by the researcher's willingness to approach the problem step by step. As the retailer gained confidence in the researcher and realized the value of the data gathered, more and more necessary information was provided.

Although such cultural differences may make survey research more difficult to conduct, it is possible. In some communities, locally prominent people could open otherwise closed doors; in other situations, professional people and local students have been used as interviewers because of their knowledge of the market. As with most of the problems of collecting primary data, the difficulties are not insurmountable to a researcher aware of their existence.

Sampling in Field Surveys.   The greatest problem of sampling stems from the lack of adequate demographic data and available lists from which to draw meaningful samples. If current, reliable lists are not available, sampling becomes more complex and generally less reliable. In many countries, telephone directories, cross-index street directories, census tract and block data, and detailed social and economic characteristics of the population being studied are not available on a current basis if at all.

To add to the confusion, in some South American, Mexican and Asian cities, street maps are unavailable, and, in some Asian metropolitan areas, streets are not identified nor are houses numbered. In contrast, one of the positive aspects of research in Japan and Taiwan is the availability and accuracy of census data on individuals. In these countries, when a household moves it is required to submit up-to-date information to a centralized government agency before it can use communal services such as water, gas, electricity and education.

The effectiveness of various methods of communication (mail, telephone and personal interview) in surveys is limited. In many countries, telephone ownership is extremely low, making telephone surveys virtually worthless unless the survey is intended to cover only the wealthy. In some countries, fewer than 5 per cent of the residents—only the wealthy—have telephones.

The problem of sampling was best summarized by one authority on research in Saudi Arabia who commented that probability sampling there was very difficult, if not impossible. The difficulties are so acute that non-probabilistic sampling becomes a necessary evil.[15] The kinds of problem encountered in drawing a random sample include:

- No officially recognized census of population.
- No other listings that can serve as sampling frames.
- Incomplete and out-of-date telephone directories.
- No accurate maps of population centres. Thus, no cluster (area) samples can be made.

Further, door-to-door interviewing in Saudi Arabia is illegal. While all the conditions described do not exist in all countries, they illustrate why the collection of primary data requires creative applications of research techniques when expanding into many foreign markets.[16]

Language and Comprehension.   The most universal survey sampling problem in foreign countries is the language barrier. Differences in idiom and the difficulty of exact translation create problems in eliciting the specific information desired and in interpreting the respondents' answers. Equivalent concepts may not exist in all languages. Family, for example, has different connotations in different countries. In Northern Europe and the United States, it generally means only the parents and children. In Italy and many Latin countries it could mean the parents, children, grandparents, uncles, aunts, cousins and so forth. The names for family members can have different meanings depending on the context within which they are used. In the Italian and many Asian cultures, aunt and uncle are different for the maternal and paternal sides of the family. The concept of affection is a universal idea but the manner in which it is manifest in each culture may differ.

Literacy poses yet another problem; in some developing countries with low literacy rates, written questionnaires are completely useless. Within countries, too, the problem of dialects and different languages can make a national questionnaire survey impractical. In India, there are 25 official languages and more than 50 unofficial ones.

The obvious solution of having questionnaires prepared or reviewed by someone fluent in the language of the country is frequently overlooked. In one such case, a German respondent was asked the number of 'washers' (washing machines) produced in Germany for a particular year; the reply reflected the production of the flat metal disc. Marketers use three different techniques, back translation, parallel translation, and decentring, to help ferret out translation errors.

- Back Translation.   In back translation the questionnaire is translated from one language to another, then a second party translates it back into the original. This pinpoints misinterpretations and misunderstandings before they reach the public. A soft-drink company wanted to use a very successful Australian advertising theme, 'Baby, it's cold inside', in Hong Kong. They had the theme translated from English into Cantonese by one translator and then retranslated by another from Cantonese into English, where the statement came out, 'Small Mosquito, on the inside it is very cold'. Although 'small mosquito' is the colloquial expression for small child in Hong Kong, the intended meaning was lost in translation.

- Parallel Translation.   Back translations may not always assure an accurate translation because of commonly used idioms in both languages. Parallel translation is used to overcome this problem. In this process, more than two translators are used for the back translation; the results are compared, differences discussed and the most appropriate translation selected.

- Decentring.   This is a successive iteration process of translation and retranslations of a questionnaire, each time by a different translator. The process is as follows: an English

MARKETING RESEARCH, DON'T LEAVE HOME WITHOUT IT

The advertising slogan for a famous credit-card company that says 'Don't leave home without it' applies equally well to marketing research. If you are going to do business in another culture, you must know your market. Effective marketing research would have helped avoid some of the following misfires.

One company, ready to launch a new peanut-packed chocolate bar aimed at giving teenagers quick energy while cramming for exams, found out in time that a Japanese old wives' tale held that eating chocolate with peanuts causes nose bleeds. The product was never marketed in Japan.

A toothpaste firm's product advertising in regions of South-east Asia stressed that the toothpaste helped enhance white teeth. For those local people who deliberately chewed betel nut to achieve the social prestige of darkly stained teeth, the ad was less than effective.

Sources: Authors' compilation and M. Katherine Glover, 'Do's and Taboos: Cultural Aspects of International Business', *Business America*, 13 August 1990, pp. 2–6.

version is translated into French and then translated back to English by a different translator. The two English versions are compared and, where there are differences, the original English version is modified and the process is repeated. If there are differences between the two English versions, the original English version of the second iteration is modified and the process of translation and back translation is repeated. The process continues to be repeated until an English version can be translated into French and back translated, by a different translator, into the same English. In this process, wording of the original instrument undergoes a change and the version that is finally used and its translation have equally comprehensive and equivalent terminologies in both languages.

Because of cultural and national differences, confusion can just as well be the problem of the researcher as of the respondent. The question itself may not be properly worded in the English version. One classic misunderstanding, which occurred in a *Reader's Digest* study of consumer behaviour in Western Europe, resulted in a report that France and Germany consumed more spaghetti than did Italy. This rather curious and erroneous finding resulted from questions that asked about purchases of 'packaged and branded spaghetti'. Italians buy their spaghetti in bulk, the French and Germans buy branded and packaged spaghetti. Because the Italians buy little branded or packaged spaghetti, the results underreported spaghetti purchases by Italians. However, the real question is what the researcher wanted to find out. Had the goal of the research been to determine how much branded and packaged spaghetti was purchased, the results would have been correct. However, because the goal was to know about total spaghetti consumption, the data were incorrect.

Multicultural Research—A Special Problem.   As companies become international marketers and seek to standardize various parts of the marketing mix across several countries, multicultural studies become more important. A company needs to determine whether standardization or adaptation of the marketing mix is appropriate. Thus, market characteristics across diverse cultures must be compared for similarities and differences before a company proceeds with a global marketing strategy. The research difficulties discussed thus far have addressed problems of conducting research within a culture. When engaging in multicultural studies, many of these same problems further complicate the difficulty of cross-cultural comparisons.

When designing multicultural studies, it is essential that the differences be taken into account. An important point to keep in mind when designing research to be applied across cultures is to ensure comparability and equivalency of results. Different methods may have varying reliabilities in different countries. It is essential that these differences be taken into account in the design of a multicultural survey. Such differences may mean that different research methods should be applied in individual countries. For example, a mail survey may have a high level of reliability in country A but not in country B, whereas a personal interview in country B will have an equivalent level of reliability as the mail survey in country A. Thus, a mail survey should be used in country A and a personal interview in country B. In collecting data from different countries, it is more important to use techniques with equivalent levels of reliability than to use the same techniques.[17]

The adaptations necessary to complete a cross-national study raise a serious question about the reliability of data gathered in cross-national research. There is evidence that insufficient attention is given not only to nonsampling errors and other problems that can exist in improperly conducted multicultural studies, but also to the appropriateness of consumer research measures that have not been tested in multicultural contexts.[18]

Analysing and Interpreting Research Information

Once data have been collected, the final steps are the analysis and interpretation of findings in light of the stated marketing problem. Both secondary and primary data collected by the market researcher are subject to the many limitations just discussed. In any final analysis, the researcher must take into consideration these factors and, despite their limitations, produce meaningful guides for management decisions.[19]

Accepting information at face value in foreign markets is imprudent. The meanings of words, the consumer's attitude towards a product, the interviewer's attitude or the interview situation can distort research findings. Just as culture and tradition influence the willingness to give information, they also influence the information given. Newspaper circulation figures, readership and listenership studies, retail outlet figures, and sales volume can all be distorted through local business practice. To cope with such disparities, the foreign market researcher must possess three talents to generate meaningful marketing information.

First, the researcher must possess a high degree of cultural understanding of the market in which research is being conducted. In order to analyse research findings, the social customs, semantics, current attitudes and business customs of a society or a subsegment of a society must be clearly understood.

Second, a creative talent for adapting research findings is necessary. A researcher in foreign markets is often travelling for a week or two and is called on to produce results under the most difficult circumstances. Ingenuity and resourcefulness, willingness to use 'catch as catch can' methods to get facts, patience, a sense of humour and a willingness to be guided by original research findings even when they conflict with popular opinion or prior assumptions are all considered prime assets in foreign marketing research.

Third, a sceptical attitude in handling both primary and secondary data is helpful. It might be necessary to check a newspaper press run over a period of time to get accurate circulation figures, or deflate or inflate reported consumer income in some areas by 25 to 50 per cent on the basis of observable socioeconomic characteristics.

GOING INTERNATIONAL 8.4

MARKETING TOOL: THE SEMANTIC DIFFERENTIAL

An important tool in attitudinal research, image studies and positioning decisions is the *semantic differential*. It was originally developed to measure the meaning that a concept—perhaps a political issue, a person, a work of art or, in marketing, a brand , product, or company—might have for people in terms of various dimensions. As first presented, the instrument consisted of pairs of polar adjectives with a seven-interval scale separating the opposite members of each pair. For example:

Extremely good   ———   Extremely bad

This instrument has been refined to obtain greater sensitivity through the use of descriptive phrases. Examples of such bipolar phrases for determining the image of a particular brand of beer are:

Something special   ———   Just another drink
Local flavour   ———   Foreign flavour
Really peps you up   ———   Somehow doesn't pep you up

The number of word pairs varies considerably but may be as many as 50 or more. Flexibility and appropriateness to a particular study are achieved by constructing tailor made word and phrase lists.

Semantic differential scales have been used in marketing to compare images of particular products, brands, firms, and stores against competing ones. The answers of all respondents can be averaged and then plotted to provide a 'profile', as shown below for three competing beers on four scales (actually, a firm would probably use more scales in such a study).

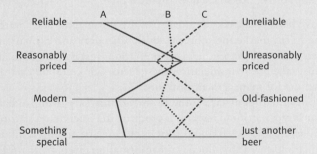

In this profile, brand A shows the dominant image over its competing brands in three of the four categories; however, the negative reaction to its price should alert the company to review pricing practices. Brand C shows a negative image especially regarding the reliability of its product. The profile indicates that brand C is perceived as being distinctive from the other two brands. Probably the weakest image of all is that of brand B; respondents viewed this brand as having no distinctive image, neither good nor bad.

Simple, easy to administer and analyse, the semantic differential is useful not only in identifying segments and positions where there might be opportunities because these are currently not well covered by competitors, but it is also useful to a well established firm—such as Coca Cola—to determine the strength and the various dimensions of attitudes towards its product. Semantic differential scales are also useful in evaluating the effectiveness of a changed marketing strategy, such as a change in advertising theme. Here the semantic differential could be administered before the campaign and again after the campaign, and any changes in perception pinpointed.

Develop eight semantic differential scales for soft drinks, and then profile Coke and Pepsi. What differences do you perceive in the two brands? Are they important? Do you see any soft-drink untapped opportunities?

Source: Robert Hartley, *Marketing Mistakes*, 6th edn (New York: Wiley, 1995), pp. 139–140.

Presenting the Findings and Results

Presentation of findings and results in a summarized and easy-to-understand manner is crucial to the success of research. The researcher has to put the research problem, the data collection and findings into a logical, consistent and persuasive report. Before writing the final report of the project, it is necessary to consider the purpose of the report and to whom it is addressed. The researcher has to convince the reader that he or she has done the job in a systematic and logical manner and that the findings are reliable. This is particularly important in international marketing research, as the results and findings are to be understood and executed by international marketers and managers.

Culturally biased and offensive conclusions need to be avoided, especially in respect of local sensitivities. The report to managers must be concise and convincing. It should include a very short, maximum two pages, executive summary explaining the major issues, some interpretations on data, collected results and managerial implications.

RESPONSIBILITY FOR CONDUCTING MARKETING RESEARCH

Depending on size and degree of involvement in foreign marketing, a company in need of foreign market research can rely on an outside foreign-based agency or on a domestic company with a branch within the country in question. It can conduct research using its own facilities or employ a combination of its own research force with the assistance of an outside agency.

Many companies have an executive specifically assigned to the research function in foreign operations; he or she selects the research method and works closely with foreign management, staff specialists and outside research agencies. Other companies maintain separate research departments for foreign operations or assign a full-time research analyst to this activity. For many companies, a separate department is too costly; the diversity of markets would require a large department to provide a skilled analyst for each area or region of international business operations.

A comprehensive review of the different approaches to multicountry research suggests that the ideal approach is to have local researchers in each country, with close coordination between the client company and the local research companies. This cooperation is important at all stages of the research project from research design, to data collection, to final analysis. Further, two stages of analysis are necessary. At the individual country level, all issues involved in each country must be identified, and at the multicountry level, the information must be distilled into a format that addresses the client's objectives. Such recommendations are supported on the grounds that two heads are better than one and that multicultural input is essential to any understanding of multicultural data. With just one interpreter of multi-cultural data, there is the danger of one's self-reference criterion (SRC) resulting in data being interpreted in terms of one's own cultural biases.[20] Self-reference bias can affect the research design, questionnaire design, and interpretation of the data.

If a company wants to use a professional marketing research firm, many are available. Most major advertising agencies and many research firms have established branch offices world-wide. There has also been a healthy growth in foreign-based research and consulting firms. A list of some of these organizations is given in Table 8.1.

An interesting aside on data collection agencies involves the changing role of the Central Intelligence Agency (CIA) since the demand for military surveillance has diminished in recent years. Members of Congress have suggested that the CIA should be active in protecting

Table 8.1   Top 25 Global Research Organizations

Rank 1996	Rank 1995	Organization	Country	No. of Subsidiaries/ Branch Offices (1)	Total Research Revenues (2) (million $)	Revenues from Outside Home Country as % of Total
1	–	AC Nielsen Corp.	USA	45	1358.6	78.9
2	–	Cognizant Corp.	USA	1	1223.8	48.8
		IMS International Inc.	*USA*	*62*	*904.4*	*65.0*
		Nielsen Media Research	*USA*	*2*	*319.4*	*3.0*
3	2	The Kantar Group Ltd	UK	1	472.9	60.1
		Research International	*UK*	*19*	*246.7*	*68.1*
		Millward Brown International	*UK*	*9*	*155.8*	*54.6*
		MRB Group Ltd.	*UK*	*5*	*70.4*	*44.2*
4	3	Information Resources Inc.	USA	17	405.6	15.0
5	4	GfK AG	Germany	31	317.6	44.8
6	5	SOFRES Group SA	France	19	276.0	54.4
7	6	Infratest Burke AG	Germany	11	167.5	35.5
8	8	IPSOS Group SA	France	11	161.4	61.3
9	10	The Arbitron Company	USA	1	153.1	—
10	9	PMSI/ Source Informatics	USA	1	152.2	28.6
		Pharmaceutical Marketing Services, Inc.	*USA*	*8*	*98.0*	*42.2*
		Source Informatics	*USA*	*5*	*54.2*	*4.0*
11	11	Westat Inc.	USA	1	146.5	—
12	7	Video Research Ltd	Japan	1	136.6*	—
13	12	Maritz Marketing Research, Inc.	USA	3	133.6	23.0
14	13	NOP Information Group	UK	5	130.9	33.7
15	14	Taylor Nelson AGB Plc	UK	5	120.6	25.9
16	17	NFO Research Inc.	USA	4	109.2	4.0
17	16	The NPD Group Inc.	USA	13	99.6	16.0
18	15	Marketing Intelligence Corp.	Japan	1	89.7	0.3
19	18	Market Facts Inc.	USA	2	83.8	7.5
20	20	Audits & Surveys Worldwide Inc.	USA	4	60.4	32.9
21	22	Sample Institute GmbH & Co. KG	Germany	7	57.1	53.8
22	21	The M/A/R/C Group, Inc.	USA	2	55.7	1.8
23	19	Dentsu Research	Japan	1	54.6	3.2
24	26	The BASES Group	USA	1	53.3	15.4
25	24	Goldfarb Consultants	Canada	7	48.5	46.9
Total					6068.8	*44.9*

(1) Includes countries which have subsidiaries with an equity interest or branch offices, or both; (2) Total revenues that include nonresearch activities for some companies are significantly higher. This information is given in the individual company profiles in the main article of the magazine (see source); (3) Rate of growth from year-to-year has been adjusted so as not to include revenue gains or losses from acquisitions. Rate of growth is based on home country currency.

*For fiscal year ending 31 March 1997.

Source: Jack Honomichi, 'Top 25 Global Firms Earn $6.1 billion in Revenue', *Marketing News*, 18 August 1997, p. H4.

FRANCE HAS STOLEN A MARCH ON THE US IN ECONOMIC INTELLIGENCE

In a report to the US Congress earlier this month, the Central Intelligence Agency named the French services, along with the Israelis, as the most active in launching operations against American interests, both inside and outside the United States. Recently, the DGSE, the French secret service, has stepped up operations in areas such as Bosnia, Algeria and Russia. In the former Soviet Union, it is credited with being the first secret service to have reached a proper diagnosis of President Boris Yeltsin's illness.

The emphasis has continued to shift towards economic intelligence. The ability to intercept secret offers made by US armament firms to Middle East countries has allowed French firms to propose better deals. In 1997, they broke into the lucrative Saudi defence market for the first time by signing a contract for the sale of 12 helicopters built by Eurocopter. The recent CIA report accused the French specifically of launching intelligence operations against US military contractors and high-technology firms. In the report, national security specialist David E. Cooper describes the intelligence-gathering of a particular country, clearly identifiable as France, which 'recruited agents at the European offices of three US computer and electronic firms'.

According to sources, IBM in Brussels and Texas Instruments were two of those targets. Clearly, France is not the only country to seek such information. In 1994, President Bill Clinton asked the FBI to launch an economic counter-intelligence programme. Former DGSE director Admiral Pierce Lacoste told *The European*:

> It is part of an indirect strategy by the US. They want all the trumps. Initially their target was Japan. But now it is France, for two main reasons. First, France is seen as one of the most vocal and active countries over the strengthening of the European Union and a single currency; and second, because this country is organizing a new economic intelligence system.

While continuing with traditional intelligence, in April 1996 Chirac set up a special economic and technological intelligence coordination body, inspired by the highly effective Japanese Ministry of International Trade and Industry. The Comité pour la Compétitivité et la Sécurité Économique (CCSE) is led by seven 'wise men', including banker Bernard Esambert, Matra boss Jean-Luc Lagardère and Henri Martre, former chairman of Aérospatiale and author of a detailed study on economic intelligence.

> 'This is essentially the start of a cultural shift on the part of French industrial and commercial intelligence. But this process will take some time to come to fruition', said Lacoste. 'Obviously, the French and future European intelligence would play some role in this. They could not allow the CIA to be the only secret service operating in that field'.

Source: *The European*, 29 August–4 September 1996.

America's economic commercial interests worldwide and in gathering international trade data to improve the information base for US businesses.

ESTIMATING MARKET DEMAND

In assessing current product demand and forecasting future demand, reliable historical data are required. As previously noted, the quality and availability of secondary data are frequently inadequate. Nevertheless, estimates of market size must be attempted in order to plan effectively. Despite limitations, there are approaches to demand estimation usable with minimum information. The success of these approaches relies on the ability of the researcher to find

INDUSTRY STATISTICS?

Considerable confusion arises when prescribed product categories overlap. If the Dutch product classifications for the printing industry specify one group comprising 'printed matter for advertising purposes' and another comprising 'calendars', where should the million-guilder printing job for the Royal Dutch Shell calendars be reported? One printing company explained: 'To balance it off, we reported one way one year and the other way the next.'

Source: 'European Market Research: Hide and Seek', *Sales Management*, vol. 102, no. 3, p. 46.

meaningful substitutes or approximations for the needed economic and demographic relationships. Some of the necessary but frequently unavailable statistics for assessing market opportunity and estimating demand for a product are current trends in market demand.

When the desired statistics are not available, a close approximation can be made using local production figures plus imports, with adjustments for exports and current inventory levels. These data are more readily available because they are commonly reported by the United Nations and other international agencies. Once approximations for sales trends are established, historical series can be used as the basis for projections of growth.[21] In any straight extrapolation, however, the estimator assumes that the trends of the immediate past will continue into the future. In a rapidly developing economy, extrapolated figures may not reflect rapid growth and must be adjusted accordingly.

Analogy.   Another technique is to estimate by *analogy*. This assumes that demand for a product develops in much the same way in all countries as comparable economic development occurs in each country. First, a relationship must be established between the item to be estimated and a measurable variable in a country that is to serve as the basis for the analogy. Once a known relationship is established, the estimator then attempts to draw an analogy between the known situation and the country in question. For example, suppose a company wanted to estimate the market growth potential for a beverage in country X, for which it had inadequate sales figures, but the company had excellent beverage data for neighbouring country Y. In country Y it is known that per capita consumption increases at a predictable ratio as per capita gross domestic product (GDP) increases. If per capita GDP is known for country X, per capita consumption for the beverage can be estimated using the relationships established in country Y. Caution must be used with analogy because the method assumes that factors other than the variable used (in this example GDP) are similar in both countries, such as the same culture, tastes, taxes, prices, selling methods, availability of products, consumption patterns and so forth. Despite the apparent drawbacks to analogy, it is useful where data are limited.

Income Elasticity.   Measuring the changes in the relationship between personal or family income and demand for a product can be used in forecasting market demand. In *income-elasticity* ratios, the sensitivity of demand for a product to income changes is measured. The elasticity coefficient is determined by dividing the percentage change in the quantity of a product demanded by the percentage change in income. With a result of less than one, it is said that the income–demand relationship is relatively inelastic and, conversely, if the result is greater than one, the relationship is elastic. As income increases, the demand for a product increases at a rate proportionately higher than income increases. For example, if income coefficient elasticity for recreation is 1.2, it implies that for each 1 per cent change in income, the demand for recreation could be expected to increase by 1.2 per cent; or if the coefficient is 0.8, then for each 1 per cent change in income, demand for recreation could be expected to increase only 0.8 per cent. The relationship also occurs when income decreases, although the rate of decrease might be greater than when income increases. Income elasticity can be very useful, too, in predicting growth in demand for a particular product or product group.

The major problem of this method is that the data necessary to establish elasticities may not be available. However, in many countries, income elasticities for products have been determined and it is possible to use the analogy method described (with all the caveats mentioned) to make estimates for those countries. Income elasticity measurements only give an indication of change in demand as income changes and do not provide the researcher with any estimate of total demand for the product.

As in the case of all methods described in this section, income elasticity measurements are no substitute for original market research when it is economically feasible and time permits. As more adequate data sources become available, as would be the situation in most of the economically developed countries, more technically advanced techniques such as multiple regression analysis or input–output analysis can be used.

MULTINATIONAL MARKETING INFORMATION SYSTEMS

Increased marketing activity by domestic and multinational firms has generated not only more data, but also a greater awareness of its need. In addition to the changes in the quantity and type of information needed, there has been an increase in competent agencies (many of them subsidiaries of Western marketing research firms) whose primary functions are to gather data. As firms become established, and their information needs shift from those necessary to make initial market investment decisions to those necessary for continuous operation, there is a growing demand for continuous sources of information both at the country operational level and at the worldwide corporate level. However, as the abundance of information increases, it reaches a point of 'information overload' and requires some systematic method of storing, interpreting and analysing data.

A company shift from decisions involving market entry to those involved in managing and controlling a number of different growing foreign markets requires greater emphasis on a continuous system designed to generate, store, catalogue and analyse information from sources within the firm and external to the firm for use as the basis of worldwide and country-oriented decision making. In short, companies have a need for a *Multinational marketing information system* (*MMIS*).

Conceptually, an MMIS embodies the same principle as any information system, that is, an interacting complex of persons, machines and procedures designed to generate an orderly flow of relevant information and to bring all the flows of recorded information into a unified

Figure 8.3   Multinational Marketing Information System

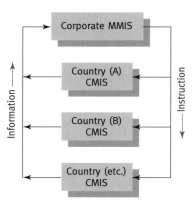

whole for decision making. The only differences from a domestic marketing information system are (1) scope—an MMIS covers more than one country—and (2) levels of information—an MMIS operates at each country level, with perhaps substantial differences among country systems, and at a worldwide level encompassing an entire international operation. The system (see Figure 8.3) includes a subsystem for each country designed for operational decision making—a country-level marketing information system. Each country system also provides information to an MMIS designed to provide for corporate control and strategic long-range planning decisions.

In developing an MMIS, it is necessary to design an adequate *Country marketing information system* (*CMIS*) for each country/market. Because of the vast differences among a company's various markets, each country/market CMIS will probably have different data requirements. Once a CMIS is set for each country/market, then an overall MMIS for the worldwide operation is designed. Each level of management has substantially different data needs because country/market systems are designed to provide information for day-to-day operations, while the MMIS is concerned with broader issues of control and long-range strategic planning. However, the country/market CMIS data are used not only for daily operations, but ultimately are transmitted to the MMIS to be included in overall planning decisions. Some of the most challenging tasks facing the developer of the MMIS are determining the kinds of data and the depth of detail necessary and analysing how it should be processed. This implies that models for decision making have been thought through and are sufficiently specific to be functional.

An MMIS can be designed as a basic system that provides only a source of information or as a highly sophisticated system that includes specific decision models. Experience has shown that success is greater when a company begins with a basic system and continues perfecting it to the desired level of sophistication.

SUMMARY

The basic objective of the market research function is providing management with information for more accurate decision making. This objective is the same for domestic and international marketing. In international marketing research, however, achieving that objective presents some problems not encountered on the domestic front.

Consumer attitudes about providing information to a researcher are culturally conditioned. Foreign market information surveys must be carefully designed to elicit the desired data and at the same time not offend the respondent's sense of privacy. Besides the cultural and managerial constraints involved in gathering information for primary data, many foreign markets have inadequate and/or unreliable bases of secondary information.

Three generalizations can be made about the direction and rate of growth of marketing research in foreign marketing. First, both home-based and foreign management are increasingly aware of and accept the importance of marketing research's role in decision making. Second, there is a current trend towards the decentralization of the research function to put control closer to the area being studied. Third, the most sophisticated tools and techniques are being adapted to foreign information gathering with increasing success. They are so successful, in fact, that it has become necessary to develop structured information systems to appreciate and utilize effectively the mass of information available.

APPENDIX: SOURCES OF SECONDARY DATA

For almost any marketing research project, an analysis of available secondary information is a useful and inexpensive first step. Although there are information gaps, particularly for detailed market information, the situation on data availability and reliability is improving. The principal agencies that collect and publish information useful in international business are presented here, with some notations of selected publications.

International Organizations

A number of international organizations provide information and statistics on international markets. *The Statistical Yearbook*, an annual publication of the United Nations, provides comprehensive social and economic data for more than 250 countries around the world. Many regional organizations, such as the Organization for Economic Cooperation and Development (OECD), Pan American Union and the European Union publish information, statistics and market studies relating to their respective regions.

Chambers of Commerce

In addition to government and organizational publications, many foreign countries maintain chamber-of-commerce offices in the European Union functioning as permanent trade missions. These foreign chambers of commerce generally have research libraries available and are knowledgeable regarding further sources of information on specific products or marketing problems.

Trade, Business and Service Organizations

Foreign trade associations are particularly good sources of information on specific products or product lines. Many associations perform special studies or continuing services in collecting comprehensive statistical data for a specific product group or industry. Although some information is proprietary in nature and available only to members of an association, non-members frequently have access to it under certain conditions. Up-to-date membership lists providing potential customers or competitors are often available to anyone requesting them, and a listing of foreign trade associations is usually annotated at the end of a specific Trade List.

Foreign service industries also supply valuable sources of information useful in international business. Service companies—such as commercial and investment banks, international advertising agencies, foreign-based research firms, economic research institutes, foreign carriers, shipping agencies and freight forwarders—generally regard the furnishing of current, reliable information as part of their service function. The banking industry in foreign countries is particularly useful as a source of information on current local economic situations. The Chase Manhattan Bank in New York periodically publishes a newsletter on such subjects as the European Union. There are several good independently published reports on techniques, trends, forecasts and other such current data. Many foreign banks publish periodic or special review newsletters relating to the local economy, providing a firsthand analysis of the economic situation of specific foreign countries. For example, the Krediet Bank in Brussels published *Belgium, Key to the Common Market*, and the Banco National Commercio Exterior in Mexico published *Mexico Facts, Figures, Trends*. Even though these publications are sometimes available without charge, they must usually be translated.

US Government

The US government actively promotes the expansion of US business into international trade. In the process of keeping US businesses informed of foreign opportunities, the US government generates a considerable amount of general and specific market data for use by international market analysts. The principal source of information from the US government is the Department of Commerce, which makes its services available to US business in a variety of ways. First, information and assistance are available either through personal consultation in Washington, DC, or through any of the US and FCS (Foreign Commercial Service) district offices of the International Trade Administration (ITA) of the Department of Commerce located in key cities in the United States. Second, the Department of Commerce works closely with trade associations, chambers of commerce and other interested associations in providing information, consultation and assistance in developing international commerce. Third, the department publishes a wide range of information available to interested persons at nominal cost.

1. International Economic Indicators.   Quarterly reports providing basic data on the economy of the United States and seven other principal industrial countries. Statistics included are gross national product, industrial production, trade, prices, finance and labour. This report measures changes in key competitive indicators and highlights economic prospects and recent trends in the eight countries.

2. Business Information Service for the Newly Independent States (BISNIS). This is a one-stop source for firms interested in obtaining assistance on selling in the markets of the Newly Independent States of the former Soviet Union. BISNIS provides information on trade regulations and legislation, defence conversion opportunities, commercial opportunities, market data, sources of financing, government and industry contacts and US government programmes supporting trade and investment in the region.

3. National Trade Data Bank (NTDB).   The Commerce Department provides a number of the data sources mentioned above and others in their computerized information system in the *National Trade Data Bank* (NTDB). The NTDB is a 'one-step' source for export promotion and international trade data collected by 17 US government agencies. Updated each month and released on two CD-ROMs, the NTDB enables a user with an IBM-compatible personal computer equipped with a CD-ROM reader to access more than 100 000 trade-related documents. The NTDB contains: (1) the latest census data on US imports and exports by commodity and country; (2) the complete Central Intelligence Agency (CIA) *World Factbook*; (3) current market research reports compiled by the US and Foreign Commercial Service; (4) the complete *Foreign Traders Index*, which contains over 55 000 names and addresses of individuals and firms abroad that are interested in importing US products; (5) State Department country reports on economic policy and trade practices; (6) the publications *Export Yellow Pages, A Basic Guide to Exporting* and the *National Trade Estimates Report on Foreign Trade Barriers*; (7) the *Export Promotion Calendar*; and many other data series. This source can be reached through internet (http:\www.stat-usa.gov/).

A number of research agencies specializing in detailed information on foreign markets provide information services on a subscription basis. A listing of commercial and investment banks in foreign countries, as well as a detailed list of special-purpose research institutes, can be found in *The Europa World Yearbook* (Europa Publications, London). Listed below are sources of information that are helpful and available for purchase or subscription.

Other Sources: Abstracts, Bibliographies and Indexes

The Economist Intelligence Unit, London. Covers Economist Intelligence publications.

F & S Index International and *F & S Europe*. Cleveland: Predicasts. Monthly with quarterly and annual cumulations. Indexes foreign companies and product and industry information with emphasis on sources giving data or statistics.

Business International. Worldwide Economic Indicators. New York. Annual: economic, demographic, trade and other statistics.

Consumer Europe. London: Euromonitor Publications. Annual: marketing indicators and trends for various markets.

European Marketing Data and Statistics. London: Euromonitor Publications. Annual.

International Marketing Data and Statistics. London: Euromonitor Publications. Annual: covers the Americas, Asia, Africa and Australia. Includes data on retail and wholesale sales, living standards and general consumer marketing data.

The Markets of Asia/Pacific: Thailand, Taiwan, Peoples Republic of China, Hong Kong, South Korea, The Philippines, Indonesia, Singapore and Malaysia. London: The Asia Pacific Centre, Ltd, New York: *Facts on File*, various years. An excellent source for data on prices, retail sales, consumer purchases and other country information.

Sources on Internet WWW

1. Michigan State University's Center for International Business, provides extensive and comprehensive links to a wide range of information sources relevant to international marketing and international business. Links are provided to numerous newspapers and journals (including academic journals) throughout the world; an extremely large number of country/market reports; information on various regional trading blocs; academic papers on international marketing/business; and numerous other linkages. This site can be reached at **http://ciber.bus.msu.edu/busres.htm**.

2. World Class Supersite, provides 'instant free access and step-by-step commentary for 1025 top business sites from 95 countries, chosen based on usefulness to world commerce,

timeliness, ease of use, and presentation.' The site comprises seven main sections covering:

- Reference (Market Guides, Regional Institutions, US Government Megasites)
- News (World Business Dailies, World Business Magazines, Business Mags by Country)
- Learning (Global MBA Elite, Notable Business Institutes)
- Money (World & US Stocks, Stocks by Country, Foreign Investment)
- Trade (World Business Directories, Cargo, Business Tools)
- Networking (Gathering Places, Bilateral Organizations, Leads and Tenders)
- World Beaters (MNC Manufacturers, MNC Services, SMEs, Trade Services)

The site can be reached at **http://web.idirect.com/~tiger/supersit.htm**.

3. Best International Trade Web Sites, which is maintained by Dolphin Marketing International, provides links to and comments on a sample of international trade sites on the WWW including the Electronic Embassy Page; International Trade Law Project; Russian Trade Connections Online; the US International Trade Commission; NAFTA Online; Asian Development Bank; International Monetary Fund; the UN Trade Development Site; the International Small Business Consortium; and several others. This site can be reached at **http://www.dmintl.com/tradelnk.html**.

4. Internet Resources for Exporters is a comprehensive list of export related resources on the 'Net' including links to MegaSites; Country and Company Information; Trade Finance, Shipping and Logistics Resources; International Legal Sites; Chamber of Commerce; International Trade Forums; and Export Reference Resources. This site can be reached at **http://www.exportusa.com/resources.html**.

5. The World Factbook provides macro- and microeconomic data by the CIA, including economic overviews of 260 countries, sectoral briefings, government and defence information. This site can be reached at **http://www.odci.gov/cia/publications/factbook/info-frame.html**.

6. The Web of Culture page is devoted to improving executives' understanding of cross-cultural communications which is a 'critical success factor' in international marketing, while the other sites reviewed here focus on the economic, business and trade environments of different countries. The site is a useful starting point for those seeking to better their understanding of different national understanding before visiting overseas markets and for students studying the cultural aspects of international marketing. This site can be reached at **http://www.webofculture.com/**.

QUESTIONS

1. Discuss how the shift from making 'market entry' decisions to 'continuous operations' decisions creates a need for different types of information and data. What assistance does an MMIS provide?

2. Using the hypothetical situation, illustrate how an MMIS might be established and how it would be used at different levels.

3. Discuss the breadth and scope of international marketing research. Why is international marketing research generally broader in scope than domestic marketing research?

4. What is the task of the international market researcher? How is it complicated by the foreign environment?

5. Discuss the stages of the research process in relation to the problems encountered. Give examples.

6. Why is the formulation of the research problem difficult in foreign market research?

7. Discuss the problems of gathering secondary data in foreign markets.

8. What are some problems created by language and the ability to comprehend in collecting primary data? How can an international market researcher overcome these difficulties?

9. Discuss how 'decentring' is used to get an accurate translation of a questionnaire.

10. Discuss when qualitative research may be more effective than quantitative research.

11. Sampling offers some major problems in market research. Discuss.

12. Select a country. From secondary sources compile the following information for at least a 10-year period prior to the present:
    Principal imports
    Principal exports
    Gross national product
    Chief of state
    Major cities and population
    Principal agricultural crop

13. 'The foreign market researcher must possess three essential capabilities to generate meaningful marketing information.' Discuss.

REFERENCES

1. Tamer Cavusgil and Pervez Ghauri, *Doing Business in Developing Countries: Entry and Negotiation Strategies* (London: Routledge, 1990).

2. For a complete discussion of marketing research in foreign environments, see Susan P. Douglas and C. Samuel Crag, *International Marketing Research* (Englewood Cliffs, NJ: Prentice-Hall, 1983).

3. John Cantwell, 'The Methodological Problems Raised by the Collection of Foreign Direct Investment Data', *Scandinavian International Business Review*, vol. 1, no. 1, 1992, pp. 86–103.

4. For another view of the complexity of marketing research practices, see Per V. Jenster and David Hover, 'A Clinical Case: How to Focus Marketing Intelligence to Serve Strategy', *Planning Review*, July–August 1992, pp. 32–37.

5. Pervez Ghauri, Kjell Grønhaug and Ivar Kristianslund, *Research Methods in Business Studies: A Practical Guide* (Hemel Hempstead: Prentice-Hall, 1994).

6. David Kiburn, 'Unilever Struggles with Surf in Japan', *Advertising Age*, 6 May 1991, p. 22.

7. Sidney J. Levy, 'What Is Qualitative Research?' in *The Dartnell Marketing Manager's Handbook*, Sidney J. Levy *et al.* (eds) (Chicago: The Dartnell Corporation, 1994), p. 275.

8. Bill Allen and Maureen Johnson, 'Taking the English Apple to Spain: The Adams' Experience', *Marketing and Research Today*, February 1994, pp. 53–61.

9. Adapted from Mahmoud Aboul-Fath and Loula Zaklama, 'Ariel High Suds Detergent in Egypt— A Case Study', *Marketing and Research Today*, May 1992, pp. 130–134.

10. Beverly Camp, 'Research Propels Innovation', *Marketing*, 27 January 1994, p. 34.

11. For an example of data available from private sources, see Amy Dockser Marcus, 'As Door Opens to Arab–Israeli Markets, Small Firm Delves into Consumer Quirks', *The Wall Street Journal*, 11 November 1993, p. A-19.

12. 'China's Faked Numbers Pile Up', *The Wall Street Journal*, 26 August 1994, p. A-6.

13. 'Chinese Call for an End to Misreported Statistics', *The New York Times*, 18 August 1994, p. C-17.

14. 'Cross-Border Market Research: Braun Battles with National Diversity', *Business Europe*, 21–27 February 1994, pp. 7–8.

15. Cecil Tuncalp, 'The Marketing Research Scene in Saudi Arabia', *European Journal of Marketing*, vol. 22, no. 5, pp. 15–22.

16. For a complete discussion of questionnaire administration and the resulting problems, see Naresh K. Malhotra, 'Administration of Questionnaires for Collecting Quantitative Data in International Marketing Research', *Journal of Global Marketing*, vol. 4, no. 2, 1991.

17. Susan P. Douglas, and C. Samuel Crag, 'Researching Global Markets', in *The Dartnell Marketing Manager's Handbook*, Sidney J. Levy, *et al.* (eds) (Chicago: The Dartnell Corporation, 1994), pp. 1278–1298.

18. An interesting report on problems in cross-cultural replications can be found in David A. Aaker, and Kevin Lane Keller, 'Interpreting Cross-Cultural Replications of Brand Extension Research', *International Journal of Research in Marketing*, March 1993, pp. 55–59.

19. 'Interpreting Research from Different Cultures', *Business Europe*, 14–20 February 1994, p. 3.

20. Monika Bhaduri, Marianne de Souza and Timm Sweeney, 'International Qualitative Research: A Critical Review of Different Approaches', *Marketing and Research Today*, September 1993, pp. 171–178.

21. An interesting report on estimating demand for beer in the Netherlands is presented in: Philip Hans Franses, 'Primary Demand for Beer in the Netherlands: An Application of ARMAX Model Specification', *Journal of Marketing Research*, May 1991, pp. 240–245.

Chapter Outline

Chapter Learning Objectives

What you should learn from Chapter 9

- The political and economic changes affecting international marketing.
- The connection between the economic level of a country and the marketing task.
- Marketing's contribution to the growth and development of a country's economy.
- New development in market behaviour.
- The growth of developing markets and their importance to regional trade.
- The political and economic factors that affect the stability of regional market groups.
- Growing trends in emerging markets.
- The marketing implications of growing homogeneous market segments.

The concept of emerging economies is relatively new and most Western managers have realized that emerging economies, besides being large markets, are also becoming competitors and sources of production for Western firms. The World Bank, IMF and *The Economist* have identified 24 emerging economies based on the size of their gross domestic products (GDP) and the capitalization of their stockmarkets. (See Table 9.1.)

Emerging markets will account for 75 per cent of the world's total trade growth in the next decade and beyond, according to estimates by the US Department of Commerce.[1] No more than a decade ago, large parts of the developing world were hostile towards foreign investment and imposed severe regulatory barriers to foreign trade. Today, the view is different. With the collapse of the Marxist–socialist, centrally planned economic model and the spectacular economic success of Taiwan, South Korea, Singapore and other Asian economies, it became apparent to many that the path to prosperity was open trade and direct investment. As a result, many developing countries are experiencing some degree of industrialization, urbanization, rising productivity, higher personal incomes and technological progress, although not all at the same level or rate of development.[2] Few nations are content with the economic *status quo*; now, more than ever, they seek economic growth, improved standards of living and an opportunity for the good life—most people want to be part of the global consumer world.[3]

Hungary, Poland, Argentina, Brazil, Mexico, Thailand, Indonesia, Malaysia and India are some of the countries undergoing impressive changes in their economies and emerging as vast markets. In these and other countries, there is an ever-expanding and changing demand for goods and services. Although the Asian crisis of 1997 has caused some setbacks in some of the Asian markets, the overall picture for emerging markets is developing positively. Markets are dynamic, developing entities reflecting the changing lifestyles of a culture. As economies grow, markets become different, larger and more demanding.

When economies grow and markets evolve beyond subsistence levels, the range of tastes, preferences and variations of products sought by the consumer increases; they demand more, better and/or different products. As countries prosper and their people are exposed to new ideas and behaviour patterns via global communications networks, old stereotypes, traditions and habits are cast aside or tempered and new patterns of consumer behaviour emerge. Sony televisions with 74 cm (29 in) screens in China, Avon cosmetics in Singapore, Wal-Mart discount stores in Argentina, Brazil, Mexico and Thailand, Volvo and BMW being assembled in Thailand, McDonald's beefless Big Macs in India, Whirlpool washers and refrigerators in Eastern Europe, Sara Lee food products in Indonesia, VW-production in the Czech Republic, and Fiat's 'Pluto' specially developed for emerging markets all represent the opportunities that are arising in these markets.

This chapter explores emerging economies and changing market patterns that are creating opportunities throughout the world. Market behaviour and a rapidly expanding middle-income class in developing and developed countries are examined in the context of a single-country market and as the basis for global market segmentation.

MARKETING AND ECONOMIC DEVELOPMENT

The economic level of a country is the single most important environmental element to which the foreign marketer must adjust the marketing task. The stage of economic growth within a country affects the attitudes towards foreign business activity, the demand for goods, distribution systems found within a country and the entire marketing process. In static economies, consumption patterns become rigid, and marketing is typically nothing more than a supply effort. In a dynamic economy, consumption patterns change rapidly. Marketing

Table 9.1   The Emerging Markets

Country[a]	Population million $ 1996	GDP billion $ 1996	GDP average annual % growth 1990–96	GNP[b] billion $ 1996	GNP average annual % growth 1990–96	GNP per capita $ 1996	GNP-PPP per capita 1996
China	1 215	815.4	12.3	906.1	10.0	750	3 330
Brazil	161	748.9	2.9	709.6	8.2	4 400	6 340
Korea, Rep.	46	484.8	7.3	483.1	6.9	10 610	13 080
Russia	148	440.6	−9.0	356.0	−5.3	2 410	4 190
India	945	356.0	5.8	357.8	6.9	380	1 580
Mexico	93	334.8	1.8	341.7	6.6	3 670	7 660
Argentina	35	294.7	4.9	295.1	4.0	8 380	9 530
Indonesia	197	225.8	7.7	213.4	7.5	1 080	3 310
Thailand	60	185.0	8.3	177.5	5.4	2 960	6 700
Turkey	63	181.5	3.6	177.5	6.8	2 830	6 060
Hong Kong	6	154.8	5.5	153.3	4.7	24 290	6 720
Poland	39	134.5	3.2	124.7	6.3	3 230	6 000
South Africa	38	126.3	1.2	132.5	2.9	3 520	7 450[c]
Greece	10	122.9	1.6	120.0	2.4	11 460	12 730
Portugal	10	104.0	1.4	100.9	2.4	10 160	13 450
Malaysia	21	99.2	8.7	89.8	8.3	4 370	10 390
Singapore	3	94.1	8.7	93.0	7.6	30 550	26 910
Israel	6	91.0[d]	6.4	90.3	2.5[e]	15 870	18 100
Philippines	72	83.8	2.9	83.3	6.9	1 160	3 550
Chile	14	74.3	7.2	70.1	10.1	4 860	11 700
Venezuela	22	67.3	1.9	67.3	−1.6	3 020	8 130
Czech Republic	10	54.9	−1.0	48.9	4.4	4 740	10 870
Hungary	10	44.8	−0.4	44.3	2.2	4 340	6 730

[a]Although considered an Emerging Market by *The Economist,* Taiwan is not included because of lack of data; [b]Calculated using the World Bank Atlas Method; [c]Estimate based on regression (others are extrapolated from the latest International Comparison Programme benchmark estimates; [d]1995; [e]1985–1995.

Source: Based on World Bank, *World Development Report 1997: The State in a Changing World,* (Oxford: Oxford University Press, 1997); World Bank, *World Development Indicators 1998,* CD-Rom.

is constantly faced with the challenge of detecting and providing for new levels of consumption, and marketing efforts must be matched with ever-changing market needs and wants.

Economic development presents a two-sided challenge. First, a study of the general aspects of economic development is necessary to gain empathy for the economic climate within developing countries. Second, the state of economic development must be studied with respect to market potential, including the present economic level and the economy's growth potential. The current level of economic development dictates the kind and degree of market potential that exists, while a knowledge of the dynamism of the economy allows the marketer to prepare for economic shifts in emerging markets.

Economic development is generally understood to mean an increase in national production that results in an increase in the average per capita GDP.[4] Besides an increase in average per capita GDP, most interpretations of the concept also imply a widespread distribution of the increased income. The term 'emerging markets', as commonly defined today, tends to mean a country with rapid economic growth—improvements achieved in decades rather than centuries—and considerable increases in consumer demand.

Stages of Economic Development

The best-known model for classifying countries by stage of economic development is that presented by Walt Rostow. He identified five stages of development; each stage is a function of the cost of labour, technical capability of the buyers, scale of operations, interest rates and level of product sophistication. Growth is the movement from one stage to another, and countries in the first three stages are considered to be economically underdeveloped. Briefly, the stages are:

Stage 1: *The traditional society.* Countries in this stage lack the capability of significantly increasing the level of productivity. There is a marked absence of systematic application of the methods of modern science and technology. Literacy is low, as are other types of social overhead.

Stage 2: *The preconditions for take-off.* This second stage includes those societies in the process of transition to the take-off stage. During this period, the advances of modern science are beginning to be applied in agriculture and production. The development of transportation, communications, power, education, health and other public undertakings are begun in a small but important way.

Stage 3: *The take-off.* At this stage, countries achieve a growth pattern which becomes a normal condition. Human resources and social overhead have been developed to sustain steady development. Agricultural and industrial modernization lead to rapid expansion in these areas.

Stage 4: *The drive to maturity.* After take-off, sustained progress is maintained and the economy seeks to extend modern technology to all fronts of economic activity. The economy takes on international involvement. In this stage, an economy demonstrates that it has the technological and entrepreneurial skills to produce not everything, but anything it chooses to produce.

Stage 5: *The age of high mass consumption.* The age of high mass consumption leads to shifts in the leading economic sectors towards durable consumers' goods and services. Real income per capita rises to the point where a very large number of people have significant amounts of discretionary income.[5]

While Rostow's classification has met with some criticism because of the difficulty of distinguishing among the five stages, it provides the marketer with some indication of the relationship between economic development, the types of products a country needs, and the sophistication of its industrial infrastructure.

Newly Industrialized Countries and Emerging Markets

Some developing countries (LDCs) have grown rapidly in the last few decades and do not fit the traditional pattern of economic development of other LDCs. These countries, referred to as *newly industrialized countries* (*NICs*), have shown rapid industrialization of targeted industries and have per capita incomes that matches with developed countries (for a classification of economies by income, see Table 9.2). They have moved away from restrictive trade practices and instituted significant free-market reforms; as a result, they attract both trade and foreign direct investment. NICs have become formidable exporters of many products including steel, automobiles, machine tools, clothing and electronics, as well as being vast markets for imported products.

Brazil is an example of the growing importance of NICs in world trade, exporting everything from alcohol to carbon steel. Brazilian orange juice, poultry, soybeans and weapons (Brazil is the world's sixth largest weapons exporter) compete with Europe and the United States for foreign markets. Embraer, the Brazilian aircraft manufacturer, provides a substantial portion of the commuter aircraft used in the Western world. Even in automobile production, Brazil is a world player; it ships more than 200 000 cars, trucks and buses to other countries annually. Volkswagen has produced more than three million VW Beetles in Brazil and is now investing more than €360 million ($400 million) in a project to produce a two-door compact, code named the AB9, aimed at the 200 million people in the Mercosur market, the free trade group formed by Argentina, Brazil, Paraguay and Uruguay.[6]

Among the other NICs, South Korea, Taiwan, Hong Kong and Singapore have had such rapid growth and export performance that they are discussed as the 'Four Tigers' of Southeast Asia. These four countries have become major world competitors as well as major suppliers of many products to Europe, the United States and Japan. Personal incomes in these countries have increased over the last decade to the point at which they are becoming major markets for industrial and consumer goods. They began their industrialization as assemblers of products for Western and Japanese companies, but are now developing their own product lines and are global competitors. South Korea, for example, exports high-tech goods such as petrochemicals, electronics, machinery and steel that are in direct competition with Japanese, European and US-made products.[7] In consumer products, Hyundai, Kia, Samsung and Lucky-Goldstar are among familiar brand names in cars, microwaves and televisions sold in the West. See Table 9.3 for a comparison of NICs and other countries.

The recent developments in the global markets and increasing growth and efficiencies in NICs and other developing countries have forced Western countries and firms to realize the existence and importance of emerging markets. Western countries will have to understand the ways of marketing in these markets because these economies, which are growing rapidly, jointly act as markets, sources and competitors. More than two-thirds of the world's population live in emerging markets. Also, the population growth rates are higher in those economies.

Infrastructure and Development

One indicator of economic development is the extent of social overhead capital or infrastructure within the economy. Infrastructure represents those types of capital goods that serve the activities of many industries. Included in a country's infrastructure are paved roads, railways, seaports, communications networks and energy supplies—all necessary to support production and marketing. The quality of infrastructure directly affects a country's economic growth potential and the ability of an enterprise to engage effectively in business.

Infrastructure is a crucial component of the uncontrollable elements facing marketers. Without adequate transportation facilities, for example, distribution costs can increase substantially, and the ability to reach certain segments of the market are impaired. In fact, a market's full potential may never be realized because of inadequate infrastructure.[8] To a marketer, the key issues in evaluating the importance of infrastructure concern the types necessary for profitable trade and the impact on a firm's ability to market effectively if a country's infrastructure is underdeveloped. In addition to the social overhead, capital type of infrastructure described, business efficiency is affected by the presence or absence of financial and commercial service infrastructure found within a country such as advertising agencies,

Table 9.2 Classification of Economies by Income and Region, 1998

Income Group	Sub-Group	Sub-Saharan Africa		Asia		Europe and Central Asia		Middle East and North Africa		
		East and Southern Africa	West Africa	East Asia and Pacific	South Asia	Eastern Europe and Central Asia	Rest of Europe	Middle East	North Africa	Americas
Low Income		Angola	Benin	Cambodia	Afghanistan	Armenia		Jemen, Rep.		Guyana
		Burundi	Burkina Faso	China	Bangladesh	Azerbaijan				Haiti
		Comoros	Camaroon	Lao PDR	Bhutan	Bosnia and Herzegovina				Honduras
		Congo, Dem. Rep.[a]	Central African Republic	Mongolia	India	Kyrgyz Republic				Nicaragua
		Eritrea	Chad	Myanmar	Nepal	Moldova				
		Ethiopia	Congo, Rep.	Vietnam	Pakistan	Tajikistan				
		Kenya	Côte d'Ivoire		Sri Lanka					
		Lesotho	Equatorial Guinea							
		Madagascar	Gambia, The							
		Malawi	Ghana							
		Mozambique	Guinea							
		Rwanda	Guinea-Bissau							
		Somalia	Liberia							
		Sudan	Mali							
		Tanzania	Mauritania							
		Uganda	Niger							
		Zambia	Nigeria							
		Zimbabwe	São Tomé and Principe							
			Senegal							
			Sierra Leone							
			Togo							

Middle Lower Income	Botswana Djibouti Nimibia Swaziland	Cape Verde	Fiji Indonesia Kiribati Korea Dem. Rep. Marshall Islands Micronesia, Fed. Sts. Papua New Guinea Philippines Samoa Solomon Islands Thailand Tonga Vanuatu	Maldives	Albania Belarus Bulgaria Estonia Georgia Kazakhstan Latvia Lithuania Macedonia FYR[b] Romania Russian Federation Turkmenistan Ukraine Uzbekistan Yugoslavia Fed Rep.[c]	Turkey	Iran, Islamic Rep. Iraq Jordan Lebanon Syrian Arab Republic West Bank and Gaza	Algeria Egypt, Arab Rep. Morocco Tunisia	Belize Bolivia Colombia Costa Rica Cuba Dominica Dominican Republic Ecuador El Salvador Grenada Guatemala Jamaica Panama Paraguay Peru St Vincent and the Grenadines Suriname Venezuela
Upper	Mauritius Mayotte Seychelles South Africa	Gabon	American Samoa Malaysia Palau		Croatia Czech Republic Hungary Poland Slovak Republic Slovenia	Isle of Man Malta	Bahrain Oman Saudi Arabia	Libya	Antigua and Barbuda Argentina Barbados Brazil Chile Guadeloupe Mexico Puerto Rico St Kitts and Nevis St Lucia Trinidad and Tobago Uruguay

Table 9.2 (continued)

Income Group	Sub-Group	Sub-Saharan Africa		Asia		Europe and Central Asia		Middle East and North Africa		Americas
		East and Southern Africa	West Africa	East Asia and Pacific	South Asia	Eastern Europe and Central Asia	Rest of Europe	Middle East	North Africa	Americas
High Income	OECD			Australia Japan Korea, Rep. New Zealand			Austria Belgium Denmark Finland France Germany Greece Iceland Ireland Italy Luxembourg The Netherlands Norway Portugal Spain Sweden Switzerland United Kingdom			Canada United States
	Non-OECD	Reunion		Brunei French Polynesia Guam Hong Kong, China[d] Macao New Caledonia			Andorra Channel Islands Cyprus Faeroe Islands Greenland Liechtenstein Monaco	Israel Kuwait Qatar United Arab Emirates		Aruba Bahamas, The Bermuda Cayman Islands French Guiana Martinique

N. Maiana Islands
Singapore

OAE[e]

The Netherlands Antilles
Virgin Islands (US)

Total 211	27	23	35	8	27	28	14	5	44

Note: This table classifies all World Bank member economies with populations of more than 30 000. Economies are divided among income groups according to 1996 GNP per capita, calculated using the World Bank Atlas method. Income groups are defined as follows: low-income, $785 or less; lower-middle-income, $786–3115; upper-middle-income, $3116–9635; and high-income, $9636 or more.

For operational and analytical purposes, the World Bank's main criterion for classifying economies is gross national product (GNP) per capita. Classification by income does not necessarily reflect development status, although low-income and middle-income economies are usually referred to as developing economies. The use of the term is convenient; it is not intended to imply that all economies in the group are experiencing similar development or that other economies have reached a preferred or final stage of development. [a]Formerly Zaire. [b]Former Yugoslav Republic of Macedonia. [c]Federal Republic of Yugoslavia (Serbia/Montenegro). [d]On 1 July 1997 China resumed its sovereignty over Hong Kong. [e]Other Asian economies—Taiwan, China.
Source: The World Bank, *World Development Indicators 1998*.

Table 9.3   Infrastructure of Selected Countries

Country	Highways* (paved km) (000)	Railways (km) (000)	Trucks and Buses in Use (000)	Electricity Production (million kwh)	Newspaper Sales (000)
United States	6 243.2	214.3	45 871.0	3 031 058	62 328
Brazil	1 670.1	22.1	2 450.0	222 195	8 100
Japan	1 115.6	20.2	22 694.4	857 273	72 524
Colombia	129.1	1.0	670.0	36 000	2 000
Germany	618.2	31.7	1 859.0	440 400	29 538
Kenya	62.6	2.7	110.0	3 000	350
Mexico	242.3	26.5	3 345.7	122 477	11 237
Spain	318.0	15.3	2 073.0	141 000	2 978

*Includes unpaved and paved.
Sources: 'Big Emerging Markets', *Business America*, Special Issue, 1994, pp. 59–65 and for additional information, see *International Marketing Data and Statistics*, 18th edn (London: Euromonitor Publications, 1994).

warehousing storage facilities, credit and banking facilities, marketing research agencies and quality-level specialized middlemen.

As trade develops, a country's infrastructure typically expands to meet the needs of the expanding economy. There is some question of whether effective marketing increases the pace of infrastructure development or whether an expanded infrastructure leads to more effective marketing. Infrastructure and effective economic development and marketing activity probably increase concurrently, although seldom progressing at the same pace. While companies continue to market in emerging and developing countries, it is usually necessary to modify offerings and the approach to meet existing levels of infrastructure.[9] See Table 9.3 for some comparisons among countries at different levels of economic development.

Objectives of Emerging Countries

A thorough assessment of economic development and marketing should begin with a brief review of the basic facts and objectives of economic development. To be capable of adjusting to a foreign economic environment, an international marketer must be able to answer questions such as: (1) What are the objectives of the developing countries? (2) What role is marketing assigned, if any, in economic growth plans? (3) What contribution must marketing make, whether overtly planned or not, for a country to grow successfully? (4) Which of the prevailing attitudes might hamper marketing strategies, development and growth? and (5) How can the market potential, present and future, be assessed?

The economic growth is not measured solely in economic goals, but also in social achievements. Because foreign businesses are outsiders, they were often feared as having goals in conflict with those of the host country. Today, foreign investors are seen as vital partners in economic development. Experience with state-owned businesses proved to be a disappointment to most governments. Instead of being engines for accelerated economic growth, state-owned enterprises (SOEs) were mismanaged, inefficient drains on state treasuries. Further, the rapid industrialization of many of the poorest Asian countries pointed towards private-sector investment as the most effective means of economic growth. Most

INCREASING DEMAND FOR WESTERN PRODUCTS

As Central and Eastern Europe's economies move out of recession, demand for West European products are soaring. From beer to aluminium furnaces or cars to mobile telephones, Western exporters have found an ever-growing market in Eastern Europe. EU exports to the countries of Central and Eastern Europe (14 states excluding the former Soviet Union but including the three Baltic States) increased by 22 per cent in 1995 to €49.3 billion ($61.6 billion) according to European Commissions Statistics. The imports from the region also increased by 23 per cent to €41.7 billion.

From 1991 to 1995, EU exports to the region have increased on average 25 per cent per year. The region accounted for 8.4 per cent of the EU's total export in 1995, as compared to 4.2 per cent in 1991. For imports the region accounts for 7 per cent of the total EU imports, growing at average at 20.8 per cent per year in the same period. While total exports to all countries from EU increased only by 8.8 per cent. According to European Commission the manufactured goods accounted for 86 per cent of exports in 1995, with industrial machinery being the biggest export category (€6.1 billion) followed by cars and vehicles (€5.3 billion).

The trade in this region is dominated by Germany which accounts for more than half of total EU trade flows (50 per cent of exports and 54 per cent imports). Italian exporters are at second place (18 per cent) followed by France (8 per cent), the Netherlands (6 per cent) and the UK at 5 per cent. Poland, the largest country of the region, is the main recipient of EU exports at 27 per cent (€13.5 billion). The Czech Republic and Hungary are also significant at €10 billion and €7 billion respectively in 1995. Other than machinery and vehicles, the fastest growing sectors include paper board and pulp, and iron and steel. The trade in these categories increased by 50 per cent in the last year. EU's trade surplus has risen from €1.5 billion in 1991 to €7.6 billion in 1995. This reflects the importance of EU trade with this region.

Source: K. Done, 'Keen Buyers for Western Products', *The Financial Times*, FT Exporter, October, 1996, p. 5.

countries deregulated industry, opened their doors to foreign investment, lowered trade barriers and began privatizing SOEs. The trend towards privatization has been a major economic phenomenon in the past two decades, in industrialized as well as in developing countries.[10]

Marketing's Contributions

How important is marketing to the achievement of a country's goals? Unfortunately, marketing (or distribution) is not always considered meaningful to those responsible for planning. Economic planners frequently are more production than marketing oriented and tend to ignore or regard distribution as an inferior economic activity. Given such attitudes, economic plans are generally more concerned with the problems of production, investment and finance than the problems of efficiency of distribution.

Imagine marketing where there is production but little disposable income, no storage, limited transportation only to the wrong markets, and no middlemen and facilitating agents to activate the flow of goods from the manufacturer to the consumer. When such conditions exist in some emerging markets, marketing and economic progress are retarded. This is, to some degree, the problem of China and many of the republics of the former Soviet Union. In China, for example, most of the 1 billion potential consumers are not accessible because of a poor distribution network. The consumer market in China is probably limited to no more than 20 per cent of those who live in the more affluent cities.

GOING INTERNATIONAL 9.2

IN EMERGING COUNTRIES, OPPORTUNITY MEANS CREATING IT

There are vast rewards in emerging markets for those with patience who offer incentives for progress and go the extra mile. For example, after 13 years of talks (patience), Nestlé was finally invited to help boost milk production in China. When Nestlé opened a powdered milk and baby cereal plant, they faced an inadequate source of milk and an overburdened infrastructure. Local trains and roads made it almost impossible to collect milk and deliver the finished product efficiently. Nestlé's solution was to develop its own infrastructure by weaving a distribution network known as the 'milk roads' between 27 villages and the factory collection points (the extra mile). Farmers pushing wheelbarrows, pedalling bicycles, or on foot delivered their milk and received payment on the spot, another innovation for China. Suddenly, the farmers had an incentive to produce milk and the district herds grew from 6000 to 9000 cows in a matter of months. To train the farmers in rudimentary animal health and hygiene, Nestlé hired retired teachers who were paid commissions on all sales to Nestlé (incentive). The result: business took off. In three years, Nestlé factory production rose from 316 tons of powdered milk and infant formula to 10 000 tons. Capacity has tripled with the addition of two factories.

Seventeen years after talks began, Nestlé's $200 million (€180 million) sales are just barely profitable (patience); however, Nestlé has exclusive rights to sell the output of their factories throughout China for 15 years (reward) and predictions are that sales will hit $700 million (€630 million) by 2000.

Source: Abstracted from Carla Rapoport, 'Nestlé's Brand Building Machine', *Fortune*, 19 September 1994, pp. 147–156.

MARKETING IN A DEVELOPING COUNTRY

A marketer cannot superimpose a sophisticated marketing programme on an underdeveloped economy. Marketing efforts must be keyed to each situation, custom tailored for each set of circumstances. A promotional programme for a population that is 80 per cent illiterate is vastly different from a programme for a population that is 80 per cent literate. Pricing in a subsistence market poses different problems than pricing in an affluent society. The distribution structure should provide an efficient method of matching productive capacity with available demand. An efficient marketing programme is one that provides for optimum utility at a single point in time, given a specific set of circumstances. In evaluating the potential in a developing country, the marketer must make an assessment of the existing level of marketing development within the country.[11]

Level of Marketing Development

The level of the marketing function roughly parallels the stages of economic development. Figure 9.1 illustrates various stages of the marketing process as they develop in a growing economy. The figure is a static model representing an idealized evolutionary process. Economic cooperation and assistance, technological change and political, social and cultural factors can and do cause significant deviations in this evolutionary process. However, the figure focuses on the logic and interdependence of marketing and economic development. The more developed an economy, the greater the variety of marketing functions demanded, and the more sophisticated and specialized the institutions become to perform marketing functions. The evolution of the channel structure illustrates the relationship between marketing development and the stage of economic development of a country.

Advertising agencies, facilities for marketing research, repair services, specialized consumer financing agencies and storage and warehousing facilities are supportive facilitating agencies created to serve the particular needs of expanded markets and economies. It is important to remember that these institutions do not come about automatically, nor does the necessary marketing institution simply appear. Part of the marketer's task when studying an economy is to determine what in the foreign environment will be useful and how much adjustment will be necessary to carry out stated objectives. In some developing countries it may be up to the marketer to institute the foundations of a modern marketing system.

Demand in a Developing Country

Estimating market potential in less-developed countries involves a myriad challenges. Most of the difficulty arises from economic dualism; that is, the coexistence of modern and traditional sectors within the economy. The modern sector is centred in the cities and has airports, international hotels, new factories and a Westernized middle class. Alongside this modern sector is a traditional sector containing the remainder of the country's population. Although the two sectors may be very close geographically, they are centuries away in production and consumption. This dual economy affects the size of the market and, in many countries, creates two distinct economic and marketing levels. Indonesia, Pakistan and India are good examples. The eleventh largest industrial economy in the world, India has a population of over 900 million, more than 250 million of whom are an affluent middle class.[12] The modern sector demands products and services similar to those available in any industrialized country; the traditional sector demands items more indigenous and basic to subsistence. As one authority on India's market observed, a rural Indian can live a sound life without many products. Toothpaste, sugar, coffee, washing soap, bath soap and kerosene are all bare necessities of life to those who live in semiurban and urban areas.[13]

In countries with dual sectors, there are at least two different market segments. Each can prove profitable but each requires its own marketing programme and products appropriate for its market characteristics. Many companies market successfully to both the traditional and the modern market segments in countries with mixed economies. The traditional sector may offer the greatest potential initially, but as the transition from the traditional to the modern takes place (i.e., as the middle-income class grows) an established marketer is better able to capitalize on the growing market.

Tomorrow's markets will include expansion in industrialized countries and the development of the traditional side of emerging and less developed countries, as well as continued expansion of the modern sectors of such countries. The greatest long-range growth potential is to be found in the traditional sector where the realization of profit may require a change in orientation and willingness to invest time and effort for longer periods. The development of demand in a traditional market sector means higher initial marketing costs, compromises in marketing methods and sometimes redesigning products but market investment today is necessary to produce profits tomorrow. The companies that will benefit in the future from emerging markets in Eastern Europe, China, Latin America, and elsewhere are the ones that invest when it is difficult and initially unprofitable.[14]

EMERGING MARKETS

The transition from socialist to market-driven economies, the liberalization of trade and investment policies in developing countries, the transfer of public-sector enterprises to the

Figure 9.1 Evolution of the Marketing Process

Stage	Substage	Examples	Marketing Functions	Marketing Institutions	Channel Control	Primary Orientation	Resources Employed	Comments
Agricultural and raw materials MK.(f) = prod.)*	Self-sufficient	Nomadic or hunting tribes	None	None	Traditional	Subsistence	Labour	Labour intensive No organized markets
	Surplus commodity producer	Agricultural economy—such as coffee bananas	Exchange	Small-scale merchants, traders, fairs, export-import	Traditional authority	Entrepreneurial Commercial	Labour	Labour and land intensive Product specialization Local markets Import oriented
Manufacturing (Mk.(f) = prod.)	Small scale	Cottage industry	Exchange Physical distribution	Merchants, wholesalers, export-import	Middlemen	Entrepreneurial Financial	Labour Land Technology Transportation	Labour intensive Product standardization and grading Regional and export markets Import oriented
	Mass production	US economy 1885–1914	Demand creation Physical distribution	Merchants, wholesalers, traders, and specialized institutions	Producer	Production and finance	Labour Land Technology Transportation Capital	Capital intensive Product differentiation National, regional, and export markets
Marketing Prod.(f) = mk.)	Commercial —transition	US economy 1915–1929	Demand creation Physical distribution Market	Large-scale and chain retailers	Producer	Entrepreneurial Commercial	Labour Land Technology Transportation Capital Communication	Capital intensive Changes in structure of distribution National, regional, and export markets

Mass distribution	US economy 1950 to present	Demand creation Physical distribution Market information Market and product planning, development	Integrated channels of distribution Increase in specialized middlemen	Producer Retailer	Marketing	Labour Land Technology Transportatiom Capital Communication	Capital and land intensive Rapid product innovation National, regional, and export markets

*Mk.(f) = prod.: Marketing is a function of production.

private sector and the rapid development of regional market alliances are changing the way countries will trade and prosper in the next century.

The US Department of Commerce estimates that over 75 per cent of the expected growth in world trade over the next two decades will come from the more than 130 developing and emerging countries. A small core of these countries will account for more than half of that growth.[15] They predict that the countries identified as big emerging markets (BEMs) alone will be a bigger import market by the end of this decade than the European Union (EU) and, by the year 2010, will be importing more than the EU and Japan combined.[16] These BEMs, as the US Department of Commerce refers to them, share a number of important traits. They:

- Are all physically large.
- Have significant populations.
- Represent considerable markets for a wide range of products.
- All have strong rates of growth or the potential for significant growth.
- Have all undertaken significant programmes of economic reform.
- Are all of major political importance within their regions.
- Are 'regional economic drivers'.
- Will engender further expansion in neighbouring markets as they grow.

While these criteria are general in nature and each country does not meet all the criteria, the US Department of Commerce identified as emerging markets: in Asia—China, Indonesia, India, Vietnam, Malaysia, Thailand and South Korea; in Latin America—Mexico, Argentina and Brazil; in Africa—South Africa; in Central Europe—the Czech Republic, Hungary and Poland; and in Southern Europe—Turkey. Although some countries in Asia, such as Malaysia, Thailand and Indonesia, have gone through an economic crisis, these countries are expected to overcome the crisis as Mexico survived the economic crisis of 1994.

These emerging markets differ from other developing countries because they import more than smaller markets and more than economies of similar size. As they embark on economic development, demand for capital goods to build their manufacturing base and develop infrastructure increases. Increased economic activity means more jobs and more income to spend on products not yet produced locally. Thus, as their economies expand, there is an accelerated growth in demand for goods and services, much of which must be imported. Emerging markets merchandise imports are expected to be nearly one trillion dollars ($1 000 000 000 000 or €902 600 000 000); if services are added, the amount jumps beyond one trillion dollars.

What is occurring in the emerging markets is analogous to the situation after World War II when tremendous demand was created during the reconstruction of Europe. As Europe rebuilt its infrastructure and industrial base, demand for capital goods exploded and, as more money was infused into its economies, consumer demand also increased rapidly. For more than a decade, Europe could not supply its increasing demand for industrial and consumer goods. During that period, the US was the principal supplier because most of the rest of the world was rebuilding or had underdeveloped economies. Meeting this demand produced one of the largest economic booms the United States had ever experienced. Now Japan, Europe and NICs will become fierce rivals in emerging markets.

Eastern Europe and the Baltic States

Eastern Europe and the Baltic states, satellite nations of the former USSR, are moving rapidly to establish free-market systems. New business opportunities are emerging almost daily and the region is described as anywhere from chaotic with big risks to an exciting place

Map 9.1   Eastern Europe and the Baltic States

with untold opportunities. Both descriptions fit as countries adjust to the political, social and economic realities of changing from the restrictions of a Marxist–socialist system to some version of free markets and capitalism. In the next century, this region will rank among the important emerging markets.[17]

Eastern Europe.   It is dangerous to generalize beyond a certain point about Eastern Europe because each of the countries has its own economic problems and is at a different

Table 9.4   Eastern European Markets

	Population (millions)	GDP ($ billions)	GDP ($ per capita)	Exports ($ millions)	Imports ($ millions)
Albania	3.28	$2.7	$820	$80	$147
Bosnia/Hercegovina*	4.36	14.0	2 454	2 000	1 900
Bulgaria	9.00	10.4	1 161	2 592	2 018
Croatia*	4.78	26.3	5 600	2 900	4 400
Czech†	10.30	28.4	2 757	12 320	12 681
Hungary	10.30	35.4	3 435	10 705	11 066
Macedonia*	2.05	4.8	2 400	578	1 100
Poland	38.40	83.6	2 178	14 046	21 549
Romania	22.80	19.4	854	4 469	5 582
Slovakia†	5.27	9.3	1 763	3 500	3 900
Slovenia*	1.96	21.0	10 700	42 900	48 800
Yugoslavia‡	9.33	81.9	8 778	13 400	14 800

*Former republics of Yugoslavia.
†Former republics of Czechoslovakia.
‡Consists of Serbia and Montenegro.
Sources: For additional data, see 'Indicators of Market Size for 115 Countries, *Crossborder Monitor*, 31 August 1994; *Business Eastern Europe*, 25 April 1994; and *International Trade Statistics Yearbook* (New York: United Nations, 1994).

point in its evolution from a socialist to a market-driven economy. Most are privatizing state-owned enterprises (SOEs), establishing free-market pricing systems, relaxing import controls, and wrestling with inflation. The Czech Republic, Poland and Hungary have made more progress towards overhauling their economies than have Bulgaria, Albania and Romania.[18]

The Commonwealth of Russian States (CIS) is still struggling with political instability and the Asian republics have different levels of ambitions and goals depending upon their location, resources and political leadership. However, in most East European countries, there are democratically elected governments that are committed to establish market economies based on a free market economy. Most of these countries are trying to attract foreign companies in order to establish technology transfer and trade links. In spite of the reluctance of Western companies to invest, there has been a considerable increase in registered joint ventures and wholly owned subsidiaries.

For the entrepreneur, freedom from communism has provided the opportunity to blossom. Nowhere is this more evident than in Poland. Reforms, coupled with the fact that Poland had a relatively large (mostly agricultural) private sector under communism, have led to an explosion of private entrepreneurial activity. For example, 20 per cent of all retail sales in 1989 were private, and by 1991 the private-sale share rose to 80 per cent. A report of a Polish trader who started a business in a warehouse to outfit retail stores typifies the entrepreneurial spirit found in many of the countries. The business, Intercommerce, has scales from Korea, cash registers from Japan, and stack upon stack of German shelves, racks, baskets, hangers, supermarket carts, bar-code readers, price-tag tape and checkout counters. When a customer wants furnishings for a new store, the owner of Intercommerce prepares a layout for the store, makes a list of what is needed, and then trucks it all to the new store. 'It takes about an hour', he says. The company's sales were €9000 ($10 000) a month in 1990 and €540 000 ($600 000) per month a year later.

Hungary and the Czech Republic, the other two emerging markets, also have promising economic prospects (Table 9.4) and, along with Poland, were the first to achieve associate status (the transitional stage before full membership) of the EU.[19] The other East European countries are trailing behind these three in their transition from communism to capitalism, and not all are successfully completing the transition to free-market economies. Monetary policy, the transfer of state-owned property to the private sector, restructuring of the legal system to include commercial law and banking reform are issues that are unresolved for many. Even though progress towards reform is spotty, an entrepreneurial class is developing rapidly and the long-term future is bright.[20]

The Baltic States.   Estonia, Latvia and Lithuania were among the first republics to declare their sovereignty and independence as the Soviet Union began to crumble. Within days of their independence, the European Parliament granted them special guest status in the EU. Trade and cooperation agreements have been signed and eventually they are expected to become associate members. The Baltic states are positioned to be a bridge for trade between the West and the former USSR. With their past experience as exporters to the USSR of manufactured goods made from Russian raw materials, the Baltic states see themselves as a logical location for Western investment seeking markets in the former Soviet Union.[21]

Eastern Europe and the Baltic states are in the sphere of influence of the EU. There is a natural tendency for them to look to the EU for assistance and, eventually, membership. As discussed, the framework for the integration of trade among countries in each of the regions is in place in Europe and the Americas.

Asia

Asia is the fastest-growing market in the world and its share of global output is projected to account for almost one-half of the increase in global output through the year 2000.[22] Both as sources of new products and technology and as vast consumer markets, the Pacific Rim and Asia are just beginning to get into their stride (see Table 9.5).

Asian Pacific Rim.   The most rapidly growing economies in this region, other than Japan, are the group of countries earlier referred to as the 'Four Tigers' (or 'Four Dragons'): Hong Kong, South Korea, Singapore and Taiwan. These were the first countries in Asia, besides Japan, to move from a status of developing countries to newly industrialized countries (NICs). They have grown from suppliers of component parts and assemblers of Western products to become major global competitors—in electronics, shipbuilding, heavy machinery, motor vehicles and a multitude of other products. In addition, each has become a major influence in trade and development in the economies of other countries within their spheres of influence.

South Korea is the centre of trade links with north China, and the Asian republics of the former Soviet Union. Although North and South Korea do not officially recognize one another, trade between the two, mostly through Hong Kong, is in excess of €112 million ($124 million) annually. There is some likelihood that the two will unite, creating a formidable regional economic power similar to that of Hong Kong and China. The Four Tigers are rapidly extending their trading activity to other parts of Asia.[23]

Japan's role in the Asian Pacific Rim is perhaps the most important in the area. While not part of a common market or any other economic cooperative alliance, Japan's influence is nevertheless increasingly dominant. Sales to Japan account for as much as 12 per cent of GDP in Malaysia and about 7 per cent of GDP in Indonesia, Thailand and South Korea.[24] That

Table 9.5 Asian Pacific Rim Markets—Economic Indicators of Selected Countries, Post-Asian Crisis

	Economic Growth (%)ᵃ				International Reserves (billion $)ᵇ	Exportsᶜ		Importsᵈ		Other Indicators	
	1996 Actual	1997 Estimate	1998 Forecast	1999 Forecast		Latest 3 Mths (billion $)	Change YoY (%)	Latest 3 Mths (billion $)	Change YoY (%)	Population Million (Year)ᵉ	Per capita GDP ($)ᶠ
China	+9.7	+8.8	+9.0	+8.6	143,73 (Feb)	43,49 (Feb–Apr)	+12.4	32,48 (Feb–Apr)	+8.1	1221,5 (95)	2 500
Hong Kong	+5.0	+5.2	−2.0	+2.4	78,51 (Mar)	40,07 (Feb–Apr)	−1.0	46,61 (Feb–Apr)	−1.6	6,31 (96)	27 500
Taiwan	+5.7	+6.8	+6.0	+6.0	83,62 (Mar)	28,40 (Feb–Mar)	+0.5	28,33 (Feb–Apr)	+2.3	21,6 (97)	13 510
Indonesia	+8.0	+4.6	−15.0	−0.6	15,49 (Feb)	12,45g (Jan–Mar)	+0.7	6,97 (Jan–Mar)	−34.1	193,75 (95)	3 500
Malaysia	+8.6	+7.8	+2.5	+3.0	21,77 (Nov)	17,19 (Nov–Jan)	−14.3	16,17 (Nov–Jan)	−18.9	20,69 (95)	9 800
Philippines	+5.7	+5.1	+2.5	+4.0	7,27 (Dec)	6,82 (Jan–Mar)	+23.8	8,31 (Jan–Mar)	−0.9	70,27 (95)	2 530
Singapore	+6.9	+7.8	+4.0	+5.5	74,42 (Nov)	29,27 (Nov–Apr)	−1.5	27,95 (Feb–Apr)	−11.4	3,04 (96)	22 900
Thailand	+5.5	+0.4	−6.0	+2.5	26,89 (Mar)	13,47 (Dec–Feb)	−0.2	11,03 (Dec–Feb)	−35.1	59,40 (95)	6 900
Japan	+3.8	+1.0	+0.3	n.a.	222,00 (Feb)	97,13 (Jan–Mar)	+3.9	74,59 (Jan–Mar)	−9.3	125,76 (96)	21 300
South Korea	+7.1	+5.5	−1.9	+2.2	29,76 (Mar)	35,66 (Mar–May)	+3.8	24,28 (Mar–May)	−36.5	45,54 (96)	13 000
India	+7.5	+4.9	+5.0	+5.1	26,26 (Mar)	8,17 (Dec–Feb)	−0.9	11,03 (Dec–Feb)	+5.06	935,74 (95)	1 500

ᵃGoldman Sachs (Asia) estimates; ᵇIMF definition of reserves minus gold except for Singapore; ᶜfob; ᵈcif; ᵉIMF, Mid-year estimate; ᶠThe World Almanac; ᵍIncluding petroleum.
Source: Based on Official Statistics, in *Far Eastern Economic Review*, 2 July 1998, pp. 66–67.

Map 9.2   Asia

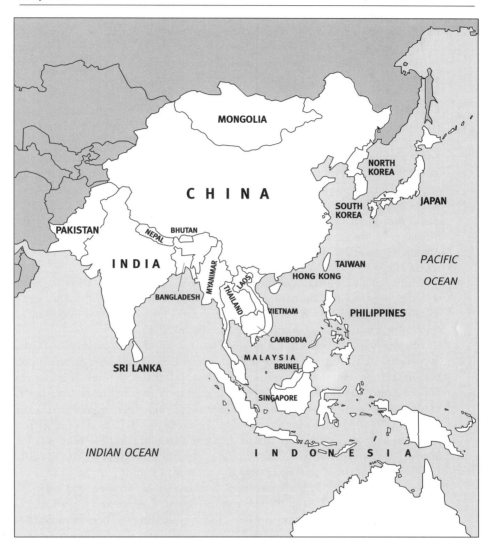

these economies influence each other was clearly seen in the 1997–98 Japanese and Asian crisis.

Other countries of Asia taking the leading position are China, Indonesia, India, Malaysia and Thailand. Malaysian planners have developed blueprints for new industries ranging from rubber sneakers to colour-television picture tubes. The most elaborate plan calls for Malaysia to become one of the world's foremost producers of word processors, answering machines and facsimile devices. Part of the idea is to limit competition among the region's countries and foster complementary patterns of development. A regional automobile industry might combine transmissions from the Philippines with steering mechanisms from Malaysia and engines from Thailand in a final assembly process in a fourth country.

As these Asian countries continue to develop, in spite of the major 1997–98 crisis, Japanese capital, technology and direction will be paramount. With Japanese leadership, the region is rapidly becoming a major economic power in global trade.[25] Japan's role among the Asian Pacific Rim countries may have the same economic trade impact for developing countries in that region as the EU provides for Eastern Europe and the United States provides for South America—investments, free-trade alliances and markets. In addition, China is gaining ground to become a major player in the world economic scene.

China.   The economic and social changes occurring in China since it began actively seeking economic ties with the industrialized world have been dramatic.[26] China's dual economic system, embracing socialism along with many tenets of capitalism, produced an economic boom with expanded opportunity for foreign investment until an internal political upheaval in 1989 cast doubt on its future. A confrontation at Tiananmen Square between the military and students demonstrating for greater personal freedom and redress against human-rights abuses led to some doubt about China's viability as a stable market. Despite the political turmoil and jockeying for power among China's leaders after the riots were quelled, official government word was that China's door was still open to foreign capital and technology. However, it was more than a year and a half before trade and direct investment resumed.

China remains a socialist economy and anyone doing business there has to contend with the trappings of both capitalist and socialist systems. In the minds of some, China's move towards free enterprise has become a free-for-all with power shifted to provinces, towns and state-owned factories—a country that lacks discipline.[27]

Anyone doing business in China must keep in mind a few fundamentals that have been overshadowed by Western euphoria. First, because of China's size, diversity, political organization and the return of Hong Kong to China, it is better to think of it as a group of seven regions rather than a single country—a grouping of regional markets rather than a single market.[28] There is no one growth strategy for China. Each region is at a different stage economically and has its own link to other regions as well as links to other parts of the world. Each has its own investment patterns, is taxed differently and has substantial autonomy in how it is governed. But while each region is separate enough to be considered individually, each is linked at the top to the central government in Beijing.

Second, distribution, manufacturing, banking, transportation and other infrastructure segments of business are out of date and inefficient. Gillette and Coca-Cola, among other companies, are making money in China, but neither can readily send profits home or bring in new equipment because of exchange and import restrictions.[29] Transportation and distribution of goods to inland China vary from good to abysmal. Roads are poor for trucking; breakdowns and delays are common for rail transportation. A World Bank official estimates it will take some 20 years to build an adequate transportation system.[30]

With the reversion of Hong Kong, a small segment, however, is becoming very wealthy. These wealthy consumers flock to new luxury shops offering Gucci handbags, Benetton sweaters and Adidas sneakers.[31] The Swiss firm Rado sold 10 000 of its top-quality watches in China (excluding Hong Kong) in a year, and many Chinese are willing to pay up to €45 000 ($50 000) for an Audi or Mercedes-Benz.[32]

China is not only a huge emerging market, but also an investor. There are thousands of Chinese companies that have invested heavily in the West, particularly Europe and the United States. A number of state-owned enterprises such as Sinochem, CITIC and COFCO have been active in real estate, manufacturing and finance. Also, a number of provincial and city companies have now set up their own Western trading, manufacturing, investment and

GOING INTERNATIONAL 9.3

LOW PER CAPITA INCOME MEANS LOW DEMAND? DON'T BE SO SURE

In China, where per capita income is less than $600 (€540), Rado is selling thousands of its $1000 (€900) watches. A Kentucky Fried Chicken dinner costs the equivalent of a day's wages, yet one of KFC's highest-volume stores is in Beijing. How can this be? There is a large wealthy group who buy the watches, but there are many others who budget and save their extra income to afford their vision of the 'good life'.

Mr Xu is a good example of China's emerging consumer market. Like millions of Chinese middle-class consumers, Mr Xu strives to afford imports from the West. He and his wife and their 22-year-old daughter live in a modest three-bedroom apartment in north Beijing with no hot water and little heat in the winter. His monthly salary as a college English professor is just over $81 (€73), and his wife, retired, contributes her $35 (€32) monthly pension to the family income. The family gets free medical care and pays a minimal $3 each month for rent. Like many Chinese, Mr Xu earns extra money by doing part-time English translation work. The additional money saved goes towards occasional family entertainment, such as a trip to McDonald's, to help his only other daughter who is studying accounting in the United States and to buy Western luxuries. They buy Hollywood brand gum, a treat for his daughter, for 70 cents, seven times the cost of a Chinese chewing gum; the family's toothpaste, Colgate, is also luxury priced at $1.41 compared to a local brand at 35 cents. He boasts, 'We haven't used a Chinese toothbrush for five years'.

Sources: Adapted from Bill Saporito, 'Where the Global Action Is', *Fortune*, Autumn–Winter 1993, p. 63, and Sheila Tefft, 'Xu's Have Western Taste', *Advertising Age*, 18 April 1994, pp. 1–10.

finance companies. Another group active in foreign investments are hybrids working through wholly owned subsidiaries in Hong Kong.[33]

India.   The wave of change that has been washing away restricted trade, controlled economies, closed markets and hostility to foreign investment in most developing countries has finally reached India. Since its independence, one of the world's largest markets had set a poor example as a model for economic growth for other developing countries and was among the last of the economically important developing nations to throw off traditional insular policies. India's growth had been constrained and shaped by policies of import substitution and an aversion to free markets. Real competition in internal markets was practically eliminated through import bans and prohibitive tariffs on foreign competition. Industry was so completely regulated that those with the proper licence could count on a specific share of the market. While other Asian countries were wooing foreign capital, India was doing its best to keep it out. Multinationals, seen as vanguards of a new colonialism, were shunned. As a result, India lost its technological connection with the rest of the world. Technological change in many manufactured products was frozen in time. Cars were protected by a complete ban on importation. The Ambassador, India's mass-produced car, has been unchanged since it was introduced 40 years ago—40 years of technological progress bypassed the Indian automotive industry. Aside from textiles, Indian industrial products found few markets abroad other than in the former Soviet Union and Eastern Europe.

Times have changed and India has embarked on the most profound transformation since it won political independence from Britain in 1947. In 1992, the new direction promised to adjust the philosophy of self-sufficiency that had been taken to extremes and to open India to world markets. India had the look and feel of the next China or Indonesia. Yet India is a mixed bag; while it did overthrow the restrictions of earlier governments, it did not move towards reforms and open markets with the same degree of vigour found in other emerging markets. Resistance to change comes from politicians, bureaucrats, union members and farmers, as well as from some industrialists who have lived comfortably behind protective tariff walls that excluded competition. Bureaucracy and rigid labour laws remain a drag on business as does corruption. One foreign oil-company executive reports having to pay off the phone repairman. 'I complained to his company, but they just laughed. The police said they would arrest him—but only for a fee.'[34] India's present problems are not economic but a mix of political, psychological and cultural attitudes. In addition, the 1998 nuclear test by India led to economic sanctions by the United States and Japan and the budget, announced a couple of weeks after the test, called once again for self-reliance and less dependence on foreign investments. These actions scared a number of foreign companies away.[35]

Despite some uncertainties, the potential of India's market is reflected by its being included among the BEMs. With a population expected to reach one billion by the year 2000, India is second in size only to China, and both contain enormous low-cost labour pools. India has a middle class numbering some 300 million, closer to the population of the EU and bigger than the United States. Among its middle class are large numbers of college graduates, 40 per cent of whom have degrees in science and engineering. India has a diverse industrial base and is developing as a centre for computer software. The magnitude of the potential is best illustrated by telecommunications: in 1997, less than 10 million telephone lines served a population of more than 900 million.

The consumer-goods sector is another important draw for the foreign investor. An estimated 300 million Indians possess sufficient disposable income to form an expanding consumer class. Imported consumer items are still banned, but foreign investment in 22 consumer sectors is now welcome. Several consumer-goods firms have recently been approved for investments, once a virtual impossibility. General Electric's application to form a €36 million ($40 million) joint venture to make refrigerators and washing machines was approved in six weeks. In the past, approval, if it came at all, would have taken three or more years. General Motors, Coca-Cola, Pepsi-Cola, McDonald's and IBM are just a few of the companies that have recently made direct investments in India.

India still presents a difficult business environment. Tariffs are well above those of developing-world norms, although they have been slashed to a maximum of 65 per cent from 400 per cent. Inadequate protection of intellectual property rights remains a serious concern. The anti-business attitudes of India's federal and state bureaucracies continue to hinder potential investors and plague their routine operations.[36]

The Americas

The North American Free Trade Agreement (NAFTA) marks the high point of a silent political and economic revolution that has been taking place in the Americas (see Map 9.3) over the last decade. Most of the countries have moved from military dictatorships to democratically elected governments, while sweeping economic and trade liberalization is replacing the economic model most Latin American countries followed for decades. Today many of them are at roughly the same stage of liberalization that launched the dynamic growth in Asia during the last two decades.[37]

The trend towards privatization of SDEs follows a period in which governments dominated economic life for most of the 20th century. State ownership was once considered the

Map 9.3   The Americas

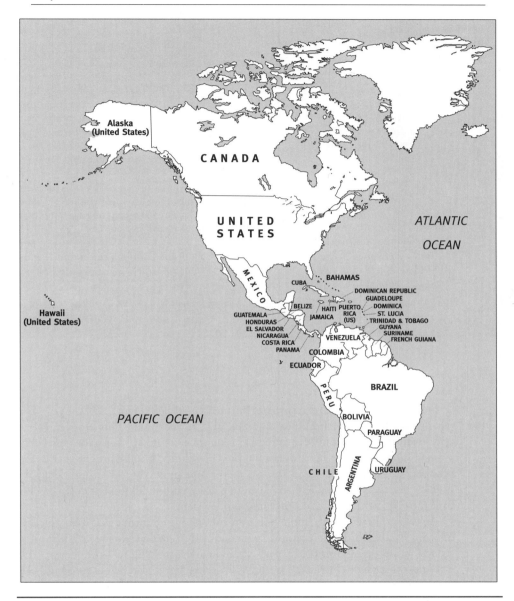

ideal engine for economic growth. Instead of economic growth, however, they got inflated public-sector bureaucracies, complicated and unpredictable regulatory environments, the outright exclusion of foreign and domestic private ownership, and inefficient public companies. A study of 35 steel companies in Brazil reported that only eight possessed a research lab and only one invested in research and development. As a consequence, productive capacity stood still for a decade.

GOING INTERNATIONAL 9.4

HISTORY REPEATS ITSELF

Some things never change. Today the United States has entered a commercial union with Latin America. A century ago, President Benjamin Harrison sought a similar free trade pact in Latin America. In some ways, the United States looked very much then as it looks now. It already had the world's second-highest per capita income, the world's largest market, and was the world's greatest foreign debtor.

A hundred years ago, the United States tried to promote less exports by proposing an inter-American customs union that excluded Latin America's traditional trade partners in Europe. Latin Americans quite naturally rejected this notion. The grand design was ultimately abandoned and an individual trade pact was signed with a number of Latin American countries, Brazil and Cuba the most prominent among them. Ironically, Mexico, the country which later proved to be the greatest Latin American market for American goods, refused to enter the agreement because of the long-standing distrust and pique at earlier insults.

This first effort to create a special trade relationship with Latin America was as unsuccessful as it was short-lived. In the three years the treaty was in force (1891–94) the volume of trade grew but the US trade deficit with Latin America grew even faster. Americans imported more sugar, coffee and hides at lower prices, but the Latin Americans found precious few US goods cheaper than goods offered by their European competitors.

Today the United States, fearful of being closed out of the European communities and of Japanese domination in Asia, is once again remembering the Latin American countries 'in our backyard', hoping to reassert US influence.

Source: Stephen C. Topik, 'Gilded Age Politics and Foreign Trade', *World Trade*, November 1991, pp. 109–110.

New leaders have turned away from the traditional closed policies of the past to implement positive market-oriented reforms and seek ways for economic cooperation. Privatization of state-owned enterprises (SOEs) and other economic, monetary and trade policy reforms show a broad shift away from inward-looking policies of import substitution (that is, manufacture products at home rather than import them) and protectionism so prevalent earlier. In a positive response to these reforms, investors are spending billions of dollars to buy airlines, banks, public works and telecommunications systems.

Argentina, Brazil, Chile and Mexico are among the countries that have quickly instituted reforms. All have brought inflation under control; Argentina has shown the most spectacular reduction, dropping from a 672 per cent annual rate in 1985 to 7 per cent in 1993. Mexico has been the leader in privatization and in lowering tariffs even before entering NAFTA. Over 750 businesses, including the telephone company, steel mills, airlines and banks, have been sold. Pemex, the national oil company, is the only major industry Mexico is not privatizing, although restrictions on joint projects between Pemex and foreign companies have been liberalized.

In addition to privatization and lowering tariffs, most Latin American countries are working at creating an environment to attract capital. Chile, Mexico and Bolivia were the first to make deep cuts in tariffs from a high of 100 per cent or more down to a maximum of 10 to 20 per cent. Taxes that act as nontariff trade barriers are being eliminated, as are restrictions on repatriation of profits. These and other changes have energized the governments, people and foreign investors.[38]

The population of nearly 460 million is one-half greater than that of the United States and

Table 9.6   Economic and Social Data for Selected Countries

Country	Consumer Spending Food ($ millions)†	Percent of Total*	Clothing ($ millions)†	Percent of Total*	Hospital Beds per (000s) Population	Number of Doctors	Literacy (percent)	Tourism Receipts ($ millions)†
United States	$741 340	18.1	$221 800	5.4	5.1	560 300	99.5	$45 579
Argentina	16 950	38.8	2 332	5.3	5.3	96 000	93.9	2 336
Brazil	81 934	31.2	12 799	4.9	3.5	169 488	77.8	1 559
Colombia	9 264	35.2	1 597	6.1	1.5	29 353	85.2	410
Mexico	57 900	33.7	12 066	7.0	0.7	130 000	76.6	4 355
Venezuela	15 501	43.2	3 679	10.2	2.6	28 400	84.7	365

*Percent of all consumer spending; †In US dollars, basis 1988.
Sources: For additional information, see *International Trade Statistics Yearbook* (New York: United Nations, 1994), *Demographic Yearbook 1994* (New York: United Nations, 1994) and *International Marketing Data and Statistics*, 18th edn (London: Euromonitor Publications, 1994).

100 million more than the European Union. Almost 60 per cent of all the merchandise trade in Latin America is transacted with countries in the western hemisphere. The United States alone provides more than 40 per cent of Latin America's imports and buys a similar share of its exports. Economic and trade policy reforms occurring in Latin American countries signify a tremendous potential for trade and investments.[39]

A study by the Institute for International Economics reported that Argentina, Brazil, Bolivia, Chile, Colombia, Paraguay, Uruguay and several Caribbean nations ranked higher on a scale of 'readiness criteria'—price stability, budget discipline, market-oriented policies and a functioning democracy—than did Mexico at the start of the NAFTA talks. Thus, they are viable candidates for a Western Hemisphere Free Trade Agreement (WHFTA) to replace NAFTA. Such an agreement would strengthen trade ties within the region, preempt a plethora of smaller trade agreements, increase trade and make economic sense for the region, the United States and Canada.[40] Table 9.6 provides some economic and social data on several countries in the Americas.

Newest Emerging Markets

The United Nations' decision to lift the embargo against South Africa, and the prospects of peace in the Middle East have created several new emerging markets. After apartheid was officially over, the United Nations lifted the economic embargo that had isolated South Africa from much of the industrialized world for more than six years, and there has been a rush of companies eager to invest in the largest economy on the continent and to participate in the pent-up demand created during the embargo. South Africa has an industrial base that will help propel it into rapid economic growth, with the possibility of doubling its GNP in as few as 10 years. The South African market also has a developed infrastructure—airports, railways, roads, telecommunications—that make it important as a base for serving nearby African markets too small to be considered individually, but viable when coupled with South Africa.[41] It is for these reasons that most sources have included South Africa among the bigger emerging markets

Table 9.7   Shrinking Economies

	GDP (billion $)		
	1996	1998[a]	1998 at PPP[b]
China	839	1063	4730
Hong Kong	154	188	190
Indonesia	226	51	1020
Malaysia	92	71	240
Philippines	84	68	240
South Korea	485	272	660
Singapore	94	92	90
Taiwan	272	269	450
Thailand	186	97	530
Total	*2432*	*2172*	*8150*

[a]Using exchange rates of 4 February 1998; [b]Purchasing-power parity.
Source: Based on EIU, Peregrine, in *The Economist*, 7 February 1998, p. 90.

CHANGING MARKET BEHAVIOUR AND MARKET SEGMENTATION

As a country develops, profound changes occur that affect its people. Incomes change, population concentrations shift, expectations for a better life adjust to higher standards, new infrastructures evolve, social capital investments are made, and foreign and domestic companies seek new markets or expand their positions in existing markets. Market behaviour changes and eventually groups of consumers with common tastes and needs (i.e. market segments) arise or disappear (see Table 9.7).

Markets evolve from a three-way interaction of the economy, the culture and the marketing efforts of companies. Markets are not, they become, that is they are not static but are constantly changing as they affect and are affected by changes in incomes, awareness of different lifestyles, exposure to new products and exposure to new ideas. Changing incomes raise expectations and the ability to buy more and different goods. The accessibility of global communications, TV, radio and print media means that people in one part of the world are aware of lifestyles in another. Global companies span the globe with new ideas on consumer behaviour and new products to try.

Emerging Market Segments

With the prosperity that results from economic growth, markets grow and distinct segments begin to emerge. A review of the literature suggests that there is a developing middle-income class, a youth market, an élite market and so on. Evidence supports the notion of an evolving worldwide middle-income class. Do these middle-income classes constitute a worldwide or at least multicountry homogeneous market segment? The evidence is less compelling, but there are some strong suggestions that—for some kinds of products—market segments across countries have more commonalties than differences. It does not, however, mean that we can standardize on marketing strategies and efforts.

Another ramification of emerging markets is the creation of a middle-class household that generates new markets for everything from disposable nappies to cars. The middle class in emerging markets differs from the Western middle class. While they do not have two cars and suburban homes, they do have discretionary income, that is, income not needed for food, clothing and shelter.

Further, large households can translate into higher disposable incomes. Young working people in Asia and Latin American usually live at home until they marry. With no rent to pay, they have more discretionary income and can contribute to household purchasing power. Low per capita incomes are potential markets for a large variety of goods; consumers show remarkable resourcefulness in finding ways to buy what really matters to them. The poorest slums of Calcutta are home to more than 70 000 VCRs and in Mexico, homes with colour televisions outnumber those with running water.

A London securities firm says a person earning €225 ($250) annually in developing countries can afford Gillette razors, and at €900 ($1000) he can become a Sony television owner. A Nissan or Volkswagen would be possible with a less than €9000 ($10 000) income. Whirlpool estimates that in Eastern Europe a family with an annual income of €900 ($1000) can afford a refrigerator and with $1800 ($2000) they can buy an automatic washer as well.

International Market Segmentation

The purpose of market segmentation is to identify relatively homogeneous groups of consumers with similar consumption patterns. A market segment has four components: (1) it must be identifiable, (2) it must be economically reachable, (3) it is more homogeneous in its characteristics than the market as a whole and (4) it is large enough to be profitable. International market segmentation is applying those criteria to market segments across country markets. Fundamentally, the international marketer is looking for an identifiable segment of consumers who have the same (or at least mostly similar) needs and wants across several country markets.

When a company does business in more than one country there are two approaches to the market. Target markets can be identified as (1) all consumers within the borders of a country or (2) global market segments—all consumers with the same needs and wants in groups of country markets. Most international marketers have traditionally viewed each country as a single market segment unique to that country.

As economies prosper and living standards improve, consumer attitudes and consumption patterns change. Retail outlets change in response to consumer demands for longer hours, shopping convenience, better service and ease of access. Hypermarkets and department stores are replacing the traditional specialty stores, and quality and service are expected as part of the product offering. Wherever economies are growing, one can expect changes in consumption patterns and the emergence of trends in market behaviour. See Table 9.8 for market indicators in selected countries.

SUMMARY

The increasing scope and level of technical and economic growth have enabled many countries to advance their standards of living by as much as two centuries in a matter of decades. As countries develop their productive capacity, all segments of their economies will feel the pressure to improve. The impact of these social and economic trends will continue to be felt throughout the world, causing significant changes in marketing practices. Marketers must focus on devising marketing plans designed to respond fully to each level of economic development. China and the former Soviet Union continue to undergo rapid political

Table 9.8   Market Indicators in Selected Countries

	Population (millions)	GDP per Capita	Cars in Use (000)	TVs in Use (000)	Telephones in Use (000)	Trucks & Buses
United States	255.0	$23 680	142 956	215 000	144 056	45 416
Argentina	33.1	6 912	4 186	7 165	3 682	1 494
Australia	17.5	16 581	7 734	8 000	8 257	1 915
Brazil	156.8	2 609	12 128	30 000	10 670	1 075
Canada	27.4	20 774	13 061	17 400	16 246	3 744
China	118.8	367	1 765	126 000	11 469	4 349
France	57.4	23 040	23 810	29 300	29 905	5 020
Germany	64.7	28 031	31 309	30 500	35 420	2 114
India	870.0	274	2 491	20 000	6 797	2 177
Indonesia	191.2	661	1 294	11 000	1 485	1 589
Italy	56.8	21 539	28 200	17 000	23 709	2 512
Japan	124.3	29 516	37 076	100 000	57 652	22 839
Mexico	89.5	3 722	6 819	56 000	6 754	3 100
Poland	38.4	2 178	5 260	10 000	3 945	1 044
South Korea	43.7	6 799	NA	9 101	1 089	NA
SPAIN	39.0	14 666	12 537	17 000	13 792	2 615
UK	57.9	18 403	22 744	20 000	26 084	3 685

Sources: For additional information see 'Indicators of Market Size for 115 Countries', *Crossborder Monitor*, 31 August 1994 and *International Trade Statistics Yearbook* (New York: United Nations, 1994).

economic changes that have resulted in opening most communist-bloc countries to foreign direct investments and international trade. And though emerging markets present special problems, they are promising markets for a broad range of products.

This ever-expanding involvement of more and more of the world's people with varying needs and wants will test old trading patterns and alliances. The foreign marketer of today and tomorrow must be able to react to market changes rapidly and to anticipate new trends within constantly evolving market segments that may not have existed as recently as last year. Many of today's market facts will probably be tomorrow's historical myths.

Emerging Markets: Challenges and Opportunities

Emerging Markets are becoming important for most international firms. In many of the emerging markets infrastructure is not as developed as in the Western world. Some countries continue working with inefficient technologies rather than let multinationals take over most sectors.

Ancient: Indians say they were growing basmati before America was born
Source: *Business Week*, 2 March 1998, p. 43.

They're boiling over rice. Indians are furious as US poachers of a famous name: Basmati rice. They want to keep multinationals out and keep on working with primitive technologies in agriculture and mining as here mining for diamonds in Madya Pradesh.

Mining in Madhya Pradesh: Locals have vowed to keep multinationals out
Source: *Business Week*, 2 March 1998, p. 43.

On one particular day more than 100 couples tie the knot. There is a baby born every two seconds in India; if this rate continues, in 50 years one in every six people will be Indian.

Source: *Business Week*, 16 June 1997, p. 31.

Cycles are still the main means of transportation in China. Distribution is a headache for Coke in China, where the traditional distribution is still the main channel.

Source: *Business Week*, 21 October 1996, p. 30.

Russia is proposing tough measures to meet tax collection targets. Here a tax policeman is confiscating clothing on sale in a market in Moscow.

Source: *Business Week*, 15 June 1998, p. 28.

Retailing in Vietnam is still dominated by mom-and-pop stores, protected by the government.

Source: *Business Week*, 6 October 1997, p. 28.

In Eastern Europe hypermarkets are taking over mom-and-pop shops. Hypermarkets, like here in Warsaw, have scores of lanes.

Source: *Business Week*, 25 May 1998, p. 43.

QUESTIONS

1. Is it possible for an economy to experience economic growth as measured by total GNP without a commensurate rise in the standard of living? Discuss fully.
2. Discuss each of the stages of evolution in the marketing process. Illustrate each stage with a particular country.
3. As a country progresses from one economic stage to another, what in general are the marketing effects?
4. Locate a country in the agricultural and raw material stage of economic development and discuss what changes will occur in marketing when it passes to a manufacturing stage.
5. Discuss the significance of economic development to international marketing. Why is the knowledge of economic development of importance in assessing the world marketing environment? Discuss.
6. Select one country in each of the five stages of economic development. For each country, outline the basic existing marketing institutions and show how the marketing strategy of a foreign company will differ in these markets.
7. The infrastructure is important to the economic growth of an economy. Comment.
8. What is marketing's role in economic development? Discuss marketing's contributions to economic development.
9. Discuss the economic and trade importance of the big emerging markets.
10. What are the traits of those countries considered to be big emerging markets? Discuss.
11. Discuss how the economic growth of BEMs is analogous to the situation after World War II.
12. One of the ramifications of emerging markets is the creation of a middle class. Discuss.
13. What are global market segments? Why are they important to global companies? Discuss.

REFERENCES

1. 'The Big Emerging Markets', *Business America*, March 1994, pp. 4–6.
2. Louis S. Richman, 'Global Growth Is on a Tear', *Fortune*, 20 March 1995, pp. 8–14.
3. For a thorough review of global consumers, see 'The Emerging Middle Class', *Business Week/21st Century Capitalism*, 1994, pp. 176–194.
4. Gross domestic product (GDP) and gross national product (GNP) are two measures of a country's economic activity. GDP is a measure of the market value of all goods and services produced within the boundaries of a nation, regardless of asset ownership. Unlike gross national product (GNP), GDP excludes receipts from that nation's business operations in foreign countries, as well as the share of reinvested earnings in foreign affiliates of domestic corporations.
5. Walt W. Rostow, *The Stages of Economic Growth*, 2d edn (London: Cambridge University Press, 1971), p. 10. For an interesting discussion see Peter Buckley and Pervez Ghauri, *Multinationals and Emerging Markets* (Oxford: Pergamon Press, 1999).
6. 'The Battle for Brazil', *Fortune*, 20 July 1998, pp. 48–53.
7. For a description of how competitive South Korea has become, see David P. Hamilton and Steve Glain, 'Silicon Duel: Koreans Move to Grab Memory-Chip Market from the Japanese', *The Wall Street Journal*, 14 March 1995, p. A-1.
8. For a discussion of the billions of dollars being invested in infrastructure, see Dave Savona, 'Remaking the Globe', *International Business*, March 1995, pp. 30–36.
9. 'Logistics: Clogged Arteries', *International Business*, July 1994, pp. 30–32.
10. For a comprehensive review of one country's move towards a more open economy, see 'Argentina Survey', *The Economist*, 26 November 1994, 18 pages unnumbered beginning on p. 62.
11. For a comprehensive review of channels of distribution in developing countries, see Saeed Samiee, 'Retailing and Channel Considerations in Developing Countries; A Review and Research Propositions', *Journal of Business Research*, vol. 23, 1993, pp. 103–130; and Janeen E. Olsen and Kent L. Granzin, 'Vertical Integration and

Economic Development: An Empirical Investigation of Channel Integration', *Journal of Global Marketing*, vol. 7, no. 3, 1994, pp. 7–39.

12. 'India: The Poor Get Richer', *The Economist*, 5 November 1994, pp. 39–40.

13. 'India's Post-Blast Gloom', *The Economist*, 11 July 1998, pp. 61–62.

14. When the US government lifted the trade embargo against Vietnam, many US companies found that their competitors had already made inroads in that market. See Marita Van Oldenborgy, 'Catch-Up Ball', *International Business*, March 1994, pp. 92–94.

15. 'The Big Emerging Markets', *Business America*, March 1994, pp. 4–6.

16. 'Big Emerging Markets' Share of World Exports Continues to Rise', *Business America*, March 1994, p. 28.

17. For a complete guide to business opportunities in Eastern Europe, see Christopher Engholm, *The Other Europe* (New York: McGraw-Hill, 1994).

18. Louis Zanga, 'Albania Optimistic about Economic Growth', RFE/RL Research Report (RFE/RL Research Institute, Munich, Germany), 18 February 1994, pp. 14–17.

19. Mark Mowrey, 'Poland: An Entrepreneurial Culture Takes Root', *Business America*, March 1994, pp. 26–27; and 'A Survey of Business in Eastern Europe', *The Economist*, 22 November 1997.

20. 'Companies Tap EE Luxury Goods Market', *Business Eastern Europe*, 28 April 1994, pp. 4–5.

21. Pervez Ghauri and Karin Holstius, 'The Role of Matching in the Foreign Market Entry Process in the Baltic States', *European Journal of Marketing*, vol. 30, no. 6, 1996, pp. 75–88.

22. John Naisbitt, *Megatrends Asia: Eight Asian Megatrends that are Reshaping Our World* (New York: Simon and Schuster, 1996).

23. Jim Rohwer, *Asia Rising, Why America will Prosper while Asia's Economics Boom* (New York: Simon and Schuster, 1995).

24. 'As Japan Goes?' *The Economist*, 20 June 1998, pp. 17–18; and 'Three Futures for Japan', *The Economist*, 21 March 1998, pp. 29–30.

25. Dan Biers, 'Now in First World, Asia's Tigers Act Like It', *The Wall Street Journal*, 28 February 1995, p. A-15.

26. 'The China Connection', *Business Week*, 5 August 1996, pp. 32–35; and 'China's WTO Accession', *Far Eastern Economic Review*, 2 July 1998, p. 38.

27. 'America's Dose of Zinophobia, Japan-Bashing Used To Be a Popular Sport in America. Now It Is More Fashionable to Worry About China', *The Economist*, 29 March 1997, pp. 67–68.

28. China is divided into 23 provinces (including Taiwan) and 5 autonomous border regions. The provinces and autonomous regions are usually grouped into six large administrative regions: Northeastern Region, Northern Region (includes Beijing), Eastern Region (includes Shanghai), South Central Region, Southwestern Region, and the Northwestern Region. After Hong Kong's reversion to China, it is considered the seventh autonomous region.

29. 'China, Hong Kong, Taiwan', *Trade & Culture*, Winter 1993–94, pp. 52–56.

30. 'A Survey of China', *The Economist*, 8 March 1997.

31. Min Chen, *Asian Management Systems* (New York: Routledge, 1995).

32. 'Exploding with Wealth', *World Press Review*, April 1993, p. 32.

33. 'The China Connection', *Business Week*, 5 August 1996, pp. 32–33.

34. 'India's Political Struggle', *The Economist*, 5 April 1997, p. 66.

35. Harak Gala, 'India: Strategies for Dealing with an Emerging Giant', *Trade & Culture*, March–April 1995, pp. 37–38; and 'Silver Lining in India', *Business Week*, 1 June 1998, p. 35.

36. 'Ludia's Political Struggle', *The Economist*, 5 April 1997, p. 66.

37. Matt Moffett, 'Seeds of Reform: Key Finance Ministers in Latin America Are Old Harvard-MIT Pals', *The Wall Street Journal*, 1 August 1994, p. 1.

38. For a review of Argentina's economic progress, see Raul Granillo Ocampo, 'Don't Cry for Me—(in) Argentina!', *The International Economy*, May 1994, pp. 52–57.

39. 'NAFTA Success May Aid New Trade Accords', *The Wall Street Journal*, 13 June 1994, p. A-1.

40. Paul Magnusson, 'With Latin America Thriving, NAFTA Might Keep Marching South', *Business Week*, 24 July 1994, p. 20.

41. 'Down with the Rand', *The Economist*, 4 July 1998, pp. 43–44.

CHAPTER

10

Multinational Market Regions and Market Groups

Chapter Learning Objectives

What you should learn from Chapter 10

- The need for economic union and how current events are affecting that need.
- The impact of the Triad power on the future of international trade.
- Patterns of multinational cooperation.
- The evolution of the European Community (EC) to the European Union (EU).
- The evolving patterns of trade as Eastern Europe and the former republics of the USSR embrace a free-market system.
- The trade linkage of NAFTA and South America and its effect on other Latin American major trade areas.
- The development of trade within the Asian Pacific Rim.
- The increasing importance of emerging markets.
- Strategic implications of regional market groups.

During the last three decades an interest for regional integration in Europe, Asia and the Americas has increased. The difficulties faced in the General Agreement on Tariffs and Trade (GATT) in the Uruguay Round and the proliferation of regional arrangements have led to renewed interest for regional integration.[1]

Among the important global trends today is the evolution of the multinational market region—those groups of countries that seek mutual economic benefit from reducing intra-regional trade and tariff barriers. Organizational form varies widely among market regions, but the universal orientation of such multinational cooperation is economic benefit for the participants. Political and social benefits sometimes accrue, but the dominant motive for affiliation is economic. The world is awash in economic cooperative agreements as countries look for economic alliances to expand their access to free markets.

Regional economic cooperative agreements have been around since the end of World War II. The most successful has been the European Union (EU), the world's largest multinational market region and foremost example of economic cooperation.

Multinational market groups form large markets that provide potentially significant market opportunities for international business. When it became apparent that the EU was to achieve its long-term goal of a single European market, a renewed interest in economic cooperation was sparked. The European Economic Area (EEA), a 17-country alliance between the EU and remaining members of the European Free Trade Area (EFTA), became the world's largest single unified market. Canada, the United States and Mexico entered into a free-trade agreement to form the North American Free Trade Agreement (NAFTA).[2] Many countries in Latin America, Asia, Eastern Europe and elsewhere are either planning some form of economic cooperation or have entered into agreements. With the dissolution of the USSR (Soviet Union) and the independence of Eastern European countries, linkages among the independent states and republics are also forming. The Commonwealth of Independent States (CIS) is an initial attempt at realignment into an economic union of some of the Newly Independent States (NIS)—former republics of the USSR.[3] The growing trend of economic cooperation is increasing concerns about the effect of such cooperation on global competition. Governments and businesses are concerned that the EEA, NAFTA and other cooperative regional groups will become regional trading blocs without trade restrictions internally but with borders protected from outsiders.[4]

Three global regions—Europe, the Americas and the Asian Pacific Rim—are involved in forging a new economic order for trade and development that will dominate world markets for years to come. In Kenichi Ohmae's book, *Triad Power*, he points out that the global companies that will be Triad powers must have significant market positions in each of the Triad regions.[5] At the economic centre of each Triad region will be an economic industrial power: in the European Triad it is Germany, in the American Triad it is the United States, in the Asian Triad it is Japan. The Triad regions are the centres of economic activity that provide global companies with a concentration of sophisticated consumer- and capital-goods markets. Within each Triad region there are strong single-country markets and/or multi-country markets (such as the European Community) bound together by economic cooperative agreements. Much of the economic growth and development that will occur in these regions and make them such important markets will result from single countries being forged into thriving free-trade areas.

The focus of this chapter is on the various patterns of multinational cooperation and the strategic marketing implications of economic cooperation for marketing.

LA RAISON D'ÊTRE

Successful economic union requires favourable economic, political, cultural and geographic factors as a basis for success. Major flaws in any one factor can destroy a union unless the other factors provide sufficient strength to overcome the weaknesses. In general, the advantages of economic union must be clear cut and significant, and the benefits must greatly outweigh the disadvantages before nations forego any part of their sovereignty. A strong threat to the economic or political security of a nation is often needed to provide the impetus for cooperation. The cooperative agreements among European countries that preceded the European Community (EC) certainly had their roots in the need for economic redevelopment after World War II. Many felt that if Europe was to survive there had to be economic unity; the agreements made then formed the groundwork for the European Community.

Economic Factors.   Every type of economic union shares the development and enlargement of market opportunities as a basic orientation; usually markets are enlarged through preferential tariff treatment for participating members and/or common tariff barriers against outsiders. Enlarged, protected markets stimulate internal economic development by providing assured outlets and preferential treatment for goods produced within the customs union, and consumers benefit from lower internal tariff barriers among the participating countries. In many cases, external as well as internal barriers are reduced because of the greater economic security afforded domestic producers by the enlarged market.

Nations with complementary economic bases are least likely to encounter frictions in the development and operation of a common market unit. However, for an economic union to survive, it must have in place agreements and mechanisms to settle economic disputes. In addition, the total benefit of economic integration must outweigh individual differences that are sure to arise as member countries adjust to new trade relationships. The European Union includes countries with diverse economies, distinctive monetary systems, developed agricultural bases and different natural resources. It is significant that most of the problems encountered by the EU have arisen over agriculture and monetary policy. In the early days of the EU, agricultural disputes were common. The British attempted to keep French poultry out of the British market, France banned Italian wine and the Irish banned eggs and poultry from other member countries. More recently, the EU, not any one country, banned British beef because of the BSE disease (also called 'mad cow disease') of British animals and its linkages with the human disease Creutzfeldt–Jakob disease (CJD). In all cases, the reason given was health and safety, but the probable motive, at least in some cases, was the continuation of the age-old policy of market protection. Such skirmishes are not unusual, but they do test the strength of the union.

The demise of the Latin American Free Trade Association (LAFTA) was caused, in part, by its economically stronger members not allowing for the needs of the weaker ones. Many of the less well-known attempts at common markets have languished because of economic incompatibility that could not be resolved and the uncertainty of future economic advantage.

Political Factors.   Political amenability among countries is another basic requisite for development of a supranational market arrangement. Participating countries must have comparable aspirations and general compatibility before surrendering any part of their national sovereignty. State sovereignty is one of the most cherished possessions of any nation and is relinquished only for a promise of significant improvement of the national position through cooperation.

Economic considerations provide the basic catalyst for the formation of a customs union group, but political elements are equally important. The uniting of the original European Community countries was partially a response to American dominance and threat of Russia's great political power; the countries of Western Europe were willing to settle their family squabbles to present a unified front. The communist threat no longer exists, but the importance of political unity to fully achieve all the benefits of economic integration has driven the EC countries to form the European Union.[6]

Geographic Proximity.   Although it is not absolutely imperative that cooperating members of a customs union have geographic proximity, such closeness facilitates the functioning of a common market. Transportation networks basic to any marketing system are likely to be interrelated and well developed when countries are close together. One of the first major strengths of the EC was its transportation network: the opening of the tunnel between England and France and a bridge between Denmark and Sweden further bound this common market. Countries that are widely separated geographically have major barriers to overcome in attempting economic fusion.

Cultural Factors.   Cultural similarity eases the shock of economic cooperation with other countries. The more similar the cultures, the more likely a market is to succeed because members understand the outlook and viewpoints of their colleagues. Although there is great cultural diversity in the EU, key members share a long-established Christian heritage and are commonly aware of being European.

Language, as a part of culture, has not created as much a barrier for EU countries as was expected. Initially there were seven major languages, but such linguistic diversity did not impede trade because European businesses historically have been multilingual. Nearly every educated European can do business in at least two or three languages; thus, in every relationship, there is likely to be a linguistic common ground. Now even countries such as France, Germany and Italy are switching over to English as a language of trade and science. A number of business schools and universities in these countries are now offering MBAs and other degree programmes in English. This was unthinkable even a decade ago.

PATTERNS OF MULTINATIONAL COOPERATION

Multinational market groups take several forms, varying significantly in the degree of cooperation, dependence and interrelationship among participating nations. There are five fundamental groupings for regional economic integration ranging from regional cooperation for development, which requires the least amount of integration, to the ultimate of integration, political union.

Regional Cooperation Groups.   The most basic economic integration and cooperation is the regional cooperation for development (RCD). In the RCD arrangement, governments agree to participate jointly to develop basic industries beneficial to each economy. Each country makes an advance commitment to participate in the financing of a new joint venture and to purchase a specified share of the output of the venture. An example is the project between Colombia and Venezuela to build a hydroelectric generating plant on the Orinoco River. They shared jointly in construction costs and they share the electricity produced.

Free-Trade Area.   A free-trade area (FTA) requires more cooperation and integration than the RCD. It is an agreement among two or more countries to reduce or eliminate

PURE GERMAN SAUSAGE BRINGS OUT WURST IN EUROPEAN UNION

A widespread suspicion among many Europeans is that many of the local-country regulations are simply disguised trade restrictions. There has been a concerted effort on the part of the European Commission to eliminate trade barriers and make the EU a true common market. The problem becomes one of deciding when restrictions are really protection of health and tradition or just more roadblocks. Consider the case for bratwurst.

At Eduard Kluehspie's snack bar in a corner of the Viktualienmarkt in Munich, the talk has turned to sausage, but not the plump and juicy bratwurst, brockwurst or currywurst that are served together with a slice of bread and a dollop of sweet Bavarian mustard. Today, the regulars are contemplating something that is totally indigestible—something less than pure German wurst.

The European Union is upset about stringent German rules that define what may or may not be put into sausage. For generations, Germans have insisted in keeping their sausage more or less pure by limiting the amount of nonmeat additives such as vegetable fat and protein. But EU bureaucrats and other European sausage-makers see the regulations as a clever German plot to keep out imports, and they are demanding change. This causes dismay among the beer-drinking regulars at the snack bar. 'I'd rather eat my dog', says one grumpy local.

Not only wurst but beer, which Bavarians call 'liquid bread', is under attack. The EU had to go to court to get Germany to drop its 'Reinheitsgebot', a medieval decree stipulating that beer may be brewed only with malt, hops, water, and yeast. It kept the beer 'pure' and just incidentally kept most other beers out of Germany.

Source: Adapted from Peter Gumbel, 'Pure German Sausage Brings Out Wurst in European Community', *The Wall Street Journal*, 9 September 1985, p. 24. Reprinted by permission of The Wall Street Journal, © 1985 Dow Jones & Company, Inc. All Rights Reserved Worldwide.

customs duties and nontariff trade barriers among partner countries while members maintain individual tariff schedules for external countries. Essentially, an FTA provides its members with a mass market without barriers that impede the flow of goods and services. The United States has free-trade agreements with Canada and Mexico (NAFTA) and separately with Israel. The seven-nation European Free-Trade Association (EFTA), among the better-known free-trade areas, still exists although three of its members also belong to the EU and five to the EEA.

Customs Union.   A customs union represents the next stage in economic cooperation. It enjoys the free-trade area's reduced or eliminated internal tariffs and adds a common external tariff on products imported from countries outside the union. The customs union is a logical stage of cooperation in the transition from an FTA to a common market. The European Community was a customs union before becoming a common market. Customs unions exist between France and Monaco, Italy and San Marino, and Switzerland and Liechtenstein.

Common Market.   A common market agreement eliminates all tariffs and other restrictions on internal trade, adopts a set of common external tariffs, and removes all restriction on the free flow of capital and labour among member nations. Thus a common market is a common marketplace for goods as well as for services (including labour) and for capital. It is a unified economy and lacks only political unity to become a political union.

Table 10.1   European Trade Areas

European Community (EC)		European Free Trade Association (EFTA)	
Belgium	Italy	Iceland	Norway
Denmark	Luxembourg	Liechtenstein	Switzerland
France	The Netherlands		
Germany	Portugal		
Greece	Spain		
Ireland	United Kingdom		

European Union (EU)		European Economic Area (EEA)	
EEC Countries and		EC Countries and	
Austria		Austria	Poland[a]
Finland		Finland	Hungary[b]
Sweden		Iceland	
		Norway	
		Sweden	

[a]Awaiting membership; [b]Seeking membership

Political Union.   Political union is the most fully integrated form of regional cooperation. It involves complete political and economic integration; it may be voluntary or enforced. The most notable enforced political union was the Council for Mutual Economic Assistance (COMECON), a centrally controlled group of countries organized by the USSR. With the dissolution of the USSR and the independence of Eastern Europe, COMECON was disbanded.

The Commonwealth of Nations is a voluntary organization providing for the loosest possible relationship that can be classified as economic integration. The British Commonwealth is comprised of Britain and countries formerly part of the British Empire. Its members recognize the British monarch as their symbolic head although Britain has no political authority over the Commonwealth. Its member states had received preferential tariffs when trading with Great Britain but, when Britain joined the European Community, all preferential tariffs were abandoned. The Commonwealth can best be described as the weakest of political unions and is mostly based on economic history and a sense of tradition. Heads of state meet every three years to discuss trade and political issues they jointly face, and compliance with any decisions or directives issued is voluntary.

GLOBAL MARKETS AND MULTINATIONAL MARKET GROUPS

The globalization of markets, the restructuring of Eastern Europe into independent market-driven economies, the dissolution of the Soviet Union into independent states, the worldwide trend towards economic cooperation, and enhanced global competition make it important that market potential be viewed in the context of regions of the world rather than country by country. Formal economic cooperation agreements such as the EC are the most notable examples of multinational market groups, but many new coalitions are forming, old ones are restructuring and the possibility of many new cooperative arrangements is on the horizon.

This section presents basic information and data on markets and market groups in Europe, the Americas, Africa, Asia and the Middle East. Existing economic cooperation agreements

Map 10.1   The European Economic Area: EU, EFTA and Associates

within each of these regions will be reviewed. The reader must appreciate that the status of cooperative agreements and alliances among nations has been extremely fluid in some parts of the world. Many are fragile and may cease to exist or may restructure into a totally different form. It will probably take the better part of a decade for many of the new trading alliances that are now forming to stabilize into semipermanent groups.

EUROPE

The European Union is the focus of the European region of the first Triad. Within Europe, every type of multinational market grouping exists. The European Union (EU), European Community (EC), European Economic Area (EEA) and the European Free Trade Association (EFTA) are the most-established cooperative groups (see Table 10.1 and Map 10.1).

Of escalating economic importance are the fledgling capitalist economies of Eastern Europe, such as Poland, Hungary and the Czech Republic, and the three Baltic states that gained independence from the USSR just prior to its breakup. Key issues centre around their economic development and eventual economic alliance with the EU.

Also within the European region is the Commonwealth of Independent States. New and untested, this coalition of 12 former USSR republics may or may not survive in its present form to take its place among the other multinational market groups.

European Union

The idea of a united Europe is centuries old, from the Roman empire to the empire of Charlemagne in the early 19th century or even to the idea of a Catholic Europe with a pope at its head, all aimed at an integrated Europe. At the third Universal Peace Congress in 1849, Victor Hugo officially presented the idea of the United States of Europe. World War I, with all its senseless bloodshed, brought about a review of the idea of a united Europe. During this period, Count Coudenhove-Kalergi, who was of Greek and Dutch descent, but was an Austro-Hungarian diplomat, started a Pan-European Union. He got support from a number of prominent political figures such as Aristide Briand, the French foreign minister, who presented a scheme to the League of Nations in the 1920s for a European Union.

World War II finally stimulated the idea of European integration. A group of European politicians worked on the idea with Jean Monet, who is often called 'Father of Europe', at its head. In addition to being a French diplomat, Monet had been the deputy secretary general of the League of Nations in the interwar years.[7]

Figure 10.1 illustrates the evolution of the EU from its beginnings after World War II to today. In 1951, six European states (France, West Germany, Italy, The Netherlands, Belgium and Luxembourg) signed the Treaty of Paris to establish the European Coal and Steel Community (ECSC). It was the forerunner of the European Community. In 1955, delegates from ECSC states met at Messina in Italy and agreed to form the European Economic Community (EEC), and in March 1957 the Treaty of Rome, formally setting up the EEC, was signed. The purpose was to achieve a customs union of the six countries and by 1969 abolish all tariffs on their mutual trade. The Treaty of Rome had three major political objectives: political unity, peace and democracy. Other objectives included integration, improvement of living standards and encouragement of trade with other countries.[8]

The European Union was created when the 12 nations of the European Community ratified the Maastricht Treaty. The members committed themselves to economic and political integration. The treaty allows for the free movement of goods, persons, services and capital throughout the member states, a common currency, common foreign and security policies, including defence, a common justice system and cooperation between police and other authorities on crime, terrorism and immigration issues. However, not all the provisions of the treaty have been universally accepted. The dismantling of border controls to permit passport-free movement between countries according to the Schengen agreement, signed in Schengen (Luxembourg) in 1995, for example, has been implemented by only 7 out of 15 EU member states.[9]

Of all the multinational market groups, none is more secure in its cooperation or more important economically than the European Union. From its beginning, it has successfully made progress towards achieving the goal of complete economic integration and, ultimately, political union. For a list of EU member countries and related economic data (see Table 10.2).

Historically, standards were used to limit market access effectively. Germany protected its

Figure 10.1   European Coal and Steel Community to European Union

1951	Treaty of Paris	European Coal and Steel Community (ECSC) (Founding members are Belgium, France, Germany, Italy, Luxembourg and the Netherlands)
1957	Treaty of Rome	Blueprint for European Economic Community (EEC)
1958	European Economic Community	Ratified by ECSC founding members. Common Market is established
1960	European Free-Trade Area	Established by Austria, Denmark, Norway, Portugal, Sweden, Switzerland and United Kingdom
1973	Expansion	Denmark, Ireland and United Kingdom join EEC
1979	European Monetary System	The European Currency Unit (ECU) is created. All members except the UK agree to maintain their exchange rates within specific margins
1981	Expansion	Greece joins EEC
1985	1992 Single Market Programme	Introduced to European Parliament 'White Paper' for action
1986	Expansion	Spain and Portugal join EEC
1987	Single European Act	Ratified with full implementation by 1992
1992	Treaty on European Union	Also known as Maastricht Treaty. Blueprint for Economic and Monetary Union (EMU)
1993	Europe 1992	Single European Act in force (1 January 1993)
1993	European Union	Treaty on European Union (Maastricht Treaty) in force with monetary union by 1999
1994	European Economic Area	The EEA was formed with EU members and Norway and Iceland
1995	Expansion	Austria, Finland and Sweden join EU
1997	Amsterdam Treaty	Established procedures for expansion to Central and Eastern Europe
1999	Monetary Union	Euro replaces all national banknotes and coins of EMU members

Source: 'Chronology of the EU', http://www.europa.eu.int/ (select Abc). Reprinted with permission from the European Communities.

beer market from the rest of Europe with a purity law requiring beer sold in Germany to be brewed only from water, hops, malt and yeast. Italy protected its pasta market by requiring that pasta be made only from durum wheat. Incidentally, both the beer and pasta regulations have been struck down by the European Court of Justice as trade violations. Such restrictive standards effectively kept competing products out of their respective markets whether from other European countries or elsewhere. Sceptics, doubtful that such cultural, legal and social differences could ever be overcome, held little hope for a unified Europe. Their scepticism has proved wrong. Today, many marvel at how far the European Union has come.[10]

WHEN ECU PLUS EMU EQUALS EURO

What will really happen when the Euro takes over from the ECU? What, apart from a few letters, distinguishes the Euro-currency of today?

First and foremost, the Euro will be a retail currency. It will replace the deutschmarks, francs, punts and guilders in your pocket, in your bank accounts and on your bills. Money earned in France, The Netherlands or the Irish Republic will be the common currency elsewhere, available to buy goods or invest in Germany vice versa. There will be Euro notes and Euro coins.

Nowhere in Europe is the ECU a domestic currency in this sense. The ECU is a weighted basket of currencies, and its principal use is in calculating the EU budget, raising levies and distributing funds (which are translated into domestic currencies). For every European domestic economy, the ECU is in effect a foreign currency, used to specify a super-national budget.

The Euro will replace the ECU in this role as well as replacing the domestic currencies of those countries that opt for monetary union. This handover from domestic central banks to the European Central Bank will be unprecedented and its danger is real.

The ECU's value and integrity will be supervised by the successor to the European Monetary Institute, which will be called the European Central Bank. (In Eurospeak: the EMI will be replaced by the ECB.) As a reflection of the weight of the German economy within Europe and of the success of the Bundesbank and the deutschmark since the Second World War, the ECB will be located in Frankfurt.

It is vital that the Euro is a sound, stable currency like the deutschmark. A sound deutschmark was a precondition for stable government in Germany after the searing experience of hyper inflation. In recent years, the strength of the deutschmark has become a source of reassurance. To people of the former East Germany, the very presence of such a currency—capable of buying things—was a reproach to the entire communist system. On the day financial unification occurred, queues of several kilometres formed on the Berlin Alexanderplatz as people waited to convert their savings into deutschmarks, real money.

Currently, the ECU has a real presence in the wholesale money and debt markets. It is here that monetary union will happen with the greatest ease and greatest speed. Almost all European governments, including the UK, have issued eco-denominated bonds. All currencies are tradable into ECUs; almost all forms of financial instruments are found in ECUs. And it is possible to buy ECU-denominated investments in equities and bonds.

The advent of the Euro will vastly enhance this presence. All of these instruments will be converted into Euros, as will the national debt of the participating nations. Assuming that Germany, France, The Netherlands, Belgium and Luxembourg enter into monetary union on 1 January 1999, the Euro will instantly become one of the world's great currencies, ranking alongside the dollar and the yen. Backed by the government guarantees and massive economic transactions, it will be traded everywhere, in every form, across the world. Its psychological effect—on the consumer and commerce—has yet to be gauged; yet it is clear it will be simply enormous. Small wonder that some anti-Europeans fear that the Euro will lead to a federal Europe. Others will fear becoming like the good citizens of the former East Germany—all the poorer for being excluded.

Source: *The European*, 1–7 August 1996, p. 17.

The Single European Act.   Europe without borders, Fortress Europe and EC 92 refer to the Single European Act—the agreement designed to finally remove all barriers to trade and make the European Community a single internal market. The ultimate goal of the Treaty of Rome, the agreement that founded the EC, was economic and political union, a United States of Europe. The Single European Act moved the EC one step closer to the goal of economic integration.

Table 10.2   European Market Regions

Association	Member	Population (millions)	GDP (US$ billions)	GDP per Capita (US$)	Imports (US$ millions)
European	Belgium	10.0	$218.9	$21 890	$124 952*
Community	Denmark	5.2	141.4	27 552	33 631
(EC)	France	57.4	1 321.8	23 040	239 239
	Germany	64.7	1 813.6	28 031	407 952
	Greece	10.3	77.9	7 562	23 152
	Ireland	3.6	50.3	14 156	22 478
	Italy	56.8	1 223.0	21 539	190 681
	Luxembourg	0.4	12.1	31 096	124 952*
	The Netherlands	15.2	320.3	21 098	130 341
	Portugal	9.9	84.2	8 546	30 193
	Spain	39.0	573.1	14 666	98 617
	United Kingdom	57.9	1 064.6	18 403	220 865
European	EC Countries	330.4	6 901.2	20 902	1 522 101
Union (EU)	Austria	7.9	185.2	23 508	54 171
	Finland	5.0	106.2	21 071	21 205
	Sweden	8.7	246.7	28 418	49 782
Central	Czech Republic	10.3	28.4	2 757	12 681
European	Hungary	10.3	35.4	3 435	11 066
Free-Trade	Poland	38.4	83.6	2 178	21 549
Area (CEFTA)	Slovakia	5.3	9.3	1 763	3 900

*Includes Luxembourg and Belgium.
Source: 'Indicators of Market Size for 115 Countries', *Crossborder Monitor*, 31 August 1994.

In addition to dismantling the existing barriers, the Single European Act proposed a wide range of new commercial policies including single European standards, one of the more difficult and time-consuming goals to achieve. Technical standards for electrical products is a good example of how overwhelming the task of achieving universal standards is. There are 29 types of electrical outlet, 10 types of plugs and 12 types of cords used by EU member countries. The estimated cost for all EU countries to change wiring systems and electrical standards to a single European standard is 80 billion European Currency Units (ECUs), or about 95 billion US dollars. Because of the time it will take to achieve uniform Eurostandards for health, safety, technical and other areas, the Single European Act provides for a policy of harmonization and mutual recognition.

Mutual recognition extends beyond technical or health standards and includes mutual recognition for marketing practices as well. The European Court of Justice's (ECJ) interpretation of Article 30, which establishes the principle of mutual recognition, is that a product put on sale legally in one member state should be available for sale in the same way in all others. The ECJ's landmark decision involved Germany's ban on the sale of Cassis de Dijon, a French liqueur. Germany claimed that selling the low-alcohol drink would encourage alcohol consumption, considered by authorities to be unhealthy. The Court of Justice rejected the argument, ruling that the restriction represented a nontariff barrier outlawed by Article 30. In other words, once Cassis de Dijon was legally sold in France, Germany was obligated, under mutual recognition, to allow its sale in Germany.[11]

Table 10.3   Top 10 Lobbying Consultancies in Europe

Consultancy	Created	Staff	Parent company	Branches
Hill & Knowlton	1967	28	WPP, UK	30 cities in Europe, 35 worldwide
GPC Government Policy Consultants	1988	28	Omnicom, US	London, Edinburgh, associate agencies all over Europe except Luxembourg and Austria
Apco Europe	1995	20	Gray Advertising, US	(With GCI) All EU member states; Washington DC, Seattle, Sacramento, Beijing, Hong Kong, Moscow
Adamson Associates	1981	16	Independent, Belgium	Geneva, Strasbourg
European Public Policy Advisers	1987	16	Private shareholders international	Austria, Belgium, Czech Republic, Finland, France, Hungary, The Netherlands, Norway, Poland, Portugal, Russia, Spain, Sweden, UK, Germany, US (with International Trade Advisers), associated offices in Ireland, Denmark, Italy, Greece
European Strategy	1990	12	Grayling Group, UK	All EU countries (except Portugal, Greece, Austria); NY
Edelman Europe	1995	10	Edelman Public Relations Worldwide, US	Nine offices in Europe, 26 in the Americas and Asia/Pacific region
Robinson, Linton and Associates	1989	9	Burson-Marsteller, US	Uses the Burson-Marsteller network (most European countries, US and Russia)
Entente International Communication	1991	6	Private shareholders	All 15 EU member states, associated offices in other countries
Charles Barker BSMG	1990	3	BSMG, US	UK

Source: Based on *The European* and *Marketing News*, several issues, 1998.

Food definition problems in particular have impeded progress in guaranteeing free circulation of food products within the EU. For example, several member states maintain different definitions of yoghurt. The French insist that anything called *yogurt* must contain live cultures; thus, they prohibited the sale of a Dutch product under the name *yoghurt* because it did not contain live cultures as does the French product. In March 1996, the European Commission decided that only goat's-milk or ewe's-milk cheese produced in Greece was entitled to be called feta. The ruling brought storms of protest from Danes, who now have five years to rename their cow's-milk feta. Greeks have a solid claim of name, backed by a thousand years of history.[12]

Some of the first and most welcome reforms were the single customs document that replaced the 70 forms originally required for transborder shipments to member countries, the elimination of cabotage rules (they kept a trucker from returning with a loaded truck after

GOING INTERNATIONAL 10.3

EURO COUNTDOWN

2–3 May 1998:
Governments picked the EMU members countries: Austria, Belgium, Finland, France, Germany, Ireland, Italy, Luxembourg, The Netherlands, Portugal and Spain. Sweden, Denmark and the UK decided not to join at this point. Greece was not allowed to join.

1 January 1999:
The European Central Bank takes over the monetary policy. National currencies remain, but stocks and government debt will be denominated in euros. Bank accounts, credit cards and prices begin to be measured in euros. Companies start accounting in euros.

1 January 2002:
The euro physically begins to replace national currencies. Retail payments are allowed only in euros.

1 July 2002:
National currencies cease to exist and are replaced by the euro in the EMU countries.

Sources: *Business Week*, 27 April 1998, p. 29; *The European*, 2–8 March 1998, p. 7; see also Figure 10.2.

delivery), and EU-wide transport licensing. These changes alone were estimated to have reduced distribution costs 50 per cent for companies doing cross-border business in the EU.

EU Structure.   The European Union was created as a result of three treaties that established the European Coal and Steel Community, The European Economic Community and the European Atomic Energy Community. These three treaties are incorporated within the European Union and serve as the community's constitution. They provide a policy framework and empower the commission and the Council of Ministers to pass laws to carry out EU policy. The union uses three legal instruments: (1) regulations binding the member states directly and having the same strength as national laws; (2) directives also binding the member states but allowing them to choose the means of execution; and (3) decisions addressed to a government, an enterprise or an individual binding the parties named.

EU Authority.   Over the years, the European Union has gained an increasing amount of authority over its member states. The Union's institutions (the European Commission, the Council of Ministers, the European Parliament and the European Court of Justice) and their decision-making processes have legal status and extensive powers in fields covered by common policies. Union institutions have the power to make decisions and execute policies in specific areas. They form a federal pattern with executive, parliamentary and judicial branches. A number of private consultant companies specialize in lobbying the different EU institutions (see Table 10.3).

■ The European Commission is a 17-member group (EEA-group) that initiates policy and supervises its observance by member states. It proposes and supervises execution of laws and policies. The Commission has a president and four vice presidents; each of its members is appointed for a four-year term by mutual agreement of EU governments. Commission members act only in the interest of the EU. They may not receive instructions from any national government and are subject to the supervision of the European Parliament. Their

Figure 10.2   Planned Timetable for the Introduction of the Euro

1994	EMI established			
1995	Madrid changeover scenario agreed			
1996	Conversion reports produced by Commission and EMI	Dublin Summit: stability pact, ERM 2, regulations on the euro		**STAGE 2**
1997	Year for which convergence data is assessed	Regulatory, organizational and logistical framework for ESCB published by EMI	Target testing begins	
1998	Participating member states chosen	ECB established	Operational decisions by ECB, testing of systems	
1999	Irrevocable locking of conversion rates; euro becomes a currency in its own right; single monetary policy commences; ECB operations and new issues of government debt all denominated in euro; wholesale financial activity expected to move rapidly to euro denomination			**STAGE 3A** *No compulsion/ no prohibition in usage of euro;*
2000				*National bank notes and coins remain legal tender*
2001	Latest date for introduction of euro bank notes and coins; beginning of mass changeover of retail activity to euro; end of legal transition period			
2002	Dual legal tender period	Bulk of public administration changeover	Latest date for withdrawal of legal tender status of national banknotes and coins	**STAGE 3B**

Source: Based on Bank of England and *The Times*, 25 March 1997, p. 31.

responsibilities are to ensure that EU rules and the principles of the common market are respected.

■ The **Council of Ministers,** one from each member country, passes laws based on commission proposals. Because the council is the decision-making body of the EU, it is their responsibility to debate and decide which proposals of the Single European Act to accept as binding on EU members. In concert with the commission's white paper, the Single European Act included the first and only amendment of the original Treaty of Rome (1957), that streamlined decision making. Under provisions in the act, the council can enact into law many of the proposals in the white paper by majority vote instead of the unanimity formerly required. Requiring only a majority vote by the council for passage of reforms was seen as a necessary change if the Single European Act was to be a reality. However, proposals for changes in tax rates on products and services still require a unanimous vote.

■ The **European Parliament** has 518 members elected every five years by universal suffrage. It is mainly a consultative body which passes on most community legislation with

OH, LIFE WOULD BE EASIER IF WE ONLY HAD A EUROPLUG

Those of you who have travelled within Europe know of the frustration with electrical plugs and other annoyances of international travel. But consider the cost to consumers and the inefficiency of production for a company that wishes to sell electrical appliances in the European 'Common' Market.

Philips, the electrical appliance manufacturer, has to produce 12 kinds of irons to serve just its European market. The problem is that Europe does not have a universal standard. The ends of domestic iron leads bristle with different plugs for different countries. Some have three prongs, others two; prongs protrude straight or angled, round or rectangular, fat, thin and sometimes sheathed. There are circular plug faces, squares, pentagons and hexagons. Some are perforated and some are notched. One French plug has a niche like a keyhole; British plugs carry fuses.

Europe's plugs and sockets are balkanized partly because different countries have different voltages and cycles. But the variety of standards also has other causes, such as protecting local manufacturers. Estimated cost for lack of universal standards is between $60 (€54) and $80 (€72) billion a year or nearly 3 per cent of the EC's total output of goods and services.

Unfortunately, there is little hope for a universal system to replace the 20 varieties of plugs in Europe and 50 around the world soon. The International Electro-Technical Commission committee has worked for more than 20 years on a design acceptable to all. Two universal standards are needed, one for the 250-volt system and one for the 125-volt system. Two standards have been proposed for the 250-volt system, but a universal 125-volt plug and socket system is still being negotiated with no apparent agreement in sight.

By the end of 1996 the EU had 6 different plugs and a common consensus was that if the nations of Europe cannot agree on something as useful as a common plug, how can they be expected to come up with a single currency and a common foreign policy.

Sources: Adapted from 'Philips Finds Obstacles to Intra-Europe Trade Are Costly, Inefficient', *The Wall Street Journal*, 7 August 1985, p. 1; Karin Davies, 'Quest for Universal Plug-and-Socket System Hardly Shocking', The Associated Press, 31 May 1994; and *The European*, 21–30 October, 1996, p. 21.

---

limited but gradually increasing budgetary powers. The Single European Act gave parliament greater powers.[13] After legislation has gone through two readings, parliament has the right on the second reading to put forward detailed alterations and amendments that, if accepted by the commission, can be rejected only by the member states and a unanimous vote of the Council of Ministers. Parliament can now influence legislation but it does not have the power to initiate legislation.

■ The European Court of Justice (ECJ) consists of 13 judges and is the Community's supreme court. Its first responsibility is challenging any measures incompatible with the Treaty of Rome when they are adopted by the commission, council or national governments. Its second responsibility is passing judgement, at the request of a national court, on interpretation or validity of points of EU law. The court's decisions are final and cannot be appealed in national courts. The Court of Justice has increased its presence in the last decade and has become very important in enforcing Union laws and regulations.

Court decisions are binding on EU members; through its judgements and interpretations, the court is helping to create a body of truly EU law that will apply to all EU institutions, member states, national courts and private citizens. Judgements of the court, in the field of EU law, overrule those of national courts. For example, the court overruled Germany's consumer protection rules that had served as a major trade barrier. Historically, German law

NO ONE SAID SETTING PRODUCT STANDARDS WOULD BE EASY

Let us now consider an issue that cuts to the very core of European economic unity. An issue that divided nations for decades took heroic efforts to resolve, and is still chewed over in conference after conference. We're talking about strawberry jam.

First, some background. The Dutch spread jam on bread for breakfast, so they like it smooth and sugary. Most Frenchmen, however, wouldn't touch smooth jam with a barge pole, much less a butter knife. They commonly eat their jam straight from the jar with a spoon and they like it lumpy and fruity. The European Community has been wrangling for more than a quarter century over the myriad bits and pieces of an issue absolutely essential to free trade throughout Europe: the development of product standards acceptable to all. The jam case and others like it (it took 14 years to set standards for toys) illustrates, in a small way, the difficulties negotiators have had to face and still face in creating a unified Europe.

The negotiators spent years getting the Dutch, who wanted more sugar in their jam, and the French, who wanted more fruit, to compromise. But just as that happened, Britain, Europe's largest jam consumer, joined the EC and tossed a monkey wrench into the works.

Its name was marmalade. It seems that low-quality jam in much of continental Europe was called marmalade, a confusion Britain refused to tolerate. After 20 years of haggling, everyone finally agreed what jam was and what should be in it, and the Eurocrats proudly unveiled a jam standard. Then, the French, who have been eating jam since the 13th century and who are extremely picky about it, decided to meditate on the matter for an additional four years.

It did not escape the Eurocrats that it had taken 25 years to decide on jam. At that rate, it could take centuries of nit-picking to do something for the many thousands of other products involved in European trade. Indeed, agreement on some of them simply couldn't be reached; the EC had to give up entirely on mayonnaise, sausage and beer because European tastes were so widely different.

Finally, an EC expert devised a brilliant shortcut. They would be content with setting basic health and safety standards, matters much easier to agree on than such issues as exactly how much nonmeat could be slipped into a sausage before it no longer deserved the name.

Source: 'Sticky Solutions: As Europeans Try to Set Standards, a Jar of Jam Becomes a Pandora's Box', *The Wall Street Journal*, 22 September 1989, p. B-1. Reprinted by permission of The Wall Street Journal, © Dow Jones & Company, Inc. All Rights Reserved Worldwide.

has frowned on, if not prohibited, any product advertising that implies medicinal benefits. Estée Lauder Cosmetics was prevented, by German courts, from selling one of its products under the name 'Clinique'. Germany claimed the name would mislead German consumers, causing them to associate the product with medical treatment. The European Court of Justice (ECJ) pointed out that the product is sold in other member states under the 'Clinique' name without confusing the consumer. Further, if the German court ruling against Estée Lauder was left to stand, it would make it difficult for companies to market their products across borders in an identical manner and thus increase the cost of advertising and packaging for the company and ultimately for the consumer.[14] This is but one example of the ECJ's power in the EU and its role in eliminating nontariff trade barriers.

The Maastricht Treaty and European Union.   The final step in the European Community's march to union was ratification of the Maastricht Treaty. The treaty provided for the Economic and Monetary Union (EMU) and European Union (EU). Under the EMU agreement, in 1998 the EU has created a European Central Bank and introduced fixed exchange rates and a single currency.[15]

Initially, there was considerable doubt about the viability of a European Union. Surrendering more sovereignty beyond that already relinquished with the provisions of the Single European Act seemed too extreme for many. Denmark and the United Kingdom were the last to ratify the treaty. Despite some last-minute hesitation, Denmark approved the treaty on a second vote, and later, with the UK's approval, the European Union became a reality, on paper at least. Within months of the ratification of the treaty, the EU was expanded when Austria, Finland and Sweden, members of the EEA, became members of the EU in 1995. Norway voted not to join the EU but will remain as a member of the European Economic Area.[16]

European Economic Area (EEA).   Because of the success of the EC and concern that they might be left out of the massive European market, five members of the European Free Trade Association (EFTA) elected to join the 12 members of the EC in 1994 to form the European Economic Area (EEA), a single market with free movement of goods, services and capital.[17] The five EFTA countries joining the EEA adopted most of the EC's competition rules and agreed to implement EC rules on company law; however, they maintain their domestic farm policies. The EEA is governed by a special Council of Ministers composed of representatives from EEA member nations.

With nearly 400 million consumers and a gross national product of €6.3 trillion ($7 trillion), the EEA is the world's largest consumer market, eclipsing the United States even after the formation of the North American Free Trade Agreement. The EEA is a middle ground for those countries that want to be part of the EU's single internal market but do not want to go directly into the EU as full members or do not meet the requirements for full membership. Of the five founding EFTA members of EEA, three joined the EU in 1995. Iceland and Norway chose not to become EU members with the other EFTA countries but will remain members of the EEA. Of the other EFTA members, Switzerland voted against joining the EEA but has formally requested membership in the EU, and Liechtenstein has not joined the EEA or requested admission to the EU. The EEA will probably be the first step for economic unification between the EU and Eastern European countries and perhaps some of the Newly Independent States. Formal requests for membership in the EEA[18] by Poland and Hungary are more than likely to be granted.

European Free-Trade Association (EFTA)

The European Free-Trade Association was conceived by the United Kingdom as a counterpart to the EC before it became a member of the EC. The original members of EFTA were Austria, Denmark, Norway, Portugal, Sweden, Switzerland and the United Kingdom. Iceland became a member in 1970, Finland in 1986, and Liechtenstein in 1991. As discussed earlier, several EFTA countries joined EC countries to form the European Economic Area, and of the original members six went on to join the EU: the United Kingdom and Denmark in 1972, Portugal in 1986, Austria, Finland and Sweden in 1995. The present members of EFTA are: Iceland, Liechtenstein, Norway and Switzerland. EFTA will most probably dissolve as its members either join the EEA or the EU.

The Commonwealth of Independent States (CIS)

The series of events after the aborted coup against Mikhail Gorbachov led to the complete dissolution of the USSR. The first to declare independence were the Baltic states, which quickly gained recognition by several Western nations. The remaining 12 republics of the

Map 10.2   The Newly Independent States (NIS)

former USSR,[19] collectively known as the Newly Independent States (NIS), regrouped into the Commonwealth of Independent States (CIS). (See Map 10.2.)

The CIS is a loose economic and political alliance with open borders but no central government. The main provisions of the commonwealth agreement are to (1) repeal all Soviet laws and assume the powers of the old regimes, (2) launch radical economic reforms, including freeing most prices, (3) keep the rouble, but allow new currencies, (4) establish a European Community-style free-trade association, (5) create joint control of nuclear weapons and (6) fulfil all Soviet foreign treaties and debt obligations.

The 12 members of the CIS share a common history of central planning, and their close cooperation could make the change to a market economy less painful, but differences over economic policy, currency reform and control of the military may break them apart. How the CIS will be organized and its ultimate importance is anyone's guess.

The three Slavic republics of Russia, the Ukraine and Belarus have interests and history in common, as do the five Central Asian Republics. But the ties between these two core groups of the CIS are tenuous and stem mainly from their former Soviet membership. The three Slavic republics are discussing the establishment of an organization modelled on the European Union to succeed the Commonwealth of Independent States. Kazakhstan and other former Soviet republics may join, which would create a trade bloc that includes most of the former Soviet Union. Moscow would dominate because Russia far outweighs the others in military might and economic resources.[20]

Central European Free-Trade Agreement (CEFTA)

The newest FTA in Europe is the CEFTA, organized in 1993 by Poland, Hungary, Slovakia and the Czech Republic. Import duties were initially removed from 60 per cent of items, and there was a commitment to abolish all duties and quotas within five years.[21] CEFTA also adopted EU regulations on the origin of goods, which will make it easier for companies in the CEFTA to conduct business in Western markets.[22] All four nations have voiced an interest in joining the EEA, and their alliance in CEFTA may be a forerunner to an eventual merger of CEFTA with the EEA and eventually the EU (for selected data on CEFTA countries, see Table 10.2). A number of CEFTA countries have already applied for EU membership, as illustrated by Table 10.4.

THE AMERICAS

The Americas, the second Triad region, has as its centre the United States. Within the Americas, the United States, Canada, Central America and South America have been natural if sometimes contentious trading partners. As in Europe, the Americas are engaged in all sorts of economic cooperative agreements.

United States–Canada Free-Trade Agreement (CFTA)

Historically, the United States and Canada have had the world's largest bilateral trade: each is the other's largest trading partner. Despite this unique commercial relationship, tariff and other trade barriers hindered even greater commercial activity. To further support trade activity, the two countries established the United States–Canada Free-Trade Area (CFTA),[23] designed to eliminate all trade barriers between the two countries.

The CFTA created a single, continental, commercial market for all goods and most services. The agreement between the United States and Canada is not a customs union such as the European Union; no economic or political union of any kind is involved. It provides only for the elimination of tariffs and other trade barriers.

The CFTA was, however, to be short-lived. Not long after both countries had ratified the CFTA, Mexico announced that it would seek free trade with the United States. Mexico's overtures were answered positively by the United States, and talks on a US–Mexico free-trade area began. Canada, initially ambivalent about joining, agreed to participate and the talks were expanded to a North American Free-Trade Agreement—Canada–United States and Mexico. The CFTA became the model after which NAFTA was designed.[24]

North American Free-Trade Agreement (NAFTA)

Mexico and the United States have been strong trading partners for decades but Mexico had never officially expressed an interest in a free trade agreement until the President of Mexico, Carlos Salinas de Gortari, announced that Mexico would seek such an agreement with the United States. Because earlier overtures to Mexico from the US had been rebuffed, Salinas' announcement was a surprise to Americans and Mexicans alike. The first signal of change came when Mexico joined the General Agreement on Tariffs and Trade, a move they had opposed earlier. Mexico was on the move readying itself to become a partner in the North American Free-Trade Agreement.

Table 10.4   Ever Wider Union?

1996 Status	Population ECU (million)	GDP ECU (billion)	GDP per person ECU	Net Contribution ECU (billion)	Net contribution per Person ECU (Rank)	
Members						
Austria	8	188.8	23 285.6	0.2	24.7	(5)
Belgium	10.1	221.0	21 649.7	−1.8	−176.3	(11)
Britain	58.1	1 248.7	21 102.9	2.3	38.9	(4)
Denmark	5.2	149.9	28 293.7	−0.2	−37.8	(9)
Finland	5.1	109.8	21 299.7	−0.1	−19.4	(8)
France	58.1	1 280.5	21 748.7	0.4	6.8	(7)
Germany	81.6	1 910.3	23 225.5	10.0	121.6	(2)
Greece	10.4	104.6	9 895.9	−4.1	−387.9	(13)
Ireland	3.5	70.2	18 993.5	−2.3	−622.3	(14)
Italy	57.2	1 049.0	18 209.0	1.3	22.6	(6)
Luxembourg	0.4	14.8	34 701.1	−0.8	−1 875.5	(15)
Netherlands	15.5	334.5	21 316.6	2.4	152.9	(1)
Portugal	9.8	89.4	9 043.1	−2.8	−283.2	(12)
Spain	39.6	492.2	12 501.6	−6.1	−154.9	(10)
Sweden	8.8	210.1	23 511.6	0.7	78.3	(3)
Non-members[a]						
Bulgaria	8.5	8.6	1 011.7			
Cyprus	0.7	n.a.	n.a.			
Czech Rep.	10.3	49.5	4 805.8			
Estonia	1.5	3.9	2 600.0			
Hungary	10.1	40.5	4 009.9			
Latvia	2.5	4.5	1 800.0			
Lithuania	3.7	7.0	1 891.8			
Poland	38.6	121.4	3 145.1			
Romania	22.7	32.0	1 409.9			
Slovakia	5.3	17.1	3 226.4			
Slovenia	1.9	16.8	8 842.1			
Norway	4.3	142.4	33 116.3			
Malta	0.4	n.a.	n.a.			
Switzerland	7.2	264.8	36 777.8			
Turkey	60.8	163.8	2 694.1			

[a]1996 figures from the World Bank.
Source: Based on Centre for European Policy Studies, Eurostat, in *The Economist*, 3 October 1998, p. 38, and World Bank, *World Development Indicators*, 1998.

Even though Mexico has an abundance of oil and a rapidly growing population, the number of new workers is increasing faster than its economy can create new jobs. The United States needs resources (especially oil), and, of course, markets. The three need each other to compete more effectively in world markets, and they need mutual assurances that their already dominant trading positions in each other's markets are safe from protectionist pressures. When the NAFTA agreement was ratified and became effective in 1994, a single market of 360 million people with a €5.4 trillion ($6 trillion) GNP emerged.

NAFTA requires the three countries to remove all tariffs and barriers to trade, but each country will have its own tariff arrangements with nonmember countries. All changes already occurring under CFTA will stand and be built on under the NAFTA agreement. Some of the key provisions of the agreement follow.

Market Access.   Within 10 years of implementation, all tariffs will be eliminated on North American industrial products traded between Canada, Mexico and the United States. All trade between Canada and the United States not already duty free will be duty free by 1998 as provided for in CFTA. Mexico will immediately eliminate tariffs on nearly 50 per cent of all industrial goods imported from the United States, and remaining tariffs will be phased out entirely within 15 years.

Nontariff Barriers.   In addition to the elimination of tariffs, countries will eliminate nontariff barriers and other trade-distorting restrictions. NAFTA also eliminates a host of other Mexican barriers such as local content, local production and export performance requirements that have limited US exports.

Rules of Origin.   NAFTA reduces tariffs only for goods made in North America. Tough rules of origin will determine whether a good qualifies for preferential tariff treatment under NAFTA. Rules of origin are designed to prevent 'free riders' from benefiting through minor processing or transshipment of non-NAFTA goods. For example, Japan could not assemble cars in Mexico and avoid US or Canadian tariffs and quotas unless the car had a specific percentage of Mexican (i.e. North American) content. For goods to be traded duty free, they must contain substantial (62.5 per cent) North American content. Table 10.5 gives a brief picture of how rules of origin work.

Customs Administration.   Under NAFTA, Canada, Mexico and the United States have agreed to implement uniform customs procedures and regulations. Uniform procedures ensure that exporters who market their products in more than one NAFTA country will not have to adapt to multiple customs procedures. Most procedures governing rules of origin documentation, record keeping and origin verification will be the same for all three NAFTA countries.

Investment.   NAFTA will eliminate investment conditions that restrict the trade of goods and service among the three countries. Among conditions eliminated are the requirements that foreign investors export a given level or percentage of goods or services, use domestic goods or services, transfer technology to competitors, or limit imports to a certain percentage of exports.

Services.   NAFTA establishes the first comprehensive set of principles governing services trade. Financial institutions are permitted to open wholly-owned subsidiaries in each other's markets, and all restrictions on the services they offer will be lifted by the year 2000.

Intellectual Property.   NAFTA will provide the highest standards of protection of intellectual property available in any bilateral or international agreement. The agreement covers patents, trademarks, copyrights, trade secrets, semiconductor integrated circuits, copyrights for North American movies, computer software and records.

Government Procurement.   NAFTA guarantees businesses fair and open competition for procurement in North America through transparent and predictable procurement procedures.

Table 10.5   How NAFTA Rules of Origin Work

Each product has a rule of origin that applies to it. The rules are organized according to the Harmonized System (HS) classification of the product. There are two types of rules; both require substantial North American processing, but they measure it differently.

Rule Type	Description	Example
Tariff-Shift Rule	Non-NAFTA imports undergo sufficient manufacture or processing to become products that can qualify under a different tariff classification.	Wood pulp (HS Chapter 47) imported from outside America is processed into paper (HS Chapter 48) within North America. The wood pulp has been transformed within NAFTA to a product eligible for distribution within NAFTA. In other words, the tariff classification shifted from HS Chapter 47 to HS Chapter 48.
Value-Content Rule	A set percentage of the value of the good must be North American (usually coupled with a tariff classification shift requirement). Some goods are subject to the value-content rule only when they fail to pass the tariff classification shift test because of non-NAFTA inputs.	If perfume (HS #3303), for example, fails the applicable tariff classification shift rule, it must contain 50–60 per cent (depending on the valuation method) North American content in order to get preferential tariff treatment.

Source: Anne M. Driscoll, 'Embracing Change, Enhancing Competitiveness: NAFTA's Key Provisions', *Business America*, 18 October 1993, p. 15.

The elimination of trade and investment barriers among Canada, Mexico and the United States creates one of the largest and richest markets in the world. Early reports on the effect of NAFTA have been positive although not without a few rough spots. In the first six months after NAFTA's inception, for example, US exports to Mexico rose to $24.5 billion, an increase of 16 per cent over the previous 12 months. Mexican exports to the United States rose 21 per cent in those first six months to €20.2 billion ($23.4 billion). Equally impressive is the increase in trade between Mexico and Canada during the same period: exports from Canada to Mexico increased 33 per cent and Mexican exports to Canada increased by 31 per cent. Trade between Canada and the United States has been increasing steadily since 1989 when the Canada Free-Trade Agreement (CFTA is now part of NAFTA) became effective. By 1995, trade between the two countries had increased since 1989 by 50 per cent.[25]

Latin-American Economic Cooperation

Prior to 1990, most Latin American market groups (Table 10.6) had varying degrees of success. The first and most ambitious, the Latin American Free Trade Association (LAFTA) gave way to LAIA (Latin American Integration Association). Plagued with tremendous foreign debt, protectionist economic systems, triple-digit inflation, state ownership of basic industries and overregulation of industry, most countries were in a perpetual state of

Table 10.6   Latin American Market Groups

Association	Member	Population (millions)	GDP (US$ billions)	GDP per Capita (US$)	Imports (US$ millions)
Andean	Bolivia	7.8	6.4	818	864
Common	Colombia	33.4	43.5	1 303	8 251
Market	Ecuador	10.7	12.7	1 181	2 825
(ANCOM)	Peru	22.5	45.3	2 016	3 744
	Venezuela	20.3	60.4	2 984	12 261
	Panama (Associate)	2.5	6.0	2 390	2 024
Central	Guatemala	9.7	10.5	1 076	2 860
American	El Salvador	5.4	6.0	1 106	1 854
Common	Costa Rica	3.1	6.5	2 106	2 682
Market	Nicaragua	4.1	1.7	408	845
(CACM)	Honduras	5.5	3.2	591	668
Caribbean	Antigua &				
Community	Barbuda	0.08	0.418	6 500	326
and Common	Barbados	0.3	1.8	7 000	1 454
Market	Belize	0.3	0.373	1 635	194
(CARICOM)	Dominica	0.09	0.170	2 000	104
	Grenada	0.08	0.238	2 800	105
	Guyana	0.8	0.4	462	353
	Jamaica	2.5	3.2	1 285	1 845
	Montserrat	0.01	–	–	25
	St. Kitts-Nevis Anguilla	0.04	88	1 544	54
	St Lucia	0.15	197	1 492	155
	St Vincent	0.12	132	1 234	87
	Trinidad-Tobago	1.3	5.4	4 314	1 415
Latin American	Argentina*	33.1	228.8	6 912	15 557
Integration	Bolivia	7.8	6.4	818	864
Association	Brazil*	156.8	409.2	2 609	23 260
(LAIA)	Chile	13.6	41.2	3 030	11 691
	Colombia	33.4	43.5	1 303	8 251
	Ecuador	10.7	12.7	1 181	2 825
	Mexico	89.5	333.3	3 722	58 545
	Paraguay*	4.5	5.9	1 299	1 237
	Peru	22.5	45.3	2 016	3 744
	Uruguay*	3.1	11.4	3 644	2 010
	Venezuela	20.3	60.4	2 984	12 261

*Mercosur countries: Southern Cone Common Market (Mercosur) is the newest common-market agreement in Latin America.
Sources: *International Trade Statistics Yearbook 1* (New York: United Nations, 1990); and *International Marketing Data and Statistics*, 18th edn (London: Euromonitor Publications, 1994).

economic chaos. Under such conditions there was not much trade or integration among member countries. But, as discussed earlier, there are significant changes occurring in Latin America. There is now a wave of genuine optimism about the economic miracle under way propagated by political and economic reforms occurring from the tip of Argentina to the Rio Grande river.

In addition to new trade agreements, many of the trade accords that have been in existence for decades, such as the Latin American Integration Association and the Andean Pact, have moved from a moribund to an active state. All of which makes the idea of a common market from Argentina to the Arctic Circle—a Western Hemisphere Free Trade Area (WHFTA)—not as unlikely as it might first appear.[26] An accord reached by Colombia, Mexico and Venezuela, the Group of Three (G-3), typifies the desire for establishing new free-trade areas in Latin America. By 2005, G-3 is scheduled to become a tariff-free zone. When approved, the accord will create a free market of 145 million people with a combined GDP of €337 billion ($373 billion).[27] The G-3 has already sparked the possibility of expansion to include Ecuador and Chile; both currently have free-trade agreements with the G-3 nations.

Latin American Integration Association (LAIA).

The long-term goal of LAIA is the establishment, in a gradual and progressive manner, of a Latin American Common Market. One of the more important aspects of LAIA is the differential treatment of member countries according to their level of economic development. Over the years, negotiations among member countries have lowered duties on selected products and eased trade tensions over quotas, local-content requirements, import licences and other trade barriers.

The Andean Common Market (ANCOM).

The Andean Pact, as it is generally referred to, has served its member nations with a framework to establish rules for foreign investment, common tariffs for nonmember countries, and the reduction or elimination of internal tariffs. The Andean Pact members agreed to go beyond a free-trade agreement and implement a customs union in 1996. This revived interest in economic integration by Andean Pact members has resulted in an evaluation of alternatives for member countries to join NAFTA and the possibility of the integration of the Andean Pact and Mercosur (see below) to form a South American Free-Trade Area (SAFTA).[28]

Southern Cone Common Market (Mercosur).

Mercosur is the newest common-market agreement in Latin America. A successful bilateral trade pact between Argentina and Brazil led to the creation of Mercosur in 1991. Argentina, Brazil, Paraguay and Uruguay are members of Mercosur and seek to achieve free circulation of goods and services, establish a regional common external tariff (targeted at 20 per cent) for third-country imports, and implement harmonized macroeconomic trade and exchange-rate policies among the four partners by 1995. Unfortunately, they were unable to meet the 1995 deadline because the leaders failed to agree on a common external tariff. The most they were able to accomplish was a customs union comprising a free-trade zone with a reduction of internal tariffs. Figure 10.3 shows the intra-Mercusor trade.

The common market envisaged by the original Mercosur accord is not likely to come into effect until 2001 or later.[29] This delay should not be viewed as failure; as history has shown in Europe, it takes time to form a common market. Even though their goals have not been met, the limited integration has had a considerable effect. As of 1995, Mercosur members had cut tariffs for each other's imports by 90 per cent. This reduction led to a 120 per cent jump in intraregional trade in three years.[30]

Figure 10.3   Fast Abroad, Faster at Home: Intra-Mercosur trade ($ billion)

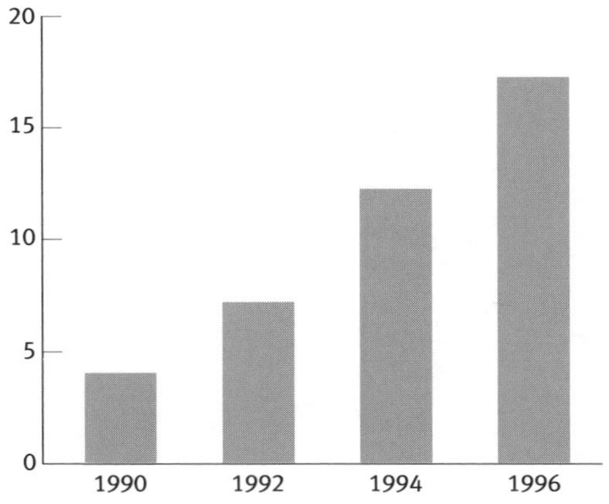

Source: Based on WTO, and *The Economist*, 22 November 1997, p. 69.

ASIA

What is happening in Asia is by far the most important development in the world today. Based on this development a new commonwealth of nations based on economic symbiosis is emerging in the Far East. The Asian continent, from Pakistan to Japan and China down to Indonesia, now accounts for more than half of the world population.[31] Countries in Asia constitute the third Triad region. Japan is at the centre of this Triad region, which also includes many of the world's newly industrialized countries (NICs) and emerging economies. After decades of dependence on the United States and Europe for technology and markets, countries in Asia are preparing for the next economic leap, driven by trade, investment and technology aided by others in the region. Though few in number, trade agreements among some of the Asian emerging countries are seen as movement towards a regionwide intra-Asian trade area. This drive was strengthened after the 1996–97 economic crisis in a number of Asian countries.

Presently, there is one multinational trade group, the Association of Southeast Asian Nations (ASEAN),[32] that has evolved into the ASEAN Free-Trade Area (AFTA), and one forum, Asia–Pacific Economic Cooperation (APEC), that meets annually to discuss regional economic development and cooperation.[33]

ASEAN.   The Association of Southeast Asian Nations (ASEAN) is the primary multinational trade group in Asia. The goals of the group are economic integration and cooperation through complementary industry programmes, preferential trading including reduced tariff and nontariff barriers, guaranteed member access to markets throughout the region, and harmonized investment incentives. Like all multinational market groups, ASEAN has experienced problems and false starts in attempting to unify their combined economies.

Most of the early economic growth came from trade outside the ASEAN group. Similarities in the kinds of products they had to export, in their natural resources and other national assets hampered earlier attempts at intra-ASEAN trade. Steps taken by ASEAN

229

Table 10.7   GDP per Head in ASEAN Countries

	Population 1996 (million)	GDP per head 1996 ($)
Members		
Indonesia	197	1 146
Vietnam	75	311
Philippines	72	1 164
Thailand	60	3 084
Malaysia	21	4 724
Singapore	3	31 354
Brunei	0.29	16 427[a]
About to join:		
Myanmar	46	97[b]
Laos	5	377
Application on hold:		
Cambodia	10	313

[a]Estimate; [b]At market exchange rate.
Source: Based on 'The Tigers' Fearful Symmetry', *The Economist*, 19 July 1997, p. 53, and 'World Development Indicators 1998', CD-Rom, World Bank.

members in the last decade to expand and diversify their industrial base have resulted in the fastest-growing economies in the region.

Four major events account for the vigorous economic growth of the ASEAN countries and their transformation from cheap-labour havens to industrialized nations: (1) the ASEAN governments' commitment to deregulation, liberalization and privatization of their economies; (2) the decision to shift their economies from commodity based to manufacturing based; (3) the decision to specialize in manufacturing components in which they have a comparative advantage (this created more diversity in their industrial output and increased opportunities for trade); and (4) Japan's emergence as a major provider of technology and capital necessary to upgrade manufacturing capability and develop new industries. As their economies became more diversified, they signed a framework agreement to create the ASEAN Free Trade Area (AFTA) by 2006. The goal of AFTA is to reduce intraregional tariffs and remove nontariff barriers over a 15-year period. Tariffs on all manufactured goods are to be reduced to 5 per cent or less by 2003.[34] The new free-trade area consists of nine countries; Brunei, Indonesia, Malaysia, The Philippines, Singapore, Thailand, Vietnam, Mynamar and Laos. It has a population of 478 million and a GDP of more than €360 billion ($400 billion). (See Table 10.7.)

APEC.   Asia–Pacific Economic Cooperation (APEC) is the other important trade group in the Asia–Pacific Rim. It provides a formal structure for the major governments of the region, including the United States and Canada, to discuss their mutual interests in open trade and economic collaboration. APEC is a unique forum that has evolved into the primary regional vehicle for promoting trade liberalization and economic cooperation. The 18-member APEC[35] includes the most powerful regional economies in the world (see Table 10.8) whose share of world trade approaches 35 per cent and, as a region, constitutes the United States' most important economic partner. APEC has as its common goal a commitment to open

Table 10.8   Comparison of Intra-Trade among Members of APEC and the EC

	Population, 1989 (millions)	Exports, 1980 (US$ millions)	Exports, 1990 (US$ millions)	GNP, 1989 (US$ billions)
APEC	1 913	296 809	832 869	10 126
North America	276	128 608	306 486	5 752
Asia	1 617	150 091	499 455	4 050
Oceania	20	18 110	26 928	324
EC	343	198 917	515 915	5 015

Sources: IMF: International Financial Statistics, Direction of Trade; OECD: National Account, EC Committee; Eurostat, etc.

trade, to increase economic collaboration, to sustain regional growth and development, to strengthen the multilateral trading system and to reduce barriers to investment and trade without detriment to other economies.

AFRICA

Africa's multinational market development activities can be characterized by a great deal of activity, but little progress. Including bilateral agreements, an estimated 200 economic arrangements exist between African countries (see Table 10.9). Despite the large number and assortment of paper organizations, there has been little actual economic integration. This is generally due to the political instability that has characterized Africa in the last decades and the unstable economic base on which Africa has had to build. Political sovereignty is a new-enough phenomenon to most African nations and they are reluctant to relinquish any part of it without specific and tangible benefits in return. Now that South Africa has changed its internal politics, one can speculate about what future role it might play in the economic integration of African countries should it decide to take a leadership position.[36]

The Economic Community of West African States (ECOWAS) is the most senior of the African regional cooperative groups and the most successful.[37] A 15-nation group, ECOWAS has an aggregate gross domestic product (GDP) of more than €52.2 billion ($57.9 billion) and is striving to achieve full economic integration. Some experts suggest the economic domination by Nigeria (45 per cent of all the market's exports) may create internal strains that cannot be overcome.

One of the groups becoming strong is the South African Development Community (SADC) with its 12 members. The members include Angola, Malawi, Tanzania, Zambia, Mozambique, Namibia, Botswana, Zimbabwe, Swaziland, Lesotho, Mauritius and South Africa. The group has a total population of 134.9 million with a GDP of €149.3 billion ($165.4 billion). In 1996, eight of these members had a growth rate above 8 per cent, while the average was above 6 per cent.

MIDDLE EAST

The Middle East has been less aggressive in the formation of successfully functioning multi-national market groups (see Table 10.10). Countries that belong to the Arab Common

Table 10.9 African Market Groups

Association	Member	Population (millions)	GDP (US$ billions)	GDP per Capita (US$)	Imports (US$ millions)
Afro-Malagasy	Benin	4.9	$1.6	$373	$288
Economic	Burkina Faso	9.5	3.2	338	515
Union	Cameroon	12.2	10.9	895	1 312
	Central African Republic	3.04	1.3	480	252
	Chad	5.7	1.1	216	419
	People's Republic of the Congo	2.4	2.8	1 193	772
	Côte d'Ivoire	12.9	11.2	866	2 465
	Gabon	1.2	5.9	4 769	1 074
	Mali	9.2	1.9	221	513
	Mauritania	2.0	0.8	453	235
	Niger	7.7	2.2	333	345
	Senegal	7.7	6.2	803	1 384
	Togo	3.5	1.1	443	487
East-Africa	Ethiopia	55.1	2.7	49	1 395
Customs	Kenya	25.7	8.0	312	2 017
Union	Sudan	25.0	9.2	398	1 000
	Tanzania	27.8	2.7	97	1 362
	Uganda	18.7	3.0	161	415
	Zambia	8.6	3.3	382	1 015
Maghreb	Algeria	26.4	46.1	1 750	8 375
Economic	Libya	4.6	22.8	5 580	4 723
Community	Tunisia	8.4	16.8	1 999	6 516
	Morocco	26.3	28.8	1 093	8 432
Casablanca	Egypt	55.2	41.8	758	13 373
Group	Ghana	16.0	6.9	431	1 680
	Guinea	5.8	2.1	335	50
	Morocco	26.3	28.8	1 093	8 432
Economic	Benin	4.9	1.6	373	288
Community	Burkina-Faso	9.5	3.2	338	515
of West	Cape Verde	0.04	0.2	510	110
Africa States	Côte d'Ivoire	12.9	11.2	866	2 465
(ECOWAS)	Gambia	0.86	0.2	261	127
	Ghana	16.0	6.9	431	1 680
	Guinea	5.8	2.1	335	50
	Guinea-Bissau	0.96	0.2	178	50
	Liberia	2.58	1.1	467	308
	Mali	9.21	1.9	221	513
	Mauritania	2.02	0.84	453	235
	Niger	7.73	2.2	333	345
	Nigeria	115.7	26.3	228	9 180
West Africa	Senegal	7.7	6.2	803	1 384
Economic	Togo	3.5	1.1	443	487
Community	Burkina-Faso	9.5	3.2	338	515
(CEAO)	Côte d'Ivoire	12.9	11.2	866	2 465
	Mali	9.2	1.9	221	513
	Mauritania	2.0	0.8	453	235
	Niger	7.7	2.2	333	345

Table 10.10   Middle East Market Groups

Association	Member	Population (millions)	GDP (US$ billions)	GDP per Capita (US$)	Imports (US$ millions)
Arab	Iraq[a]	19	22 000	1 140	647
Common	Kuwait[b]	1.7	26 650	15 676	7 784
Market	Jordan	4	7 343	1 836	3 698[b]
	Syria[b]	14.1	16 783	1 190	4 616[b]
	Egypt	59	67 691	1 147	11 739[b]
Economic	Pakistan	134	64 846	484	11 461[b]
Cooperation	Iran[a]	62	59 700	970	23 916
Organization	Turkey	63	181 464	2 880	35 710[b]
(ECO)	Azerbaijan	8	3 650	456	955[b]
	Turkmenistan	5	4 310	862	n.a.
	Uzbekistan	23	25 198	1 095	3 598[b]
Gulf	Bahrain	0.577[b]	n.a.	n.a.	n.a.
Cooperation	Kuwait[b]	1.7	26 650	15 676	7 784
Council	Oman[b]	2.2	12 102	5 500	4 248
(GCC)	Quatar	0.642[b]	n.a.	n.a.	n.a.
	Saudi Arabia[b]	19.0	125 501	6 605	27 458
	United Arab Emirates[b]	2.5	39 107	15 642	21 024[c]

[a]1990/1994 figures; [b]1995 figures; [c]Estimate
Source: *International Trade Statistics Yearbook 1* (New York: United Nations), 1990;
International Marketing Data and Statistics, 18th edn (London: Euromonitor Publications, 1994); *World Development Report 1997*; and *World Development Indicators 1998*, World Bank.

Market have set goals for free internal trade but have not achieved them. With the possibility of continuing peace in the Middle East, the prospect of a meaningful trade group has improved.

FUTURE MULTINATIONAL MARKET GROUPS

With the advent of a single European market and the North American Free Trade Agreement (NAFTA), and with the general concern that these two formidable market groups may be the forerunners of many other regional trading blocs, there is speculation about future alliances.

A conjectural free-trade agreement that has emerged is one between the United States and the European Union. Europe fears it will be isolated by free-trade agreements that the United States is trying to form with Latin American and Asian countries; the United States is concerned by the fact that Mexico is trying to negotiate its own free-trade accord with Europe and that Europe is seeking to establish free-trade ties with the countries of Mercosur. No official talks have taken place but informal discussions lead some to speculate that a United States–Europe agreement is possible within the next decade.[38]

Another more speculative trade group centres around the political and economic unification of China, Taiwan and Hong Kong. Although currently at odds politically, economic

Table 10.11   The Chinese Empire Overseas

	Chinese Population		Business Output	
	as % of total local population	million	as % of total local economy	GDP contribution $ billion
Hong Kong	98	6	80	120
Singapore	76	2	76	62
Taiwan	99	21	95	255
Malaysia	32	6	60	48
Indonesia	4	8	50	98
Philippines	1	1	40	30
Thailand	10	6	50	80
Vietnam	1	1	20	4
Total		51		697

Source: Based on 'A Survey of Business in Asia', *The Economist*, 9 March 1996, p. 10.

integration between Hong Kong, Taiwan and the coastal provinces of Southern China, often unofficially referred to as the *Chinese Economic Area* (*CEA*), has advanced rapidly in recent years. The current expansion of the triangular economic relationship can be attributed to a steady transfer of labour-intensive manufacturing operations from Taiwan and Hong Kong to the Chinese mainland. China provides a supply of cheap, abundant labour, and Taiwan and Hong Kong provide capital, technology and management expertise. Hong Kong, now formally part of China, also plays an important role as the financier, investor, supplier and provider of technology and as a port of entry for China as a whole.[39]

As an economic region, the CEA's economic importance should not be undervalued. Combined exports of the CEA were valued at €254.1 billion ($281.5 billion), accounting for 7.6 per cent of the world's exports and ranking fourth worldwide, behind the United States, Germany and Japan. Their combined imports totalled €240 billion ($266 billion), accounting for 6.9 per cent of the world's imports and ranking third, behind the United States and Germany.[40] The Chinese business empire extends beyond Hong Kong and Taiwan and China itself (see Table 10.11).

STRATEGIC IMPLICATIONS FOR MARKETING

The complexion of the entire world marketplace has been changed significantly by the coalition of nations into multinational market groups. To international business firms, multinational groups spell opportunity in bold letters through access to greatly enlarged markets with reduced or abolished country-by-country tariff barriers and restrictions. Production, financing, labour and marketing decisions are affected by the remapping of the world into market groups.

As goals of the EEA and NAFTA are reached, new marketing opportunities are created; so are new problems. World competition will intensify as businesses become stronger and more experienced in dealing with large market groups. European and non-European multinationals are preparing to deal with the changes in competition in a fully integrated Europe. In an integrated Europe, industries and markets are being restructured. Mergers, acquisitions and joint ventures consolidate operations of European firms in anticipation of the benefits of a single European market. International managers will still be confronted by individual national markets with the same problems of language, customs and instability, even though they are packaged under the umbrella of a common market.

Opportunities.   Economic integration creates large mass markets for the marketer. Many national markets, too small to bother with individually, take on new dimensions and significance when combined with markets from cooperating countries. Large markets are particularly important to businesses accustomed to mass production and mass distribution because of the economies of scale and marketing efficiencies that can be achieved. In highly competitive markets, the benefits derived from enhanced efficiencies are often passed along as lower prices which lead to increased purchasing power.

Another major saving will result from the billions of dollars wasted in developing different versions of products to meet a hodgepodge of national standards. Philips and other European companies invested a total of €18 billion ($20 billion) to develop a common switching system for Europe's 10 different telephone networks. This compares with €2.7 billion ($3 billion) spent in the United States for a common system and €1.35 billion ($1.5 billion) in Japan for a single system.

Market Barriers.   The initial aim of a multinational market is to protect businesses that operate within its borders. An expressed goal is to give an advantage to the companies within the market in their dealings with other countries of the market group. Analysis of the intra-regional and international trade patterns of the market groups indicates that such goals have been achieved. Trade does increase among member nations and decrease with nonmember nations.

Local preferences certainly spell trouble for the exporter located outside the market. Companies willing to invest in production facilities in multinational markets may benefit from such protection as they become a part of the market. Exporters, however, are in a considerably weaker position. This prospect confronts many US exporters faced with the possible need to invest in Europe to protect their export markets in the European Community. Recent heavy investments by Japanese (Toyota, Honda and Nissan), American (MCI, GM and Procter & Gamble) and Korean companies (Lucky Goldstar and Samsung) are good examples of such investments.

Ensuring EU Market Entry

Whether or not the European Union will close its doors to outsiders, firms who want to be competitive in the EU will have to establish a presence there. There are four levels of involvement that a firm may have *vis-à-vis* the EU: (1) firms based in Europe with well-established manufacturing and distribution operations in several European countries; (2) firms with operations in a single EU country; (3) firms that export manufactured goods to the EU from an offshore location; and (4) firms that have not actively exported to EU countries. The strategies for effective competitiveness in the EU are different for each type of firm.

The first firm, fully established in several EU countries with local manufacturing, is the best positioned. However, the competitive structure will change under a single Europe. Marketers will have to exploit the opportunities of greater efficiencies of production and distribution that result from lowering the barriers. They will also have to deal with increased competition from European firms as well as other MNCs that will be aggressively establishing market positions. A third area of change will require companies to learn how their customers are changing and, thus, how best to market to them.

European retailers and wholesalers as well as industrial customers are merging, expanding and taking steps to assure their success in this larger market. Nestlé has bought Rowntree, a UK confectionery company, and Britone, the Italian food conglomerate, to strengthen their ties to EU market firms. European banking is also going through a stage of mergers. In one 18-month period, 400 banks and finance firms merged, took stock in one another, or devised joint marketing ventures to sell stocks, mutual funds, insurance or other financial instruments. These mergers are viewed as necessary to compete with Japanese, US and Swiss financial institutions.

A second type of firm—with operations in one European country—is vulnerable when barriers come down and competitors enter the company's market. The firm's biggest problem in this situation is not being large enough to withstand the competition from outside the country. The answer is to become larger, or withdraw. There are several choices for this firm: expand through acquisition or merger, enter a strategic alliance with a second company, or expand the company beyond being a local single-country firm to being a pan-European competitor.

Marketing Mix Implications

Companies are adjusting their marketing mix strategies to reflect anticipated market differences in a single European market. In the past, companies often charged different prices in different European markets. Nontariff barriers between member states supported price differentials and kept lower-priced products from entering those markets where higher prices were charged. Colgate-Palmolive Company has adapted its Colgate toothpaste into a single formula for sale across Europe at one price. Before changing its pricing practices, Colgate sold its toothpaste at different prices in different markets. Badedas Shower Gel, for example, is priced in the middle of the market in Germany and as a high-priced product in the United Kingdom. As long as products from lower-priced markets could not move to higher-priced markets, such differential price schemes worked. Now, however, under the EU rules, companies cannot prevent the free movement of goods, and parallel imports from lower-priced markets to higher-priced markets are more apt to occur. Some price standardization among country markets will be one of the necessary changes to avoid the problem of parallel imports.[41]

In addition to initiating uniform pricing policies, companies are reducing the number of brands they produce to focus advertising and promotion efforts. For example, Nestlé's current three brands of yoghurt in the EU will be reduced to a single brand.

A major benefit from an integrated Europe is competition at the retail level. Europe lacks an integrated and competitive distribution system that would support small and midsize outlets. The elimination of borders could result in increased competition among retailers and the creation of Europe-wide distribution channels. Retail giants such as France's Carréfour, Germany's Aldi group and Holland's Ahold are planning huge hypermarkets with big advertising budgets.

SUMMARY

The experience of the multinational market groups developed since World War II points up both the possible successes and the hazards such groups encounter. The various attempts at economic cooperation represent varying degrees of success and failure, but, almost without regard to their degree of success, the economic market groups have created great excitement among marketers.

Economic benefits possible through cooperation relate to more efficient marketing and production: marketing efficiency is effected through the development of mass markets, encouragement of competition, the improvement of personal income and various psychological market factors. Production efficiency derives from specialization, mass production for mass markets and the free movement of the factors of production. Economic integration also tends to foster political harmony among the countries involved; such harmony leads to stability, which is beneficial to the marketer.

The marketing implications of multinational market groups may be studied from the standpoint of firms located inside the market or of firms located outside that wish to sell to the markets. For each viewpoint the problems and opportunities are somewhat different; but regardless of the location of the marketer, multinational market groups provide great opportunity for the creative marketer who wishes to expand volume. Market groupings make it economically feasible to enter new markets and to employ new marketing strategies that could not be applied to the smaller markets represented by individual countries.

The success of the European Union, the creation of the Canada–Mexico–United States free-trade area (NAFTA), the expansion of ASEAN to the ASEAN Free-Trade Area (AFTA) and the new Mercosur suggest the growing importance of economic cooperation and integration. Such developments will continue to challenge the international marketer by providing continually growing market opportunities.

QUESTIONS

1. Elaborate on the problems and benefits for international marketers from multinational market groups.
2. Explain the political role of multinational market groups. Identify the factors on which one may judge the potential success or failure of a multinational market group.
3. Explain the marketing implications of the factors contributing to the successful development of a multinational market group.
4. Differentiate between a free-trade area and a common market. Explain the marketing implication of the differences.
5. Select any three countries that might have some logical basis for establishing a multinational market organization. Identify the various problems that would be encountered in forming multinational market groups of such countries.
6. US exports to the European Union are expected to decline in future years. What marketing actions may a US company take to counteract such changes?

7. 'Because they are dynamic and because they have great growth possibilities, the multinational markets are likely to be especially rough and tumble for the external business.' Discuss.
8. Why have African nations had such difficulty in forming effective economic unions?
9. Discuss the implications of the European Union on marketing strategy in Europe.
10. Discuss the United States–Canada Free-Trade Agreement and compare it with the European Union.
11. What are some of the possibilities for other multinational marketing groups forming? Discuss the implications to global marketing if these groups should develop.
12. Using the factors that serve as the basis for success of an economic union (political, economic, social and geographic), evaluate the potential success of the EU, NAFTA, ASEAN, AFTA and Mercosur.

REFERENCES

1. UNCTAD, *Companies without Borders: Transnational Corporations in the 1990s* (London: Thomson Business Press, 1996).

2. Jay L. Camillo, 'Mexico: NAFTA Opens Door to US Business', *Business America*, March 1994, pp. 14–21.

3. Suzanne Crow, 'Russia Promotes the CIS As an International Organization', RFE/RL Research Report, 18 March 1994, pp. 33–36.

4. Clinton Shiells, 'Regional Trade Blocs: Trade Creating or Diverting?' *Finance & Development*, March 1995, pp. 30–32.

5. Kenichi Ohmae, *Triad Power* (New York: The Free Press, 1985), p. 220.

6. The European Community still exists as a legal entity within the broader framework of the European Union.

7. Keith Perry, *Business and the European Community* (Oxford: Butterworth-Heinemann, 1994).

8. 'Ever Closer Union, 40 Years On', *The Economist*, 29 March 1997, p. 31.

9. Alan Cowell, '7 Members of the European Union Launch a Passport-Free Zone', *New York Times*, 27 March 1995, p. A-4.

10. Lionel Barber, 'From the Heart of Europe', *Europe*, July–August 1994, pp. 14–17; and 'Pondering Europe's Union', *The Economist*, 20 June 1998, p. 32.

11. 'Ambiguous Pointers from the ECJ', *Business Europe*, 28 March–3 April 1994, p. 3.

12. *The European*, Magazine, 20–26 June 1996, pp. 16–17

13. 'The EP's Legislative Veto', *Business Europe*, 7–13 March 1994, p. 1.

14. 'Advertising: Awaiting the Commission's Green Paper', *Business Europe*, 28 March–3 April 1994, pp. 2–3.

15. 'The Euro: Will It Create A New European Economy?' *Business Week*, Special Issue, 27 April 1998.

16. John Darnton, 'Vote in Norway Blocks Joining Europe's Union', *The New York Times*, 29 November 1994, p. A1.

17. EFTA countries joining the EEA were Austria, Finland, Iceland, Norway and Sweden.

18. 'Inside Europe: Support for Polish Membership', *Europe*, May 1994, p. 2.

19. The 12 republics of the former USSR, collectively referred to as the Newly Independent States (NIS), are: Russia, Ukraine, Belarus (formerly Byelorussia), Armenia, Moldova (formerly Moldavia), Azerbaijan, Uzbekistan, Turkmenistan, Tajikistan, Kazakhstan, Kyrgystan (formerly Kirghiziya) and Georgia. These same countries, the NIS, are also members of the CIS.

20. Suzanne Crow, 'Russia Promotes the CIS As an International Organization', RFE/RL Research Report, 18 March 1994, pp. 33–37.

21. 'What CEFTA Means', *Business Eastern Europe*, 7 March 1994, p. 1.

22. 'Companies Weigh CEFTA Strategy', *Business Eastern Europe*, 7 March 1994, pp. 1–2.

23. Jonathan P. Doh, 'Canada Is an Important NAFTA Partner Too!' *Business America*, 18 October 1993, pp. 30–32.

24. Duane Kujawa, Suk H. Kim and Kim Hang-Joe, 'A North American Free-Trade Agreement: The First Step toward One America', *Multinational Business Review*, Fall 1993, pp. 12–18.

25. Lori Ioannou, 'NAFTA's Promised Land', *International Business*, January 1995, pp. 22–23; and 'Meanwhile, to the North, NAFTA Is a Smash', *Business Week*, 27 February 1995, p. 66.

26. Paul Magnusson, 'With Latin America Thriving, NAFTA Might Keep Marching South', *Business Week*, 24 July 1994, p. 20.

27. 'G-3 Success', *Business Latin America*, 23 May 1994, pp. 1–2.

28. Paul W. Moore and Rebecca K. Hunt, 'The Andean Pact: In the Forefront of the Integration Movement', *Business America*, May 1994, pp. 10–11.

29. 'Mercosur: Up and Running', *Business Latin America*, 30 January 1995, pp. 4–5.

30. 'Mercosur Takes Off', *World Press Review*, March 1995, p. 23.

31. John Naisbitt, *Mega Trends in Asia* (New York: Simon & Schuster, 1996).

32. ASEAN countries are: Brunei, Indonesia, Malaysia, The Philippines, Singapore and Thailand. Vietnam entered ASEAN in 1996.

33. 'A Great Slide Backward in Southeast Asia', *Business Week*, 5 August 1996, p. 23.

34. 'ASEAN to Speed Trade Area', *The Wall Street Journal*, 22 September 1994, p. A-10.

35. APEC members are: Australia, Brunei, Canada, Chile, China, Hong Kong, Indonesia, Japan, The Republic of Korea, Malaysia, Mexico, New Zealand, the Philippines, Papua New Guinea, Singapore, Chinese Taipei (Taiwan), Thailand and the United States.

36. 'Opening South Africa; It Should Act Now to Rid Itself and the Region of Apartheid's Economic Remnants', *The Economist*, 8 March 1997, p. 17.

37. 'ECOWAS: Last Month ECOWAS Celebrated Its 19th Anniversary', *West Africa*, 18 July 1994, pp. 1258–1263.

38. Nathaniel C. Nash, 'Is A Trans-Atlantic Pact Coming Down the Pike?' *The New York Times*, 15 April 1995, p. 18.

39. 'The Chinese Economic Area: A Fast-Growing Region in Asia', *Business America*, March 1994, pp. 7–8.

40. Kenichi Ohmae, 'The New World Order: The Rise of the Region-State', *The Wall Street Journal*, 8 August 1994, p. A-12.

41. For a comprehensive report on strategy for the EU, see Colin Egan and Peter McKiernan, *Inside Fortress Europe: Strategies for the Single Market* (Reading, MA: Addison-Wesley, 1994).

Developing International Marketing Strategies

CHAPTER

11

Developing International Marketing Strategies

Chapter Learning Objectives

What you should learn from Chapter 11

- How international marketing management differs from global marketing.

- Is adaptation necessary?

- When can we use standardized marketing?

- The importance of total quality management (TQM) in international competition.

- The definition of quality as it relates to products and their use.

- The importance of collaborative relationships.

- The increasing importance of strategic international alliances.

- The need for strategic planning to achieve company goals.

- The important factors that influence alternative market-entry strategies.

Confronted with increasing global competition for expanding markets, multinational companies are changing their marketing strategies. Their goals are to enhance their competitiveness and to assure proper positioning in order to capitalize on opportunities in the global marketplace.

A recent study of North American and European corporations indicated that nearly 75 per cent of the companies are revamping their business processes, that most have formalized strategic-planning programmes and that the need to stay cost competitive was considered to be the most important external issue affecting their marketing strategies.[1] Change is not limited to the giant multinationals but includes small- and medium-sized firms as well.[2] In fact, the flexibility of a smaller company may enable it to reflect the demands of international markets and redefine its programmes more quickly than larger multinationals. Acquiring a global perspective is easy, but the execution requires planning, organization and a willingness to try new approaches, from engaging in collaborative relationships to redefining the scope of company operations.[3]

This chapter discusses global marketing management, competition in the global marketplace, strategic planning and alternative market-entry strategies.

INTERNATIONAL MARKETING MANAGEMENT

Determining a firm's overall international strategy to achieve goals and objectives is the central task of international marketing management that defines the level of international integration of the company. Companies must deal with a multitude of strategic issues including the extent of the internationalization of operations.

As discussed in Chapter 1, a company's international orientation can be characterized as one of three operating concepts: (1) under the *Domestic Market Extension Concept*, foreign markets are extensions of the domestic market and the domestic marketing mix is offered, as is, to foreign markets; (2) with the *Multidomestic Market Concept*, each country is viewed as being culturally unique and an adapted marketing mix for each country market is developed; and (3) with the *Global Market Concept*, the world is the market and, wherever cost- and culturally effective, an overall standardized marketing strategy is developed for entire sets of country markets, while only marketing mix elements are adapted wherever necessary.

The selection of any one of the approaches to internationalization produces different effects on subsequent product, promotion, distribution and pricing decisions and strategies.

Global versus International Marketing Management

The primary distinction between global marketing management and international marketing management is orientation[4] (see Table 11.1). Global marketing management is guided by the global marketing concept which views the world as one market and is based on identifying and targeting cross-cultural similarities. International marketing management is based on the premise of cross-cultural differences and is guided by the belief that each foreign market requires its own culturally adapted marketing strategy. Although consumers in New Delhi dining at McDonald's and Western teens plugged into their Sony Walkman are a reality, the idea of marketing a standardized product with a uniform marketing plan around the world remains 'purely theoretical'.[5]

As discussed in an earlier chapter, there is still debate about the extent of global markets today. A reasonable question concerns whether a global marketing strategy is possible and whether a completely standardized marketing mix can be achieved. Keep in mind that global

Table 11.1   A Comparison of Assumptions about Global and Multinational Companies

	Multinational Companies	*Global Companies*
Product Life Cycle	Products are in different stages of the product life cycle in each nation.	Global product life cycles. All consumers want the most advanced products.
Design	Adjustments to products initially designed for domestic markets.	International performance criteria considered during design stage.
Adaptation	Product adaptation is necessary in markets characterized by national differences.	Products are adapted to global wants and needs. Restrained concern for product suitability.
Market Segmentation	Segments reflect differences. Customised products for each segment.	Segments reflect group similarities. Group similar segments together.
	Many customized markets	Fewer standardized markets.
	Acceptance of regional/national differences.	Expansion of segments into world-wide proportions.
Competition	Domestic/national competitive relationships.	Ability to compete in national markets is affected by a firm's global position.
Production	Standardization limited by requirements to adapt products to national tastes.	Globally standardized production. Adaptations are handled through modular designs.
The Consumer	Preferences reflect national differences	Global convergence of consumer wants and needs.
Product	Products differentiated on the basis of design, features, functions, style and image.	Emphasis on value-enhancing distinction.
Price	Consumers willing to pay more for a customized product.	Consumers prefer a globally standardized good if it carries a lower price.
Promotion	National product image, sensitive to national needs.	Global product image, sensitive to national differences and global needs.
Place	National distribution channels.	Global standardization of distribution.

Sources: Adapted with the authors' permission from Gerald M. Hampton and Erwin Buske, 'The Global Marketing Perspective', *Advances in International Marketing*, vol. 2, S. Tamer Cavusgil, ed. (Greenwich, Conn.: JAI Press, 1987), pp. 265–266.

marketing strategy, as used in this text, and the globalization of markets are two separate, although interrelated, ideas. One has to do with efficiency of operations, competitiveness and orientation, the other with the homogeneity of demand across cultures.[6] There are at least three points that help define a global approach to international marketing: (1) the world is viewed as the market (that is, sets of country markets); (2) homogeneous market segments are

BENEFITS OF GLOBALIZATION

The transfer of experience and technology among international divisions is often cited as a benefit a company gains when it has a global orientation. Here are some examples. Whirlpool developed a super-efficient, chlorofluorocarbon-free refrigerator that won 'most efficient refrigerator' in a contest sponsored by a group of utility companies. Several divisions contributed: insulation technology from the European operation, compressor technology from the Brazilian affiliates and manufacturing and design expertise from the US operation. In an Italian consumer study, Whirlpool found that microwave ovens would sell better if they had a model that would brown food. Swedish researchers developed the VIP Crisp which became a bestseller in Europe and the United States.

A Nestlé division in Thailand faced flat coffee sales; the market was not growing at an expected rate. A cold coffee drink, Nestlé Shake, was borrowed from a Nestlé Greek summer promotion and adapted to the Thai market. A plastic container to mix the drink was designed; a dance, the Shake, was invented to popularize the drink and a Miss Shake-Girl contest was held. Coffee sales in Thailand jumped from $25 million (€23 million) in 1987 to $100 million (€90 million) in 1994.

Sources: Adapted from Regina Fazio Maruca, 'The Right Way to Go Global', *Harvard Business Review*, March–April 1994, p. 145; 'Call It Worldpool', *Business Week*, 28 November 1994, p. 99; and Carla Rapoport, 'Nestlé's Brand Building Machine', *Fortune*, 19 September 1994, p. 150.

sought across country market sets; and (3) standardization of the marketing mix is sought wherever possible but adapted whenever culturally necessary.

Standardization versus Adaptation

Why globalize? Several benefits are derived from globalization and standardization of the marketing mix. *Economies of scale in production and marketing* are the most frequently cited benefits. Black & Decker Manufacturing Company (electrical hand tools, appliances and other consumer products) realized significant production cost savings when they adopted a global strategy. They were able to reduce not only the number of motor sizes for the European market from 260 to 8, but also 15 different models to 8. Ford estimates that by globalizing its product development, purchasing, and supply activities it can save up to €2.7 billion ($3 billion) a year.[7] The savings in the standardization of advertising can be substantial. Colgate-Palmolive Company introduced its Colgate tartar-control toothpaste in over 40 countries, each of which could choose one of two ads. The company estimates that for every country where the standardized commercial runs, it saves €0.9 ($1) to €1.8 ($2) million in production costs.

Transfer of experience and know-how across countries through improved coordination and integration of marketing activities is also cited as a benefit of globalization. Unilever, NV, successfully introduced two global brands originally developed by two subsidiaries. Their South African subsidiary developed Impulse body spray and a European branch developed a detergent that cleaned effectively in European hard water. These are examples of how coordination and transfer of know-how from a local market to a world market can be achieved.

The most important benefit derived from globalization is a *uniform international image*. Global recognition of brand accelerates new product introductions and increase the efficiency and effectiveness of advertising. Uniform global images are increasingly important as satellite communications spread throughout the world. Brands such as Sony, Volvo, Shell, IBM and Ericsson are good examples. Philips International, an electronics manufacturer, had enormous impact with a global product image when it sponsored the soccer World Cup in 1994—the same advertisement was seen in 44 countries with voice-over translations in six languages. Adidas acquired the same benefits when it sponsored the soccer World Cup in 1998, which was seen in more then 60 countries.

Global marketing also made a marked difference in accelerating a 3M product launch on a global scale. For example, a high-grade super VHS videotape was introduced in Japan one month, and in the United States three months later; it appeared in Europe just six months after its introduction in Japan. In the past, it would have been impossible to get effective media coverage and introduce a new 3M product in all its markets in such a short time.[8] Another example was Microsoft's Windows 95 that was launched simultaneously all over the world, from Chicago to Singapore.

Without doubt, market differences seldom permit complete standardization. Government and trade restrictions, differences in the availability of media, differences in customer interests and response patterns and the whole host of cultural differences presented in earlier chapters preclude complete standardization of a global marketing mix.

COMPETITION IN THE GLOBAL MARKETPLACE

Global competition is placing new emphasis on some basic tenets of business. It is reducing time frames and focusing on the importance of quality, competitive prices and innovative products. Time is becoming a precious commodity for business, and expanding technology is shortening product life cycles and creating greater opportunities for innovative products. A company can no longer introduce a new product with the expectation of dominating the market for years while the idea spreads slowly through world markets. Consider the effect on Hewlett-Packard's strategies and plans when, in any given year, two-thirds of its revenue comes from products introduced in the prior three years. Shorter product life cycles mean that a company must maximize sales rapidly to recover development costs and generate a profit by offering its products globally. Along with technological advances have come enhanced market expectations for innovative products at competitive prices. Today, strategic planning must include emphasis on quality, technology and cost containment.

Quality and Competitive Marketing

As global competition increases for most businesses, many industry and government leaders have warned that a renewed emphasis on quality is a necessity for doing business in growing global markets. In most global markets the cost and quality of a product are among the most important criteria by which purchases are made. Further, the market has gradually shifted from a seller's market to a buyer's market. All over the world, customers have more power because they have more choices as more companies compete for their attention.

Total Quality Management (TQM) Defined.

Quality is an important criterion for success, but what does quality mean? For many companies, quality is defined internally from the firm's view and is measured in terms of compliance with predetermined product specifications or standards and with minimum defects. The concept that quality is measured in terms of conformance to products specifications works if the specifications meet the needs of the market and if the product is delivered to the customer in a manner that fills the customer's needs. The assumption is that a product conforming to exact standards is what the market wants. There is, however, some evidence that quality viewed from within a company may result in 'quality for quality's sake' and yet not fully meet customer expectations of a quality product.[9]

Conformance to standards is absolutely necessary for quality, but a customer's perception of quality includes more. A study of the differences between businesses with a poor quality image and those with a good quality image found that businesses with poor quality images relative to that of competitors:

- Downgraded the customer's viewpoint.
- Made high quality synonymous with tight tolerance.
- Tied quality objectives to manufacturing flow.
- Expressed quality objectives as number of defects per unit.
- Formalized quality control systems only for the manufacturing function.

By contrast, businesses praised by customers for a positive quality image:

- Identified customer's real needs through market research.
- Emphasized real rather than imagined customer expectations.
- Formulated quality control systems for all functions, not just manufacturing.[10]

Total quality management (TQM) is a corporate strategy that focuses total company efforts on manufacturing superior products with continuous technological improvement and zero defects that satisfy customer needs. Defining quality as customer satisfaction means the marketer must continually monitor the customer's changing requirements as well as competitive offerings and adjust product offerings as needed, because the customer evaluates a company's product relative to competing products. Your product may be the 'best engineered' in the market with zero defects, but if it does not fulfil all your customer's expectations as well as a competitor's does, the competition wins.

Cost Containment and International Sourcing

As global competition intensifies, profit margins are squeezed. To stay profitable, companies seek ways to keep costs within a range that permits competitive pricing. Global sourcing, a major driving force behind companies producing goods around the world, is used to minimize costs and risks. It is rapidly becoming a prerequisite to competing in today's marketplace.

Lower costs are not the only advantage to global sourcing; flexibility and dependability are also important benefits. Worldwide sources strengthen the reliability of quality and supply. Companies can achieve technical supremacy by securing access to innovative technology from offshore sources and perhaps prevent competitors from obtaining the technology as well. The uniqueness of a company's needs and their availability lead a company to source globally. To establish a foothold in markets that might otherwise be closed, companies may source some goods to comply with a country's local-content requirements.

Collaborative Relationships

The accelerating rate of technological progress, market demand created by global industrialization, and the creation of new middle classes will result in tremendous potential in global markets. But along with this surge in global demand comes an increase in competition as technology and management capabilities spread beyond global companies to new competitors from Asia, Europe and Latin America.[11]

GOING INTERNATIONAL 11.2

BENETTON'S STRATEGY

Benetton has achieved its retail distribution through an unusual arrangement with 'agents', first in Italy and other European countries, and now in emerging economies. According to one of the company's marketing executives, the term 'franchising' in describing Benetton is a misnomer. Agents of the company are assigned vast territories, largely through verbal agreements, in which they try to develop Benetton retail outlets. They find smaller investors and store operators exhibiting a 'Benetton mentality' to form individual partnerships. An individual agent might supervise and hold an interest in a number of stores. In 1982, Benetton conducted business with 35 agents. Store owners are neither required to pay Benetton a fee nor a royalty for using its name. They are required to carry only Benetton merchandise, maintain a minimum sales level (equivalent to orders for about 3500 garments per year), adhere to suggested mark-ups of about 80 per cent above cost and pay for their orders within 90 days.

Although global markets offer tremendous potential, companies seeking to function effectively in a fragmented global market of five billion people are being forced to stretch production, design and marketing resources and capabilities because of the intensity of competition and the pace of technology. Improving quality and staying on the cutting edge of technology are critical and basic for survival but often are not enough. Restructuring, reorganizing and downsizing are all avenues being taken by firms to strengthen their competitive positions.

Additionally, many multinational companies are realizing they must develop long-term, mutually beneficial relationships throughout the company and beyond: to competitors, suppliers, governments and customers. In short, multinational companies are developing orientations that focus on building collaborative relationships to promote long-term alliances, and they are seeking continuous, mutually beneficial exchanges instead of one-time sales or events.

These collaborative relationships are a mindset characterizing an approach to management that can be described as relational exchanges. Relational exchanges occur (1) internally among functional departments, business units, subsidiaries and employees and (2) externally among customers (both intermediary and final), suppliers of goods and services, competitors, government agencies and related businesses where a mutually beneficial goal is sought.[12]

Collaborative relationships[13] can be grouped into two broad categories: relationship marketing—those relationships that focus on the marketing process; and strategic business alliances— those relationships that encompass the other activities of the business enterprise.[14]

A study of CEOs of multinational companies on strategies for the year 2000 and beyond revealed that most felt that just satisfying the customer will not be enough. The focus will have to be more on the customer, who will be the strongest influence on the corporation.[15] Companies must rid themselves of the one-time-sale orientation and focus instead on servicing the consumer's needs over time.

Strategic International Alliances (SIA)

Strategic international alliances are sought as a way to shore up weaknesses and increase competitive strengths. Opportunities for rapid expansion into new markets, access to new technology, more efficient production and marketing costs and additional sources of capital are motives for engaging in strategic international alliances.

An SIA is a business relationship established by two or more companies to cooperate out of mutual need and to share risk in achieving a common objective. A strategic international alliance implies (1) that there is a common objective, (2) that one partner's weakness is offset by the other's strength, (3) that reaching the objective alone would be too costly, take too much time or be too risky and (4) that together their respective strengths make possible what otherwise would be unattainable. In short, an SIA is a synergistic relationship established to achieve a common goal where both parties benefit.

Opportunities abound the world over, but to benefit, firms must be current in new technology, have the ability to keep abreast of technological change, have distribution systems to capitalize on global demand, have cost-effective manufacturing and have capital to build new systems as necessary. Other reasons to enter into strategic alliances are to:[16]

1. Acquire needed current market bases.
2. Acquire needed technological bases.
3. Utilize excess manufacturing capacity.
4. Reduce new market risk and entry costs.
5. Accelerate product introductions demanded by rapid technological changes and shorter product life cycles.
6. Achieve economies of scale in productions, research and development or marketing.
7. Overcome cultural and trade barriers.
8. Extend the existing scope of operations.

The scope of what a company needs to do and what it can do is at a point where even the largest firms engage in alliances to maintain their competitiveness. Table 11.2 and Figure 11.1 show the different alliances in the airline industry and in the European television broadcast market.[17]

A company enters a strategic alliance to acquire the skills necessary to achieve its objectives more effectively, at a lower cost or with less risk than if it acted alone.[18] For example, a company strong in research and development skills and weak in the ability or capital to successfully market a product will seek an alliance to offset its weakness—one partner to provide marketing skills and capital and the other to provide technology and a product. The majority of alliances today are designed to exploit markets and/or technology.[19]

Many companies are entering SIAs to be in a strategic position to be competitive and to benefit from the expected growth in the single European market. One example is General Mills which wants a share of the rapidly growing breakfast-cereal market in Europe. It could be worth hundreds of millions of dollars as health-conscious Europeans change their breakfast diet from eggs and bacon to dry cereal. Kellogg has been in Europe since 1920 and controls about half of the market. General Mills, Kellogg's major US competitor, has set its sights on a 20 per cent share of the EU market and it plans to achieve that goal with Cereal Partners Worldwide (CPW), a joint venture between General Mills and Nestlé.

It would be extremely costly to enter the market from scratch. Although the cereal business uses cheap commodities as its raw materials, it is both capital and marketing intensive; sales

Table 11.2   The Biggest Airline Alliances

Alliance	Aircraft Fleet	Turnover (billion € [$])	Passengers (million)	GDP Kilometre* (million)	Close Relationships With:
Oneworld American Airlines British Airways Cathay Pacific (Hong Kong) Quantas (Australia) Canadian Airlines	1 157	64 (71)	159.4	390	Aerolineas (Arg); Avianca (Col); Taca, Tam (Brazil); LanChile; Iberia (Spain); Finair; Lot (Poland); Japan Airlines; US Airways
Star Alliance United Airlines (US) Lufthansa (Germany) SAS (Sweden) Air Canada Thai Airways Varig (Brazil)	578	58.7 (65)	188.5	335	Singapore Airlines; Air New Zealand; Ansett (Australia)
Northwest-KLM Northwest Airlines KLM Alitalia Continental Airlines	989	31 (34.4)	134.0	253	Kenya Airways; (*35%*) Japan Air System, Nippon Cargo (Japan); Malaysian Airline System (*16 mln passengers*); America West; Aces (Col); Braathens (Nor); Eurowings (Ger); (talking to China Airlines)
Global Alliance Delta Airlines (US) Swissair Sabena (Belgium) THY Turkish Airlines TAP Air Portugal Austrian Airlines AOM (France)	830	25.3 (28)	149.5	194	Aeromexico; AeroPeru; Air France

*A 'passenger-kilometre' is one kilometre flown with one passenger. The figures give the total amount of 'passenger-kilometre' flown by the alliance.
Source: Based on 'Vier Allianties Beheersen Helft van Luchtvaart', *De Volkskrant*, 22 September, p. 16, and 'Clubable Class Books Slots for Take-off', *The European*, 28 September–4 October 1998, pp. 18–19.

volume must be high before profits begin to develop. Only recently has Kellogg's earned significant profits in Europe.

General Mills wanted a part of this large and rapidly growing market. To reach its goal would have required a manufacturing base and a massive salesforce. Further, Kellogg's stranglehold on supermarkets would have been difficult for an unknown to breach easily. The

Figure 11.1   Europe's Major Pay-TV Players

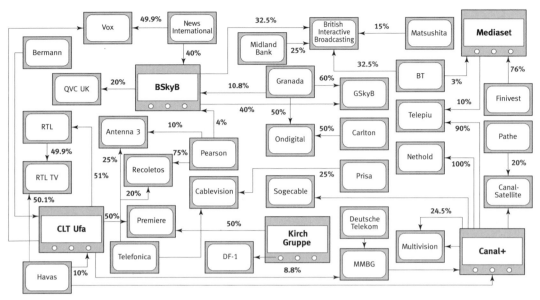

The tangled web. A look at major movers and shakers reveals some of the alliances they have formed. It also shows the variety of players entering the market, ranging from broadcasters such as CLT-Ufa to telcos such as BT to banks such as Midland. Companies are competing and cooperating at the same time. In Britain, News International and Granada are partners in GSkyB, but Granada's stake in the planned Ondigital service will be in direct competition with BSkyB, part-owned by News International. The arrows point towards subsidiaries and the percentages show the stake held in the subsidiaries — a complicated picture.

Source: ARC Chart, *The European*, 10–16 August 1998, p. 10.

solution was a joint venture with Nestlé. Nestlé had everything General Mills lacked—a well-known brand name, a network of plants, a powerful distribution system—except the one thing General Mills could provide—strong cereal brands.[20]

Of course, not all SIAs are successful; some fail and others are dissolved after reaching their goals. Failures can be attributed to a variety of reasons, but all revolve around lack of perceived benefits to one or more of the partners. Benefits may never have been realized in some cases, and different goals and management styles have caused dissatisfaction in other alliances. Such was the case with an alliance between Rubbermaid and the Dutch chemical company, DSM; the two differed on management and strategic issues. Rubbermaid wanted to invest in new products and expansion to combat sluggish demand as the result of a European recession, while DSM baulked at any new investments.[21] In other cases, an alliance may have outlived its usefulness even though the alliance was successful.[22]

Relationship Marketing

Relationship marketing is the category of collaborative relationships that focuses on the marketing process. Like all relational collaborations, relationship marketing has as its focus the creation, development and support of successful relational exchanges throughout the marketing process. The ultimate goal is to achieve a competitive advantage by establishing long-term, mutually beneficial associations with loyal, satisfied customers.[23]

To build a sustainable relationship with customers, businesses are changing their attitudes towards internal relationships and between themselves and traditional competitors, suppliers, distributors and retailers. It becomes a matter of working with customers and all others involved to produce goods that best serve the customers' needs.

The Whirlpool Corporation, as one example, has formal agreements with Procter & Gamble and Unilever to exchange basic information and ideas. Together they are involved at the engineering and technology levels of product development. The basic rationale for this relationship is that the two industries, washing machines and detergents, are codependent—'they can't be designing detergents 10 years out for washing machines that can't use them'—and Whirlpool cannot design satisfactory washing machines without knowledge of the detergents that will be available. Whirlpool also develops relationships with suppliers; instead of working with five steel suppliers, for example, they have partnerships with one or two. They are seeking agreements that give them access to supplier technologies so they can work together on process improvements.[24]

Why relationship marketing?   It helps cement customer loyalty, which means repeat sales and referrals and, thus, market share and revenue growth. A consulting company study estimates that a decrease in customer defection rate of 5 per cent can boost profits by 25 to 95 per cent. The adage that 20 per cent of your customers account for 50 to 80 per cent of your profits has some merit. It has always been good business to focus company resources on the best customers rather than those who are strictly price shoppers.[25] Relationship marketing strengthens that focus.

National Semiconductor Corporation, the multinational chip manufacturer, is forging a partnership with Federal Express Corporation, noted for its worldwide electronic communications and air–truck network. The partnership will allow the chip manufacturer to close its costly global warehouse system, to guarantee just-in-time delivery from its Singapore plant to thousands of customers worldwide within 48 hours, to plan product deliveries precisely and even to divert product to new locations at short notice.

STRATEGIC PLANNING

Strategic planning is a systematized way of relating to the future. It is an attempt to manage the effects of external, uncontrollable factors on the firm's strengths, weaknesses, objectives and goals to attain a desired end. Further, it is a commitment of resources to a country market to achieve specific goals. In other words, planning is the job of making things happen that may not otherwise occur.

Is there a difference between strategic planning for a domestic company and for an international company? The principles of planning are not in themselves different, but the intricacies of the operating environments of the multinational corporation (host country, home and corporate environments), its organizational structure, and the task of controlling a multicountry operation, create differences in the complexity and process of international planning.

Strategic planning allows for rapid growth of the international function, changing markets, increasing competition and the ever-varying challenges of different national markets. The plan must blend the changing parameters of external country environments with corporate objectives and capabilities to develop a sound, workable marketing programme. A strategic

GOING INTERNATIONAL 11.3

STRATEGIC ALLIANCES IN JAPANESE AUTO INDUSTRY

Company	Product	Plants	Alliances	Possible suitors/ mergers	Future
Toyota (annual production: 4 890 000)	Cars, light commercials, trucks	Asia, US, Europe, South America, South Africa, China, Australia, New Zealand	Owns 33% of Daihatsu; marketing of VW/Audi cars in Japan	None foreseeable	Big enough to weather the current storm
Nissan (annual production: 2 743 000)	Cars, 4×4s, light commercials, trucks	Japan, US, Europe, South America, Asia, New Zealand, South Africa	Joint venture with Ford	Daimler-Chrysler (trucks), Ford	Although selling well in Europe, problems at home and high levels of investment in America have caused profit problems. Likely to sell stake in Nissan Diesel to Daimler-Chrysler.
Honda (annual production: 2 300 000)	Cars, 4×4s, light commercials, motorcycles, power products, marine engines	Asia, US, Europe, New Zealand, South America, South Africa	Joint venture with Mercedes in South Africa; Daewoo in Korea	BMW	Hugely profitable and with a strong product range. Is the time right to merge with BMW, a like-minded company?
Mitsubishi (annual production: 1 980 000)	Cars, light commercials, trucks	Japan, US, Europe, Australia	Joint venture Chrysler in US and Volvo in Europe; technical exchanges with Mercedes-Benz in Europe; component production for Ford, GM and Toyota in Australia. Owns 20% of Hyundai, 40% of Proton	Daimler-Chrysler, Volvo	Part of huge Mitsubishi Corporation, so long-term strength is guaranteed
Suzuki (annual production: 1 820 000)	Cars, light commercials, motorcycles, power products, marine engines	Asia, US, Europe, Australia	Small stake of Suzuki owned by GM (5.7%). Produces badge-engineered cars from Subaru and GM	GM	Likely to stay independent, though might forge more joint ventures with GM

GOING INTERNATIONAL 11.3 (continued)

Company	Product	Plants	Alliances	Possible suitors/ mergers	Future
Mazda (annual production: 1 100 000)	Cars, light commercials	Asia, US	Ford owns 33% of Mazda	Ford	Maybe it is time for Mazda to concentrate on niche cars such as the MX and Xedos ranges
Daihatsu (annual production: 900 000)	Cars, micro cars, 4×4s, light commercials	Asia	33% owned by Toyota and builds some Toyota-badged cars. Joint venture with Paggio in Italy to produce some small van, with Briggs and Stratton in America to build industrial engines	Toyota	Unlikely to get much bigger. Safely tucked under Toyota's wing
Subaru (annual production: 554 300)	Cars, 4×4s	Asia, US, Europe	Part of Fuji heavy industries. Badges Hungarian-made 4×4 Suzuki Swift as a Subaru Justy	Rally successes would be an asset to a performance car division, which Daimler-Chrysler lacks	Organic growth only unless snapped up by a multinational
Isuzu (annual production: 349 000)	4×4s, light commercials, trucks	Asia, US	Partly owned by GM (37.8%). Joint partner in IBC in Luton, UK, with GM	GM	When the going gets tough, Isuzu's future will look shaky

Source: Based on 'Japan's Road to Mega-mergers', *The European*, 18–24 May 1998, p. 23.

plan commits corporate resources to products and markets to increase competitiveness and profits.

Planning relates to the formulation of goals and methods of accomplishing them, so it is both a process and a philosophy. Structurally, planning may be viewed as corporate, strategic and/or tactical. International planning at the corporate level is essentially long-term, incorporating generalized goals for the enterprise as a whole. Strategic planning is conducted at the highest levels of management and deals with products, capital and research, and long- and short-term goals of the company. Tactical planning or market planning pertains to specific actions and to the allocation of resources used to implement strategic planning goals in specific markets. Tactical plans are made at the local level and address marketing and advertising questions.

A major advantage to a company involved in strategic planning is the discipline imposed by the process. An international marketer who has gone through the planning process has a framework for analysing marketing problems and opportunities and a basis for coordinating information from different country markets. The process of planning may be as important as the plan itself because it forces decision makers to examine all factors that affect the success of a marketing programme and involves those who will be responsible for its implementation.

Company Objectives and Resources

Evaluation of a company's objectives and resources is crucial in all stages of planning for international operations. Each new market entered can require a complete evaluation, including existing commitments, relative to the parent company's objectives and resources. As markets grow increasingly competitive, as companies find new opportunities, and as the cost of entering foreign markets increases, companies need such planning.

Foreign market opportunities do not always parallel corporate objectives; it may be necessary to change the objectives, alter the scale of international plans or abandon them. One market may offer immediate profit but have a poor long-run outlook, while another may offer the reverse. Only when corporate objectives are clear can such differences be reconciled effectively.

International Commitment

The strategic planning approach taken by an international firm affects the degree of internationalization to which management is philosophically committed. Such commitment affects the specific international strategies and decisions of the firm. After company objectives have been identified, management needs to determine whether it is prepared to make the level of commitment required for successful international operations—commitment in terms of resources to be invested, personnel for managing the international organization and determination to stay in the market long enough to realize a return on these investments.

The Planning Process

Whether a company is marketing in several countries or is entering a foreign market for the first time, planning is a major factor of success. The first-time foreign marketer must decide what products to develop, in which markets, and with what level of resource commitment. For the company already committed, the key decisions involve allocating effort and resources among countries and product, deciding on new markets to develop or old ones to withdraw from, and which products to develop or drop. Guidelines and systematic procedures are essential for evaluating international opportunities and risks and for developing strategic plans to take advantage of such opportunities. The process illustrated in Figure 11.2 offers a systematic guide to planning for the multinational firm operating in several countries.

Phase 1—Preliminary Analysis and Screening. Matching Company/Country Needs.   Whether a company is new to international marketing or heavily involved, an evaluation of potential markets is the first step in the planning process. A critical first

Figure 11.2   International Planning Process

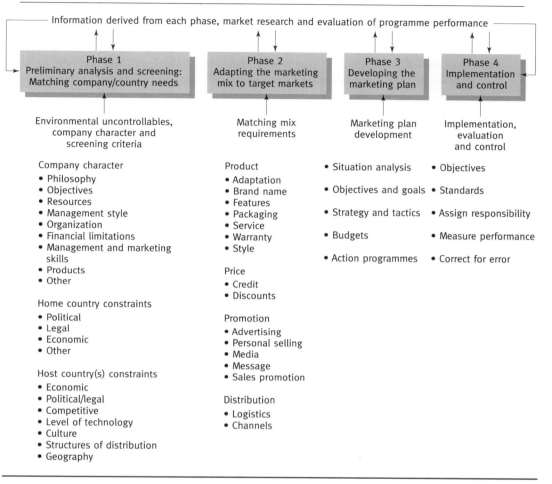

Information derived from each phase, market research and evaluation of programme performance

| Phase 1 Preliminary analysis and screening: Matching company/country needs | Phase 2 Adapting the marketing mix to target markets | Phase 3 Developing the marketing plan | Phase 4 Implementation and control |

Environmental uncontrollables, company character and screening criteria

Matching mix requirements

Marketing plan development

Implementation, evaluation and control

Company character
- Philosophy
- Objectives
- Resources
- Management style
- Organization
- Financial limitations
- Management and marketing skills
- Products
- Other

Home country constraints
- Political
- Legal
- Economic
- Other

Host country(s) constraints
- Economic
- Political/legal
- Competitive
- Level of technology
- Culture
- Structures of distribution
- Geography

Product
- Adaptation
- Brand name
- Features
- Packaging
- Service
- Warranty
- Style

Price
- Credit
- Discounts

Promotion
- Advertising
- Personal selling
- Media
- Message
- Sales promotion

Distribution
- Logistics
- Channels

- Situation analysis
- Objectives and goals
- Strategy and tactics
- Budgets
- Action programmes

- Objectives
- Standards
- Assign responsibility
- Measure performance
- Correct for error

question in the international planning process is deciding in which existing country market to make a market investment. A company's strengths and weaknesses, products, philosophies and objectives must be matched with a country's constraining factors as well as limitations and potential. In the first part of the planning process, countries are analysed and screened to eliminate those that do not offer sufficient potential for further consideration.

The next step is to establish screening criteria against which prospective countries can be evaluated. These criteria are ascertained by an analysis of company objectives, resources and other corporate capabilities and limitations. It is important to determine the reasons for entering a foreign market and the returns expected from such an investment. A company's commitment to international business and objectives for going international are important in establishing evaluation criteria. Minimum market potential, minimum profit, return on investment, acceptable competitive levels, standards of political stability, acceptable legal requirements and other measures appropriate for the company's products are examples of the evaluation criteria to be established.

Once evaluation criteria are set, a complete analysis of the environment within which a company plans to operate is made. The environment consists of the uncontrollable elements discussed earlier and includes both home-country and host-country restraints, marketing objectives and any other company limitations or strengths that exist at the beginning of each planning period. Although an understanding of uncontrollable environments is important in domestic market planning, the task is more complex in foreign marketing because each country under consideration presents the foreign marketer with a different set of unfamiliar environmental constraints. It is this stage in the planning process that more than anything else distinguishes international from domestic marketing planning.

The results of phase 1 provide the marketer with the basic information necessary to: (1) evaluate the potential of a proposed country market, (2) identify problems that would eliminate the country from further consideration, (3) identify environmental elements which need further analysis, (4) determine which part of the marketing mix must be adapted to meet local market needs and (5) develop and implement a marketing action plan.

Information generated in phase 1 helps a company avoid the mistakes that plagued Radio Shack Corporation, a leading merchandiser of consumer electronic equipment in the United States, when it first went international. Radio Shack's early attempts at international marketing in Western Europe resulted in a series of costly mistakes that could have been avoided had it properly analysed the uncontrollable elements of the countries targeted for the first attempt at multinational marketing. The company staged its first Christmas promotion for 25 December in The Netherlands, unaware that the Dutch celebrate St Nicholas Day and gift giving on 5 December. Legal problems in various countries interfered with some of their plans; they were unaware that most European countries have laws prohibiting the sale of citizen-band radios, one of the company's most lucrative US products and one they expected to sell in Europe. A free flashlight promotion in German stores was promptly stopped by German courts because giveaways violate German sales laws. In Belgium, the company overlooked a law requiring a government tax stamp on all window signs, and poorly selected store sites resulted in many of the new stores closing shortly after opening.[26]

Phase 2—Adapting the Marketing Mix to Target Markets. A more detailed examination of the components of the marketing mix is the purpose of phase 2. When target markets are selected, the market mix must be evaluated in light of the data generated in phase 1. In which ways can the product, promotion, price and distribution be standardized and in which ways must they be adapted to meet target market requirements? Incorrect decisions at this point lead to costly mistakes through efficiency loss from lack of standardization, products inappropriate for the intended market and/or costly mistakes in improper pricing, advertising, and promotional blunders. The primary goal of phase 2 is to decide on a marketing mix adjusted to the cultural constraints imposed by the uncontrollable elements of the environment that effectively achieves corporate objectives and goals.

An example of the type of analysis done in phase 2 is the process used by the Nestlé Company. Each product manager has a country fact book that includes much of the information suggested in phase 1. The country fact book analyses in detail a variety of culturally related questions. In Germany, the product manager for coffee must furnish answers to a number of questions. How does a German rank coffee in the hierarchy of consumer products? Is Germany a high or a low per capita consumption market? (These facts alone can be of enormous consequence. In Sweden the annual per capita consumption of coffee is 18 pounds, while in Japan it's half a gram!) How is coffee used—in bean form, ground or powdered? If it is ground, how is it brewed? Which coffee is preferred—Brazilian Santos blended with Colombian coffee or robusta from the Ivory Coast? Is it roasted? Do the people prefer dark roasted or blonde coffee? (The colour of Nestlé's soluble coffee must resemble as closely as possible the colour of the coffee consumed in the country.) As a result of the answers to these and other questions, Nestlé produces 200 types of instant coffee (Nescafé), from the dark robust espresso preferred in Latin countries to the lighter blends popular in the United States.

Almost €45 million ($50 million) a year is spent in four research laboratories around the world experimenting with new shadings in colour, aroma and flavour. Do the Germans drink coffee after lunch or with their breakfast? Do they take it black or with cream or milk? Do they drink coffee in the evening? Do they sweeten it? (In France, the answer is clear: in the morning, coffee with milk; at noon, black coffee—i.e. two totally different coffees.) At what age do people begin drinking coffee? Is it a traditional beverage as in France? Is it a form of rebellion among the young as in England where coffee drinking has been taken up in defiance of tea-drinking parents? Or is it a gift as in Japan? There is a coffee boom in tea-drinking Japan where Nescafé is considered a luxury gift item; instead of chocolates and flowers, Nescafé is toted in fancy containers to dinners and birthday parties. With such depth of information, the product manager can evaluate the marketing mix in terms of the information in the country fact book.

Phase 2 also permits the marketer to determine possibilities for standardization. By grouping all countries together and looking at similarities, market characteristics that can be standardized become evident.

Frequently, the results of the analysis in phase 2 indicate that the marketing mix would require such drastic adaptation that a decision not to enter a particular market is made. For example, a product may have to be reduced in physical size to fit the needs of the market, but the additional manufacturing cost of a smaller size may be too high to justify market entry. Also the price required to show a profit might be too high for a majority of the market to afford. If there is no way to reduce the price, sales potential at the higher price may be too low to justify entry.

On the other hand, additional research in this phase may provide information that can suggest ways to standardize marketing programmes among two or more country markets. This was the case for Nestlé when research revealed that young coffee drinkers in England and Japan had identical motivations. As a result, Nestlé now uses principally the same message in both markets.

The answers to three major questions are generated in phase 2: (1) Which elements of the marketing mix can be standardized and where is standardization not culturally possible? (2) Which cultural/environmental adaptations are necessary for successful acceptance of the marketing mix? (3) Will adaptation costs allow profitable market entry? Based on the results in phase 2, a second screening of countries may take place with some countries dropped from further consideration. The next phase in the planning process is development of a marketing plan.

Phase 3—Developing the Marketing Plan.   At this stage of the planning process, a marketing plan is developed for the target market—whether a single country or a global market set. It begins with a situation analysis and culminates in a specific action programme for the market. The specific plan establishes what is to be done, by whom, how it is to be done and when. Included are budgets and sales and profit expectations. Just as in phase 2, a decision not to enter a specific market may be made if it is determined that company marketing objectives and goals cannot be met.

Phase 4—Implementation and Control.   A 'go' decision in phase 3 triggers implementation of specific plans and anticipation of successful marketing. However, the planning process does not end at this point. All marketing plans require coordination and control (phase 4) during the period of implementation. Many businesses do not control marketing plans as thoroughly as they could even though continuous monitoring and control could increase their success. An evaluation and control system requires performance objective action, that is, to bring the plan back on track should standards of performance fall short. A global orientation facilitates the difficult but extremely important management tasks of coordinating and controlling the complexities of international marketing.

While the model is presented as a series of sequential phases, the planning process is a dynamic, continuous set of interacting variables with information continuously building among phases. The phases outline a crucial path to be followed for effective, systematic planning. Furthermore, it provides the basis for viewing all country markets and their inter-relationships as an integrated global unit.[27] By following the guidelines presented in Part VI, 'The Country Notebook—A Guide for Developing a Marketing Plan', the international marketer can put the strategic planning process into operation.[28]

ALTERNATIVE MARKET-ENTRY STRATEGIES

When a company makes the commitment to go international, it must choose an entry strategy. This decision should reflect an analysis of market potential, company capabilities, and the degree of marketing involvement and commitment management is prepared to make. A company's approach to foreign marketing can require minimal investment and be limited to infrequent exporting with little thought given to market development. Or a company can make large investments of capital and management effort to capture and maintain a permanent, specific share of world markets.[29] Both approaches can be profitable.

There is a variety of foreign market entry strategies from which to choose. Each has particular advantages and shortcomings, depending on company strengths and weaknesses, the degree of commitment the company is willing or able to make and market characteristics, as depicted by Figure 11.3.

Exporting

A company might decide to enter the international arena by exporting from the home country. This means of foreign market development is the easiest and most common approach employed by companies taking their first international step because the risks of financial loss can be minimized. Exporting is a common approach for the mature international company as well. Several companies engage in exporting as their major market-entry method. Generally, early motives are to skim the cream from the market or gain business to absorb overhead. Even though such motives might appear opportunistic, exporting is a sound and permanent form of operating in international marketing. The mechanics of exporting and the different middlemen available to facilitate the exporting process are discussed in detail in the next chapters.

Licensing

A means of establishing a foothold in foreign markets without large capital outlays is licensing. Patent rights, trademark rights and the rights to use technological processes are granted in foreign licensing. It is a favourite strategy for small- and medium-sized companies although by no means limited to such companies. Not many confine their foreign operations to

Figure 11.3   Factors Influencing Market Entry Strategies

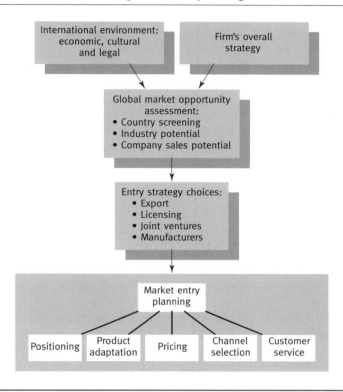

licensing alone; it is generally viewed as a supplement to exporting or manufacturing, rather than the only means of entry into foreign markets. The advantages of licensing are most apparent: when capital is scarce, when import restrictions forbid other means of entry, when a country is sensitive to foreign ownership, or when it is necessary to protect patents and trademarks against cancellation for nonuse. Although this may be the least profitable way of entering a market, the risks and headaches are less than for direct investments; it is a legitimate means of capitalizing on intellectual property in a foreign market.

Licensing takes several forms. Licences may be granted for production processes, for the use of a trade name, or for the distribution of imported products. Licences may be closely controlled or be autonomous, and they permit expansion without great capital or personnel commitment if licensees have the requisite capabilities. Not all licensing experiences are successful because of the burden of finding, supervising and inspiring licensees.

Joint Ventures

Joint ventures (JVs), one of the more important types of collaborative relationship, have accelerated sharply during the past 20 years. Besides serving as a means of lessening political and economic risks by the amount of the partner's contribution to the venture, joint ventures provide a less risky way to enter markets that pose legal and cultural barriers than would be the case in an acquisition of an existing company.

In the Asian Pacific Rim, US companies face less-familiar legal and cultural barriers than they find in Western Europe, and thus prefer joint ventures to buying existing businesses. In 1993, for example, US companies acquired 225 European firms and entered into 67 joint ventures, whereas in Asia, US firms acquired only 27 existing companies but formed 97 joint ventures.[30]

Local partners can often lead the way through legal mazes and provide the outsider with help in understanding cultural nuances. A joint venture can be attractive to an international marketer (1) when it enables a company to utilize the specialized skills of a local partner, (2) when it allows the marketer to gain access to a partner's local distribution system, (3) when a company seeks to enter a market where wholly-owned activities are prohibited, (4) when it provides access to markets protected by tariffs or quotas and (5) when the firm lacks the capital or personnel capabilities to expand its international activities.

In China, a country considered to be among the riskiest in Asia, there have been 49 400 joint ventures established in the first 15 years since they began allowing JVs. Among the many reasons JVs are so popular is that they offer a way of getting around high Chinese tariffs, allowing a company to gain a competitive price advantage over imports. By manufacturing locally with a Chinese partner rather than importing, China's high tariffs (the tariff on motor vehicles is 200 per cent, 150 per cent on cosmetics and the average on miscellaneous products is 75 per cent) are bypassed and additional savings are achieved by using low-cost Chinese labour.[31] Many Western brands are manufactured and marketed in China at prices that would not be possible if the products were imported.

A joint venture is differentiated from other types of strategic alliances or collaborative relationships in that a joint venture is a partnership of two or more participating companies that have joined forces to create a separate legal entity. Joint ventures should also be differentiated from minority holdings by an MNC in a local firm. Four factors are associated with joint ventures: (1) JVs are established, separate, legal entities; (2) they acknowledge intent by the partners to share in the management of the JV; (3) they are partnerships between legally incorporated entities, such as companies, chartered organizations or governments, and not between individuals; (4) equity positions are held by each of the partners.

Nearly all companies active in world trade participate in at least one joint venture somewhere; many number their joint ventures in the dozens. A recent Conference Board study indicated that more than 50 per cent of Fortune 500 companies were engaged in one or more international joint ventures. In Japan alone, Royal Dutch Shell has more than 30 joint ventures; IBM has more than 35.[32]

Franchising

Franchising is a rapidly growing form of licensing in which the franchiser provides a standard package of products, systems and management services, and the franchisee provides market knowledge, capital and personal involvement in management. The combination of skills permits flexibility in dealing with local market conditions and yet provides the parent firm with a reasonable degree of control. The franchiser can follow through on marketing of the products to the point of final sale. It is an important form of vertical market integration. Potentially, the franchise system provides an effective blending of skill centralization and operational decentralization, and has become an increasingly important form of international marketing. In some cases, franchising is having a profound effect on traditional businesses. In England, for example, it is estimated that annual franchised sales of fast foods is nearly €1.8 billion ($2 billion), which accounts for 30 per cent of all foods eaten outside the home.

Prior to 1970, international franchising was not a major activity. A survey by the International Franchising Association revealed that only 14 per cent of its member firms had franchises outside of the United States, and the majority of those were in Canada. By the 1990s, more than 30 000 franchises of US firms were located in countries throughout the world. Franchises include soft drinks, motels, retailing, fast foods, car rentals, automotive services, recreational services and a variety of business services from print shops to sign shops. Franchising is the fastest-growing market-entry strategy. It is often among the first types of foreign retail business to open in the emerging market economies of Eastern Europe, the former republics of Russia and China. McDonald's is in Moscow (their first store seats 700 inside and has 27 cash registers), and Kentucky Fried Chicken is in China (the Beijing KFC store has the highest sales volume of any KFC store in the world).

There are three types of franchise agreements used by franchising firms: master franchise, joint venture and licensing, any one of which can have a country's government as one partner. The master franchise is the most inclusive agreement and the method used in more than half of the international franchises. The master franchise gives the franchisee the rights to a specific area (many are for an entire country) with the authority to sell or establish subfranchises. McDonald's franchise in Moscow is a master agreement owned by a Canadian firm and its partner, the Moscow City Council Department of Food Services.[33]

Consortia

The consortium and syndicate are similar to the joint venture and could be classified as such except for two unique characteristics: (1) they typically involve a large number of participants; (2) they frequently operate in a country or market in which none of the participants is currently active. Consortia are developed for pooling financial and managerial resources and to lessen risks. Often, huge construction projects are built under a consortium arrangement in which major contractors with different specialties form a separate company specifically to negotiate for and produce one job. One firm usually acts as the lead firm or the newly formed corporation may exist quite independently of its originators.

Manufacturing

Another means of foreign market development and entry is manufacturing within a foreign country. A company may manufacture locally to capitalize on low-cost labour, to avoid high import taxes, to reduce the high costs of transportation to market, to gain access to raw materials, and/or as a means of gaining market entry. Seeking lower labour costs offshore is no longer an unusual strategy. A hallmark of global companies today is the establishment of manufacturing operations throughout the world. This is a trend that will increase as barriers to free trade are eliminated and companies can locate manufacturing wherever it is most cost effective.

There are three types of manufacturing investments by firms in foreign countries: (1) market seeking; (2) resource seeking; (3) efficiency seeking. Investments in China, for example, are of first kind, where companies are attracted by the size of the market. Investment in India, especially by a number of fashion garment producers such as Mexx and Marc O' Polo are of second type. While investments in Malaysia and Singapore by electronics manufacturers such as Philips and Motorola are of third type.

Countertrade

Countertrade deals are now on the increase and represent a significant proportion of world trade. Countertrade ties the export and other foreign sales to an undertaking from the seller to purchase products from the buyer or a third party in the buyer's country. There are several reasons behind the demand for countertrade, such as promotion of local exports, saving scarce foreign exchange, balancing trade flows and/or ensuring guaranteed supplies. The terms and conditions for countertrade are not standardized and may be different from market to market. Other terms used for countertrade include counterpurchase, buyback, compensation and offset and barter. In the 1960s, Eastern European countries started demanding counter-trade to achieve a balance in foreign trade. Nowadays, however, it is common practice in developing as well as in developed markets, and there are a number of companies that specialize in advising on countertrade and a number of trading houses that act as clearing houses for countertrade products.[33]

SUMMARY

Expanding markets around the world have increased competition for all levels of inter-national marketing. To keep abreast of the competition and maintain a viable position for increasingly competitive markets, a global perspective is necessary. Global competition also requires quality products designed to meet ever-changing customer needs and rapidly advancing technology. Cost containment, customer satisfaction and a greater number of players mean that every opportunity to refine international business practices must be examined in the light of company goals. Collaborative relationships, strategic international alliances, strategic planning and alternative market-entry strategies are important avenues to global marketing that must be implemented in the planning of global marketing management.

QUESTIONS

1. Define strategic planning. How does strategic planning for international marketing differ from domestic marketing?
2. Discuss the benefits to an MNC of accepting the global market concept.
3. Define the concept of quality. How do the concept of quality and TQM relate?
4. Cost containment and technological improvement are said to be the basis for competition. Why? Discuss.
5. Discuss how consumer satisfaction and quality relate.
6. Explain the three points that define a global approach to international marketing.
7. Discuss the effect of shorter product life cycles on a company's planning process.
8. What is the importance of collaborative relationships to competition?
9. Discuss what is meant by relationship marketing and how it does differ from traditional marketing.

10. In phases 1 and 2 of the international planning process, countries may be dropped from further consideration as potential markets. Discuss some of the conditions in each phase that may exist in a country that would lead a marketer to exclude a country.
11. Assume that you are the director of international marketing for a company producing refrigerators. Select one country in Asia and one in Europe and develop screening criteria to use in evaluating the two countries. Make any additional assumptions that are necessary about your company.
12. How will entry into a developed foreign market differ from entry into a relatively untapped market?
13. Explain the popularity of joint ventures.

REFERENCES

1. 'Ford's Reorganization: Another New Model', *The Economist*, 7 January 1995, pp. 52–53.

2. See, for example, Tamir Agmon and Richard Drobnick (eds), *Small Firms in Global Competition* (New York: Oxford University Press, 1994).

3. 'It's A Small (Business) World', *Business Week*, 17 April 1995, pp. 96–101.

4. Cyndee Miller, 'Chasing Global Dream', *Marketing News*, 2 December 1996, pp. 1–2

5. Eugene H. Fram and Riad Ajami, 'Globalization of Markets and Shopping Stress: Cross-Country Comparisons', *Business Horizons*, January–February 1994, pp. 17–23.

6. 'Ford: Alex Trotman's Daring Global Strategy', *Business Week*, 3 April 1995, pp. 94–104.

7. For other examples, see Lawrence W. Tuller, *Going Global: New Opportunities for Growing Companies to Compete in World Markets* (Homewood, IL: Business One Irwin, 1991), p. 238.

8. 'Quality: How To Make It Pay', *Business Week*, 8 August 1994, pp. 54–59.

9. Bradley T. Gale and Robert D. Buzzell, 'Market-Perceived Quality: Key Strategic Concept', *IEEE Engineering Management Review*, March 1990, pp. 41–42.

10. 'Tearing Up Today's Organization Chart', *Business Week*, 21st Century Capitalism Issue, 1994, pp. 80–82.

11. This section draws from Robert M. Morgan and Shelby D. Hunt, 'The Commitment-Trust Theory of Relationship Marketing', *Journal of Marketing*, July 1994, pp. 20–38.

12. The authors prefer to use the term *collaborative relationship* to refer to all forms of collaborative efforts between a company and its customers, markets, suppliers, manufacturing partners, research and development partners, government agencies and all other types of alliances. Consumer orientation, Keiretsu and strategic alliances can all be grouped under the broad rubric of collaborative relationships. All seek similar universal 'truths'—participant satisfaction, long-term ties, loyalty and mutually beneficial exchanges. Yet, there are some fundamental differences among them.

13. Regina Fazio Maruca, 'The Right Way to Go Global: An Interview with Whirlpool CEO David Whitwam', *Harvard Business Review*, March–April 1994, p. 143.

14. 'MNCs of Year 2000: Corporate Strategies for Success', *Crossborder Monitor*, 23 March 1994, pp. 1–2.

15. Julie Chohen Mason, 'Strategic Alliances: Partnering for Success', *Management Review*, May 1993, pp. 10–15.

16. For a useful guide on SIAS, see e.g. David Faulkner, *International Strategic Alliances; Co-operating to Compete* (London: McGraw Hill, 1995).

17. For a complete discussion of the logic of SIAs, see Kenichi Ohmae, *The Borderless World* (New York: Harper Business, 1990), Chap. 8, 'The Global Logic of Strategic Alliances', pp. 114–136; and Kenichi Ohmae, 'Putting Global Logic First', *Harvard Business Review*, January 1995, pp. 119–125.

18. Roger Kashlak, Rajan Chandran and Anthony Di Benedetto, 'Reciprocity in International Business: A Study of Telecommunications Alliances and Contracts', *Journal of International Business Studies*, vol. 29, no. 2, 1998, pp. 281–304.

19. John Tagliabue, 'Spoon-to-Spoon Combat Overseas', *The New York Times*, 1 January 1995, p. 17.

20. Anne Field, 'Keep in Touch, You Hear?' *International Business*, June 1994, pp. 26–28.

21. Raju Narisetti, 'Rubbermaid Brings to End Europe Venture', *The Wall Street Journal*, 1 June 1994, p. A-4.

22. J. Daniel McCort, 'A Framework for Evaluating the Relational Extent of a Relationship Marketing Strategy: The Case of Nonprofit Organizations', *Journal of Direct Marketing*, Spring 1994, p. 54.

23. Rahul Jacob, 'Why Some Customers Are More Equal than Others', *Fortune*, 19 September 1994, p. 216.

24. Nicolle Coviello and Hugh Munro, 'Network Relationships and the Internationalization Process of Small Software Firms', *International Business Review*, vol. 6, no. 4, 1997, pp. 361–386.

25. Ram Mudambi, 'The Role of Duration in Multinational Investment Strategies', *Journal of International Business Studies*, vol. 29, no. 2, 1998, pp. 239–262.

26. For a thought-provoking discussion of scenario planning as a tool for strategic planning, see Paul J.H. Schoemaker, 'Scenario Planning: A Tool for

Strategic Thinking', *Sloan Management Review*, vol. 36, issue 2, 1995, pp. 25–40.

27. Students engaged in class projects involving a country analysis should see the Country Notebook section in Part VI of this text for a set of guidelines on developing cultural, economic and market analyses of a country.

28. S. Tamer Cavusgil and Shaoming Zou, 'Marketing Strategy-Performance Relationship: An Investigation of the Empirical Link in Export Market Ventures,' *Journal of Marketing*, January 1994, pp. 1–21.

29. Preet Aulakh, Tamer Cavusgil and M.B. Sarkar, 'Compensation in International Licensing Agreements', *Journal of International Business Studies*, vol. 29, no. 2, 1998, pp. 409–420.

30. Steve Lanier, 'China: Joint Ventures Are Not Just for Giants', *Trade & Culture*, September–October 1994, pp. 17–18.

31. Joel Bleeke and David Ernst (eds), *Collaborating to Compete* (New York: Wiley, 1993).

32. This section draws from a comprehensive review of franchising by Peng S. Chan and Robert T. Justis, 'Franchise Management in East Asia', *Academy of Management Executive*, vol. 4, no. 2, 1990, pp. 75–85.

33. For further details on this topic see: Michael Row, *Countertrade* (London: Euromoney Books, 1989).

Globalization and Competition

Japan, Microsoft's Most Important International Market

Microsoft has been involved in international markets from its earliest years. Today the company has some 48 offices and more than 8000 of its 25 000 employees working in other countries. Of its $11.4 billion in revenues generated in 1997, 58 per cent were from international sales. Microsoft products are available in more than 30 languages and sold in more than 50 countries.

Japan has always been Microsoft's single most important international market. Chairman/CEO Bill Gates reports in his book, *The Road Ahead* (New York: Viking, 1995), even as early as ' . . . 1979 almost half our business was coming from Japan . . . ' (p. 41).

'A simple addition is not enough.'

These four ads are for specific products. Notice the company slogan and some of the other material in English. By 1997 the 'Where do you want to go today?' was a global aspect of the print presentation. Packaging as represented in the lower right-hand corner was also common across countries.

Notice how the background colours of these next three ads are consistent with the puzzle pieces in the first ad. Also, notice how the 'Where do you want to go today?' theme is reflected in the backgrounds—the pyramids in Egypt, the Gaudi Cathedral in Barcelona, Spain, and the Great Wall of China.

'A path to the future.'

'This is the software developer's destination.'

Germany, Another Crucial Foreign Language Market for Microsoft

Notice the 'Windows' colours reflected in the Office 97 and Encarta 97 ads but not in the earlier Office 95 ad. Also, flip back to the first page and see the differences between the Japanese and German versions of the Office 97 ads. Of the four major language categories, Japanese was the last to become part of Microsoft's globalization efforts in advertising copy. What's global and local about the broad reach campaign on the previous pages? Global: the Microsoft 'soft' colours, the messages, the slogan (except in French), and the images. Local: languages used in most of the text (no English in the French ads), the diversity of the people represented in the ads in English, and the Web sites referenced.

'Pay attention investors.' Also the word *inklusive* means *'everything included'* in German.

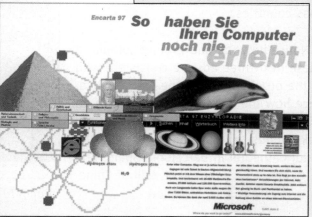

'Use all the information of the world for your business.' Notice the German spelling of *klick*.

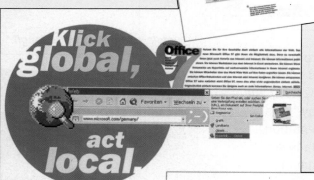

'You have never experienced your computer like this.'

To tap the American market, Mercedes-Benz invested $300 million in a plant in Tuscaloosa, Atlanta, to produce a brand-new car for the local market.

Source: *Business Week*, 31 March 1997, p. 57.

With an investment of $65 million, Kellogg is having a tough time in weaning Indians from hot veggie breakfast to Kellogg's cereals. It has introduced new products to match the local taste.

Source: *Business Week*, 11 August 1997, p. 26.

Foreign brands like Coca-Cola are having tough times in competing with local brands in India (left) and the Philippines (below).

Source: *Business Week*, 14 April 1997, p. 27.

Source: *Business Week*, 11 August 1997, p. 25.

Global brands serve global markets: over the past four and a half years ESPRIT has opened 108 stores in China.

Source: *Business Week*, 11 August 1997, p. 52.

Increasing competition is forcing industrial product companies to be more efficient. DELL computers claims a turnaround time between customer order and delivery of 36 hours.

Source: *Business Week*, 7 April 1997, p. 52.

IKEA's new line of children's furniture and toys put it ahead of its rivals.,

Source: *Business Week*, 6 October 1997, pp. 46 and 47.

Export Trade Mechanics and Logistics

Chapter Outline

Chapter Learning Objectives

What you should learn from Chapter 12

- The added steps necessary to move goods across country borders.

- How various import restrictions are used politically.

- Means of reducing import taxes to remain competitive.

- The mechanics of export documents and their importance.

- The logistics and problems of the physical movement of goods.

- Exporting is an indispensable part of all international business, whether the company markets in one country or is a global marketer.

- Goods manufactured in one country, destined for another, must be moved across borders to enter the distribution system of the target market.

Most countries control the movement of goods crossing their borders, whether leaving (exports) or entering (imports). Export and import documents, tariffs, quotas and other barriers to the free flow of goods between independent sovereignties are requirements that must be met by either the exporter or importer, or both.

The mechanics of exporting adds extra steps and costs to an international marketing sale that are not incurred when marketing domestically. In addition to selecting a target market, designing an appropriate product, establishing a price, planning a promotional programme and selecting a distribution channel, the international marketer must meet the legal requirements of moving goods from one country to another. The exporting process (see Table 12.1) includes the licences and documentation necessary to leave the country, an international carrier to transport the goods, and fulfilment of the requirements necessary to get the shipment legally into another country. These mechanics of exporting are sometimes considered the essence of foreign marketing. Although their importance cannot be minimized, they should not be seen as the primary task of international marketing.

The rules and regulations that cover the exportation and importation of goods and the physical movement of those goods between countries are the special concerns of this chapter.

REGULATIONS AND RESTRICTIONS OF EXPORTING AND IMPORTING

There are many reasons why countries impose some form of regulation and restriction on the exporting and importing of goods. Export regulations can be designed to conserve scarce goods for home consumption or to control the flow of strategic goods to actual or potential enemies. Import regulations may be imposed to protect health, conserve foreign exchange, serve as economic reprisals, protect home industry or provide revenue in the form of tariffs. To comply with various regulations, the exporter may have to acquire licences or permits from the home country and ascertain that the potential customer has the necessary permits for importing goods.

Export Controls

Delivering a product or service is a vital aspect of marketing and product availability is an important part of customer satisfaction. In case of EC crossborder restrictions, the Single Europe Act (1986) was quite clear; from 31 December 1992 the EC will be 'an area without internal frontiers, in which free movement of goods, persons, services and capital is ensured'. In this respect real progress has been made. Single Administrative Document was already introduced in 1993 to replace a number of customs documents. There are no foreign exchange restrictions on transactions across Europe. There are standardized rules and regulations for transport methods and working conditions. However, civil law codes vary across Europe and implication of contract law is not the same in EU countries. It is thus advised that each contract should specify which country's law is to apply.

The major trends over the last few years include: an increased volume of trade using road transport, more use of special cargoes instead of bulk trade and a shift from rail or road transport to a combination of road, rail, air and sea transport to cover the distances more efficiently and to provide door-to-door service.[1]

Import Restrictions

When an exporter plans a sale to a foreign buyer, it is necessary to examine the export restrictions of the home country as well as the import restrictions and regulations of the importing

GOING INTERNATIONAL 12.1

EXPORT SUBSIDIES UNDER REVIEW

The UK's earnings from world trade amounted to £320 billion ($524 billion/€473 billion) in 1996, making it the fifth largest exporter of goods after the US, Germany, Japan and France.

Small UK companies usually approach their local Business Links, the regional advice organization for business, for information about opportunities outside UK. Links, in turn, access the UK-based DTI (Department of Trade and Industry's export promotion arm) which has specialist knowledge of particular markets and foreign office staff at embassies and consulates. In 1997–98 the Foreign Office and DTI spent £220 million ($360 million/€325 million) on export promotion. In the post-cold-war global market, the Foreign Office regarded export promotion as part of its natural job. The department defended its budget of £1 billion ($1.6 billion/€1.5 billion) by claiming that further cuts would endanger Britain's ability to explore new markets in Latin America, China and Eastern Europe. The Foreign Office spent £90 million ($147 million/€133 million) in 1992, more than £100 million ($164 million/€148 million) in 1995 and closer to £150 million ($245 million/€222 million) in 1997 and the same amount in 1998.

In the United States, the companies are subsidized by about $2 billion (€1.8 billion) a year, as claimed by the European Commission. These subsidies are often given as tax exemptions for exports through foreign sales corporations (FSCs). On 1 July 1998, the European Commission made a formal request to the World Trade Organization Panel to investigate US export subsidies that lead to a significant distortion of international trade violating WTO rules.

Source: Based on *The Financial Times*, 2 July 1998 and 4–5 July 1998.

Table 12.1   The Exporting Process

Leaving the Exporting Country	Physical Distribution	Entering the Importing Country
Licences	International shipping	Tariffs, taxes
General	and logistics	Nontariff barriers
Validated	Packing	Standards
Documentation	Insurance	Inspection
Export declaration		Documentation
Commercial invoice		Quotas
Bill of lading		Fees
Consular invoice		Licences
Special certificates		Special certificates
Other documents		Exchange permits
		Other barriers

country. Although the responsibility for import restrictions may rest with the importer, the exporter does not want to ship goods until it is certain that all import regulations have been met. Goods arriving without proper documentation can be denied entry.

There are many types of trade restriction besides import tariffs imposed by the foreign country. A few examples of the 30 basic barriers to exporting considered important by *Business International* include: (1) import licences, quotas and other quantitative restrictions; (2) currency restrictions and allocation of exchange at unfavourable rates on payments for imports; (3) devaluation; (4) prohibitive prior import deposits, prohibition of collection-basis sales and insistence on cash letters of credit; (5) arbitrarily short periods in which to apply for import licences; and (6) delays resulting from pressure on overworked officials or from

FREE TRADE OR HYPOCRISY?

Much has been written about trade problems between the United States, Europe and other countries. The impression is that high tariffs, quotas and export trade subsidies are restrictions used by other countries—that the United States is a free, open market while the rest of the world's markets are riddled with trade restrictions. Neither impression is completely true. The United States does engage in trade restrictions. One estimate is that over 25 per cent of manufactured goods sold in the United States are affected by trade barriers. The cost to US consumers is $50 billion (€45 billion) more annually than if there were no restrictions. Consider a sample of US trade hypocrisy:

Quotas: Sugar quotas imposed by the United States result in a pound of sugar costing 10 cents in Canada versus 35 cents in the United States. US beef quotas cost consumers $873 million (€788 million) a year in higher prices. There are quotas with all major clothing-producing nations and on steel with the EU.

Tariffs: Tariffs average 26 per cent of the value of imported clothing, 40 per cent on orange juice, 40 per cent on peanuts, 115 per cent on low-priced watch parts imported from Taiwan and 40 per cent on leather imports from Japan.

Shipping: Foreign ships are barred from carrying passengers or freight between any two US ports. Food donations to foreign countries cost an extra $100 million (€90 million) because they must be shipped on US carriers.

Subsidies: The United States provided export subsidies to US farmers of 111 per cent for poultry exports, 78 per cent for wheat and flour and more than 100 per cent for rice.

Many of these restrictions will begin to disappear as the provisions of the Uruguay Round of GATT and the WTO apply, but even then countries will have tariffs, quotas and other barriers to trade.

Sources: Abstracted from 'Import Tariffs Imposed by a Protectionist US', *Fortune*, 12 December 1991, p. 14, and James Bovard, 'A US History of Trade Hypocrisy', *The Wall Street Journal*, 8 March 1994, p. 36.

competitors' influence on susceptible officials. The most frequently encountered trade restrictions, besides tariffs, are such nontariff barriers as exchange permits, quotas, import licences, boycotts, standards and voluntary agreements.

The various market barriers that exist among members of the European Union create a major impediment to trade. One study of 20 000 EU exporting firms indicated that the most troublesome barriers were administrative roadblocks, border-crossing delays and capital controls. One such barrier was imposed by the French government against Japanese VCRs. All Japanese VCRs were directed to land only at one port where only one inspector was employed; hence, only 10 or 12 VCRs could enter France each day.[2]

As the EU becomes a single market, many of the barriers that existed among member countries have been erased. The single European market has no doubt made trade easier among its member countries, but there is a rising concern that a fully integrated EU will become a market with even stronger protectionist barriers towards nonmember countries.

Tariffs.   Tariffs are the taxes or customs duties levied against goods imported from another country. All countries have tariffs for the purpose of raising revenue and protecting home industries from the competition of foreign-produced goods. Tariff rates are based on value or quantity or a combination of both.

The EU is the largest member of GATT/WTO in terms of trade, including intra-EU trade, it accounts for almost 40 per cent of world merchandise trade. However, with increasing integration the EU's trade with third countries is decreasing. The Treaty of Rome required the EC to develop a Common Commercial Policy (CCP), the aim of which is to liberalize world trade. The key element of CCP is the Common External Tariff (CET) which all member states must apply. The community has a number of preferential trade agreements, for example with EFTA and Turkey. But at the same time, it has variable levies on imported food and quotas on imported textiles through the Multi-Fibre Agreement (MFA), as well as a number of other restrictions on imports that harm sensitive domestic industries such as agriculture and cars. On the other hand, the Clinton administration created a climate of uncertainty for a number of EU firms. The government proposed that no federal agencies should award contracts to companies from a number of EU states. The Clinton government also proposed that all four-wheel-drive cars should be considered as trucks and thus pay 25 per cent tariff instead of 2.5 per cent as cars. Although, the main purpose was to stop Japanese four-wheel-drive cars, the EU manufacturers such as Land Rover, Mercedes-Benz and Volkswagen would also be affected. It was also feared that the Clinton administration would increase tariffs on 'gas-guzzling' cars. This would directly influence Rolls-Royce, BMW, Jaguar and Mercedes-Benz.

Exchange Permits.   Especially troublesome to exporters are exchange restrictions placed on the flow of currency by some foreign countries. To conserve scarce foreign exchange and alleviate balance-of-payment difficulties, many countries impose restrictions on the amount of their currency they will exchange for the currency of another country. In effect, they ration the amount of currency available to pay for imports. Exchange controls may be applied in general to all commodities, or a country may employ a system of multiple exchange rates based on the type of import. Essential products might have a very favourable exchange rate, while nonessentials or luxuries would have a less favourable rate of exchange. South Africa, for example, until recently had a two-tier system for foreign exchange, commercial rand and financial rand. At times, countries may not issue any exchange permits for certain classes of commodities.

In countries that use exchange controls, the usual procedure is for the importer to apply to the control agency of the importing country for an import permit; if the control agency approves the request, an import licence is issued. On presentation to the proper government agency, the import licence can be used to have local currency exchanged for the currency of the seller.

Receiving an import licence, or even an exchange permit, however, is not a guarantee that a seller can exchange local currency for the currency of the seller. If local currency is in short supply—a chronic problem in some countries—other means of acquiring home-country currency are necessary. For example, in a transaction between the government of Colombia and a US truck manufacturer, there was a scarcity of US currency to exchange for the 1000 vehicles Colombia wanted to purchase. The problem was solved through a series of exchanges. Colombia had a surplus of coffee that the truck manufacturer accepted and traded in Europe for sugar; the sugar was traded for pig iron, and finally the pig iron for US dollars.

This somewhat complicated but effective countertrade transaction has become more common. As discussed in other chapters, countertrade deals are often a result of the inability to convert local currency into home-country currency and/or the refusal of a government to issue foreign exchange.

EXPORT METHODS NEED TO BE CONSTANTLY REASSESSED AND ADJUSTED

All companies need to rethink their export strategy periodically. A surprising number of firms and small potential exporters need to develop one for the first time. This means tailoring marketing and product strategies to the markets they work or want to penetrate. In Europe in order to succeed it is vital, at least in some industries, to be less dependent on the home market. According to Chris Walkey, Rover's director for external affairs: 'As recently as 1991 Rover allocated no resources to exploring markets overseas. Now we are exporters investing resources to find opportunities in international markets and we are now making substantial adaptations for foreign markets.' Paul Brauklin, from Oxford Instruments and an export promoter for UK firms seeking opportunities in Japan, considers top management's commitment as an essential for exporting. He argues: 'They must have a clear strategy, an effective management team and they must be continually monitoring progress. . . . If you come across a company not doing well in, say, Japan, it is because one of these elements is missing.'

The London-based Institute of Export recommends that its members follow six points of strategy:

1. Know the market by conducting extensive market research.
2. Know the documentation, sales executives often neglect to build in the cost of documentation and squeeze margins to the point where the deal becomes problematic and future orders are endangered.
3. Examine the potential for currency fluctuations. UK exporters should not necessarily invoice in sterling.
4. Consider credit insurance. It may prove expensive for a small company working on 10–15 per cent margins.
5. Ensure staff are fully trained. This can range from one-day courses to long-term professional qualifications.
6. Use official bodies such as the Department of Trade and Industry (DTI) in the UK or Export Promotion Bureaus in other countries. In some cases financial support for business development will be available.

Source: *The Financial Times: FT Exporter*, Autumn 1995, p. 11.

Quotas.   Countries may also impose limitations on the quantity of certain goods imported during a specific period. These quotas may be applied to imports from specific countries or from all foreign sources in general. Most European Union countries, for example, have specific quotas for importing cotton, tobacco, textiles and cars; in the case of some of these items, there are also limitations on the amount imported from specific countries.

The most important reasons to set quotas are to protect domestic industry and to conserve foreign exchange. Some importing countries also set quotas to ensure an equitable distribution of a major market among friendly countries.

Import Licences.   As a means of regulating the flow of exchange and the quantity of a particular imported commodity, countries often require import licences. The fundamental difference between quotas and import licences as a means of controlling imports is the greater flexibility of import licences over quotas. Quotas permit importing until the quota is filled; licensing limits quantities on a case-by-case basis.

Boycott.   A boycott is an absolute restriction against trade with a country, or trade of specific goods. Countries can refuse to trade (buy or sell) with other countries; for example,

Table 12.2   Top textile-producing countries (% of total)

Country	1975*	1997*
China	11	21
United States	17	15
India	6	8
Pakistan	2	5
Taiwan	2	4
South Korea	2	4
Japan	7	4
Former Soviet Union	14	4
Italy	3	4
Indonesia	1	3

*Estimate.

Source: Textiles Intelligence; based on: Casting off Clothes', *The Economist, A Survey of Manufacturing*, 20 June 1998, p. 5.

the United States imposed, with the help of the United Nations, a boycott on trade with Libya, which was respected by most countries. The United Nations also imposed a boycott on trade with Iraq after the Gulf War. The United States also has had a boycott on trade with Cuba, due to its communist regime. This boycott was also respected by Western European countries. However, lately the WTO and the European Union want to open trade with Cuba.

Standards.   Health standards, safety standards and product quality standards are necessary to protect the consuming public, and imported goods are required to comply with local laws. Unfortunately, standards can also be used to slow down or restrict the procedures for importing to the point that the additional time and cost required to comply become, in effect, trade restrictions. Safety standards are a good example. Most countries have safety standards for electrical appliances and require that imported electrical products meet local standards. However, the restrictiveness of safety standards can be escalated to the level of an absolute trade barrier by manipulating the procedures used to determine if products meet the standards. The simplest process for the importing nation is to accept the safety standard verification used by the exporting country. In some industries, such as clothing, most parties are familiar with these standards and there are hardly any problems arising due to this fact. Table 12.2 lists the major textile-producing companies.

Voluntary Agreements.   Foreign restrictions of all kinds abound and the United States can be counted among those governments using restrictions. For over a decade, US government officials have been arranging 'voluntary' agreements with the Japanese steel and automotive industries to limit sales to the United States. Japan entered these voluntary agreements under the implied threat that if it did not voluntarily restrict the exports of automobiles or steel to an agreed limit, the United States might impose even harsher restrictions including additional import duties. Similar negotiations with the governments of major textile producers have limited textile imports as well. It is estimated that the cost of tariffs, quotas and voluntary agreements on all fibres is as much as €36 billion ($40 billion) at the retail level. This works out to be a hidden tax of almost €450 ($500) a year for every American family.

GOING INTERNATIONAL 12.4

UNDERWEAR, OUTERWEAR AND POINTED EARS—WHAT DO THEY HAVE IN COMMON?

What do underwear, outerwear and pointed ears have in common? Quotas, that's what!

Call the first one *The Madonna Effect*. Madonna, the voluptuous pop star, has affected the interpretation of outerwear/underwear. A shipment of the 880 bustiers was stopped at the US border by the ever-vigilant US Customs Service. The problem was quota and tariff violations. The shipper classified them as underwear. Underwear comes into the United States without quota and tariff, whereas outerwear imports are controlled by a quota. The Customs official classified the fashion item inspired by Madonna as 'outerwear' and demanded the appropriate quota certificates.

'It was definitely outerwear. I've seen it; and I've seen the girls wearing it, and they're wearing it as outerwear.' It took the importer three weeks to obtain sufficient outerwear quota allowances to cover the shipment; by that time, several retailers had cancelled their orders.

Call the second *The Vulcan Effect*. 'Beam me up, Scotty'. The European Union bureaucracy has gone mad. EU officials have applied the Vulcan death grip to Star Trek hero Spock. Likenesses of the point-eared Spock and other 'nonhuman creatures' have fallen victim to an EU quota on dolls made in China. The EU Council of Ministers slapped a quota equivalent to $81.7 million (€73.7 million) on nonhuman dolls from China. But it left human dolls alone.

British customs officials are in the unusual position of debating each doll's humanity. They have blacklisted teddy bears but cleared Batman and Robin. Although they have turned away Spock because of his Vulcan origins, they have admitted Star Trek's Captain Kirk.

The Official Fan Club for Star Trek said the customs officials 'ought to cut Spock some slack' because his mother, Amanda, was human. But Britain's customs office said, 'We see no reason to change our interpretation. You don't find a human with ears that size.'

Sources: Abstracted from Rosalind Resnick, 'Busting Out of Tariff Quotas', *North American International Business* (now published as *International Business*), February 1991, p. 10; and Dana Milbank, 'British Customs Officials Consider Mr Spock Dolls to Be Illegal Aliens', *The Wall Street Journal*, 2 August 1994, p. B-1.

Other Restrictions.   Restrictions may be imposed on imports of harmful products, drugs, medicines and immoral products and literature. Products must also comply with government standards set for health, sanitation, packaging and labelling. For example, in The Netherlands all imported hen and duck eggs must be marked in indelible ink with the country of origin; in Spain, imported condensed milk must be labelled to show fat content if it is less than 8 per cent fat; and in European Union countries, all animals imported from outside the European Union must be accompanied by a sanitary certificate issued by an approved veterinary inspector, even then the animals have to spend a specified period in quarantine. Failure to comply with regulations can result in severe fines and penalties.

While sanitation certificates, content labelling and other such regulations serve a legitimate purpose, countries can effectively limit imports by using such restrictions as additional trade barriers. Most of the economically developed world encourages foreign trade and works through GATT/WTO to reduce tariffs and nontariff barriers to a reasonable rate. Yet, in times of economic recession, countries revert to a protectionist philosophy and seek ways to restrict the importing of goods. Nontariff barriers have become one of the most potent ways for a country to restrict trade. The elimination of nontariff barriers has been a major concern of GATT negotiations in the Uruguay Round and the next session of WTO will emphasize more on these issues as well as on tariffs and trade in services.[3]

FREE-TRADE ZONES BOOM IN RUSSIA AND EASTERN EUROPE

St Petersburg, Russia hosted a conference aimed at turning the entire city into a free-trade zone (FTZ) where manufacturers can assemble their products without paying tariffs on the imported parts until they enter a country and are for sale. The Russian republics are attempting to create several of these special zones designed to boost industrial production, especially for export, and to create employment. Their efforts are inspired by China's Special Economic Zones (SEZs), which encompass entire regions, rather than the smaller FTZ that may be simply a warehouse or factory.

Bulgaria, Hungary, Poland and Romania are also in the process of setting up FTZs. Some countries designate a factory or a warehouse where goods can be stored or assembled; others designate an entire area as an FTZ. Hungary, for example, has no plans to design special industrial enclaves as FTZs but, instead, will designate factories as FTZs.

Special zones for export processing have existed in the developed world for decades—the United States has some 200. Volkswagen and Nissan operate large automobile assembly plants in an FTZ in Barcelona; Ireland has had an FTZ near Shannon Airport since 1959.

Source: Abstracted from 'Free-Trade Zones in Europe: A Boom in the East, a Burden in the West', *EuroSphere*, KPMG Peat Marwick, August–September 1991, pp. 2–3.

CUSTOMS-PRIVILEGED FACILITIES

To facilitate export trade, countries designate areas within their borders as customs-privileged areas, that is, areas where goods can be imported for storage and/or processing with tariffs and quota limits postponed until the products leave the designated areas. Foreign-trade zones (also known as free-trade zones), free ports and in-bond arrangements are all types of customs-privileged facilities that countries use to promote foreign trade.

Foreign-Trade Zones

The number of countries with foreign-trade zones (FTZs) has increased as trade liberalization has spread through Latin America, Eastern Europe and other parts of Europe and Asia. Most FTZs function in a similar manner regardless of the host country. The FTZs extend their services to thousands of firms engaged in a spectrum of international trade-related activities ranging from distribution to assembly and manufacturing.

In situations where goods are imported into a country to be combined with local-made goods and reexported, the importer or exporter can avoid payment of local import duties on the foreign portion and eliminate the complications of applying for a 'drawback', that is, a request for a refund from the government of the duties paid on imports later reexported. Other benefits for companies utilizing foreign-trade zones include: (1) lower insurance costs due to the greater security required in FTZs; (2) more working capital since duties are deferred until goods leave the zone; (3) the opportunity to stockpile products when quotas are filled or while waiting for ideal market conditions; (4) significant savings on goods or materials rejected, damaged or scrapped for which no duties are assessed; and (5) exemption from paying duties on labour and overhead costs incurred in an FTZ which are excluded in determining the value of the goods.

The Special Economic Zone in Shenzhen, China, is an example of China's economic development programme that established Special Economic Zones as a means of attracting foreign capital and technology. In 10 years, Shenzhen's population grew from 30 000 to over 1 million. Hundreds of thousands of Chinese work in a Special Economic Zone (SEZ). Hourly manufacturing labour costs in China are very low compared with the Western minimum wage; average per capita labour costs, including benefits, run between €54 ($60) and €81 ($95) per month.

EXPORT DOCUMENTS

Each export shipment requires various documents to satisfy government regulations controlling exporting as well as to meet requirements for international commercial payment transactions. The most frequently required documents are export declarations, consular invoices or certificates of origin, bills of lading, commercial invoices and insurance certificates. In addition, documents such as import licences, export licenses, packing lists and inspection certificates for agricultural products are often necessary.

The paperwork involved in successfully completing a transaction is considered by many to be the greatest of all nontariff trade barriers. Generally, preparation of documents can be handled routinely, but their importance should not be minimized; incomplete or improperly prepared documents lead to delays in shipment. In some countries, there are penalties, fines and even confiscation of goods as a result of errors in some of these documents. Export documents are the result of requirements imposed by the exporting government, of requirements set by commercial procedures established in foreign trade and, in some cases, of the supporting import documents required by the foreign government. Descriptions of the principal export documents follow.

Export Declaration.   To maintain a statistical measure of the quantity of goods shipped abroad and to provide a means of determining whether regulations are being met, most countries require shipments abroad to be accompanied by an export declaration. Usually such a declaration, presented at the port of exit, includes the names and addresses of the principals involved, the destination of the goods, a full description of the goods and their declared value.

Bill of Lading.   The bill of lading is the most important document required to establish legal ownership and facilitate financial transactions. It serves the following purposes: (1) as a contract for shipment between the carrier and shipper; (2) as a receipt from the carrier for shipment; and (3) as a certificate of ownership or title to the goods. Bills of lading are issued in the form of straight bills, which are nonnegotiable and are delivered directly to a consignee, or order bills, which are negotiable instruments. Bills of lading are frequently referred to as being either clean or foul. A clean bill of lading means the items presented to the carrier for shipment were properly packaged and clear of apparent damage when received; a foul bill of lading means the shipment was received in damaged condition and the damage is noted on the bill of lading.

Commercial Invoice.   Every international transaction requires a commercial invoice, that is, a bill or statement for the goods sold. This document often serves several purposes; some countries require a copy for customs clearance, and it is one of the financial documents required in international commercial payments.

Insurance Policy or Certificate.   The risks of shipment due to political or economic unrest in some countries, and the possibility of damage from sea and weather, make it absolutely necessary to have adequate insurance covering loss due to damage, war or riots. Typically the method of payment or terms of sale require insurance on the goods, so few export shipments are uninsured. The insurance policy or certificate of insurance is considered a key document in export trade.

Licences.   Export or import licences are additional documents frequently required in export trade. In those cases where import licences are required by the country of entry, a copy of the licence or licence number is usually required to obtain a consular invoice. Whenever a commodity requires an export licence, it must be obtained before an export declaration can be properly certified.

Others.   Sanitary and health inspection certificates attesting to the absence of disease and pests may be required for certain agricultural products before a country allows goods to enter its borders. Packing lists with correct weights are also required in some cases.

TERMS OF SALE

Terms of sale, or trade terms, differ somewhat in international marketing from country to country. In some countries it is customary to ship FOB (free on board, meaning that the price is established at the door of the factory), while in others CIF (cost, insurance and freight) is more common. International trade terms often sound similar to those used in domestic business but generally have different meanings. International terms indicate how buyer and seller divide risks and obligations and, therefore, the costs of specific kinds of international trade transactions. When quoting prices, it is important to make them meaningful. The most commonly used international trade terms include:

CIF   (cost, insurance, freight) to a named overseas port of import. A CIF quote is more meaningful to the overseas buyer because it includes the costs of goods, insurance and all transportation and miscellaneous charges to the named place of debarkation.

C&F   (cost and freight) to named overseas port. The price includes the cost of the goods and transportation costs to the named place of debarkation. The cost of insurance is borne by the buyer.

FAS   (free alongside) at a named port of export. The price includes cost of goods and charges for delivery of the goods alongside the shipping vessel. The buyer is responsible for the cost of loading onto the vessel, transportation and insurance.

FOB   (free on board) at a named inland point of origin; at a named port of exportation; or a named vessel and port of export. The price includes the cost of the goods and delivery to the place named.

EX   (named port of origin). The price quoted covers costs only at the point of origin (example, EX Factory). All other charges are the buyer's concern.

A complete list of terms and their definitions can be found in *Incoterms*, a booklet published by the International Chamber of Commerce. It is important for the exporter to understand exactly the meanings of terms used in quotations. A simple misunderstanding regarding delivery terms may prevent the exporter from meeting contractual obligations or make that person responsible for shipping costs he or she did not intend to incur. Table 12.3 indicates who is responsible for a variety of costs under various terms.

Table 12.3 Who's Responsible for Costs Under Various Terms?

Cost Items/Terms	FOB (Free on Board) Inland Carrier at Factory	FOB (Free on Board) Inland Carrier at Point of Shipment	FAS (Free Alongside) Vessel or Plane at Port of Shipment	CIF (Cost, Insurance, Freight) at Port of Destination
Export packing*	Buyer	Seller	Seller	Seller
Inland freight	Buyer	Seller	Seller	Seller
Port charges	Buyer	Buyer	Seller	Seller
Forwarder's fee	Buyer	Buyer	Buyer	Seller
Consular fee	Buyer	Buyer	Buyer	Buyer†
Loading on vessel or plane	Buyer	Buyer	Buyer	Seller
Ocean freight	Buyer	Buyer	Buyer	Seller
Cargo insurance	Buyer	Buyer	Buyer	Seller
Customs duties	Buyer	Buyer	Buyer	Buyer
Ownership of goods passes	When goods on board an inland carrier (truck, rail, etc.) or in hands of inland carrier	When goods unloaded by inland carrier	When goods alongside carrier, in hands of air or ocean carrier	When goods on board air or ocean carrier at port of shipment

*Who absorbs export packing? This charge should be clearly agreed on. Charges are sometimes controversial.
†The seller has responsibility to arrange for consular invoices (and other documents requested by buyer's government). According to official definitions, buyer pays fees, but sometimes, as a matter of practice, seller includes in quotations.

Packing and Marking

Special packing and marking requirements must be considered for shipments destined to be transported over water, subject to excessive handling or destined for parts of the world with extreme climates or unprotected outdoor storage. Packing adequate for domestic shipments often falls short for goods subject to the conditions mentioned. Protection against rough handling, moisture, temperature extremes and pilferage may require heavy crating, which increases total packing costs as well as freight rates because of increased weight and size. Since some countries determine import duties on gross weight, packing can add a significant amount to import fees. To avoid the extremes of too much or too little packing, the marketer should consult export brokers, export freight forwarders or other specialists.

Export Shipping

Whenever and however title to goods is transferred, those goods must be transported. Shipping goods to another country presents some important differences from shipping to a domestic site. The goods can be out of the shipper's control for longer periods of time than in domestic distribution, more shipping and collections documents are required, packing must be suitable and shipping insurance coverage is necessarily more extensive. The task is to match each order of goods to the shipping modes best suited for swift, safe and economical delivery. Ocean shipping, air freight, air express and parcel post are all possibilities. Ocean shipping is usually the least expensive and most frequently used method for heavy bulk shipment. For certain categories of goods, air freight can be the most economical and certainly the speediest.

Shipping costs are an important factor in a product's price in export marketing; the transportation mode must be selected in terms of the total impact on cost. One estimate is that logistics account for between 19 and 23 per cent of the total cost of a finished product sold internationally. In ocean shipping, one of the important innovations in reducing or controlling the high cost of transportation is the use of containerization. Containerized shipments, in place of the traditional bulk handling of full loads or breakbulk operations, has resulted in intermodal transport between inland points, reduced costs and simplified handling of international shipments.

With increased use of containerization, rail container service has developed in many countries to provide the international shipper with door-to-door movement of goods under seal, originating and terminating inland. This eliminates several loadings, unloadings and changes of carriers and reduces costs substantially as illustrated in Table 12.4. Containerized cargo handling also reduces damage and pilferage in transit.

For many commodities of high unit value and low weight and volume, international air freight has become important. Air freight has shown the fastest growth rate for freight transportation even though it accounts for only a fraction of total international shipments.[4] While air freight can cost two to five times surface charges for general cargo, some cost reduction is realized through reduced packing requirements, paperwork, insurance and the cost of money tied up in inventory. Although usually not enough to offset the higher rates charged for air freight, if the commodity has high unit value or high inventory costs, or if there is concern with delivery time, air freight can be a justifiable alternative. Many products moving to foreign markets meet these criteria.

The selection of transportation mode has an important bearing on the cost of export shipping, but it is not the only cost involved in the physical movement of goods from point of origin to ultimate market. Indeed, the selection of mode, the location of inventory,

Table 12.4   Examples of Distribution Costs from Paris to Denver via New York (US dollars per metric tonne)

Conventional Cargo Handling	Commodity A per Metric Tonne	Commodity B per Metric Tonne
Domestic carrier	$0.95	$0.95
Inland warehouse, 1 month including handling and delivery	12.14	12.14
Transport to port	12.78	12.78
Ship's agent	1.89	5.18
Port forwarder	0.97	2.66
Port warehouse (average 4 days) including handling	2.92	2.92
Stevedore	3.93	5.70
Sea carrier	21.67	80.70
Stevedore + port warehouse	6.32	6.32
Ship's agent	0.94	2.59
Port forwarder	0.79	0.79
Inland transport	46.64	46.64
Unloading	11.50	11.50
Totals	$123.44	$190.87

Containerized Cargo Handling	Commodity A per Metric Tonne	Commodity B per Metric Tonne
Domestic carrier	$0.95	$0.95
Inland warehouse, 1 month including handling and delivery	12.14	12.14
Transport to port	5.97	5.97
Ship's agent	1.69	4.65
Port forwarder	0.87	2.39
Stevedore	1.60	1.60
Sea carrier	23.07	78.35
Stevedore + port warehouse	6.32	6.32
Ship's agent	0.85	2.32
Forwarder	0.79	0.79
Inland transport	33.45	35.49
Unloading	11.50	11.50
Totals	$99.20	$162.47

Note: Commodity A = Industrial cooking oil in 10-gallon containers (low-tariff cargo).
    Commodity B = Industrial chemicals, harmless (high-tariff cargo).

warehouses and so forth, all figure in the cost of the physical movement of goods. A narrow solution to physical movement of goods is the selection of transportation; a broader application is the concept of logistics management or physical distribution.

LOGISTICS

When a company is primarily an exporter from a single country to a single market, the typical approach to the physical movement of goods is the selection of a dependable mode of transportation which ensures safe arrival of the goods within a reasonable time for a reasonable carrier cost. As a company becomes global, such a solution to the movement of products could prove costly and highly inefficient for seller and buyer. At some point in the growth and expansion of an international firm, costs other than transportation are such that an optimal cost solution to the physical movement of goods cannot be achieved without thinking of the physical distribution process as an integrated system. When a foreign marketer begins producing and selling in more than one country and becomes a global marketer, it is time to consider the concept of logistics management, that is, a total systems approach to management of the distribution process that includes all activities involved in physically moving raw material, in-process inventory and finished goods inventory from the point of origin to the point of use or consumption.[5]

Interdependence of Physical Distribution Activities

Distribution viewed as a system involves more than the physical movement of goods. It includes location of plants and warehousing (storage), transportation mode, inventory quantities and packing. The concept of physical distribution takes into account that the costs of each activity are interdependent and a decision involving one affects the cost and efficiency of one or all others.[6]

The idea of interdependence can be illustrated by the classic example of air freight. Figure 12.1 is an illustration of an actual company's costs of shipping 44 000 peripheral boards worth €6.9 million ($7.7 million) from a Singapore plant to the US West Coast using two modes of transportation—ocean freight and the more expensive air freight. When total costs are calculated, air freight is actually less costly than ocean freight. When considering only rates for transportation and carrying costs for inventory in transit, air transportation costs are approximately €51 000 ($57 000) higher than ocean freight. However, there are other costs involved. To offset the slower ocean freight and the possibility of unforeseen delays and still ensure prompt customer delivery schedules, the company has to continuously maintain 30 days of inventory in Singapore and another 30 days inventory at the company's distribution centres. Costs of financing 60 days of inventory and additional warehousing costs at both points—that is, real physical distribution costs—would result in the cost of ocean freight exceeding air by more than €67,000 ($75 000). There may even be additional costs associated with ocean freight—for example, higher damage rate, higher insurance and higher packing rates for ocean freight. Substantial savings can result from systematic examination of logistics costs and the calculation of total physical distribution costs.[7]

Although a cost difference will not always be the case, the example serves to illustrate the interdependence of the various activities in the physical distribution mix and the total cost. A change of transportation mode affected a change in packaging and handling, inventory costs, warehousing time and cost, and delivery charges.

Distribution problems confronting the international marketer are compounded by additional variables and costs that are also interdependent and must be included in the total physical distribution decision. As the international firm broadens the scope of its operations, the additional variables and costs become more crucial in their effect on the efficiency of the distribution system.

One of the major benefits of the European unification is the elimination of transportation barriers among member countries. Instead of approaching Europe on a country-by-country basis, a centralized logistics network can be developed. Studies indicate that companies operating in Europe may be able to cut 20 warehousing locations to three and maintain the same level of customer service.[8] A German white goods manufacturer was able to reduce its

Figure 12.1   Real Physical Distribution Costs between Air and Ocean Freight—
Singapore to the United States

In this example 44 000 peripheral boards worth €6.9 million ($7.7 million) are shipped from a Singapore plant to the US West Coast. Cost of capital to finance inventories is 10 per cent annually: $2109 per day to finance $7.7 million.

	Ocean	Air
Transport costs	$31 790 (in transit 21 days)	$127 160 (in transit 3 days)
In-transit inventory financing costs	$44 289	$6 328
Total transportation costs	$76 079	$133 487
Warehousing inventory costs, Singapore and US	(60 days @ $2 109 per day) $126 540	
Warehouse rent	$6 500	
Real physical distribution costs	$209 119	$133 487

Source: Adapted from 'Air and Adaptec's Competitive Strategy', *International Business*, September 1993, p. 44.

European warehouses from 39 to 10 as well as improve its distribution and enhance customer service. By cutting the number of warehouses, it reduced total distribution and warehousing costs, brought down staff numbers, held fewer items of stock, provided greater access to regional markets, made better use of transport networks and improved service to customers, all with a 21 per cent reduction of total logistics costs.[9]

Benefits of Physical Distribution Systems

A physical distribution system may also result in better (more dependable) delivery service to the market; when production occurs at different locations, companies are able to quickly determine the most economical source for a particular customer. As companies expand into multinational markets and source these markets from multinational production facilities, they are increasingly confronted with cost variables that make it imperative to employ a total systems approach to the management of the distribution process to achieve efficient operation. Finally, a physical distribution system can render the natural obstructions created by geography less economically critical for the multinational marketer.

THE FOREIGN-FREIGHT FORWARDER

The foreign-freight forwarder, licensed by the government, arranges for the shipment of goods as the agent for an exporter. The forwarder is an indispensable agent for an exporting firm that cannot afford an in-house specialist to handle paperwork and other export trade mechanics. Even in large companies with active export departments capable of handling documentation, a forwarder is useful as a shipment coordinator at the port of export or at the destination port. Besides arranging for complete shipping documentation, the full-service foreign-freight forwarder provides information and advice on routing and scheduling, rates and related charges, consular and licensing requirements, labelling requirements and export restrictions. Further, the agent offers shipping insurance, warehouse storage, packing and

Figure 12.2   Major Services Rendered by International Freight Forwarders

- Develops most economic methods of shipment. Figures costs, FOB, CIF, etc.
- Arranges export licences or import permits.
- Arranges transport from plant to port/airport and beyond.
- Prepares export declaration, bill of lading and other necessary documents.
- Arranges and executes formalities with authorities such as port and customs.
- Prepares or arranges documents in foreign language, if necessary.
- Assembles all documents necessary for export/import and presents them to relevant authorities when required
- Prepares and presents documents to the bank for letter of credit or payment.

Source: Based on Subhash Jain, *Export Strategy, Westpol* (Connecticut: Quorum, 1989).

containerization, and ocean cargo or air freight space. Both large and small shippers find freight forwarders' wide range of services useful and well worth the fees normally charged. In fact, for many shipments, forwarders can save on freight charges because they can consolidate shipments into larger, more economical quantities. Experienced exporters regard the foreign-freight forwarder as an important addition to in-house specialists. (See Figure 12.2.)

SUMMARY

An awareness of the mechanics of export trade is indispensable to the foreign marketer who engages in exporting goods from one country to another. Although most marketing techniques are open to interpretation and creative application, the mechanics of exporting are very exact; there is little room for interpretation or improvisation with the requirements of export licences, quotas, tariffs, export documents, packing, marketing and the various uses of commercial payments. The very nature of the regulations and restrictions surrounding importing and exporting can lead to frequent and rapid change. In handling the mechanics of export trade successfully, the manufacturer must keep abreast of all foreign and domestic changes in requirements and regulations pertaining to the product involved. For firms unable to maintain their own export staffs, foreign-freight forwarders can handle many details for a nominal fee.

With paperwork completed, the physical movement of goods must be considered. Transportation mode affects total product cost because of the varying requirements of packing, inventory levels, time requirements, perishability, unit cost, damage and pilfering losses and customer service. Transportation for each product must be assessed in view of the interdependent nature of all these factors. To assure optimum distribution at minimal cost, a physical distribution system determines everything from plant location to final customer delivery in terms of the most efficient use of capital investment, resources, production, inventory, packing and transportation.

QUESTIONS

1. Explain the reasoning behind the various regulations and restrictions imposed on the exportation and importation of goods.
2. What is the purpose of an import licence? Discuss.
3. Explain foreign-trade zones and illustrate how they may be used by an exporter. By an importer. How do foreign-trade zones differ from bonded warehouses?

4. Explain each of the following export documents:
   a. Bill of lading
   b. Consular invoice or certificate of origin
   c. Commercial invoice
   d. Insurance certificate
5. Why would an exporter use the services of a foreign-freight forwarder? Discuss.
6. Besides cost advantages, what are the other benefits of an effective physical distribution system?

REFERENCES

1. Pervez Ghauri, 'Recent Trends in Global Business and the Asian Crisis: Cooperation vs. Competition', *KELOLA*, Journal of Gajah Mada University, Indonesia, 1998, 18/VII, pp. 1–15.
2. Fahri Karakaya, 'Barriers to Entry in International Markets', *Journal of Global Marketing*, vol. 7, no. 1, 1993, p. 10.
3. Alan Rugman and Alain Verbeke, 'Multinational Enterprises and Public Policy', *Journal of International Business Studies*, vol. 29, no. 1, 1998, pp. 115–136.
4. John Gorsuch, 'Air Cargo', *Trade & Culture*, March–April 1995, pp. 21–26.
5. Gregory L. Miles, 'Mastering the Logistics Labyrinth', *International Business*, January 1994, pp. 46–48.
6. Constantine Katsikeas, Ali Al-Khalifa and Dave Crick, 'Manufacturer's Understanding of their Overseas Distributors: The Relevance of Export Involvement', *International Business Review*, vol. 6, no. 2, 1997, pp. 147–164.
7. Gregory L. Miles, 'Why Air Transport Is Taking Off', *International Business*, September 1993, pp. 40–46.
8. 'Cross-Border Logistics: A Challenge for the Mid-1990s', *Business Europe*, 23–29 May 1994, pp. 2–3.
9. 'Cross-Border Logistics: How Bosch-Siemens Saved Time and Costs', *Business Europe*, 23–29 May 1994, p. 7.

CHAPTER

13

Developing Consumer Products for International Markets

Chapter Learning Objectives

What you should learn from Chapter 13

- The importance of offering a product suitable to the intended market.

- The current dichotomy of standardized versus differentiated products in international marketing.

- The relationship between product acceptance and the market into which it is introduced.

- Country of origin effect on product image.

- Physical, mandatory and cultural requirements for product evaluation.

- Physical, mandatory and cultural requirements for product adaptation.

- The need to view all attributes of a product in order to overcome or modify resistance to its acceptance.

- The impact of environmental awareness on product decisions.

- The increasing importance of quality in international marketing.

The opportunities and challenges for international marketers of consumer goods today have never been greater or more diverse. New consumers are springing forth in emerging markets from Eastern Europe, the Commonwealth of Independent States, China, India, other Asian countries and Latin America—in short, globally.[1] While some of these emerging markets have little purchasing power today, they promise to be huge markets in the future.[2] In the more mature markets of the industrialized world, opportunity and challenge also abound as consumers' tastes become more sophisticated and complex and as increases in purchasing power provide them with the means of satisfying new demands.

Never has the question 'Which products should we sell?' been more critical than it is today. For the company with a domestic-market-extension orientation, the answer generally is: 'Whatever we are selling at home'. The company with a multidomestic-market orientation develops different products to fit the uniqueness of each country market; the global orientation seeks commonalties in needs among sets of country markets and responds with a somewhat global product.

All three strategies are appropriate somewhere but, because of the enormous diversity in international markets, the appropriate strategy for a specific market is determined by the company's resources, the product and the target market. Consequently, each country market must be examined thoroughly or a firm risks marketing poorly conceived products in incorrectly defined markets with an inappropriate marketing effort.[3]

The trend for larger firms is towards becoming global in orientation and strategy. However, product adaptation is as important a task in a smaller firm's marketing effort as it is for global companies. As competition for world markets intensifies and as market preferences become more global, selling what is produced for the domestic market in the same manner as it is sold at home proves to be increasingly less effective. Most products cannot be sold at all in foreign markets without modification; others may be sold as is but their acceptance is greatly enhanced when tailored specifically to market needs. In a competitive struggle, quality products that meet the needs and wants of a market at an affordable price should be the goal of any marketing firm. For some product category groups and some country markets, this means differentiated products for each market. Other product groups and country market segments do well competitively with a global or standardized product but, for both, an effective marketing is essential. Even standardized products may have to be sold by different and adapted marketing strategies.

This chapter explores some of the relevant issues facing an international marketer when planning and developing consumer products for international markets. The questions about product planning and development range from the obvious—which product to sell—to the more complex—when, how and if products should be adapted for different markets.

INTERNATIONAL MARKETS AND PRODUCT DEVELOPMENT

There is a recurring debate about product planning and development that focuses on the question of standardized or global products marketed worldwide versus differentiated products adapted, or even redesigned, for each culturally unique market. One extreme position is held by those with strong production and unit-cost orientation who advocate global standardization, while at the other extreme are those, perhaps more culturally sensitive, who propose a different or adapted product for each market.[4]

Underlying the arguments offered by the proponents of standardized products is the premise that global communications and other worldwide socializing forces have fostered a homogenization of tastes, needs and values in a significant sector of the population across all

GOING INTERNATIONAL 13.1

IKEA'S NEW GAME PLAN

Ingvar Kamprad, the 71-year-old founder, set up IKEA—an acronym for Ingvar Kamprad Elmtaryd Agunnaryd—in 1943. With the name Elmtaryd, the name of his family's farm and Agunnaryd, his village in Sweden, he started selling furniture in the 1950s, with 'well-designed furniture at low prices' as his slogan.

When it started its first store in the US market (Philadelphia) in 1985, it sold European-size curtains that did not fit American windows. In 1990, it snapped up five stores owned by Store Furnishings International in California. The new stores were a big fiasco and analysts said that IKEA came in with a certain arrogance, without adapting its products or marketing for the American market. So in 1995 and 1996, it shook up its North American operations shutting two of its 21 stores and slashing office staff. Now it designs about one-third of its products especially for the US market; sofas are firmer and kitchen cabinets are deeper to match American appliances. In 1996, the North American unit turned a profit on $859 million (€775 million) sales.

For the year ending August 1997, IKEA's sales jumped 21 per cent. Although its furniture, toys and housewares are priced from 20 per cent to 30 per cent below rivals, its sales per square metre are three times the industry average and its 8 per cent to 10 per cent pretax margin is twice as high.

Now IKEA has launched a big expansion into new products and markets. It is rolling out a major new product line of children's furniture and toys. It is opening up eight new stores from Shanghai to Warsaw, thus going beyond its traditional Western European base. It envisions an IKEA that grabs customers in childhood and holds on to them for life. In the past two decades, IKEA has grown more than tenfold, to 139 stores in 28 countries. Kamprad is still the chief strategy officer and he embodies the company's value and vision. As he hustles to expand his empire, Kamprad is also acting to protect it from his own family. He decided long ago that none of his three sons, although working as IKEA managers, would ever control the company. So he transferred 100 per cent of his IKEA equity to a Dutch-based charitable foundation as an irrevocable gift in 1984. IKEA is valued by the analysts at more than $6 billion (€5.4 billion) or 18 times its earnings of $340 million (€307 million) in 1997.

Source: Julia Flynn and Lori Bongiorno, 'IKEA's New Game Plan', *Business Week*, 6 October 1997, pp. 99–100.

---

cultures. This has resulted in a large global market with similar needs and wants that demands the same reasonably priced products of good quality and reliability.[5]

In support of this argument, a study found that products targeted for urban markets in less developed countries needed few changes from products sold to urban markets in developed countries. 'Modern products usually fit into lifestyles of urban consumers wherever they are.'[6] Other studies identify a commonality of preferences among population segments across countries. Families in New York need the same dishwashers as families in Paris, and families in Rome make similar demands on a washing machine as do families in London. However, the sizes, colours, voltage requirements, switches and advertising may need to be adapted to each market.

Although recognizing some cultural variations, advocates of standardization believe that product standardization leads to production economies and other savings that permit profits at prices that make a product attractive to the global market. Economies of production, better planning, more effective control and better use of creative managerial personnel are the advantages of standardization. Such standardization can result in significant cost savings but it makes sense only when there is adequate demand for the standardized product.

Those who hold the opposing view stress that substantial cultural variation among countries dictates a need for differentiated products to accommodate the uniqueness of cultural norms and product use patterns. For example, Electrolux, the appliance manufacturer, finds the refrigerator market among European countries far from homogeneous. Northern Europeans want large refrigerators because they shop only once a week in supermarkets; Southern Europeans prefer small ones because they pick through open-air markets almost daily. Northerners like their freezers on the bottom, Southerners on top. And Britons, who devour huge quantities of frozen foods, insist on units with 60 per cent freezer space. Further, 100 appliance makers compete for that market. To be competitive, Electrolux alone produces 120 basic designs with 1500 variations. Compare such differences to the relatively homogeneous United States market where most refrigerators are standardized, have freezers on top, and come in only a few sizes, and where 80 per cent are sold by four firms. Can Electrolux standardize their refrigerator line for the European market? Management thinks not, so long as the market remains as it is.[7]

The issue between these two extremes cannot be resolved with a simple either/or decision since the prudent position probably lies somewhere in the middle. Most astute marketers concede that there are definable segments across country markets with some commonality of product preferences, and that substantial efficiencies can be attained by standardizing, but they also recognize there may be cultural differences that remain important. The key issue is not whether to adapt or standardize, but how much adaptation is necessary and to what point a product can be standardized.

Most products are adapted, at least to some degree, even those traditionally held up as examples of standardization. Although the substantial portion of their product is standardized worldwide, McDonald's does not sell beefburgers but includes vegetarian and lambburgers in its Indian stores, to accommodate dietary and religious restrictions, and wine and beer in European stores. In Norway, it sells a salmonburger which is not sold in other markets. In Indonesia and the Philippines it sells chicken and rice meals. Pepsi Cola reformulated its diet cola to be sweeter and more syrupy, and changed its name from Diet Pepsi to Pepsi Light and Pepsi Max to appeal to international markets where the idea of 'diet' is often shunned and a sweeter taste is preferred.[8]

Even if different products are necessary to satisfy local needs, as in the case of Electrolux, it does not exclude a standardization approach. A fully standardized product may not be appropriate, but some efficiencies through standardizing some aspects of the product may be achieved. Whirlpool faced this problem when it acquired NV Philips, a division of Philips, the European appliance manufacturer whose approach to the European market was to make a different product for each country market. Whirlpool found that the Philips' German plant produced feature-rich washing machines that sold at higher prices, while washers from the Italian plants ran at lower RPMs and were less costly. Each plant operated independently of the other and produced customized products for their respective markets. The washing machines made in the Italian and German facilities differed so much that 'they did not have one screw in common', yet the reality was that the insides of the machines were very similar. Immediate steps were taken to standardize and simplify both the German and Italian machines by reducing the number of parts and using as many common parts as possible. New products were developed in a way to ensure that a wide variety of models could be built on a standardized platform. The same approach was taken for dryers and other product categories. Although complete standardization could not be achieved, efficiencies were attained by standardizing the platform (the core product) and customizing other features to meet local preferences.[9]

As companies gain more experience with the idea of global markets, the approach is likely

FIAT DEVELOPS A CAR FOR EMERGING MARKETS

Until now manufacturers have traditionally recycled old models to the Third World—sometimes even shipping over entire production lines. Renault, for example, is assembling its 15-year-old Renault 9 in Argentina. Fiat's Uno, which went out of production in Italy in 1993, is being assembled in Morocco and India.

Fiat has now developed a new Fiat, Palio, meant only for emerging markets and is spending US $2 billion (€1.8 billion) to set up production plants for Palio in Brazil and Argentina. The model is based on a single modular platform, allowing it to spread the car's $1.2 billion (€1.1 billion) development costs, over many different production sites. The Palio's toughened chassis is designed for the rough terrains and harsh climates of the emerging markets.

In 1996 Palio's started rolling out of Fiat plants in Poland. In 1997, production of station wagon versions started at a new $600 million (€540 million) factory in Argentina. Fiat is also negotiating partnerships with Johannesburg-based automakers, Bombay-based Premier automobiles and Turkey's Koc Group to build the car. It has already reached agreements to produce in Morocco and Algeria. It plans to have six or seven production plants all over the world and the production is expected to reach 900 000 units by the end of the decade. That number can jump drastically if the company manages to strike a deal with China.

Source: 'Can Fiat Drive the Palio Around the World?', *Business Week*, 22 April 1996.

to be to standardize where possible and adapt where necessary. To benefit from standardization as much as possible and still provide for local cultural differences, companies are using an approach to product development that allows for such flexibility. The idea is to develop a core platform containing the essential technology, and then base variations on this platform. Sony of Japan has used this approach for its Walkman. The basic Walkman platform gives them the flexibility to rapidly adjust production to shifts in market preference. It is interesting to speculate on the possibilities of using this approach for standardizing the refrigerators discussed above.

To differentiate for the sake of differentiation is not a solution, nor is adaptation for the sake of adaptation or standardization for the sake of standardization. Realistic business practice requires that a company strives for uniformity in its marketing mix whenever and wherever possible, while recognizing that cultural differences may demand some accommodation if the product is to be competitive.[10]

Global Brands

Hand in hand with global products are global brands. A global brand is defined as the worldwide use of a name, term, sign, symbol, design or combination thereof intended to identify goods or services of one seller and to differentiate them from those of competitors. Much like the experience with global products, there is no single answer to the question of whether or not to establish global brands. There is, however, little question of the importance of a brand name.

A successful brand is the most valuable resource a company has. The brand name encompasses the years of advertising, good will, quality evaluation, product experience and the other beneficial attributes the market associates with the product. The value of Philips, Kodak, Sony, Coca-Cola, McDonald's, Nike, Adidas, Toyota and Shell is indisputable. One estimate of the value of 112-year-old Coca-Cola, the world's most valuable brand, places it at over $35 billion.[11]

GOING INTERNATIONAL 13.3

BUILDING BRAND AWARENESS IN CHINA

If you stroll around in any residential area in a Chinese city, sooner or later you will encounter a senior citizen with a red arm band observing strangers suspiciously. These senior citizens are the pensioners who are staff members of neighbourhood committees and work as watchdogs for the ruling party. They supervise an area with up to 200 families.

In Shanghai some of these senior citizens have been signed up by Coca-Cola. Coke approached 14 neighbourhood committees in 1996 with a proposal to get its product to the customer. In George Chu's, head of Coke, words: 'We told them: you have some old people who aren't doing much. Why don't we stock our products in your office? Then you can sell it and earn some commission.'

So since 1996 the party workers are now selling Cokes as a Coca-Cola salesforce. They do not handle big volume but they have proved to be a useful vehicle for building brand awareness.

In a society that seems to conspire against foreign enterprise, Coke's Shanghai initiative is a good example of working with the system.

Source: Based on Richard Tomlinson, 'The China Card: Building Brand Awareness Is Always Easier When You Have the Ruling Party's Eyes and Ears Working for You', *Fortune*, 25 May 1998, p. 41.

Naturally, companies with such strong brands strive to use those brands globally. Even for products that must be adapted to local market conditions, a global brand can be successfully used. Philips produces several models of TVs and vacuum cleaners for different markets using the same brand name. Toyota markets several models in different countries using the same brand names. And Sony is, of course, a global brand.

A global brand generally means substantial cost savings and gives a company a uniform worldwide image that enhances efficiency and cost savings when introducing other products associated with the brand name, but not all companies believe a global approach is the best. Except for companies like Philips, Kodak, Coca-Cola, Caterpillar, Sony and Levi's that use the same brands worldwide, other multinationals such as Nestlé, Mars, Procter & Gamble, Unilever and Gillette have some brands that are promoted worldwide and others that are country specific. Unilever never uses the name 'Unilever' for any of its products. Among companies that have faced the question of whether or not to make all their brands global, not all have followed the same path.

Companies that already have successful country-specific brand names must balance the benefits of a global brand against the risk of losing the benefits of an established brand. The cost of reestablishing the same level of brand preference and market share for the global brand that the local brand had, must be offset against the long-term cost savings and benefits of having only one brand name worldwide.

A different strategy is followed by the Nestlé Company which has a stable of global and country-specific brands in its product line. The Nestlé name itself is promoted globally but its global brand expansion strategy is two-pronged. It acquires well-established local brands when it can and builds on their strengths; in other markets where there are no strong brands it can acquire, it uses global brand names. The company is described as preferring brands to be local, people regional and technology global. It does, however, own some of the world's largest global brands; Nescafé is but one.

Unilever is another company that follows a similar strategy of a mix of local and global brands. In Poland, Unilever introduced its Omo brand detergent (sold in many other

Figure 13.1   Nestlé's Branding Strategy

Level 1	10 worldwide corporate brands	*For example:* Nestlé; Carnation; Buitoni; Maggi; Perrier
Level 2	45 worldwide strategic brands	*For example:* Kitkat; Polo; Cerelac; Baci; Mighty Dog; Smarties; After Eight; Coffee-Mate
Level 3	140 regional strategic brands	*For example:* Mackintosh; Vittel; Contadina; Stouffer's; Herta; Alpo; Findus
Level 4	7500 local brands	*For example:* Texicana; Brigadeiro; Rocky; Solis

Source: Based on Andrew Parsons, 'Nestlé: The Visions of Local Managers', An Interview with Peter Brabeck-Letmathe, CEO Nestlé', *The McKinsey Quarterly*, 2 November 1996, pp. 5–29.

countries), but it also purchased a local brand, Pollena 2000. Despite a strong introduction of two competing brands, Omo by Unilever and Ariel by Procter & Gamble, a refurbished Pollena 2000 had the largest market share a year later. Unilever's explanation was that Eastern European consumers are leery of new brands; they want brands that are affordable and in keeping with their own tastes and values. Pollena 2000 is successful not just because it is cheaper but because it chimes with local values.[12]

Country-of-Origin Effect and Global Brands

As discussed earlier, brands are used as external cues to taste, design, performance, quality, value, prestige and so forth. In other words, the consumer associates the value of the product with the brand. The brand can convey either a positive or a negative message about the product to the consumer and is affected by past advertising and promotion, product reputation and product evaluation and experience. In short, many factors affect brand image, and one factor that is of great concern to multinational companies that manufacture worldwide is the country-of-origin effect (COE) on the market's perception of the product.[13]

Country-of-origin effect (COE) can be defined as any influence that the country of manufacture has on a consumer's positive or negative perception of a product. Today a company competing in global markets will manufacture products worldwide and, when the customer is aware of the country of origin, there is the possibility that the place of manufacture will affect product/brand image.

The country, the type of product and the image of the company and its brands all influence whether or not the country of origin will engender a positive or negative reaction. There is a variety of generalizations that can be made about-country-of-origin effects on products and brands. Consumers tend to have stereotypes about products and countries that have been formed by experience, hearsay and myth. Following are some of the more frequently cited generalizations.

Consumers have broad but somewhat vague stereotypes about specific countries and specific product categories that they judge 'best': English tea, French fashion garments and perfumes, Chinese silk, Italian leather, Japanese electronics, Jamaican rum and so on. Stereotyping of this nature is typically product specific and may not extend to other categories of products from these countries.

FOREIGN NAMES ADD FLAIR

Petit Patapon, despite its flavour of French, is a successful Portuguese brand of children's clothing. Scottwool, founded in 1982, a label invoking centuries of Celtic tradition, belongs to a Portuguese producer of knitwear. Maconde, another Portuguese garment producer, owns the Macmodex brand which it franchises to other countries of Europe as do Petit Patapon and Scottwool. Petit Patapon, for example, has franchises operating in Spain, France and the United States.

Linguistic borrowings such as these reflect how the Portuguese clothing industry is responding to a powerful advantage enjoyed by competitors in Italy, France and, to some extent, the United States and United Kingdom; their national cultures are strongly associated with fashion and alluring lifestyle. National images are an asset less related to economic resources. For example, Spain and Germany, despite strong efforts, have not been able to achieve a name in the clothing industry. Portugal has learned the lesson, instead of aspiring to prominence in the fashion world as a garment producer, it is seeking to establish itself as a valuable fashion partner for foreign companies that do have a reputation and resources to market fashion products successfully.

Most of the companies in garment industry are smaller companies. Scottwool employs 320 workers and supplies knitwear to more than 20 international labels sold from Harrods in London to Bloomingdale's in New York. The advantage of being small is that companies can react quickly to the demands and wishes of their customers. The disadvantage is that they lack an international profile and resources to launch and market international brands. A way of overcoming this disadvantage is franchising which is successfully used by a number of Portuguese companies.

Source: *The Financial Times, FT Exporter*, Autumn 1995 p. 18.

Ethnocentrism can also have country-of-origin effects; feelings of national pride—the 'buy American' effect, for example—can influence attitudes towards foreign products. Honda, which manufactures one of its models almost entirely in the United States, recognizes this phenomenon and points out how many component parts are made in America in some of its advertisements. On the other hand, others have a stereotype of Japan as producing the 'best' cars. A recent study found that US car producers may suffer comparatively tarnished in-country images regardless of whether they actually produce superior products.[14]

Countries are also stereotyped on the basis of whether they are industrialized, in emerging or less developed. These stereotypes are less country-product specific; they are more a perception of the quality of goods in general produced within the country. Industrialized countries have the highest quality image, and there is generally a bias against products from developing countries. However, within countries grouped by economic development there are variations of image. For example, one study of COE between Mexico and Taiwan found that a microwave oven manufactured in Mexico was perceived as significantly more risky than an oven made in Taiwan. However, for jeans there was no difference in perception between the two countries.[15]

One might generalize that the more technical the product, the less positive is the perception of one manufactured in a less developed country. There is also the tendency to favour foreign-made products over domestic-made ones in less-developed countries. Not all foreign products fare equally well because consumers in developing countries have stereotypes about the quality of foreign-made products even from industrialized countries. A survey of consumers in the Czech Republic found that 72 per cent of Japanese products were considered to be of the highest quality, German goods followed with 51 per cent, Swiss goods

GOING INTERNATIONAL 13.5

CREAM OF SNAKE SOUP? IT MIGHT SELL!

Prepared food may be the toughest product to sell overseas. It isn't as universal or as easily marketed as, say, soap, cigarettes or coca-cola. Regional tastes are involved and food flavours do not necessarily travel well.

Campbell found that Italians, unsurprisingly, shudder at canned pasta, so Franco-American SpaghettiOs don't fly there. The average Pole consumes five bowls of soup a week—three times the American average—but 98 per cent of Polish soups are homemade, and Mum is one tough competitor. To get around that problem, Campbell advertises to working Polish mothers looking for convenience, which just might work. But Campbell realizes it can't just shove a can in the consumer's face and replace Mum. To encourage customers to ease into canned soups, it typically launches a basic meat or chicken broth which consumers can doctor with meats, vegetables and spices. Then it brings out more sophisticated soups created to appeal to distinctly regional tastes.

To help develop these new soups, the company taste tests with consumers around the world. On any weekday morning, a dozen consumers take the elevator to the 19th floor of Cornwall House, home to Campbell Soup Co.'s Hong Kong taste kitchen opened to help get the right flavours to reach 2 billion Asian consumers. Chosen carefully to get the right demographic mix, such groups are assembled to taste the offerings that Campbell hopes will ignite consumer interest in China and other parts of Asia. There, they split off into carrels and take their seats before bowls of soup and eager food scientists.

Campbell has a couple of hits to its credit: scallop and ham soups came out of the Hong Kong lab and watercress and duck-gizzard soup out of a US test kitchen. Local ingredients are always considered, but Campbell draws the line on some Asian favourites. Dog soup is out, as is shark's fin, since most species of shark are endangered. But the staff keeps an open mind. Snake, for example. One researcher admits: 'I have tasted it.' Who knows? Campbell's cream of snake could emerge as the chicken noodle of the future. Hmm! Good!!

Sources: Adam Heller, 'A Recipe for Success?' *The China Business Review*, July–August 1993, pp. 30–32; Susan Warner, 'Campbell Soup Tries New Recipes to Cater to Asian Market', *Journal of Commerce and Commercial*, 13 July 1993, p. 9-A. 'Campbell: Now It's M-M-Global', *Business Week*, 15 March 1994, pp. 52–54; and ' "Hmm. Could Use a Little More Snake" ', *Business Week*, 15 March 1994, p. 53.

with 48 per cent, Czech goods with 32 per cent, and, last, the United States with 29 per cent.[16]

One final generalization about COE involves fads that often surround products from particular countries or regions in the world. These fads are most often product specific and generally involve goods that are themselves faddish in nature. European consumers are apparently enamoured with a host of American-made products ranging from Jeep Cherokees, Budweiser beer and Jim Beam bourbon to Bose sound systems.[17] In the 1970s and 80s, there was a backlash against anything American, but in the 1990s American is in. In China, anything Western seems to be the fad. If it is Western it is in demand, even at prices three or four times higher than domestic products.[18] In most cases, such fads wane after a few years as some new fad takes over.

Country stereotyping can be overcome with good marketing. The image of Korean electronics improved substantially in Western countries once the market gained positive experience with Korean brands. All of which stresses the importance of building strong global brands like Sony, General Electric, Samsung and Levi's. Brands effectively advertised and products properly positioned can help ameliorate a less-than-positive country stereotype. Consumers perceive pioneering brands more positively than follower brands, irrespective of COE. Sony Walkman is a good example.[19]

Own Brands

Growing as challenges to manufacturers' brands, whether global or country-specific, are brands owned by retailers. In the food-retailing sector in Britain, The Netherlands and many European countries, manufacturers' brands are increasingly confronted by brands owned by national retailers. From blackberry jam, coffee, tea and vacuum-cleaner bags to smoked salmon and sun-dried tomatoes, own-brand products dominate grocery stores in Britain and in many of the hypermarkets of Europe. It is estimated that own-brand products have captured nearly 30 per cent of the British and Swiss markets and more than 20 per cent of the French and German markets. In some European markets, own-brand market share has doubled in just the past five years.

Sainsbury, for example, one of Britain's largest grocery retailers with 420 stores, reserves the best shelf space for its own brands. A typical Sainsbury's store has about 16 000 products, of which 8000 are Sainsbury's own brands. The company avidly develops new products, launching 1400 to 1500 new own-brand items each year, and weeds out hundreds of others that are no longer popular. It launched its own Novon-brand laundry detergent and, in the first year, its sales climbed past Procter & Gamble's and Unilever's top brands to make it the top-selling detergent in Sainsbury's stores and the second-best seller nationally with a 30 per cent market share.[20] The 15 per cent margin on own-brand labels that chains such as Sainsbury boast about helps explain why their operating profit margins are as high as 8 per cent, or eight times the profit margins of their US counterparts.

Own-brand penetration has traditionally been high in Britain and, more recently, high in Europe as well. Own brands, with their high margins, will become even more important as the trend in consolidation of retailers continues and as discounters such as Ahold of The Netherlands, Aldi of Germany, Wal-Mart of the United States and Carréfour of France expand throughout Europe, putting greater pressure on prices.

As it stands now, own brands are formidable competitors. They provide the retailer with high margins, they receive preferential shelf space and strong in-store promotion and, perhaps most important for consumer appeal, they are quality products at low prices. Contrast that with manufacturers' brands which traditionally are premium priced and offer the retailer lower margins than they get from their own brands.

To maintain market share, global brands will have to be priced competitively and provide real consumer value. Global marketers must examine the adequacy of their brand strategies in the light of such competition. This may make cost and efficiency benefits of global brands even more appealing.

PRODUCTS AND CULTURE

To appreciate the complexity of standardized versus adapted products, one needs to understand how cultural influences are interwoven with the perceived value and importance a market places on a product. A product is more than a physical item; it is a bundle of satisfactions (or utilities) the buyer receives. This includes its form, taste, colour, odour and texture, how it functions in use, the package, the label, the warranty, manufacturer's and retailer's servicing, the confidence or prestige enjoyed by the brand, the manufacturer's reputation, the country of origin and any other symbolic utility received from the possession or use of the goods. In short, the market relates to more than a product's physical form and primary function. (See Figure 13.2.)

Figure 13.2 Factors Influencing International Product Decisions

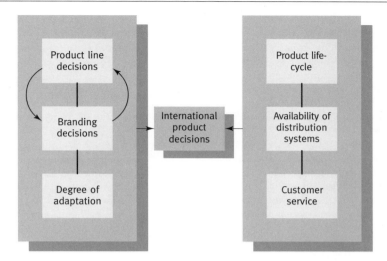

Its physical attributes generally are required to create the primary function of the product. The primary function of a car, for example, is to move passengers from point A to point B. This ability requires an engine, transmission and other physical features to achieve its primary purpose. The physical features and primary function of a car are generally in demand in all cultures where there is a desire to move from one point to another other than by foot or animal power. Few changes to the physical attributes of a product are required when moving from one culture to another. However, a car has a bundle of psychological features as important in providing consumer satisfaction as its physical features. Within a specific culture, other features (colour, size, design, brand name) have little to do with the car's primary function, the movement from point A to B, but do add value to the satisfaction received.

The meaning and value imputed to the psychological attributes of a product can vary among cultures and are perceived as negative or positive. To maximize the bundle of satisfactions received and to create positive product attributes rather than negative ones, adaptation of the nonphysical features of a product may be necessary.

Coca-Cola, frequently touted as a global product, found it had to change Diet Coke to Coke Light when it was introduced in Japan and a number of European countries. Japanese women do not like to admit to dieting and, further, the idea of diet implies sickness or medicine. This also applies in some European countries. So, instead of emphasizing weight loss, 'figure maintenance' is stressed.

The adoption of some products by consumers can be affected as much by how the product concept conflicts with norms, values and behaviour patterns as by its physical or mechanical attributes. As one authority states:

> In short, it is not just lack of money, nor even differences in the natural environment, that constitutes major barriers to the acceptance of new products and new ways of behaving. A novelty always comes up against a closely integrated cultural pattern, and it is primarily this that determines whether, when, how and in what form it gets adopted.

GOING INTERNATIONAL 13.6

HERE COMES KELLOGG—CAUSING CULTURAL CHANGE

Marketers become cultural change agents by accident or by design. In Latvia, cultural change is being planned.

As a column of creamy white milk cascades into a bowl of Corn Flakes in the television ad, a camera moves in for a tight shot and the message 'eight vitamins' flashes across the screen.

Kellogg Company of Battle Creek, Michigan, is trying to change the way hundreds of millions of Latvians and other former Soviet citizens start their day. Historically, the favourite breakfast in Latvia and in much of the former Soviet Union has been a hearty plate of sausage, cold cuts, potatoes, eggs and a few slices of thick, chewy bread slathered with wonderfully high-cholesterol butter.

Kellogg is out to change all that and is pressing ahead with one of the more ambitious education programmes in the annals of eating. 'We have to teach people a whole new way to eat breakfast', said a specialist in Soviet affairs for Kellogg. To win converts, Kellogg is relying mainly on slick television advertisements showing a family joyfully digging into its Corn Flakes, and on demonstrations in grocery stores that the company refers to as 'taste testing'.

Kellogg's marketing plans are best summarized in a Kellogg Company representative's comment, 'It took 40 years to develop the Latin American market; Latvia is going to be part of long-term growth'. Any wonder that Kellogg has the world's most successful cereal companies with 51 per cent of the market? Latvia is the 18th international facility and Kellogg plans to open plants in India and China. Today, you would have a hard time finding a store in Latvia that doesn't have Kellogg's Corn Flakes.

Source: Adapted from Joseph B. Treaster, 'Kellogg Seeks to Reset Latvia's Breakfast Table', *New York Times*, 19 May 1994, p. C-1.

The Japanese have always found all body jewellery repugnant. The Scots have a decided resistance to pork and all its associated products, apparently from days long ago when such taboos were decided by fundamentalist interpretations of the Bible.[21]

When analysing a product for a second market, the extent of adaptation required depends on cultural differences in product use and perception between the market the product was originally developed for and the new market. The greater these cultural differences between the two markets, the greater the extent of adaptation necessary.

An example of this involves an undisputed American leader in cake mixes which tacitly admitted failure in the English market by closing down operations after five unsuccessful years. Taking its most successful mixes in the US market, the company introduced them into the British market. A considerable amount of time, money and effort was expended to introduce its variety of cake mixes to this new market. Hindsight provides several probable causes for the company's failure. The British eat most of their cake with tea instead of dinner and have always preferred dry sponge cake, which is easy to handle; the fancy, iced cakes favoured in the United States were the type introduced. Fancy, iced cakes are accepted in Britain, but they are considered extra special and purchased from a bakery or made with much effort and care at home. Homemakers felt guilty about not even cracking an egg, and there was suspicion that dried eggs and milk were not as good as fresh ones. Therefore, when the occasion called for a fancy cake, an easy cake mix was simply not good enough.

When instant cake mixes were introduced in Japan, the consumers' response was less than enthusiastic. Not only do Japanese reserve cakes for special occasions, they prefer them to be beautifully wrapped and purchased in pastry shops. The acceptance of instant cakes was further complicated by another cultural difference—most Japanese homes do not have ovens.

GOING INTERNATIONAL 13.7

GILLETTE IN CHINA

In 1992, Gillette established a $43 million (€39 million) joint venture with the state-owned Shanghai Razor & Blade Factory (SRBF). At the time SRBF enjoyed 70 per cent of the market share at the low-end blade market and Gillette hoped to capitalize on this consumer base and to build up consumer demand towards a more sophisticated and expensive razor where the margins are higher.

Gillette has used this strategy all around the world but in China the progress has been frustratingly slow, according to Ian Jackson, the head of Asia Pacific Division, Gillette's market research was too optimistic about the Chinese consumers. In China, about one billion blades are sold annually, out of which 400 million are the cheapest double-edged variety at about 2 cents per unit. Gillette hoped that if it could persuade even a fraction of those low-end customers to move up to more expensive blades, it could make good profits. Its Contour brand sells for around 50 cents. And once it starts selling Mach 3, currently priced at $1.50 in the United States, it can make good money.

Gillette has, however, discovered that it is not so easy to convince the customers to climb the consumption ladder. Chinese men do not shave as often as Westerners and they are quite happy with cheaper blades. What Gillette has learned is to adapt its sales and marketing strategy according to local consumer behaviour.

Another mistake Gillette has made is that when it entered in a joint venture with SRBF, it assumed that the local partner had an effective salesforce and distribution channels. But it realized that SRBF's sales and distribution network was not of much use. SRBF's wholesalers, often state-owned, literally collected their blade quota at the factory gate. There was no need to market the product because the market, as we perceive it, did not exist. Gillette is now building a 1000 men-strong national sales and distribution team from scratch.

Gillette has thus learned that in a market like China, you have to give full attention to details. Focusing only on the big picture and overall strategy leads definitely to problems.

Source: Richard Tomlinson, 'Why So Many Western Companies Are Coming Down with China Fatigue', *Fortune*, 25 May 1998, pp. 60–64.

Innovative Products and Adaptation

An important first step in adapting a product to a foreign market is to determine the degree of newness perceived by the intended market. How people react to newness and how new a product is to a market must be understood. In evaluating the newness of a product, the international marketer must be aware that many products successful in Western countries, having reached the maturity or even decline stage in their life cycles, may be perceived as new in another country or culture and, thus, must be treated as innovations. A new product would therefore demand a different type of marketing strategy than the one used at home, for a rather mature product.

Whether or not a group accepts an innovation and the time it takes depends on its characteristics. Products new to a social system are innovations, and knowledge about the diffusion (i.e. the process by which innovation spreads) of innovation is helpful in developing a successful product strategy.

Another US cake mix company entered the British market but carefully eliminated most of the newness of the product. Instead of introducing the most popular American cake mixes, the company asked 500 British housewives to bake their favourite cake. Since the majority baked a simple, very popular dry sponge cake, the company brought to the market a similar easy mix. The sponge cake mix represented familiar tastes and habits that could be translated into a convenience item, and did not infringe on the emotional aspects of preparing a fancy product for special occasions. Consequently, after a short period of time, the second company's product gained 30 to 35 per cent of the British cake-mix market. Once the idea of a mix for sponge cake was acceptable, the introduction of other flavours became easier.

The goal of a foreign marketer is to gain product acceptance by the largest number of consumers in the market in the shortest span of time. However, as many of the examples cited have illustrated, new products are not always readily accepted by a culture; indeed, they often meet resistance. Although they may ultimately be accepted, the time it takes for a culture to learn new ways, to learn to accept a new product, are of critical importance to the marketer since planning reflects a time frame for investment and profitability.

Diffusion of Innovations

There is ample evidence of the fact that product innovations have a varying rate of acceptance. Some diffuse from introduction to widespread use in a few years, others take decades. Microwave ovens, introduced in the 1950s, reached widespread acceptance in the 1980s. The contraceptive pill was introduced during that same period and gained acceptance in a few years. There is also a growing body of evidence that the understanding of diffusion theory may provide ways in which the process of diffusion can be accelerated. Knowledge of this process may provide the foreign marketer with the ability to assess the time it takes for a product to diffuse—before it is necessary to make a financial commitment.

At least three extraneous variables affect the rate of diffusion of an object: the degree of perceived newness, the perceived attributes of the innovation, and the method used to communicate the idea. Each variable has a bearing on consumer reaction to a new product and the time needed for acceptance. An understanding of these variables can produce better product strategies for the international marketer.

Degree of Newness

As perceived by the market, varying degrees of newness categorize all new products. Within each category, myriad reactions affect the rate of diffusion. In giving a name to these categories, one might think of (1) congruent innovations, (2) continuous innovations, (3) dynamically continuous innovations and (4) discontinuous innovations.

1. A *congruent* innovation is actually not an innovation at all because it causes absolutely no disruption of established consumption patterns. The product concept is accepted by the culture and the innovativeness is typically one of introducing variety and quality or functional features, style or perhaps an exact duplicate of an already existing product—exact in the sense that the market perceives no newness, such as cane sugar versus beet sugar.

2. A *continuous* innovation has the least disruptive influence on established consumption patterns. Alteration of a product is almost always involved rather than the creation of a new product. Generally, the alterations result in better use patterns—perceived improvement in the satisfaction derived from its use. Examples include fluoride toothpaste, disposable razors and flavours in coffee. A continuous improvement in Gillette and Wilkinson Sword razors is another example.

3. A *dynamically continuous* innovation has more disruptive effects than a continuous innovation, although it generally does not involve new consumption patterns. It may mean the creation of a new product or considerable alteration of an existing one designed to fulfil new needs arising from changes in lifestyles or new expectations brought about by change. It is generally disruptive and therefore resisted because old patterns of behaviour must change if

GOING INTERNATIONAL 13.8

ICED TEA FOR THE BRITISH—'IT WAS BLOODY AWFUL'

After sampling one of the new canned iced teas, the response by one Brit was, 'It tasted like stewed tea that had been left in the pot. It was bloody awful.' Such are the challenges faced by iced-tea makers in Britain, a culture where tea, served hot, is the national drink and cold tea borders on the sacrilegious. . . .

Unilever and PepsiCo with Liptonice and Snapple Beverage Corp. with Snapple believe they can eventually convince the British that iced tea isn't just hot tea that has got cold, but a plausible alternative to soft drinks. Each company is approaching this mammoth task differently.

To distinguish iced tea from cold dregs left in the pot, Liptonice is carbonated. 'We've tried to bring people around to the idea of looking at tea in a different way.' Public reaction is mixed. One response: 'Let's say it was unusual. I've never quite tasted anything like it actually. I'll stick with Coke.' Actually, this is the second time Unilever has tried iced tea in the British market. The previous attempt 'flopped'. The product itself wasn't the problem, 'it was just ahead of its time'. Now, Unilever points to the growth of carbonated flavoured water as an indication that consumers are increasingly receptive to new types of beverages.

Snapple's approach is to ease British consumers into drinking iced tea by enticing them to sample other Snapple products first. Lemonade and other fruit-flavoured drinks, including raspberry, peach and orange, were sold in Britain for about a year before iced tea was introduced. Its goal is to persuade a nation of tea-lovers to sample a line anchored by a beverage that is not served hot or with milk. When you ask people if they want to try cold tea, their immediate reaction is no. Snapple's approach is to saturate the market to gain awareness by making Snapple available in 15 000 retail outlets from minuscule confectionery, news and tobacco stores to huge supermarkets. Coupled with extensive distribution, Snapple will offer 250 000 samples in tiny Snapple-labelled cups in all kinds of outlets, including hundreds of service stations. In its first major sales promotion, 'Tea for Two', Snapple tackles the tea issue head-on. In point-of-sale displays at 750 Esso service stations, Snapple shows colourful photos of the product and brand name, offering customers who buy two Snapple fruit-flavoured drinks a free one-pint tea drink. All of this is supported with advertising.

The third member of the big iced-tea companies, Nestlé with Nestea, introduced its product in several European countries but not Britain. Because there is no history of consumption of iced tea in England, changing consumer perception is going to take a long time. Nestlé prefers to wait and see, although there is speculation that it will enter the British market soon.

Two companies with the same goal—change British attitudes about drinking iced tea—and two different strategies. Which will win? Maybe both, maybe neither.

Sources: Adapted from: Tara Parker-Pope, 'Will the British Warm Up to Iced Tea? Some Big Marketers Are Counting on It', *The Wall Street Journal*, 22 August 1994, p. B-1; and Elena Bowes and Laurel Wentz, 'Snapple Beverage War Spills Onto Continent', *Advertising Age*, 18 April 1994, p. I-1.

---

consumers are to accept and perceive the value of the dynamically continuous innovation. Examples include electric toothbrushes, electric haircurlers, central air-conditioning and frozen dinners.

4. A *discontinuous innovation* involves the establishment of new consumption patterns and the creation of previously unknown products. It introduces an idea or behaviour pattern where there was none before. Examples include television, the computer, the fax machine, the electric car and microwave ovens.

The extent of a product's diffusion and its rate of diffusion are partly functions of the particular product's attributes. Each innovation has characteristics by which it can be

GILLETTE IS BETTING A BILLION DOLLARS ON A NEW RAZOR BLADE

After more than a decade's work and $750 million (€677 million) in development and tooling costs, Gillette introduced its new razor, the Mach 3, on 14 April 1998. Gillette is also to spend another $300 million (€270 million) on advertising and marketing over the next 15 months.

Mach 3 will be sold at a 35 per cent higher price than Sensor Excel, Gillette's top of the line product. Analysts said that was a big risk as the consumers were highly satisfied with existing products as compared to the time when Gillette introduced Sensor in 1989. They also believe that Mach 3 will generate annual revenues of $1 billion (€900 million) by the year 2001.

Mach 3 is so complex that Gillette had to develop a new manufacturing process for it. The development process went as follows:

1985: Serious research began on developing the first new edge for Gillette's blades since 1969.
1988: Gillette researchers managed to arrange three blades in a progressive alignment, meaning the first blade sticks out less than the second and the third blade.
1992: An advanced prototype, Manx, beats Sensor Excel, Gillette's most advanced razor, in shave tests.
1995: Gillette board gave green light to develop Manx.
1996: Gillette's engineers developed a method to assemble Manx's cartridge that was three times faster than Sensor Excel production.
1997: Board approved final stage of $750 million (€677 million) investment. Production started.
1998: Mach 3 launched (14 April).

Source: 'How much would you spend on a blade?' *Business Week*, 27 April 1998, p. 23.

described, and each person's perception of these characteristics can be utilized in explaining the differences in perceived newness of an innovation. These attributes can also be utilized in predicting the rate of adoption, and the adjustment of these attributes or product adaptation can lead to changes in consumer perception and thus to altered rates of diffusion. Emphasis given to product adaptation for local cultural norms and the overall brand image created are critical marketing decision areas.

Physical or Mandatory Requirements and Adaptation

A product may have to change in a number of ways to meet physical or mandatory requirements of a new market; they can range from simple package changes to total redesign of the physical core product. Some changes are obvious with relatively little analysis; a cursory examination of a country will uncover the need to rewire electrical goods for a different voltage system, simplify a product when the local level of technology is not high, or print multilingual labels where required by law. Electrolux, for example, offers a cold-wash-only washing machine in Asian countries in which electric power is expensive or scarce.[22]

Legal, economic, technological and climatic requirements of the local marketplace often dictate product adaptation. Specific package sizes and safety and quality standards are usually set by laws that vary among countries. To make a purchase more affordable in low-income countries, the number of units per package may have to be reduced from the typical quantities offered in high-income countries. Razor blades, cigarettes, chewing gum and other multiple-pack items are often sold singly or two to a pack instead of the more customary 10 or 20.

Figure 13.3   Product Life Cycle for a Product in Different Markets

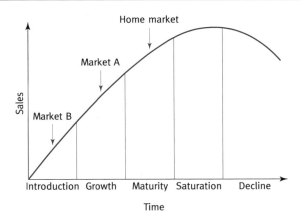

Changes may also have to be made to accommodate climatic differences. General Motors of Canada, for example, experienced major problems with several thousand Chevrolet cars shipped to a Middle East country; it was quickly discovered they were unfit for the hot, dusty climate. Supplementary air filters and different clutches had to be added to adjust for the problem. Even peanuts and crackers have to be packaged in tins for humid areas.

The less economically developed a market is, the greater degree of change a product may need for acceptance. One study found only 1 in 10 products could be marketed in developing countries without modification of some sort. Of the modifications made, nearly 25 per cent were mandatory; the other modifications were made to accommodate variations in cultures.[23]

PRODUCT LIFE CYCLE AND ADAPTATION

Even between markets with few cultural differences, substantial adaptation could be necessary if the product is in a different stage of its life cycle in each market. Product life cycle and the marketing mix are interrelated; a product in a mature stage of its life cycle in one market can have unwanted and/or unknown attributes in a market where the product is perceived as new and thus in its introductory stage. Marketing history is replete with examples of mature products in one market being introduced in another and failing. (See Figure 13.3.)

Certainly an important approach in analysing products for foreign markets is determining the stage of the product's life cycle. All subsequent marketing plans must then include adaptations necessary to correspond to the stage of the product life cycle in the new market.

The success of these alternatives depends on the product and the fundamental need it fulfils, its characteristics, its perception within the culture and the associated costs of each programme. To know that foreign markets are different and that different product strategies may be needed is one thing; to know when adaptation of your product line and marketing programme is necessary is another and more complicated problem.

CAN HONDA BUILD A GLOBAL CAR

The Accord makes almost half of Honda's sales in the US, its biggest market. Worldwide Honda devotes more than a quarter of its production to Accord. It competes in the middle of the world's biggest car segment, the family sedan. The sporty restyled Accord which was launched in 1990, was not successful at all. It was too cramped for US drivers and not stylish enough for the Japanese. In 1994 Honda started remodelling its Accord which was launched in 1996, the market surged in the US by 12 per cent nearly topping Ford Taurus, America's top-seller. But it was not successful in Japan. Honda thus had to completely overhaul its Accord, which was launched in the US and Japan on 25 September 1997 and in Europe in the Spring of 1998. The American Accord will be big, matching Ford Taurus, while the Japanese Accord will be smaller, sportier and compact and the European version will be short and narrow featuring stiff and sporty ride.

The success factor is that with its versatile new platform as a base, Honda plans to build vastly different cars geared to local markets around the world. Here's what's coming:

September 1997—At 189 inches long and 70 inches wide, the new US Accord is a midsize competitor to Ford's Taurus. A raised roof provides extra headroom and a roomy interior for this conservative family car.

September 1997—Six inches shorter, four inches thinner and with a lower roof than its US cousin, the new Japanese Accord is a sporty and compact loaded with high-tech gizmos beloved by Japanese professionals.

Spring 1998—The European Accord will be launched with a short, narrow body geared to tiny streets. It's expected to have the stiffer, sportier ride Old World drivers prefer.

Fall 1998—By enlarging the frame even more, Honda will build a minivan for the US as big as the market-leading Dodge Caravan.

Fall 1999—Next up, a sport-utility vehicle for the US market. At 200 inches long, it will rival the big Chevrolet Tahoe in size.

Fall 1998 and Fall 1999—Two Acura luxury cars – the TL sedan and CL coupe – will be launched in the US off the same platform.

Source: 'Can Honda Build A World Car?' *Business Week* (cover story), 8 September 1997, pp. 38–41.

SCREENING PRODUCTS FOR ADAPTATION

Evaluating a product for marketing in another country requires a systematic method of screening products to determine if there are cultural resistances to overcome and/or physical or mandatory changes necessary for product acceptance. Only when the psychological (or cultural) and physical dimensions of the product, as determined by the country market, are known can the decision for adaptation be made. Products can be screened on two different bases by using the 'Analysis of Characteristics of Innovations' to determine if there are cultural-perceptual reasons why a product will be better accepted if adapted, and/or 'Analysis of Product Components' to determine if there are mandatory or physical reasons why a product must be adapted.

Analysis of Characteristics of Innovations

Attributes of a product that cause market resistance to its acceptance and affect the rate of acceptance can be determined if a product is analysed by the five characteristics of an innovation: (1) relative advantage—the perceived marginal value of the new product relative to the old; (2) compatibility—its compatibility with acceptable behaviour, norms, values and so forth; (3) complexity—the degree of complexity associated with product use; (4) trialability—the degree of economic and/or social risk associated with product use; and (5) observability—the ease with which the product benefits can be communicated.[24] In general, it can be postulated that the rate of diffusion is positively related to relative advantage, compatibility, trialability and observability, but negatively related to complexity.

The evaluator must remember it is the perception of product characteristics by the potential adopter, not the marketer, that is crucial to the evaluation. A market analyst's self-reference criterion may cause a perceptual bias when interpreting the characteristics of a product. Thus, instead of evaluating product characteristics from the foreign user's frame of reference, it is analysed from the marketer's frame of reference, leading to a misinterpretation of the cultural importance.

Once the analysis has been made, some of the perceived newness or cause for resistance can be minimized through adroit marketing. The more congruent with current cultural values perceptions of the product can be, the less the probable resistance and the more rapid the diffusion or acceptance of the product. A product can frequently be modified physically to improve its relative advantage over competing products, enhance its compatibility with cultural values and even minimize its complexity. Its relative advantage and compatibility also can be enhanced and some degree of complexity lessened through advertising efforts. Small sizes, samples, packaging and product demonstrations are all sales promotion efforts that can be used to alter the characteristics of an innovative product and accelerate its rate of adoption.

Analysis of Product Components

In addition to cultural resistance to product acceptance which may require adaptation, physical attributes can influence the acceptance or rejection of a product. A product is multi-dimensional, and the sum of all its features determines the bundle of satisfactions received by the consumer. To identify all the possible ways a product may be adapted to a new market, it helps to separate its many dimensions into three distinct components as illustrated in Figure 13.4, the Product Component Model. The core component, packaging component and support services component include all a product's tangible and intangible elements and provide the bundle of utilities the market receives from use of the product. By analysing a product along the dimensions of its three components, the marketer focuses on different levels of product adaptation.

The Core Component.   This component consists of the physical product—the platform that contains the essential technology—and all its design and functional features. It is on the product platform that product variations can be added or deleted to satisfy local differences. Major adjustments in the platform aspect of the core component may be costly because a change in the platform can affect product processes and thus require additional capital investment. However, alterations in design, functional features, flavours, colour and other aspects can be made to adapt the product to cultural variations. In Japan, both Nestlé and Kellogg sold the same kind of Corn Flakes and Sugar Pops that they sold in the Western countries, but Japanese children ate them mostly as snacks instead of for breakfast. In order to move their product into the large breakfast market, Nestlé reformulated its cereals to fit Japanese taste more closely. The Japanese traditionally eat fish and rice for breakfast, so Nestlé

Figure 13.4 Product Component Model

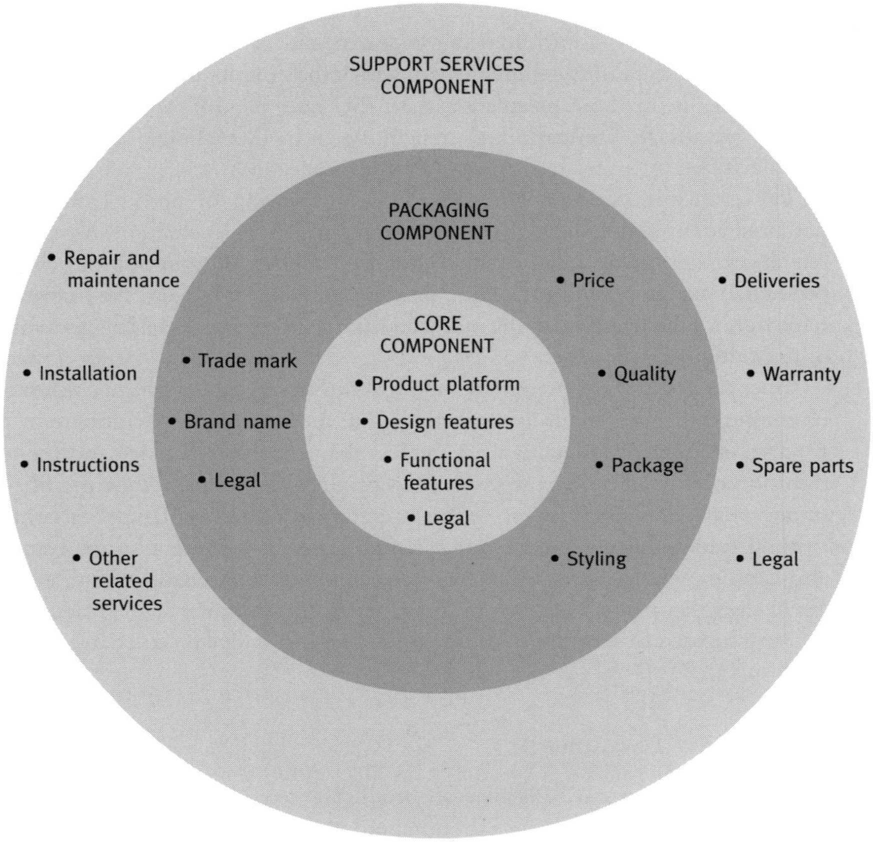

developed cereals with familiar tastes—seaweed, carrots and zucchini, and coconuts and papaya. The result was a 12 per cent share of a growing market.[25]

Functional features can be added or eliminated depending on the market. In markets where hot water is not commonly available, washing machines have heaters as a functional feature. In other markets, automatic soap and bleach dispensers may be eliminated to cut costs and/or to minimize repair problems. Additional changes may be necessary to meet safety and electrical standards or other mandatory requirements. The physical product and all its functional features should be examined as potential candidates for adaptation.

The Packaging Component. The packaging component includes style features, packaging, labelling, trademarks, brand name, quality, price and all other aspects of a product's package. As with the core component, the importance of each of these elements in the eyes of the consumer depends on the need that the product is designed to serve. Packaging components frequently require both discretionary and mandatory changes. For example, some countries require labels to be printed in more than one language while others forbid the use of any foreign language. Elements in the packaging component may incorporate symbols which convey an unintended meaning and thus must be changed. One company's red-circle trademark was popular in some countries but was rejected in parts of Asia where it conjured up images of the Japanese flag. Yellow flowers used in another company trademark were rejected in Mexico where a yellow flower symbolizes death or disrespect.

Care must be taken to ensure that corporate trademarks and other parts of the packaging component do not have unacceptable symbolic meanings. Particular attention should be given to translations of brand names and colours used in packaging. White, the colour for purity in Western countries, is the colour for mourning in others. When Coca-Cola went to China, translators chose characters that sounded like Coca-Cola, but to the Chinese they read, 'bite the wax tadpole'.

There are countless reasons why a company might have to adapt a product's package. In some countries, specific bottle, can and package sizes are stipulated by law, as are measurement units. Such descriptive words as 'giant' or 'jumbo' on a package or label may be illegal. High humidity and/or the need for long shelf life because of extended distribution systems may dictate extra-heavy packaging for some products. A poorly packaged product conveys an impression of poor quality. It is also important to determine if the packaging has other uses in the market. Again in Japan, Lever Brothers sells Lux soap in stylish boxes because in Japan more than half of all soap cakes are purchased during the two gift-giving seasons. Size of the package is also a factor that may make a difference to success in Japan. Soft drinks are sold in smaller-size cans than in the United States and Western Europe to accommodate local consumption patterns and the smaller Japanese hand.

Labelling laws vary from country to country and do not seem to follow any predictable pattern. In Saudi Arabia, for example, product names must be specific. 'Hot Chilli' will not do, it must be 'Spiced Hot Chilli'. Prices are required to be printed on the labels in many countries, but in Chile it is illegal to put prices on labels or in any way suggest retail prices. Coca-Cola ran into a legal problem in Brazil with its Diet Coke. Brazilian law interprets diet to have medicinal qualities. Under the law, producers must give daily recommended consumption on the labels of all medicines. Coke had to get special approval to get around this restriction.

The Support Services Component.   This component includes repair and maintenance, instructions, installation, warranties, deliveries and the availability of spare parts. Many otherwise-successful marketing programmes have ultimately failed because little attention was given to this product component. Repair and maintenance are especially difficult problems in developing countries. In Europe and the United States, a consumer has the option of company service as well as a score of competitive service retailers ready to repair and maintain anything from cars to lawn mowers. Equally available are repair parts from company-owned or licensed outlets or the local hardware store. Consumers in a developing country and many developed countries may not have even one of the possibilities for repair and maintenance available in the West.

Literacy rates and educational levels of a country may require a firm to change a product's instructions. A simple term in one country may be incomprehensible in another. In rural Africa, for example, the consumer had trouble understanding that Vaseline Intensive Care lotion is absorbed into the skin. Absorbed was changed to soaks into, and the confusion was eliminated. The Brazilians have successfully overcome low literacy and technical skills of users of the sophisticated military tanks it sells to Third World countries. They include video-cassette players and videotapes with detailed repair instructions as part of the standard instruction package. They also minimize spare parts problems by using standardized, off-the-shelf parts available throughout the world.

GREEN MARKETING AND PRODUCT DEVELOPMENT

From the Earth Summit Conference (1992) in Rio de Janeiro to local city governments, the world and its people are becoming increasingly aware of the importance of protecting the environment.[26] The 21st century has been dubbed 'the century of environmental awareness'. Consumers, business people and public administrators must now demonstrate a sense of 'green' responsibility by integrating environmental habits into individual behaviour.

Europe has been at the forefront of the 'green movement,' with strong public opinion and specific legislation favouring environmentally friendly marketing. Green marketing is a term used to identify concern with the environmental consequences of a variety of marketing activities. The European Union, concerned that national restrictions on waste would create 15 different codes that could become clear barriers to trade, has passed legislation to control all kinds of packaging waste throughout the EU. Two critical issues that affect product development are the control of the packaging component of solid waste and consumer demand for environmentally friendly products.[27]

Germany has a strict eco-labelling programme to identify, for the concerned consumer, products that have a lesser impact on the environment than similar products. Under German law, a manufacturer is permitted to display a logo, called the 'Blue Angel', on all products that comply with certain criteria that make it environmentally friendly. More than 3200 products in 58 product categories have been examined and given the Blue Angel logo. While it is difficult to judge the commercial value of a Blue Angel designation, manufacturers are seeking the eco-label for their products in response to growing consumer demand for environmentally friendly products. Similar national labels are under discussion in France, Denmark, The Netherlands and the United Kingdom. One report has speculated that if all these national proposals for labelling legislation were to be passed, a French plastic trash bag, consisting of 85 per cent recycled polyethylene (that would qualify it as environmentally friendly) to be sold in all 15 European countries would be covered with logos from France, Belgium, The Netherlands and so on.

Partly to offset an onrush of eco-labels from every European country, the European Commission issued guidelines for eco-labelling that became operational in October 1992. Under the EC directive, a product is evaluated on all significant environmental effects throughout its life cycle, from manufacturing to disposal—a cradle-to-grave approach.[28] Companies will be encouraged to continuously update their environmental technology because eco-labels will be granted for a limited period. As more environmentally friendly products come onto the market, the standards will become tougher, and products that have not been improved will lose their eco-labels.[29] (See Figure 13.5.)

The Blue Angel and similar eco-labels are awarded on the basis of a product's environmental friendliness, that is, how 'friendly' it is when used and when its residue is released into the environment (see Table 13.1). A detergent formulated to be biodegradable and not to pollute would be judged more friendly than a detergent whose formulation would be harmful when discharged. Aerosol propellants that do not deplete the ozone layer are another example of environmentally friendly products. No country's laws yet require products to carry an 'eco-label' for them to be sold. The designation that a product is 'environmentally friendly' is voluntary and its environmental success depends on the consumer selecting the 'eco-friendly' product. However, laws that mandate systems to control solid waste, while voluntary in one sense, do carry penalties, albeit indirect ones.

Germany's law requires that packaging materials through all levels of distribution, from the manufacturer to the consumer, must be recycled or reused. Each level of the distribution chain is responsible for returning, back upstream, all packaging, packing and other waste

Table 13.1   How Long Will Litter Last?

	Number of years
Cigarette butts	1–5
Aluminium cans and tabs	500
Glass bottles	1000
Plastic bags	10–20
Plastic coated paper	5
Plastic film containers	20–30
Nylon fabric	30–40
Leather	up to 50
Orange and banana peels	up to 2
Tin cans	50
Plastic holders	100
Plastic bottles and Styrofoam	indefinitely

Source: Based on Grame Pole, *Au Altitude Super Guide: Canadian Rockies* (Vancouver: Altitude Publishing, 1993), p. 29.

Figure 13.5   Examples of EC Environmental Symbols

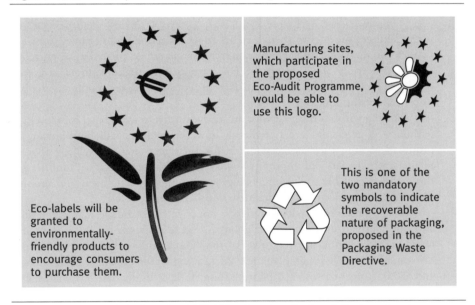

Manufacturing sites, which participate in the proposed Eco-Audit Programme, would be able to use this logo.

This is one of the two mandatory symbols to indicate the recoverable nature of packaging, proposed in the Packaging Waste Directive.

Eco-labels will be granted to environmentally-friendly products to encourage consumers to purchase them.

Source: Catherine Vial, 'Why Policy Will Affect American Business', *Business America*, 8 March 1993, p. 27.

materials. The biggest problem is with the packaging the customer takes home; by law the retailer must take back all packaging from the customer if no central recycling locations are available. To save retailers from having to shoulder the burden of the recovery of sales packaging alone, a parallel or dual waste collection system is part of the German law. For the

PACKAGE LAW YIELDS RETURNS

Packaging used by German industry and retailers has decreased by 10 per cent. Since the law was introduced forcing companies to collect it back from consumers for recycling. Before the 'Packaging Ordinance' was passed in 1991, consumption of packaging from paper, glass, aluminum, tin and plastic had risen by 26 per cent in the previous three years to 13 million tons. In 1995 half of the packaging material was collected back through the 'Grüne Punkt' licensing system.

Under the German law 60–70 per cent of each material must be recycled except that which is incinerated, land-filled or returned for reuse. Between 1991 and 1995, packaging used by households and small businesses fell by 900 000 tons to 6.7 million tons, or 12 per cent. More than 5 million tons, 79 per cent, of this was dropped in 'Grüne Punkt', about 65 kg per person.

As a result, 82 per cent of all glass was recycled, 90 per cent of paper and cardboard, 70 per cent of aluminum and 50–60 per cent of plastics, tin plate and other material. The German government is in the process of further tightening up of the system, as legal provisions are still missing for many sectors. On 7 October 1996 a new product recycling and waste management act is passed. This act makes companies responsible for all their products from the point of raw material supply, not just at disposal. The trend to use less packaging material is catching up across the European Union.

Source: *The European*, 31 October–6 November 1996, p. 19.

manufacturer's product to participate in direct collection and not have to be returned to the retailer for recycling, the manufacturer must guarantee financial support for kerbside or central collection of all materials. For participating manufacturers, a green dot can be displayed on the package which signals to the consumer that a product is eligible for kerbside or central-location pickup.

Packaging without the green dot must be returned to the retailer for recycling. Goods sold without the green dot are not illegal; however, retailers will be reluctant to stock such products because they are responsible for their recycling. It is likely that the market— retailers, wholesalers and importers—will refuse packaged goods without the green dot, even those with recyclable packaging. The growing public and political pressure to control solid waste is a strong incentive for manufacturers to comply.

Packaging used by fast-food outlets is not covered by the German green dot programme, and one German city, concerned about its waste disposal, imposed a tax on all fast-food containers. The local law requires fast-food restaurants to pay a tax equivalent to €0.27 (30 cents) for each paper plate, €0.22 (25 cents) for each can or nonreturnable bottle, and €0.05 (6 cents) for each plastic spoon, fork or knife. The law was challenged by two McDonald's restaurants and two vending machine companies, but the German court upheld the tax. The impact has led some snack bars and fast-food outlets to adopt new packaging techniques. Cream is now served in reusable metal pitchers and jam and yoghurt in glass jars. French fries are sold in plates made of edible wafers, and soft drinks are offered in returnable bottles rather than in cans. The city is happy with the results.[30]

To stave off a multitude of individual country laws controlling solid waste disposal, the European Commission has issued a global packaging directive. This law is considered weaker than the German law, but the limits of the law on total recovery of solid waste are seen as more workable than the German law and collection of sales packaging materials by retailers is not mandated. The law leaves rules on collection up to individual member states, so the German 'green dot' programme is permissible.[31]

QUALITY PRODUCTS

The debate about product standardization versus product adaptation is not just a textbook exercise. It can mean the difference between success and failure in today's markets. As discussed in an earlier chapter, a quality product is one that satisfies consumer needs, has minimum defects, and is priced competitively. Gone are the days when the customer's knowledge was limited to one or at best just a few different products. Today the customer knows what is best, cheapest and best quality.[32] The power in the marketplace is shifting from a seller's market to the customers who have more choices because there are more companies competing for their attention. It is the customer who defines quality in terms of his or her needs and resources. Quality is not just desirable, it is essential for success in today's competitive international market, and the decision to standardize or adapt a product is crucial in delivering quality.

SUMMARY

The growing globalization of markets that gives rise to standardization must be balanced with the continuing need to assess all markets for those differences that might require adaptation for successful acceptance. Each product must be viewed in light of how it is perceived by each culture with which it comes in contact. What is acceptable and comfortable within one group may be radically new and resisted within others depending on the experiences and perceptions of each group. Understanding that an established product in one culture may be considered an innovation in another is critical in planning and developing consumer products for foreign markets. Analysing a product as an innovation and using the Product Component Model may provide the marketer with important leads for adaptation.

QUESTIONS

1. Debate the issue of global versus adapted products for the international marketer.
2. Define the country-of-origin effect and give examples.
3. The text discusses stereotypes, ethnocentrism, degree of economic development and fads as the basis for generalizations about country-of-origin effect on product perception. Explain each and give an example.
4. Discuss how different stages in the life cycle of a product can influence the standardization/adaptation decision. Give three examples.
5. Discuss the different promotional/product strategies available to an international marketer.
6. Assume you are deciding to 'go international', and outline the steps you would take to help you decide on a product line.
7. Products can be adapted physically and culturally for foreign markets. Discuss.
8. What are the three major components of a product? Discuss their importance to product adaptation.
9. How can a knowledge of the diffusion of innovations help a product manager plan international investments?
10. Discuss the characteristics of an innovation that can account for differential diffusion rates.
11. Give an example of how a foreign marketer can use knowledge of the characteristics of innovations in product adaptation decisions.
12. Discuss 'environmentally friendly' products and product development.

REFERENCES

1. Rahul Jacob, 'The Big Rise: Middle Classes Explode Around the Globe Bringing New Markets and New Prosperity', *Fortune*, 30 May 1994, pp. 74–90; and 'Consumers Have Money to Burn', *Business Week*, 20 April 1998, pp. 30–31.

2. 'Brazil's New Look: A Sounder Economy is Emerging', *Business Week*, 4 May 1998, pp. 22–26.; and 'What to do about Asia', *Business Week*, 26 January 1998, pp. 48–50.

3. For an empirical study of the debate, see David M. Szymanski, Sundar G. Bharadwaj and Rajan P. Varadarajan, 'Standardization versus Adaptation of International Marketing Strategy: An Empirical Investigation', *Journal of Marketing*, October 1993, pp. 1–17.

4. For a balanced view, see S. Tamer Cavusgil, Shaoming Zou and G.M. Naidu, 'Product and Promotion Adaptation in Export Ventures: An Empirical Investigation', *Journal of International Business Studies*, Third Quarter 1993, pp. 479–506.

5. Gregory L. Miles, 'Tailoring a Global Product', *International Business*, March 1995, pp. 50–52.

6. An interesting comment on the increasing importance of consistency in product design for the European market is covered in 'Cross-Border Design', *Business Europe*, 9–15 January 1995, pp. 6–7; and Pervez Ghauri, 'Recent Trends in Global Business and the Asian Crisis: Cooperation vs. Competition', *KELOLA*, Journal of Gajah Mada University, Indonesia, 1998, 18/VII, pp. 1–15.

7. William Echikson, 'Electrolux: The Trick to Selling in Europe', *Fortune*, 20 September 1993, p. 82.

8. Laurie M. Grossman, 'PepsiCo Plans Big Overseas Expansion in Diet Cola Wars with Its Pepsi Max', *The Wall Street Journal*, 4 April 1994, p. B-4.

9. Regina Fazio Maruca, 'The Right Way to Go Global', *Harvard Business Review*, March–April 1994, p. 136.

10. Adrian Palmer, 'Relationship Marketing: Local Implementation of Universal Concept', *International Business Review*, vol. 4, no. 4, 1995, pp. 471–482.

11. Valuations are based on branded products' worldwide sales, profitability and growth potential minus costs such as plants, equipment and taxes. For the valuation of other global products, see Keith J. Kelly, 'Coca-Cola Shows That Top-Brand Fizz', *Advertising Age*, 11 July 1994, p. 3.

12. 'Unilever Chief: Refresh Brands', *Advertising Age*, 19 July 1994, pp. 1–20.

13. For a comprehensive review of the literature on country-of-origin effects, see e.g. Warren Bilky and Erik Nes, 'Country-of-Origin Effects in Product Evaluations', *Journal of International Business Studies*, 1982, vol. 13, no. 1, pp. 89–99; Aysegul Ozsomer and Tamer Cavusgil, 'Country-of-Origin Effects on Product Evaluation: A Sequel to Bilky and Nes Review', in M.C. Gilly *et al.* (eds), *Proceedings of the American Marketing Association, Annual Conference, 1991*, pp. 69–77; and Robert Peterson and Alain Jolibert, 'A Meta Analysis of Country-of-Origin Effects', *Journal of International Business Studies*, vol. 26, no. 4, 1996, pp. 883–900.

14. David Strutton, Lou E. Pelton and James R. Lumpkin, 'Internal and External Country of Origin Stereotypes in the Global Marketplace for the Domestic Promotion of US Automobiles', *Journal of Global Marketing*, vol. 7, no. 3, 1994, pp. 61–77.

15. Jerome Witt and C.P. Rao, 'The Impact of Global Sourcing on Consumers: Country-of-Origin Effects on Perceived Risk', *Journal of Global Marketing*, vol. 6, no. 3, 1992, pp. 105–128.

16. 'Czech Republic: Consumers Think Foreign Goods Are Overpriced', *Crossborder Monitor*, 3 August 1994, p. 4.

17. Dana Milbank, 'Made In American Becomes a Boast in Europe', *The Wall Street Journal*, 19 January 1994, p. B-1.

18. Sheila Tefft, 'China's Savvy Shoppers Load Carts with Expensive Imported Goods', *Advertising Age*, 20 June 1994, pp. 1–21.

19. See Frank Alpert and Michael Kamins, 'An Empirical Investigation of Consumer Memory, Attitude, and Perceptions Towards Pioneer and Follower Brands', *Journal of Marketing*, vol. 59, no. 4, 1995, pp. 34–45.

20. Eleena de Lisser and Kevin Helliker, 'Private Labels Reign in British Groceries', *The Wall Street Journal*, 3 March 1994, p. B-1.

21. D.E. Allen, 'Anthropological Insights into Customer Behaviour', *European Journal of Marketing*, vol. 5, no. 3, p. 54.

22. 'Electrolux Targets Southeast Asia', *Dow Jones News Service*, 4 January 1995.

23. Jagdish Sheth and Babwari Mittal, 'A Framework for Managing Customer Expectations', *Journal of Market Focused Management*, vol. 1, no. 2, 1996, pp. 137–158.

24. Susan Hart, 'Dimensions of Success in New Product Development: An Exploratory Investigation', *Journal of Marketing Management*, vol. 9, 1993, pp. 23–41.

25. John Marcolm Jr, 'Feed the World', *Forbes*, 1 October 1990, p. 111.

26. Joseph Sirgy and Dong-Jim Lee, 'Setting Socially Responsible Marketing Objectives: A Quality of A Life Approach', *European Journal of Marketing*, 1996, vol. 30, no. 5, pp. 20–34.

27. Lynn S. Amine, 'The Need For Moral Champions in Global Marketing', *European Journal of Marketing*, vol. 30, no. 5, 1996, pp. 81–94.

28. 'EC Wants Public as Environmental Watchdogs', *Business Europe*, 10 January 1992, pp. 1–2.

29. Kirsten Bergstrom, 'The Eco-Label and Exporting to Europe', *Business America*, 29 November 1993, p. 21.

30. Stephen Kinzer, 'Germany Upholds Tax on Fast-Food Containers', *The New York Times*, 22 August 1994, p. C-2.

31. See, for example, Dagmar Mussey, 'Buyers Want Better Value in E. Europe', *Advertising Age*, 17 April 1995, p. I-18.

CHAPTER

14

Marketing Industrial Products and Business Services

Chapter Learning Objectives

What you should learn from Chapter 14

- The relationship between a country's environment and its industrial market needs.

- How demand is affected by technology.

- Characteristics of an industrial product.

- What is meant by quality in industrial products?

- ISO 9000 certification.

- Importance of relationship marketing in industrial products.

- Importance of trade shows in promoting industrial goods.

- The growth of business services and their fundamental characteristics.

- How to market services internationally.

The interest in industrial marketing, also referred to as business to business marketing or interorganizational buying and selling, got real momentum in the 1970s. It is argued that marketing of industrial products is different from marketing of consumer products. In industrial markets buyers are well-informed, highly organized and sophisticated in their purchasing behaviour. Moreover, multiple influences participate actively in purchasing decisions. While in consumer marketing buyers are often passive and the relationship between the buyers and sellers is indirect. In industrial marketing, the buyer most often is not the end user of the product and sells it to the next stage in the supply chain, as it is, or as a part of a package/product assembled or produced by him. In this type of markets, interaction between the organizations and a network of relationships is considered more important than finding a marketing mix.[1]

Industrial products and services from computers and photocopiers to machine tools and air freight or telecommunications, are different in nature. Firstly, industrial goods are goods and services often used in the process of creating other goods and services. Consumer goods are in their final form and are consumed by individuals. Secondly, the motives are different: industrial buyers are seeking profits while final consumers are seeking satisfaction. Moreover, while in consumer markets the number of customers is huge, in industrial markets the number of buyers and sellers is small. These factors are manifest in specific buying patterns and demand characteristics, and in special emphasis on relationship marketing as a tool.[2]

Industrial goods can be categorized in a variety of ways. A typical scheme involves, construction material, heavy equipment, light equipment, components and subassemblies, raw materials, processed materials, maintenance materials and operating supplies.[3]

Along with industrial goods, business services are a highly competitive growth market seeking quality and value. Manufactured products generally come to mind when we think of international trade. Yet the most-rapidly-growing sector of international trade today consists of business and consumer services—accounting, advertising, banking, consulting, construction, hotels, insurance, law, transportation, travel, television programmes and films sold internationally. The intangibility of business services creates a set of unique problems to which the service provider must respond. A further complication is a lack of uniform laws that regulate market entry. Protectionism, while prevalent for industrial goods, can be much more pronounced for the business service provider, such as airlines and telecommunications.[4]

This chapter discusses the special problems in marketing industrial goods and business services internationally, the increased competition and demand for quality in those goods and services, and the implications for the international marketer.

THE INDUSTRIAL PRODUCT MARKET

Technology and Market Demand

Not only is technology the key to economic growth, for many products it is the competitive edge in today's global markets. As precision robots, sophisticated computer programs and digital control systems take over the factory floor, manufacturing is becoming more science-oriented and access to inexpensive labour and raw materials is becoming less important. The ability to develop the latest technology and to benefit from its application is a critical factor in international competitiveness of countries and companies.[5]

Demand and Technology.   Three interrelated trends will spur demand for technologically advanced products: (1) expanding economic and industrial growth in emerging markets;

(2) the liberalization of Eastern Europe; and (3) the privatization of government-owned industries.

The economic development of Japan and many Asian countries have been in a state of rapid economic growth over the last 25 years. Japan has become the most advanced industrialized country in the region, while South Korea, Hong Kong, Singapore and Taiwan (the 'four tigers') have successfully moved from being cheap-labour sources to industrialized nations. The emerging markets of Brazil, Mexico, Malaysia, Thailand and Indonesia are exporters of semimanufactured and manufactured products to Japan, Europe and the United States, but they are methodically gearing up for greater industrialization.[6]

Besides demand for goods to build new manufacturing plants, many of the emerging countries are making much-needed investments in infrastructure.[7]

As a market economy develops in the Newly Independent States (former republics of the USSR) and other Eastern European countries, new privately-owned businesses are creating a demand for the latest technology to revitalize and expand manufacturing facilities. The big emerging markets (BEMs) are estimated to account for more than €1.3 trillion ($1.5 trillion) of trade by 2010.[8] These countries are demanding the latest technology to expand their industrial bases and build modern infrastructures. Telmex, a €3.6 billion ($4 billion) joint venture between Southwestern Bell, France Telecom and Telefonos de Mexico, has invested hundreds of millions of dollars to bring the Mexican telephone system up to the most advanced standards. Telmex is only one of scores of new privatized companies from Poland to Patagonia that are creating a mass market for the most advanced technology.

ATTRIBUTES OF PRODUCT QUALITY

As discussed earlier, the concept of quality encompasses many factors, and the perception of quality rests solely with the customer. The level of technology reflected in the product, compliance with standards that reflect customer needs, support services and follow through and the price relative to competitive products are all part of a customer's evaluation and perception of quality. As noted, these requirements are different for ultimate consumers and for industrial customers because of differing end uses. The factors themselves also differ among industrial goods customers because their needs are varied.

Industrial marketers frequently misinterpret the concept of quality. Good quality is not the same as technically good quality. For example, an African government had been buying hand-operated dusters to distribute pesticides in cotton fields; the dusters were loaned to individual farmers. The duster supplied was a finely machined device requiring regular oiling and good care. But the fact that this duster turned more easily than any other on the market was relatively unimportant to the farmers. Furthermore, the requirement for careful oiling and care simply meant that in a relatively short time of inadequate care the machines froze up and broke. The result? The local government went back to an older type of French duster that was heavy, turned with difficulty and gave a poorer distribution of dust, but which lasted longer because it required less care and lubrication. In this situation, the French machine possessed more relevant quality features and therefore in marketing terms, possessed the higher quality for the particular customer.

It must be kept in mind that the concept of quality is not an absolute measure but one relative to use patterns and/or predetermined standards. Best quality is best because the product adheres exactly to specified standards that have been determined by expected use of the product. Since use patterns are frequently different from one buyer to another, standards vary so that superior quality for one customer falls short of superior quality as determined by

GOING INTERNATIONAL 14.1

INDIA'S DIAMOND-STUDDED DILEMMA

Geological and historical clues about Indian diamonds are tantalizing. The 109-carat Koh-i-noor diamond, now a jewel in the British crown, came from India, a country with a 3000-year mining history. And the discovery of the Kimberlité pipes—the host rock for diamonds—in Madya Pradesh and other states in recent years has whetted investors' interest, says Alan Campbell, chief executive officer of De Beers' Indian subsidiary.

In 1997, four executives from De Beers Consolidated Mines flew to Raipur, one of India's poorest districts, to view what many believe to be the site of a vast, untapped diamond deposit. Instead they were greeted by 500 angry locals, many of whom had been illegally digging for diamonds. Local law enforcement officials, fearing violence, quickly hustled the executives back onto their plane.

The confrontation reflects the passion aroused by foreign companies that are eyeing prospects in India. Although without sufficient mining technology or financial backing, Indians have been unable to explore systematically for diamonds in Madya Pradesh. That's why state officials invited the world mining power-house to take on the job. Yet conditions set out by the state government so far leave potential investors cold. While most global mining ventures pay royalties to host governments averaging 5 per cent to 7 per cent of the value of their output, Madya Pradesh officials want a minimum of 10 per cent and they encourage competition among bidders to offer more. Moreover, companies are required to set up joint mining ventures in which the state will hold an 11 per cent share. Both South African De Beers and Anglo-Australian Rio Tinto PLC have submitted bids to explore the area but the winner is sure to face major opposition from the locals.

Source: *Business Week*, 2 March 1998, p. 43.

the needs of another customer. Total quality management (TQM) includes customer satisfaction as well as conformance to standards. Customer needs are as much a part of the concept of quality as are standards. One research report examining the purchase decision variables of import managers found that product quality, including dependability of suppliers and timely delivery, were the most important variables influencing purchase decisions.

Price–Quality Relationship

There is a price–quality relationship that exists in an industrial buyer's decision. One important dimension of quality is how well a product meets the specific needs of the buyer. When a product falls short of performance expectations, its poor quality is readily apparent. However, it is less apparent but nonetheless true that a product that exceeds performance expectations is also of poor quality. A product whose design exceeds the wants of the buyer's intended use generally means a higher price that reflects the extra capacity. Quality for many goods is assessed in terms of fulfilling specific expectations, no more and no less. A product that produces 20 000 units per hour when the buyer needs one that produces only 5000 units per hour is not a quality product in that the extra capacity of 15 000 units is unnecessary to meet the buyer's use expectations.

This does not mean quality is unimportant or that the latest technology is not sought by some buyers. Rather, it means that those buyers require products designed to meet their specific needs, not products designed for different uses and expectations, especially if the additional features result in higher prices. This attitude was reflected in a study of purchasing behaviour of Chinese import managers who ranked product quality first, followed in importance by price. Timely delivery was third and product style/features ranked eleventh out of 17 variables studied.[9] Hence, a product whose design reflects the needs and expectations of the buyer—no more, no less—is a quality product.

Product Design–Quality Relationship

Industrial marketers must keep in mind that buyers of industrial goods judge products by their contribution to profit or to the improvement of the buyer's own products and production processes. Consequently, products designed to meet the needs of individual industrial users are critical to competitive advantage. Competitors from Japan, the US and even of the emerging countries stand ready to provide the customer with a product that fits its exact needs and is offered at a competitive price.

The design of a product must be viewed from all aspects of use. Extreme variations in climate create problems in designing equipment that is universally operable. Products that function effectively in Western Europe may require major design changes to operate as well in the hot, dry Sahara region or the humid, tropical rainforests of Latin America. Trucks designed to travel the autobahns of Germany almost surely will experience operational difficulties in the mountainous regions of Asia on roads that barely resemble jeep trails. Manufacturers must consider many variations in making products that will be functional in far-flung markets.

In the light of today's competition, a company must consider the nature of its market and the adequacy of the design of its products. Effective competition in global markets means that overengineered and overpriced products must give way to products that meet the specifications of the customer at competitive prices. Success is in offering products that fit a customer's needs, technologically advanced for some and less sophisticated for others, but all of high quality. In most industrial markets, especially for components and parts, the buyer normally decides and gives specifications for design and other characteristics of the product.

Service and Replacement Parts

Effective competition abroad not only requires proper product design but effective service, prompt deliveries and the ability to furnish spare and replacement parts without delay.[10] In highly competitive markets such as Japan, for example, it is imperative to give the same kind of service a domestic company or a Western company can give.

For many technical products, the willingness of the seller to provide installation and training may be the deciding factor for the buyers in accepting one company's product over another's. South Korean and other Asian businesspersons are frank in admitting they prefer to buy from Western firms, but the Japanese get the business because of service. Frequently heard tales of conflicts between Western and foreign firms over assistance expected from the seller are indicative of the problems of after-sales service and support. A South Korean businessman's experiences with a German engineer and some Japanese engineers typify the situation. The Korean electronic firm purchased semiconductor-chip-making equipment for a plant expansion. The German engineer was slow in completing the installation; he stopped work at five o'clock and would not work at the weekends. The Japanese, installing other equipment, understood the urgency of getting the factory up and running; without being asked they worked day and night until the job was finished.

Unfortunately this is not an isolated case; Hyundai Motor Company bought two multi-million-euro presses to stamp body parts for cars. The 'presses arrived late, the engineers took much longer than promised to set up the machines, and Hyundai had to pay the Western workers extra to get the machines to work right.' The impact of such problems translates into

GOING INTERNATIONAL 14.2

WINNERS FOR 1997: THE DESIGN FIRMS AND CORPORATIONS WHOSE PRODUCTS WON INDUSTRIAL DESIGN EXCELLENCE AWARDS IN 1997

Design Firms	Awards Gold	Silver	Bronze	Total
IDEO	3	4	3	10
Fitch		3	4	7
Pentagram Design	1	3	2	6
Frogdesign	2	1	2	5
Lunar Design		2	3	5
Ziba Design	2	1	2	5
Altitude		1	2	3
E-Lab		2	1	3
R. Applebaum Associates		1	1	2
Carlson Technology		1	1	2
HF/ID			2	2
ION Design		1	1	2
Coco Raynes Associates		1	1	2
Worktools		1	1	2
Corporations				
Apple Computer			4	4
Compaq Computer		2	2	4
Steelcase	1	2	1	4
Samsung Electronics		1	3	4
Black & Decker			3	3
Pitney Bowes		1	2	3
Coleman		1	1	2
First Alert			2	2
Heartstream		1	1	2
Harman/JBL			2	2
Microsoft			2	2
NCR			2	2
NV Philips		1	1	2
Rubbermaid			2	2

Source: *Business Week*, 2 June 1997, p. 40.

lost business for Western firms. Samsung Electronics Company, Korea's largest chip maker, used Western equipment for 75 per cent of its first memory-chip plant. When it outfitted its most recent chip plant, it bought 75 per cent of the equipment from Japan.

Technical training is rapidly becoming a major after-sales service when selling technical products in countries that demand the latest technology but do not always have trained personnel. China demands the most advanced technical equipment but frequently has untrained people responsible for products they do not understand. Heavy emphasis on training programmes and self-teaching materials to help overcome the common lack of skills to operate technical equipment is a necessary part of the after-sales service package in much of the developing world.

A recent study of international users of heavy construction equipment revealed that, next to the manufacturer's reputation, quick delivery of replacement parts was of major importance in purchasing construction equipment. Furthermore, 70 per cent of those questioned indicated they bought parts not made by the original manufacturer of the equipment because of the difficulty of getting original parts. Smaller importers complain of Western exporting firms not responding to orders or responding only after extensive delay. It appears that the importance of timely availability of spare parts to sustain a market is forgotten by some Western exporters. When companies are responsive, the rewards are significant.

Some international marketers also may be forgoing the opportunity of participating in a lucrative aftermarket. Certain kinds of machine tools use up five times their original value in replacement parts during an average lifespan and thus represent an even greater market. One international machine tool company has capitalized on the need for direct service and available parts by changing its distribution system from the 'normal' to one of stressing rapid service and readily available parts. Instead of selling through independent distributors, as do most machine tool manufacturers in foreign markets, this company established a series of company stores and service centres similar to those found in the home market. This company can render service through its system of local stores, while most competitors dispatch service people from their home-based factories. The service people are kept on tap for rapid service calls in each of its network of local stores, and each store keeps a large stock of standard parts available for immediate delivery. The net result of meeting industrial needs quickly is keeping the company among the top suppliers in foreign sales of machine tools.

Universal Standards

A lack of universal standards is another problem in international sales of industrial products. The United Kingdom and the United States have two major areas of concern for the industrial goods exporter: one is a lack of common standards for manufacturing highly specialized equipment such as machine tools and computers, and the other is the use of the inch-pound or English system of measurement.[11] Domestically, the use of the inch-pound and the lack of a universal manufacturing standard are minor problems, but they have serious consequences when affected products are scheduled for export. Conflicting standards are encountered in test methods for materials and equipment, quality control systems and machine specifications. In the telecommunications industry, the vast differences in standards among countries create enormous problems for expansion of that industry. Efforts are being made through international organizations to create international standards; for example, the International Electrotechnical Commission (IEC) is concerned with standard specifications for electrical equipment for machine tools.

In addition to industry and international organizations setting standards, countries often have standards for products entering their markets. Saudi Arabia has been working on setting standards for everything from light bulbs to lemon juice, and it has asked its trading partners for help. The standards will most likely be adopted by the entire Arab world. Most countries sent representatives, even New Zealand sent a representative to help write the standards for the shelf life of lamb.

ISO 9000 Certification

With quality becoming the cornerstone of global competition, companies are requiring assurance of standard conformance from suppliers just as their customers are requiring the same from them. ISO 9000, a series of five international industrial standards (ISO 9000–9004) originally designed to meet the need for product quality assurances in purchasing agreements, is becoming a quality assurance certification programme that has competitive and legal ramifications when doing business in the European Union and elsewhere.[12]

ISO 9000 refers to the registration and certification of a manufacturer's quality system. It is a certification of the existence of a quality control system a company has in place to ensure it can meet published quality standards. ISO 9000 standards do not apply to specific products. They relate to generic system standards that enable a company, through a mix of internal and external audits, to provide assurance that it has a quality control system. It is a certification of the production process only, and does not guarantee a manufacturer produces a 'quality' product. The series describes three quality system models, defines quality concepts and gives guidelines for using international standards in quality systems.[13]

A company requests a certifying body (a third party authorized to provide an ISO 9000 audit) to conduct a registration assessment, that is, an audit of the key business processes of a company. The assessor asks questions about everything from blueprints to sales calls to filing. 'Does the supplier meet promised delivery dates?' and 'Is there evidence of customer satisfaction?' are some of the questions asked and the issues explored. The object is to develop a comprehensive plan to ensure minute details are not overlooked. The assessor helps management create a quality manual which will be made available to customers wishing to verify the organization's reliability. When accreditation is granted, the company receives certification. A complete assessment for recertification is done every four years with inter-mediate evaluations during the four-year period.

ISO 9000 is not a legal requirement for access to the European market, but ISO 9000 certification is required under EU law for product certification on a few highly regulated, high-risk products such as medical devices, telecommunication terminal equipment, gas appliances and personal protective equipment.

Although ISO 9000 is voluntary, except for regulated products, the EU Product Liability Directive puts pressure on all companies to become certified. The directive holds that a manufacturer, including an exporter, will be liable, regardless of fault or negligence, if a person is harmed by a product that fails because of a faulty component. Thus, customers in the EU need to be assured that the components of their products are free of defects or deficiencies. A manufacturer with a well-documented quality system will be better able to prove that products are defect-free and thus minimize liability claims.

A strong level of interest in ISO 9000 is being driven more by 'marketplace' requirements than by government regulations, and ISO 9000 is becoming an important competitive marketing tool in Europe. As the market demands quality and more and more companies adopt some form of TQM (total quality management), manufacturers are increasingly requiring ISO 9000 registration of their suppliers. Companies manufacturing parts and com-ponents in China are quickly discovering that ISO 9000 certification is a virtual necessity. More and more buyers, particularly those in Europe, are refusing to buy from manufacturers that do not have internationally recognized third-party proof of their quality capabilities.[14]

Outside of regulated product areas, the importance of ISO 9000 registration as a competitive market tool in the EU varies from sector to sector. In some sectors, European companies may require suppliers to attest that they have an approved quality system in place as a condition for purchase. ISO 9000 may be used to serve as a means of differentiating different 'classes' of suppliers (particularly in high-tech areas) where high product reliability is crucial. In other words, if two suppliers are competing for the same contract, the one with ISO 9000 registration may have a competitive edge.

Manufacturers in developing countries are seeking ISO certification to offset concern among buyers about their quality capabilities. In Brazil, over 400 companies have been certified, compared with only 18 three years earlier. ISO certification has been credited as a major contributor to Brazil's positive trade surplus.[15] If a company practises total quality management (TQM), the system probably meets ISO 9000 standards but it would have to be audited and certified as such.[16]

RELATIONSHIP MARKETING

Relationship marketing has gained considerable attention in recent years. A number of studies on relational selling (key account management, database marketing, etc.), customer and supplier retention (in industrial as well as consumer products), cooperative marketing arrangements (cobranding, just-in-time, supplies, EDI, shared logistics, etc.) and strategic partnerships (comarketing, codesign, coproduction, joint R&D, etc.) have appeared in this area. Scholars from all parts of the world, Europe, America, Asia and Australia, are stressing relationship marketing.[17]

While traditional transactional marketing is believed to be based on competition and self-interest, relationship marketing is based more on mutual cooperation, trust and joint benefits.[18] The purpose of relationship marketing is considered to enhance marketing productivity by achieving efficiency and effectiveness.[19] Through interdependence and partnering, a lower cost and competitive advantages are achieved.

Relationship marketing is believed to be useful both for consumer products as well as industrial or business-to-business products. The relationship of consumers to business organizations is best described as that of membership.[20] The differences in the type of relationship and interdependence between the parties in business-consumer versus business-to-business relationships is explained in Table 14.1. The table reveals that while business-to-consumer and business-to-business relationships have similarities, there are also major differences. It seems that the latter type of relationship is more long-term and thus demands a higher level of relationship and commitment.

The marketing strategy of a firm will depend upon the nature of its products (the more complex the product the more need there is for the relationship), the nature of its customers (according to the importance individuals attach to the economic versus social aspects of exchange, e.g. in different cultures) and on the nature of the organizations involved (orientation of the organizations towards networks and collaborations).

Relationship marketing is not new, but it has become increasingly important in international marketing activities. The importance of relationships in China, so called *guanxi* (connections) has been reported by a number of scholars, where a business relationship often started with social relationship. The development of a good relationship 'with a friend', was usually considered as a prerequisite for a business relationship. Due to recent decentralization of economic decision making in China, relationships have become even more important.[21]

The characteristics that define the uniqueness of industrial products discussed above lead naturally to relationship marketing.[22] The long-term relationship with customers which is at the core of relationship marketing fits the characteristics inherent in industrial products and is a viable strategy for industrial goods marketing. The first and foremost characteristic of industrial goods markets is the motive of the buyer—to make a profit. Industrial products fit into a business or manufacturing process, and their contributions will be judged on how well they contribute to that process. In order for an industrial marketer to fulfil the needs of its customer, the marketer must understand those needs as they exist today and how they will change as the buyer strives to compete in global markets that call for long-term relationships.[23]

Table 14.1   Comparison of Business-to-Consumer and Business-to-Business Relationships

Characteristics	Business to-Consumer	Business-to-Business
1. Relationship form	Membership	Working partnership, just-in-time exchange, comarketing, alliance, strategic alliance, distribution channel relationship
2. Average sale size; potential lifetime value of the customer to the selling firm	Normally small sale size; relatively small and predictable lifetime value of the customer; limit on the amount of investment in relationship for any single customer	Normally large and consequential; allows for large and idiosyncratic investments in single relationship
3. Number of customers	Large number; requires large overall investments in relationship management, but low investment per customer	Relatively fewer customers to spread investments in relationships over; investments often idiosyncratic
4. Seller's ability and cost to replace lost customer	Can normally be replaced quickly and at relatively low cost	Large customers can be difficult and time consuming to replace
5. Seller's dependence on buyer	Low for any single customer	Varies based on customer size; can be devastating
6. Buyer dependence on seller	Normally has viable alternatives, low switching costs and switch can be made quickly	Viable alternatives can take time to find, switching costs can be high and changes impact multiple people in the organization
7. Purchasing time frame, process, and buying centre complexity	Normally a short time frame, simple process, and simple buying centre, where one or two individuals fill most buying roles	Often a long time frame, complex process; may have multiple individuals for a single buying role; may be subject to organization budget cycles
8. Personal knowledge of other party	Relatively few contact points with seller, even when loyal user; seller's knowledge of buyer often limited to database information	Multiple personal relationships; multiple inter-organizational linkages
9. Communication means to build and sustain relationships	Dependence on non-personal means of contact; seller's knowledge generally limited to database information of customer	Emphasis on personal selling and personal contact; customer knowledge held in different forms and places
10. Relative size	Seller normally larger than buyer	Relative size may vary
11. Legal	Consumer protection laws unbalanced to favour consumer	Relationships governed by prevailing contract law as well as industry standard regulations and ethics

Source: Thomas Gruen, 'The Outcome of Relationship Marketing in Consumer Markets', *International Business Review*, vol. 4, no. 4, pp. 447–469.

INTEL INSIDE

In microprocessors Intel has a kind of monopoly that any company would be proud to control. More than 85 per cent of all personal computers (PCs) rely on Intel technology. Intel's current and very challenging goal is to maintain its 'PC' monopoly while dominating the market for the new high-performance chips that promise to put PCs at par with high-end workstations. Many computer analysts think that Intel could eventually control more than 90 per cent of the desktop market, including workstations.

By aggressively promoting the Pentium processor in the media, Intel bypassed its traditional customers—the computer manufacturers—and directly targeted PC users. This 'awareness campaign' for its processors has led the majority of PC buyers—especially business users—to specifically demand an Intel processor in their computers. In turn this has created an additional barrier for Intel's competitors: they not only have to deliver processors that are faster and cheaper than Intel's, but, more importantly, convince consumers that their products are fully compatible with Intel's. Andy Grove, Intel's chairman, and until recently the CEO says, 'It was an attitude change, a change we actually stimulated, but one whose impact we did not fully comprehend'.

However, as Intel's business model is essentially based around selling a continuous stream of faster microprocessors, its investment in production, R&D and marketing have reflected this at every stage. But growth in high-powered (read high-margin) Pentium II chips has slowed down, mainly as consumers have flocked to sub-thousand dollar PCs. In this price-sensitive segment, Pentium's premium image doesn't stand for much. Customers look at the best price-performance. This is where AMD seems to have a slight edge; and only time will tell if Intel can manage to repeat its success in this highly cut-throat market with its recently introduced Celeron processors.

Source: *European Business Report*, Spring 1Q, 1998, p. 31.

Relationship marketing ranges all the way from gathering information on customer needs to designing products and services, channelling products to the customer in a timely and convenient manner, and following up to make sure the customer is satisfied. For example, SKF, the bearing manufacturer, seeks strong customer relations with after-sales follow-through. The end of the transaction is not delivery; it continues as SKF makes sure the bearings are properly mounted and maintained. This helps customers reduce downtime, thus creating value in the relationship with SKF. SKF marketing efforts encompass an array of activities to support long-term relationships which go beyond ' . . . merely satisfying the next link in the distribution chain to meeting the more complex needs of the end user, whether those needs are technical, operational, or financial'.[24]

The industrial customer's needs in global markets are continuously changing, and suppliers' offerings must also continue to change. The need for the latest technology means that it is not a matter of selling the right product the first time but one of continuously changing the product to keep it right over time. The objective of relationship marketing is to make the relationship an important attribute of the transaction, thus differentiating oneself from competitors. It shifts the focus away from price to service and long-term benefits. The reward is loyal customers that translate into substantial profits.

Relationship marketing can often give a company the competitive edge when a customer's ultimate success depends on more than technical expertise. For example, Pacific Telesis Group (Pactel), the San Francisco Baby Bell, won the right to build and partly own a €1.4 billion ($2 billion) cellular-phone network in Germany. Other bidders had the technical expertise to build the system, but the Pactel unit offered after-sale support systems, such as accounting software, management information systems and customer service procedures, critical to building the business and making it user-friendly.[25]

IBM of Brazil stresses stronger ties with its customers by offering planning seminars that address corporate strategies, competition, quality and how to identify marketing opportunities. One of these seminars showed a food import/export firm how it could increase efficiency by decentralizing its computer facilities to better serve its customers. The company's computers were centralized at headquarters while branches took orders manually and mailed them to the home office for processing and invoicing. It took several days before the customer's order was entered and added several days to delivery time. The seminar helped the company realize it could streamline its order processing by installing branch office terminals that were connected to computers at the food company's headquarters. A customer could then place an order and receive an invoice on the spot, shortening the delivery time by several days or weeks. Not all participants who attend the 30 different seminars offered annually become IBM customers, but it creates a continuing relationship among potential customers. 'So much so', as one executive commented, 'that when a customer does need increased computer power, he will likely turn to us.'[26]

PROMOTING INDUSTRIAL PRODUCTS

The promotional problems encountered by foreign industrial marketers are little different from the problems faced by domestic marketers. Until recently there has been a paucity of specialized advertising media in many countries. In the last decade, however, specialized industrial media have been developed to provide the industrial marketer with a means of communicating with potential customers, especially in Western Europe and to some extent in Eastern Europe, the Commonwealth of Independent States (CIS) of the former USSR, and China. In addition to advertising in print media and reaching industrial customers through catalogues and direct mail, the trade show has become the primary vehicle for doing business in many foreign countries.

Industrial Trade Shows

One of the most powerful international promotional media is the trade show or trade fair. As part of their international promotion activities, the European Union, Germany and the US Department of Commerce and many other countries sponsor trade fairs in many cities around the world. Additionally, there are annual trade shows sponsored by local governments in most countries. African countries, for example, host more than 70 industry-specific trade shows.

Trade shows serve as the most important vehicles for selling products, reaching prospective customers, contacting and evaluating potential agents and distributors, and marketing in most countries. They have been at the centre of commerce in Europe for centuries and are where most prospects are found. European trade shows attract high-level decision makers who are not attending just to see the latest products but are there to buy.[27] The importance of trade shows to Europeans is reflected in the percentage of their media budget spent on participating in trade events. On average, Europeans spend 22 per cent of their total annual media budget on trade events, while American firms typically spend less than 5 per cent. The Hannover Industry Fair (Germany), the largest trade fair in the world, has nearly 6000 exhibitors who show a wide range of industrial products to 600 000 visitors.

Trade shows provide the facilities for a manufacturer to exhibit and demonstrate products to potential users. They are an opportunity to create sales and establish relationships with agents and distributors that can lead to more-permanent distribution channels in foreign markets. In fact, a trade show may be the only way to reach some prospects. Trade show experts estimate that 80 to 85 per cent of the people seen on a trade-show floor never have a salesperson call on them.

The number and variety of trade shows is such that almost any target market in any given country can be found through this medium. In the CIS, fairs and exhibitions offer companies the opportunity to meet new customers, including private traders, young entrepreneurs and representatives of non-state organizations. The exhibitions in the CIS offer a cost-effective way of reaching a large number of customers who might otherwise be difficult to target through individual sale calls. Specialized fairs in individual sectors such as computers, the automotive industry, fashion and home furnishings regularly take place.[28]

Thirty-nine American firms participated in a seven-day electronics production equipment exhibition in Osaka, Japan, and came home with €1.4 million ($1.6 million) in confirmed orders along with estimates for the following year of €9 million ($10 million). Five of the companies were seeking Asian agent/distributors through the show, and each was able to sign a representative before the show closed. Trade shows and trade fairs are scheduled periodically and any interested business can reserve space to exhibit.[29]

Countertrade—A Pricing Tool

Willingness to accept countertrades, the inclusive term used to describe transactions where all or partial payment is made in kind rather than cash, is an important price advantage in international trade.[30] While not unique to industrial-goods markets, countertrading will continue to be important when marketing to the emerging markets—in Eastern Europe, the former republics of Russia, China and some countries in Asia and South America.[31] In most rapidly industrializing countries, there is a shortage of hard currencies, and those that exist are reserved for top-priority projects; goods of less importance, and even some priority goods, are acquired with some form of countertrade. A marketer unwilling to accept countertrades will probably lose the sale to a competitor who already includes countertrading as an important pricing tool.

MARKETING SERVICES GLOBALLY

The service sector in many industrial nations collectively account for up to 70 per cent of the gross national product. It includes a broad range of industries as well as many government and non-profit activities. The changing patterns of government regulations, privatization of public corporations and non-profit organizations, computerization and technological innovations and the internationalization of service businesses are some of the factors that are transforming service sectors in the European Union, the United States, Japan and many emerging economies. In many cases services are competing with products as they provide similar benefits. For example, buying a service may be an alternative to doing it yourself, jobs such as lawn care, equipment maintenance, etc. Using a rental service is an alternative to buying a product. Moreover, the service content of a number of products ranging from fast-food restaurants to automobile manufactures is increasing.[32]

Unlike merchandise trade that requires a declaration of value when exported, most services do not have to have an export declaration nor do they always pass through a tariff or customs barrier when entering a country. Consequently, an accurate tally of service trade exports is difficult to determine. Services not counted include advertising, accounting,

GOING INTERNATIONAL 14.4

KEYS TO SUCCESS IN THE EURO ENTERTAINMENT MARKET

Despite increased competition throughout the industry, Europe still is an attractive market for entertainment companies. This is partly due to more vacation days (the European Union standard is 20 days), higher disposable incomes and leisure developments encouraged by city and county planning authorities.

Europe has a long, extensive history of theme parks and attractions, which historically were family-owned, small-scale operations. Although many of these mum-and-dad parks and attractions have disappeared, Europe still boasts the oldest operating amusement park—in Bakken, Denmark.

Many family entertainment projects—such as Disneyland Paris, Port Aventura in Spain and LegoLand in Windsor, England—emerged within the last decade through various public and privately funded bodies.

Their success in Europe often is driven by weather considerations, the addition of rides and attractions and retail propositions linked to a park, movie or intellectual property that enhance the overall brand.

Based on our work with many US entertainment companies, we have developed a 'Top 10 Predictors of Success' of an entertainment venture in Europe:

10. Do your homework. Make sure you are aware of past case studies, regional and national consumer tastes, preferences and traditions.
9. Get your relationship right with HQ. Strike a balance between the amount of autonomy or control your headquarters and European teams are given, and develop a reporting structure that enables all involved to share best marketing practices with colleagues across geographic boundaries.
8. Manage expectations within your company about when your European activities will start showing a profit (or, at least, break even).
7. 'Glocalize' your concepts, striking the balance between how much of your US ideas should be brought to Europe, while still making it appeal to 'local' European tastes.
6. Set realistic payback periods.
5. Understand that the different business customs across these 15 distinct markets means that you have at least 15 different customer tastes, and therefore need to consider how 'entertainment' is defined by and made relevant to such a disparate population.
4. There is no such thing as the 'United States of Europe'. Because of differing consumer tastes, the implementation of your marketing plans within each of the EU countries will vary significantly.
3. Use local experts wherever possible, to ensure you've been given an accurate, current picture of your target market trends and concerns.
2. Test your concepts and ideas with your target guests to learn what they like, their propensity to pay various entry fees, promotional tie-ins and other marketing activities.
1. Plan, plan, plan!

Source: Allyson L. Stewart-Allen, 'Marketing Perspective', *Marketing News*, 17 August 1998, p. 9. For Europe's largest entertainment groups and their global ranking see Table 14.2.

management consulting, legal services and most insurance; ironically, these are among the fastest growing.[33]

Characteristics of Services

In contrast to industrial and consumer goods, services are distinguished by unique characteristics and thus require special consideration. Products are classified as tangible or intangible.

Table 14.2   Europe's Largest Entertainment Groups

Rank	Company	Country	Revenue 1996 ($m)	Global Ranking
1	Bertelsmann	Germany	13 700	3
2	Havas	France	8 800	6
3	Polygram	UK/Neth.	5 530	9
4	EMI	UK	5 453	10
5	Kirch Group	Germany	4 000ᵃ	14
6	Granada Group	UK	3 587	17
7	Rank Organisation	UK	3 584	18
8	United News & Media	UK	2 930	22
9	Pearson	UK	2 836	23
10	Carlton Communications	UK	2 447	25

[a]Estimate.
Source: *Variety*, September 1996 and *The European*, 12–18 September 1996, p. 27.

Cars, computers, furniture, etc., are examples of *tangible products* that have a physical presence; they are a thing or object that can be stored and possessed, and whose intrinsic value is embedded within its physical presence. Insurance, dry cleaning, hotel accommodation and airline passage or freight service are *intangible products* whose intrinsic value is the result of a process, a performance or an occurrence that only exists while it is being created. The intangibility of services results in characteristics unique to a service: it is *inseparable* in that its creation cannot be separated from its consumption; it is *heterogeneous* in that it is individually produced and is thus virtually unique; it is *perishable* in that once created it cannot be stored but must be consumed simultaneously with its creation. Contrast these characteristics with a tangible product that can be produced in one location and consumed elsewhere, that can be standardized, whose quality assurance can be determined and maintained over time, and which can be produced and stored in anticipation of fluctuations in demand.[34]

Services can be classified as being either consumer or industrial in nature. Additionally, the same service can be marketed both as industrial and consumer, depending on the motive of, and use by, the purchaser. For example, travel agents and airlines sell industrial services to a businessperson and a consumer service to a tourist. Financial services, hotels, insurance, legal services and others all may be industrial or consumer services.

These fundamental characteristics explain why it is important that services be discussed separately from industrial and consumer goods and why their very nature affects the manner in which they are marketed internationally.

Entering International Markets

Client Followers and Market Seekers.   Most Western service companies entered international markets to service their Western clients, business travellers and tourists. Banks, accounting and advertising firms were among the earlier companies to establish branches or acquire local affiliations abroad to serve their Western multinational clients. Hotels and car-rental agencies followed the business traveller and tourist to fill their needs.[35] Their primary purpose for marketing their services internationally was to service home-country clients. Once established, many of these *client followers*, as one researcher refers to them, expanded

Table 14.3   Entry Motive by Type of Service offered (per cent selected as follower or seeker)

Entry Motive	Advertising, Accounting	Computer Needs	Engineering, Architecture	Management Consulting	Consumer	Bank	Misc.
Client followers	46.15%	22.01%	24.35%	21.48%	00.0%	30.77%	27.45%
Market seekers	53.65	77.99	75.65	78.52	100.0	69.23	72.55
Total: 100%							

Source: M. Krishna Erramilli, 'Entry Mode Choice in Service Industries', *International Marketing Review*, vol. 7, no. 5, 1991, p. 58.

their client base to include local companies. As global markets grew, creating greater demand for business services, service companies became *market seekers* in that they actively sought customers for their services worldwide. One study of select types of service industries shows that the relative importance of client following or market seeking as a motive for entry into foreign markets varies by type of service.[36]

Table 14.3 shows that today the most important motive for engaging in international business for most business service firms is to seek new markets. The notable exceptions are accounting and advertising firms whose motives are about equally divided between being client followers and market seekers.

Entry Modes.   Because of the varied characteristics of business services, not all of the traditional methods of market entry discussed earlier are applicable to all types of services.

Although most services have the inseparability of creation and consumption just discussed, there are those where these occurrences can be separated. Such services are those whose intrinsic value can be 'embodied in some tangible form (such as a blueprint or document) and thus can be produced in one country and exported to another'. Data processing and data analysis services are other examples. The analysis or processing is completed on a computer located in a Western country and the output (the service) is transmitted via satellite to a distant customer. Some banking services could be exported from one country to another on a limited basis through the use of ATMs (automatic teller machines). Architecture and engineering consulting services are exportable when the consultant travels to the client's site and later returns home to write and submit a report or a blueprint. In addition to exporting as an entry mode, these services also use franchising, direct investment (joint ventures and wholly owned subsidiaries) and licensing.

Most other services—car rentals, airline services, entertainment, hotels and tourism, to name a few—are inseparable and require production and consumption to occur almost simultaneously, and thus, exporting is not a viable entry method for them. The vast majority of services enter foreign markets by licensing, franchising and/or direct investment.[37]

Market Environment for Business Services

Service firms face most of the same environmental constraints and problems confronting merchandise traders. Protectionism, control of transborder data flows, competition and the protection of trademarks, processes and patents are possibly the most important problems confronting the MNC in today's international services market.

GARBAGE COLLECTION AN INTERNATIONAL SERVICE?

The service industry in Western societies has a bright future with a variety of services to sell. Ten thousand house-hungry Londoners signed up for more than €450 million ($500 million) of mortgages. A Wall Street subsidiary of Salomon Brothers has European executives eager to get a package from Amsterdam to Atlanta. Increasingly, they are turning to Federal Express, a US company whose international revenues have been doubling every year since it began operating overseas. That is only part of the story; there are many services we don't hear about. For example, Hospital Corporation of America, the biggest operator of private hospitals in the United States, has acquired 28 hospitals abroad and signed contracts to operate 9 others.

Having persuaded hundreds of local governments in the United States to contract out street cleaning and rubbish collection, WMX Technologies is collecting rubbish, cleaning streets and constructing sanitary landfills in 20 countries, including Argentina, New Zealand and Saudi Arabia. It also has a 15-year contract to run a hazardous-waste treatment plant that will process all of Hong Kong's industrial waste.

Sources: Adapted from Richard I. Kirkland, Jr, 'The Bright Future of Service Exports', *Fortune*, 8 June 1987, pp. 32 and 38; and Ralph T. King, Jr, 'Quiet Boom: US Service Exports Are Growing Rapidly, but Almost Unnoticed', *The Wall Street Journal*, 21 April 1993, p. A-6.

Protectionism. The most serious threat to the continued expansion of international services trade is protectionism. The growth of international services has been so rapid during the last decade that it has drawn the attention of domestic companies and governments. As a result, direct and indirect trade barriers have been imposed to restrict foreign companies from domestic markets. Every reason, from the protection of infant industries to national security, has been used to justify some of the restrictive practices. The General Agreement on Trade in Services (GATS), part of the Uruguay Round package, provides for most-favoured-nation treatment, national treatment, market access, transparency and the free flow of payments and transfers.[38]

Until the GATT and WTO agreements there were few international rules of fair play governing trade in services. Service companies faced a complex group of national regulations that impeded the movement of people and technology from country to country. The industrialized nations want their banks, insurance companies, construction firms and other service providers to be allowed to move people, capital and technology around the globe unimpeded.

Restrictions designed to protect local markets range from not being allowed to do business in a country to requirements that all foreign professionals pass certification exams in the local language before being permitted to practice.

The European Union is making considerable progress towards establishing a single market for services.[39] Legal services and the film industry seem to be two that are very difficult to negotiate. A directive regarding Transfrontier Television Broadcasting created a quota for European programmes requiring EU member states to ensure that at least 50 per cent of entertainment air time is devoted to 'European works'. The EU argues that this set-aside for domestic programming is necessary to preserve Europe's cultural identity. The consequences for the US film industry are significant because over 40 per cent of US film industry profits come from foreign revenues.

Transborder Data Flow. Restrictions on transborder data flows are potentially the most damaging to both the communications industry and other multinationals who rely on data transfers across borders to conduct business. Some countries impose tariffs on the transmission of data and many others are passing laws forcing companies to open their computer files to inspection by government agencies. This situation, however, is changing as the telecommunications industry all over the world is being restructured.[40]

Most countries have a variety of laws to deal with the processing and electronic transmission of data across borders. There is intense concern about how to deal with this relatively new technology. In some cases, concern stems from not understanding how best to tax transborder data flows and, in other cases, there is concern over the protection of individual rights when personal data are involved. The European Commission is concerned that data on individuals (such as income, spending preferences, debt repayment histories, medical records and employment data) are being collected, manipulated and transferred between companies with little regard to the privacy of the individuals on whom the data are collected. A proposed directive by the Commission would require the consent of the individual before data are collected or processed. A wide range of foreign service companies would be affected by such a directive; insurance underwriters, banks, credit reporting firms, direct marketing companies and tour operators are a few examples. The directive would have a wide-ranging effect on data-processing and data-analysis firms because it will prevent a firm from transferring information electronically to other countries for computer processing if it concerns individual European consumers.

Competition. As mentioned earlier, competition in all phases of the service industry is increasing as host-country markets are invaded by many foreign firms. The practice of following a client into foreign markets and then expanding into international markets is followed by German, British, Japanese, Swedish, American and service firms from other countries. Telecommunications, banking, advertising, construction and hotels are services that face major global competition, not only among European and Japanese companies but also from representatives of Brazil, China and other parts of the world.

Protection of Intellectual Property. An important form of competition difficult to combat is pirated trademarks, processes and patents. Computer design and software, trademarks, brand names and other intellectual properties are easy to duplicate and difficult to protect.[41] The protection of intellectual property rights is a major problem in the services industries. Countries seldom have adequate—or any—legislation; any laws they do have are extremely difficult to enforce. The Trade Related Intellectual Property Rights part of the GATT agreement obligates all members to provide strong protection for copyright and related rights, patents, trademarks, trade secrets, industrial designs, geographic indications and layout designs for integrated circuits.

The TRIPS agreement is helpful in protection of services but the key issue is that enforcement is very difficult without full cooperation of host countries. The situation in China has been especially slow because that country has only recently been trying to enforce rights of intellectual property.[42] The total annual cost for US businesses of pirated software, CDs, books and films in China alone totals more than €2235 million ($2476 million). Industry estimates are that Western companies lost over €54 billion ($60 billion) annually on piracy of all types of intellectual property. As it is so easy to duplicate electronically recorded music and films, pirated copies are often available within a few days of their release. In Thailand, for example, illegal copies of films are available within 10 days of their release in the Western markets. (See Figure 14.1.)

Things are, however, improving. Beijing authorities have destroyed 800 000 pirated videos and audio cassettes and more than 40 000 software programs. In one particular year, they have

Figure 14.1   Europe's Black Economy

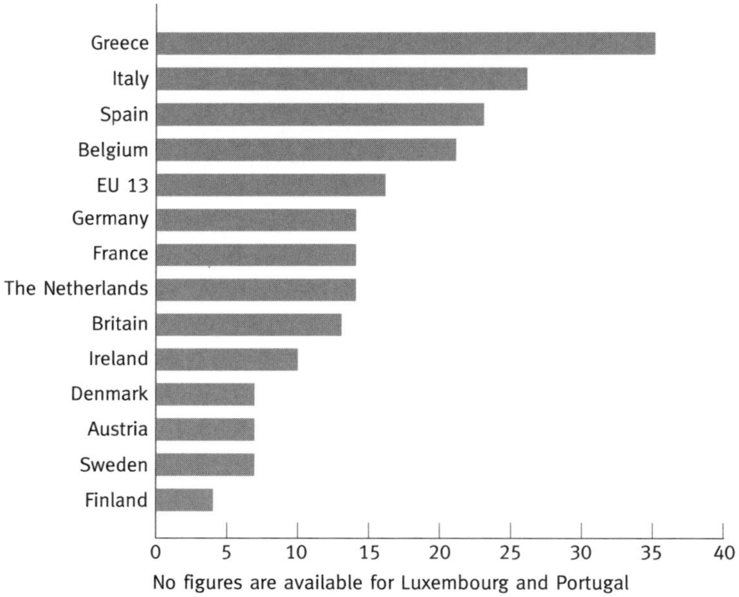

No figures are available for Luxembourg and Portugal

Source: EU, *The European*, 6–12 April 1998, p. 27.

also fined some €2.7 million ($3 million) in connection with some 9000 cases of trademark violation.

SUMMARY

Industrial goods marketing requires close attention to the exact needs of customers. Basic differences across various markets are less than for consumer goods but the motives behind purchases differ enough to require a special approach. Global competition has risen to the point that industrial goods marketers must pay close attention to the level of economic and technological development for each market to determine the buyer's assessment of quality. Companies that adapt their products to these needs are the ones that should be the most effective in the marketplace. Industrial markets are lucrative and continue to grow as more countries strive for at least a semblance of industrial self-sufficiency.

One of the fastest-growing areas of international trade is business services. This segment of marketing involves all countries at every level of development; even the least-developed countries are seeking computer technology and sophisticated data banks to aid them in advancing their economies. Their rapid growth and profit profile make them targets for protectionism and piracy.

QUESTIONS

1. What are the differences between consumer and industrial goods and what are the implications for international marketing? Discuss.
2. 'The adequacy of a product must be considered in relation to the general environment within which it will be operated rather than solely on the basis of technical efficiency.' Discuss the implications of this statement.
3. What role do service, replacement parts and standards play in competition in foreign marketing? Illustrate.
4. Discuss the part industrial trade fairs play in international marketing of industrial goods.
5. Describe the reasons an MNC might seek an ISO 9000 certification.
6. What ISO 9000 legal requirements are imposed on products sold in the EC? Discuss.
7. Discuss how the characteristics that define the uniqueness of industrial products lead naturally to relationship marketing. Give some examples.
8. Select several countries, each at a different stage of economic development, and illustrate how the stage affects the usage of relationship marketing.

REFERENCES

1. For a discussion on networks in industrial marketing see e.g. Pervez Ghauri (ed.), *Advances in International Marketing: From Mass Marketing to Relationships and Networks* (Greenwich, NY: JAI Press, 1999).
2. Hans Gemünden, Thomas Ritter and Achim Walter (eds), *Relationships and Networks in International Markets* (Oxford: Pergamon), 1997.
3. Frederick Webster, *Industrial Marketing Strategy*, 3rd edn (New York: Wiley, 1991).
4. Karin Venetis, Service Quality and Customer Loyalty in Professional Business Service, Ph.D. dissertation, Maastricht University, 1997.
5. John Naisbitt, *Mega Trends Asia* (New York: Simon & Schuster, 1996).
6. Philippe Lasserre and Helmut Schütte, *Strategies for Asia Pacific* (London, Macmillan, 1995).
7. Gregory Ingram and Christine Kessides, 'Infrastructure for Development', *Finance & Development*, September 1994, pp. 18–21.
8. 'The Big Emerging Markets', *Business America*, March 1994, pp. 4–6.
9. Kyung-Il Ghymn, Paul Johnson and Weijiong Zhang, 'Chinese Import Managers' Purchasing Behavior', *Journal of Asian Business*, vol. 9, no. 3, Summer 1993, pp. 35–45.
10. For a report on after-sales service in Russia, see 'Service with a Smile', *Business Eastern Europe*, 20 February 1995, p. 1.
11. Tom Reilly, 'The Harmonization of Standards in the European Union and the Impact on US Business', *Business Horizons*, March–April 1995, pp. 28–34.
12. Neil Morgan and Nigel Piercy, 'Interactions Between Marketing and Quality at the SBU Level: Influences and Outcomes', *Journal of the Academy of Marketing Science*, vol. 26, no. 3, 1998, pp. 190–208.
13. Robert W. Peach (ed.), *The ISO 9000 Handbook*, 2nd edn (Fairfax, VA: CEEM Information Services, 1994).
14. 'Quality: ISO 9000 Certification Standardization', *Business China*, 30 May 1994, p. 4.
15. James Brooke, 'A New Quality in Brazil's Exports', *The New York Times*, 21 October 1994, p. C-1.
16. 'Quality Control-ISO 9000: A Program in Transition', *Trade & Culture*, September–October 1994, pp. 24–28.
17. Jagdish Sheth and Atul Parvatiyar, 'The Evolution of Relationship Marketing', *International Business Review*, vol. 4, no. 4, 1995, pp. 397–418.
18. R.M. Morgan and S.D. Hunt, 'The Commitment-Trust Theory of Relationship Marketing', *Journal of Marketing*, vol. 58, July 1994, pp. 20–38.
19. J.N. Sheth and R. Sisodia, 'Improving the Marketing Productivity', in *Encyclopedia of Marketing for the Year 2000* (Chicago, IL: American Marketing Association-NTC, 1995).
20. Thomas Gruen, 'The Outcome Set of Relationship Marketing in Consumer Markets', *International Business Review*, vol. 4, no. 4, 1995, pp. 447–469.
21. See, e.g. Ingemar Björkman and Sören Kock, 'Social Relationships and Business Networks: the Case of Western Companies in China', *International Business Review*, vol. 4, no. 4, 1995, pp. 519–535.

22. Adrian Palmer, 'Relationship Marketing: Local Implementation of a Universal Concept', *International Business Review*, vol. 4, no. 4, 1995, pp. 471–481.

23. For a comprehensive review of relationship literature, see Robert M. Morgan, and Shelby D. Hunt, 'The Commitment-Trust Theory of Relationship Marketing,' *Journal of Marketing*, July 1994, pp. 20–38 and a special issue of *International Business Review on Relationship Marketing*, vol. 4, no. 4, 1995.

24. Rahul Jacob, 'Why Some Customers Are More Equal than Others', *Fortune*, 19 September 1994, p. 215.

25. Ralph T. King, Jr, 'US Service Exports Are Growing Rapidly, but Almost Unnoticed', *The Wall Street Journal*, 21 April 1993, p. A-1.

26. 'Brazil: Relationship-Building', *Business Latin America*, 7 February 1994, p. 6.

27. Marnik G. Dekimpe, Pierre François, Srinath Gopalakrishna, Gary L. Lilien and Christophe van den Bulte, 'Generalizing About Trade Show Effectiveness: A Cross-National Comparison', *Journal of Marketing*, vol. 61, no. 4, 1997, pp. 55–64.

28. 'Trade Fairs: Is Exhibiting Worth It?' *Business Eastern Europe*, 23 May 1994, pp. 6–7; and Valeri Akopov, 'Making a Name for Your Product in the New Russia', *Trade & Culture*, March–April 1995, pp. 47–48.

29. 'Africa: Marketing through Trade Shows', *Trade & Culture*, Spring 1994, pp. 55–56.

30. Countertrades are discussed in depth in Chapter 18.

31. 'Financing CIS Sales: Reinventing Countertrade', *Business Eastern Europe*, 17 January 1994, pp. 1–2.

32. Christopher Lovelock, 'Service Marketing: Text, Cases and Readings', 2nd edn (Englewood Cliffs, NJ: Prentice-Hall, 1991).

33. 'Service Exports', *Business America*, Annual Report to the US Congress, October 1994, p. 87.

34. Lee D. Dahringer, Charles D. Frame, Oliver Yau and Janet McColl-Kennedy, 'Consumer Involvement in Services: An International Evaluation', *Journal of International Consumer Marketing*, vol. 3, no. 2, 1991, pp. 61–77.

35. Christine Domegan, 'The Adoption of Information Technology in Customer Service', *European Journal of Marketing*, vol. 30, no. 6, 1996, pp. 52–69.

36. Jiatao Li, 'International Strategies of Service MNCs in the Asia-Pacific Region', *The International Executive*, May–June 1994, pp. 305–325.

37. For an insightful study of entry-mode choice by service firms, see M. Krishna Erramilli and C.P. Rao, 'Service Firms' International Entry-Mode Choice: A Modified Transaction-Cost Analysis', *Journal of Marketing*, July 1993, pp. 19–38.

38. James I. Walsh, 'NAFTA: A "Bill of Rights" for US Service Providers', *Business America*, May 1994, p. 26.

39. 'A Single Market for Services', *Business Europe*, January–February 1994, pp. 1–2.

40. 'Concert: The Shape of Rings to Come', *The European*, 7–13 November 1996, p. 21.

41. Kyle Pope, 'Software Piracy Is Big Business in East Europe', *The Wall Street Journal*, 27 April 1995, p. A-10.

42. 'Slapping Piracy Sanctions on Beijing May Help Save MFN Status', *Business Week*, 8 April 1996, p. 16.

Chapter Outline

Chapter Learning Objectives

What you should learn from Chapter 15

- The variety of distribution channels and how they affect cost and efficiency in marketing.
- The Japanese distribution structure and what it means to Western customers and to competing importers of goods.
- How distribution patterns affect the various aspects of international marketing.
- The growing importance of direct-mail distribution in foreign markets.
- The functions, advantages and disadvantages of various middlemen.
- The importance of middlemen to a product's success and the importance of selecting and maintaining middlemen.

If expected marketing goals are to be achieved, a product must be made accessible to the target market in an efficient manner. In many markets, the biggest constraint to successful marketing is distribution.[1] Getting the product to the target market can be a costly process if inadequacies within the distribution structure cannot be overcome. Forging an efficient and reliable channel of distribution may be the most critical and challenging task facing the international marketer.

Each market contains a distribution network with many channel choices whose structures are unique and, in the short run, fixed. In some markets, the distribution structure is multilayered, complex and difficult for new marketers to penetrate; in others, there are few specialized middlemen except in major urban areas; and in yet others, there is a dynamic mixture of traditional and new, evolving distribution institutions available. Regardless of the predominating distribution structure, competitive advantage will reside with the marketer best able to build the most efficient channel from among the alternatives available.

This chapter discusses the basic points involved in making channel decisions: (1) channel structures; (2) available alternative middlemen; (3) locating, selecting, motivating and terminating middlemen; and (4) controlling the channel process.

CHANNEL OF DISTRIBUTION STRUCTURES

In every country and in every market, urban or rural, rich or poor, all consumer and industrial products eventually go through a distribution process. The process includes the physical handling and distribution of goods, the passage of ownership (title), and—most important from the standpoint of marketing strategy—the buying and selling negotiations between producers and middlemen and between middlemen and customers.[2]

A host of policy and strategy channel-selection issues confronts the international marketing manager. These issues are not in themselves very different from those encountered in domestic distribution, but the resolution of the issues differs because of different channel alternatives and market patterns.

Each country market has a channel structure through which goods pass from producer to user. Within this structure are a variety of middlemen whose customary functions, activities and services reflect existing competition, market characteristics, tradition and economic development. In short, the behaviour of channel members is the result of the interactions between the cultural environment and the marketing process.[3] Channel structures range from those with little developed marketing infrastructure found in many emerging markets to the highly complex, multilayered system found in Japan.

Import-Oriented Distribution Structure

Traditional channels in developing countries evolved from economies with a strong dependence on imported manufactured goods. Typically, an importer controls a fixed supply of goods and the marketing system develops around the philosophy of selling a limited supply of goods at high prices to a small number of affluent customers. In the resulting seller's market, market penetration and mass distribution are not necessary because demand exceeds supply and, in most cases, the customer seeks the supply. This produces a channel structure with a limited number of middlemen.

Contrast this with the mass consumption–distribution philosophy which prevails in Europe and other industrialized nations. In these markets, supply is not dominated by one supplier, supply can be increased or decreased within a given range, and profit maximization occurs at or near production capacity. Generally a buyer's market exists and the producer strives to penetrate the market and push goods out to the consumer, resulting in a highly developed channel structure that includes a variety of intermediaries.

This import-oriented philosophy permeates all aspects of market activities and behaviour. For example, a Brazilian bank had ordered piggy banks for a local promotion; because it went better than expected, the banker placed a reorder of three times the original. The local manufacturer immediately increased the price and, despite arguments pointing out reduced production costs and other supply-cost factors, could not be dissuaded from this action. True to an import-oriented attitude, the notion of economies of scale and the use of price as a demand stimulus escaped the manufacturer who was going on the theory that with demand up, the price also had to go up. A one-deal mentality of pricing at retail and wholesale levels exists because in an import-oriented market, goods come in at a landed price and pricing is then simply an assessment of demand and diminishing supply. If the producer or importer has control of supply, then the price is whatever the market will bear.

This attitude affects the development of intermediaries and their functions. Distribution systems are local rather than national in scope and the relationship between the supplier and any middleman in the marketplace is considerably different from that found in a mass-marketing system. The idea of a channel as a chain of intermediaries performing specific activities and each selling to a smaller unit beneath it until the chain reaches the ultimate consumer is not common in an import-oriented system.[4]

European Distribution Structure

The unified Europe has a larger population than the United States or Japan, yet most of the manufacturers and consumers live and work within a radius of 800 km. They are located in an area which is only 12 per cent of the land area of the United States. In spite of this concentration, transportation in the EU was overburdened with regulations and administrative routines. A truck from Glasgow to Athens was spending 30 per cent of its time on border crossings, waiting and filling out some 200 forms. These inefficiencies are now gone and now only one piece of paper is required to move goods between EU member states. Transit documents have been simplified and custom formalities have been eliminated. As a result companies are now working with centralized warehouses and distribution centres. More and more companies are implementing just-in-time (JIT) production and purchasing methods. Pan-European franchising has increased following the removal of trade barriers. Retailers and supermarkets have undergone some restructuring, and companies like Marks & Spencer, A-hold, Aldi and Carréfour are now present in most major cities around Europe. As distribution becomes easier concentration of production is becoming common. Nestlé, for example, is now producing candy bars in Berlin for distribution throughout Europe. The distributor's power is thus increasing.

United States and Japanese Distribution Structure

In the United States, the distribution system is most advanced and it is not difficult to reach all corners of the market. The huge size of the market has led to large-sized retailers who often buy direct from manufacturers. At the same time many manufacturers have their own distribution channels or retail stores.

Distribution in Japan has long been considered the most effective nontariff barrier to the Japanese market.[5] The distribution system is different enough from its United States or European counterparts that it should be carefully studied by anyone contemplating entry.

GOING INTERNATIONAL 15.1

NORWAY'S SUNDAY BEST

In some countries in Europe, questions such as how to regulate the retail trade seem to have taken over from religion and ideology for public debate. To encourage people to think beyond materialistic values and to strengthen the family, the ruling Christian People's Party, with the support of the opposition labour party (which is concerned about shop-workers' rights) has passed a law that will stop larger shops opening on Sunday.

This has led to an open debate. The leading retailers are devising more ingenious forms of resistance. Stein Erik Hagen, the owner of RIMI, the biggest supermarket chain in Norway, has noticed that the new law allows all but the biggest stores to open on Sundays. Hence he announced on 23 July, that in partnership with a Swedish retailer, ICA, he would buy petrol stations from Statoil, the national oil company, for $3.4 billion (€3 billion). As most filling stations carry groceries in Norway.

The rivals at REMA, the country's second largest supermarket chain, plans to either build new petrol stations or start selling car accessories in its existing shops. Its lawyers argue that to qualify as a petrol station, you do not really have to sell fuel; serving motorists in other ways is good enough.

Petrol stations are now offering an ever-widening range of food and household goods. Some shopkeepers say they will cut off parts of their premises to ensure that they are small enough to be allowed to stay open on Sundays. Others are planning to install a petrol pump at the door. One group that will not be affected is the immigrant retailers—mostly from the Balkan or Indian subcontinent—who work all the hours they can in small corner shops and are under the size limit for opening.

Source: Based on *The Economist*, 1 August 1998, p. 25.

The Japanese system has four distinguishing features: (1) a structure dominated by many small wholesalers dealing with many small retailers; (2) channel control by manufacturers; (3) a business philosophy shaped by a unique culture; and (4) laws that protect the foundation of the system—the small retailer.[6]

High Density of Middlemen.   There is a density of middlemen, retailers and wholesalers in the Japanese market unparalleled in any Western industrialized country. The traditional structure serves consumers who make small, frequent purchases at small, conveniently located stores. Figure 15.1 illustrates the contrast between shorter US channels and the long Japanese channels.

In Japan, small stores (95.1 per cent of all retail food stores) account for 57.7 per cent of retail foods sales, whereas in the United States small stores (69.8 per cent of all retail food stores) generate 19.2 per cent of food sales. A disproportionate percentage of nonfood sales are made in small stores in Japan as well. In the United States, small stores (81.6 per cent of all stores) sell 32.9 per cent of nonfood items; in Japan, small stores (94.1 per cent of all stores) sell 50.4 per cent.[7]

Channel Control.   Manufacturers depend on wholesalers for a multitude of services to other members of the distribution network.[8] Financing, physical distribution, warehousing, inventory, promotion and payment collection are provided to other channel members by wholesalers. The system works because wholesalers and all other middlemen downstream are tied to manufacturers by a set of practices and incentives designed to ensure strong marketing support for their products and to exclude rival competitors from the channel.[9]

Figure 15.1   Comparison of Distribution Channels between the United States and Japan

Car parts: Japan

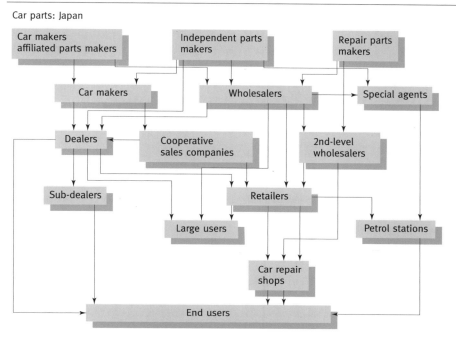

Car parts: United States

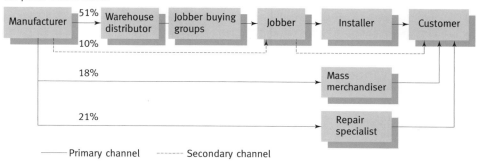

—————Primary channel   - - - - - Secondary channel

Source: McKinsey Industry Studies.

Business Philosophy.   Coupled with the close economic ties and dependency created by trade customs and the long structure of Japanese distribution channels is a unique business philosophy that emphasizes loyalty, harmony and friendship. The value system supports long-term dealer/supplier relationships that are difficult to change as long as each party perceives economic advantage. The traditional partner, the insider, generally has the advantage.

A general lack of price competition, the provision of costly services, and other inefficiencies render the cost of Japanese consumer goods among the highest in the world. For example, a

GOING INTERNATIONAL 15.2

MITSUKOSHI DEPARTMENT STORE, ESTABLISHED 1611—BUT WILL IT BE THERE IN 2011?

Japanese department stores have a long history in Japanese retailing. Mitsukoshi department store, the epitome of Japanese retailing, began as a dry goods store in 1611. To visit a Japanese department store is to get a glimpse of Japanese life. In the basements and subbasements, food abounds with everything from crunchy Japanese pickles to delicate French pastry and soft-coloured, seasonally changing forms of Japanese candies. Besides the traditional floors for women's and men's clothing and furniture, most stores have a floor devoted to kimonos and related accessories and another floor dedicated to children's needs and wants. On the roof there may be miniature open-air amusement parks for children.

But wait, there's more. Department stores are not merely content to dazzle with variety, delight with imaginative displays and accept large amounts of yen for clothes and vegetables. They also seek to serve up a bit of culture. Somewhere between the floors of clothing and the roof, it is likely that you will find a banqueting hall, an art gallery, an exhibition hall and one or two floors of restaurants serving everything from *doria* (creamy rice with cheese) to *tempura*. Department stores aim to be 'total lifestyle enterprises', says one manager. 'We try to be all-inclusive, with art, culture, shopping and fashion. We stress the philosophy of *i-shoku-ju*, the three big factors in life: what you wear, what you eat and how you live.'

Japanese retailing is dominated by two kinds of stores, giant department stores like Mitsukoshi and small neighbourhood shops, both kept alive by a complex distribution system that translates into high prices for the Japanese consumer. In exchange for high prices, the Japanese consumer gets variety, services and, what may be unique to Japanese department stores, cultural enlightenment.

But there are winds of change. Sales for department stores have been down. The Japanese like the amenities of department stores but they are beginning to take notice of the wave of 'new' discount stores that are challenging the traditional retail system by offering quality products at sharply reduced prices. Aoyama Trading Company, which opened a discount men's suit store in the heart of Ginza, where Tokyo's most prestigious department stores are located, may be the future. The owner says he can sell suits for two-thirds the department store price by purchasing directly from manufacturers. Another omen may be Toys "R" Us which has opened 16 discount toy stores in Japan. Department store response has been to discount toy prices, for the first time, by as much as 30 per cent. As one discounter after another 'cherry pick' item after item to discount, can department stores continue to be 'total lifestyle enterprises'? Will there be a Mitsukoshi, as we know it today, in 2011?

Sources: 'A World in Themselves', *Look Japan*, January 1994, pp. 40–42; and 'From Men's Suits to Sake, Discounting Booms in Japan', *Advertising Age International*, 21 March 1994, p. I-4.

bottle of 96 aspirin tablets sells for $20, and not just because of the strong yen.[10] Additionally, Japanese law gives the small retailer enormous advantage over the development of larger stores and competition.[11]

Large-Scale Retail Store Law.   Competition from large retail stores has been almost totally controlled by *Daitenho*—the Large-Scale Retail Store Law. Designed to protect small retailers from large intruders into their markets, the law requires that any store larger than 500 square metres (5382 square feet) must have approval from the prefectural government to be 'built, expanded, stay open later in the evening, or change the days of the month they must remain closed.'[12]

Agreements between the European Union, the United States and Japan have had a profound impact on the Japanese distribution system by leading to deregulation of retailing

NEW CHALLENGES FOR GLOBAL RETAILING

One of the most problematic trends in today's retail industry is globalization. The global arena has proved extremely difficult for many retailers over the past two decades. Retailers' performance in local markets is highly influenced by variations in consumer behaviour. Entrants in markets such as Brazil, Indonesia and Thailand find pronounced differences in consumer tastes, buying behaviour and spending patterns. These differences are prevalent not only in far-away markets but also within so-called Western markets:

Galeries Lafayette attempted to export a high-end Parisian fashion concept to the United States. It was not perceived exclusive enough for the highly competitive Manhattan market and the concept failed. Marks & Spencer introduced a new retail concept to Canada: clothing plus food. Both in the local shopping areas and in the malls it tried to operate with its proven and successful UK formula and own brands, which few Canadians recognized or liked. Marks & Spencer had to adapt its products and strategies to achieve some market position.

There are other encouraging examples where the retailers are able to restructure their business systems using a mix of global, regional and local processes. IKEA, for example, first establishes a relationship with its customers educating them to assemble furniture, which also helps it to cut manufacturing and distribution costs. It builds up a rather consistent but locally adapted line of Scandinavian inspired furniture. It has transformed its relationship with its suppliers across the globe. It educates its supplier to achieve quality standards decreasing supply risks. And, finally, IKEA has invested in global information systems to manage logistics across more than 120 stores, a dozen of distribution centres and 2300 suppliers in 70 countries.

Retailers like Bodyshop, Wall Mart, Makro, Carréfour, Aldi and A-hold are starting to recognize and adopt this approach.

Source: Karen Barth, Nancy Karels, Kathleen McLaughlin and Christina Smith Shi, 'Global Retailing: Tempting Trouble?' *The McKinsey Quarterly*, no. 1, 1996, p. 117–125 and *The Economist*, 2 May 1998, p. 69.

and by strengthening rules on monopoly business practices.[13] The retailing law has been relaxed to permit new outlets as large as 1000 square meters without prior permission. Limits on store hours and business days per year have also been lifted.[14] Officially relaxing laws and regulations on retailing is but one of the important changes signalling the beginning of profound changes in how the Japanese shop.[15]

Trends—From Traditional to Modern Channel Structures

Today, few countries are so sufficiently isolated that they are unaffected by global economic and political changes. These currents of change are altering all levels of economic fabric, including the distribution structure. Traditional channel structures are giving way to new forms, new alliances and new processes—some more slowly than others, but all changing. Pressures for change in a country come from within and without. Multinational marketers are seeking ways to profitably tap market segments that are served by costly, traditional distribution systems. Direct marketing, door-to-door selling hypermarkets, discount houses, shopping malls, catalogue-selling and selling through the Internet are being introduced in an attempt to provide efficient distribution channels.[16]

In anticipation of a single European market, national and international retailing networks are developing throughout Europe. An example is Sainsbury's, the UK supermarket giant, which has entered an alliance with Esselunga of Italy (supermarkets), Docks de France

Figure 15.2   Cutting Out the Middlemen

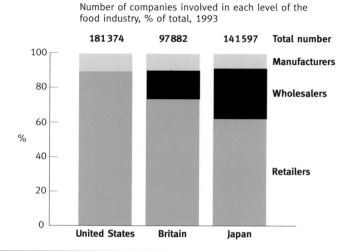

Number of companies involved in each level of the
food industry, % of total, 1993

Source: McKinsey.

(hypermarkets, supermarkets and discount stores), and Belgium's Delhaize (supermarkets). The alliance provides the opportunity for the four to pool their experience and buying power and prepare to expand into other European markets.[17] A-hold (Albert Heijn) of the Netherlands is expanding globally from the United States to Asia. More than 60 per cent of its revenue is coming from abroad. While European retailers see a unified Europe as an opportunity for pan-European expansion, foreign retailers are attracted by the high margins and prices characterized as 'among the most expensive anywhere in the world'. Costco, the US-based warehouse retailer, saw the high gross margins British supermarkets command, 7 to 8 per cent compared with 2.5 to 3 per cent in the United States, as an opportunity. Costco prices will be 10 to 20 per cent cheaper than rival local retailers. The impact of these and other trends is to change traditional distribution and marketing systems, leading to greater efficiency in distribution.[18] Competition will translate those efficiencies into lower consumer prices. Figure 15.2 gives you an idea of the relative importance of different types of middlemen in the United States, Britain and Japan.

Electronic Commerce

The Internet has connected hundreds of millions of the world's people through a seamless digital network. A store placed on the Internet anywhere is in fact everywhere. If the store sells digital products, such as Netscape, it can deliver the products as easily as handing them over the counter. Cisco Computers, a network equipment maker, is already selling products from its website at the rate of $1 billion (€900 million) a year. General Electric is saving a fortune by buying $1 billion (€900 million) worth of components from its suppliers on-line. Dell computer is selling more than $1 million worth of PCs a day on the web.

According to surveys by Nielsen and from international data, 73 per cent of Internet users had used the web for shopping in 1997. It is estimated that by the year 2000, some 50 million consumers will be buying on-line, in America alone, spending at average of $50 (€45) a year.

Electronic commerce not only means buying on-line—many consumers search their purchase on-line and then buy in another way. The Internet is just one source of electronic commerce. Credit cards, automatic teller machines, telephone banking, electronic data interchange (EDI) and other commercial on-line services from France's Minitel to Compuserve are all electronic commerce. All these have changed their own markets and competition in a radical way.

Credit cards initiated home shopping by creating a virtual payment system that transcended national borders. The Internet extends this beyond the transaction itself to everything that comes before and after, from marketing to product display to order-tracking and even delivery. And, unlike the commercial services which are open only to their subscribers, the Internet is open to everyone. If we consider e-mail, it is much the same as a regular mail but it is faster. It is so much faster that it has reshaped companies, curtailed distances and has revitalized letter writing.

Electronic commerce has already had a profound impact on retailing. There are now two thousand on-line shopping malls, supermalls and malls-of-malls which are directly competing with traditional retailers.

Other than financial services, travel and adult entertainment, retailing has been affected most by electronic commerce. The most obvious advantage of electronic shops is that their costs are lower and they are less constrained for space as compared to traditional retailers. A number of traditional retailers have also opened their electronic shops on the Internet but their offerings are often limited, hard to find and slow to download or see on the screen. Building an on-line shopping site that is attractive and convenient to buyers is not an easy task.

Advertising and marketing, although not strictly in the category of electronic commerce have also been profoundly affected by this development. Unlike traditional advertising, Internet advertising is interactive and can be customized for each viewer. Internet advertising cannot replace mass advertising in other media but is a good alternative to direct mail, which is normally quite expensive. The Internet makes it easier to both communicate with and target potential customers.[19]

Financial services and travel are two of many sectors that are already using the Internet for marketing and customer services. An Internet advertising banner provides a direct link to the advertiser's website for more information and alternatives. Compare it with television advertising where a customer sees the advertisement for a minute or less and may have to remember it for days until he or she next goes shopping. The Internet advertisement allows for not only more information, but also for an immediate response or purchase. The total advertising revenues were $267 million (€241 million) as compared to $33 billion (€30 billion) for television advertising in America alone.

It is not only retailers who believe that the traditional shop may soon become a rarity, manufacturers are equally worried. Procter & Gamble, one of the largest advertisers in the world, has revealed that it is considering moving 80 per cent of its $3 billion (€2.7 billion) advertising budget to the Internet. The Internet is considered the most important marketing media in history.

The amount of goods and services sold through electronic commerce is growing at an amazing rate. In 1998, goods and services sold on-line in Europe and United States exceeded $5 billion (€4.5 billion), double the figure for 1997.[20] It is estimated that on-line commerce will be worth around $65 billion (€59 billion) in the year 2001.

MAKING A GLOBAL WEB SITE

By the end of 1998, an estimated 97.3 million people had access to the World Wide Web. That number is expected to swell to a staggering 319.8 million in just four years, according to estimates from International Data Corp. in Framingham, MA (USA).

Unfortunately, the World Wide Web silences the 'If we build it, they will come' mantra. Building a site that's accessible to a global audience means more than simply establishing a presence on the Web. It means revising your on-line communications-strategy.

You must write lively copy that takes into account the cultural and linguistic makeup of your potential audience, and then use graphics effectively. Here are some guidelines to get you started:

- *Use simple language and avoid complicated sentence structures.*
  Strive for clear, concise language by choosing a shorter word over a longer one, for example, whenever possible. Keep the tone simple and straightforward.
- *Use the active voice.*
  Active voice, which helps achieve concise copy, is especially important on the Web where readability is essential. For example, instead of 'The ad was designed by the creative team', write 'The creative team designed the ad.'
- *Avoid culturally specific idioms or references.*
  Expressions such as 'putting all your eggs in one basket' or 'looking for a needle in a haystack' may not be understood by all your readers.
- *Avoid humour.*
  Humour is rooted in cultural norms. No matter how clever your tagline or cartoon seems, it likely will elude, and possibly offend, a percentage of your audience.
- *Consider dates, time and geography.*
  If you write Oct. 4, 1998, as '10/04/98', Americans will read it correctly, but Asians and Europeans will understand 10 April 1998. If weights, measures or temperatures form part of your message, provide both American units and metric equivalents. Consider expressing time in military format (16.00 for 4 p.m.) to avoid confusion.
- *Define acronyms and abbreviations.*
  Remember that acronyms such as TQM may not be clear to all of your readers. If a name is long or cumbersome, spell it out in the first reference with the acronym in parentheses, then abbreviate all subsequent instances. For example, write 'Efficient Consumer Response (ECR)' the first time, then simply 'ECR' thereafter.

Across Europe, electronic commerce has become a reliable alternative to traditional shopping. It has revived catalogue shopping, which was earlier considered a down-market and lower-quality provider that would take weeks or months to arrive. With the help of the Internet, this method has become trendy for buying anything from a dress to computers. The Internet offering promises delivery within 24–48 hours.

Two years of research by the Consumer Direct Cooperative (CDC), a consortium of 31 organizations including Coca-Cola, Nabisco and Procter & Gamble identified six major groups of potential on-line shoppers:

1. *Shopping avoiders:* Customers who dislike the routine of regular grocery shopping.
2. *Necessity users:* People who are limited in their ability to go shopping, due to their working hours or having young children.
3. *New technologists:* Younger customers who are eager to embrace and feel comfortable with new technologies.
4. *Time-starved:* People who do not worry much about the price and are willing to pay extra to save time.

GOING INTERNATIONAL 15.4 (continued)

- *Consistency is key.*
  Consistency is the essence of all corporate communications, but it bears repeating for the purposes of the Web. Use the same tense throughout your site, and refer to products, events and people in the same way every time. If your Web site consists of sections written by different people, hire an experienced editor to make the site speak in 'one voice' so it will project a unified corporate image.
- *Use graphics to assist in communicating written concepts.*
  Never underestimate the power of graphics, which are especially important in the face of language barriers. In your Web site, for example, replace the link 'Contact us' with an image of an envelope. Use other internationally understood graphical icons for ease in navigating your site.
- *Double-check photographs and illustrations.*
  Always avoid representing cultural stereotypes or metaphors. Remove any pictures that include hand gestures, no matter how benign they may seem to you.

For your site to be truly global, it must be multilingual. It's true that English is the global language of business, and there's a strong bias towards English on the Web. An estimated 55 million English speakers currently access the Internet, including residents of North America, Britain, Australia, New Zealand and India. Still, potential customers among the 9 million Japanese speakers, 6.9 million German speakers and 5.3 million Spanish speakers on-line should not be dismissed.

If many of your customers are overseas, it pays to have your site 'localized' so that it reflects not only the native language but the local norms of weights and measures, time, currency and so on. Localization is essential if you want your customers abroad to find you using keyword searches in their native languages and order your products in their currency.

Seeking examples of effective global sites on the Web? Look not to corporate America but to papal Rome. At the Vatican home page (http://www.vatican.va), everything is in place: concise text, effective graphics, six different languages and links to sites of specialized interest.

Source: Laura Morelli, 'Writing for a global audience on the Web', *Marketing News*, 17 August 1998, p. 17.

5. *Responsibles*: Customers who have a lot of free time and enjoy shopping.
6. *Traditional customers*: Often older people who normally avoid new technologies and enjoy shopping in high street shops.

According to this research, the first four groups are real potential on-line shoppers as they see a clear advantage in electronic commerce. The latter two groups are initially reluctant, but CDC believes, even they will change over time.

DISTRIBUTION PATTERNS

International marketers need a general awareness of the patterns of distribution that confront them in world marketplaces. Nearly every international trading firm is forced by the structure of the market to use at least some middlemen in the distribution arrangement. It is all too easy to conclude that, because the structural arrangements of foreign and domestic distribution seem alike, foreign channels are the same as or similar to domestic channels of the

GOING INTERNATIONAL 15.5

MASS CUSTOMIZATION IS CHANGING THE WAY PRODUCTS ARE SOLD

A revolution is taking place in the way products and services are made and sold. Companies with millions of customers are starting to build products designed just for you. You can buy a Dell computer assembled to your exact specifications and you can buy Levi's jeans cut exactly to fit your body. You can also buy pills with the exact blend of vitamins, minerals and taste you like. You can get glasses made to fit just your face, CDs with music tracks that you choose, cosmetics to match your skin tone, textbooks whose chapters are picked out by your professor and a night in a hotel where every employee knows your favourite food and wine.

Companies such as BMW, Dell computers, Levi Strauss, McGraw-Hill and Mattel are adopting mass customization to maintain their competitive edge. Mass customization is more than just manufacturing, delivery or marketing strategy. It is an organizing principle of business in the next century, just as mass production was the organizing principle for this one.

The two principles are quite different from each other. Mass producers dictate one-to-many relationships, while mass customizers require continual dialogue with customers. Mass customization has two major advantages over mass production: it is at the service of the customer and it makes full use of cutting-edge technology.

The Internet is making customization easier and faster. Anything you can digitize, you can customize. The net makes it easier for companies to conduct an ongoing, one-to-one dialogue with each of its customers, to learn about and respond to their exact preferences. In many markets choice then becomes a higher value than brand. Dell computers is the best example, it builds only those PCs that have been ordered. Companies like IBM and Compaq are trying to copy Dell. Dell is now selling more PCs than IBM, its sales were up 54 per cent in the 2nd quarter of 1998 and earnings soared 62 per cent.

Amazon.Com has three million relationships. It sells books on-line and now is moving into music. Every time a customer orders a book, Amazon learns her taste and suggests other titles she might enjoy. About 60 per cent of its customers are repeat-customers.

Source: 'The Customized Economy', *Fortune*, 28 September 1998, pp. 68–74.

same name. This is misleading. Only when the varied intricacies of actual distribution patterns are understood can the complexity of the distribution task be appreciated. The following description should convey a sense of the variety of distribution patterns.

General Patterns

Generalizing about internal distribution channel patterns of various countries is almost as difficult as generalizing about behaviour patterns of people. Despite similarities, marketing channels are not the same throughout the world. Marketing methods taken for granted in most European Union markets are rare in many countries. Even within Europe there are differences, as illustrated by Table 15.1.

Middlemen Services.   Service attitudes of tradespeople vary sharply at both the retail and wholesale levels from country to country. In Egypt, for example, the primary purpose of the simple trading system is to handle the physical distribution of available goods. On the other hand, when margins are low and there is a continuing battle for customer preference, both wholesalers and retailers try to offer extra services to make their goods attractive to consumers. When middlemen are disinterested in promoting or selling individual items of

Table 15.1   Shopping Around—Permitted Shopping Hours in Europe

Country	Monday–Friday	Saturday	Sunday
Austria	07.00–19.30	07.00–13.00	Closed (exceptions in tourist areas)
Belgium	05.00–20.00	05.00–20.00	05.00–13.00
Britain	No restriction	No restriction	No restriction (large shops can open for only six hours)
Denmark	05.00–17.00	06.00–17.00	Closed (except small shops)
Germany	06.00–20.00	06.00–16.00	Closed (except small shops)
Finland	07.00–21.00	07.00–18.00	Closed (except 12.00–21.00 in June to August and December)
France	No restriction	No restriction	No restriction (but no obligation for employees to work)
Ireland	No restriction	No restriction	No restriction
Italy	09.00–20.00*	09.00–20.00	Closed
Luxembourg	06.00–20.00	06.00–18.00	06.00–13.00
Netherlands	06.00–22.00	06.00–22.00	Closed (shops may open 12 Sundays a year)
Norway	06.00–20.00	06.00–18.00	Closed
Sweden	No restriction	No restriction	No restriction

*Must close for half a day once a week.
Source: Based on 'Il Sole 24 Ore', *The Economist*, 14 March 1998, p. 41.

merchandise, the manufacturer must provide adequate inducement to the middlemen, or undertake much of the promotion and selling effort.

Line Breadth.   Every nation has a distinct pattern relative to the breadth of line carried by wholesalers and retailers. The distribution system of some countries seems to be characterized by middlemen who carry or can get everything. In others, every middleman seems to be a specialist dealing only in extremely narrow lines. Government regulations in some countries limit the breadth of line that can be carried by middlemen, and licensing requirements to handle certain merchandise are not uncommon.

Costs and Margins.   Cost levels and middleman margins vary widely from country to country, depending on the level of competition, services offered, efficiencies or inefficiencies of scale, and geographic and turnover factors related to market size, purchasing power, tradition and other basic determinants. In India, competition in large cities is so intense that costs are low and margins thin; but in rural areas, the lack of capital has permitted the few traders with capital to gain monopolies with consequent high prices and wide margins.

Channel Length.   Some correlation may be found between the stage of economic development and the length of marketing channels. In every country, channels are likely to be shorter for industrial goods and for high-priced consumer goods than for low-priced products. In general, there is an inverse relationship between channel length and the size of the purchase. Combination wholesaler–retailers or semi-wholesalers exist in many countries, adding one or two links to the length of the distribution chain. In China, for example, the

EUROPE'S ICE-CREAM MARKET IS A BATTLEGROUND

Two companies, one European and one American, have been at war for seven years over ice cream. Unilever, the Anglo-Dutch group, Europe's powerful retailer, is the biggest ice-cream producer in the world and has 40 per cent of sales in Europe. It delivers its products to customers in its own freezer cabinets which are strictly off-limit to competitor products. Mars, the US's largest privately owned company, finds it hard to get its products into European shops where all the space is taken over by Unilever freezer cabinets. Mars is fighting back and is hoping that the European Commission (EC) will rule against the practice of Unilever and others, of excluding rival products from freezer cabinets.

The EC has to decide about Unilever's operations in Ireland, where its subsidiary has 80 per cent of the market. Ireland is a test case and the ruling will provide a precedent for the rest of Europe. For Unilever, it's an important decision as ice cream is one of its dominating products, accounting for more than 11 per cent of the group's £34 billion (€50 billion) annual turnover and even higher proportion of profit. The EC regulators suspect that ice-cream producers are defending their market shares by building up dedicated distribution chains such as exclusive freezer cabinets. Mars is behaving as a small firm being oppressed by the giant Unilever. It introduced its ice cream in 1989 and was taken to court by Unilever in Ireland for inducing retailers to stock its products in Unilever cabinets. Unilever won the case and the decision has been lingering through the appeals process ever since.

In March 1991, Mars complained to the EC that Unilever was breaking EU competition rules in Germany and Ireland. In the German case, retailers were exclusively tied to one supplier. It was found against the rules. According to Unilever, exclusive freezers allow Unilever to control the quality of its product and to offer retailers a 24-hour service. While Mars is trying to get into the market with a limited range of products, 'hitching a ride on the industry'.

Mars argues that it is the consumers who lose out from the present arrangement because there is less choice in the shops. Also that there is no reason that ice cream should be different from other impulse products such as sweets and cigarettes.

Europe's Ice Cream Rivals (Market Shares 1997)

	Germany (%)	UK (%)	France (%)	Spain (%)	Netherlands (%)	Italy (%)
Unilever	48	50	34	25	37	27
Nestlé	4	8	14	28	5	15
Häagen-Dazs	–	6	3	4	5	–
Mars	1	4	4	–	8	–
Others	47	32	45	43	45	58
	100	*100*	*100*	*100*	*100*	*100*

Preliminarily, the EC decided that exclusive cabinets are anti-competition in 1993. Unilever headed off censure in 1995 by promising to sell 1750 cabinets in Ireland to retailers, allowing them to use them to store competitor products. But most shopkeepers were unwilling to take the offer. Unilever decided to appeal to the European Court against any ban on freezer exclusivity, a process that could take three years.

Source: Based on John William, 'Cold Cabinet Warriors', *The Financial Times*, 1 January 1998, p. 12.

traditional distribution system for over-the-counter drugs consists of large local wholesalers divided into three levels. First-level wholesalers supply drugs to major cities such as Beijing and Shanghai. Second-level ones service medium-sized cities, while the third level distributes to counties and cities with 100 000 people or less. It can be profitable for a company to sell directly to the two top-level wholesalers and leave them to sell to the third level, which is so small that it would be unprofitable for the company to seek out.[21]

Nonexistent Channels.   One of the things companies discover about international channel-of-distribution patterns is that, in many countries, adequate market coverage through a simple channel of distribution is nearly impossible. In many instances, appropriate channels do not exist; in others, parts of a channel system are available but other parts are not. Several distinct distribution channels are necessary to reach different segments of a market; channels suitable for distribution in urban areas seldom provide adequate rural coverage.

Eastern Europe presents a special problem. When communism collapsed, so did the government-run distribution system. Local entrepreneurs are emerging to fill the gap but they lack facilities, training and product knowledge and they are generally undercapitalized. Companies that have any hope of getting goods to customers profitably must be prepared to invest heavily in distribution.[22]

Blocked Channels.   International marketers may be blocked from using the channel of their choice. Blockage can result from competitors' already-established lines in the various channels and trade associations or cartels having closed certain channels. Associations of middlemen sometimes restrict the number of distribution alternatives available to a producer. Drug manufacturers in many countries have inhibited distribution of a wide range of goods through any retail outlets except pharmacies. The pharmacies, in turn, have been supplied by a relatively small number of wholesalers who have long-established relationships with their suppliers. Thus, through a combination of competition and association, a producer may be kept out of the market completely.

Stocking.   The high cost of credit, danger of loss through inflation, lack of capital and other concerns cause foreign middlemen in many countries to limit inventories. This often results in out-of-stock conditions and sales lost to competitors. Physical distribution lags intensify their problem so that, in many cases, the manufacturer must provide local warehousing or extend long credit to encourage middlemen to carry large inventories. Considerable ingenuity, assistance and, perhaps, pressure are required to induce middlemen in most countries to carry adequate or even minimal inventories.

Power and Competition.   Distribution power tends to concentrate in countries where a few large wholesalers distribute to a mass of small middlemen. Large wholesalers generally finance middlemen downstream. The strong allegiance they command from their customers enables them to effectively block existing channels and force an outsider to rely on less effective and more costly distribution.

Retail Patterns

Retailing shows even greater diversity in its structure than does wholesaling. In Italy and Morocco, retailing is composed largely of specialty houses that carry narrow lines, while in Finland most retailers carry a more general line of merchandise. Retail size is represented at one end by Japan's giant Mitsukoshi, which reportedly enjoys the patronage of more than 100 000 customers every day. The other extreme is represented in the market of Ibadan, Nigeria, where some 3000 one- or two-person stalls serve not many more customers.

THE EURO EFFECT: THE RACE TO RULE RETAILING HEATS UP

European retailers are on a buying spree. In January France's no. 5 retailer, Promodés, announced it will buy Belgium's no. 1 grocery chain, GB, for $293 million (€264 million). A day earlier, Marks & Spencer PLC of Britain announced it had bought a Frankfurt store from rival Hertie Waren und Kaufhaus, and announced 30 new locations it plans to open on the continent in the next three years.

The race to dominate retailing in the next century is getting red-hot, as all the big players are rushing to create Europeanwide store networks. When the euro kicks in, easier comparison shopping will induce consumers across borders to look for bargains on big items such as refrigerators and televisions. Many European countries restrict large new stores to protect smaller retailers. In France for example, any store bigger than 300 square metres must be approved by a special commission.

Retailers are looking beyond borders for sales growth. Hypermarket chain, Auchan (France), merged its Italian operations with Gruppo Rinascente, Italy's largest department store in a $900 million (€812 million) deal. One reason for this enhanced activity is that North American retailers are on the march in Europe. Wal-Mart, the world's biggest retailer with sales of $117 billion (€105 billion) announced it would buy Wertkauf, a private chain of 21 stores in Germany. Analysts figure that Wertkauf is Wal-Marts first step in Europe.

All this restructuring takes place due to the fact that the introduction of the euro accelerates a European shift from fragmented national markets toward an integrated one. Efficient giants such as Carréfour of France and A-hold of the Netherlands enjoy economies of scale and purchasing clout which will boost their cost advantage over rivals.

Speciality retailers such as the Swedish group Hennes & Maurits and Benetton have already successfully established themselves in most European markets due to the same advantages. Hennes & Maurits opened 50 new stores in 1997 and planned to open 50 more in 1998.

Small- and medium-sized companies are the losers. In Germany, for example, 42 per cent of shoes and apparel sales occur at small chains or individual shops.

Source: 'The Euro Effect', *Business Week*, 19 January 1998, pp. 16–17.

Size Patterns.   The extremes in size in retailing are similar to those that predominate in wholesaling. Table 15.2 dramatically illustrates some of the variations in size and number of retailers per person that exist in some countries. The retail structure and the problems it engenders cause real difficulties for the international marketing firm selling consumer goods. In Italy, official figures show there are 865 000 retail stores, or one store for every 66 Italians. Of the 340 000 food stores, fewer than 1500 can be classified as large. Thus, middlemen are a critical factor in adequate distribution in Italy.

Emerging countries present similar problems. Among the large supermarket chains in South Africa there is considerable concentration. One thousand of the country's 31 000 stores control 60 per cent of all grocery sales, leaving the remaining 40 per cent of sales to be spread among 30 000 stores. It may be difficult to reach the 40 per cent of the market served by those 30 000 stores. Predominantly in black communities, retailing is on a small scale—cigarettes are often sold singly, and the entire fruit inventory may consist of four apples in a bowl.[23]

Direct Marketing.   Retailing around the world has been in a state of active ferment for several years. The rate of change appears to be directly related to the stage and speed of economic development, and even the least-developed countries are experiencing dramatic changes. Supermarkets of one variety or another are blossoming in developed and developing countries alike. Discount houses that sell everything from powdered milk and canned chilli

Table 15.2   Retail Patterns

Country	Retail Outlets (000)	Population per Outlet	Employees per Outlet
Argentina	787.0	40	3
Canada	134.5	185	9
South Korea	716.8	60	2
Australia	160.2	100	6
India	3140.0	259	–
Malaysia	148.3	124	9
Mexico	825.0	109	3
Philippines	118.5	531	29
USA	1872.5	228	11
Japan	1821.0	68	3

Sources: *International Marketing Data and Statistics*, 18th edn (London: Euromonitor Publications, 1994), and 'Indicators of Market Size for 117 Countries', *Crossborder Monitor*, 31 August 1994.

Table 15.3   Undercutting the Competition

Product	Average Tokyo Retail Price	Shop America Catalogue Price
Audiocassette	$11–$14	$6–$8
Auto-Reverse Walkman	70	50
Braun juicer	32	20
Canon Autoboy camera	260	180
Chanel No. 5 (½ oz)	153	85
Compact disk	15–20	8–11
Lady Remington shaver	86	46
Rolex watch	4857	3078

Source: Shop America Ltd as quoted in 'Can This Catalog Company Crack the Japanese Marketing Maze?', *Business Week*, 19 March 1990, p. 60.

to Korean TVs and VCRs are thriving and expanding worldwide. Selling directly to the consumer through the mail, by telephone or door-to-door is becoming the distribution-marketing approach of choice in markets with insufficient and/or underdeveloped distribution systems. Avon has successfully expanded into Eastern Europe, Latin America and Asia with its method of direct marketing. Companies that enlist individuals to sell their products, such as Avon, are proving to be especially popular in Eastern Europe and other countries where many are looking for ways to become entrepreneurs.

Direct sales through catalogues have proved to be a successful way to enter foreign markets. In Japan, it has been an important way to break the trade barrier imposed by the Japanese distribution system. For example, a US mail-order company, Shop America, has teamed up with 7-Eleven in Japan to distribute catalogues in its 4000 stores. Shop America sells items such as compact discs, Canon cameras, Rolex watches for 30 to 50 per cent less than Tokyo stores (see Table 15.3).

Resistances to Change.   Efforts to improve the efficiency of the distribution system, new types of middlemen, and other attempts to change traditional ways are typically viewed

GOING INTERNATIONAL 15.8

BEIJING'S BAN ON DIRECT SELLING IS A DIRECT HIT ON AMERICAN DIRECT SELLERS

Direct selling took off rapidly after China opened its market in 1990. Estimates of total revenues from direct selling in China rang up to $2 billion (€1.8 billion) annually. The authorities are irritated because it is not only Western companies but also many local and regional companies from Taiwan and Hong Kong that engage in questionable practices such as pyramids and ponzi and stealing the savings of common people, and also because a number of teachers and civil servants have taken up these jobs to supplement their income.

Alarmed by a rise in pyramid schemes by some direct sellers and uneasy about the big sales meetings that these sellers hold, Beijing gave directions to all companies on 22 April 1998 that they must convert their direct selling licences to retail outlets or shut down by 31 October. But it may be too late to halt direct selling. An estimated 20 million Chinese are involved in direct sales, with more turning to the business as unemployment rises.

The ban could also spark a US–China trade dispute. The move particularly threatens sales of American companies: Avon, for example, sells for about $75 million (€68 million) a year. The three dominating American companies, Avon, Amway and Mary Kay's, combined China investment is about $180 million (€162 million) as shown below:

Companies affected by China's ban on direct sales

	Avon	Amway	Mary Kay
Sales in China	$75 (€68) million	$178 (€161) million	$25 (€23) million
Growth	10%	N/A	39%
Sales Reps	50 000	80 000	8 000
Investment in China	$75 (€68) million	$100 (€90) million	$8 (€7) million

According to the US Trade Representative in China, 'It is a serious matter when a government simply bans the operations of legitimate invested companies'.

Source: Dexter Roberts and Kathleen Kerwin, 'Ultimatum for the Avon Lady', *Business Week*, 11 May 1998, p. 26.

as threatening and thus resisted. Laws abound that protect the entrenched in their positions. In Italy, a new retail outlet must obtain a licence from a municipal board composed of local trades people. In a two-year period, some 200 applications were made and only 10 new licences granted. Opposition to retail innovation prevails everywhere, yet in the face of all the restrictions and hindrances, self-service, discount merchandising, liberal store hours[24] and large-scale merchandising continue to grow because they offer the consumer convenience and a broad range of quality product brands at advantageous prices.

ALTERNATIVE MIDDLEMAN CHOICES

A marketer's options range from assuming the entire distribution activity (by establishing its own subsidiaries and marketing directly to the end user) to depending on intermediaries for distribution of the product. Channel selection must be given considerable thought since, once initiated, it is difficult to change, and if it proves inappropriate, future growth of market share may be affected.[25]

Figure 15.3 shows some of the possible channel-of-distribution alternatives. The arrows

Figure 15.3   International Channel-of-Distribution Alternatives

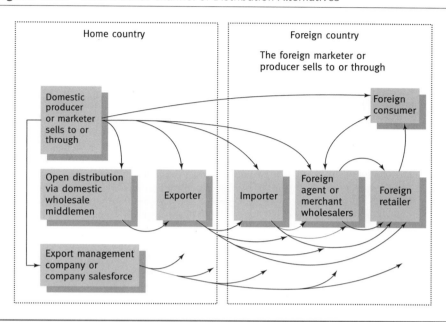

show those to whom the producer and each of the middlemen may sell. In the home country, the seller must have an organization (generally the international marketing division of a company) to deal with channel members needed to move goods between countries. In the foreign market, the seller must supervise the channels that supply the product to the end user.

Once the marketer has clarified company objectives and policies, the next step is the selection of specific intermediaries needed to develop a channel. External middlemen are differentiated on whether or not they take title to the goods. Agent middlemen represent the principal rather than themselves, and merchant middlemen take title to the goods and buy and sell on their own account. The distinction between agent and merchant middlemen is important because a manufacturer's control of the distribution process is affected by who has title to the goods in the channel.

■ Agent middlemen work on commission and arrange for sales in the foreign country but do not take title to the merchandise. By using agents, the manufacturer assumes trading risk but maintains the right to establish policy guidelines and prices and to require its agents to provide sales records and customer information.

■ Merchant middlemen actually take title to manufacturers' goods and assume the trading risks, so they tend to be less controllable than agent middlemen. Merchant middlemen provide a variety of import and export wholesaling functions involved in purchasing for their own account and selling in other countries. Because merchant middlemen are primarily concerned with sales and profit margins on their merchandise, they are frequently criticized for not representing the best interests of a manufacturer. Unless they have a franchise or a strong and profitable brand, merchant middlemen seek goods from any source and are likely to have low brand loyalty. Ease of contact, minimized credit risk and elimination of all

SUPERHIGHWAY OFFERS FIRMS A ROAD TO RICHES

Bob Richards, a Californian wine grower, was over in Madrid last week talking to an aspiring European agent. Juan Martin knew the product and its market. The conversation was a meeting of minds and commercial interests. Terms were agreed and final details were being ironed out until a problem arose. Martin did not have an electronic mail address. The American would not be able to do business with a company that did not have an e-mail facility because he felt that the time difference across the Atlantic would make communicating by any other means inconvenient and slow. Even within Europe, companies lacking e-mail can find it is a stumbling block to furthering commercial relationships. But the benefits of having it are manifold.

Not least, e-mail is likely to cut more expensive business-to-business conventional postal communications by up to a third if trends in the United States are matched. The more advanced Internet, of which e-mail is just a component, is also growing in importance. Various introductory courses will help beginners familiarize themselves with the often hermetic terminology and mechanics of using this valuable resource. The European Commission in Brussels is making its databases available free of charge on the Internet. There are numerous Web sites to search, including the main one called Europa, which is concerned with the EC's policies and aims.

The I'M Europe site and the Cordis site, which are linked, contain information about forthcoming calls for proposals for EC grants. The Espirit project, which covers the main funding activities for the summer and autumn, is a major technology research, transfer and development programme. A pot of ECU 26 million ($33 million) is available for companies bidding with software technology innovations. Companies developing technology for components and subsystems can command up to ECU 70 million, with ECU 20 million available for multimedia systems and ECU 25 million for long-term research.

ECU 35 million is up for grabs for high-performance computing and networking projects and ECU 28 million is available for business process technologies.

Find Europa at *http://europa.eu.int* and I'M Europe at *http://www.echo.lu*

Source: *The European*, 15–21 August 1996.

merchandise handling outside the home market are some of the advantages of using merchant middlemen.

Middlemen are not clear-cut, precise, easily defined entities. It is exceptional to find a firm that represents one of the pure types identified here. What functions are performed by the British middleman called a *stockist*, or one called an *exporter* or *importer*? One company engages in both importing and exporting, acts as an agent and a merchant middleman, operates from offices in the United States, Germany and the United Kingdom, provides financial services and acts as a freight forwarder. It would be difficult to put this company into an appropriate pigeonhole. Many firms work in a single capacity, but the conglomerate type of middleman described here is a major force in some international business.

Only by analysing middlemen functions in skeletal simplicity can the nature of the channels be determined. Three alternatives are presented: first, middlemen physically located in the manufacturer's home country, next, middlemen located in foreign countries and finally, a company-owned system.

Home Country Middlemen

Home country, or domestic, middlemen, located in the producing firm's country, provide marketing services from a domestic base. By selecting domestic middlemen as intermediaries

Figure 15.4   How Does an EMC Operate?

Most export management companies offer a wide range of services and assistance, including:

Researching foreign markets for a client's products.

Travelling overseas to determine the best method of distributing the product.

Appointing distributors or commission representatives as needed in individual foreign countries, frequently within an already existing overseas network created for similar goods.

Exhibiting the client's products at international trade shows, such as US Department of Commerce-sponsored commercial exhibitions at trade fairs and US Export Development Offices around the world.

Handling the routine details in getting the product to the foreign customer—export declarations, shipping and customs documentation, insurance, banking and instructions for special export packing and marking.

Granting the customary finance terms to the trade abroad and assuring payment to the manufacturer of the product.

Preparing advertising and sales literature in cooperation with the manfuacturer and adapting it to overseas requirements for use in personal contacts with foreign buyers.

Corresponding in the necessary foreign languages.

Making sure that goods being shipped are suitable for local conditions, and meet overseas legal and trade norms, including labelling, packaging, purity and electrical characteristics.

Advising on overseas patent and trademark protection requirement.

Source: 'The Export Management Company', US Deptartment of Commerce, Washington, DC.

in the distribution processes, companies relegate foreign-market distribution to others. Domestic middlemen offer many advantages for companies with a small international sales volume, those inexperienced with foreign markets, those not wanting to become immediately involved with the complexities of international marketing and those wanting to sell abroad with minimum financial and management commitment. A major trade-off for using domestic middlemen is limited control over the entire process. Domestic middlemen are most likely to be used when the marketer is uncertain and/or desires to minimize financial and management investment. A brief discussion of the more frequently used domestic middlemen follows.

Export Management Companies.   The export management company (EMC) is an important middleman for firms with relatively small international volume or for those unwilling to involve their own personnel in the international function. EMC firms range in size from one person up to 100 and handle about 10 per cent of the manufactured goods exported.

Whether handling 5 clients or 100, the EMC's stock-in-trade is personalized service. Typically, the EMC becomes an integral part of the marketing operations of the client companies. Working under the names of the manufacturers, the EMC functions as a low-cost, independent marketing department with direct responsibility to the parent firm. The working relationship is so close that customers are often unaware they are not dealing directly with the export department of the company. (See Figure 15.4.)

Two of the chief advantages of EMC's are (1) minimum investment on the part of the company to get into international markets and (2) no company personnel or major expenditure of managerial effort. The result, in effect, is an extension of the market for the firm with negligible financial or personnel commitments.

Trading Companies. Trading companies have a long and honourable history as important intermediaries in the development of trade between nations. Trading companies accumulate, transport and distribute goods from many countries. In concept, the trading company has changed little in hundreds of years.

The British firm, Gray MacKenzie and Company, is typical of companies operating in the Middle East. It has some 70 salespeople and handles consumer products ranging from toiletries to outboard motors and Scotch whisky. The key advantage to this type of trading company is that it covers the entire Middle East.

Large, established trading companies are generally located in developed countries; they sell manufactured goods to developing countries and buy raw materials and unprocessed goods. Japanese trading companies (*sogo shosha*), dating back to the early 1700s, operate both as importers and exporters. Some 300 are engaged in foreign and domestic trade through 2000 branch offices outside Japan and handle over $1 trillion (€0.9 trillion) in trading volume annually.[26]

Complementary Marketers. Companies with marketing facilities or contacts in different countries with excess marketing capacity or a desire for a broader product line sometimes take on additional lines for international distribution; although the generic name for such activities is complementary marketing, it is commonly called *piggybacking*.[27] General Electric Company has been distributing merchandise from other suppliers for many years. It accepts products that are noncompetitive but complementary and that add to the basic distribution strength of the company itself.

Most piggyback arrangements are undertaken when a firm wants to fill out its product line or keep its seasonal distribution channels functioning throughout the year. Companies may work either on an agency or merchant basis, but the greatest volume of piggyback business is handled on an ownership (merchant) purchase–resale arrangement.

The selection process for new products for piggyback distribution determines whether (1) the product relates to the product line and contributes to it, (2) the product fits the sales and distribution channel presently employed, (3) there is an adequate margin to make the undertaking worthwhile and (4) the product will find market acceptance and profitable volume. If these requirements are met, piggybacking can be a logical way of increasing volume and profit for both the carrier and the piggybacker.

Manufacturer's Export Agent. The manufacturer's export agent (MEA) is an individual agent middleman or an agent middleman firm providing a selling service for manufacturers. Unlike the EMC, the MEA does not serve as the producer's export department but has a short-term relationship, covers only one or two markets, and operates on a straight commission basis. Another principal difference is that MEAs do business in their own names rather than in the name of the client.

Home Country Brokers. The term *broker* is a catchall for a variety of middlemen performing low-cost agent services. The term is typically applied to import–export brokers who provide the intermediary function of bringing buyers and sellers together and who do not have a continuing relationship with their clients. Most brokers specialize in one or more commodities for which they maintain contact with major producers and purchasers throughout the world.

Buying Offices. A variety of agent middlemen may be classified simply as buyers or buyers for export. Their common denominator is a primary function of seeking and

GOING INTERNATIONAL 15.10

CORDIS DATABASE ACTS AS MATCHMAKER FOR EURO FIRMS

A company in Greece has invented an image-sensing quality control system for processing fruit and other difficult-to-handle consumer items.

A French firm has a simulator for trainees using a sheet-fed offset printer which teaches good diagnostic practice and quality control.

A team in Italy has been working on a sampling device for pesticides in soil or water.

And Cranfield Institute of Technology in the UK has developed a clever pocket-sized device that delivers the precision and accuracy of a laboratory analyser at a price of only ECU 30 ($38).

All these advances were made possible with a share of the European Commission's ECU 12 billion ($13.3 billion) grant budget for the fourth framework which runs until 1999. European funding typically provides just 50 per cent of the costs of development and research.

Now these companies and many others are looking for corporate partners, further financing or marketing expertise, for example, which could provide small businesses with lucrative opportunities.

The European Commission is acting as a matchmaker in an attempt to put companies together through one of its huge databases. The community research and development information service (Cordis) contains information on tens of thousands of research projects which could point towards new products or processes for your company. While the Commission is not necessarily offering further funding there are clear chances for commercial exploitation of existing programmes.

The service has nine databases, which range from news about research matters to a listing of acronyms to thousands of pages of Commission documentation. But it is the research and technical development projects database which is the starting point. Judith Sorensen, promotion coordinator of Cordis in Luxembourg, says the database is underused.

> Companies do not realize the opportunities. Cordis offers a list of firms and their work, with a profile of what they do and their projects, results, potential partners and contact details.

Cordis can be contacted on tel: +352 40 116 240; or fax: +352 40 116 2248; or e-mail: *helpdesk@cordis.lu*.

Source: Abstracted from: *The European*, 12–18 September 1996, p. 39.

---

purchasing merchandise on request from principals; as such, they do not provide a selling service. In fact, their chief emphasis is on flexibility and the ability to find merchandise from any source. They do not often become involved in continuing relationships with domestic suppliers and do not provide a continuing source of representation.

Norazi Agent.   Norazi agents are unique middlemen specializing in shady or difficult transactions. They deal in contraband materials, such as hazardous waste products or war materials, and in providing strategic goods to countries closed to normal trading channels. The Norazi is also likely to be engaged in black-market currency operations and untaxed liquor, narcotics, industrial espionage and other illicit traffic. The Norazi exists because tariffs, import taxes, import/export regulations and excise taxes make illegal movements of goods more profitable than legal movements. The 100 per cent tax imposed by China on televisions and VCRs creates the right opportunity for the Norazi agent operating in duty-free Hong Kong. Estimates are that half of all VCRs and colour TV sets sold in Hong Kong are smuggled to mainland China.[28] The volume of business transacted by Norazi is unknown but estimates are in excess of €90 billion ($100 billion), not counting illegal drugs.

Export Merchants.   Export merchants are essentially domestic merchants operating in foreign markets. As such, they operate much like the domestic wholesaler. Specifically, they purchase goods from a large number of manufacturers, ship them to foreign countries and take full responsibility for their marketing. Sometimes they utilize their own organizations, but, more commonly, they sell through middlemen. They may carry competing lines, have full control over prices, and maintain little loyalty to suppliers although they continue to handle products as long as they are profitable.

Export Jobbers.   Export jobbers deal mostly in commodities; they do not take physical possession of goods but assume responsibility for arranging transportation. Because they work on a job-lot basis, they do not provide a particularly attractive distribution alternative for most producers. Table 15.4 summarizes information pertaining to the major kinds of domestic middlemen operating in foreign markets. No attempt is made to generalize about rates of commission, markup or pay because so many factors influence compensation.

Foreign Country Middlemen

The variety of agent and merchant middlemen in most countries is similar to those in Europe and the United States. An international marketer seeking greater control over the distribution process may elect to deal directly with middlemen in the foreign market. They gain the advantage of shorter channels and deal with middlemen in constant contact with the market. As with all middlemen, particularly those working at a distance, effectiveness is directly dependent on the selection of middlemen and on the degree of control the manufacturer can and/or will exert.

Using foreign-country middlemen moves the manufacturer closer to the market and involves the company more closely with problems of language, physical distribution, communications and financing. Foreign middlemen may be agents or merchants; they may be associated with the parent company to varying degrees; or they may be temporarily hired for special purposes. Some of the more important foreign-country middlemen are manufacturers' representatives and foreign distributors.

Manufacturers' Representatives.   Manufacturers' representatives are agent middlemen who take responsibility for a producer's goods in a city, regional market area, entire country or several adjacent countries. When responsible for an entire country, the middleman is often called a sole agent. The well-chosen, well-motivated, well-controlled manufacturer's representative can provide excellent market coverage for the manufacturer in certain circumstances. The manufacturer's representative is widely used in distribution of industrial goods overseas and is an excellent representative for any type of manufactured consumer goods.

Foreign manufacturers' representatives have a variety of titles, including sales agent, resident sales agent, exclusive agent, commission agent and indent agent. They take no credit, exchange or market risk but deal strictly as field sales representatives. They do not arrange for shipping or for handling and usually do not take physical possession. Manufacturers who wish the type of control and intensive market coverage their own salesforce would afford, but who cannot field one, may find the manufacturer's representative a satisfactory choice.

Distributors.   A foreign distributor is a merchant middleman. This intermediary often has exclusive sales rights in a specific country and works in close cooperation with the manufacturer. The distributor has a relatively high degree of dependence on the supplier companies, and arrangements are likely to be on a long-term, continuous basis. Working through distributors permits the manufacturer a reasonable degree of control over prices, promotional effort, inventory, servicing and other distribution functions. If a line is profitable for distributors, they can be depended on to handle it in a manner closely approximating the desires of the manufacturer.

Foreign-Country Brokers.   Like the export broker discussed earlier, brokers are agents who deal largely in commodities and food products. The foreign brokers are typically part of small brokerage firms operating in one country or in a few contiguous countries. Their strength is in having good continuing relationships with customers and providing speedy market coverage at a low cost.

Managing Agents.   A managing agent conducts business within a foreign nation under an exclusive contract arrangement with the parent company. The managing agent in some cases invests in the operation and in most instances operates under a contract with the parent company. Compensation is usually on the basis of cost plus a specified percentage of the profits of the managed company.

Dealers.   Generally speaking, anyone who has a continuing relationship with a supplier in buying and selling goods is considered a dealer. More specifically, dealers are middlemen selling industrial goods or durable consumer goods direct to customers; dealers are the last step in the channel of distribution. Dealers have continuing, close working relationships with their suppliers and exclusive selling rights for their producer's products within a given geographic area. Finally, they derive a large portion of their sales volume from the products of a single supplier firm. Usually a dealer is an independent merchant middleman, but sometimes the supplier company has an equity in its dealers.

Some of the best examples of dealer operations are found in the farm equipment, earthmoving and automotive industries. These categories include Massey Ferguson, with a vast, worldwide network of dealers; Caterpillar Tractor Company, with dealers in every major city of the world; and the various car companies.

Import Jobbers, Wholesalers and Retailers.   Import jobbers purchase goods directly from the manufacturer and sell to wholesalers and retailers and to industrial customers. Large and small wholesalers and retailers engage in direct importing for their own outlets and for redistribution to smaller middlemen. The combination retailer–wholesaler is more important in foreign countries than in the Western countries. It is not uncommon to find large retailers wholesaling goods to local shops and dealers. Table 15.5 summarizes the characteristics of foreign-country middlemen.

Government-Affiliated Middlemen

Marketers must deal with governments in every country of the world. Products, services and commodities for the government's own use are always procured through government purchasing offices at federal, regional and local levels. As more and more social services are undertaken by governments, the level of government purchasing activity escalates. In The Netherlands, the state's purchasing office deals with more than 10 000 suppliers in 20 countries. About one-third of the products purchased by that agency are produced outside The Netherlands; 90 per cent of foreign purchases are handled through Dutch representatives. The other 10 per cent are purchased directly from producing companies. In Sweden and Norway, the state has a monopoly on all alcoholic drinks and they can only be bought in state-monopoly stores.

Table 15.4 Characteristics of Domestic Middlemen Serving Overseas Markets

Type of Duties	Agent					Merchant				
	EMC	MEA	Broker	Buying Offices	Selling Groups	Norazi	Export Merchant	Export Jobber	Importers and Trading Companies	Complementary Marketers
Take title	No*	No	No	No	No	Yes	Yes	Yes	Yes	Yes
Take possession	Yes	Yes	No	Yes	Yes	Yes	Yes	No	Yes	Yes
Continuing relationship	Yes	Yes	No	Yes	Yes	No	No	Yes	Yes	Yes
Share of foreign output	All	All	Any	Small	All	Small	Any	Small	Any	Most
Degree of control by principal	Fair	Fair	Nil	Nil	Good	Nil	None	None	Nil	Fair
Price authority	Advisory	Advisory	Yes (at market level)	Yes (to buy)	Advisory	Yes	Yes	Yes	No	Some
Represent buyer or seller	Seller	Seller	Either	Buyer	Seller	Both	Self	Self	Self	Self
Number of principals	Few—many	Few—many	Many	Small	Few	Several per transaction	Many sources	Many sources	Many sources	One per product
Arrange shipping	Yes	Yes	Not usually	Yes	Yes	Yes	Yes	Yes	Yes	Yes
Type of goods	Manufactured goods and commodities	Staples and commodities	Staples and commodities	Staples and commodities	Complementary to their own lines	Contraband	Manufactured goods	Bulky and raw materials	Manufactured goods	Complementary to line
Breadth of line	Specialty—wide	All types of staples	All types of staples	Retail goods	Narrow	n.a.	Broad	Broad	Broad	Narrow

Handle competitive lines	No	No	Yes	Yes	Yes	No	Yes—utilizes many sources	Yes	No	No
Extent of promotion and selling effort	Good	Good	Nil	Nil	Nil	Good	n.a.	One shot	Good	Good
Extend credit to principal	Occasionally Fair	Occasionally Fair	No	Occasionally	Seldom	Seldom	Seldom	Seldom	Seldom	Seldom
Market information	Good	Fair	No	Nil	Nil	Good	For principal not for manufacturer	Price and market conditions	Fair	Good

Note: n.a. = not available.
*The EMC may take title and thus becomes a merchant middleman.

Table 15.5 Characteristics of Domestic Middlemen in Foreign Countries

Type of Duties	Agent				Merchant			
	Broker	Manufacturer's Representative	Managing Agent	Comprador	Distributor	Dealer	Import Jobber	Wholesaler and Retailer
Take title	No	No	No	No	Yes	Yes	Yes	Yes
Take possession	No	Seldom	Seldom	Yes	Yes	Yes	Yes	Yes
Continuing relationship	No	Often	With buyer, not seller	Yes	Yes	Yes	No	Usually not
Share of foreign output	Small	All or part for one area	n.a.	All one area	All, for certain countries	Assignment area	Small	Very small
Degree of control by principal	Low	Fair	None	Fair	High	High	Low	Nil
Price authority	Nil	Nil	Nil	Partial	Partial	Partial	Full	Full
Represent buyer or seller	Either	Seller	Buyer	Seller	Seller	Seller	Self	Self
Number of principals	Many	Few	Many	Few	Small	Few major	Many	Many
Arrange shipping	No	No	No	No	No	No	No	No
Type of goods	Commodity and food	Manufactured goods	All types manufactured goods	Manufactured goods	Manufactured goods	Manufactured goods	Manufactured goods	Manufactured consumer goods
Breadth of line	Broad	Allied lines	Broad	Varies	Narrow to broad	Narrow	Narrow to broad	Narrow to broad
Handle competitive lines	Yes	No	Yes	No	No	No	Yes	Yes
Extent of promotion and selling effort	Nil	Fair	Nil	Fair	Fair	Good	Nil	Nil usually
Extend credit to principal	No	No	No	Sometimes	Sometimes	No	No	No
Market information	Nil	Good	Nil	Good	Fair	Good	Nil	Nil

Note: n.a. = not available.

Figure 15.5   Factors Influencing Choice of Channels

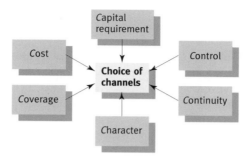

FACTORS AFFECTING CHOICE OF CHANNELS

The international marketer needs a clear understanding of market characteristics and must have established operating policies before beginning the selection of channel middlemen. The following points should be addressed prior to the selection process.

1. Identify specific target markets within and across countries.
2. Specify marketing goals in terms of volume, market share and profit margin requirements.
3. Specify financial and personnel commitments to the development of international distribution.
4. Identify control, length of channels, terms of sale and channel ownership.

Once these points are established, selecting among alternative middlemen choices to forge the best channel can begin. Marketers must get their goods into the hands of consumers and must choose between handling all distribution or turning part or all of it over to various middlemen. Distribution channels vary depending on target market size, competition and available distribution intermediaries.

Although the overall marketing strategy of the firm must embody the company's profit goals in the short and long run, channel strategy itself is considered to have six specific strategic goals. These goals can be characterized as the six Cs of channel strategy—cost, capital, control, coverage, character and continuity as illustrated in Figure 15.5.

Cost

In forging the overall channel-of-distribution strategy, each of the six Cs must be considered in building an economical, effective distribution organization within the long-range channel policies of the company.

There are two kinds of channel cost: the capital or investment cost of developing the channel and the continuing cost of maintaining it. The latter can be in the form of direct expenditure for the maintenance of the company's selling force or in the form of margins, markup or commissions of various middlemen handling the goods. Marketing costs (a substantial part of which is channel cost) must be considered as the entire difference between the factory price of the goods and the price the customer ultimately pays for the merchandise.

The costs of middlemen include transporting and storing the goods, breaking bulk, providing credit and the cost of local advertising, sales representation and negotiations.

Capital Requirement

The financial ramifications of a distribution policy are often overlooked. Critical elements are capital requirement and cash-flow patterns associated with using a particular type of middleman. Maximum investment is usually required when a company establishes its own internal channels, its own salesforce. Use of distributors or dealers may lessen the cash investment, but manufacturers often provide initial inventories on consignment, loans, floor plans or other arrangements.

Control

The more involved a company is with the distribution, the more control it exerts. A company's own salesforce affords the most control but often at a cost that is not practical. Each type of channel arrangement provides a different level of control and, as channels grow longer, the ability to control price, volume, promotion and types of outlet diminishes. If a company cannot sell directly to the end user or final retailer, an important selection criterion of middlemen should be the amount of control the marketer can and wants to maintain.

Coverage

Another major goal is full-market coverage to (1) gain the optimum volume of sales obtainable in each market, (2) secure a reasonable market share and (3) attain satisfactory market penetration. Coverage may be assessed on geographic and/or market segments. Adequate market coverage may require changes in distribution systems from country to country or time to time. Coverage is difficult to develop both in highly developed areas and in sparse markets—the former because of heavy competition and the latter because of inadequate channels.

Many companies do not attempt full-market coverage but seek significant penetration in major population centres. In some countries, two or three cities constitute the majority of the national buying power. For instance, 60 per cent of the Japanese population lives in the Tokyo–Nagoya–Osaka market area, which essentially functions as one massive city.[29]

In China, for example, the often-quoted 1 billion person market is, in reality, fewer than 25 to 30 per cent of the population of the most affluent cities. Even as personal income increases in China, distribution inadequacies limit marketers in reaching all those who have adequate incomes.

Character

The channel-of-distribution system selected must fit the character of the company and the markets in which it is doing business. Some obvious product requirements, often the first considered, relate to perishability or bulk of the product, complexity of sale, sales service required and value of the product.

Channel commanders must be aware that channel patterns change; they cannot assume that once a channel has been developed to fit the character of both company and market that no more need be done. The United Kingdom, for example, has epitomized distribution through specialty-type middlemen, distributors, wholesalers and retailers; in fact, all middlemen have traditionally worked within narrow product specialty areas. In recent years, however, there has been a trend towards broader lines, conglomerate merchandising and mass marketing.

Continuity

Channels of distribution often pose longevity problems. Most agent middlemen firms tend to be small institutions. When one individual retires or moves out of a line of business, the company may find it has lost its distribution in that area. Wholesalers, and especially retailers, are not noted for their continuity in business either. Most middlemen have little loyalty to their vendors. They handle brands in good times when the line is making money, but quickly reject such products within a season or a year if they fail to produce during that period. Distributors and dealers are probably the most loyal middlemen, but even with them manufacturers must attempt to build brand loyalty downstream in a channel lest middlemen shift allegiance to other companies or other inducements.

LOCATING, SELECTING AND MOTIVATING CHANNEL MEMBERS

The actual process of building channels for international distribution is seldom easy and many companies have been stopped in their efforts to develop international markets by their inability to construct a satisfactory system of channels.

Despite the chaotic condition of international distribution channels, international marketers can follow a logical procedure in developing channels. After general policy guides are established, marketers need to develop criteria for the selection of specific middlemen. Construction of the middleman network includes seeking out potential middlemen, selecting those who fit the company's requirements and establishing working relationships with them.

In international marketing, the channel-building process is hardly routine. The closer the company wants to get to the consumer in its channel contact, the larger the salesforce required. If a company is content with finding an exclusive importer or selling agent for a given country, channel building may not be too difficult; but if it goes down to the level of subwholesaler or retailer it is taking on a tremendous task and must have an internal staff capable of supporting such an effort.

Locating Middlemen

The search for prospective middlemen should begin with study of the market and determination of criteria for evaluating middlemen servicing that market. The company's broad policy guidelines should be followed, but expect expediency to override policy at times. The checklist of criteria differs according to the type of middlemen being used and the nature of their relationship with the company. Basically, such lists are built around four subject areas: (1) productivity or volume; (2) financial strength; (3) managerial stability and capability; and (4) the nature and reputation of the business. Emphasis is usually placed on either the actual or potential productivity of the middleman.

Selecting Middlemen

Finding prospective middlemen is less a problem than determining which of them can perform satisfactorily. Most prospects are hampered by low volume or low potential volume, many are underfinanced, and some simply cannot be trusted. In many cases, when a manufacturer is not well-known abroad, the reputation of the middleman becomes the reputation of the manufacturer, so a poor choice at this point can be devastating.

Screening.   The screening and selection process itself should follow this sequence: (1) a letter including product information and distributor requirements in the native language to each prospective middleman; (2) a follow-up to the best respondents for more specific information concerning lines handled, territory covered, size of firm, number of salespeople, and other background information; (3) check of credit and references from other clients and customers of the prospective middleman; and (4) if possible, a personal check of the most promising firms.

One source suggests that the only way to select a middleman is to go personally to the country and talk to ultimate users of your product to find whom they consider to be the best distributors. Visit each one before selecting the one to represent you; look for one with a key man who will take the new line of equipment to his heart and make it his personal objective to make the sale of that line a success.

The Agreement.   Once a potential middleman has been found and evaluated, there remains the task of detailing the arrangements with that middleman. So far the company has been in a buying position, now it must shift into a selling and negotiating position to convince the middleman to handle the goods and accept a distribution agreement that is workable for the company. Agreements must spell out the specific responsibilities of the manufacturer and the middleman including an annual sales minimum. The sales minimum serves as a basis for evaluation of the distributor and failure to meet sales minimums may give the exporter the right of termination.

Some experienced exporters recommend that initial contracts be signed for one year only. If the first year's performance is satisfactory, they should be reviewed for renewal for a longer period. This permits easier termination and, more important, after a year of working together in the market, a more workable arrangement can generally be reached.

Motivating Middlemen

Once middlemen are selected, a promotional programme must be started to maintain high-level interest in the manufacturer's products. A larger proportion of the advertising budget must be devoted to channel communications than in the head office because there are so many small middlemen to be contacted. Consumer advertising is of no avail unless the goods are actually available. On all levels, there is a clear correlation between the middleman's motivation and sales volume. The hundreds of motivational techniques that can be employed to maintain middleman interest and support for the product may be grouped into five categories: financial rewards, psychological rewards, communications, company support and corporate rapport.

Obviously, margins or commissions must be competitive and set to meet the needs of the middleman and may vary according to the volume of sales and the level of services offered. Without a combination of adequate margin and adequate volume, a middleman cannot afford to give much attention to a product.

Being human, middlemen and their salespeople respond to psychological rewards and recognition for the jobs they are doing. A trip to the parent company's home or regional office is a great honour. Publicity in company media and local newspapers also builds esteem and involvement among foreign middlemen.

Terminating Middlemen

When middlemen do not perform up to standards or when market situations change, requiring a company to restructure its distribution, it may be necessary to terminate relationships with certain middlemen or certain types of middlemen. In the Western markets, it is usually a simple action regardless of the type of middlemen—agent or merchant; they are simply dismissed. However, in other parts of the world, the middleman typically has some legal protection that makes it difficult to terminate relationships. Some companies give all middlemen contracts for one year, or for another specified period, to avoid such problems. But as many experienced international marketers know, the best rule is to avoid the need to terminate distributors by screening all prospective middlemen carefully. A poorly chosen distributor may not only fail to live up to expectations but may also adversely affect future business and prospects in the country.

Controlling Middlemen

The extreme length of channels typically used in international distribution makes control of middlemen particularly difficult. Some companies solve this problem by establishing their own distribution systems; others issue franchises or exclusive distributorships in an effort to maintain control through the first stages of the channels.

Until the various world markets are more highly developed, most international marketers cannot expect to exert a high degree of control over their international distribution operations. Although control is difficult, a company that succeeds in controlling distribution channels is likely to be a successful international marketer.

Some manufacturers have lost control through 'secondary wholesaling'—when rebuffed discounters have secured a product through an unauthorized outlet. A manufacturer may then find some of the toughest competition from its own products that have been diverted through other countries or manufactured by subsidiaries and exported or bootlegged into markets the parent would prefer to reserve. Such action can directly conflict with exclusive arrangements made with distributors in other countries and may undermine the entire distribution system by harming relationships between manufacturers and their channels.[30]

SUMMARY

From the foregoing discussion, it is evident that the international marketer has a broad range of alternatives for developing an economical, efficient, high-volume international distribution system. To the uninitiated, however, the variety may be overwhelming.

Careful analysis of the functions performed suggests more similarity than difference between international and domestic distribution systems; in both cases there are three primary alternatives of using agent middlemen, merchant middlemen or a company's own sales and distribution system. In many instances, all three types of middlemen are employed on the international scene, and channel structure may vary from nation to nation or from continent to continent. The neophyte company in international marketing can gain strength from the knowledge that information and advice are available relative to the structuring of international distribution systems and that many well-developed and capable middleman firms exist for the international distribution of goods. Within the past decade, international middlemen have become more numerous, more reliable, more sophisticated and more readily available to marketers in all countries. Such growth and development offer an ever-wider range of possibilities for entering foreign markets, but the international business-person should remember that it is just as easy for competitors.

QUESTIONS

1. Discuss the distinguishing features of the European distribution system.
2. Discuss the ways Japanese manufacturers control the distribution process from manufacturer to retailer.
3. Discuss how the globalization of markets, especially in the European Union, affects retail distribution.
4. To what extent, and in what ways, do the functions of domestic middlemen differ from those of their foreign counterparts?
5. Why is the EMC sometimes called an independent export department?
6. Discuss how physical distribution relates to channel policy and how they affect one another.
7. Explain how and why distribution channels are affected as they are when the stage of development of an economy improves.
8. In what circumstances is the use of an EMC logical?
9. Predict whether the Norazi agent is likely to grow or decline in importance.
10. In which circumstances are trading companies likely to be used?
11. How is distribution-channel structure affected by increasing emphasis on the government as a customer and by the existence of state trading agencies?
12. Review the key variables that affect the marketer's choice of distribution channels.
13. Account, as best you can, for the differences in channel patterns that might be encountered in a highly-developed country and an emerging country.
14. One of the first things companies discover about international channels-of-distribution patterns is that in most countries it is nearly impossible to gain adequate market coverage through a simple channel-of-distribution plan. Discuss.
15. Discuss the various methods of overcoming blocked channels.

REFERENCES

1. For a detailed review of changes in retail distribution, see 'Change at the Check-out', *The Economist* (*A Survey of Retailing*), 4 March 1995, pp. 1–18.
2. Bert Rosenbloom and Trina L. Larsen, 'International Channels of Distribution and the Role of Comparative Marketing Analysis', *Journal of Global Marketing*, vol. 4, no. 4, 1991, pp. 39–54.
3. Sudhir H. Kale, 'How National Culture, Organizational Culture and Personality Impact Buyer-Seller Interactions', in Pervez Ghauri and Jean-Claude Usunier, *International Business Negotiations* (Oxford: Pergamon, 1996), pp. 21–38.
4. For a report on research on a nation's level of economic development and marketing channels, see Janeen E. Olsen and Kent L. Granzin, *Journal of Global Marketing*, vol. 7, no. 3, 1994, pp. 7–39.
5. Constantine Katsikeas, Ali Al-Khalifa and Dave Crick, 'Manufacturers' Understanding of their

Overseas Distributors: The Relevance of Export Involvement', *International Business Review*, vol. 6, no. 2, 1997, pp. 147–164
6. A comprehensive review of the changing character of the Japanese distribution system is presented in John Fahy and Fuyuki Taguchi, 'Reassessing the Japanese Distribution System', *Sloan Management Review*, Winter 1995, pp. 49–61.
7. Arieh Goldman, 'Japan's Distribution System: Institutional Structure, Internal Political Economy, and Modernization', *Journal of Retailing*, Summer 1991, pp. 156–161.
8. Ibid, p. 164.
9. Gregory L. Miles, 'Unmasking Japan's Distributors', *International Business*, April 1994, pp. 30–42.
10. Emily Thornton, 'Revolution in Japanese Retailing', 7 February 1994, p. 143.
11. 'Japan's Shoppers Bring a New Era to Economy', *The Wall Street Journal*, 20 June 1994, p. A-1.
12. Robert E. Weigand, 'So You Think Our Retailing

Laws Are Tough?' *The Wall Street Journal*, 13 November 1989, p. A-12; and 'The Euro Effect: The Race to Rule Retailing Heats Up as New Currency Looms', *Business Week*, 19 January 1998, pp. 16–17.

13. Masami Kogayu, 'Fair Is Free and Free Is Fair', *Look Japan*, July 1994, pp. 12–13; and Marnik G. Dekimpe, Pierre François, Srinath Gopalakrishna, Gary L. Lilien and Christophe van den Bulte, 'Generalizing About Trade Show Effectiveness: A Cross-National Comparison', *Journal of Marketing*, vol. 61, no. 4, 1997, pp. 55–64.

14. Fumio Matsuo, 'Trade with a Moral Compass', *The Wall Street Journal*, 6 December 1994, p. A-20.

15. Alma Mintu-Wimsatt, Dazumi Lino and Hector R. Lozada, 'A Unique Distribution System: The Case of Toys "R" Us in Japan', *Advances in Marketing 1994* (Proceedings: Southwestern Marketing Association), pp. 275–280.

16. 'Colombian Retailing: Battling the Bodega and Beyond', *Business Latin America*, 30 January 1995, pp. 3–4.

17. 'Stores Form New Euro-Retail Alliance', *Business Europe*, 18–24 April 1994, pp. 7–8.

18. Carla Rapoport and Justin Martin, 'Retailers Go Global', *Fortune*, 20 February 1995, pp. 102–108.

19. Electronic Commerce Survey', *The Economist*, 10 May 1997.

20. 'Death of the Shop', *The European, Retailing*, 24–30 August 1998, pp. 18–19.

21. 'Moving Goods in Beijing and Tianjin: Market Making,' *Business China*, 5 September 1994, pp. 8–9.

22. 'Poland: Stocking the Corner Shop', *Business Eastern Europe*, 9 January 1995, p. 1.

23. Gillian Ann Findlay, 'Sticky Situation for Uncle Ben's in South Africa', *Advertising Age*, 18 April 1994, p. I-15.

24. 'Europe Shops for Longer Store Hours', *Advertising Age*, 17 January 1994, p. I-8.

25. See, for example, 'Consumer Marketing in Indonesia: A Market Too Far', *Business Asia*, 14 February 1994, pp. 6–7.

26. Yukio Onuma, 'Myths and Realities of the Sogo-Shosha', *Trade & Culture*, September–October 1994, pp. 33–34.

27. 'Piggybacking Your Way to Internationalization', *The International Executive*, March–April 1991, pp. 45–46.

28. Peter Fuhrman and Andrew Tanzer, 'The Tai Fei Know the Way', *Forbes*, 21 December 1992, pp. 172–175.

29. 'Distribution', *Business Asia*, 17 January 1994, p. 7.

30. See Chapter 18 for a discussion of parallel imports; and Christopher Heath, 'From "Parker" to "BBS"—The Treatment of Parallel Imports in Japan', *ICC: International Review of Industrial Property and Copyright Law*, April 1993, pp. 179–188.

CHAPTER

16

The International Advertising and Promotion Effort

Chapter Learning Objectives

What you should learn from Chapter 16

- Local market characteristics which affect the advertising and promotion of products.
- Is Pan-European advertising possible?
- When global advertising is most effective; when modified advertising is necessary.
- The effects of a single European market on advertising.
- The effect of limited media, excessive media, and government regulations on advertising and promotion budgets.
- Creative challenges in international advertising.
- Sales promotions.
- The communication process and advertising misfires.

Advertising, sales promotion, personal selling and public relations, the mutually reinforcing elements of the promotional mix, have as their common objective successful sale of a product or service. Once a product is developed to meet target market needs and is properly distributed, intended customers must be informed of the product's value and availability. Advertising and promotion are basic ingredients in the marketing mix of an international company (see Figure 16.1).

Of all the elements of the marketing mix, decisions involving advertising are those most often affected by cultural differences among country markets. Consumers respond in terms of their culture, its style, feelings, value systems, attitudes, beliefs and perceptions.[1] Because advertising's function is to interpret or translate the need/want-satisfying qualities of products and services in terms of consumer needs, wants, desires and aspirations, the emotional appeals, symbols, persuasive approaches and other characteristics of an advertisement must coincide with cultural norms if it is to be effective. Because advertising is mainly based on language and images, it is influenced by culture.[2]

Reconciling an international advertising and sales promotion effort with the cultural uniqueness of markets is the challenge confronting the international marketer. The basic framework and concepts of international promotion are essentially the same wherever employed. Six steps are involved: (1) study the target market(s); (2) determine the extent of worldwide standardization; (3) determine the promotional mix (the blend of advertising, personal selling, sales promotions and public relations) by national or global markets; (4) develop the most effective message(s); (5) select effective media; and (6) establish the necessary controls to assist in monitoring and achieving worldwide marketing objectives. (See Figure 16.2.)

A review of some of the global trends that can impact international advertising is followed by a discussion of global versus modified advertising. A survey of problems and challenges confronting international advertisers—including basic creative strategy, media planning and selection, sales promotions and the communications process—conclude the chapter.

INTERNATIONAL ADVERTISING

Intense competition for world markets and the increasing sophistication of foreign consumers have led to a need for more sophisticated advertising strategies. Increased costs, problems of coordinating advertising programmes in multiple countries, and a desire for a common worldwide company or product image have caused companies to seek greater control and efficiency without sacrificing local responsiveness. In the quest for more effective and responsive promotion programmes, the policies covering centralized or decentralized authority, use of single or multiple foreign or domestic agencies, appropriation and allocation procedures, copy, media and research are being examined.

One of the most widely debated policy areas pertains to the degree of specialized advertising necessary from country to country.[3] One view sees advertising customized for each country or region because every country is seen as posing a special problem. Executives with this viewpoint argue that the only way to achieve adequate and relevant advertising is to develop separate campaigns for each country. At the other extreme are those who suggest that advertising should be standardized for all markets of the world and overlook regional differences altogether.[4]

Debate on the merits of standardization compared to modification of international advertising has been going on for decades. Theodore Levitt's article, 'The Globalization of Markets', caused many companies to examine their international strategies and to adopt a

Figure 16.1   World Advertising Spending

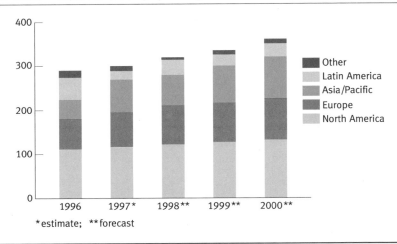

*estimate;   **forecast

Figure 16.2   A Framework for International Promotion

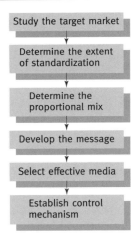

Source: 'Zenith Media', *The Economist*, 17 January 1998, p. 102.

global marketing strategy.[5] Levitt postulated the existence and growth of the global consumer with similar needs and wants, and advocated that international marketers should operate as if the world were one large market, ignoring superficial regional and national differences. In our opinion, although we do have some global products and brands, we need to adopt our marketing approach and tactics according to cultural differences and segments. Even in the EU, a truly integrated market, the buying behaviour for global products, such as Sony TVs or Philips vacuum cleaners, is different.

Another example is Gillette Company that sells 800 products in more than 200 countries. Gillette has a consistent worldwide image as a masculine, sports-oriented company, but its

ECONOMISTS ASSUME THAT PEOPLE KNOW WHAT THEY WANT. ADVERTISERS ASSUME THAT THEY DO NOT. WHO IS RIGHT?

Companies such as Coca-Cola, Kodak and McDonald's believe that the huge sums they spend on advertising are an investment in their valuable brands. They are not the only ones, however, who pay close attention to advertising. To economists—the official sponsors of rational decision making—the motives and methods of advertisers raise doubts about a fundamental claim: that people are good at making decisions for themselves.

In the economist's view of the world there is little need for firms to spend so much money cajoling consumers into buying their wares. Of course, people need good information to make good choices and it is often too costly or time-consuming to collect it themselves. So advertising a product's features, its price or even its existence can provide genuine value. But many ads seem to convey no such 'hard' information. Moreover, most advertising firms place a huge emphasis on creativity and human psychology when designing campaigns.

Economists need to explain, therefore, why a rational consumer would be persuaded by an ad that offers nothing but an enticing image or a good laugh. If consumers are rational, they should ignore such obvious gimmicks. If producers are rational, they should not waste money on ads that consumers will ignore.

Companies such as Kodak and McDonald's are willing to spend huge sums convincing people their products are the best around. This explanation was first developed by Phillip Nelson, in a classic paper written in 1974. He argued that a great deal of seemingly wasteful advertisement is in fact intended to send a 'signal' to consumers—that even though a product's quality is hard to verify in advance, it really is one of the best on the market. From this perspective, it does not matter what an advertisement says—so long as consumers can see the firm spending big sums on advertising.

On the whole, economists find Nelson's account convincing. But they believe that he had only half the story: companies need pricing as well as advertising to convey quality to consumers. However, they have not been able to agree how prices and advertising should be related.

Part of the problem is that it is extremely difficult to measure the amount firms spend on advertising 'hard' information about a product's price, say, or how it works, as opposed to their spending on 'signal' advertising of the touchy-feely sort. Moreover, some kinds of products — those whose quality can be verified only through experience—should have more 'signal' advertising. But what is quality? And can an economist tell how easily it can be verified? In fact, two economists recently conducted a different kind of study which suggests that the 'signalling' theory may be wrong. Sridhar Moorthy and Scott Hawkins ran an experiment in which people read foreign-language magazines with ads for unfamiliar brands in several product categories: cookware, overcoats, nasal spray and yoghurt. The ads were real, but the magazines were altered to change the frequency with which they appeared.

Although they did not understand the ads' content, the subjects associated a high frequency of advertising with high quality. However, a control group saw each ad only once, with a message attached telling them how often it appeared in other magazines. Even though the control group could remember the frequency of the ads, they did not assume—as their peers had done—that more ads meant higher quality. This suggests that people do indeed associate more ads with higher quality, but not because they have a sophisticated understanding of the signal companies are trying to send. They simply see lots of ads for a product and want to buy it. The distinction is crucial. If seeing is truly believing, then even low-quality firms may be able to create the impression of high quality by advertising, confounding the signal. Or perhaps not.

Sources: Phillip Nelson, 'Advertising as information', *Journal of Political Economy*, July 1974; Sridhar Moorthy and Scott Hawkins, 'Advertising Repetition and Quality Perceptions', Working Paper, February 1998; *The Economist*, 14 February 1998, p. 92.

products have no such consistent image. Its razors, blades, toiletries and cosmetics are known by many names. Trac II blades in the United States are more widely known worldwide as G-II, and Atra blades are called Contour in Europe and Asia. Silkience hair conditioner is known as Soyance in France, Sientel in Italy and Silkience in Germany. Whether or not a global brand name could have been chosen for Gillette's many existing products is speculative. However, Gillette's current corporate philosophy of globalization provides for an umbrella statement, 'Gillette, the Best a Man Can Get', in all advertisements for men's toiletries products in the hope of providing some common image.

A similar situation exists for Unilever NV that sells a cleaning liquid called Vif in Switzerland, Viss in Germany, Jif in Britain and Greece and Cif in France. This situation is a result of Unilever marketing separately to each of these countries. At this point, it would be difficult for Gillette or Unilever to standardize their brand names since each brand is established in its market. Yet, with such a diversity of brand names it is easy to imagine the problem of coordination and control and the potential competitive disadvantage against a company with global brand recognition.

As discussed earlier, there is a fundamental difference between a multidomestic marketing strategy and a global marketing strategy. One is based on the premise that all markets are culturally different and a company must adapt marketing programmes to accommodate the differences, whereas the other assumes similarities as well as differences and standardizes where there are similarities but adapts where culturally required. Further, it may be possible to standardize some parts of the marketing mix and not others. Also, the same standardized products may be marketed globally but, because of differences in cultures, target segments or stages in the product life cycle, have a different advertising appeal in different markets.[6]

Parker Pen Company sells the same pen in all markets, but advertising differs dramatically from country to country. Print ads in Germany simply show the Parker pen held in a hand that is writing a headline—'This is how you write with precision'. In the United Kingdom, where it is the brand leader, the exotic processes used to make pens, such as gently polishing the gold nibs with walnut chips, is emphasized. In the United States, the ad campaign's theme is status and image. The headlines in the ads are, 'You walk into a boardroom and everyone's naked. Here's how to tell who's boss', and 'There are times when it has to be a Parker'. The company considers the different themes necessary because of the different product images and different customer motives in each market. On the other hand, their most expensive Duofold Centennial pen (about €180, or $200), created to coincide with the company's 100th anniversary and targeted for an upscale market in each country, is advertised the same way throughout the world. The advertising theme is designed to convey a statement about the company as well as the pricey new product.

The seasoned international marketer or advertiser realizes the decision for standardization or modification depends more on motives for buying than on geography. Advertising must relate to motives. If people in different markets buy similar products for significantly different reasons, advertising must focus on such differences. An advertising programme developed by Chanel, the perfume manufacturer, failed in the United States although it was very popular in Europe. Admitting failure in their attempt to globalize the advertising, one fragrance analyst commented, 'There is a French–American problem. The French concept of prestige is not the same as America's.'[7]

Pattern Advertising—Plan Globally, Act Locally

As discussed in Chapter 13, a product is more than a physical item; it is a bundle of satisfactions the buyer receives. This package of satisfactions or utilities includes the primary function of the product along with many other benefits imputed by the values and customs of the culture. Different cultures often seek the same value or benefits from the primary function of a product; for example, the ability of a car to get from point A to point B, a camera to take a picture or a wristwatch to tell time. But while agreeing on the benefit of the primary function of a product, other features and psychological attributes of the item can have significant differences.

Consider the different market-perceived needs for a camera. In the United Kingdom, excellent pictures with easy, foolproof operation are expected by most of the market; in most countries of Europe, the United States and Japan, a camera must take excellent pictures but the camera must also be state-of-the-art in design. In Africa, where penetration of cameras is less than 20 per cent of the households, the concept of picture-taking must be sold. In all three markets, excellent pictures are expected (i.e. the primary function of a camera is demanded) but the additional utility or satisfaction derived from a camera differs among cultures. There are many products that produce these different expectations beyond the common benefit sought by all. Thus, many companies follow a strategy of pattern advertising, a global advertising strategy with a standardized basic message allowing some degree of modification to meet local situations. As the popular saying goes, 'Think Globally, Act Locally'. In this way, some economies of standardization can be realized while specific cultural differences are accommodated.[8]

Evidence indicates that no generalized recommendation can be made about whether to adapt or standardize international advertising. The only answer is 'it depends'. It depends on the product, the culture, use patterns and so on.[9] A review of business practices indicates that few companies adopt either extreme of adapting or standardizing all their advertising efforts and those that have are moving towards a more centralist position; standardize where possible and adapt where necessary, which generally translates into pattern advertising.[10]

Global Advertising and World Brands

Global brands generally are the result of a company that elects to be guided by a global marketing strategy. Global brands carry the same name, same design, and same creative strategy everywhere in the world; Sony, Philips, Marks & Spencer, Jaguar, BMW, Volvo, Coca-Cola, Pepsi-Cola and McDonald's are a few of the global brands. Even when cultural differences make it ineffective to have a standardized advertising programme or a standardized product, a company may have a world brand. Nescafé, the world brand for Nestlé Company's instant coffee, is used throughout the world even though advertising messages and formulation (dark roast and light roast) vary to suit cultural differences. In Japan and the United Kingdom, advertising reflects each country's preference for tea; in France, Germany and Brazil, cultural preferences for ground coffee call for a different advertising message and formulation.[11]

The Colgate-Palmolive Company announced it was decentralizing its advertising; marketing in future would be tailored specifically to local markets and countries. An industry analyst reported that 'There will be little, if any, global advertising'. This appeared to be a reversal for Colgate, one of the first companies to embrace worldwide standardized advertising.[12] The seeming reversal in the earlier policy to decentralize advertising represents what is happening in many companies which initially took extreme positions on standardizing their marketing efforts. Companies have discovered that the idea of complete global standardization is more myth than reality.

As discussed earlier, markets are constantly changing and are in the process of becoming more alike, but the world is still far from being a homogeneous market with common needs

SELLING LEVI'S AROUND THE WORLD

Levi's are sold in more than 70 countries, with different cultural and political aspects affecting advertising appeals. Here are some of the appeals used:

In Indonesia, ads show Levi's-clad teenagers cruising around Dubuque, Iowa, in 1960s convertibles.

In the United Kingdom, ads emphasize that Levi's is an American brand and star an all-American hero, the cowboy, in fantasy Wild West settings.

In Japan, local jeans companies had already positioned themselves as American. To differentiate Levi's, the company positioned itself as legendary American jeans with commercials themed 'Heroes Wear Levi's', featuring clips of cult figures such as James Dean. The Japanese responded—awareness of Levi's in Japan went from 35 per cent to 95 per cent as a result of this campaign.

In Brazil, the market is strongly influenced by fashion trends emanating from the Continent rather than from America. Thus, the ads for Brazil are filmed in Paris, featuring young people, cool amidst a wild Parisian traffic scene.

In Australia, commercials were designed to build brand awareness with product benefits. The lines 'fit looks tight, doesn't feel tight, can feel comfortable all night' and 'a legend doesn't come apart at the seams' highlighted Levi's quality image, and 'since 1850 Levi's jeans have handled everything from bucking broncos . . . ' stressed Levi's unique positioning.

Sources: Adapted from 'Exporting a Legend', *International Advertiser*, November–December 1981; and 'For Levi's, a Flattering Fit Overseas', *Business Week*, 5 November 1990, p. 76.

and wants for all products. Myriad obstacles to strict standardization remain. Nevertheless, the lack of commonality among markets should not deter a marketer from being guided by a global strategy, that is a marketing philosophy that directs products and advertising towards a worldwide rather than a local or regional market, seeking standardization where possible and modifying where necessary. To achieve global advertising huge sums are being spent on worldwide events such as the Olympic Games (see Table 16.1).

Pan-European Advertising

The attraction of a single European market will entice many companies to standardize as much of their promotional effort as possible. As media coverage across Europe expands, it will become more common for markets to be exposed to multiple advertising messages and brand names of the same product. To avoid the confusion that results when a market is exposed to these, as well as for reasons of efficiency, companies will strive for harmony in brand names, advertising and promotions across Europe.[13]

Mars, the confectionery company, traditionally used several brand names for the same product but recently has achieved uniformity by replacing them with a single name. A chocolate bar sold in some parts of Europe under the brand name Raider was changed to Twix, the name used in the United States and the United Kingdom.

Along with changes in behaviour patterns, legal restrictions are gradually being eliminated, and viable market segments across country markets are emerging. While Europe will never be a single homogeneous market for every product, it does not mean that companies should shun the idea of developing European-wide promotional programmes especially for global,

Table 16.1   Big Television Broadcasting Deals in Europe and America

Event	Date	Buyer	€ bn	($ bn)
Olympic Games	1996–2008*	NBC	3.6	(4)
World Cup soccer	2002–2006	Kirch	2.13	(2.36)
NCAA basketball	1995–2002	CBS	1.56	(1.73)
National Football League (NFL)	1995–1998†	Fox	1.43	(1.58)
Olympic Games	1996–2008	EBU	1.3	(1.44)
English Premier League soccer	1997–2001†	BSkyB	0.87	(0.96)
NFL	1995–1998†	ABC	0.83	(0.92)
NFL	1995–1998†	NBC	0.79	(0.87)
National Basketball Association	1995–1998†	NBC	0.68	(0.75)
Dutch Premier League soccer	1996–2004	Sport 7	0.59	(0.65)

*1998 Winter Games bought by CBS.
†Season ending.
Source: Broadcasting & Cable and Kagan World Medias in *The Economist*, 20 July 1996,
p. 18.

European brands and for corporate image. A Pan-European promotional strategy would mean identifying a market segment across all European countries and designing a promotional concept appealing to market segment similarities.

International Market Segmentation and Promotional Strategy

Rather than approach a promotional strategy decision as having to be either standardized or adapted, a company should first identify market segments. Market segments can be defined within country boundaries or across countries. Global market segmentation involves identifying homogeneous market segments across groups of countries.

Procter & Gamble is an example of a company that identified mass market segments across the world and designed brand and advertising concepts that apply to all. The company's shampoo positioning strategy, 'Pro-V vitamin formula strengthens the hair and makes it shine', was developed for the Taiwan market, and then successfully launched in several other countries with only minor adaptation for hair types and languages.[14] L'Oreal's 'It's expensive and I'm worth it' brand position also works well worldwide. Unilever's fabric softener's teddy bear brand concept has worked well across borders, even though the 'Snuggle' brand name changes in some countries; it is *Kuschelweich* in Germany, *Coccolino* in Italy and *Mimosin* in France.[15]

Other companies have identified niche segments too small for country-specific development but, when taken in aggregate, they have become profitable markets. The luxury brand luggage, Vuitton, is an example of a product designed for a niche segment. It is marketed as an exclusive, high-priced, glamorous product worldwide to relatively small segments in most countries.

While there are those who continue to argue the merits of standardization versus adaptation, most will agree that identifiable market segments for specific products exist across country markets, especially in some types of product, and that companies should approach promotional planning from a global perspective, standardize where feasible and adapt where necessary.

CHALLENGES OF INTERNATIONAL ADVERTISING

The growing intensity of international competition, coupled with the complexity of marketing multinationally, demands that the international advertiser function at the highest creative level. Advertisers from around the world have developed their skills and abilities to the point that the advertisements from different countries reveal basic similarities and a growing level of sophistication. To complicate matters further, boundaries are placed on creativity by legal, tax, language, cultural, media, production and cost limitations.

Legal and Tax Considerations

Laws that control comparative advertising vary from country to country in Europe. In Germany, it is illegal to use any comparative terminology; you can be sued by a competitor if you do. Belgium and Luxembourg explicitly ban comparative advertising, whereas it is clearly authorized in the United Kingdom, Sweden, Ireland, Spain and Portugal. The European Commission is issuing several directives to harmonize the laws governing advertising. Many fear that if the laws are not harmonized, member states may close their borders to advertising that does not respect their national rules. The directive covering comparative advertising will allow implicit comparisons that do not name competitors, but will ban explicit comparisons between named products. In Asia, an advertisement showing chimps choosing Pepsi over Coke was banned from most satellite television. The term 'the leading cola' was accepted only in the Philippines.[16]

Advertising on television is strictly controlled in many countries. In Kuwait, the government-controlled TV network allows only 32 minutes of advertising per day, in the evening.[17] Commercials are controlled to exclude superlative descriptions, indecent words, fearful or shocking shots, indecent clothing or dancing, contests, hatred or revenge shots and attacks on competition. It is also illegal to advertise cigarettes, lighters, pharmaceuticals, alcohol, airlines and chocolates or other sweets. In the United States advertising pharmaceuticals is allowed (see Figure 16.3).

Some countries have special taxes that apply to advertising which might restrict creative freedom in media selection. The tax structure in Austria best illustrates how advertising taxation can distort media choice by changing the cost ratios of various media. In federal states, with the exception of Bergenland and Tyrol, there is a 10 per cent tax on ad insertions; for posters, there is a 10–30 per cent tax according to state and municipality. Radio advertising carries a 10 per cent tax, except in Tyrol where it is 20 per cent. In Salzburg, Steiermark, Karnten and Voralbert, there is no tax. There is a uniform tax of 10 per cent throughout the country on television ads. Cinema advertising has a 10 per cent tax in Vienna, 20 per cent in Bergenland and 30 per cent in Steiermark. There is no cinema tax in the other federal states.

Language Limitations

Language is one of the major barriers to effective communication through advertising. The problem involves different languages of different countries, different languages or dialects within one country and the subtler problems of linguistic nuance and vernacular.

Incautious handling of language has created problems in nearly every country. Some examples suffice. Chrysler Corporation was nearly laughed out of Spain when it translated the US theme advertising, 'Dart Is Power'. To the Spanish, the phrase implied that buyers sought but lacked sexual vigour. The Bacardi Company concocted a fruity bitters with a made-up name, 'Pavane', suggestive of French chic. Bacardi wanted to sell the drink in

Figure 16.3   Hard Sell—Direct to Consumer Prescription-drug Advertising in the United States

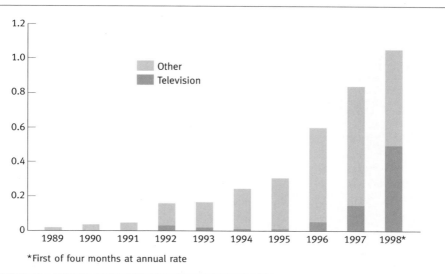

*First of four months at annual rate

Source: 'Competitive Media Reporting', *The Economist*, 8 August 1998, p. 58.

Germany, but 'Pavane' is perilously close to 'pavian', which means 'baboon'. A company marketing tomato paste in the Middle East found that in Arabic the phrase 'tomato paste' translates as 'tomato glue'. In Spanish-speaking countries you have to be careful of words that have different meanings in the different countries. The word 'ball' translates in Spanish as 'bola'. Bola means ball in one country, revolution in another, a lie or fabrication in another and in yet another it is an obscenity.[18] Tropicana brand orange juice was advertised as 'jugo de China' in Puerto Rico, but when transported to Miami's Cuban community it failed. To the Puerto Rican, 'China' translated into orange, but to the Cuban it was 'China' and the Cubans were not in the market for Chinese juice.[19] One Middle East advertisement features a car's new suspension system that, in translation, said the car was 'suspended from the ceiling'. Since there are at least 30 dialects among Arab countries, there is ample room for error. What may appear as the most obvious translation can come out wrong. 'A whole new range of products' in a German advertisement came out as 'a whole new stove of products'.

Low literacy in many countries seriously impedes communications and calls for greater creativity and use of verbal media. Multiple languages within a country or advertising area provide another problem for the advertiser. Even a tiny country such as Switzerland has four separate languages. The melting-pot character of the Israeli population accounts for some 50 languages. A Tel Aviv commentator says that even though Hebrew 'has become a negotiable instrument of daily speech, this has yet to be converted into advertising idiom'. As revealed by one study:

> In industrialized countries such as Canada and Sweden, advertising copy in general contains more writing and technical information, because most consumers have a high level of literacy and education and like to compare technical details and specifications. Comparative shopping practices are limited in Turkey, and the general level of education

377

GOING INTERNATIONAL 16.3

NAMING PROBLEMS

The car industry has had its share of naming problems. Rolls-Royce had to change the name of Silver Mist in Germany when it found out that 'Mist' means 'manure' and is a mild expletive in Germany. Ford's Fiera means 'ugly old woman' in Spanish, and Pinto in Portuguese is slang for a small male organ. General Motors 'Nova' means 'It doesn't go' if pronounced 'no-va' in Spanish speaking countries. American Motors' 'Matador' suggests not only strength, but a 'killer'—not a positive image when traffic fatalities are high. And Esso had difficulties in the Japanese market because, phonetically, 'Esso' means 'stalled car'.

Source: David Ricks, *Big Business Blunders* (Homewood, IL: Dow Jones-Irwin, 1993).

is not that high. Unlike Canada and Sweden most of the advertising copy used by the Turkish agencies is persuasive in nature rather than informative or comparative.[20]

Language translation encounters innumerable barriers that impede effective, idiomatic translation and thereby hamper communication. This is especially apparent in advertising materials. Abstraction, terse writing and word economy, the most effective tools of the advertiser, pose problems for translators. Communication is impeded by the great diversity of cultural heritage and education that exists within countries and that causes varying interpretations of even single sentences and simple concepts. Some companies have tried to solve the translation problem by hiring foreign translators who live in the West, but often this is not satisfactory; both the language and the translator change, so the expatriate in the West is out of touch after a few years. Everyday words have different meanings in different cultures. Even pronunciation causes problems: Wm. Wrigley, Jr., Company had trouble selling Spearmint gum in Germany until it changed the spelling to Speermint.

Cultural Diversity

The problems of communicating to people in diverse cultures is one of the great creative challenges in advertising. Communication is more difficult because cultural factors largely determine the way various phenomena are perceived. If the perceptual framework is different, perception of the message itself differs.

International marketers are becoming accustomed to the problems of adapting from culture to culture. Knowledge of differing symbolisms of colours is a basic part of the international marketer's encyclopaedia. An astute marketer knows that white in Europe is associated with purity but in Asia it is commonly associated with death. The marketer must also be sophisticated enough to know that the presence of black in the West or white in Eastern countries does not automatically connote death. Colour is a small part of the communications package, but if the symbolism in each culture is understood, the marketer has an educated choice of using or not using various colours.

Knowledge of cultural diversity must encompass the total advertising project. Existing perceptions based on tradition and heritage are often hard to overcome. Marketing researchers in Hong Kong found that cheese is associated with *Yeung-Yen* (foreigners) and rejected by some Chinese. The concept of cooling and heating the body is important in Chinese thinking; malted milk is considered heating, while fresh milk is cooling; brandy is sustaining, whisky harmful. A soap commercial featuring a man touching a woman's skin while she bathes, a theme used in some European countries and in the United States, would be rejected in countries where the idea of a man being in the same bathroom with a female would be taboo.

As though it were not enough for advertisers to be concerned with differences among nations, they find subcultures within a country require attention as well. In India, there are several patterns of breakfast eating. The youth of a country almost always constitute a different consuming culture from the older people, and urban dwellers differ significantly from rural dwellers. Besides these differences, there is the problem of changing traditions. In all countries, people of all ages, urban or rural, cling to their heritage to a certain degree but are willing to change some areas of behaviour.[21]

Production and Cost Limitations

Creativity is especially important when a budget is small or where there are severe production limitations, poor-quality printing and a lack of high-grade paper. For example, the poor quality of high-circulation glossy magazines and other quality publications has caused Colgate-Palmolive to depart from its customary heavy use of print media in the West for other media in Eastern Europe.[22] The necessity for low-cost reproduction in small markets poses another problem in many countries. For example, hand-painted billboards must be used instead of printed sheets because the limited number of billboards does not warrant the production of printed sheets. In Western societies, the increasing cost of advertising in television and radio is forcing companies to look for alternative advertising methods. The increasing advertising through sports events is illustrated by the Olympic broadcast rights fees over the years (Figure 16.4).

MEDIA PLANNING AND ANALYSIS

Tactical Considerations

Although nearly every sizeable nation essentially has the same kind of media, there are a number of specific considerations, problems and differences encountered from one nation to another. In international advertising, an advertiser must consider the availability, cost and coverage of the media. Local variations and lack of market data provide areas for additional attention.

Imagine the ingenuity required of advertisers confronted with these situations:

1. TV commercials are sandwiched together in a string of 10–50 commercials within one station break in Brazil.
2. In many countries, national coverage means using as many as 40–50 different media.
3. Specialized media reach small segments of the market only. In some countries of Europe, there are socialist, neutral and other specialized broadcasting systems.
4. In Germany, TV scheduling for an entire year must be arranged by 30 August of the

Figure 16.4   Chariots for Hire—Olympic Broadcast Rights Fees* ($ billion)

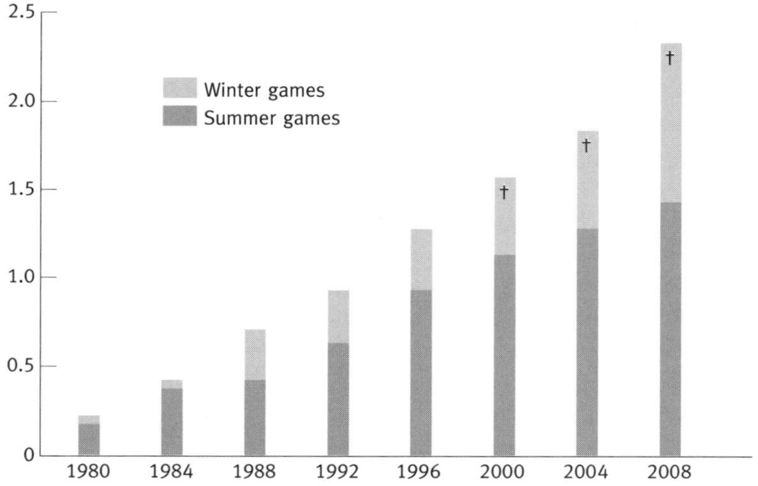

*Rights for 2000–2008 Games negotiated to March 1996; †two years earlier

Source: 'IOC', *The Economist*, 20 July 1996, p. 17.

preceding year, and there is no guarantee that commercials intended for summer viewing will always be run in the specified period.

5. In Vietnam, advertising in newspapers and magazines will be limited to 10 per cent of space and to 5 per cent of time, or three minutes an hour, on radio and TV.[23]

As European Commission directives become effective, many of the European restrictions may be eliminated, or at least harmonized, among the member states.[24]

Availability.   One of the contrasts of international advertising is that some countries have too few advertising media and others have too many. In some countries, certain advertising media are forbidden by government edict to accept some advertising materials. Such restrictions are most prevalent in radio and television broadcasting. In many countries, there are too few magazines and newspapers to run all the advertising offered to them. Conversely, some nations segment the market with so many newspapers that the advertiser cannot gain effective coverage at a reasonable cost. Gilberto Sozzani, head of an Italian advertising agency, comments about his country: 'One fundamental rule. You cannot buy what you want.'

Cost.   Media prices are susceptible to negotiation in most countries. Agency space discounts are often split with the client to bring down the cost of media. The advertiser may find the cost of reaching a prospect through advertising depends on the agent's bargaining ability. The per-contract cost varies widely from country to country. One study showed the cost of reaching a thousand readers in 11 different European countries ranged from €1.43 ($1.58) in Belgium to €5.33 ($5.91) in Italy; in women's service magazines, the page cost per thousand circulation ranged from €2.27 ($2.51) in Denmark to €9.81 ($10.87) in Germany. In some markets, shortages of advertising time on commercial television have caused substantial price increases.[25]

GOING INTERNATIONAL 16.4

TELEPHONE BELLE CINDY GRABBED BY AUSTRIANS

A fevered market has sprung up following the launch of Austrian Post's latest phonecard, which carries an image of the model and aspiring film actress Cindy Crawford in a green swimsuit; 100 000 of the cards, which cost Sch95 ($9), have been produced, and a telephone company spokesman reported that many customers are finding the card impossible to get hold of as post offices have sold out.

Palmers, the Austrian lingerie firm which sponsors the card, said the response had been fantastic. Palmers first sponsored a telephone card using Cindy Crawford in August last year. This showed her modelling a black bra and knickers, and all 100 000 phone cards sold out within three weeks. These cards are now available only at phone card collectors' fairs where they fetch four to five times the original asking price.

After the initial success of the Cindy card, Palmers—which operates across Europe and in the Middle East—sponsored a second card in July using a Danish model named Therese Garga wearing a white brassiere. The response was comparatively poor, however, which is why Palmers returned to the original inspiration. The only subject that has matched the response for Crawford featured the Disney film *The Lion King*.

Company spokesman Angela Pengl said: 'Of all the sponsored cards that the Austrian Post Office produced last year, ours featuring Cindy in a bra and panties was the only one to sell out completely, and that was within a few weeks. It's incredible.' Palmers pays about one schilling for each card, making the phonecard one of the most cost-effective campaigns in European advertising.

A spokesman for Austrian Post, Brigitte Brunner, said: 'Telephone cards are not usually a big part of our business, but at the moment it is the only thing the customers are interested in. I have lost count of how many I have sold'.

Source: *The European*, 12–18 September 1996.

Coverage.   Closely akin to the cost dilemma is the problem of coverage. Two points are particularly important: one relates to the difficulty of reaching certain sectors of the population with advertising and the other to the lack of information on coverage. In many world marketplaces, a wide variety of media must be used to reach the majority of the markets. In some countries, large numbers of separate media have divided markets into uneconomical advertising segments. With some exceptions, a majority of the native population of developing countries cannot be reached readily through the medium of advertising. In Brazil, an exception, television is an important medium with a huge audience. One network, in fact, can reach 90 per cent of Brazil's more than 17 million TV households.

Because of the lack of adequate coverage by any single media in Eastern European countries, it is necessary for companies to resort to a multimedia approach. In the Czech Republic, for example, TV advertising rates are high and unavailable prime-time spots have forced companies to use billboard advertising. Outdoor advertising has become popular and in Prague alone billboards have increased from 50 in 1990 to over 5000 in 1996.[26]

Lack of Market Data.   Verification of circulation or coverage figures is a difficult task. Even though many countries have organizations similar to the Audit Bureau of Circulation, accurate circulation and audience data are not assured. For example, the president of the Mexican national Advertisers Association charged that newspaper circulation figures are 'grossly exaggerated'. He suggested that 'as a rule agencies divide these figures in two and take the result with a grain of salt'. The situation in China is no better: surveys of habits and

GOING INTERNATIONAL 16.5

HOW DO WE MEASURE THE EFFECTIVENESS OF ADVERTISING?

A firm can spend millions of dollars for advertising, and it is only natural to want some feedback of the results of such an expenditure: To what extent did the advertising really pay? Yet, many problems confront the firm trying to measure this.

Most of the methods for measuring effectiveness focus not on sales changes but on how well the communication is remembered, recognized or recalled. Most evaluative methods simply tell which ad is the best among those being appraised. But even though one ad may be found to be more memorable or to create more attention than another, that fact alone gives no assurance of relationship to sales success. A classic example of the dire consequences that can befall advertising people as a result of the inability to directly measure the impact of ads on sales occurred in December 1970:

In 1970, the Doyle Dane Bernbach advertising agency created memorable TV commercials for Alka-Seltzer, such as the 'spicy meatball man', and the 'poached oyster bride'. These won professional awards as the best commercials of the year and received high marks for humour and audience recall. But in December the $22 million (€20 million) account was abruptly switched to another agency. The reason? Alka-Seltzers sales had dropped somewhat. Of course, no one will ever know whether the drop might have been much worse without these notable commercials.

So, how do we measure the value of millions of dollars spent for advertising? Not well. Nor can we determine what is the right amount to spend for advertising, versus what is too much or too little.

Can a business succeed without advertising? Why or why not?

Source: Robert Hartley, *Marketing Mistakes*, 6th edn (New York: Wiley, 1995), p. 134.

penetration are available only for the cities of Beijing, Shanghai and Guangzhou.[27] Radio and television audiences are always difficult to measure, but at least in most countries, geographic coverage is known.

Specific Media Information

An attempt to evaluate specific characteristics of each medium is beyond the scope of this discussion. Furthermore, such information would quickly become outdated because of the rapid changes in the international advertising media field. It may be interesting, however, to examine some of the unique international characteristics of various advertising media.[28] In most instances, the major implications of each variation may be discerned from the data presented.

Newspapers. The newspaper industry is suffering in some countries from lack of competition and choking because of it in others. Most European cities have just one or two major daily newspapers but, in many countries, there are so many newspapers an advertiser has trouble reaching even partial market coverage. Uruguay, population 3 million, has 21 daily newspapers with a combined circulation of 553 000. Norway on the other hand, with a population of more than 4 million has only one national daily morning newspaper. Turkey has 380 newspapers, and an advertiser must consider the political position of each newspaper so the product's reputation is not harmed through affiliations with unpopular positions. Japan has only five national daily newspapers, but the complications of producing a Japanese-language newspaper are such that they each contain just 16–20 pages. Connections are necessary to buy advertising space; *Asahi*, Japan's largest newspaper, has been known to turn down over a million dollars a month in advertising revenue.

Separation between editorial and advertising content in newspapers provides another basis for contrast on the international scene. In some countries, it is possible to buy editorial space for advertising and promotional purposes. The news columns are for sale not only to the government but to anyone who has the money. Since there is no indication that the space is paid for, it is impossible to tell exactly how much advertising appears in a given newspaper.

Magazines.   The use of foreign national consumer magazines by international advertisers has been notably low for many reasons. Few magazines have large circulations or provide dependable circulation figures. Technical magazines are used extensively to promote export goods; but, as in the case of newspapers, paper shortages cause placement problems.

Increasingly, Western publications are publishing overseas editions. *Reader's Digest International* has added a new Russian-language edition to its more than 20 languages. Other print media available in international editions range from *Playboy* to *The Economist*. Advertisers have three new magazines to reach females in China: Hachette Filipacfchi Presse, the French publisher, is expanding Chinese-language editions of *Elle*, a fashion magazine; *Woman's Day* is aimed at China's 'busy modern' woman; and *L'Événement Sportif* is a sports magazine.[29] These media offer alternatives for multinationals as well as for local advertisers.

Radio and Television.   Possibly because of their inherent entertainment value, radio and television have become major communications media in most nations. Most populous areas have television broadcasting facilities. In some markets, such as Japan, television has become almost a national obsession and thus finds tremendous audiences for its advertisers. In China, for example, virtually all homes in major cities have a television and most adults view television and listen to radio daily.[30] Radio has been relegated to a subordinate position in the media race in countries where television facilities are well developed. In many countries, however, radio is a particularly important and vital advertising medium when it is the only one reaching large segments of the population.

Entrepreneurs in the radio–television field have discovered that audiences in commercially restricted countries are hungry for commercial television and radio, and that marketers are eager to bring their messages into these countries. A major study in 22 countries revealed that the majority were favourable towards advertising. Individuals in former communist countries were among the more enthusiastic supporters. In a 22-country survey, Egypt was the only one where the majority of responses were anti-advertising. Only 9 per cent of Egyptians surveyed agreed that many TV commercials are enjoyable, compared to 80 per cent or more in Italy, Uruguay and Bulgaria.[31] Italy, which had no private/local radio or TV until 1976, currently has some 300 privately owned stations.

Satellite and Cable TV.   Of increasing importance in TV advertising is the growth and development of satellite TV broadcasting. Sky Channel, a UK-based commercial satellite TV station, beams its programmes and advertising into most of Europe via cable TV subscribers. New technology now permits households to receive broadcasts directly from the satellite via a dish the 'size of a dinner plate' costing about €315 ($350). This innovation adds possibilities of greater coverage and the ability to reach all of Europe with a single message.[32]

Parts of Asia and Latin America receive TV broadcasts from satellite television networks. Univision and Televisa are two Latin-American satellite television networks broadcasting via a series of affiliate stations in each country to most of the Spanish-speaking world, including the United States. 'Sabado Gigante', a popular Spanish-language programme broadcast by

Univision, is seen by tens of millions of viewers in 16 countries.[33] Star TV, a new Pan-Asian satellite television network, has a potential audience of 2.7 billion people, living in 38 countries from Egypt through India to Japan, and from the Soviet Far East to Indonesia. Star TV was the first to broadcast across Asia but was quickly joined by ESPN and CNN. The first Asian 24-hour all-sports channel was followed by MTV Asia and a Mandarin Chinese-language channel that delivers dramas, comedies, films and financial news aimed at the millions of overseas Chinese living throughout Asia. Programmes are delivered through cable networks but can be received through private satellite dishes.

Direct Mail.   Direct mail is a viable medium in many countries. It is especially important when other media are not available. As is often the case in international marketing, even such a fundamental medium is subject to some odd and novel quirks. Despite some limitations with direct mail, many companies have found it a meaningful way to reach their markets. The Reader's Digest Association has used direct-mail advertising in many countries to successfully market its magazines.

In South-east Asian markets where print media are scarce, direct mail is considered one of the most effective ways to reach those responsible for making industrial goods purchases, even though accurate mailing lists are a problem in Asia as well as in other parts of the world. Industrial advertisers are heavy mail users and rely on catalogues and sales sheets to generate large volumes of international business. Even in Japan, where media availability is not a problem, direct mail is successfully used by marketers such as Nestlé Japan and Dell Computer. To promote its Buitoni fresh chilled pasta, Nestlé is using a 12-page colour direct-mail booklet of recipes, including Japanese-style versions of Italian favourites.[34]

Other Media.   Restrictions on traditional media or their availability cause advertisers to call on lesser media to solve particular local-country problems. The cinema is an important medium in many countries, as are billboards and other forms of outside advertising. Billboards are especially useful in countries with high illiteracy rates.

In Haiti, sound trucks equipped with powerful loudspeakers provide an effective and widespread advertising medium. Private contractors own the equipment and sell advertising space much as a radio station would. This medium overcomes the problems of illiteracy, lack of radio and television set ownership, and limited print media circulation. In Ukraine, where the postal service is unreliable, businesses have found that the most-effective form of direct business-to-business advertising is direct faxing.[35]

SALES PROMOTION

Other than advertising, personal selling and publicity, all marketing activities that stimulate consumer purchases and improve retailer or middlemen effectiveness and cooperation are sales promotions. In-store demonstrations, samples, coupons, gifts, product tie-ins, contests, sweepstakes, sponsorship of special events, such as concerts and fairs, and point-of-purchase displays are types of sales promotion devices designed to supplement advertising and personal selling in the promotional mix. Multinational companies spend millions of dollars to get exposure through big events such as the soccer World Cup (see Table 16.2).

Sales promotions are short-term efforts directed to the consumer and/or retailer to achieve such specific objectives as: (1) consumer–product trial and/or immediate purchase, (2) consumer introduction to the store, (3) gaining retail point-of-purchase displays, (4) encouraging

GOING INTERNATIONAL 16.6

JAPAN TURNS TO MAIL ORDER

The Japanese market is never the easiest to crack, but importers of consumer goods have gained an inside track through catalogue sales. Mail-order shopping or *kojin yunyu*—Japanese for personal imports—is booming. Every day hundreds of consumers can be found turning the pages in the catalogue library at the World Import Mart Building in Ikebukuro in Tokyo.

'The prices are reasonable and you get more choice', said housewife Fuyumi Endo, choosing clothes for her eight-year-old daughter. Despite the soaring yen in the late 1980s, prices of foreign manufactured goods in Japanese stores did not fall. Consumers found it was cheaper to buy direct from catalogues. One of the first arrivals, and still the largest mail-order company exporting to Japan, is US clothing company LL Bean. Around 300 LL Bean packages arrive in Japan every day, and the company has set up a local distribution centre.

More than three million small packages, most of them from mail-order companies, were registered by the postal system last year. The Manufactured Imports Promotion Organization (Mipro) expects a substantial rise this year. The US is by far the biggest mail-order exporter to Japan, followed by Britain and France. Mipro set up the catalogue library, which has catalogues from 1500 companies. In March Mipro hosted an international fair in Tokyo to promote overseas mail-order companies.

Children's clothes are among the most popular products, but European mail-order firms export success across a range of goods. A US journalist said his Japanese wife orders Darjeeling tea for tea ceremony classes from the UK's Fortnum and Mason catalogue because it is cheaper than buying Darjeeling in Japan.

One company was glad it was contracted by Mipro is Scandinavish Glass of Copenhagen, which sells glassware and ceramics. 'We sent some brochures, and it is now a very important part of our business', said spokesman Per Anker. French mail-order clothes firm La Redoute sells through a joint venture with one of Japan's largest catalogue firms, Nissen, which carries several pages of La Redoute's catalogue inside its own. Jean-Michel Laot, La Redoute's export manager, said Japan is perfect for mail-order because of its efficient postal service and strong brand loyalty.

But some mail-order firms still hesitate about going to Japan. Mipro executive director Tadao Yamazaki said: 'Many European companies are worried about the language. But you don't have to put the entire catalogue in Japanese, you just do a few pages explaining how much an item will cost after postage and packing.

Source: *The European*, 28 March–3 April 1996, p. 21.

Table 16.2   World Cup Sponsor Confusion

Eleven Multinationals Paid up to $30 million to be Global Sponsors . . .	*. . . But Eight Companies Paid the French Organizers a Total of $100 million to be 'Suppliers'*
Coca-Cola	Crédit Agricole
Adidas	Danone
Opel	EDS
Mastercard	France Telecom
Canon	Hewlett-Packard
Fujifilm	French Post Office
Gillette	Manpower
JVC	Sybase
McDonald's	
Philips	
Snickers	

Source: Based on FIFA, in *Business Week*, 8 June 1998, p. 19.

PROMOTIONS—WHEN THEY ARE GOOD, THEY ARE VERY GOOD— WHEN THEY ARE BAD, THEY COST LIKE THE DICKENS

Contests, lotteries and all those schemes designed to get the consumer to buy your product for a chance to win a prize can be effective promotions, when they work right. The operative words here are 'work right'. Two recent events, Hoover appliances in London and Pepsi-Cola in the Philippines, didn't exactly 'work right'.

Hoover, the appliance and vacuum cleaner manufacturer, launched a promotion campaign in the United Kingdom and Ireland to build sales and brand awareness. Hoover offered two round-trip flights to Europe or America free with the purchase of $150 worth of Hoover appliances. (The cheapest airline tickets to New York were $750.) The company expected people to be attracted by the free tickets, but didn't expect many to follow through because of restrictions on travel times and hotel accommodations. No way. It didn't take a rocket scientist to figure out the key—buy the least-expensive appliance and go to the States. Over 200 000 did. It cost the company an estimated $72 million (€65 million) to make good on its offer.

Coca-Cola and Pepsi-Cola were fighting for market share and Pepsi needed a boost. 'Number Fever', a cash prize promotion, looked like the winning ticket. It had worked in 10 Latin American countries and it combined the Filipinos' penchant for gambling and the lure of instant wealth. Buyers of Pepsi products would look under the bottle caps for a three-digit number from 001 to 999, to win a cash prize ranging from 1000 pesos (€36/$40) to 1 million pesos (€36 000/$40 000), and a 7-digit security code. Pepsi would announce the winning three digits daily. Although all caps were imprinted with cash prizes, purchasers would not know if they had won until the three-digit number was announced. The more caps they collected, the greater their chance of winning. Over a three-month period, Pepsi seeded 60 winning numbers for cash prizes amounting to a total of 25 million pesos (€0.9 million/$1 million).

Number Fever was an immediate success. Sales and market share of Pepsi products rose and within a month, increased sales covered the $4 million (€3.6 million) in prize money and advertising costs budgeted for the promotion.

At the end of six weeks, Pepsi's market share had risen to 24.9 per cent. The success prompted the company to extend Number Fever for five more weeks. Twenty-five new winning numbers were picked by computer. The consultants were convinced that a non-winning number in the original promotion period would not come up as a winning number in the extension. They were wrong. They announced 349 as the winning number for 26 May.

A jobless man, married with one child, couldn't sleep the night 349 was announced as a winner. He had bottle caps good for 3 million pesos. He dreamed about the house he would buy and the business he might start. There were as many as 800 000 who could be holding 349 from the first contest. Paying the winners would have cost the company $1.6 billion (€1.4 billion). Pepsi's first move was to replace 349 with a new winning number. The claimants organized, lobbied, boycotted, sued and even bombed delivery trucks. Pepsi offered to pay all holders of 349 caps 500 pesos as a compromise. Five hundred thousand came forward to claim the 500 pesos, costing the company $10 million (€9 million). The 349 debacle sapped employee morale, ruined Pepsi's image, scared off potential retail distributors, cost the firm all its market share gains, and nine executives were arrested for swindling. The last news was that the Philippine Supreme Court upheld arrest warrants for nine executives of the Manila subsidiary of PepsiCo accused of refusing to pay all holders of winning bottle caps.

Sources: Adapted from 'Hoover Hopes to Sweep Up Mess from Flights Promotion', Associated Press release, 5 March 1993; 'Pepsi's Philippine Fiasco', *World Press Review*, July 1994, pp. 40–41; 'Pepsi in the Philippines: Putting the Fizz Back', *Crossborder Monitor*, 6 April 1994, p. 8; 'Court Upholds Arrest Warrants', Reuters release, 30 September 1994.

stores to stock the product and (5) supporting and augmenting advertising and personal sales efforts. An example of sales promotion is the African cigarette manufacturer who, in addition to regular advertising, sponsors musical groups and river explorations and participates in local fairs in attempts to make the public aware of the product. Procter & Gamble's introduction of Ariel detergent in Egypt included the 'Ariel Road Show'. The puppet show was taken to local markets in villages where more than half of the Egyptian population still live. The show drew huge crowds, entertained people, told about Ariel's better performance without the use of additives, and sold the brand through a distribution van at a nominal discount. Beside creating brand awareness for Ariel, the road show helped overcome the reluctance of the rural retailers to handle the premium-priced Ariel.[36]

An especially effective promotional tool when the product concept is new or has a very small market share is product sampling. Nestlé Baby Foods faced such a problem in France in its attempt to gain share from Gerber, the leader. The company combined sampling with a novel sales promotion programme to gain brand recognition and to build goodwill.

Most Frenchmen take off for a long vacation in the summertime. They pile the whole family into the car and roam around France, or head for Spain or Italy, staying at well-maintained campgrounds found throughout the country. It's an inexpensive way to enjoy the month-long vacation. However, travelling with a baby still in nappies can be a chore. Nestlé came up with a way to dramatically improve the quality of life for any parent and baby on the road.

Nestlé provides rest-stop structures along the road where parents can feed and change their babies. Sparkling clean Le Relais Bébés are located along main travel routes. Sixty-four hostesses at these rest stops welcome 120 000 baby visits and dispense 600 000 samples of baby food each year. There are free disposable nappies, a changing table and high chairs for the babies to sit in during meals.[37] A strong tie between Nestlé and French mothers developed as a result of Le Relais Bébé. The most-recent market research survey showed an approval rating of 94 per cent and Nestle's share of market has climbed to more than 43 per cent—close to a 24 share-point rise in less than seven years.

As is true in advertising, the success of a promotion may depend on local adaptation. Major constraints are imposed by local laws which may not permit premiums or free gifts to be given. Some countries' laws control the amount of discount given at retail, others require permits for all sales promotions and in at least one country no competitor is permitted to spend more on a sales promotion than any other company selling the product. Effective sales promotions can enhance the advertising and personal selling efforts and, in some instances, may be effective substitutes when environmental constraints prevent full utilization of advertising.[38]

GLOBAL ADVERTISING AND THE COMMUNICATIONS PROCESS

Promotional activities (advertising, personal selling, sales promotions and public relations) are basically a communications process. All the attendant problems of developing an effective promotional strategy in domestic marketing plus all the cultural problems discussed earlier must be overcome to have a successful international promotional programme. A major consideration for foreign marketers is to ascertain that all constraints (cultural diversity, media limitations, legal problems and so forth) are controlled so the right message is communicated to and received by prospective consumers. International communications may fail for a variety of reasons: a message may not get through because of media inadequacy, the message may be received by the intended audience but not be understood because of different cultural

Figure 16.5   The International Communication Process

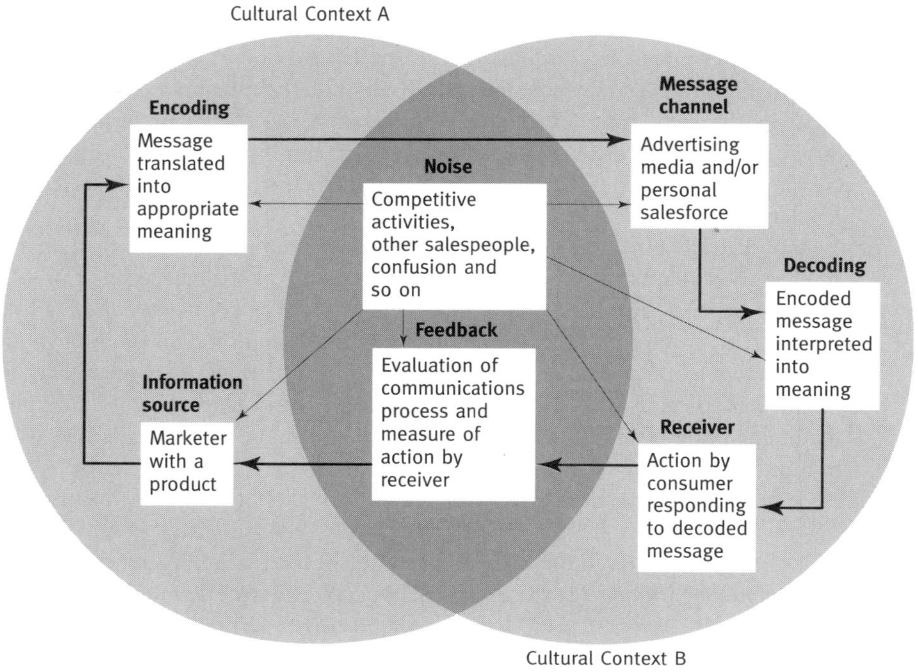

Cultural Context A

Encoding
Message translated into appropriate meaning

Noise
Competitive activities, other salespeople, confusion and so on

Message channel
Advertising media and/or personal salesforce

Decoding
Encoded message interpreted into meaning

Feedback
Evaluation of communications process and measure of action by receiver

Information source
Marketer with a product

Receiver
Action by consumer responding to decoded message

Cultural Context B

interpretations or the message may reach the intended audience and be understood but have no effect because the marketer did not correctly assess the needs and wants of the target market.

The effectiveness of promotional strategy can be jeopardized by so many factors that a marketer must be certain no influences are overlooked. Those international executives who understand the communications process are better equipped to manage the diversity they face in developing an international promotional programme.

In the communications process, each of the seven identifiable segments can ultimately affect the accuracy of the process. As illustrated in Figure 16.5, the process consists of: (1) an information source—an international marketing executive with a product message to communicate; (2) encoding—the message from the source converted into effective symbolism for transmission to a receiver; (3) a message channel—the salesforce and/or advertising media which conveys the encoded message to the intended receiver; (4) decoding—the interpretation by the receiver of the symbolism transmitted from the information source; (5) receiver—consumer action by those who receive the message and are the target for the thought transmitted; (6) feedback—information about the effectiveness of the message which flows from the receiver (the intended target) back to the information source for evaluation of the effectiveness of the process; and, to complete the process; and (7) noise—uncontrollable and unpredictable influences such as competitive activities and confusion detracting from the process and affecting any or all of the other six steps.

Unfortunately, the process is not as simple as just sending a message via a medium to a receiver and being certain that the intended message sent is the same one perceived by the receiver. In Figure 16.5, the communications-process steps are encased in Cultural Context A and Cultural Context B to illustrate the influences complicating the process when the message is encoded in one culture and decoded in another. If not properly considered, the different cultural contexts can increase the probability of misunderstandings. According to one researcher, effective communication demands that there exist a psychological overlap between the sender and the receiver; otherwise a message falling outside the receiver's perceptual field may transmit an unintended meaning. It is in this area that even the most experienced companies make blunders.[39]

Most promotional misfires or mistakes in international marketing are attributable to one or several of these steps not properly reflecting cultural influences and/or a general lack of knowledge about the target market. A review of some of the points discussed in this chapter serves to illustrate this. The information source is a marketer with a product to sell to a specific target market. The product message to be conveyed should reflect the needs and wants of the target market; however, as many previous examples have illustrated, the marketer's perception of market needs and actual market needs do not always coincide. This is especially true when the marketer relies more on the self-reference criterion (SRC) than on effective research. It can never be assumed that 'if it sells well in one country, it will sell in another!' Bicycles designed and sold in the United States to consumers fulfilling recreational-exercise needs are not as effectively sold for the same reasons in a market where the primary use of the bicycle is transportation. From the onset of the communications process, if basic needs are incorrectly defined, communications fail because an incorrect or meaningless message is received even though the remaining steps in the process are executed properly.

The encoding step causes problems even with a proper message. At this step such factors as colour, values, beliefs and tastes can cause the international marketer to symbolize the message incorrectly. For example, the marketer wants the product to convey coolness so the colour green is used; however, people in the tropics might decode green as dangerous or associate it with disease. Another example of the encoding process misfiring was a perfume presented against a backdrop of rain which, for Europeans, symbolized a clean, cool, refreshing image, but to Africans was a symbol of fertility. The ad prompted many viewers to ask if the perfume was effective against infertility.

Message channels must be carefully selected if an encoded message is to reach the consumer. Media problems are generally thought of in terms of the difficulty in getting a message to the intended market. Problems of literacy, media availability and types of media create problems in the communications process at this step. Errors such as using television as a medium when only a small percentage of an intended market is exposed to TV, or using print media for a channel of communications when the majority of the intended users cannot read, are examples of ineffective media channel selection in the communications process. Decoding problems are generally created by improper encoding, causing such errors as a translation that was supposed to be decoded as 'hydraulic ram' but was instead decoded as 'wet sheep'.[40]

Decoding errors may also occur accidentally. In some cases, the intended symbolism has no meaning to the decoder. One soft drink manufacturer's advertisement promised a thirst-quenching reward based on the concepts 'Glacier Fresh' or 'Avalanche of Taste' in a part of the world where wintry mountain temperatures are an unknown experience. Errors at the receiver end of the process generally result from a combination of factors: an improper message resulting from incorrect knowledge of use patterns, poor encoding producing a meaningless message, poor media selection that does not get the message to the receiver or inaccurate decoding by the receiver so that the message is garbled or incorrect.

SOME ADVERTISING MISSES AND NEAR-MISSES

When translating an advertisement into another language, several missteps are possible: some words may be euphemisms in another language, a literal translation does not convey the intended meaning, phonetic problems may result in brand names sounding like a different word or symbols become inappropriate or project an unintended message. Here are a few examples that have shown up on advertisements.

Incorrect translation of phrases
   Stepping stone translated into *stumbling block.*
   Car wash translated into *car enema.*
   High rated translated into *over rated.*
   On leather translated into *naked.*

Phonetic problems with brand names
   Bardok sounds like the word for brothel in Russian.
   Misair sounds like the word for misery in French.

Symbols
   Owl used in an advertisement for India. Owl is bad luck there.
   Elephant used in an ad for India was an African elephant, not Indian.

Unintended message
   Soiled clothes on left—soap in middle—clean clothes on right. Fine, unless you read from right to left. Then the ad seems to say: take clean clothes, use our soap, and they will be soiled.

   Telephone company ad in the Middle East showing executive talking on telephone with his feet on the desk. You don't sit in a way that would show the soles of your shoes to anyone.

Source: Compilation by the authors.

Finally, the feedback step of the communications process is important as a check on the effectiveness of the other steps. Companies that do not measure their communications efforts are apt to allow errors of source, encoding, media selection, decoding or receiver to continue longer than necessary. In fact, a proper feedback system allows a company to correct errors before substantial damage occurs.

In addition to the problems inherent in the steps outlined, the effectiveness of the communications process can be impaired by noise. Noise comprises all other external influences such as competitive advertising, other sales personnel and confusion at the receiving end that can detract from the ultimate effectiveness of the communications. Noise is a disruptive force interfering with the process at any step and is frequently beyond the control of the sender or the receiver. The significance is that one or all steps in the process, cultural factors, or the marketer's SRC, can affect the ultimate success of the communication. In designing an international promotional strategy, the international marketer can effectively use this model as a guide to help assure all potential constraints and problems are considered so that the final communication received and the action taken correspond with the intent of the source.

THE ADVERTISING AGENCY

Just as manufacturing firms have become international, US, Japanese and European advertising agencies are expanding internationally to provide sophisticated agency assistance worldwide. Local agencies also have expanded as the demand for advertising services by MNCs has developed. Thus, the international marketer has a variety of alternatives available. In most commercially significant countries, an advertiser has the opportunity to employ (1) a local domestic agency, (2) its company-owned agency or (3) one of the multinational advertising agencies with local branches.

A local domestic agency may provide a company with the best cultural interpretation in situations where local modification is sought, but the level of sophistication can be weak. Another drawback of local agencies is the difficulty of coordinating a worldwide campaign. One drawback of the company-owned agency is the possible loss of local input when it is located outside the area and has little contact within the host country. The best compromise is the multinational agency with local branches because it has the sophistication of a major agency with local representation. Further, the multinational agency with local branches is better able to provide a coordinated worldwide advertising campaign. This has become especially important for firms doing business in Europe. With the interest in global or standardized advertising, many agencies have expanded to provide worldwide representation. Many companies with a global orientation employ one, or perhaps two, agencies to represent them worldwide.

Compensation arrangements for advertising agencies throughout the world are based on 15 per cent commissions. However, agency commission patterns throughout the world are not as consistent as they are in Europe or the United States; in some countries, agency commissions vary from medium to medium. Services provided by advertising agencies also vary greatly but few foreign agencies offer the full services found in Western agencies.

INTERNATIONAL CONTROL OF ADVERTISING

European Community officials are establishing directives to provide controls on advertising as cable and satellite broadcasting expands. Deception in advertising is a major issue because most member countries have different interpretations of what constitutes a misleading advertisement. Demands for regulation of advertising aimed at young consumers is a trend appearing in both industrialized and developing countries.

Decency and the blatant use of sex in advertisements are also receiving public attention. One of the problems in controlling decency and sex in ads is the cultural variations around the world. An ad perfectly acceptable to a Westerner may be very offensive to someone from the United States or, for that matter, a Spaniard. Standards for appropriate behaviour as depicted in advertisements vary from culture to culture. Regardless of these variations, there is growing concern about decency, sex and ads that demean women and men.

The difficulty that business has with self-regulation and restrictive laws is that sex can be powerful in some types of advertisements. European advertisements for Häagen-Dazs, a premium ice cream, and LapPower, a Swedish laptop computer company, received criticism for their ads as being too sexy. Häagen-Dazs's ad shows a couple, in various stages of undress, in an embrace feeding ice cream to one another. Some British editorial writers and radio commentators were outraged. One commented that 'the ad was the most blatant and inappropriate use of sex as a sales aid'.[41] The ad for LapPower personal computers that the Stockholm Business Council on Ethics condemned featured the co-owner of the company with an 'inviting smile and provocative demeanour displayed'. (She was bending over a LapPower computer in a low-cut dress.)

The bottom line for both these companies was increased sales. In the United Kingdom, sales soared after the 'Dedicated to Pleasure' ads appeared, and in Sweden the co-owner stated

GOING INTERNATIONAL 16.9

HARMONIZATION OF EC RULES FOR CHILDREN'S ADVERTISEMENTS

Creating one advertising campaign for the European market is almost impossible with the plethora of rules that govern children's advertising. One estimate is that in all of Europe there are at least 50 different laws restricting advertising to children. Here are some samples.

■ In the Netherlands, confectionery ads must not be aimed at children, can't be shown before 8 p.m. or feature children under the age of 14. Further, a toothbrush must appear on the screen, either at the bottom during the entire spot or filling the whole screen for the last 1½ seconds.
■ War toys cannot be advertised in Spain or Germany.
■ French law prohibits children from being presenters of a product or to appear without adults. A Kellogg Company spot that runs in the UK featuring a child assigning a different day to each box could not be used in France.
■ Sweden prohibits TV spots aimed at children under 12 and no commercials of any kind can be shown before, during or after children's programmes. It's interesting to note that Sweden passed the law at least a year before commercial television was permitted.

Look for many of these laws to be struck down and replaced with EC-wide rules. Advertisers are concerned that the harmonization of laws governing children's ads may be too restrictive and through the EAAA (European Association of Advertising Agencies) they have proposed a 12-point self-regulatory code. The code allows children to appear in ads but not verbally endorse a product or act as presenters. Children could not request products or make product comparisons in ads but could handle or consume the product.

Source: Adapted from Laurel Wentz, 'Playing By the Same Rules', *Advertising Age*, 2 December 1991, p. S-2.

that 'Sales are increasing daily'. Whether laws are passed or the industry polices itself, there is an international concern about advertising and its effect on people's behaviour.

The advertising industry is sufficiently concerned with the negative attitudes of consumers and governments and with the poor practices of some advertisers that the International Advertising Association and other national and international industry groups have developed a variety of self-regulating codes. Sponsors of these codes feel that unless the advertisers themselves come up with an effective framework for control, governments will intervene. This threat of government intervention has spurred interest groups in Europe to develop codes to ensure that the majority of ads conform to standards set for 'honesty, truth and decency'. In those countries where the credibility of advertising is questioned and in those where the consumerism movement exists, the creativity of the advertiser is challenged.[42]

In many countries, there is a feeling that advertising and especially TV advertising, is too powerful and persuades consumers to buy what they do not need. South Korea, for example, has threatened to ban advertising of bottled water because the commercials may arouse public mistrust of tap water.[43]

SUMMARY

Global advertisers face unique legal, language, media and production limitations in every market that must be considered when designing a promotional mix. As the world and its markets become more sophisticated, there is greater emphasis on international marketing strategy. The current debate among marketers is the effectiveness of standardized versus modified advertising for culturally varied markets. And, as competition increases and markets expand, greater emphasis is being placed on global brands and/or image recognition.

The most logical conclusion seems to be that, when buying motives and company objectives are the same for various countries, the advertising orientation can be the same. When they vary from nation to nation, the advertising effort will have to reflect these variations. In any case, variety in media availability, coverage and effectiveness will have to be taken into consideration in the advertiser's plans. If common appeals are used, they may have to be presented by a radio broadcast in one country, by cinema in another, and by television in still a third.

A skilled advertising practitioner must be sensitive to the environment and alert to new facts about the market. It is also essential for success in international advertising endeavours to pay close attention to the communications process and the steps involved.

QUESTIONS

1. 'Perhaps advertising is the side of international marketing with the greatest similarities from country to country throughout the world. Paradoxically, despite its many similarities, it may also be credited with the greatest number of unique problems in international marketing.' Discuss.
2. Discuss the difference between advertising strategy when a company follows a multidomestic strategy rather than a global market strategy.
3. With satellite TV able to reach many countries, discuss how a company can use satellite TV and deal effectively with different languages, different cultures, and different legal systems.
4. Outline some of the major problems confronting an international advertiser.
5. Defend either side of the proposition that advertising can be standardized for all countries.
6. Review the basic areas of advertising regulation.
7. How can advertisers overcome the problems of low literacy in their markets?

8. What special media problems confront the international advertiser?
9. Discuss the reason for pattern advertising.
10. Will the ability to broadcast advertisements over TV satellites increase or decrease the need for standardization of advertisements? What are the problems associated with satellite broadcasting? Comment.
11. 'Foreign newspapers cannot be considered homogeneous advertising entities.' Elaborate.
12. What is sales promotion and how is it used in international marketing?
13. Show how the communications process can help an international marketer avoid problems in international advertising.
14. Take each of the steps of the communications process and give an example of how cultural differences can affect the final message received.
15. Discuss the problems created because the communications process is initiated in one cultural context and ends in another.

REFERENCES

1. Laurent Gallissot, 'The Cultural Significance of Advertising: A General Framework of the Cultural Analysis of the Advertising Industry in Europe', *International Sociology*, March 1994, pp. 13–28.

2. Jean-Claude Usunier, *Marketing Across Cultures* (Hemel Hempstead: Prentice-Hall , 1996).

3. Michael G. Harvey, 'Point of View: A Model to Determine Standardization of the Advertising Process in International Markets', *Journal of Advertising Research*, July–August 1993, pp. 57–63.

4. Isabelle Maignan, 'International Advertising: Standardization or Localization?', *Advances in Marketing, Proceedings of the Southwestern Marketing Association 1994*, pp. 384–392; and Nigel Piercy, 'Marketing Implementation: The Implications of Marketing Paradigm Weakness for the Strategy Execution Process', *Journal of the Academy of Marketing Science*, vol. 26, no. 3, 1998, pp. 222–236.

5. Theodore Levitt, 'The Globalization of Markets', *Harvard Business Review*, May–June 1983, pp. 92–102.

6. Siva Balasubramanian and V. Kumar, 'Explaining Variations in the Advertising & Promotional Costs/Sales Ratio: A Reanalysis', *Journal of Marketing*, vol. 61, no. 1, 1997, pp. 85–92.

7. Penelope Rowlands, 'Global Approach Doesn't Always Make Scents,', *Advertising Age*, 17 January 1994, p. I-1.

8. 'The Money in the Message', *The Economist*, 14 February 1998, p. 92.

9. For the results of a comprehensive study addressing the issue of product and promotion adaptations, see S. Tamer Cavusgil and Shaoming Zou, 'Product and Promotion Adaptation in Export Ventures: An Empirical Investigation', *Journal of International Business Studies*, Third Quarter 1993, pp. 479–506.

10. 'Estee's Many Faces', *Fortune*, 25 May 1998, pp. 48–52.

11. Carla Rapoport, 'Nestlé's Brand Building Machine', *Fortune*, 19 September 1994, pp. 147–156.

12. 'How Colgate-Palmolive Crafts Ad Strategies in Eastern Europe', *Crossborder Monitor*, 2 March 1994, p. 8.

13. Juliana Koranteng, 'EU Membership Spurs New Ads', *Advertising Age*, 23 January 1995, p. 10.

14. John Wade, 'PG Sees Success in Policy of Transplanting Ad Ideas', *Advertising Age*, 19 July 1993, p. I-2.

15. Ashish Banerjee, 'Global Campaigns Don't Work; Multinationals Do', *Advertising Age*, 18 April 1994, p. 23.

16. 'Pepsi Spots Banned in Asia', *Advertising Age International*, 21 March 1994, p. I-2.

17. 'Satellite Bans Signal Worry: Western Channels Program with Caution in Middle East', *Advertising Age*, 6 May 1994, p. 16.

18. Roger E. Axtell, *The Do's and Taboos of International Trade* (New York: Wiley, 1994), p. 221; and Robert Hartley, *Marketing Mistakes*, 6th edn (New York: Wiley, 1995).

19. 'Slips of the Tongue Result in Classic Marketing Errors', *Advertising Age*, 20 June 1993, p. I-5.

20. Erdener Kaynak and Pervez Ghauri, 'A Comparative Analysis of Advertising Practices in Unlike Environments: a Study of Agency–Client Relationship', *International Journal of Advertising*, vol. 5, 1986, pp. 121–146, 127.

21. 'Companies Face Advertising Restrictions', *Business Eastern Europe*, 21 March 1994, p. 1; and 'How Pepsi Outfoxed Coke in India', *Fortune*, 27 April 1998, p. 34.

22. 'How Colgate-Palmolive Crafts Ad Strategies in Eastern Europe', *Crossborder Monitor*, 2 March 1994, p. 8.

23. For additional restrictions imposed by Vietnam, see 'Selling to Vietnam's Masses', *Business Asia*, 13 February 1995, pp. 1–2.

24. 'EU to Fine Offenders', *The Wall Street Journal*, 6 July 1994, p. A-15; and 'Competitive Media Reporting', *The Economist*, 8 August 1998, p. 58.

25. 'Study: Pan Euro TV Not a Hot Commodity', *Advertising Age*, 25 February 1991, p. 32.

26. 'Czech Republic: Billboards Gain Momentum', *Business Eastern Europe*, 7 March 1994.

27. 'Media Madness', *Business China*, 11 July 1994, p. 7.

28. Singapore has very restrictive legislation governing the use of media. See, for example, Ian Stewart, 'Singapore Attracts Media Despite Rules', *Advertising Age*, 20 February 1995, p. I-6.

29. 'Glamour and Glitz Sparks a Magazine Blitz', *The Wall Street Journal*, 27 May 1994, p. B-1.

30. 'Advertising Spending Expands: Going Slick', *Business China*, 11 July 1994, pp. 6–7.

31. Laurel Wentz, 'Major Global Study Finds Consumers Support Ads', *Advertising Age*, 11 October 1993, p. I-1.

32. Shawn Tully, 'Bad Box Office', *Fortune*, 24 January 1994, p. 24.

33. Jeffrey D. Zbar, 'Latin Pay TV Shines as Gold

Advertising: Standardization vs. Adaptation

Advertising: standardization vs. Adaptation

International marketers strive for efficiency in their advertising—they standardize where possible and adapt according to cultural preferences.

Even a standardized product like perfumes need adaptations in marketing.

Source: Svende Hollensen, *Global Marketing: A Market Responsive Approach* (London: Prentice-Hall, 1998), Plate 6, Figure 6.10.

MTV claims to reach more than 100 million Asians and Latin Americans mixing American music with local acts. Here in India and Brazil.

Source: *Business Week*, 23 June 1997, p. 23.

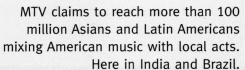

Source: *Business Week*, 9 February 1997, p. 50.

You need a different marketing message when selling toys in Asia, where parents are more concerned with the educational values than play and fun.

Coke uses pricing as one of the marketing slogans in India.

Source: *Business Week*, 21 October 1996, p. 31.

Nescafé uses different advertising and packing for each market since one campaign cannot address market differences. The only constant is the Nescafé brand name.

In Israel, Nestlé faced a unique problem; Nescafé was used generically for instant coffee. Before Nescafé the Israeli market had been exposed only to low-quality powdered coffee. To overcome the generic connotation of Nescafé, whenever Nescafé was mentioned it was always presented as 'Nescafé of Nestlé'.

In Japan, principally a tea-drinking country, the market has to be converted not just to coffee but to instant coffee.

Mine for Ads', *Advertising Age International*, 20 September 1994, p. I-19.

34. David Kilburn, 'Direct Mail Defies Japan's Ad Recession', *Advertising Age International*, 18 April 1994, p. I-8.

35. 'Advertising in Ukraine', *Business Eastern Europe*, 4 April 1994, pp. 8–9.

36. Mahmoud Aboul-Fath and Loula Zaklama, 'Ariel High Suds Detergent in Egypt—A Case Study', *Marketing and Research Today*, May 1992, p. 134.

37. 'European Prototype Shows Credible Communication with Consumer Is Key to Future, Nestlé Exec Says', *Advertising Age*, 25 October 1993, p. S-6.

38. See, for example, 'Unilever Takes a Promo Across Europe's Borders', *Crossborder Monitor*, 18 January 1995, p. 8.

39. Sudhir H. Kale, 'How National Culture, Organizational Culture and Personality Impact Buyer–Seller Interactions', in Pervez Ghauri and Jean-Claude Usunier (eds), *International Business Negotiations* (Oxford: Pergamon, 1996).

40. Gary P. Ferraro, *The Cultural Dimension of International Business*, 2nd edn (Englewood Cliffs, NJ: Prentice-Hall, 1994), p. 43.

41. 'No Sexy Sales Ads, Please—We're Brits and Swedes', *Fortune*, 21 October 1991, p. 13.

42. Nowhere is there greater need for self-control in advertising than in China. See, for example, 'Advertising in China: Hard Sell', *The Economist*, 4 March 1995, pp. 67–68.

43. Yoo-Lim Lee, 'South Korea Threatens to Pull Plug on Water Ads', *Advertising Age*, 17 April 1995, p. I-6.

CHAPTER

17

Personal Selling and Negotiations

Chapter Learning Objectives

What you should learn from Chapter 17

- The importance of relationship in selling.
- Understanding the nuances of cross-cultural communications.
- The attributes of each classification of international sales personnel.
- The problems unique to selecting and training foreign sales staffs.
- The changes in future personnel selection that are a result of global marketing.
- The importance of skill in a foreign language.
- The factors influencing cross-cultural negotiation.
- The art of international sales negotiation.

There are four ways of achieving marketing communication: advertising, sales promotions, personal selling and public relations. Cultural differences as well as the type of product have a major impact on how an optimal mix is found among the above mentioned four ways to achieve the objectives of a company. People who want to take into account cultural differences have to be relationship centred rather than purely deal-centred.[1]

The salesperson provides a company's most direct contact with the customer and, in the eyes of most customers, the salesperson is the company. As the presenter of the company's offerings and gatherer of customer information, the salesperson is the final link in the culmination of a company's marketing and sales effort.

The tasks of building, training, compensating and motivating an international marketing group generate unique problems at every stage of management and development. This chapter discusses the importance of communications and negotiations in building marketing relationships with international customers.

SELLING IN INTERNATIONAL MARKETS

Increased global competition coupled with the dynamic and complex nature of international business increases the need for closer ties with both customers and suppliers. Selling in international marketing, built on effective communications between the seller and buyer, focuses on building long-term alliances rather than treating each sale as a one-time event.[2] This approach is becoming increasingly important for successful international marketers, especially in industrial buyer–seller interactions.[3] In personal selling, persuasive arguments are presented directly in a face-to-face relationship between sellers and potential buyers. To be effective, salespeople must be certain that their communication and negotiation skills are properly adapted to a cross-cultural setting.

In many countries a low status is associated with selling. It is associated with the negative connotation of taking money out of people rather than usefully bringing products and services to them. Seller status can also be associated with a particular group of people, e.g. Chinese, Dutch or Lebanese. In this perception, the seller's role is to convince and show the buyer the worth of the product on offer. In marketing, however, one of the seller's roles is to recognize the customer's needs and make them known to his or her company. The style of selling is often related to national culture, but it also depends upon the personality of the salesperson and the type of industry. Selling styles can also depend upon which type of results or achievements are sought, for example, whether it is to win a new customer or maintaining an old relationship. According to Usunier, when preparing arguments, a salesperson has two main concerns: one is for the customers and their needs, the other is for achieving the sales.[4] This is illustrated in Figure 17.1.

If we separate the seller's role from that of the negotiator, the role of the salesperson is mainly persuasion. There are, however, differences between persuasion and rather insistent and annoying behaviour. The main issue here is to understand what arguments will be best and quickest to persuade a particular customer.

In addition to the above factors, the two main components of personal selling are content and style. Content refers to the substantive aspects of the interaction for which the buyer and the seller come together. It includes suggesting, offering and negotiating. Style refers to the rituals, format, mannerisms and ground rules that the buyer and the seller follow in their encounter. A satisfactory interaction between the buyer and the seller is contingent upon buyer–seller compatibility with respect to both the content and the style of communication. The level of this compatibility is determined by cultural and personality factors.[5] The

Figure 17.1   Selling Orientations

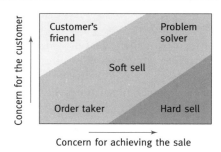

Source: Jean-Claud Usunier, *Marketing Across Cultures* (Hemel Hempstead: Prentice-Hall, 1996), p. 464.

effectiveness of personal selling in international marketing is influenced by a number of factors such as: the nature of salesperson–customer relationship, the behaviour of the salesperson, the resources of the salesperson and the nature of the customer's buying task, as illustrated by Figure 17.2.

The Nature of Salesperson–Customer Relationship.   The salesperson–customer relationship is very important in international marketing as keeping a salesforce in a foreign market means that the company is concerned about the continuity in the relationship with its customers and that it wants to meet people face-to-face rather than through printed material and advertising. The relationship development thus becomes very important. The salesperson has to develop a relationship of trust and friendship with its customers. In most relationships one party is more dominant than the other, this is also true in salesperson–customer relationship.

   Here the salespersons should seek to create a balance in this power/dependence situation. Depending on the above and the nature of the relationship, the parties perceive it as cooperative or conflicting. This issue is directly related to the bargaining power of the parties. The salesperson's job is to drive the relationship towards a cooperative one. The nature of this relationship and willingness to cooperate also depends on what the parties expect from each other in the future. The more they anticipate a future beneficial interaction, the more the relationship is improved.

Behaviour of the Salesperson.   The behaviour of the salesperson in international marketing interaction is highly dependent upon his or her awareness of the local culture, values and norms. Due to this, companies normally use a local salesforce. Whether the salesperson is an expatriate or a local, the sales message, approach and behaviour to the customer should be adapted in terms of language, level of argument and local norms. A relationship orientation instead of a one-shot deal orientation is essential in interaction with customers. In fact, this is often the main reason behind having a salesforce. Salespersons should also use the influential techniques mentioned earlier and in the negotiation section of this chapter. One should be aware that these techniques can be different in different markets, depending upon culture, type of product and company.

Figure 17.2   Factors Influencing the Effectiveness of Personal Selling

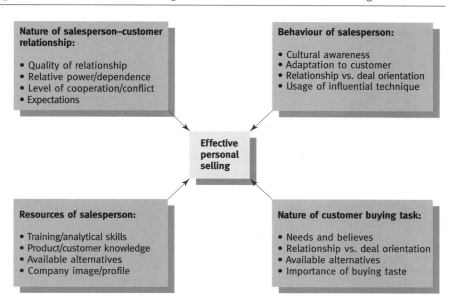

Resources of the Salesperson.   The salesperson to be used in international marketing needs to be trained not only for a particular market/culture but also for general skills such as analytical techniques and negotiation. These skills are essential for international marketing activities and for developing relationships with customers. The salesforce should be fully aware of the company's products and customer's needs and how these two could be matched together. A holistic view of the company capabilities and resources is essential for representing the company fully and efficiently. The salesperson should have full knowledge of the market and customer segmentation, not only of existing customers. Having a full picture of all available alternatives is a good resource which helps customer relationships. The image and positioning of a company in a particular market is of the utmost importance and is good baggage for the salesperson. There should be some consistency in the company image and the message a salesperson is taking to its customers.

Nature of Customer's Buying Task.   One of the factors, external to the salesperson, is the nature and characteristic of the customer's buying task. Although it is beyond the salesperson's control, he or she can in fact influence it. One way is to make the customer believe that there is a perfect match between his or her needs and what the salesperson is offering. Another way is to work with the customer in defining those needs. The relationship orientation from both sides is thus crucial, as it can allow the salesperson to get involved at an early stage of the customer's buying process. The number of alternatives available to customers would influence this aspect. The more options a customer has, the harder the salesperson has to work to convince the customer. The importance of the buying task in the customer's organization is also valuable information a salesperson should have. The more important the buying task, the earlier the customer should be directed towards relationship orientation, which will lead to an earlier involvement of the sales organization in the customer's internal decision making.

'TUBELESS TYRES YOU SAID . . .'

A consumer bought a leading European make of tyre for his car. He asked his garage to fit the tyres. In fact they fitted tubeless tyres since they were supposed to be cheaper (as they did not need air chambers). These tyres, however, kept deflating. When complaining for the first time, the customer was told by the garage to be slightly more careful in inflating the tyres. They had to be reinflated roughly twice a week. The customer contacted his garage again but was merely told that it 'didn't usually happen'. The customer asked if the tyre manufacturer would take back the defective tyres but the garage told him that was impossible and that in any case the tyres did at least stay inflated for a couple of days.

Finally, after going backwards and forwards several times, the customer had air chambers put into the tyres. The problem immediately ceased. When he spoke to his garage, they informed him that the wheel rims had warped slightly owing to the 30 000 miles (48 000 km) that the car had done. Other cars (the garage mentioned a German make) had rims made out of a thicker steel which was more resistant and therefore did not warp. Such a car could have tubeless tyres fitted successfully, whatever its age. The customer asked the garage to pass on this information to the tyre manufacturer so that it could inform tyre centres which cars were not suitable for tubeless tyres after a certain mileage had been covered. The garage said that this was impossible.

The information was not passed on. Tubeless tyres continue to deflate in a fair number of cases. Customers either fit air chambers or buy a different car . . . or they change their make of tyre.

Source: Jean-Claude Usunier, *Marketing across Cultures* (Hemel Hempstead, Prentice-Hall, 1996).

The International Selling Sequence

Knowing the customer in international sales means more than understanding the customer's product needs. It includes knowing the customer's culture. A cosmopolitan salesperson will become more adept at cross-cultural selling if given a thorough grounding in the sequence that should be followed. Figure 17.3 presents a flowchart of international selling transactions. This step-by-step approach can be utilized for salesforce planning and training.[6]

The selling sequence starts with a self-appraisal, which is quite similar to the self-reference criteria (SRC) discussed in earlier chapters. The aim of self-appraisal is to develop a frame of reference whereby one's own communication preferences with regard to content and style could be understood. Dimensions of SRC, that is, an unconscious reference to one's own cultural values, experience and knowledge, serve as a basis for self-awareness (see Chapter 1).

Impression formation involves understanding the buyer's cultural position. Typically, national culture and organizational culture can be assessed even before the seller meets with the buyer. Hofstede provides scores and ranks for 50 countries on the basis of positions on the four dimensions of national culture.[7] The organizational culture of most large- and medium-sized companies can be gleaned from their press releases, annual reports and from popular literature. A trained salesperson can assess a buyer's temperament with a fair degree of accuracy in a relatively short period of interaction. An accurate impression of the buyer in terms of national culture, organizational culture and temperament lays the foundation for relationship building, which is so critical to successful selling.

In the third step, the seller goes through the mental exercise of 'discrepancy identification'. This involves comparing the buyer's estimated position on the various dimensions of culture with one's own. This alerts the seller to potential problem areas in communication arising out of differences in temperament and cultural conditioning.

Figure 17.3   The International Selling Sequence

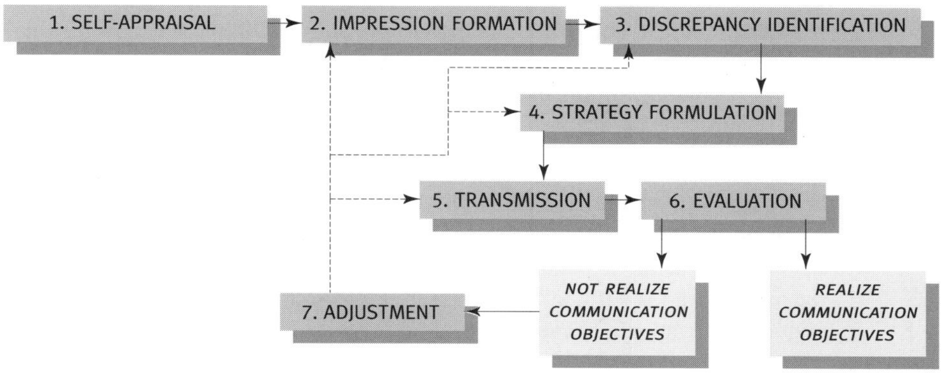

Source: Sudhir Kalé, 'How National Culture, Organizational Culture and Personality Impact Buyer–Seller Interactions', Pervez Ghauri and Jean-Claud Usunier, *International Business Negotiations* (Oxford: Pergamon, 1996), p. 35.

Strategy formulation involves minimizing the impact of problem areas identified in the earlier step. For instance, if the buyer is a feeler, and the seller is a thinker, the seller needs to modify his persuasion style. While his preferred persuasion style is logical and impersonal, this may not fit well with the buyer. The appropriate style in this instance would be to appeal to the buyer's feelings and emotions, and to point out the people-benefits behind the seller's offering. Similar adjustments need to be made on other dimensions as well where discrepancies exist between the seller and the buyer.

Transmission involves implementation of the communication/persuasion strategy. During the course of transmission, the seller should be sensitive to the verbal and nonverbal feedback received from the buyer. If the seller has correctly identified the seller's mindset based on temperament and culture, the strategy should be on target and the feedback received from the buyer will be encouraging.

Assessing the effect of the communication strategy constitutes the 'evaluation' phase. If the seller's communication objectives are realized, then the encounter has been successful. If not, the seller goes through the 'adjustment' process where buyer impressions, discrepancies and strategy are reevaluated and the transmission is modified. At the evaluation and adjustment phase, the seller always has the choice of cutting short the encounter, and trying again at some time in the future. Regardless of the outcome, every encounter adds to the seller's repertoire of experiences, skills, strategies and alternative transmission approaches.

Understanding the Nuances of Cross-Cultural Communications

Communications and the art of persuasion, knowledge of the customer and product, the ability to close a sale and after-sale service are all necessary for successful selling. These are the attributes sought when hiring an experienced person and those taught to new employees. Since culture impacts on the international sales effort just as it does on international advertising and promotion, the marketer must be certain that all international sales personnel have an understanding of the influence of culture on communications. After all, selling is communication and, unless the salesperson understands the overtones of cross-cultural communications, the sales process could be thwarted.

Effective communication requires an understanding of the nuances of the spoken language as well as the silent language.[8] Perhaps more important than language nuances are the meanings of different silent languages spoken by people from different cultures. They may think they are understanding one another when, in fact, they are misinterpreting one another. For example:

> A Briton visits a Saudi official to convince him to expedite permits for equipment being brought into the country. The Saudi offers the Briton coffee which is politely refused (he had been drinking coffee all morning at the hotel while planning the visit). The latter sits down and crosses his legs, exposing the sole of his shoe. He passes the documents to the Saudi with his left hand, enquires after the Saudi's wife and emphasizes the urgency of getting the needed permits.

In less than three minutes, the Briton unwittingly offended the Saudi five times. He refused his host's hospitality, showed disrespect, used an 'unclean' hand, implied an unintended familial familiarity and displayed impatience with his host. He had no intention of offending his host and probably was not aware of the rudeness of his behaviour. The Saudi might forgive his British guest for being ignorant of local custom, but the forgiven salesperson is in a weakened position.

Knowing your customer in international sales means more than knowing your customer's product needs; it includes knowing your customer's culture. One international consultant suggests five rules of thumb for successful selling abroad:

1. **Be Prepared** and do your homework. Learn about the host's culture, values, geography, religion and political structure. In short, do as complete a cultural analysis as possible to avoid cultural mistakes.
2. **Slow Down**. Westerners are slaves to the clock. Time is money to a Westerner but, in many countries, emphasis on time implies unfriendliness, arrogance and untrustworthiness.
3. **Develop Relationships** and trust before getting down to business. In many countries, business is not done until a feeling of trust has developed.
4. **Learn the Language**, its nuances and the idiom, and/or get a good interpreter. There are just too many ways for miscommunication to occur.
5. **Respect the Culture**. Manners are important. You are the guest, so respect what your host considers important.[9]

Anyone being sent into another culture as a salesperson or company representative should receive training to develop the cultural skills discussed. In addition, they should receive *specific* schooling on the customs, values and social and political institutions of the host country.

In international sales and purchase transactions, the responsibilities need to be clearly defined. For example, who is responsible for freight and insurance and from which point (ex-factory, on board, etc.) to which point are crucial issues and if ignored can lead to serious problems. What are the penalties for delays, and how is responsibility for delays to be determined, for example, in the case of strike, accident or fire? What if the goods do not correspond to the agreed sample or specifications? What if the payment is not made on time? Although a number of middlemen, such as clearing agents, are available to handle these issues, the salesperson is solely responsible to negotiate these terms. The price or terms might be different with different responsibilities.

RECRUITMENT OF INTERNATIONAL SALES FORCE

The number of marketing management personnel from the home country assigned to foreign countries varies according to the size of the operation and the availability of qualified locals. Increasingly, the number of home-country nationals (expatriates) assigned to foreign posts is smaller as the pool of trained, experienced locals grows.

The largest personnel requirement abroad for most companies is the salesforce, drawn from three sources: expatriates, local nationals and third-country nationals. A company's staffing pattern may include all three types in any single foreign operation, depending on qualifications, availability and a company's needs.

Expatriates.   The number of companies relying on expatriate personnel is declining as the volume of world trade increases and as more companies use locals to fill marketing positions. However, when products are highly technical, or when selling requires an extensive background of information and applications, an expatriate salesforce remains the best choice. The expatriate salesperson may have the advantages of greater technical training, better knowledge of the company and its product line and proven dependability and effectiveness. And, because they are not locals, expatriates sometimes add to the prestige of the product line in the eyes of local customers.

Local Nationals.   The historical preference for expatriate managers and salespeople from the home country is giving way to a preference for locals. At the sales level, the picture is clearly biased in favour of the locals because they transcend both cultural and legal barriers. More knowledgeable about a country's business structure than an expatriate would be, local salespeople are better able to lead a company through the maze of unfamiliar distribution systems. Furthermore, there is now a pool of qualified local personnel available that costs less to maintain than a staff of expatriates. In Asia, many locals will have earned Master or MBA degrees in Europe or the United States; thus you get the cultural knowledge of the local meshed with an understanding of Western business management. Although expatriates' salaries may be no more than those of their national counterparts, the total cost of keeping comparable groups of expatriates in a country can be considerably higher because of special cost-of-living benefits, moving expenses, taxes and other costs associated with keeping an expatriate abroad.

Third-Country Nationals.   The internationalization of business has created a pool of third-country nationals (TCNs), expatriates from their own countries working for a foreign company in a third country. The TCNs are a group whose nationality has little to do with where they work or for whom. An example would be a German working in Malaysia for a US company. Historically, there have been a few expatriates or TCNs who have spent the majority of their careers abroad, but now a truly 'global executive' has begun to emerge. The recently appointed chairman of a division of a major Netherlands company is a Norwegian who gained that post after stints in the United States, where he was the US subsidiary's chairman, and in Brazil, where he held the position of general manager. At one time, Burroughs Corporation's Italian subsidiary was run by a Frenchman, the Swiss subsidiary by a Dane, the German subsidiary by an Englishman, the French subsidiary by a Swiss, the Venezuelan subsidiary by an Argentinean, and the Danish subsidiary by a Dutchman. The CEO of Up John-Pharmacia, an American–Swedish Pharmaceutical multinational with its head office in Michigan, is a Pakistani.

Development of TCN executives reflects not only a growing internationalization of business but also acknowledges that personal skills and motivations are not the exclusive property of one nation.[10] TCNs are often sought because they speak several languages and know an industry or foreign country well. More and more companies are realizing that talent flows to opportunity regardless of the nationality.

Host Country Restrictions.   The host governments' attitudes towards foreign workers complicate flexibility in selecting expatriate nationals or local nationals. Concern about foreign corporate domination, local unemployment and other issues causes some countries to restrict the number of non-nationals allowed to work within the country. Most countries have specific rules limiting work permits for foreigners to positions that cannot be filled by a national. Further, the law often limits such permits to periods just long enough to train a local for a specific position. Such restrictions mean that MNCs have fewer opportunities for sending home-country personnel to sales positions abroad.

Selecting an International Salesforce

To select personnel for international positions effectively, management must define precisely what is expected of its people. A formal job description can aid management in expressing those desires for long-range needs as well as for current needs. In addition to descriptions for each marketing position, the criteria should include special requirements indigenous to various countries.[11]

People operating in the home country need only the attributes of effective salespersons, whereas a transnational manager can require skills and attitudes that would challenge a diplomat. Personnel requirements for various positions vary considerably, but despite the range of differences, some basic requisites leading to effective performance should be considered because effective executives and salespeople, regardless of in what foreign country they are operating, share certain characteristics. Special personal characteristics, skills and orientations are demanded for international operations.

Maturity is a prime requisite for expatriate and third-country personnel. Sales personnel working abroad typically must work more independently than their domestic counterparts. The company must have confidence in their ability to make decisions and commitments without constant recourse to the home office, or they cannot be individually effective.

Also, salespeople operating in foreign countries need *considerable breadth of knowledge of many subjects both on and off the job*. The ability to speak several languages is becoming a necessity. In addition to the intangible skills necessary in handling interpersonal relationships, international marketers must also be effective salespeople. Every marketing person in a foreign position is directly involved in the selling effort and must possess a sales sense that cuts through personal, cultural and language differences and deals effectively with the selling situation.

The marketer who expects to be effective in the international marketplace needs to have a positive outlook on an international assignment. People who do not like what they are doing and where they are doing it stand little chance of success. Failures are usually the result of overselling the assignment, showing the bright side of the picture, and not warning about the bleak side.

Successful adaptation in international affairs is based on a combination of attitude and effort. A careful study of the customs of the market country should be initiated before the marketer arrives, and should continue as long as there are facets of the culture that are not clear. One useful approach is to listen to the advice of national and foreign business people

GOING INTERNATIONAL 17.2

THE VIEW FROM THE OTHER SIDE

The globalization of US markets means that more foreign managers are coming to the United States to live. The problem of cultural adaptation and adjustment is no less a problem for them than for Americans going to their countries to live. Here are a few observations from the other side—from foreigners in the United States.

'There are no small eggs in America,' says a Dutchman. 'There are only jumbo, extra large, large and medium.' This is no country for humility.

'If you are not aggressive, you're not noticed.' 'For a foreigner to succeed in the United States . . . he needs to be more aggressive than in his own culture because Americans expect that.'

Young Japanese have difficulty addressing American superiors in a manner that shows self-confidence and an air of competence. The essential elements are posture and eye contact, but the Japanese simply cannot stand up straight, puff up their chests, look the Americans in the eyes and talk at the same time.

Schedules and deadlines are taken very seriously. How quickly one does a job is often as important as how well one does the job. Japanese, who are experts at being members of teams, need help in learning to compete, take initiative and develop leadership skills.

A Latin American has to refrain from the sort of socializing he would do in Latin countries, where rapport comes before deal making. 'Here that is not necessary', he says. 'You can even do business with someone you do not like.' He still feels uncomfortable launching right into business, but Americans become frustrated when they think they are wasting time.

Americans say, 'Come on over sometime', but the foreigner learns—perhaps after an awkward visit—that this is not really an invitation.

'Living alone in the United States is very sad, so much loneliness. Of course, living alone in Japan is also lonely, but in this country we can't speak English so fluently, so it is difficult to find a friend. I miss my boyfriend. I miss my parents. I miss my close friends.'

Source: Adapted from Lennie Copeland, 'Managing in the Melting Pot', *Across the Board*, June 1986, pp. 52–59.

operating in that country. Cultural empathy is clearly a part of basic orientation because it is unlikely that anyone can be effective if antagonistic or confused about the environment.

The personal characteristics, skills and orientation that identify the potentially effective salesperson have been labelled in many different ways. Each person studying the field has a preferred list of characteristics, yet rising above all the characteristics there is an intangible something that some have referred to as a 'sixth sense'. This implies that, regardless of the individual attributes, there is a certain blend of personal characteristics, skills and orientation that is hard to pinpoint and that may differ from individual to individual, but that produces the most effective overseas personnel.

Getting the right person to handle the job is a primary function of personnel management. It becomes especially important in the selection of locals to work for foreign companies within their home country. Most developing countries and many European countries have stringent laws protecting workers' rights. These laws are specific as to penalties for the dismissal of employees.

Training and Motivating

The nature of a training programme depends largely on whether expatriate or local personnel are being trained as salespeople. Training for the expatriates focuses on the customs and the special foreign sales problems that will be encountered, whereas local personnel require greater emphasis on the company, its products, technical information and selling methods. In training either type of personnel, the sales training activity is burdened with problems stemming from long-established behaviour and attitudes. Local personnel cling to habits continually reinforced by local culture. Nowhere is the problem greater than in China, where the legacy of the communist tradition lingers. The attitude that whether you work hard or not, you get the same rewards, has to be changed if training is going to hold. Expatriates as well are captives of their own habits and patterns. Before any training can be effective, open-minded attitudes must be established.

Continual training may be more important in foreign markets than in domestic ones because of the lack of routine contact with the parent company and its marketing personnel. One aspect of training is frequently overlooked; home-office personnel dealing with international marketing operations need training designed to make them responsive to the needs of the foreign operations. In most companies, the requisite sensitivities are expected to be developed by osmosis in the process of dealing with foreign affairs; a few companies send home-office personnel abroad periodically to increase their awareness of the problems of the foreign operations.[12]

Marketing is a business function requiring high motivation regardless of the location of the practitioner. Marketing managers and sales managers typically work hard, travel extensively and have day-to-day challenges. Selling is hard, competitive work wherever undertaken, and a constant flow of inspiration is needed to keep personnel functioning at an optimal level. National differences must always be considered in motivating the marketing force. One company found its salespeople were losing respect and had low motivation because they did not have girls to pour tea for customers in the Japanese branch offices. The company learned that when male personnel served tea, they felt they lost face; tea girls were authorized for all branches.

The behaviour of a salesforce is dependent upon a number of factors such as: *Background*: their education, general knowledge and ability to speak more than one language. It is also important how they dress and talk and that they deal tactfully with people. *Well informed*: first of all about the product and company they are selling. Buyers are never satisfied with information they get from brochures and ask the salespeople all kinds of questions. If the latter are not well-informed they will not be able to provide satisfactory information to the customer. Salespeople should also have full knowledge of the local market, competing products and new developments in the field. *Morale*: to keep people going, their morale should be kept high. A common complaint among international salespeople is that their head office does not understand them. They often feel left alone or deserted. Their morale can be boosted through realistic sales targets, giving them full support and making them feel that the head office is fully behind them. Their achievements should be properly rewarded in accordance with their career goals. *Job stability*: salespeople often have an uneasy feeling that while they are on the road other people at the office are getting all the benefits with regard to promotions and job stability. They may also be afraid about what will happen if they do not meet their target. Salespeople worried about these issues cannot be very effective, it is thus very important to select salespeople with care, train them and then support them with confidence and backing.

As the cultural differences reviewed in earlier chapters affect the motivational patterns of a salesforce, a manager must be extremely sensitive to the personal behaviour patterns of employees. Individual incentives that work effectively in the West can fail completely in other cultures. For example, with Japan's emphasis on paternalism and collectivism and its system of lifetime employment and seniority, motivation through individual incentive does not work because Japanese employees seem to derive the greatest satisfaction from being comfortable members of a group. Thus, an offer of financial reward for outstanding work could be turned

CROSS-CULTURAL SELLING

Some stereotypes of selling styles are often associated with different markets. Here are some examples.

In Asian countries, where arrogance and showing of extreme confidence are not appreciated, salespeople should make modest, rational, down-to-earth points. They should avoid trying to win arguments with the customers, who could suffer from a 'loss-of-face' and react negatively.

In Italy, on the contrary, the lack of self-confidence would be perceived as a clear sign of lack of personal credibility and reliability; thus one needs to argue strongly in order to be taken seriously.

In Switzerland, you have to speak precisely and your words will be taken quite literally.

In the United Kingdom, it is advisable to use the *soft sell* approach. Do not be pushy and try to 'chat' and convince.

In Germany, you should use the *hard sell* approach by being persistent. Make visits, offer trials and be very visible.

down because an employee would prefer not to appear different from peers and possibly attract their resentment.

Blending company sales objectives and the personal objectives of the salespeople is a task worthy of the most skilled manager. The Western manager must be constantly aware that many of the techniques used to motivate Western personnel and their responses to these techniques are based on Western cultural premises and may not work in other countries.

CROSS-CULTURAL NEGOTIATIONS

The keystone of effective marketing and buyer–seller interactions is effective negotiations. Poorly conducted negotiations can leave the seller and the buyer frustrated and do more to destroy effective relationships than anything else can do. Negotiation should be handled in such a way that a long-term relationship between buyer and seller is ensured.[13]

The basic elements of business negotiations are the same in every country; they relate to the product, its price and terms, services associated with the product and, finally, friendship between vendors and customers. Selling is often thought of as a routine exchange with established prices and distribution networks from which there is little deviation. But, particularly in international sales, the selling transaction is almost always a negotiated exchange. Price, delivery dates, quality of goods or services, volume of goods sold, financing, exchange rate risk, shipping mode, insurance, and so on, are all set by bargaining or negotiations. Such negotiations should not be conducted in a typical 'win-lose' situation but as a shared benefit that will ensure a long-term relationship.[14]

Simply stated, to negotiate is to confer, bargain or discuss with a view towards reaching an agreement. It is a sequential rather than simultaneous give-and-take discussion resulting in a mutually beneficial understanding. Most authorities on negotiating include three stages in the negotiating process: (1) pre-negotiation stage; (2) negotiation stage; and (3) post-negotiation stage. In the pre-negotiation stage parties attempt to understand each others needs and offers,

Figure 17.4   The Process of International Sales Negotiations

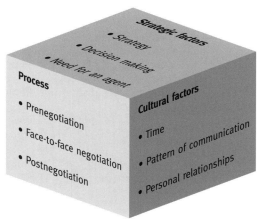

which is done through informal meetings and arrangements. The negotiation stage refers to face-to-face negotiations and the post-negotiation stage refers to the stage when parties have agreed to most of the issues and are to agree on contract language and format and signing of the contract, and how it leads to more business and relationship development.

In addition to these stages, the process of international business negotiation has two more dimensions; (1) strategic factors and (2) cultural factors (see Figure 17.4).

As explained earlier, cultural factors play an important role in each and every stage of the international negotiation process. Cultural factors include time, pattern of communication and emphasis on personal relationships. While time is 'money' in Western cultures, it has no such value attached to it in Asia, Latin America and Africa. Knowing whether the other party is looking for a collective solution or an individual benefit is very important. According to Hofstede's studies, we can place different countries on different scales of individual and collective behaviour.[15] Different cultures have different patterns of communication as regards direct versus indirect and explicit versus implicit communication. Some languages are traditionally vague, others exaggerate, which makes communication difficult for those from outside who are not familiar with the language. And finally, different cultures give different importance to personal relations in negotiations. In the West, the negotiators are more concerned with the issue at hand, irrespective of who is representing the other side.

Before entering an international negotiation process, the two parties should know which type of decision-making procedure is going to be followed by the other party and which type of strategy should be used to match it. How should a party present its offer and capabilities? The formal versus informal and argumentative versus informative presentation style is very distinct in many countries. If not prepared, negotiators can make serious blunders. In negotiations people refer to different type of strategies such as tough, soft or intermediate. In this respect also it is important to have information on the other party's strategy, so that you can match with it. Furthermore, it is important to know who makes the decisions, and whether the negotiators taking part in the negotiation have decision-making powers.

Under strategic factors, it is also important to evaluate your position and realize whether there is a need for an agent or consultant for a particular negotiation process. It is a generally held opinion that the more unfamiliar or complex the other party or market is, the greater is the need for an agent or consultant.

Business people have to understand the cultural context of negotiations. An authoritative source on cross-cultural negotiating suggests that one of the major difficulties in any cross-cultural negotiation is that expectations about the normal process of negotiations differ among cultures. Two important areas where differences can arise in cross-cultural negotiating are rapport and the degree of emphasis placed on each of the stages in the negotiating process by those involved in a negotiation.[16]

Pre-Negotiation Stage

In the pre-negotiation stage the parties gather as much relevant information as possible on each other. Some informal meetings are held to check each other's positions and capabilities. This stage is often more important than the formal negotiation stage, as buyers and sellers can develop social, informal relationships. Trust and confidence gained from these relationships increase the chances of an agreement.

The most important issue at this stage, however, is to do the preparation thoroughly. An insight into buying behaviour of the customer and his or her priorities is crucial, as it is necessary to present the product/service in a manner consistent with those priorities and behaviour. For a new customer, the amount of homework to be done is quite heavy, but it will help in subsequent interactions. The idea is to read the map before getting lost. The necessary first step in getting started in an overseas venture is to 'study the map' and learn as much as possible about the target country, culture and individuals before leaving home. Preparation on some practical details such as availability of office equipment and computers in the new country or the necessity of having an agent, etc., are also some of the essentials of this stage.

Face-to-Face Negotiation Stage

In the formal face-to-face negotiation stage, parties evaluate alternatives. The differences in preferences and expectations are explored and possibilities of coming closer to each other are sought. Negotiators give and take and come to their final positions. In this stage, a balance between firmness and credibility is important and parties give and receive signals for further movement in the process.

Time plays an important role in cross-cultural negotiation. In a culture, where time is money, little importance is given to relationship building and small talk. In the West, people are constantly on the move, while Asians believe that a considerable time should be spent in building general understanding, trust and relationships. Selling in international markets takes much longer than in domestic transactions, not only due to culture, but also because the tempo is generally slower. In some countries, there are long religious or national holidays. In Muslim countries, the Ramadan months are not really appropriate for negotiations. In Europe, the months of July and August are not suitable as most people are away. In the United States, the period between Thanksgiving and New Year is considered difficult. And so on. All these aspects need to be considered while planning for negotiations.

While negotiating in other countries a combination of solid know-how, experience and common sense is required to master the process. Now that an extensive literature on such negotiations exists, it is possible to acquire this know-how and learn from other's experience. Some of the literature that is available is general in nature, but there are also specialist books on regional negotiation styles.[17]

NOW, THAT'S SALESMANSHIP

The *Export Times* of London sponsored the Vladivar Vodka Incredible Export Award to honour capitalist ingenuity. Here are some winners.

1. *Tom-toms to Nigeria*: The Premier Drum Company of Leicester won first prize with their sale of four shipments of tom-toms to Nigeria, including complete kits for the Nigerian Police Band and the country's top band (Dr Victor Oliyia and his all-star orchestra). Premier also sold maracas to South America and xylophones to Cuba.
2. *Oil to the Arabs*: Second place went to Permaflex Ltd of Stoke-on-Trent, which exports £50 000 of petroleum a year to the Arab states in the form of lighter fluid.
3. *Sand to Abu Dhabi*: Eastern Sands and Refractories of Cambridge shipped 1800 tons of sand to sand-rich Abu Dhabi, which needed sand grains of a special shape for water filtration.
4. *Snowplough to Arabia*: The defence force of the Arab sheikdom of Dubai purchased from Bunce Ltd of Ashbury, Wiltshire, one snowplough. It is to be used to clear sand from remote roads.
5. *Coals to Newcastle*: Timothy Dexter (1747–1806), an American merchant prince and eccentric who once published a book without punctuation, actually sent a shipload of coal to Newcastle, known as a centre for shipping coal out. The coal arrived just as Newcastle was paralysed by a coal strike and there was a shortage of fuel for the citizenry. Dexter came away with enormous profits.
6. *Peking ducks to China*: Cherry Valley Duck Farms signed a 10-year contract in Canton to sell British-bred Peking ducks to a farm at Tai Ling Shan, China.
7. *Vodka to Russia*: A Dutch firm exports 200 000 litres of vodka to Russia. There is such global demand for Russian vodka at premium prices that Russian exports have caused a serious shortage of vodka in Russia.

Sources: Abstracted from *Export Times*, London, and ' "Da" for Dutch Vodka', *World Press Review*, November 1993, p. 42.

The following are some general recommendations:

1. **Understand the Value of the Particular Deal.** The first step in each negotiation process is to realize the implication of that deal in the short run as well as in the long run. Unless you have a clear picture of the deal you cannot formulate a true strategy towards transactions versus relational approach.
2. **Evaluate the Competition.** If you know what range of alternatives the other party has, you can see more clearly how important the deal is for them. In this way, you can create arguments and alternatives that match or compete with the alternatives the other party has.
3. **Check your Language and Communication Capabilities.** Depending upon the other party and the market/country involved you have to decide how best you can manage the communication process. The messages should be adopted to the level and culture of the other party. Also consider nonverbal communication, especially those things you cannot/should not do.[18]
4. **Understand the Decision-Making Process**, your own and of the other party. It is clear that you can make all decisions while you are out there. Do you know that the negotiators coming from the other side can make all decisions? Who in their team or head office is in fact the decision maker?

5. **Patience Is an Asset in International Business Negotiations.** In many cultures, Asian, Middle Eastern and even in Eastern Europe, things take their time. Negotiators from these cultures are not to be hurried; they really need to feel the negotiation process before they are ready to make a decision. In such cases it is not useful to push them to make a decision.

Post-Negotiation Stage

In the post-negotiation stage the contract is drawn up. Experience shows that writing the contract and its language and formulations can be a negotiation process in itself as meanings and values differ between the two parties. If not properly handled, this stage can lead to renewed face-to-face negotiations. The best way to avoid this is to make sure that both parties thoroughly understand what they have agreed upon before leaving each negotiation session.

SUMMARY

An effective international salesforce constitutes one of the international marketer's greatest concerns. The company salesforce represents the major alternative method of organizing a company for foreign distribution and, as such, is on the front line of a marketing organization.

The role of marketers in both domestic and foreign markets is rapidly changing, along with the composition of international managerial teams and salesforces. These last two have many unique requirements that are being filled by expatriates, locals, third-country nationals, or a combination of the three. In recent years, the pattern of development has been to place more emphasis on local personnel operating in their own countries.

The importance of negotiations is more evident in international as compared to domestic marketing. The salesforce needs to be trained in cross-cultural communication and negotiation for successful marketing performance.

QUESTIONS

1. What are the factors that influence the effectiveness of personal selling in international marketing? Explain.
2. How can a salesperson plan a selling sequence while selling to foreign markets? Explain the selling sequence in international seller–buyer interaction.
3. Why may it be difficult to adhere to set job criteria in selecting foreign personnel? What compensating actions might be necessary?
4. Under which circumstances should expatriate salespeople be utilized?
5. Discuss the problems that might be encountered in having an expatriate salesperson supervising foreign salespeople.
6. 'It is costly to maintain an international salesforce.' Comment.
7. Adaptability and maturity are traits needed by all salespeople. Why should they be singled out as especially important for international salespeople?
8. Discuss the stages in cross-cultural negotiations. How can you effectively manage an international negotiation process? Discuss.
9. Why is sound negotiation the keystone to effective relationship marketing? Discuss.

REFERENCES

1. Jean-Claude Usunier, *Marketing Across Cultures* (Hemel Hempstead: Prentice Hall, 1996).

2. Jagdish Sheth and Atul Parvatiyar, 'The Evolution of Relationship Marketing', *International Business Review*, vol. 4, no. 4, 1995, pp. 379–418.

3. Harald Biong and Fred Selnes, 'Relational Selling Behavior and Skills in Long-Term Industrial Buyer-Seller Relationships', *International Business Review*, vol. 4, no. 4, 1995, pp. 483–498.

4. Jean-Claude Usunier, *Marketing Across Cultures* (Hemel Hempstead: Prentice-Hall, 1996).

5. Jagdish Sheth, 'Cross-Cultural Influences on the Buyer-Seller Interaction/Negotiation Process', *Asia Pacific Journal of Management*, vol. 1, no. 1, 1983, pp. 46–55.

6. This section is based on Sudhir Kalé, 'How National Culture, Organizational Culture and Personality Impact Buyer-Seller Interactions', in Pervez Ghauri and Jean-Claude Usunier, *International Business Negotiations* (Oxford: Pergamon, 1996), pp. 21–37.

7. Geert Hofstede, 'National Cultures in Four Dimensions: A Research-based Theory of Cultural Differences Among Nations', *International Studies of Management and Organization*, vol. xii, nos. 1–2, 1983, pp. 46–74.

8. See, for example, 'Nonverbal Negotiation in China: Cycling in Beijing', *Negotiation Journal*, January 1995, pp. 11–18.

9. This section draws on Lennie Copeland, 'The Art of International Selling', *Business America*, 25 June 1984, pp. 2–7; and Roger E. Axtell, *The Do's and Taboos of International Trade* (New York: Wiley, 1994).

10. 'Business Globalization Stimulates Increases in Foreign Assignments', *The Wall Street Journal*, 14 June 1994, p. A-1

11. Lori Ioannou, 'Catching Global Managers', *International Business*, March 1994, pp. 60–67.

12. For a comprehensive review of the difference between human resource management in Europe and the United States, see Chris Brewster, 'Towards a "European Model of Human Resource Management" ', *Journal of International Business Studies*, First Quarter 1995, pp. 1–21.

13. This section draws on Pervez Ghauri and Jean-Claude Usunier, *International Business Negotiations* (Oxford: Pergamon, 1996).

14. A comprehensive review of culture and negotiating is included in Geert Hofstede, 'Hofstede's Dimensions of Culture and Their Influence on International Business Negotiations', in Pervez Ghauri and Jean-Claude Usunier, *International Business Negotiations* (Oxford: Pergamon, 1996).

15. Geert Hofstede, 'National Cultures in Four Dimensions: A Research-based Theory of Cultural Differences Among Nations', *International Studies of Management and Organization*, vol. xii, nos. 1–2, 1983, pp. 46–74.

16. Sabine Urban, 'Negotiating International Joint Ventures', in Pervez Ghauri and Jean-Claude Usunier, *International Business Negotiations* (Oxford: Pergamon, 1996), pp. 231–252.

17. See, for example, Lennie Copeland and Lewis Griggs, *Going International* (New York: Plume, 1985); John L. Graham and Yoshihiro Sano, *Smart Bargaining: Doing Business with the Japanese*, rev. edn (New York: Harper, 1990); and Pervez Ghauri and Jean-Claude Usunier, *International Business Negotiations* (Oxford: Pergamon, 1996).

18. See, for example 'Nonverbal Negotiation in China: Cycling in Beijing', *Negotiating Journal*, January 1995, pp. 11–18.

Chapter Outline

Chapter Learning Objectives

What you should learn from Chapter 18

- Components of pricing as competitive tools in international marketing.
- The pricing pitfalls directly related to international marketing.
- How to control pricing in parallel imports or grey markets.
- Factors influencing international pricing strategy.
- Price escalation and how to minimize its effect.
- How firms use transfer pricing for their benefits.
- The mechanics of price quotations.
- Countertrading and its place in international marketing policies.

Even when the international marketer produces the right product, promotes it correctly and initiates the proper channel of distribution, the effort fails if the product is not properly priced. Setting the right price for a product can be the key to success or failure. While the quality of Western products is widely recognized in global markets, foreign buyers, like domestic buyers, balance quality and price in their purchase decisions. A product's price must reflect the quality/value the consumer perceives in the product. Of all the tasks facing the international marketer, determining what price to charge is one of the most difficult decisions. It is further complicated when the company sells its product to customers in different country markets.[1]

A unified Europe, economic reforms in Eastern Europe, the Newly Independent States and the economic growth in Asian and Latin American countries are creating new marketing opportunities with enhanced competition. As global companies vie for these markets, price becomes increasingly important as a competitive tool. Whether exporting or managing overseas operations, the international marketing manager is responsible for setting and controlling the actual price of goods as they are traded in different markets. The marketer is confronted with new sets of variables to consider with each new market: different tariffs, costs, attitudes, competition, currency fluctuations, methods of price quotation and the marketing strategy of the firm.

This chapter focuses on pricing considerations of particular concern in the international marketplace. Basic pricing policy questions that arise from the special cost, market and competitive factors in foreign markets are reviewed. A discussion of price escalation and its control and factors associated with price setting is followed by a review of the mechanics of international price quotation.

PRICING POLICY

Active marketing in several countries compounds the number of pricing problems and variables relating to price policy. Unless a firm has a clearly thought-out, explicitly defined price policy, prices are established by expediency rather than design. Pricing activity is affected by the country in which business is being conducted, the type of product, variations in competitive conditions and other strategic factors. Price and terms of sale cannot be based on domestic criteria alone.[2]

Parallel Imports

The broader the product line and the larger the number of countries involved, the more complex the process of controlling prices to the end user. Besides having to meet price competition country by country and product by product, companies have to guard against competition from within the company and by their own customers. If a large company does not have effective controls, it can find its products in competition with its own subsidiaries or branches. Because of different prices that can exist in different country markets, a product sold in one country may be exported to another and undercut the prices charged in that country. For example, to meet economic conditions and local competition, a British pharmaceutical company sells its drugs in a developing country at a low price only to discover that these discounted drugs are exported to a third country where they are in direct competition with the same product sold for higher prices by the same firm.[3] These *parallel imports* (sometimes called a grey market) upset price levels and result from ineffective management of prices and lack of control.

Table 18.1   Showroom Tactics—New Car Prices (Cheapest European Country Equals 100)

	Germany	Spain	France	Italy	UK
VW Golf	107.4	102.6	103.9	106.7	130.9
VW Passat	125.3	104.3	108.6	111.1	126.9
Opel Corsa	109.3	102.8	102.7	101.9	124.1
Opel Astra	116.3	100.0	105.2	108.3	121.5
Opel Vectra	119.5	100.0	108.0	112.2	114.1
Ford Escort	125.3	115.0	113.1	120.5	133.3
Ford Mondeo	119.0	100.0	117.4	127.7	123.9
Renault Clio	107.3	107.3	114.8	103.0	124.0
Renault Mégane	101.2	109.3	115.8	106.0	129.8
Peugeot 306	110.3	104.4	123.6	114.9	137.6
Fiat Punto	126.2	107.5	100.0	113.3	127.3
Fiat Bravo	115.2	108.3	107.1	123.2	135.9

Source: Based on the European Commission, in *The European*, 2–8 February 1998, p. 22.

Parallel imports develop when importers buy products from distributors in one country and sell them in another to distributors who are not part of the manufacturer's regular distribution system. This practice is lucrative when wide margins exist between prices for the same products in different countries (see Table 18.1). A variety of conditions can create the profitable opportunity for a parallel market.

Variations in the value of currencies between countries frequently lead to conditions that make parallel imports profitable. When the dollar was high relative to the German mark, Cabbage Patch dolls were purchased from German distributors at what amounted to a discount and resold in the United States.

Purposefully restricting the supply of a product in a market is another practice that causes abnormally high prices and thus makes a parallel market lucrative. Such was the case with the Mercedes-Benz cars whose supply was limited in the United States. The grey market that evolved in Mercedes cars was partially supplied by Americans returning to the United States with cars they could sell for double the price they paid in Germany. This situation persisted until the price differential that had been created by limited distribution evaporated.

Restrictions brought about by import quotas and high tariffs can lead to parallel imports and make illegal imports attractive. India has a three-tier duty structure on computer parts ranging from 50–80 per cent on imports. As a result, estimates are that as much as 35 per cent of India's domestic computer hardware sales are accounted for by the grey market.[4]

Large price differentials between country markets is another condition conducive to the creation of parallel markets. Japanese merchants have long maintained very high prices for consumer products sold within the Japanese market. As a result, prices for Japanese products sold in other countries are often lower than they are in Japan. For example, the Japanese can buy Canon cameras from New York catalogue retailers and have them shipped to Japan for a price below that of the camera purchased in Japan. In addition to the higher prices for products at home, the rising value of the yen makes these price differentials even wider. When the New York price for Panasonic cordless telephones was €54.10 ($59.95), they cost

---

GOING INTERNATIONAL 18.1

DRIVING A GOLF THROUGH THE GREY MARKET

Estimates of the grey market's current share of car sales range from 3 per cent to 10 per cent, depending on the country. Assuming a conservative 5 per cent, the total only in Europe, in one year could hit 600 000 vehicles worth $12 billion (€10.8 billion). The biggest source of grey-market cars is Italy, where more than 10 per cent of the cars sold, or roughly 185 000 end up in other countries. Re-importers also handle cars from the Netherlands and even from countries outside the European Union, such as Canada. The major destination is Germany, where about 330 000 grey market cars are sold annually. The grey market has benefited consumers while giving fits to traditional dealers and car makers. Competition from the grey market is forcing dealers to negotiate lower prices, while producers have cancelled or delayed planned price increases. Because most of the re-importers are legitimate, the car manufacturers only hope of stopping them is to block renegade dealers from selling to the grey market. In 1994, for example, Peugeot asked the European Commission to ban sales to re-importers, but was not successful.

Car makers can withdraw a dealer's franchise, as Peugeot yanked its dealer in Italy. But it is almost impossible to spot and stop these side deals. Golf is a typical example, VW ships Golf from its plant in Wolfsburg, Germany, to a VW distributor in Italy, pricing it low to compete locally. The distributor sells the car to a franchised VW dealer in, let's say, Florence. An independent re-importer buys the car from the Italian dealer and ships it back to Germany. A German consumer then buys the car from the re-importer for some DM 6000–7000 less than it would cost at a German VW dealer.

Source: 'Carmakers Think Monetary Union is The Answer', *Business Week*, 20 November 1995, p. 21.

€137.20 ($152) in Tokyo, and when the Sony Walkman was €80.30 ($89), it was €149.14 ($165.23) in Tokyo.

Foreign companies doing business in Japan generally follow the same pattern of high prices for the products they sell in Japan, thus creating an opportunity for parallel markets in their products. Eastman Kodak prices its film higher in Japan than in other parts of Asia. Enterprising merchants buy Kodak film in South Korea for a discount and resell it in Japan at 25 per cent less than the authorized Japanese Kodak dealers. For the same reason, Coca-Cola imported from the United States sells for 27 per cent less through discounters than Coke's own made-in-Japan product.[5]

The possibility of a parallel market occurs whenever price differences are greater than the cost of transportation between two markets. In Europe, because of different taxes and competitive price structures, prices for the same product vary between countries. When this occurs, it is not unusual for companies to find themselves competing in one country with their own product imported from another country at lower prices. Presumably such price differentials will cease to exist once all restrictions to trade are eliminated in the European Union and a full monetary union is achieved, stabilizing prices in the EU countries.[6]

Perfume and designer brands such as Gucci and Cartier are especially prone to grey markets. To maintain the image of quality and exclusivity, prices for such products traditionally include high profit margins at each level of distribution, differential prices among markets, and limited quantities, as well as distribution restricted to upmarket retailers. In the United States, wholesale prices for exclusive brands of fragrances are often 25 per cent more than wholesale prices in other countries. These are the ideal conditions for a lucrative grey market for unauthorized dealers in other countries who buy more than they need at wholesale prices lower than US wholesalers pay. They then sell the excess at a profit to unauthorized

GOING INTERNATIONAL 18.2

GREY MARKET RULING BY EU

In 1995, Silhouette, an upmarket Austrian sunglasses manufacturer, sold 21 000 pairs of an older model, to a Bulgarian company on a promise that these glasses would be sold in Bulgaria or the former Soviet Union. However, within a couple of months, the sunglasses were back in Austria and were sold at the discount chain Hartlauer at a very low price. Silhouette took Hartlauer to court. Eventually the case was referred to the European Court of Justice, which ruled in favour of Silhouette on 16 July 1998, giving it the right to choose its distributor.

The implication of this ruling extends far beyond sunglasses. Brand owners from clothing to cars are now reviewing their policies to tackle with the so-called grey market. Levi Strauss UK described the ruling as 'most helpful', it said, 'the parallel goods from the US are now unlawful when traded by dealers without our consent'. Retailers, particularly in the United Kingdom, have increasingly used their parallel imported goods to gain price differences and promotional advantages.

Tesco's global nonfood sourcing, claims that the ruling encourages the practice by brand owners for restricting supply to ensure higher prices. 'The ruling means that they are setting up a European price cartel. That is what we are lobbying against.' Adidas said that there were advantages for consumers in a restricted distribution network. 'We make an important commitment to our customers that our products will be consistently of high quality.' The European Commission claims that allowing trademark owners to keep control of their product distribution offered some advantages to consumers such as guaranteed product quality and after sales service.

Source: Based on 'Grey market ruling delights brand owners', *The Financial Times*, 17 July 1998, p. 8.

US retailers, but at a price lower than the retailer would have to pay to an authorized US distributor.

To prevent parallel markets from developing when such marketing and pricing strategies are used, companies must maintain strong control systems. These control systems are difficult to maintain and there remains the suspicion that some companies are less concerned with controlling grey markets than they claim. For example, in one year a French company exported €36 million ($40 million) of perfume to Panamanian distributors. At that rate, Panama's per capita consumption of that one brand of perfume alone was 35 times that of the European Union.

Skimming versus Penetration Pricing

Firms must also decide when to follow a skimming or a penetration-pricing policy. Traditionally, the decision on which policy to follow depends on the level of competition, the innovativeness of the product, and market characteristics (see Figure 18.1).[7]

A company skims when the objective is to reach a segment of the market that is relatively price-insensitive and thus willing to pay a premium price for the value received. If limited supply exists, a company may follow a skimming approach in order to maximize revenue and to match demand to supply. When a company is the only seller of a new or innovative product, a skimming price may be used to maximize profits until competition forces a lower price. Skimming is often used in those markets where there are only two income levels, the wealthy and the poor. Costs prohibit setting a price that will be attractive to the lower income market so the marketer charges a premium price and directs the product to the high-income,

Figure 18.1 Skimming Versus Penetration Strategies in Marketing

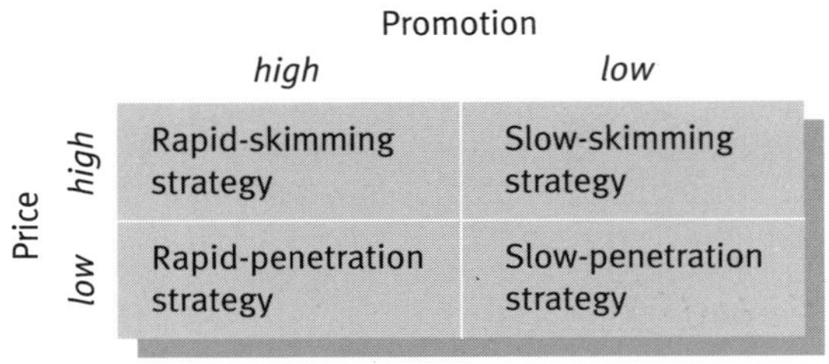

relatively price-inelastic segment. Today, such opportunities are fading away as the disparity in income levels is giving way to growing middle-income market segments.

A penetration price policy is used to stimulate market growth and capture market share by deliberately offering products at low prices. Penetration pricing is most often used to acquire and hold share of market as a competitive manoeuvre. However, in country markets experiencing rapid and sustained economic growth and where large parts of the population move into middle-income classes, penetration pricing may be used to stimulate market growth even with minimum competition. Penetration pricing may be a more profitable strategy than skimming if it maximizes revenues and builds market share as a base for the competition that is sure to come.

As many of the potential market growth trends that were set in place in the early 1990s begin to pay dividends with economic growth and a more equitable distribution of wealth within local economies, and as distinct market segments emerge within and across country markets, global companies will have to make more sophisticated pricing decisions than were made when companies directed their marketing efforts only towards single market segments.

Leasing in International Markets

An important selling technique to alleviate high prices and capital shortages for capital equipment is the leasing system. The concept of equipment leasing has become increasingly important as a means of selling capital equipment in overseas markets. In fact, it is estimated that €45 billion ($50 billion) worth (original cost) of foreign-made equipment is on lease in Western Europe.

The system of leasing used by industrial exporters is quite simple. Terms of the leases usually run from one to five years, with payments made monthly or annually; included in the rental fee are servicing, repairs and spare parts. Just as contracts for domestic and overseas leasing arrangements are similar, so are the basic motivations and the shortcomings. For example:

1. Leasing opens the door to a large segment of nominally financed foreign firms that can be sold on a lease option but might be unable to buy for cash.
2. Leasing can ease the problems of selling new, experimental equipment, because less risk is involved for the users.
3. Leasing helps guarantee better maintenance and service on overseas equipment.
4. Equipment leased and in use helps to sell other companies in that country.
5. Lease revenue tends to be more stable over a period of time than direct sales would be.

HOW DO LEVI'S 501s GET TO INTERNATIONAL MARKETS?

Levi Strauss sells in international markets, how else do 501s get to market? Well, there is another way via the grey market or 'diverters'. These diverters are enterprising people who buy 501s legally at retail prices, usually during sales, and then resell them to foreign buyers. It is estimated that millions of dollars of Levi's are sold abroad at discount prices—all sales authorized by Levi Strauss. In Germany, for example, Levi's 501s are sold to authorized wholesalers for about $40 (€36) and authorized retailers sell them at about $80 (€72), compared with US retail prices of $30 (€27) to $40 (€36) a pair. The difference of $40 (€36) or so makes it economically possible for a diverter to buy 501s in the US and sell them to unauthorized dealers who sell them for $60 (€54) to $70 (€63), undercutting authorized German retailers. Similar practices happen in Japan and other countries around the world. How do these diverters work?

One way is to buy 501s legally at retail prices. A report on diverters in Portland, Oregon, is an example of what is repeated in city after city all over the United States. 'They come into a store in groups and buy every pair of Levi's 501 jeans they can', says one store manager. He says he has seen two or three vans full of people come to the store when there is a sale and buy the six-pair-a-day limit, and return day after day until the sale is over. In another chain store having a month-long store-wide sale, Levi's were eliminated as a sale item after only two weeks. A group of 'customers' was visiting each store daily to buy the limit, and the store wanted to preserve a reasonable selection for its regular customers. All these Levi's are channelled to a diverter who exports them to unauthorized buyers throughout the world. What makes this practice feasible is the lower markups and prices US retailers have compared with the higher costs (Levi's have a higher wholesale price for foreign sales than for domestic sales) and the resulting higher markups and prices retailers charge in many other countries.

Retail prices in the US are often more competitive than in other countries where, historically, price competition is not as widely practised and markups along the distribution chain are often higher. Thus, prices for imported goods frequently are substantially higher in foreign markets than in domestic markets. One recent study of retail prices in Britain reported that some of the differences in prices between the United States and Britain were 'staggering'. For example, besides blue jeans which sell for $90 (€81) in Britain versus $30 (€27) in the United States, disposable contact lenses are $225 (€203) versus $87 (€79) and a tennis racket is $225 (€203) versus $78 (€70). Some, but not all, of the price differences can be attributed to price escalation, that is, tariffs, shipping and other costs associated with exporting, but that portion of the difference attributable to higher margins creates an opportunity for profitable diverting.

Sources: Jim Hill, 'Flight of the 501s', *The Oregonian*, 27 June 1993, p. G-1; and 'Consumers in Britain Pay More', *The Wall Street Journal*, 2 February 1994, p. A-13.

The disadvantages or shortcomings take on an international flavour. Besides the inherent disadvantages of leasing, some problems are compounded by international relationships. In a country beset with inflation, lease contracts that include maintenance and supply parts, as most do, can lead to heavy losses towards the end of the contract period. Further, countries where leasing is most attractive are those where spiralling inflation is most likely to occur. The added problems of currency devaluation, expropriation or other political risks are operative longer than if the sale of the same equipment is made outright. In the light of these perils, there is greater risk in leasing than in outright sale; however, there is a definite trend towards increased use of this method of selling internationally.[8]

Figure 18.2   Factors Influencing International Pricing

FACTORS INFLUENCING INTERNATIONAL PRICING

People travelling abroad are often surprised to find goods that are relatively inexpensive in their home country priced outrageously higher in other countries. It is also possible that goods priced reasonably abroad may be priced enormously high in the home market. Beginning with the import tariff, each time a product changes hands an additional cost is incurred. First, the product passes through the hands of an importer, then to the company with primary responsibility for sales and service, then to a secondary or even a tertiary local distributor and finally to the retailer and the consumer. The factors influencing pricing in international markets include, the objective of the firm in a particular market, price escalation, competition, target customer segment and pricing control (see Figure 18.2).

Pricing Objectives

In general, price decisions are viewed two ways: pricing as an active instrument of accomplishing marketing objectives or pricing as a static element in a business decision. If the former view is followed, the company uses price to achieve a specific objective, whether a targeted return on profits, a targeted market share or some other specific goal. The company that follows the second approach probably exports only excess inventory, places a low priority on foreign business and views its export sales as passive contributions to sales volume. Profit is by far the most important pricing objective. Pricing objectives should be consistent with the marketing objectives of the firm in a particular market as well as the overall strategy of the firm. Essentially, objectives are defined in terms of profit, market share or positioning.

The more control a company has over the final selling price of a product, the better it is able to achieve its marketing goals. However, it is not always possible to control end prices, and in this case, companies may resort to 'mill net pricing', that is, the price received at the plant.

Price Escalation

Excess profits do exist in some international markets, but generally the cause of the disproportionate difference in price between the exporting country and the importing country, here termed *price escalation*, is the added costs incurred as a result of exporting products from one country to another. Specifically, the term relates to situations where ultimate prices are raised by shipping costs, insurance, packing, tariffs, longer channels of distribution, larger middle-

Figure 18.3   Factors Influencing Price Escalation

men margins, special taxes, administrative costs and exchange-rate fluctuations (see Figure 18.3). The majority of these costs arise as a direct result of moving goods across borders from one country to another and combine to escalate the final price to a level considerably higher than in the domestic market.

Taxes, Tariffs and Administrative Costs.   'Nothing is surer than death and taxes' has a particularly familiar ring to the ears of the international trader because taxes include tariffs, and tariffs are one of the most pervasive features of international trading. Taxes and tariffs affect the ultimate consumer price for a product and, in most instances, the consumer bears the burden of both. Sometimes, however, the consumer benefits when manufacturers selling goods in foreign countries reduce their net return to gain access to a foreign market. Absorbed or passed on, taxes and tariffs must be considered by the international business-person.

A tariff, or duty, is a special form of taxation and, like other forms of taxes, may be levied for the purpose of protecting a market or for increasing government revenue. A tariff is a fee charged when goods are brought into a country from another country. The level of tariff is typically expressed as the rate of duty and may be levied as specific, ad valorem, or a combination. A *specific* duty is a flat charge per physical unit imported, such as 15 cents per bushel of rye. *Ad valorem* duties are levied as a percentage of the value of the goods imported, such as 20 per cent of the value of imported watches. *Combination* tariffs include both a specific and an *ad valorem* charge, such as €1 per camera plus 10 per cent of its value.

In addition to taxes and tariffs, there is a variety of administrative costs directly associated with exporting and importing a product. Acquiring export and import licences and other documents and the physical arrangements for getting the product from port of entry to the buyer's location mean additional costs. While such costs are relatively small, they add to the overall cost of exporting.

Inflation.   The effect of inflation on cost must be taken into account. In countries with rapid inflation or exchange variation, the selling price must be related to the cost of goods sold and the cost of replacing the items. Goods are often sold below their cost of replacement plus overhead, and sometimes are sold below replacement cost. In these instances, the company would be better off not to sell the products at all. When payment is likely to be delayed for several months or is worked out on a long-term contract, inflationary factors must be figured into the price.

Table 18.2   Pricing Strategies under Varying Currency Conditions

When Domestic Currency is WEAK...	When Domestic Currency is STRONG...
Stress price benefits	Engage in nonprice competition by improving quality, delivery and after-sale service
Expand product line and add more-costly features	Improve productivity and engage in vigorous cost reduction
Shift sourcing and manufacturing to domestic market	Shift sourcing and manufacturing overseas
Exploit export opportunities in all markets	Give priority to exports to relatively strong-currency countries
Conduct conventional cash-for-goods trade	Deal in countertrade with weak-currency countries
Use full-costing approach, but use marginal-cost pricing to penetrate new/competitive markets	Trim profit margins and use marginal-cost pricing
Speed repatriation of foreign-earned income and collections	Keep the foreign-earned income in host country, slow collections
Minimize expenditures in local, host-country currency	Maximize expenditures in local, host-country currency
Buy needed services (advertising, insurance, transportation, etc.) in domestic market	Buy needed services abroad and pay for them in local currencies
Minimize local borrowing	Borrow money needed for expansion in local market
Bill foreign customers in domestic currency	Bill foreign customers in their own currency

Source: S. Tamer Cavusgil, 'Unraveling the Mystiques of Export Pricing', Chapter 71 in Sidney J. Levy *et al.* (eds), *Marketing Manager's Handbook* (New York: The Dartnell Corporation, 1994), Figure 2, p. 1362.

Because inflation is beyond the control of companies, they use a variety of techniques to inflate the selling price to compensate for inflation pressure and price controls. They may charge for extra services, inflate costs in transfer pricing, break up products into components and price each component separately or require the purchase of two or more products simultaneously and refuse to deliver one product unless the purchaser agrees to take another, more expensive item as well. Table 18.2 focuses on the different price strategies a company might employ under a weak or strong domestic currency.

Exchange-Rate Fluctuations.   At one time, world trade contracts could be easily written and payment was specified in a relatively stable currency. The American dollar was the standard and all transactions could be related to the dollar. Now that all major currencies are floating freely relative to one another, no one is quite sure of the value of any currency in the future. Increasingly, companies are insisting that transactions be written in terms of the vendor company's national currency, and forward hedging is becoming more common. If

Table 18.3   The Gaps that the Euro Could Close—Prices on Selected Goods and Services ($)

	Belgium	France	Germany	Italy	Spain
1.5 litre bottle of Coca-Cola	$2.05	$1.05	$1.89	$1.65	$1.14
Big Mac	2.86	3.08	2.67	2.48	2.38
Volkswagen Golf GL[a]	13 553	16 317	13 999	17 056	17 356
Litre of unleaded petrol	0.93	1.03	0.87	0.94	0.73
Dry-cleaned men's shirt	3.68	4.67	2.43	2.75	2.92
Subway or bus ticket	1.32	1.20	2.10	0.83	0.82
Pair of Levi's 501 jeans	71	83	81	69	70
Compaq Pressario 2240 computer	1 316	1 348	917	1 208	1 267[c]
One-day rental care Mercedes C-class[b]	154	110	103	243	113
One hour of translation	89	104	78	55	39

[a]Two-door model; [b]Without insurance; [c]Model 4504.
Source: *Business Week*, 27 April 1998, p. 44.

exchange rates are not carefully considered in long-term contracts, companies find themselves unwittingly giving 15–20 per cent discounts. The added cost incurred as exchange rates fluctuate on a day-to-day basis must be taken into account, especially where there is a significant time lapse between signing the order and delivery of the goods. Exchange-rate differentials mount up. Due to exchange rate fluctuations in one year, Nestle lost a million dollars in six months, while other companies have lost and gained even larger amounts. In June 1996, the £ sterling was worth 2.55 Dutch Guilders while in June 1997 it was worth 3.50, which created huge problems for British and Dutch firms selling in each others market (see Table 18.3).

Varying Currency Values.   In addition to risks from exchange-rate variations, other risks result from the changing values of a country's currency relative to other currencies. Consider the situation in Germany for a purchaser of US manufactured goods from the mid-1980s to the mid-1990s. During this period, the value of the US dollar relative to the German mark went from a very strong position ($1 US to 2.69 DM) in the late 1980s to a weaker position in 1996 ($1 US to 1.49 DM). A strong dollar produces price resistance because it takes a larger quantity of local currency to buy a US dollar. Conversely, when the US dollar is weak, demand for US goods increases because fewer units of local currency are needed to buy a US dollar. The weaker Us dollar, compared to most of the world's stronger currencies, that existed in the mid-1990s created a boom in US exports.[9]

When the value of the dollar is weak relative to the buyer's currency (i.e. it takes fewer units of the foreign currency to buy a dollar), companies generally employ cost-plus pricing. To remain price competitive when the dollar is strong (i.e. when it takes more units of the foreign currency to buy a dollar), companies must find ways to offset the higher price caused by currency values. By comparing the price of a relatively standardized product, it is possible to gain an insight into the under or over valuation of currencies (see Table 18.4).

Table 18.4   The Hamburger Pricing Standards

| | Big Mac Prices | | | | |
	In Local Currency	In Dollars	Implied PPP of the Dollar	Actual Exchange Rate 7/4/97	Local currency Under (−)/over (+) Valuation, + %
United States	$2.42	2.42	–	–	–
Argentina	Peso 2.50	2.50	1.03	1.00	+3
Australia	A$ 2.50	1.94	1.03	1.29	−20
Austria	Sch 34.00	2.82	14.0	12.0	+17
Belgium	BFr 109	3.09	45.0	35.3	+28
Brazil	Real 2.97	2.81	1.23	1.06	+16
Britain	£1.81	2.95	1.34++	1.63++	+22
Canada	C$ 2.88	2.07	1.19	1.39	−14
Chile	Peso 1200	2.88	496	417	+19
China	Yuan 9.70	1.16	4.01	8.33	−52
Czech Republic	CKr 53.0	1.81	21.9	29.2	−25
Denmark	DLr 25.72	3.95	10.6	6.25	+63
France	FFr 17.5	3.04	7.23	5.76	+26
Germany	DM 4.90	2.86	2.02	1.71	+18
Hong Kong	HK$ 9.90	1.28	4.09	7.75	−47
Hungary	Forint 271	1.52	112	178	−37
Israel	Shekel 11.5	3.40	4.75	3.38	+40
Italy	Lire 4600	2.73	1.901	1.683	+13
Japan	¥294	2.34	121	126	−3
Malaysia	M$ 3.87	1.55	1.60	2.50	−36
Mexico	Peso 14.9	1.89	6.16	7.90	−22
Netherlands	Fl 5.45	2.83	2.25	1.92	+17
New Zealand	NZ$ 3.25	2.24	1.34	1.45	−7
Poland	Zloty 4.30	1.39	1.78	3.10	−43
Russia	Rouble 11.000	1.92	4.545	5.739	−21
Singapore	S$ 3.00	2.08	1.24	1.44	−14
South Africa	Rand 7.80	1.76	3.22	4.43	−27
South Korea	Won 2.300	2.57	950	894	+6
Spain	Pta 375	2.60	155	144	+7
Sweden	SKr 26.0	3.37	10.7	7.72	+39
Switzerland	SFr 5.90	4.02	2.44	1.47	+66
Taiwan	NT$ 68.0	2.47	28.1	27.6	+2
Thailand	Baht 46.7	1.79	19.3	26.1	−26

Source: McDonald's cited in *The Economist*, 12 April 1997, p. 81.

Middleman.   Channel length and marketing patterns vary widely. In some countries, channels are longer and middleman margins higher than is customary. The diversity of channels used to reach markets and the lack of standardized middleman markups leave many producers unaware of the ultimate price of a product.

Besides channel diversity, the fully integrated marketer operating abroad faces various unanticipated costs because marketing and distribution channel infrastructures are under-developed in many countries. The marketer can also incur added expenses for warehousing and handling of small shipments, and may have to bear increased financing costs when dealing with underfinanced middlemen. Because no convenient source of data on middleman costs is available, the international marketer must rely on experience and marketing research to ascertain middleman costs.

Transportation.   Exporting also incurs increased transportation costs when moving goods from one country to another. If the goods go over water, there are additional costs for insurance, packing and handling not generally added to locally produced goods. Such costs add yet another burden because import tariffs in many countries are based on the landed cost that includes transportation, insurance and shipping charges. These costs add to the inflation of the final price. The next section details how a reasonable price in the home market may more than double in the foreign market.

Table 18.5 illustrates some of the effects these factors may have on the end price of a consumer item. Because costs and tariffs vary so widely from country to country, a hypothetical but realistic example is used. It assumes (1) that a constant net price is received by the manufacturer, (2) that all domestic transportation costs are absorbed by the various middlemen and reflected in their margins and (3) that the foreign middlemen have the same margins as the domestic middlemen. In some instances, foreign middlemen margins are lower, but it is equally probable that these margins could be greater. In fact, in many instances, middlemen use higher wholesale and retail margins for foreign goods than for similar domestic goods.

Notice that the retail prices in Table 18.5 range widely, illustrating the difficulty of price control by manufacturers in overseas retail markets. No matter how much the manufacturer may wish to market a product in a foreign country for a price equivalent to €9, there is little opportunity for such control. Even assuming the most optimistic conditions for Foreign Example 1, the producer would need to cut net by more than one-third to absorb freight and tariff costs if the goods are to be priced the same in both foreign and domestic markets.

Unless price escalation can be reduced, marketers find that the only buyers left are the wealthier ones. If marketers are to compete successfully in the growth of markets around the world, cost containment must be among their highest priorities. If costs can be reduced anywhere along the chain from manufacturer's cost to retailer markups, price escalation will be reduced. A discussion of some of the approaches to lessening price escalation follows.

Approaches to Lessening Price Escalation.   There are four efforts whereby costs may be reduced in attempting to lower price escalation: (1) lower the cost of goods; (2) lower the tariffs; (3) lower the distribution costs; and (4) using foreign trade zones.

■ Lower Cost of Goods.   If the manufacturer's price can be lowered, the effect is felt throughout the chain. One of the important reasons for manufacturing in a third country is an attempt to reduce manufacturing costs and, thus, price escalation. The impact can be profound if you consider that the hourly cost of skilled labour in India is less than €1.8 ($2) an hour including benefits, compared with more than €13 ($15) in Germany.

For US General Electric Company, the costs of manufacturing a typical microwave oven are GE €197 ($218), compared to €140 ($155) for Samsung, a Korean manufacturer. A breakdown of costs revealed that assembly labour cost GE €7.2 ($8) per oven and the Korean firm only €0.57 ($0.63). Overhead labour for supervision, maintenance and setup was €27 ($30) per GE oven and €0.66 ($0.73) for the Korean company. The largest area of difference was for line and central management; that came to €18 ($20) per oven for GE versus €0.02 ($0.02) for Samsung. Perhaps the most disturbing finding was that Korean labourers delivered more for less cost. GE produced four units per person whereas the Korean company produced nine.

Table 18.5 Sample Causes and Effects of Price Escalation

	Domestic Example	Foreign Example 1: Assuming the Same Channels with Wholesaler Importing Directly	Foreign Example 2: Importer and Same Margins and Channels	Foreign Example 3: Same as 2 but with 10 per cent Cumulative Turnover Tax
Manufacturing net	$5.00	$5.00	$5.00	$5.00
Transport cif	n.a.	6.10	6.10	6.10
Tariff (20 per cent cif value)	n.a.	1.22	1.22	1.22
Importer pays	n.a.	n.a.	7.32	7.32
Importer margin when sold to wholesaler (25 per cent) on cost	n.a.	n.a.	1.83	1.83
				+0.73 turnover tax
Wholesaler pays landed cost	5.00	7.32	9.15	9.88
Wholesaler margin (33⅓ per cent on cost)	1.67	2.44	3.05	3.29
				+0.99 turnover tax
Retailer pays	6.67	9.76	12.20	14.16
Retail margin (50 per cent on cost)	3.34	4.88	6.10	7.08
				+1.42 turnover tax
Retail price	$10.01	$14.64	$18.30	$22.66

Notes: *a.* All figures in US dollars; cif = cost, insurance and freigns; n.a. = not applicable.
b. The table assumes that all domestic transportation costs are absorbed by the middleman.
c. Transportation, tariffs and middleman margins vary from country to country, but for purposes of comparison, only a few of the possible variations are shown.

Lowering manufacturing costs can often have a double benefit—the lower price to the buyer may also mean lower tariffs, since most tariffs are levied on an *ad valorem* basis.

■ **Lower Tariffs.**   When tariffs account for a large part of price escalation, as they often do, companies seek ways to lower the rate. Some products can be reclassified into a different, and lower, customs classification. An American company selling data communications equipment in Australia faced a 25 per cent tariff which affected the price competitiveness of its products. It persuaded the Australian government to change the classification for the type of products the company sells from 'computer equipment' (25 per cent tariff) to 'telecommunication equipment' (3 per cent tariff). Like many products, this company's products could be legally classified under either category.

There are often differential rates between fully assembled, ready-to-use products and those requiring some assembly, further processing, the addition of locally manufactured component parts or other processing that adds value to the product and can be performed within the foreign country. A ready-to-operate piece of machinery with a 20 per cent tariff may be subject to only a 12 per cent tariff when imported unassembled. An even lower tariff may apply when the product is assembled in the country and some local content is added.

■ **Lower Distribution Costs.**   Shorter channels can help keep prices under control. Designing a channel that has fewer middlemen may lower distribution costs by reducing or eliminating middlemen markup. Besides eliminating markups, fewer middlemen may mean lower overall taxes. Some countries levy a value-added tax on goods as they pass through channels. Each time goods change hands, they are taxed. The tax may be cumulative or non-cumulative. The cumulative value-added tax is based on total selling price and is assessed every time the goods change hands. Obviously, in countries where value-added tax is cumulative, tax alone provides a special incentive for developing short distribution channels. Where that is achieved, tax is paid only on the difference between the middleman's cost and the selling price.

■ **Using Foreign-Trade Zones.**   Some countries have established foreign or free-trade zones (FTZ) or free ports to facilitate international trade. There are more than 300 of these facilities in operation throughout the world where imported goods can be stored or processed. As free-trade policies in Asia, Eastern Europe and other developing regions expand, there has been an equally rapid expansion in the creation and use of FTZs. In a free port or FTZ, payment of import duties is postponed until the product leaves the FTZ area and enters the country. An FTZ is, in essence, a tax-free enclave and not considered part of the country as far as import regulations are concerned. When an item leaves an FTZ and is officially imported into the host country of the FTZ, all duties and regulations are imposed.[10]

By shipping unassembled goods to an FTZ in an importing country, a marketer can lower costs in a variety of ways:

1. Tariffs may be lower because duties are typically assessed at a lower rate for unassembled versus assembled goods.
2. If labour costs are lower in the importing country, substantial savings may be realized in the final product cost.
3. Ocean transportation rates are affected by weight and volume, thus, unassembled goods may qualify for lower freight rates.
4. If local content, such as packaging or component parts, can be used in the final assembly, there may be a further reduction of tariffs.

All in all, an FTZ is an important method for controlling price escalation. Incidentally, all the advantages offered by an FTZ for an exporter are also advantages for an importer. These

HOW ARE FOREIGN-TRADE ZONES USED?

There are more than 100 foreign-trade zones (FTZs) in the United States and FTZs exist in many other countries as well. Companies use them to postpone the payment of tariffs on products while they are in the FTZ. Here are some examples of how FTZs in the United States are used.

- A Japanese firm assembles motorcycles, jet skis and three-wheel all-terrain vehicles for import as well as for export to Canada, Latin America and Europe.
- A US manufacturer of window blinds and miniblinds imports and stores fabric from Holland in a FTZ, thereby postponing a 17 per cent tariff until the fabric leaves the FTZ.
- A manufacturer of hair dryers stores its product in a FTZ, which it uses as its main distribution centre for products manufactured in Asia.
- A European-based medical supply company manufactures kidney dialysis machines and sterile tubing using raw materials from Germany and US labour. It then exports 30 per cent of its products to Scandinavian countries.
- A Canadian company assembles electronic teaching machines using cabinets from Italy, electronics from Taiwan, Korea and Japan, and labour from the United States, for export to Colombia and Peru.

In all these examples, tariffs are postponed until the products leave the FTZ and enter the US. Further, in most situations the tariff is at the lower rate for component parts and raw materials versus the higher rate that would have been charged if imported directly as finished goods. If the finished products are not imported into the US from the FTZ, but shipped to another country, no US tariffs apply.

Sources: Lewis E. Leibowitz, 'An Overview of Foreign Trade Zones', Europe, Winter–Spring 1987, p. 12; and 'Cheap Imports', *International Business*, March 1993, pp. 98–100.

zones are used in many countries in the West as well as in the emerging markets. Over 100 FTZs in the United States are used by US importers to help lower their costs of imported goods.[11]

Competition

The nature of market structure in particular is an important determinant of price. It refers to the number of competing firms, their size and relative position. In the case of an oligopoly structure, the entering firm would have little freedom to choose a price. Depending upon the income levels, a certain market can take only a certain level of pricing. The prices have thus to be set at the level of the competing products. A company can also use competitors' prices as a landmark for positioning its products as compared to competitors. For example, if it wants to position its product as being of higher quality than its competitors, it has to price it accordingly. On the other hand, if a company decides to compete with its competitors on price, it has to set a competitive price. While entering a market and using competitive pricing, a company needs also to check on the cost structure of its competitors. The price is just one of the elements of marketing mix and has thus to be matched with other elements of it. When a higher price is charged, the company should be able to convince the market that it has a better product, thereby justifying its higher price.

Target Customer

Marketers have to evaluate and understand a particular segment or a target customer group in the market that they are entering. A knowledge of demand elasticity and price is essential and how customers would react in the case of price change. Demand for a product is *elastic* if demand can be considerably increased by lowering the price. If a decrease in price would not have much effect on demand, it will be considered *inelastic*. Other than the buying behaviour, the ability of customers to buy, prices of substitute and competing products and the nature of nonprice competition are of the utmost importance. In the case of undifferentiated products, the competition is more on pricing, but with differentiated products, however, market share of a company can even be enhanced through higher prices. Brand names and an image of high quality are two of the factors that characterize differentiated products that can be sold at premium prices.

Pricing Controls

Companies doing business in foreign countries encounter a number of different types of government price setting. To control prices, governments may establish margins, set prices and floors or ceilings, restrict price changes, compete in the market, grant subsidies or act as a purchasing monopsony or selling monopoly. The government may also influence prices by permitting, or even encouraging, businesses to collude in setting manipulative prices.

In most countries, governments regulate pricing. All these rules and regulations need to be considered while setting prices. A number of governments, although liberal on price setting, restrict price changes. A company entering a foreign market with a penetration strategy with a lower price, hoping to increase the price after achieving a certain market share might not be able to change its price. In Europe, a number of rules and regulations are being changed and standardized. Price controls are normally exercised for political and social reasons such as to control inflation, protect consumers from unjustified price increases, and stimulate equal distribution of wealth. Price controls are not only limited to developing countries. In the 1980s, countries such as France, Sweden and the United States enforced price freezes to control inflation and balance of payments. To cover against the impact of price-freezes and controls, firms should regularly review prices in inflationary markets. Firms should watch out for such measures and preempt such controls. One way out of them is to keep introducing new products. Another way is to review payment terms and other conditions of sale such as discounts and credits.

ADMINISTERED PRICING

Administered pricing relates to attempts to establish prices for an entire market. Such prices may be arranged through the cooperation of competitors, through national, state or local governments or by international agreement. The legality of administered pricing arrangements of various kinds differs from country to country and from time to time. A country may condone price fixing for foreign markets but condemn it for the domestic market.

In general, the end goal of all administered pricing activities is to reduce the impact of price competition or eliminate it. Price fixing by business is not viewed as an acceptable practice but when governments enter the field of price administration, they presume to do it for the general good to lessen the effects of 'destructive' competition.

Price Setting by Industry Groups

The pervasiveness of price-fixing attempts in business is reflected by the diversity of the language of administered prices; pricing arrangements are known as agreements, arrangements, combines, conspiracies, cartels, communities of profit, profit pools, licensing, trade associations, price leadership, customary pricing or informal interfirm agreements. The arrangements themselves vary from the completely informal with no spoken or acknowledged agreement to highly formalized and structured arrangements. Any type of price-fixing arrangement can be adapted to international business; but of all the forms mentioned, the three most directly associated with international marketing are licensing, cartels and trade associations.

Licensing Agreements.   In industries where technological innovation is especially important, patent or process agreements are the most common type of international combination. In most countries, licensing agreements are legally acceptable because the owners of patents and other processes are granting an exclusive licence to someone in another country to produce a product. By contractual definition, a patent holder can control territorial boundaries and, because of the monopoly, can control pricing. Often such arrangements go beyond a specific licensing agreement to include a gentlemen's agreement to give their foreign counterparts first rights on patents and new developments. Such arrangements can lead to national monopolies that significantly restrict competition and thereby raise product prices. Like so many other agreements related to restricting competition, the legality of licensing agreements is difficult to discuss outside the context of a specific situation. Licensing arrangements have been an important factor in international marketing in the past and continue to be important despite numerous restrictions.

Cartels.   A cartel exists when various companies producing similar products work together to control markets for the types of goods they produce. Generally, a cartel involves more than a patent licensing agreement and endows the participants with greater power. The cartel association may use formal agreements to set prices, establish levels of production and sales for the participating companies, allocate market territories and even redistribute profits. In some instances, the cartel organization itself takes over the entire selling function, sells the goods of all the producers and distributes the profits.

The economic role of cartels is highly debatable, but their proponents argue that they eliminate cut-throat competition and 'rationalize' business, permitting greater technical progress and lower prices to consumers. However, in the view of most experts, it is doubtful that the consumer benefits very often from cartels.

The Organization of Petroleum Exporting Countries (OPEC) is probably the best-known international cartel. Its power in controlling the price of oil resulted from the percentage of oil production they controlled. In the early 1970s, when OPEC members provided the industrial world with 67 per cent of its oil, OPEC was able to quadruple the price of oil. The sudden rise in price from $10 (€9) or $12 (€11) a barrel to $50 (€45) or more a barrel was a primary factor in throwing the world into a major recession. Non-OPEC oil exporting countries benefited from the price increase while net importers of foreign oil suffered economic downturns. Among less developed countries, those producing oil prospered while oil importers suffered economically from the high prices.[12]

The legality of cartels at present is not clearly defined. Domestic cartelization is illegal in the United States, and the European Union has provisions for controlling cartels. The United States, however, does permit firms to take cartel-like actions in foreign markets. Increasingly, it has become apparent that many governments have concluded they cannot ignore or destroy cartels completely, so they have chosen to establish ground rules and regulatory agencies to oversee the cartel-like activities of businesses within their jurisdiction.

Trade Associations.   The term *trade association* is so broad it is almost meaningless. Trade associations may exist as hard, tight cartels or merely informal trade organizations having nothing to do with pricing, market share or levels of production. In many countries, trade associations gather information about prices and transactions within a given industry. Such associations have the general goal of protecting and maintaining the pricing structure most generally acceptable to industry members.

In most industrial nations manufacturers' associations frequently represent 90 to 100 per cent of an industry. The association is a club one must join for access to customers and suppliers. It often handles industrywide labour negotiations and is capable of influencing government decisions relating to the industry.

International Agreements

Governments of producing and consuming countries seem to play an ever-increasing role in the establishment of international prices for certain basic commodities. There are, for example, an international coffee agreement, an international cocoa agreement and an international sugar agreement. The world price of wheat has long been at least partially determined by negotiations between national governments.

Despite the pressures of business, government and international price agreements, most marketers still have wide latitude in their pricing decisions for most products and markets.

TRANSFER PRICING

As companies increase the number of worldwide subsidiaries, joint ventures, company-owned distributing systems and other marketing arrangements, the price charged to different affiliates becomes a preeminent question. Prices of goods transferred from operations or sales units in one country to a company's units elsewhere may be adjusted to enhance the ultimate profit of the company as a whole. The benefits are:

1. Lowering duty costs by shipping goods into high-tariff countries at minimal transfer prices so duty base and duty are low.
2. Reduction of income taxes in high-tax countries by overpricing goods transferred to units in such countries; profits are eliminated and shifted to low-tax countries. Such profit shifting may also be used for 'dressing up' financial statements by increasing reported profits in countries where borrowing and other financing are undertaken.
3. Facilitation of dividend repatriation. When dividend repatriation is curtailed by government policy, invisible income may be taken out in the form of high prices for products or components shipped to units in that country.
4. To show more or less profit in crucial times, for example in the case of new emission, government rules, to please shareholders or to show the good performance of new/old management.

The tax and financial manipulation possibilities of transfer pricing have not been overlooked by government authorities. Transfer pricing can be used to hide subsidiary profits and to escape foreign market taxes. Transfer pricing is managed in such a way that profit is taken in the country with the lowest tax rate. For example, a foreign manufacturer makes a VCR for €45 ($50), sells it to its European subsidiary for €135 ($150). The European subsidiary sells it to a retailer for €180 ($200), but it spends €45 ($50) on advertising and shipping so it shows no profit and pays no taxes. Meanwhile, the parent company makes a €90 ($100) gross margin on each unit and pays at a lower tax rate in the home country. If the tax rate was lower in the country where the subsidiary resides, the profit would be taken there and no profit taken in the home country.[13]

The overall objectives of the transfer pricing system include: (1) maximizing profits for the corporation as a whole, (2) facilitating parent-company control and (3) offering management at all levels, both in the product divisions and in the international divisions, and an adequate basis for maintaining, developing and receiving credit for their own profitability.

An intracorporate pricing system should employ sound accounting techniques and be defensible to the tax authorities of the countries involved. All of these factors argue against a single uniform price or even a uniform pricing system for all international operations.

Four arrangements for pricing goods for intracompany transfer are:

1. Sales at the local manufacturing cost plus a standard markup.
2. Sales at the cost of the most efficient producer in the company plus a standard markup.
3. Sales at negotiated prices.
4. Arm's-length sales using the same prices as quoted to independent customers.

Of the four, the arm's-length transfer is most acceptable to tax authorities and most likely to be acceptable to foreign divisions, but the appropriate basis for intracompany transfers depends on the nature of the subsidiaries and market conditions.

DUMPING

A logical outgrowth of a market policy in international business is goods priced competitively at widely differing prices in various markets. Marginal (variable) cost pricing, as discussed above, is one way prices can be reduced to stay within a competitive price range. The market and economic logic of such pricing policies can hardly be disputed, but the practices are often classified as dumping and are subject to severe penalties and fines (see Table 18.6). *Dumping* is defined differently by various economists. One approach classifies international shipments as dumped if the products are sold below their cost of production. The other approach characterizes dumping as selling goods in a foreign market below the price of the same goods in the home market. Even rate cutting on cargo shipping has been called dumping.

In the 1960s and 1970s, dumping was hardly an issue because world markets were strong. As the decade of the 1980s began, dumping became a major issue for a large number of industries. Excess production capacity relative to home-country demand caused many companies to price their goods on a marginal-cost basis figuring that any contribution above variable cost was beneficial to company profits. In a classic case of dumping, prices are maintained in the home-country market and reduced in foreign markets. For example, the European Union charged that differences in prices between Japan and EU countries ranged from 4.8 to 86 per cent. To correct for this dumping activity, a special import duty of 33.4 per cent was imposed on Japanese computer printers.

Assembly in the importing country is one way companies attempt to lower prices

Table 18.6   Antitrade—Summary of Anti-dumping Actions, 1996

	New Actions	Measures in Force*
South Africa	30	31
Argentina	23	30
EU	23	153
United States	21	311
India	20	15
Australia	17	47
Brazil	17	24
Korea	13	14
Indonesia	8	n.a.
Israel	6	n.a.
Canada	5	96
Peru	5	4
New Zealand	4	27
Chile	3	0
Mexico	3	95
Venezuela	3	3
Malaysia	2	n.a.
Colombia	1	7
Guatemala	1	n.a.
Thailand	1	1
Japan	—	3
Singapore	—	2
Turkey	—	37
Total	*206*	*900*

*31 December 1996.
Source: Based on WTO, *The Economist*, 8 November 1997.

and avoid dumping charges. However, these screwdriver plants, as they are often called, are subject to dumping charges if the price differentials reflect more than the cost savings that result from assembly in the importing country. The increased concern and enforcement in the European Union reflects the changing attitudes among all countries towards dumping. The EU has had anti-dumping legislation from its inception, but the first anti-dumping duties ever imposed were on Taiwanese bicycle chains in 1976. Since then, the Department of Trade of the EU has imposed duties on a variety of products.

PRICE QUOTATIONS

In quoting the price of goods for international sale, a contract may include specific elements affecting the price, such as credit, sales terms and transportation. Parties to the transaction must be certain that the quotation settled on appropriately locates responsibility for the goods during transportation and spells out who pays transportation charges and from what point. Price quotations must also specify the currency to be used, credit terms and the type of

GOING INTERNATIONAL 18.5

ANTI-DUMPING LAWS IN EUROPE

According to World Trade Organization rules, anti-dumping action may be brought if a product is sold for export at a lower price than that for which it is sold at home, or for less than its production costs at home plus a 'reasonable' addition for selling costs and profit. An industry in the importing country must also show that it has been caused injury by this dumping. There is, however, no reference to price at home or abroad. But how is it practised? Here is one example:

In November 1996, the European Commission imposed anti-dumping duties on imports of unbleached cotton fabrics from China, Egypt, Indonesia, Pakistan and Turkey. On 13 July, eight EU countries, led by France, complained against the decision. In fact, the French president made several telephone calls to the president of the European Commission.

The issue is that the price of cotton, including unbleached cotton, fell by 36 per cent between May and August 1995. The commission used this fall as an argument that the fabric was dumped. It calculated the difference between the 'right' price and the 'dumped' price disregarding the losses or below-cost sales in the home markets as well. It also disregarded the high price sales in export markets arguing that they were an artificial front to hide dumping.

These types of calculations are also used by the American International Trade Administration (ITA) resulting in the fact that in most of the cases brought in the EU (about 75 per cent) and in America (96 per cent) firms are found guilty. A number of scholars in Europe and the Cato Institute in Washington have thus been arguing that anti-dumping policy should be, well, dumped. It is theoretically as well as practically faulty, as at the bottom, the policy reposes on the prejudice that foreign producers should be subject to different laws from domestic ones. Normal competition law (the EU treaties article 86) takes care of predatory pricing; the attempt to drive competitors out of business by undercutting them. It is, however, difficult to understand why there should be a different law for domestic predators and a different one for foreign ones. A recent study of EU anti-dumping cases between 1980 and 1997 concluded that only 2 per cent of the cases filed were 'possible candidates for a closer examination of possible predatory behaviour'. In the world as a whole, there were 1558 cases recorded between 1980–1989 alone. In one US case, the ITA ruled that the mere threat of competition in super computers would damage Cray, a US producer. However, Cray had provided more than 25 per cent of the 500 fastest computers in the world, while its rivals Fujitsu and NEC, whom ITC found guilty of dumping, had only 10 per cent combined.

Source: 'Dumping anti-dumping laws', *The European*, 20–26 July 1998, p. 7.

documentation required. Finally, the price quotation and contract should define quantity and quality. A quantity definition might be necessary because different countries use different units of measurement.[14]

COUNTERTRADES AS A PRICING TOOL

The challenges of countertrade must be viewed from the same perspective as all other variations in international trade. Marketers must be aware of which markets will be likely to require countertrades just as they must be aware of social customs and legal requirements. Assessing this factor along with all other market factors will enhance a marketer's competitive position.

Ben and Jerry's Homemade Ice Cream Inc., a well-known US ice-cream vendor, is manufacturing and selling ice cream in Russia. With the roubles they earn, they are buying Russian walnuts, honey and matryoshky (Russian nesting dolls) to sell in the United States.

This is the only means of getting their profit out of Russia because there is a shortage of hard currencies in Russia making it difficult to convert roubles to dollars. Pepsi-Cola sells Pepsi to Russians in exchange for the exclusive rights to sell Stolichnaya vodka in the United States. In neither transaction does cash change hands; these are barter deals, a type of countertrade. Although cash may be the preferred method of payment, countertrades are becoming an important part of trade with Eastern Europe, China and, to a varying degree, some Latin American and African nations.[15] Today, an international company must include in its market-pricing toolkit some understanding of countertrading.

Types of Countertrade

Countertrade includes four distinct transactions: barter, compensation deals, counterpurchase and buy-back.[16]

■ Barter is the direct exchange of goods between two parties in a transaction. One of the largest barter deals to date involved Occidental Petroleum Corporation's agreement to ship superphosphoric acid to the former Soviet Union for ammonia urea and potash under a 2-year, €18 billion ($20 billion) deal. No money changed hands nor were any third parties involved. Obviously, in a barter transaction, the seller (Occidental Petroleum) must be able to dispose of the goods at a net price equal to the expected selling price in a regular, for-cash transaction. Further, during the negotiation stage of a barter deal, the seller must know the market and the price for the items offered in trade. In the Russian barter trade example, the price and a market for the ammonia urea and potash were established because Occidental could use the products in its operations. But bartered goods can range from hams to iron pellets, mineral water, furniture or olive oil—all somewhat more difficult to price and market when potential customers must be sought.

■ Compensation deals involve payment in goods and in cash. A Western seller delivers lathes to a buyer in Pakistan and receives 70 per cent of the payment in convertible currency and 30 per cent in tanned hides and raw cotton. In an actual deal, General Motors Corporation sold €11.8 million ($12 million) worth of locomotives and diesel engines to Yugoslavia and took cash and €3.6 million ($4 million) in Yugoslavian cutting tools as payment.

An advantage of a compensation deal over barter is the immediate cash settlement of a portion of the bill; the remainder of the cash is generated after successful sale of the goods received. If the company has a use for the goods received, the process is relatively simple and uncomplicated. On the other hand, if the seller has to rely on a third party to find a buyer, the cost involved must be anticipated in the original compensation negotiation if the net proceeds to the seller are to be equal to the market price.

■ Counterpurchase or offset trade is probably the most frequently used type of countertrade. For this trade, two contracts are negotiated. The seller agrees to sell a product at a set price to a buyer and receives payment in cash. However, the first contract is contingent on a second contract that is an agreement by the original seller to buy goods from the buyer for the total monetary amount involved in the first contract or for a set percentage of that amount. This arrangement provides the seller with more flexibility than the compensation deal because there is generally a time period—6 to 12 months or longer—for completion of the second contract. During the time that markets are sought for the goods in the second contract, the seller has received full payment for the original sale. Further, the goods to be purchased in the second contract are generally of greater variety than those offered in a compensation deal.

The *offset trades*, as they are sometimes called, are becoming more prevalent among economically weak countries. Several variations of a counterpurchase or offset have developed

MAY I PAY WITH CANNED MUSHROOMS?

China, Russia, Eastern Europe and Latin America are huge markets, but a shortage of hard currency in these countries makes it difficult for a company to collect for sales. Barter, or countertrade, is one means companies use to convert local currencies to US dollars.

Pepsi-Cola Company has had a long history of using countertrade in Russia, so its World Trade, Inc., a trading arm founded to find barter deals in the Soviet Union, was ready when the need arose in China. Pepsi buys $20 million (€18 million) of goods annually in China. This includes goods such as canned mushrooms, some of which are used in its Pizza Hut chain, plastic cartoon characters given away in promotional campaigns at Kentucky Fried Chicken outlets, and spices used by Pizza Hut. Not all the goods Pepsi receives in countertrade deals are used by the company. It regularly receives and markets through PepsiCo World Trade surgical gauze and surgical instruments, leather goods and cat food.

It is not unusual for companies doing business in cash-poor countries to have to resort to some sort of countertrade. Xerox Corporation exports Brazilian steel to Europe and venetian blinds worth $100 million (€90 million) annually to the United States. H.J. Heinz Company's operation in Zimbabwe bakes and cans kidney beans and other foods for local consumption and raises scarce currency by exporting the beans to Botswana, Britain and other parts of the world. Companies regard such strategies as far from perfect but necessary if they are to do business in these countries.

Sources: Louis Kraar, 'How to Sell to Cashless Buyers', *Fortune*, 7 November 1988, pp. 147–152 and 'Learn from Russia', *Business China*, 5 September 1994, pp. 1–2.

to make it more economical for the selling company. For example, the Lockheed Corporation goes so far as to build up offset trade credits before a counterpurchase deal is made. Knowing that some type of countertrade would have to be accepted to make aircraft sales to Korea, they actively sought the opportunity to assist in the sale of Hyundai personal computers even though there was no guarantee that Korea would actually buy aircraft from them. Lockheed has been involved in countertrades for over 20 years. During that time countertrade agreements have totalled over €1.2 billion ($1.3 billion) and have included everything from tomato paste to rugs, textiles and automotive parts.

■ Product buy-back agreement is the last of the four countertrade transactions. This type of agreement is made when the sale involves goods or services that produce other goods and services, that is, production plant, production equipment or technology. The buy-back agreement usually involves one of two situations: the seller agrees to accept as partial payment a certain portion of the output, or the seller receives full price initially but agrees to buy back a certain portion of the output. When Massey Ferguson, a British farm equipment manufacturer, sold a tractor plant to Poland it was paid part in hard currency and the balance in Polish-built tractors. In another situation, General Motors built a motor vehicle manufacturing plant in Brazil and was paid under normal terms but agreed to the purchase of resulting output when the new facilities came on stream. Levi Strauss took Hungarian made blue jeans, which it sells abroad, in exchange for setting up a jeans factory near Budapest.[17]

A major drawback to product buy-back agreements comes when the seller finds that the products bought back are in competition with its own similarly produced goods. On the other hand, some have found that a product buy-back agreement provides them with a supplemental source in areas of the world where there is demand but where they have no available supply.[18]

CUTTLEFISH—WHO WANTS CUTTLEFISH?

For effective international pricing you need a working knowledge of countertrade. You can almost bet that with certain countries something other than money will be offered in a deal. Here's what happened to a US businessman.

The businessman figured he would make about $1 million (€0.9 million) on the deal, a $2.5 million (€2.3 million) contract with the Republic of China. He started looking for a loan to pay expenses; 10 local banks turned him down. The problem: his deal had a catch—instead of cash the Chinese wanted to pay him in cuttlefish.

'A lot of countries don't pay money', he says, 'They pay in countertrade of commodities'. He had only started his company two years before and this type of deal was new to him. The banks found it hilarious. 'I saw dollars, the bankers saw fish', he says. 'One banker said he had never heard anything so ridiculous in his life.'

After it was too late, he found there were banks with experience in countertrading deals that might have approved his financing. He also learned he could have instantly sold the cuttlefish in Indonesia. But it was too late. 'I lost out on a fine deal because I did not know how to handle it. I didn't know anything about countertrade.'

Source: Adapted from 'Going Global', *Denver Business*, April 1988, p. 44.

Western Firms and Countertrade

Countertrade transactions are on the increase in world trade; some estimates of countertrade in international trade go as high as 30 per cent. More conservative estimates place the amount closer to 20 per cent. Regardless, a significant amount of all international trade now involves some type of countertrade transaction, and this percentage is predicted to increase substantially in the near future. Much of that increase will come in trading with emerging countries; in fact, some require countertrades of some sort with all foreign trade. Countertrade arrangements are involved in an estimated 50 per cent or more of all international trade with Eastern European and developing countries.[19]

Western European and Japanese firms have the longest history of countertrade. Western Europe has traded with Eastern Europe and Japan through its *soga shosha* (trading companies) worldwide.[20]

The crucial problem confronting a seller in a countertrade negotiation is determining the value of and potential demand for the goods offered. Frequently there is inadequate time to conduct a market analysis; in fact, it is not unusual to have sales negotiations almost completed before countertrade is introduced as a requirement in the transaction.

Although such problems are difficult to deal with, they can be minimized with proper preparation. In most cases where losses have occurred in countertrades, the seller has been unprepared to negotiate in anything other than cash. Some preliminary research should be done in anticipation of being confronted with a countertrade proposal. Countries with a history of countertrading are easily identified and the products most likely to be offered in a countertrade can often be ascertained.[21]

Barter houses specialize in trading goods acquired through barter arrangements and are the primary outside source of aid for companies beset by the uncertainty of a countertrade. While barter houses, most of which are found in Europe and Asia, can find a market for bartered goods, it requires time, which puts a financial strain on a company because capital is tied up longer than in normal transactions. Seeking loans to tide it over until sales are completed usually solves this problem.

There are many examples of companies losing sales to competitors who were willing to enter into countertrade agreements. A Western oilfield equipment manufacturer claims it submitted the lowest dollar bid in an Egyptian offer but lost the sale to a bidder who offered a counter purchase arrangement. Incidentally, the successful company was Japanese with a sizeable established trading company to dispose of the Egyptian goods received in the counterpurchase arrangement.

Proactive Countertrade Strategy

Some authorities suggest that companies should have a defined countertrade strategy as part of their marketing strategy rather than be caught unprepared when confronted with a countertrade proposition. Currently most companies have a reactive strategy, that is, they use countertrade when they believe it is the only way to make a sale. Even when these companies include countertrade as a permanent feature of their operations, they use it to react to a sales demand rather than using countertrade as an aggressive marketing tool for expansion.[22]

Successful countertrade transactions require that the marketer (1) accurately establishes the market value of the goods being offered and (2) disposes of the bartered goods once they are received. Most countertrades judged unsuccessful result from not properly resolving one or both of these factors.

In short, unsuccessful countertrades are generally the result of inadequate planning and preparation. One experienced countertrader suggests answering the following questions before entering into a countertrade agreement: (1) Is there a ready market for the goods bartered? (2) Is the quality of the goods offered consistent and acceptable? (3) Is an expert needed to handle the negotiations? (4) Is the contract price sufficient to cover the cost of barter and net the desired revenue?

SUMMARY

Pricing is one of the most complicated decision areas encountered by international marketers. Rather than deal with one set of market conditions, one group of competitors, one set of cost factors and one set of government regulations, international marketers must take all these factors into account, not only for each country in which they are operating, but often for each market within a country. The continuing growth of the less developed country markets coupled with their lack of investment capital has increased the importance of countertrades for most marketers, making it an important tool to include in pricing policy.

Market prices at the consumer level are much more difficult to control in international than in domestic marketing, but the international marketer must still approach the pricing task on a basis of objectives and policy, leaving enough flexibility for tactical price movements. Pricing in the international marketplace requires a combination of intimate knowledge of market costs and regulations, an awareness of possible countertrade deals, infinite patience for detail and a shrewd sense of market strategy.

QUESTIONS

1. Discuss the causes of and solutions for parallel imports and their effect on price.
2. Why is it so difficult to control consumer prices when selling overseas?
3. What are the causes of price escalation? Do they differ for exports and goods produced and sold in a foreign country?
4. Why is it seldom feasible for a company to absorb the high cost of international transportation and reduce the net price received?
5. Price escalation is a major pricing problem for the international marketer. How can this problem be counteracted? Discuss.
6. Changing currency values have an impact on pricing strategies. Discuss.
7. 'Regardless of the strategic factors involved and the company's orientation to market pricing, every price must be set with cost considerations in mind.' Discuss.
8. 'Price fixing by business is not generally viewed as an acceptable practice (at least in the domestic market); but when governments enter the field of price administration, they presume to do it for the general welfare to lessen the effects of destructive' competition.' Discuss.
9. Do value-added taxes discriminate against imported goods?
10. Explain specific tariffs, ad valorem tariffs, and combination tariffs.
11. Suggest an approach a marketer may follow in adjusting prices to accommodate exchange-rate fluctuations.
12. Why has dumping become such an issue in recent years?
13. Discuss the various ways in which governments set prices. Why do they engage in such activities?
14. Discuss the alternative objectives possible in setting transfer prices.
15. Why do governments so carefully scrutinize transfer pricing arrangements?
16. Why are costs so difficult to assess in marketing internationally?
17. Discuss why countertrading is on the increase.
18. Discuss the major problems facing a company that is countertrading.
19. If a country you are trading with has a shortage of hard currency, how should you prepare to negotiate price?
20. Of the four types of countertrades discussed in the text, which is the most beneficial to the seller? Explain.
21. Why should a 'knowledge of countertrades be part of an international marketer's pricing toolkit'? Discuss.

REFERENCES

1. For a comprehensive review of pricing and the integration of Europe, see Wolfgang Gaul and Ulrich Luz, 'Pricing in International Marketing and Western European Economic Integration', *Management International Review*, vol. 34, no. 2, 1994, pp. 101–124.

2. S. Tamer Cavusgil, 'Unraveling the Mystiques of Export Pricing', in Sidney J. Levy, *et al.* (eds), *Marketing Manager's Handbook* (New York: Dartnell, 1994), pp. 1357–1374; and 'The Debate on Export Subsidies', *European Business Report*, Spring IQ, 1998, p. 58.

3. For a complete and thorough discussion of parallel markets, see Robert E. Weigand, 'Parallel Import Channels—Options for Preserving Territorial Integrity', *The Columbia Journal of World Business*, Spring 1991, pp. 53–60.

4. 'Indian Computer Makers Say Smugglers Are Taking Business', Reuters News Service release, 2 February 1994.

5. 'Coca-Cola Faces a Price War in Japan and the Enemy Is Itself', *The Wall Street Journal*, 7 July 1994, p. A-1.

6. 'Cross-border Pricing: Is the Price Right?' *Business Europe*, 6–12 February 1995, pp. 6–7; and 'Showroom Tactics: New Car Prices', *The European*, 2–8 February 1998, p. 22.

7. For a comprehensive review of pricing in foreign markets, see James K. Weekly, 'Pricing in Foreign Markets: Pitfalls and Opportunities', *Industrial Marketing Management*, May 1992, pp. 173–179.

8. See, for example, Joseph Neu, 'Profiting from Leasing Abroad', *International Business*, April 1995, pp. 56–58.

9. 'US-Based MNCs Say Weak Dollar Is Nothing to Cry About', *Crossborder Monitor*, 20 July 1994, pp. 1–2.

10. 'Special Section: FTZs', *Global Trade and Transportation*, September 1994, pp. 24–27.

11. D. Scott Freeman, 'Foreign Trade Zones: An Underutilized US Asset', *Trade & Culture*, September–October 1994, pp. 94–95.

12. 'Oil Prices', *The Wall Street Journal*, 15 March 1995, p. C-14.

13. 'Transfer Pricing Is Alive and Well', *International Business*, June 1994, p. 95.

14. D. Gary McKinnon, 'Export Sales—The Importance of Setting Competitive Payments Terms', *Business America*, February 1995, pp. 6–8

15. Most countertrade is found in countries with shortages of foreign exchange, which is often given as the reason why countertrades are mandated by these countries. An interesting study, however, casts some doubt on this thesis and suggests instead that countertrades may be a reasonable way for countries to minimize transaction costs. For an insightful report on this research, see Jean-Francois Hennart, and Erin Anderson, 'Countertrade and the Minimization of Transaction Costs: An Empirical Examination', *The Journal of Law, Economics, & Organization*, vol. 9, no. 2, 1993, pp. 290–313.

16. A variety of terms are used to describe the transactions the authors classify as countertrades. Switch trading, parallel trades, offset trades, and clearing agreements are other terms used to describe countertrade, but they are only variations of the four types mentioned here. In order not to further confuse the issue but to help standardize terminology, the authors have used the terms developed by Business International.

17. Rosalind Resnick, 'Barter Boom: How to Trade with Eastern Europe', *International Business*, October 1993, pp. 19–20.

18. 'Financing CIS Sales: Reinventing Countertrade', *Business Eastern Europe*, 17 January 1994, pp. 1–2.

19. A report on risk sharing in countertrade is found in Erwin Amann and Dalia Marin, 'Risk-Sharing in International Trade: An Analysis of Countertrade', *The Journal of Industrial Economics*, March 1994, pp. 63–77.

20. For an interesting study on Japanese trading companies and countertrade, see Aspy P. Palia, 'Countertrade Practices in Japan', *Industrial marketing Management*, May 1993, pp. 125–132.

21. See, for example, the study by Aspy P. Palia and Heon Deok Yoon, 'Countertrade Practices in Korea', *Industrial Marketing Management*, July 1994, pp. 205–214, which examines the kinds of countertrade practices most appropriate in Korea.

22. Sam C. Okoroafo, 'Implementing International Countertrade: A Dyadic Approach', *Industrial Marketing Management*, July 1994, pp. 229–234.

Financing and Managing International Marketing Operations

Part Outline

Financial Requirements for International Marketing: A Major Concern for Smaller Firms

Chapter Learning Objectives

What you should learn from Chapter 19

- The components of international marketing that create the need for increased capital.

- What market penetration costs are.

- Available sources of funding and support designed to aid the export of goods.

- Sources of government funding for international marketing and how to use them.

- The mechanics of international payment for goods.

- The types of financial risks peculiar to foreign marketing and the management of those risks.

When companies decide to market internationally, additional financing is one of the important resources. An often-cited reason for companies not reaching international business objectives is insufficient capital to fund the additional investments necessary for success. This is particularly true for small- and medium-sized (SMEs) companies. Marketing and finance are inextricably intertwined with overall corporate planning, goals and objectives; policies and decisions in either one have a profound effect on the other. Without proper financial support, marketing activities cannot achieve their ultimate potential.

As a company moves more deeply into the international arena, the interdependence of marketing and financial activities increases and places greater demands on the company. This means (1) an increased need for working capital, (2) assuring timely international payments, (3) enhanced financial risk resulting from fluctuating exchange rates and (4) implementing methods of minimizing risks.[1]

This chapter emphasizes the financial requirements of international marketing; it discusses the need for increased funds especially for SMEs, the sources of those funds, the financial risks involved and methods of minimizing those risks. The entire treatment is concerned with the strategic marketing implications related to finance.

CAPITAL NEEDS FOR INTERNATIONAL MARKETING

Distance, time lags, tariffs, taxes, financial participation requirements, exchange restrictions, fluctuating monetary values and adequate local financial strength are all elements differentiating the problems of financing international marketing activities from those related to domestic marketing. Effective management of the financial functions of marketing can be a strategic factor affecting profits and having great impact on the company's ability to develop marketing channels.

Time lags caused by distance and crossing international borders add cost elements to international marketing that make cash-flow planning especially important. Even in a relatively simple transaction, money may be tied up for months while goods are being shipped from one part of the world to another; customs clearance may add days, weeks or months; payment may be held up while the international payment documents are being transferred from one nation to another; and breakage, commercial disputes or governmental restrictions can add further delay. One study done by a credit management association found that the time required for foreign firms to collect on the average bill from international customers ranged from 54 days for payment from Germany and to a high of 337 days from Iran.[2] In countries where shortages of hard currency exist and countertrades are necessary, capital requirements are even greater since full receipts are not collectible until the countertraded goods are sold. Nearly every international transaction encounters some time lag during which marketing financing must be provided.

For smaller firms, in addition to greater demands for working capital, the international marketer may have to make long-term capital investments. In some instances, markets are closed to a foreign business unless all or some portion of the product is manufactured locally. Thus, international marketing activities frequently require supplemental financing for working capital and capital investment.

Working Capital Requirements

Because of time lags, shipping costs, duties, higher start-up costs, inventory cost, market penetration costs and increased financial needs for trade and channel credit, international operations typically require higher levels of working capital than domestic activities operating at the same volume levels. Travel costs alone can consume working capital funds; in one instance, a small firm discovered it was spending more on travel in a foreign market than on salaries.

Start-Up Costs.   Start-up costs for a company entering new international markets frequently require large amounts of working capital. Such costs can come as a surprise to the firm accustomed to operating in a familiar domestic market. A firm may find it must pay for information assumed or acquired without cost in the home country. Also part of start-up costs are legal fees, establishing an office, purchase of licences, and so on. Marketing research can become a major expense, particularly if a company has to research three or four countries before embarking on a business enterprise in any one of them.

Inventory.   The marketer's effectiveness in managing inventories has considerable impact on the financial requirements of this function. Adequate servicing of overseas markets frequently requires goods to be inventoried in several locations; one company that uses two factory warehouses for the entire continental Europe needed six foreign distribution points that together handled less merchandise than either European outlet. One of the advantages of a single European market is the use of fewer inventory storage points than were required when there were 15 different countries, with rules that hampered speedy delivery.[3] Most other markets are not so integrated.

Slower transportation and longer distances when shipping over water mean inventory turnover can be lengthened considerably over the customary time for domestic operations. Add loading and unloading time, and the time in transit for an overseas shipment from a British manufacturer in Europe to an Asian market, for example Indonesia, can be as much as two months or longer. If your product is entering a congested port, there may be a week's delay just for unloading. The additional time required for delivery increases the capital requirements needed to finance inventories.

Market Penetration Costs

A variety of costs is associated with market penetration. In many cases these costs are higher, relative to sales, in foreign markets than in domestic markets, thereby increasing the capital needs for international marketing.

Promotion and advertising costs, similar in domestic and foreign markets, are generally higher relative to actual sales. Markets are smaller, media usually more expensive and multiple media generally required; these and similar factors increase investment needs.

Manufacturers of durable goods have found they often must provide funds for service facilities before their products are accepted. Japanese carmakers met with little success in Europe until they invested in adequate service facilities and expanded spare parts inventories.

It is never inexpensive to establish a channel of distribution, but again, the complications of international distribution can require extra-large channel investments. Foreign middlemen are seldom adequately financed and may require extensive long-term credit if they are to carry adequate inventories and offer their customers adequate credit.

Channel credit requirements have surprised many Western firms. Most of the world's middlemen are woefully underfinanced, and if they are to buy goods in economical quantities, interim credit must be provided by the producers. The international finance director of a machinery and equipment company says he expects increasing foreign sales volume to require additional working capital to 'support from 50 per cent to 75 per cent of the sales increase'.

GOING INTERNATIONAL 19.1

EURO GAINS FOR THE CONSUMER

Not only companies but also consumers stand to benefit from the single European currency. The euro will pinpoint existing differences in the prices of consumer goods between the various EU countries and thus help to eliminate them. This will also be of advantage to consumers in Germany, a country where consumer prices are high. The convergence of long-term interest rates in the EU is accompanied by a similar convergence of inflation rates. According to the harmonized CPI compiled by Eurostat, the European Union's Statistical Office, inflation in all EU member states except Greece ranged between 1 and 2 per cent in 1997. National price levels, on the other hand, are far from uniform.

The consumer-price parity shows how many units of the domestic currency are needed to buy the same quantity of goods of a certain quality which one can get abroad for a given number of foreign units. True, consumer-price parity alone does not show whether a country's price level is high or low. If the relative price level is to be determined, the bilateral exchange rate must also be taken into account.

A consumer-price parity exceeding the exchange rate means that the cost of living in the foreign country is lower. For example, the average consumer-price parity between the Netherlands and Germany in 1996 was 100 guilders to DM95.30. However, the average exchange rate—DM89.24 for 100 guilders—was below the consumer-price parity. In other words, the price in Dutch guilders of an item costing DM95.30 equalled DM89.24. Hence on an average Dutch prices in 1996 were lower (by 6.8 per cent) than those in Germany.

This will not cause any problems for the likely participants in the first wave of EMU, as the current exchange rates are very close to present ECU central rates. As regards the United Kingdom and Sweden, two countries which, for reasons of domestic policy, will remain outside EMU for the time being, it is difficult to compare prices by this method. The British pound, which does not participate in the EMS, merely has an 'imaginary' ECU central rate, which, in addition, is significantly below the current exchange rate.

The Swedish krona has no ECU central rate, as it is not included in the ECU basket. The entry rates of these two currencies would therefore have to be fixed through political bargaining. The Swedish krona's current exchange rate looks more realistic than the British pound's, and—following the pound's latest run-up—Britain would, for competitive reasons, probably want the entry rate to be set at a lower level. A low entry rate is of great advantage to a country, as such a 'devaluation' does not pose inflationary risks (imported inflation). Moreover, the gain in competitiveness thus achieved *vis-à-vis* the other EMU participants is a permanent one.

Smaller firms' competitive position may be weaker in world markets than in domestic markets because of the number of competitors vying for customers in certain product lines. One UK company that marketed insecticides in Spain through seven local distributors found that within less than three years, six of those distributors had been purchased, or partially purchased, by competitive firms, thus blocking the initial supplier's distribution. The company found similar situations in Latin America, South Africa, Australia and Asia. To retain a competitive position, the company in question was virtually forced to make major investments in buying distributors throughout the world. While many of these ventures are profitable, it requires a huge infusion of funds to maintain market position. In the home market, such investments would probably not have been necessary.

Accounts-receivable financing imposes great strains on international working capital. Middlemen and industrial customers both have learned they are in a position to pressure manufacturers into continuously longer and longer credit extensions because credit terms are such an important marketing weapon in the battle for competitive position in international markets. Marketing and product advantages are being offset by more-advantageous financial terms from competing foreign suppliers. To get goods into the channel of distribution,

GOING INTERNATIONAL 19.1 (continued)

Germany will be among the high-price countries in the European Monetary Union. Among the inaugural group of countries, only Austria (+11.2 per cent) and Finland (+12.6 per cent) will have significantly higher prices. The price level in France, Belgium and Portugal is similar to that in Germany. All other EMU countries have lower price levels. Spain will be EMU's 'bargain basement': Spanish consumer prices are, on average, 11.3 per cent below those in Germany.

Prices in the Netherlands, Italy, Ireland and Luxembourg are more than 8 per cent lower. Denmark which will not yet join EMU has the highest consumer prices. Danish prices are almost one-quarter (23.4 per cent) above the prices in Germany and almost 40 per cent higher than those in Spain. In the case of some products, the gap is even wider.

Differences in taxation are one of the reasons for the disparate national price levels. Denmark, for example, has the value-added tax in the EU (25 per cent) as well as stiff excise duties on oil, tobacco and alcohol. But the impact of taxes should not be overrated. Germany, a country where consumer prices are comparatively high, has currently the lowest VAT rate in the EU (16 per cent), while countries such as Italy and Ireland, where consumer goods are cheaper than in Germany, have VAT rates of 20 and 21 per cent respectively.

The heterogeneity of demand is probably an even more important factor. Differences in consumer preferences, e.g. for certain brands, domestic or imported products, have up to now allowed companies to differentiate prices. This is a particularly common phenomenon in branded consumer products.

For example, Nivea face cream costs DM10.59 in Germany, which is almost twice its price in France (DM5.77) at the current exchange rate. A 400-g jar of Nutella chocolate spread sells at the equivalent of DM4.68 in Britain, which exceeds the price in Germany by roughly one-half. Pampers nappies (diapers), on the other hand, are cheaper in Britain than in Germany (DM16.88 vs. DM24.98).

Price differences between national markets, which reflect disparities in economic conditions and taxation, are quite normal. In the EMU countries, however, they will shrink, at least as far as tradeable goods are concerned. Despite market deregulation and harmonization in the single European market, these differences have largely been concealed from consumers. The multitude of exchange rates and their frequent ups and downs impair the necessary price transparency.

Source: *European Business Report*, Spring, 1Q, 1998, pp. 12–13.

marketers may have to compensate for the middlemen's lack of capital by providing consignment merchandise, floor-plan financing or long-term credit. Without such financial assistance, most foreign middlemen cannot handle adequate inventories.

A decade or two ago, international marketers had little concern about credit because terms tended to be cash in advance. Many small agricultural marketers or exporters continue to rely on these terms; but, in today's intensely competitive world marketplace, no major marketer can afford a cash-only posture. Middlemen may require both extensive and intensive credit availability to develop the type of distribution systems requisite to international marketing. When Daewoo entered the European market with its cars, it offered two to three years interest free credit in a number of European countries.

Capital Investment

Some markets are closed to foreign business unless they produce goods locally. The French government, for example, gave notice to Ford Motor Company that if it expected to keep its large volume of sales in France, it had to produce there; Ford prudently agreed to build its next European plant in France. Ford, Toyota, Sony or Siemens can easily adhere to these type of demands from local governments. The situation is, however, different for smaller firms. In such cases, the production facility itself is a crucial element to market entry and may be considered part of the marketing system because market requirements alone dictated the expenditure. In addition, such marketing facilities as warehouses, shipping docks, retail stores and sales offices require significant capital investment in physical facilities. In considering financial implications, the cost of the production facility as well as costs of marketing facilities may logically be related to marketing as a cost of market entry.

An important financial issue facing international marketers from smaller firms is the availability and source of capital to finance the additional working capital needed. Besides a company's own resources, there are a variety of public funds available.

SOURCES OF GOVERNMENT FUNDS FOR INTERNATIONAL MARKETING OPERATIONS

Working capital for international marketing operations is usually derived from the assets of the company engaging in international trade or exporting. However, private external sources may be used for financing inventory, accounts receivable, construction of physical facilities, and other financing needs. Public sources of funds are likely to play a more important role in financing marketing operations internationally than they do domestically. A number of supranational agencies are engaged in financing international development and marketing activities, plus the foreign marketer may turn to foreign, national, state and local governments for various kinds of financial assistance.

The great majority of sources of public funds for international business are oriented to industrial development activities. Some agencies, however, interpret industrial development broadly and make funds available for a wide range of business activities.

Export Credit Banks.   In most Western countries, there are specialized banks for export credit. Also, most well-established banks in these countries finance export activities of their clients. Other than these private banks, a number of government or semi-government agencies provide funds for international trade and investments. These agencies operate as loan guarantee programmes. Loans are made through commercial banks and guaranteed by these agencies.[4] Some banks specialize in different regions such as the European Bank for Reconstruction and Development (EBRD) for Eastern Europe and the Asian Development Bank for Asia.

International Development Agencies (IDA).   These agencies provide loans and grants to less developed countries for both developmental and foreign policy reasons. Developmental loans are extended to support recipient-country development in key economic sectors in agriculture and nutrition, health, training and education, and energy. Foreign policy loans are extended to developing countries and are used to pay for imports needed to run their economies. A significant portion of each loan or grant is used to finance Western exports.[5] Almost all Western countries have their international development agencies that fund or partly finance exports and franchising for all exports that can be related to development sectors such as education, health and infrastructure development.

Eurodollar Market.   The Eurodollar market is one of the more important sources of debt capital available to the MNC. The term *Eurodollar* refers to a deposit liability banked outside

DAVID AND GOLIATH IN ESTONIA

Borås Wäveri (BW), a small textile manufacturer from Sweden, has taken over Kreenholm Holding (KH), Estonia's biggest industrial group and one of the largest textile plants in Europe. At its peak in the 1980s, Kreenholm employed 12 000 people and produced around 220 million square metres of fabric a year—ten times as much as Borås Wäveri. Lars Mauritzon, the CEO of BW, wants to transform KH from an inefficient Soviet monolith to a lean and competitive actor on the world market.

There has been a dramatic shift since 1995, when BW took over, productivity has increased, some 90 per cent of the output is now exported mainly to the US and the Nordic market. Mauritzon says, when he first saw the plant, he was daunted by its size: 116 buildings spread over 80 000 square metres of land, but the plant was quite modern and technically of high quality. Moreover, it had a knowledge base of 125 years in textile business. BW took over 75.5 per cent of a new company, while KH and Estonian State took the balance. The price was US$10.5 million (€9.5 million) for fixed assets and $20 million (€18 million) for receivables. The Estonian State provided a credit for the purchase, offering BW a 10-year loan at 6.4 per cent interest. All BW needed was a $5 million (€4.5 million) loan as working capital. BW turned to the European Bank for Reconstruction and Development (EBRD) but talks were bogged down. EBRD wanted more detailed budget forecasts and marketing plans. BW felt that was not realistic at that stage. BW then turned to a consortium of Nordic Banks, comprising Sweden's Swedfund, Helsinki based Nordic Investment Bank and the Estonian Investment Bank. Again BW's request was turned down due to lack of detailed projections and marketing plans. Eventually the finance was provided by a Swedish factoring company financed by Skandinaviska Enskilda Banken of Sweden. BW was quite sore about the financial difficulties but accepts that there was a clash between its industrialist mentality and the bank's financial mentality.

After the take over, the biggest job, according to BW, was to change the mentality of KH. Their attitude was 'customers have to buy what we produce'. The plant is now totally by local (Estonian) management, partly because it is difficult to find good Westerners to move to Narva, a grim former military base at the border with Russia, and partly it was deliberate policy. However, a number of management training courses have been run for top and middle level management to upgrade the local staff.

Source: 'David and Goliath in Estonia', *The Financial Times*, 6 May 1996, p. 8.

---

the United States, that is, dollars banked in Germany or any country other than the United States. While the Eurodollar market refers to dollars, the Eurodollar market includes other national currencies banked outside their countries of origin. Because the Eurodollar market includes other than US currencies, it is sometimes referred to as the Eurocurrency market, even though the predominant currency is the US dollar. These currencies serve as a ready source of cash that holding banks can use as an asset on which a dollar-denominated loan can be made to someone else. Similar markets in Asia and the Caribbean consist of national currencies deposited in banks outside the country of origin.

Debt–Equity Swaps.   Another source of funds for companies operating in countries with high external debt are *debt–equity swaps*. Banks wanting to lower their debt portfolios, and countries wanting to lower their debt burdens without using scarce foreign exchange, participate in favourable debt–equity swaps with foreign companies. For foreign companies, it is a way to finance business activity in a country at discount rates. Debt–equity swaps have been used to finance joint ventures, to acquire working capital, to buy raw materials and to invest in new facilities.[6]

FOREIGN COMMERCIAL PAYMENTS

The sale of goods in other countries is further complicated by additional risks encountered when dealing with foreign customers. There are risks from inadequate credit reports on customers, problems of currency exchange controls, distance and different legal systems, and the cost and difficulty of collecting delinquent accounts which require a different emphasis on payment systems.[7] Terms of sales are typically arranged between the buyer and seller at the time of the sale. Type of merchandise, the amount of money involved, business custom, the credit rating of the buyer, the country of the buyer, and whether the buyer is a new or old customer must be considered in establishing the terms of sale. The five basic payment arrangements—(1) letters of credit, (2) bills of exchange, (3) cash in advance, (4) open accounts and (5) forfaiting—are discussed in this section.

Letters of Credit

Most exports are handled by export letters of credit opened in favour of the seller by the buyer. Letters of credit shift the buyer's credit risk to the bank issuing the letter of credit. When a letter of credit is employed, the seller ordinarily can draw a draft against the bank issuing the credit and receive cash by presenting proper shipping documents. Except for cash in advance, letters of credit afford the greatest degree of protection for the seller.

The procedure for a letter of credit begins with completion of the contract when the buyer goes to a local bank and arranges for the issuance of a letter of credit; the buyer's bank then notifies its correspondent bank in the seller's country that the letter has been issued. After meeting the requirements set forth in the letter of credit, the seller can draw a draft against the credit (in effect, the bank issuing the letter) for payment for the goods. The precise conditions of the letter of credit are detailed in it and usually also require presentation of certain documents with the draft before the correspondent bank will honour it. The documents usually required are (1) a commercial invoice, (2) a consular invoice (when requested), (3) a clean bill of lading and (4) an insurance policy or certificate.

Letters of credit can be revocable or irrevocable. Irrevocable means that once the credit has been accepted by the seller, it cannot be altered in any way by the buyer without permission of the seller. Added protection is gained if the buyer is required to confirm the letter of credit through a foreign bank. This irrevocable, confirmed letter of credit means that a foreign bank accepts responsibility to pay regardless of the financial situation of the buyer or buyer's domestic bank. From the seller's viewpoint, this eliminates the foreign political risk and replaces the commercial risk of the buyer's bank with that of the confirming bank. Payment against a confirmed letter of credit is assured by the confirming bank. As soon as the documents are presented to the bank, the seller receives payment.

Bills of Exchange

Another important international commercial payment form is sight or time drafts (bills of exchange) drawn by sellers on foreign buyers. In letters of credit, the credit of one or more banks is involved, but in the use of bills of exchange, the seller assumes all risk until the actual cash is received. The typical procedure is for the seller to draw a draft on the buyer and present it with the necessary documents to the seller's bank for collection. The documents required are principally the same as for letters of credit. On receipt of the draft, the bank forwards it with the necessary documents to a correspondent bank in the buyer's country; then the buyer is presented with the draft for acceptance and immediate or later payment.

With acceptance of the draft, the buyer receives the properly endorsed bill of lading that is used to acquire the goods from the carrier.

Bills of exchange have one of three time periods—sight, arrival or date. A sight draft requires acceptance and payment on presentation of the draft and often before arrival of the goods. An arrival draft requires payment be made on arrival of the goods. Unlike the other two, a date draft has an exact date for payment and in no way is affected by the movement of the goods. There may be time designations placed on sight and arrival drafts stipulating a fixed number of days after acceptance when the obligation must be paid. Usually this period is 30 to 120 days, thus providing a means of extending credit to the foreign buyer.

Bills of exchange have advantages for the seller because an accepted draft frequently can be discounted at a bank for immediate payment. Banks, however, usually discount drafts only with recourse, that is, if the draft is not honoured by the buyer, the bank returns it to the seller for payment.

Cash in Advance

The volume of business handled on a cash-in-advance basis is not large. Cash places unpopular burdens on the customer and typically is used when credit is doubtful, when exchange restrictions within the country of destination are such that the return of funds from abroad may be delayed for an unreasonable period, or when the exporter for any reason is unwilling to sell on credit terms.

Although payment in advance is infrequently employed, partial payment (from 25 to 50 per cent) in advance is not unusual when the character of the merchandise is such that an incomplete contract can result in heavy loss. For example, complicated machinery or equipment manufactured to specification or special design would necessitate advance payment which would be, in fact, a nonrefundable deposit.

Open Accounts

Sales on open accounts are not generally made in foreign trade except to customers of long standing with excellent credit reputations, or to a subsidiary or branch of the exporter. Open accounts obviously leave sellers in a position where most of the problems of international commercial finance work to their disadvantage. It is generally recommended that sales on open account should not be made when it is the practice of the trade to use some other method, when special merchandise is ordered, when shipping is hazardous, when the country of the importer imposes difficult exchange restrictions or when political unrest requires additional caution.

Forfaiting

Inconvertible currencies and cash-short customers can kill an international sale if the seller cannot offer long-term financing. Unless the company has large cash reserves to finance its customers, a deal may be lost. Forfaiting is a financing technique for such a situation.

In a forfait transaction, the seller makes a one-time arrangement with a bank or other financial institution to take over responsibility for collecting the account receivable. The basic idea of a forfaiting transaction is fairly simple. The exporter offers a long financing term to its buyer, but intends to sell its account receivable, at a discount, for immediate cash. The forfaiter buys the debt, typically a promissory note or bill of exchange, on a nonrecourse basis. Once the exporter sells the paper, the forfaiter assumes the risk of collecting the importer's

A LETTER-OF-CREDIT TRANSACTION

Here is what typically happens when payment is made by an irrevocable letter of credit confirmed by a Western bank.

1. After you and your customer agree on the terms of sale, the customer arranges for his or her bank to open a letter of credit. (Delays may be encountered if, for example, the buyer has 'insufficient funds'. In many developing countries, foreign currencies may be scarce.)
2. The buyer's bank prepares an irrevocable letter of credit, including all instructions.
3. The buyer's bank sends the irrevocable letter of credit to a Western bank requesting confirmation. (Foreign banks generally select the nearest one to the exporter.)
4. The Western bank prepares a letter of confirmation to forward to you, along with the irrevocable letter of credit.
5. You review carefully all conditions in the letter of credit, in particular, shipping dates. If you cannot comply, alert your customer at once. (Your freight forwarder can help advise you.)
6. You arrange with your freight forwarder to deliver your goods to the appropriate port or airport. If the forwarder is to present the documents to the bank (a wise move for new-to-export firms), the forwarder will need copies of the letter of credit.
7. After the goods are loaded, the forwarder completes the necessary documents (or transmits the information to you).
8. You (or your forwarder) present documents indicating full compliance to the Western bank.
9. The bank reviews the documents. If they are in order, it issues you a cheque. The documents are airmailed to the buyer's bank for review and transmitted to the buyer.
10. The buyer (or agent) gets the documents which may be needed to claim the goods.

Source: 'A Basic Guide to Exporting', US Department of Commerce, International Trade Administration, Washington, DC, 1994.

payments. The forfaiting institution also assumes any political risk present in the importer's country.

Forfaiting is similar to factoring but is not the same. In factoring, a company has an ongoing relationship with a bank that routinely buys its short-term accounts receivable at a discount—the bank is acting as a collections department for its client. In forfaiting, the seller makes a one-time arrangement with a bank to buy a specific account receivable.[8]

FINANCIAL RISK AND RISK MANAGEMENT

Several types of financial risk are encountered in international marketing; the major problems include commercial, political and foreign-exchange risk. Some risks are similar to domestic risks although usually intensified, while others are uniquely international. Every business should deal with the fact of risk through a structured risk-management programme. Such a programme may call for assuming risks, engaging in some type of risk avoidance and/or initiating risk-shifting behaviour.

Commercial Risk

Commercial risks are handled essentially as normal credit risks encountered in day-to-day business. They include solvency, default or refusal to pay bills. The major risk is

GOING INTERNATIONAL 19.4

THE DEBATE ON EXPORT SUBSIDIES

The Arrangement on Guidelines for Officially Supported Export Credits, as its name suggests, sets out guidelines to regulate officially supported (i.e. government-backed) export credit guarantees and insurance against the risk of non-repayment. An export credit arises whenever a foreign buyer of exported goods or services is allowed to defer payment. Export-credit insurance and guarantees may take the form of 'supplier' or 'buyer' credits where the exporter's bank or other financial institution lend to the buyer or his bank respectively.

The Arrangement also regulates official financing support where the government provides such loans directly, offers refinancing or supports interest rates. The institutions which undertake these official activities, for or on behalf of governments, are export-credit agencies (ECAs). There are several types of such agencies: they can be government-owned (as with the Export Credits Guarantee Department (ECGD) in the United Kingdom, which is a government department), or privately-owned institutions which administer an account, separate from their commercial business, backed by the state (such as COFACE in France).

The Arrangement on Guidelines for Officially Supported Export Credits, then commonly known as 'the Consensus', was formerly established in 1978. The Arrangement applies to officially supported export credits with a repayment term of two years or more (most short-term business is now underwritten by the private sector) and sets out, *inter alia*, maximum repayment terms and, where official financing support is involved, minimum interest rates. From April 1999, the disciplines will also encompass minimum risk-based premium fees for country and sovereign risk.

The Arrangement details the circumstances in which trade-related tied and partially untied aid may be given in transactions where aid funds are provided on the condition that the goods/ services being supported are purchased from the country providing the aid money (a restriction which is sometimes extended to a limited number of other countries).

One of the most noteworthy developments of recent years has been the agreement on the 'pricing' of official support reached in June 1997, the so-called 'Knaepen Package'. In essence, these ground-breaking new rules, which will come into force in April 1999, provide for minimum risk-based premium fees which should be adequate to cover the risk of non-repayment by an overseas country/government in markets in which OECD exporters are active.

The overall flexibility of the Arrangement allows it to reflect political and market developments. A main issue now under negotiation is complementary guidelines for agricultural products. Although currently exempted from the provisions of the Arrangement, such guidelines will go a long way to preventing subsidies and distortions of competition.

Another major issue facing the participants is that of project financing, a technique that is used increasingly, particularly for infrastructure projects, where loan repayments are made from the revenue generated by the projects themselves. As current guidelines, which require equal semi-annual loan repayments beginning at six months after the start of the credit, do not reflect the revenue-generating potential of many of the projects, the industrialized countries are set to negotiate flexibility in the Arrangement which will accommodate the structure of such deals better.

Source: *European Business Report*, Spring 1Q, 1998, p. 58.

competition which can only be dealt with through consistently effective management and marketing.

One unique risk encountered by the international marketer involves financial adjustments. Such risk is encountered when a controversy arises about the quality of goods delivered (but not accepted), a dispute over contract terms or any other disagreement over which payment is withheld. For example, a British company shipped several hundred tons of dehydrated potatoes to a distributor in Germany. The distributor tested the shipment and declared it to be below acceptable taste and texture standards (not explicitly established). The alternatives for the exporter of reducing the price, reselling the potatoes or shipping them home again involved considerable cost. Although there is less risk of substantial loss in the adjustment situation, it is possible for the selling company to have large sums of money tied up for relatively long periods of time until the client accepts the controversial goods, if ever. In some cases, goods must be returned or remanufactured, and in other instances, contracts may be modified to alleviate the controversies. All such problems are uninsurable and costly.

Political Risk

Political risk is related to the problems of war or revolution, currency inconvertibility, expropriation or expulsion, and restriction or cancellation of import licences. One of the most frequently encountered political risks arises when a country refuses to allow local currency to be converted to any other currency. This often happens when countries are experiencing economic difficulties and want to conserve scarce supplies of hard currencies, that is, currencies that are easily exchangeable for goods or other currencies. For example, when someone in Russia wants to purchase goods from a company in another country, the seller would probably be reluctant to accept payment in roubles because roubles have a history of rapid erosion as a result of hyperinflation. The Russian buyer has to convert roubles into a hard currency, the US dollar, euro, British pound or any other currency that is freely accepted for payment by most of the world.

There are times when it is not possible to avoid political risks, so marketers must be prepared to handle them or avoid doing business in risky markets.[9] Some types of political risk are insurable by agencies mentioned in the risk-management section that follows.

Foreign-Exchange Risk

Until 1973, the international monetary system operated under an agreement (Bretton Woods Agreement) that pegged exchange rates for currencies of the industrialized countries to a gold exchange standard. During the period of the Bretton Woods Agreement, most hard currencies were relatively stable and fluctuations were infrequent and small. Thus, a firm's transactions in foreign currencies were fairly secure in terms of exchange rates to other currencies because devaluations of major currencies were infrequent and usually anticipated. Since the abandonment of the Bretton Woods Agreement, currencies are allowed to float freely and exchange rates fluctuate daily. Figure 19.1 illustrates the volatility that has occurred in some major currencies between 1990 and 1998. It is not hard to imagine the foreign-exchange risk problems of companies that deal with large quantities of foreign currencies at any given point. Depending on the specific time span, a firm could suffer the loss of substantial sums of money from too much exposure to fluctuating currencies.[10] Floating exchange rates have forced all marketers to be especially aware of exchange-rate fluctuation and the extent of their transaction exposure.

Transaction exposure occurs at any time a company has assets denominated in some currency other than that of its home country and expects to convert the foreign currency to its home currency to realize a profit. When a Western company sells in a foreign country, it sometimes must accept payment in the buyer's currency to be competitive. The seller then has to exchange the currency received for pounds or dollars. Between the time price is agreed on and payment is actually received and converted to pounds or dollars, the company's transaction is exposed to exchange-rate fluctuations; that is, the company experiences transaction exposure.

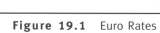

GOING INTERNATIONAL 19.5

THE EFFECTS OF TRANSACTION EXPOSURE

In long-term transactions (even those of two or three years), exchange-rate fluctuations can have extreme effects and at times can far exceed the profitability of a given transaction. Consider the following example of the cost of money in a strongly fluctuating money market.

22 July 1995
US firm borrows 10 000 000 pounds sterling. Interest rate: 14 per cent. Exchange rate: 1 pound sterling = $1.5990 US. Company secures $15 990 000.

21 July 1996
US firm owes $11 400 000 pounds sterling. Exchange rate: 1 pound sterling = $1.7093 US. Company requires $19 486 020.

Transaction cost
$3 496 020 to use $15 990 000 for 1 year; 21.86 per cent effective cost of money for 1 year.

Because of exchange rate exposure, a loan expected to cost 14 per cent increased to a rate of 21.86 per cent, a substantial increase in the cost of doing business.

Figure 19.1   Euro Rates

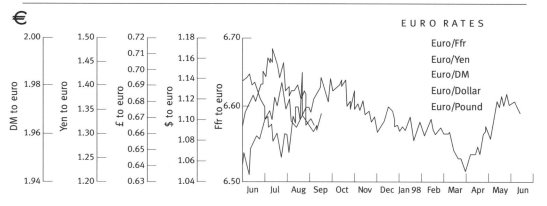

Source: 'The Euro Currencies—Bank Reserves Send Gold Towards 18-Year Low', *The European*, 15–21 June 1998, p. 60.

Transaction exposure occurs when a company:

1. Has assets in one currency that it expects to convert to another to realize a profit.
2. Has assets denominated in one currency that must be converted into another at some expected value.
3. Borrows money in one currency that, when repaid, must be exchanged to make repayment.
4. Purchases goods for resale in one currency, sells them in another and needs to convert the proceeds into a third currency to realize planned profits.

A large MNC might encounter several or all of these situations in the course of normal business activity. Most firms try to minimize exchange risks. The most obvious way is to demand payment in the home-country currency, but competitively that is not always possible. When a company demands payment in home-country currency, the exchange risk is shifted to the buyer, who is then similarly exposed. In a fluctuating exchange market such as the one that has existed since the early 1970s, there is a tendency for each party in a transaction to attempt to shift the exchange risk to the other. Thus, demand for payment in the seller's currency may not always be possible. More formal methods of risk avoidance are discussed in the following section on financial-risk management.

MANAGING FINANCIAL RISKS

When financial risks become too high, companies either stop doing business in high-risk situations or seek ways to minimize potential loss. There are various tools available to manage risks, although none provides perfect protection.

Commercial and political risks are insurable through a variety of government agencies. The principal agencies are: (1) Overseas Private Investment Corporations (OPIC), (2) The Foreign Credit Insurance Association (FCIA), (3) the Export Credit Bank and (4) the Multilateral Investment Guarantee Agency (MIGA), a World Bank affiliate.[11] Protection against risks resulting from exchange-rate fluctuations is not available from any government agency. It comes only from effective financial-risk management. Some companies avoid risks by refusing to enter transactions not denominated in home-country currency; others accept the consequences of currency oscillations as a condition of doing business.

Hedging

Hedging in money is essentially no different from any other kind of hedging in the marketplace. It consists of forward sale of a currency in danger of devaluation for dollars or euros, or another stable monetary unit.

The same techniques used to buy futures in wheat, soybeans and cattle can be used to reduce risks associated with fluctuations in the values of currencies. The process consists of offsetting risk incurred in the actual sale with buying a futures contract in that currency.

Hedging does not always afford complete protection against price changes. Sometimes factors operate to prevent a hedge from offering complete protection. The primary reason for there being no perfect hedge (i.e. where the spot and future yields would be the same) is that the spread between the spot and futures markets does not always move at the same rate. The two prices may move in the same direction but at different degrees and different speeds. Thus a company which hedges can receive an unexpected profit or incur an unexpected loss. However, in situations where exchange rates are fluctuating, the profits or losses are comparatively smaller than they would have been without a hedge.[12]

Foreign-Exchange Options

In addition to buying foreign-exchange futures to hedge against exchange risk, the international marketer has the alternative of buying foreign-exchange options. An option is an agreement between two parties in which one party grants the other the right, but not the obligation, to buy or sell foreign exchange under specific conditions. With a futures contract, there is an obligation to buy or sell foreign exchange. The foreign currency option market

Table 19.1 European Currency Unit (ECU)

European Community Currencies Are Included in the ECU 'Basket' in the Following Amounts (based on September 1989 ECU value)*

National Currency	Amount in ECU Currency	Share (%)
German mark	0.6242	30.4
French franc	1.332	19.3
British pound sterling	0.08748	12.6
Dutch guilder	0.2198	9.5
Italian lira	151.8	9.9
Belgian/Luxembourg franc	3.431	8.1
Danish krone	0.1976	2.5
Irish punt	0.008552	1.1
Greek drachma	1.440	0.7
Spanish peseta	6.885	5.2
Portuguese escudo	1.393	0.8

*The value of each country's currency amount is revised every five years. The last revision occurred in 1995.

functions in much the same manner as options for commodities or stocks. Although using options to hedge can often be more expensive than buying futures contracts, there are circumstances when it would be better to hedge with options. Because hedging with futures contracts or with options is a complicated financial process, the international department of a major bank should be consulted.

European Currency Units

Some of the volatility of European currencies can be minimized by denominating contracts in the European Currency Unit (ECU). The ECU (renamed as euro in 1999), originally introduced in 1975 as the European Unit of Account, represents a composite of 15 European currencies (Table 19.1). The ECU was developed to promote monetary stability among European currencies. Intended originally as a unit of account for central banks of EC-member countries and as a unit of account for all EC budgetary purposes, it gradually grew as a private payment medium. The euro is freely convertible into all major currencies and is used to price, invoice and settle transactions involving goods and services.

The major advantage of the euro is the stability relative to any one of the major European currencies. Because there is relative stability, contracts denominated by euros have potentially less financial risk than contracts denominated in any one of the currencies included in the determination of the euro. Future contracts for euros can be purchased, making the euro available for forward buying and hedging. It is expected that in the future most business will be done in one of the three currencies dollar, euro or yen. The relative importance of the currencies and the countries behind it is shown in Table 19.2.

Since the beginning, the ECU has continued to gain importance in commercial transactions and is replaced by euro in 1999. Coins and bank notes have now been introduced.[13] A significant provision of the Maastricht Treaty, which established the European Union, was

Table 19.2   A Tale of Three Currencies

	Dollarland (USA)	Euroland (EU 11ª)	Yenland (Japan)
Population (millions)	267.1	288.9	125.1
Population growth rate (average between 1985–95)	1%	0.4%	0.3%
Population under the age of 15	22%	16.5%	16.2%
GDP (billions)	$8 457.2	$6 326.3	$4 071.8
Average annual growth rate in real GDP 1985–95	2.5	2.5	3.1
GDP per head	$26 580	$20 599	$39 687
Price of a Big Mac	$2.56	$2.64	$2.08
Unemployment	5.6%	10.7%	3.2%
Consumer price inflation	2.9%	2.2%	0.1%
Average annual inflation 1989–96	3.6%	3.8%	1.5%
Total exports (billions)	$575.9	$1 626.6ᵇ	$443
Total imports (billions)	$749.4	$1 515.7	$336.1

ªGermany, France, Italy, Spain, Belgium, Luxembourg, Netherlands, Austria, Portugal, Finland, Ireland'; ᵇIncludes inter-EU trade.
Source: Based on *The European*, 4–10 May 1998, p. 9.

the creation of a common currency to be established by 1997.[14] The 1997 date was postponed to 1999 which has been achieved, at least in eleven EU countries.

UNBLOCKING PROFITS

International marketing executives are plagued with a problem unknown to their domestic counterparts; they must not only sell the goods but also find ways to repatriate payment for the goods and profits from operations to the parent company. Countries have long controlled the holding and purchasing of currency within their borders. Due to the global debt crisis that has plagued the developing world and the opening of many countries to the free-enterprise system after decades of socialism, foreign-exchange controls have spread as countries allocate scarce hard-currency reserves for specific imports or to pay interest on foreign debt.[15]

The result is that international companies often have problems repatriating earnings. Funds for both capital and profit repatriation are often blocked by a host country.[16] The solution to this problem for many is to use some form of countertrade.[17] One English company sold €4.5 million ($5 million) worth of airplanes to Brazil and was paid entirely in coffee, which it later sold in another country. Uganda wanted 18 helicopters to help stamp out elephant and rhino poaching, but did not have the €22.6 million ($25 million) to pay for them. McDonnell-Douglas Helicopters' countertrade division helped set up several local projects that generated hard currency, including a plant to catch and process Nile perch, a factory to turn pineapples and passion fruit into concentrates, and the marketing of these products in Europe.[18] Other financial alternatives to repatriation include reinvestment in other local enterprises and expanding operations in the country. Many franchise operations invest locally earned profits in new units to expand their competitive base within the market while waiting for more favourable expatriation terms. Investing local profits in companies that produce products for export is another indirect way companies can repatriate earnings.[19]

MANAT, KROON, LATS OR A GRIVNA—EXOTIC ANIMALS?

No! They are new currencies created by the Newly Independent States (NIS) of the former USSR.

When the USSR dissolved into the many NIS, one of their first tasks was to decide whether to retain the Russian rouble or create their own currencies. Many have created those new currencies, which is the easy part; giving it value is the difficult part.

Different nations took different paths: Estonia pegged the value of its kroon to the Deutsche Mark; Latvia (lats) and Kyrgyzstan (som) let their currencies' values float. Currency crises exist in Ukraine's karbovanet, which had an inflation rate over 70 per cent a month; as a result, prices for most staples have increased 300 to 500 per cent. The Russian rouble has not done well either. Monthly inflation in 1994 was as high as 18 per cent and the value of the rouble against the US dollar dropped from about 1200 per dollar to nearly 4500 between January and October 1994. Currency fluctuations are a major problem for a foreign marketer who must either demand payment in a hard currency or accept monetary risk.

Sources: Adapted from 'Not-so-Funny Money', *International Business*, February 1994, p. 113; and Adi Ignatius, 'Ruble's Plunge Prompts Yeltsin to Fire Finance Chief, Seek to Oust Bank Head', *The Wall Street Journal*, 13 October 1994, p. A-2.

SUMMARY

Although it is not their formal domain, marketing executives of small- and medium-sized enterprises (SMEs) should be acquainted with the requirements, sources, problems and opportunities associated with the financing of international marketing operations. The financial needs of international marketing differ considerably from those of the domestic market. Most specifically, the international marketer must be prepared to invest larger-than-normal amounts of working capital in inventories, receivables, channel financing and consumer credit. It is possible that market entry may require capital financing of production facilities for purely marketing reasons. International marketers need to be willing to undertake additional financial burdens to operate successfully in foreign countries. Indeed, adequate financing may spell the difference between success and failure in foreign operations. The willingness of marketers to carry adequate inventories in strategic locations and/or to provide consumer or channel credit that they would not be likely to furnish in their home country may be key elements in market development.

Financial risks associated with international marketing are greater than those encountered domestically, but such risk-taking is necessary for effective operations. Many companies have been so conservative in their credit and payment terms that they have succeeded in alienating foreign customers. These risks, as well as those of exchange availability or fluctuation and the various political risks, can be accommodated in an effective financial-risk management programme.

QUESTIONS

1. Explain why marketers should be concerned with the financial considerations associated with international marketing.

2. Explain how a debt–equity swap works for a company that wants to make an investment in a country.

3. Identify the financial requirements for marketing internationally most likely to concern a smaller company.

4. Discuss the differences between financial requirements for export marketers and for overseas marketing operations.

5. What are the extra problems and risks faced by a smaller international marketer?

6. Review some of the ways financial requirements can be reduced by variations in marketing policies or strategies.

7. In which ways are marketing financial requirements of exporters different from those of full-scale international marketers?

8. What significance do government sources of funds have for marketers?

9. 'The principles of international credit are basically no different from those of domestic credit.' Elaborate.

10. Compare the advantages and disadvantages of bills of exchange and letters of credit.

11. Review the types of financial risk involved in international operations and discuss how each may be reduced.

12. Using exchange data in *The Financial Times* on a date assigned by your instructor, calculate the foreign exchange gain or loss on this transaction: a British firm borrows 5 million Swiss francs one year before the assigned date, converts those to British pounds, pays 9 per cent interest per annum. How many pounds will be required to repay the loan and interest?

13. Discuss the ways a company can reduce exchange risk.

14. Discuss the ways a company can reduce the risk of exchange-rate fluctuations. Give examples of each.

15. What is the European Currency Unit (ECU) and how might it be used in managing financial risks?

REFERENCES

1. 'Brazilian FX Gets Real', *Business Latin America*, 13 June 1994, pp. 1–2; and 'The Tale of Three Currencies', *The European*, 4–10 May, 1998, p. 9.

2. Michael Selz, 'Small Firms Hit Foreign Obstacles in Billing Overseas', *The Wall Street Journal*, 8 December 1992, p. B-2.

3. 'Cross-Border Logistics: How Bosch-Siemens Saved Time and Costs', *Business Europe*, 23–29 May 1994, p. 7.

4. 'Sources of Export Financing', *Business America*, February 1995, pp. 23–26.

5. Michael Williams, 'How to Secure Funding for Entrepreneurial Projects', *Trade & Culture*, September–October 1994, pp. 52–53.

6. Joseph Ganitsky, 'Investing in Developing Nations Using Debt–Equity Swaps', *The International Executive*, May–June 1991, pp. 14–19.

7. 'Congratulations, Exporter! Now about Getting Paid', *Business Week*, 27 January 1994, p. 98.

8. Elnora Uzzelle, 'Forfaiting Should Not Be Overlooked as an Innovative Means of Export Finance', *Business America*, February 1995, pp. 20–22.

9. Nilly Landau, 'Watch Your Step: How to Put the Best Foot Forward When Managing Your Company's Financial Risks', *International Business*, February 1994, pp. 92–94.

10. 'Harsh New Currency World', *International Business*, April 1995, pp. 16–18.

11. 'Investment Insurance: Guaranteed Return', *Business China*, 30 May 1994, pp. 2–3.

12. For a complete discussion of financial risk management, see David K. Eiteman and Arthur I. Stonehill, *Multinational Business Finance*, 8th edn (Reading, MA: Addison-Wesley, 1998).

13. 'Europe Takes Flight', *The Economist*, 2 May 1998, p. 11.

14. 'ECU—Sounder', *The Economist*, 8 April 1995, p. 45.

15. 'Russia: How MNCs Get Around New Forex Ban', *Crossborder Monitor*, 2 March 1994, p. 1; and *European Business Report*, Spring 1Q, 1998, p.58.

16. For a comprehensive review of countertrade practices, see Erwin Amann and Marin Dalia, 'Risk-Sharing in International Trade: An Analysis of Countertrade', *The Journal of Industrial Economics*, March 1994, pp. 63–77.

17. 'Financing CIS Sales: Reinventing Countertrade', *Business Eastern Europe*, 17 January 1994, pp. 1–2.

18. Most East European countries' currencies are not convertible to other currencies. However, this is changing and the Czech Republic is moving rapidly towards convertibility of its koruna. For a discussion of these changes, see 'Czech Republic/Slovakia: Currency Converts', *Business Eastern Europe*, 9 January 1995, pp. 5–6.

19. 'Asia, Watch Out! There is more trouble to come', *Business Week*, 17 August 1998, pp. 32–35.

CHAPTER

20

Organizing International Marketing Activities

Chapter Learning Objectives

What you should learn from Chapter 20

- The importance of organization in international marketing activities.
- The factors that influence structure in an international firm/organization.
- How to prepare personnel in foreign markets.
- How to manage personnel in foreign markets.
- The changing profile of an international manager and is it realistic?
- How management is practised in different parts of the world.

An international marketing plan should optimize the resources committed to stated company objectives. The organization plan includes the type of organizational arrangements to be used and the scope and location of responsibility. Many ambitious multinational plans meet with less than full success because of confused lines of authority, poor communications and lack of cooperation between headquarters and the subsidiary organization.

In building an organization, important considerations include the level of policy decisions, length of chain of command, staff support, source of natural and personnel resources, degree of control, centralization and the degree of involvement of marketing.

A company may be organized by product line, but have geographical subdivisions under the product categories. Both may be supplemented by functional staff support. Figure 20.1 shows such a combination. Modifications of the basic arrangements are used by a majority of large companies doing business internationally. Companies are usually structured around one of these three alternatives: global product divisions responsible for products sales throughout the world, geographical divisions responsible for all products and functions within a particular geographical area or a matrix organization consisting of either of these arrangements with centralized sales and marketing run by centralized functional staff or a combination of area operations and global product management.

The extent to which a company can be successful in its international marketing efforts depends upon two major factors: first, the nature and suitability of marketing strategy used and, second, the efficient organization of the firm's international activities. The importance of organizational issues is often not fully recognized or is only partly dealt with. One reason is the underestimation of organizing and coordination of different units operating in different markets. These units are of different sizes, type and complexity. At the same time, these units are staffed by people with different backgrounds and abilities. The extent of international marketing success thus forces companies to constantly restructure their organizations. There is no 'right' structure that an international organization can adopt to be successful. What companies need is to strike the right balance or 'fit' between the companies' objectives, strategies and the local environment or customer needs. The structure that allows this 'fit' and takes care of the ever-changing international marketing environment is the most suitable.[1]

MARKETING AND ORGANIZATION

Organization development is an instrument that is used to achieve marketing objectives and not an end itself. An organization that looks neat and elegant on a chart is not necessarily the right organization for a firm in a particular market. A company should thus first establish its goals and marketing strategies and then explore what type of organization can help it to achieve those goals and strategies. To achieve the goals of the marketing strategies each function of marketing needs to be properly organized in regard to who will plan and who will perform different tasks, and how these tasks can be performed and coordinated best. As shown by Figure 20.2 some of these tasks are more crucial than others. Some of these tasks can be performed outside the company and some activities demand special capabilities, for example research and advertising. First, an organization has to realize whether it has its own capabilities to do research or whether it should get it done from outside. Second, the marketing objectives in regard to product, process, distribution, selling and promotion in a particular market would lead to a certain type of organization. Third, marketing operations such as advertising, salesforce management, sales administration, deliveries and after-sales service are to be organized by the firm. Finally, sales control, distribution cost analysis, measurement of advertising effectiveness and other evaluation would give feedback to the

Figure 20.1   Schematic Marketing Organization Plan Combining Product, Geographic and Functional Approaches

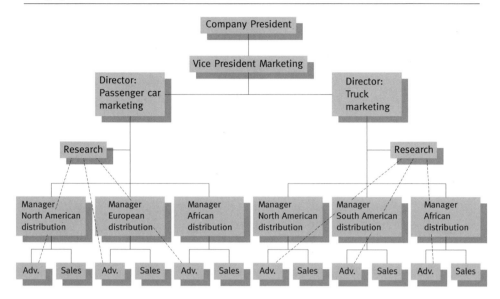

Source: 'An Ever-Quicker Trip from R&D to Customer', *Business Week*, Special 21st Century Capitalism Issue, 1994, p. 88.

organization for further development and organizational change. A firm has to accommodate these different marketing activities into its structure. The degree of complexity enhances with the number of markets a firm is active in and the number of products it is selling.[2]

ISSUES INFLUENCING A STRUCTURE

The effectiveness and quality of an organization can only be measured by its ability to achieve its overall goals and marketing strategies. Although there is no best structure available, nonetheless there are a number of considerations an international marketer should bear in mind while designing an organization. These issues include centralization vs. decentralization, communication, position of marketing in an organization, coordination and the availability of personnel.

Centralization versus Decentralization

Considerations of where decisions will be made, by whom, and by which method constitute a major element of organization strategy. Management policy must be explicit about which decisions are to be made by the head office and which at local offices. Most companies also limit the amount of money to be spent at local levels. Some multinationals have regional offices and some decision making is done at regional headquarters. Most multinational decisions are made at the head office (centralized) or local offices (decentralized). The chief

Figure 20.2   Organizing Marketing Activities

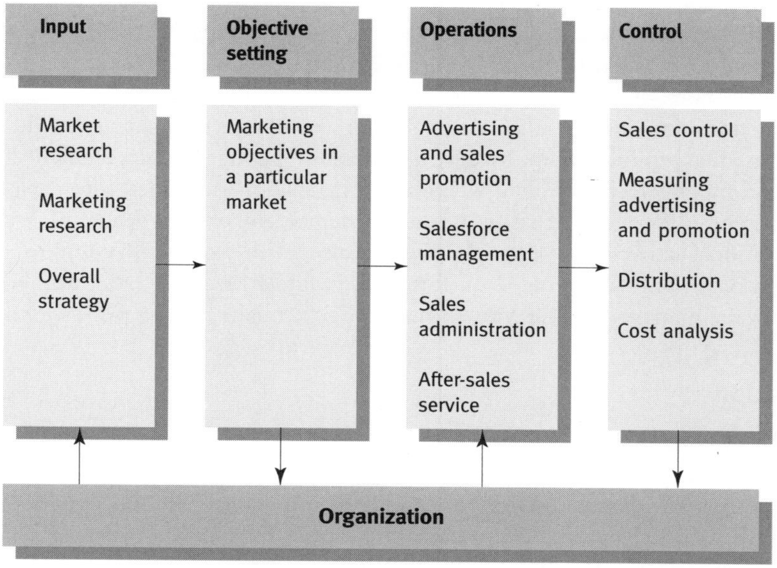

Source: Based on Simon Majaro, *International Marketing* (London: Unwin Hyman, 1987).

advantages of centralization are availability of experts at one location, the ability to exercise a high degree of control on planning and implementation and centralization of all records and information.

In a number of companies strategic decisions are centralized and operational decisions are decentralized. The choice between centralization vs. decentralization is basically a choice between control and delegation, to strike the right balance is often very difficult. The factors that influence this decision are the importance of international activities, the size of the firm, the cruciality of technology/patents involved, the distance between head office and the local office and the cultural and management style of a particular company. According to one author, the more a company has an ethnocentric orientation the more it tends to be centralized.[3]

Communication Flows

Communication is considered to be one of the most important issues influencing international organizations and their efficient functioning. Coordination beyond national boundaries becomes increasingly difficult due to communication problems such as misinterpretations, ambiguities and costs. An efficient and speedy communication flow is thus essential for an effective international organization. When discussing the choice of a particular organizational design and structure, consideration of its communication implications is extremely important. Grouping together of some offices/subsidiaries under a regional office, all of which have language and cultural closeness, is one such example.

Position of Marketing

Different organizations have different 'centres of gravity'—some companies are technology oriented and thereby have their technical side, engineering and design, as their centre of gravity. On the other hand, companies that are market oriented tend to have marketing as their centre of gravity. The differences of degree in these two orientations would influence the organization design and structure. In the second type of organization the structure might be based on product groups because of different types of customer segments. This can be seen in a company such as Volvo, where the organization is divided into cars, trucks and aircraft engine divisions. The structure is also dependent on the degree of involvement in international activities. For example, a firm dealing with exports to a couple of markets might have an organic structure based on functions, while a firm that has a number of subsidiaries in several markets, dealing with several products, might have to work with a matrix structure.

Coordination

Coordination is perhaps the most important task of an internationally scattered company. Whatever the level of decentralization and independence of the local offices and subsidiaries, an international firm needs to coordinate and consolidate the activities of its several units. Other than centralized decision making, this is the only way firms can exercise some control on their international activities. From the perspective of the subsidiary, it can easily be considered as permanent pressure from the head office for a constant stream of reports and statements. The dilemma for head office is to apply some sort of standardized tools to measure the performance of the subsidiaries and managers and at the same time allow some freedom or openness to let subsidiaries use their local systems of evaluation and rewards. The coordination of purchasing, production and most of the marketing activities can influence cost structure and efficiency of the company to a great extent. Who is responsible for what and who reports to whom, leads to an overall coordination of a firm's activities.

Availability of Personnel

For an efficient running of local operations and subsidiaries, firms have to employ locals as well as expatriates. Structures are not just boxes and positions, these boxes have to be manned by efficient personnel. The first issue here is the availability of such personnel in each market. Experienced and skilled marketing personnel are a scarce resource in many foreign markets. Besides availability, whether a firm decides to employ local people or send people from head office depends upon the company culture and the extent of control. Whatever course of action is taken, a company has to make the people familiar with the company, its product, its culture and working morale. Some companies thus face enormous difficulties in recruiting and training local staff in their subsidiaries. Hiring nationals from third countries has recently become quite common, which is a real alternative to local recruitment problems. The problems related to recruitment, training and motivation of personnel are discussed in the next section.

PREPARING WESTERN PERSONNEL FOR FOREIGN ASSIGNMENTS

Estimates of the annual cost of sending and supporting a manager and the family on a foreign assignment range from 150 to 400 per cent of base salary at home. The cost in money and morale increases substantially if the expatriate requests a return home before completing the normal tour of duty (a normal stay is two to four years). In addition, if repatriation into domestic operations is not successful and the employee leaves the company, an indeterminately high cost in low morale and loss of experienced personnel results. To reduce these problems, international personnel management has increased planning for expatriate personnel to move abroad, remain abroad, and then return to the home country. The planning process must begin prior to the selection of those who go abroad and extend to their specific assignments after returning home. Selection, training, compensation and career development policies (including repatriation) should reflect the unique problems of managing the expatriate.

Besides the job-related criteria for a specific position, the typical candidate for an international assignment is married, has one or two school-aged children, is expected to stay overseas three years, and has the potential for promotion into higher management levels. These characteristics of the typical selectee are the basis of most of the difficulties associated with getting the best qualified to go overseas, keeping them there and assimilating them on their return.

Overcoming Reluctance to Accept a Foreign Assignment

Concerns for career and family are the most frequently mentioned reasons for a manager to refuse a foreign assignment. The most important career-related reservation is the fear that a two- or three-year absence will adversely affect opportunities for advancement. This 'out of sight, out of mind' fear is closely linked to the problems of repatriation. Without evidence of advance planning to protect career development, better-qualified and ambitious personnel may decline the offer to go abroad. However, if candidates for expatriate assignments are picked thoughtfully, returned to the home office at the right moment and rewarded for good performance with subsequent promotions at home, companies find recruiting of executives for international assignments eased.

Even though the career development question may be adequately answered with proper planning, concern for family may interfere with many accepting an assignment abroad. Initially, most potential candidates are worried about uprooting a family and settling into a strange environment. Questions about the education of the children,[4] isolation from family and friends, proper health care and, in some countries, the potential for violence reflect the misgivings a family faces when relocating in a foreign country. Special compensation packages have been the typical way to deal with this problem. A hardship allowance, allowances to cover special educational requirements that frequently include private schools, housing allowances and extended expensive holidays are part of compensation packages designed to overcome family-related problems with an overseas assignment.

Once the employee and family accept the assignment abroad, the next problem is keeping them there for the assigned time. The attrition rate of those selected for overseas positions can be very high. One Western firm with a hospital management contract experienced an annualized failure rate of 20 per cent—not high when compared with the construction contractor who started out in Saudi Arabia with 155 Americans and was down to 65 after only two months.

A study of personnel directors of over 300 international firms found that the inability of the manager's spouse to adjust to a different physical or cultural environment was the primary reason for an expatriate's failure to function effectively in a foreign assignment. One researcher estimated that 75 per cent of families sent to a foreign post experience adjustment problems with children or have marital discord. One executive suggests that there is so much pressure on the family that if there are any cracks in the marriage and you want to save it, think long and hard about taking a foreign assignment.[5]

Dissatisfaction is caused by the stress and trauma of adjusting to new and often strange cultures. The employee has less trouble adjusting than family members; a company's expatriate moves in a familiar environment even abroad and is often isolated from the cultural differences that create problems for the rest of the family. Family members have far greater daily exposure to the new culture but are often not given assistance in adjusting. Family members frequently cannot be employed and, in many cultures, female members of the family face severe social restrictions.

Developing Cultural Awareness

Throughout the text, the need to adapt to the local culture has been stressed over and over. Developing cultural sensitivity is necessary for all international marketers. Personnel can be selected with great care, but if they do not possess or are not given the opportunity to develop some understanding of the culture to which they are being assigned, there is every chance they will develop culture shock, inadvertently alienate those with whom they come in contact in the new culture, and/or make all the cultural mistakes discussed in this text.

Many businesses focus on functional skills needed in international marketing, overlooking the importance of cultural knowledge. Just as the idea 'if a product sells well in London it will sell well in Jakarta' is risky, so is the idea 'a manager who excels in London will excel in Jakarta'. Most expatriate failures are not caused by lack of management skills but by lack of an understanding of cultural differences and their effect on management skills.

Just as we remark that someone has achieved good social skills (i.e. an ability to remain poised and be in control in all social situations), so good cultural skills can be developed. These skills serve a similar function in varying cultural situations; they provide the individual with the ability to relate to a different culture even when the individual is unfamiliar with the details of that particular culture. People with cultural skills can: (1) communicate respect and convey verbally and nonverbally a positive regard and sincere interest in people and their culture, (2) tolerate ambiguity and cope with cultural differences and the frustration that frequently develops when things are different and circumstances change, (3) display empathy by understanding other people's needs and differences from their point of view, (4) be non-judgemental by not judging the behaviour of others by their own value standards, (5) recognize and control the SRC, that is, recognize their own culture and values as an influence on their perceptions, evaluations and judgement in a situation and (6) laugh things off—a good sense of humour helps when frustration levels rise and things do not work as planned.

Compensation

Developing an equitable and functional compensation plan that combines balance, consistent motivation and flexibility is extremely challenging in international operations. This is especially true when a company operates in a number of countries, when it has individuals who work in a number of countries or when the force is composed of expatriate and local personnel. Fringe benefits play a major role in many countries. Those working in high-tax countries prefer liberal expense accounts and fringe benefits which are nontaxable instead of direct income subject to high taxes. Fringe-benefit costs are high in Europe, ranging from 35 to 60 per cent of salary.

Conglomerate operations that include domestic and foreign personnel cause the greatest problems in compensation planning. Expatriates tend to compare their compensation with what they would have received at the home office at the same time, and local personnel and expatriate personnel are likely to compare notes on salary. Although any differences in the compensation level may easily and logically be explained, the group receiving the lower amount almost always feels aggrieved and mistreated.

An important trend questions the need for expatriates to fill foreign positions. Many companies now feel that the increase in the number and quality of managers in other countries means many positions being filled by expatriates could be filled by locals and/or third-country nationals who would require lower compensation packages. Several major multinationals, including PepsiCo, Philips, Shell, Alcatel, Black & Decker and Hewlett-Packard, have established policies to minimize the number of expatriate personnel they post abroad. With more emphasis being placed on the development of local and third-country nationals for managerial positions, companies find they can reduce compensation packages.

THE CHANGING PROFILE OF THE GLOBAL MANAGER

The executive recently picked to head Procter & Gamble's US operations is a good example of the effect globalization is having on businesses and the importance of experience, whether in Japan, Europe or elsewhere. The head of all P&G's US business was born in The Netherlands, received an MBA from Rotterdam's Erasmus University, then rose through P&G's marketing ranks in Holland, the United States and Austria. After proving his mettle in Japan, he moved to Cincinnati to direct P&G's push into East Asia and then to his new position.

Fewer companies today limit their search for senior-level executive talent to their home countries. Coca-Cola's former CEO Guizetta, who began his ascent to the top in his native Cuba, and the former IBM vice-chairman, a Swiss national who rose through the ranks in Europe, are two prominent examples of individuals who rose to the top of firms outside their home countries.

Businesses are placing a greater premium on international experience.[6] In the past, a foreign assignment might have been considered a ticket to nowhere, but such experience has now come to represent the fast track to senior management in a growing number of MNCs. The truly global executive, an individual who takes on several consecutive international assignments and eventually assumes a senior management position at headquarters, is beginning to emerge. For example, of the eight members of the executive committee at Whirlpool, five have had international postings within three years of joining the committee. In each case, it was a planned move that had everything to do with their executive development.

The executives of the year 2010, as one report speculates, will be completely different from the CEOs of today's corporations. They will come from almost anywhere, with an education that will include an undergraduate degree in French literature as well as a joint management/engineering degree. Starting in research, these executives for the 21st century will quickly move to marketing and then onto finance. Along the way there will be international assignments taking them to China, India or Brazil, where turning around a failing joint venture will be the first real test of ability that leads to the top. These executives will speak English, Portuguese, Spanish and French, and will be on a first-name basis with commerce ministers in half a dozen countries.

While this description of tomorrow's business leaders is speculative, there is mounting evidence that the route to the top for tomorrow's executives will be dramatically different from today's. A Whirlpool Corporation executive was quoted as saying that the CEO of the

GOING INTERNATIONAL 20.1

KOREANS LEARN FOREIGN WAYS—GOOF OFF AT THE MALL

The Samsung Group is one of Korea's largest companies and it wants to be more culturally sensitive to foreign ways. To that end, the company has launched an internationalization campaign. Cards are taped up in bathrooms each day to teach a phrase of English or Japanese. Overseas-bound managers attend a month-long boot camp where they are awakened at 5:30 a.m. for a jog, meditation and then lessons on table manners, dancing and avoiding sexual harassment. About 400 of its brightest junior employees are sent overseas for a year. Their mission, goof off! They know international exposure is important, but they feel you also have to develop international taste. To do this you have to do more than visit. You have to goof off at the mall and watch people. The payoff? One executive of Samsung remarked, after reading a report of 'goofing off' by an employee who spent a year's sabbatical in Russia, ' . . . in 20 years, if this man is representing Samsung in Moscow, he will have friends and he will be able to communicate, and then we will get the payoff'.

Japanese companies have a similar programme of exposure to foreign markets which comes early in the employees' careers. The day he was hired by Mitsubishi in 1962, a new employee was asked if he wanted to go overseas. Mitsubishi did not need his services abroad immediately but the bosses were sorting out who, over the next 40 years, would spend some time overseas. Japanese executives have long accepted the fact that a stint overseas is often necessary for career advancement. Because foreign tours are so critical for promotions, Japanese companies do not have to offer huge compensation packages to lure executives abroad. The new employee who was asked to go abroad back in 1962 is now on his third US tour and has spent a total of 10 years in the United States.

Sources: Abstracted from 'Sensitivity Kick: Korea's Biggest Firm Teaches Junior Execs Strange Foreign Ways', *The Wall Street Journal*, 30 December 1992, p. A-1; and 'Why Japan's Execs Travel Better', *Business Week*, November 1993, p. 68.

21st century 'must have a multienvironment, multicountry, multifunctional, and maybe even multicompany, multiindustry experience'.

Some companies, such as Colgate-Palmolive, believe that it is important to have international assignments early in a person's career, and international training is an integral part of their entry-level development programmes. Colgate recruits its future managers from the world's best colleges and business schools. Acceptance is highly competitive and successful applicants have a degree, often in business/management, with proven leadership skills, fluency in at least one language besides English and some experience living abroad.

Trainees begin their careers in a two-year, entry-level, total-immersion programme that consists of stints in various Colgate departments. A typical rotation includes time in the finance, manufacturing and marketing departments and an in-depth exposure to the company's marketing system. During that phase, trainees are rotated through the firm's ad agency, marketing research and product management departments and then work seven months as a field salesperson. At least once during the two years, trainees accompany their mentors on business trips to a foreign subsidiary. The company's goal is to develop in their trainees the skills they need to become effective marketing managers, domestically or globally.

On completion of the programme, trainees can expect a foreign posting, either immediately after graduation or soon after an assignment in their home country. The first positions are not in London or Paris, as many might hope, but in emerging markets such as Brazil, Indonesia or maybe South Africa. Because international sales are so important to Colgate

GOING INTERNATIONAL 20.2

A LOOK INTO THE FUTURE—TOMORROW'S INTERNATIONAL LEADERS? AN EDUCATION FOR THE 21st CENTURY

A school supported by the European Community teaches Britons, French, Germans, Dutch and others to be future Europeans. The European School in a suburb of Brussels has students from 12 nations who come to be educated for life and work, not as products of motherland or fatherland but as Europeans. The EC runs nine European Schools in Western Europe, enrolling 15 000 students from kindergarten to 12th grade. Graduates emerge superbly educated, usually trilingual, and very, very European.

The Schools are a linguistic and cultural melange. There are native speakers of 36 different languages represented in one school alone. Each year students take fewer and fewer classes in their native tongue. Early on, usually in first grade, they begin a second language, known as the 'working language', which must be English, French or German. A third language is introduced in the seventh year and a fourth may be started in the ninth.

By the time students reach their 11th year, they are taking history, geography, economics, advanced maths, music, art and gym in the working language. When the students are in groups talking, they are constantly switching languages to 'whatever works'.

Besides language, students learn history, politics, literature and music from the perspective of all the European countries—in short, European culture. The curriculum is designed to teach the French, German, Briton and other nationalities to be future Europeans.

Source: Abstracted from Glynn Mapes, 'Polyglot Students Are Weaned Early Off Mother Tongue', *The Wall Street Journal*, 6 March 1990, p. A-1. Reprinted by permission of THE WALL STREET JOURNAL, ©1990 Dow Jones & Company, Inc. All Rights Reserved Worldwide.

(60 per cent of its total revenues are generated abroad), a manager may not return to his home country after the first foreign assignment but moves from one overseas post to another, developing into a career internationalist, which could open to a CEO's position. Commenting on the importance of international experience to Colgate's top management, the director of management and organization said: 'The career track to the top—and I'm talking about the CEO and key executives—requires global experience. . . . Not everyone in the company has to be a global manager, but certainly anyone who is developing strategy does.'

Companies whose foreign receipts make up a substantial portion of their earnings, and who see themselves as global companies rather than as domestic companies doing business in foreign markets, are the most active in making the foreign experience an integrated part of a successful corporate career. Their global orientation permeates the entire organization from personnel policies to marketing and business strategies. Such is the case with Gillette, which made a significant recruitment and management-development decision when it decided to develop managers internally. Gillette's international human resources department implemented its international-trainee programme, designed to supply a steady stream of managerial talent from within its own ranks. Trainees are recruited from all over the world, and when their training is complete they will return to their home countries to become part of Gillette's global management team.[7]

FOREIGN LANGUAGE SKILLS

It is now widely agreed that a second language is of utmost importance for an international career. Proponents of language skills argue that learning a language improves cultural understanding and business relationships. Others point out that, to be taken seriously in the business community, the expatriate must be at least conversational in the host language. Perhaps the Director General of Northern Telecom, Mexico, put it best when he commented, 'A lot of Mexican executives will speak English with you and they are very good. That's great at the beginning when you come and you don't know Spanish, but later it does become an obstacle, a burden. You become an outsider, because you can't get inside that way; and it is not the way to sustain a long-term business relationship.'[8]

Most recruiters in Europe want candidates who speak at least one foreign language, even if the language will not be needed in a particular job. Having learned a second language is a strong signal to the recruiter that the candidate is willing to get involved in someone else's culture.

The authors feel strongly that language skills are of great importance; if you want to be a major player in international business in the future, learn to speak other languages, or you might not make it—your competition will be those European students described earlier. There is a joke that foreigners tell about language skills. It goes something like this: What do you call a person who speaks three or more languages? Multilingual. What do you call a person who speaks two languages? Bilingual. What do you call a person who speaks only one language? An Englishman!

MANAGING INTERNATIONAL PERSONNEL

Several vital questions arise when attempting to manage in other cultures. How much does a different culture affect management practices, processes and concepts used in the home market? Will practices that work well at home be equally effective when customs, values and life-styles differ? Transferring management practices to other cultures without concern for their exportability is no less vulnerable to major error than assuming a product successful in the home market will be successful in other countries. Management concepts are influenced by cultural diversity and must be evaluated in terms of local norms. Whether or not any single management practice needs adapting depends on the local culture.[9]

Impact of Cultural Values on Management

Because of the unlimited cultural diversity in the values, attitudes and beliefs affecting management practices, only those fundamental premises on which Western management practices are based are presented here for comparison. International managers must analyse normally used management practices to assess their transferability to another culture. The purpose of this section is to heighten the reader's awareness of the need for adaptation of management practices rather than to present a complete discussion of Western culture and management behaviour.

There are many divergent views on the most important ideas on which normative Western business cultural concepts are based. Those that occur most frequently in discussions of cross-cultural evaluations are represented by the following: (1) 'master of destiny' viewpoint; (2) independent enterprise—the instrument of social action; (3) personnel selection on merit; (4) decisions based on objective analysis; (5) wide sharing in decision making; and (6) neverending quest for improvement.

The *master of destiny* philosophy underlies much of management thought and is a belief held by many in Western culture. Simply stated: people can substantially influence the future; we are in control of our own destinies. This viewpoint also reflects the attitude that although luck may influence an individual's future, on balance, persistence, hard work, a commitment to fulfil expectations and effective use of time give people control of their destinies. In contrast, many cultures have a fatalistic approach to life—individual destiny is determined by a higher order and what happens cannot be controlled. It is very close to uncertainty avoidance in Hofstede's dimension of culture.[10]

Approaches to planning, control, supervision, commitment, motivation, scheduling and deadlines are all influenced by the concept that individuals can control their futures. In cultures with more fatalistic beliefs, these good business practices may be followed but concern for the final outcome is different.

NON-WESTERN MANAGEMENT STYLES

The acceptance of the idea that *independent enterprise* is an *instrument for social action* is the fundamental concept of Western corporations. A corporation is recognized as an entity that has rules and continuity of existence, and is a separate and vital social institution. This recognition of the corporation as an entity can result in strong feelings of obligation to serve the company. In fact, the enterprise can take priority over personal preferences and social obligations because it is viewed as an entity that must be protected and developed. This concept ties into the master-of-destiny concept in that, for a company to work and for individuals to control their destinies, they must feel a strong obligation to fulfil the requirements necessary to the success of the enterprise. Indeed, the company may take precedence over family, friends or other activities which might detract from what is best for the company.

Consistent with the view that individuals control their own destinies is the belief that *personnel selection is made on merit.* The selection, promotion, motivation or dismissal of personnel by Western managers emphasizes the need to select the best-qualified persons for jobs, retaining them as long as their performance meets standards of expectations, and continuing the opportunity for upward mobility as long as those standards are met. Indeed, the belief that anyone can become the corporate president prevails among management personnel within Europe and the United States. Such presumptions lead to the belief that striving and making accomplishments will be rewarded and, conversely, the failure to do so will be penalized. The penalty for poor performance could be dismissal. The reward and penalty scheme is a major basis for motivating Western personnel.[11]

This scientific approach is not necessarily the premise on which foreign executives base decisions. In fact, the infallibility of the judgement of a key executive in many foreign cultures may be more important in the decision process than any other single factor. If one accepts scientific management as a fundamental basis for decision making, then attitudes towards accuracy and promptness in reporting data, availability and openness of data to all levels within the corporation and the willingness to express even unpopular judgements become important characteristics of the business process. Thus, in Western business, great emphasis is placed on the collection and free flow of information to all levels within the organization and on frankness of expression in the evaluation of business opinions or decisions. In other cultures, such high value on factual and rational support for decisions is not as important; the accuracy of data and even the proper reporting of data are not prime prerequisites. Further, existing data frequently are for the eyes of a select few. The frankness of expression and openness in dealing with data characteristic of Western businesses do not fit easily into some cultures.

Although today fewer barriers to trade exist than at any time in the recent past, the efforts of GATT, WTO, the European Union, the US government and other countries to improve global trade relations and lower tariffs have not yet provided a level playing field for international trade. Some companies are deriving a substantial competitive advantage not only from protective tariffs but from the way they are organized and their relationship to other companies. A number of studies have revealed that more and more companies develop a network of relationships with a number of related companies such as suppliers, distributors, banks and even competitors. In Japan similar networks are called Keiretsu, in South Korea Chaebol and in India these are dominated by one family and often called groups such as Tatas and Birlas.

Management in Former Socialist Countries

The wave of capitalism sweeping through Eastern Europe, the Commonwealth of Independent States and China is opening up greater foreign investment and the need to work with managers from these countries. Besides cultural differences and the lack of opportunity to observe firsthand the different management systems that have evolved in these socialist countries, the expatriate businessperson needs to pay particular attention to understanding how best to manage personnel where profit and performance have not been a part of the work ethic. One study of management practices in China reported that the Chinese attitude and ethic towards work were 'superficial, not serious; they have little pride in their work; they stress quantity over quality'. Differing cultural assumptions, a shoddy work ethic and a general lack of technical and management skills are all frustrations facing the Western businessperson in China and many former Eastern bloc countries.[12]

Expatriate managers need more than a superficial understanding of their counterparts' management system, work styles and practices. We often have distorted views of management techniques in former socialist countries. What we urgently need is to have a clear understanding of the effectiveness of all management practices in order to combine complementary strengths. According to one author foreign firms managing in China, first of all, should attempt to reduce complexity through imposing routines and standards. Secondly, firms should use Chinese capabilities to absorb complexities of Chinese management system. For example by being careful in partner/employee selection. The Chinese partners/employees are often willing to accept foreign leadership. Finally, the companies need to create a balance between forces for global integration and those for local responsiveness.[13]

Japanese Keiretsu

The keiretsu, a unique form of business organization that links companies together in industrial groups, may be providing Japanese business with a substantial competitive edge over non-keiretsu organizations. Keiretsus are descended from the zaibatsus, huge industrial conglomerates that virtually controlled the Japanese economy before World War II. Four of the largest zaibatsus, Mitsubishi, Mitsui, Sumitomo and Yasuda, accounted for about a quarter of all Japanese industrial assets.[14] Zaibatsus were outlawed after World War II and keiretsus emerged as a variation. Today there are 6 major industrial keiretsu groups and 11 lesser ones. Together, the sales in these groups are responsible for about 25 per cent of the activities of all Japanese companies, and keiretsus account for 78 per cent of the value of all shares on the Tokyo Stock Exchange.[15]

Figure 20.3 illustrates the range and complexity of the relationships among the members of the Mitsubishi Group. It is led by Mitsubishi Bank and Mitsubishi Heavy Industries, the country's largest machinery manufacturer, with interests ranging from aircraft to air-conditioning equipment. Altogether, the Mitsubishi Group, with annual sales of

Figure 20.3   The Core Members of the Mitsubishi Keiretsu*

The Flagship Members
Mitsubishi Corporation (32%)
Mitsubishi Bank (25%)
Mitsubishi Industries (20%)

Twenty-Five Core members
Mitsubishi Paper Mills (32%)
Mitsubishi Kasei (23%)
Mitsubishi Plastics Industries (57%)
Mitsubishi Petrochemical (37%)
Mitsubishi Gas Chemical (24%)
Kirin Brewery (19%)
Mitsubishi Oil (41%)
Mitsubishi Steel Manufacturing (38%)
Mitsubishi Cable Industries (48%)
Mitsubishi Estate (25%)
Mitsubishi Warehousing and Transportation (40%)
Mitsubishi Metal (21%)
Mitsubishi Construction (100%)
Asahi Glass (28%)
Mitsubishi Rayon (25%)
Mitsubishi Electric (17%)
Mitsubishi Kakoki (37%)
Mitsubishi Aluminium (100%)
Mitsubishi Mining & Cement (37%)
Tokyo Marine & Fire Insurance (24%)
Meiji Mutual Life Insurance (0%)
Mitsubishi Trust & Banking (28%)
Nippon Yusen (25%)
Mitsubishi Motors (55%)
Nikon Corp. (27%)
and
Hundreds of other Mitsubishi-related companies.

*Percentages represent shares of each company held by others in the group.
Source: Adapted from 'Mighty Mitsubishi Is on the Move', *Business Week*, 24 September 1990, p. 99; and 'Why Japan Keeps on Winning', *Fortune*, 15 July 1991, pp. 76 and 81.

€156 billion ($175 billion), involves 160 companies, of which 124 are listed on the Tokyo Stock Exchange. Each is entirely independent with its own board of directors.

Keiretsus are collections of dozens of major companies spanning several industries and held together by cross-shareholding, old-boy networks, interlocking directorates, long-term business relationships and social and historical links. At the hub of each keiretsu is a bank or cash-rich company that provides low-cost, 'patient' (long-term, low-interest) capital. The six top Japanese financial-based keiretsus and the number of core industries within each are:

- Dai-Ichi Kangin—47 core companies.
- Fuyo—29 core companies.
- Mitsui Group—24 core companies.
- Sanwa—44 core companies.
- Sumitomo—20 core companies.
- Mitsubishi—28 core companies.

Figure 20.4   Ties that Bind: Japanese Keiretsu and Toyota

Toyota has a typical keiretsu family with financial ties to its most important suppliers. Some of those companies, with the percentage of each that Toyota owns:

Lighting—Koito Mfg.	19 %
Rubber—Toyoda Gosel	41.4
Disc brakes—Akebona	13.9
Transmissions, clutches, brakes—Aisin Seiki	22
Clocks—Jeco	34
Electronics—Nippondenso	23.6
Seat belts, switches—Tokai Rika	28.2
Steel—Aichi Steel Works	21.0
Upholstery material—Kyowa Leather	33.5
Door sashes, moulding—Shiroki	13.2
Painting—Trinity	30.2
Mufflers—Futaba Industrial	13.2

Source: Adapted from 'Japan: All in the Family', *Newsweek*, 10 June 1991, p. 38.

There are three types of keiretsus: (1) financial; (2) production; and (3) sales–distribution. The *financial keiretsus* are loose federations of powerful, independent firms clustered around a core bank that provides funds to a general trading company and other member firms. They are linked together by cross-holdings of shares, by sales and purchases within the group and by formal and informal consultations.

The *production*, or *vertical*, *keiretsu* is a web of interlocking, long-term relationships between a big manufacturer and its main suppliers. Vertical keiretsus are pyramids of companies that serve a single master—a manufacturer that dictates virtually everything, including prices it will pay to hundreds of suppliers who are often prohibited from doing business outside the keiretsu. At the pyramid's bottom is a swarm of job shops and family ventures with primitive working conditions and subsistence-level pay and profits.

Production keiretsus are typically found in the automotive industry and consist of vertically integrated systems—from the manufacturer to suppliers. Rather than produce the majority of parts in-house as American auto companies do (GM, Chrysler and Ford produce 60 per cent of their parts in-house), keiretsus depend on their supplier partners. A large manufacturing firm will have a group of primary subcontractors, which in turn farm out work to thousands of little firms. All subcontractors are integrated into the manufacturer's production process and receive extensive technological, managerial and financial support. Manufacturers and their subcontractors are tied by reciprocal obligation: the subcontractor to high quality and low costs; the manufacturer to providing a steady flow of financial and technical resources. Figure 20.4 illustrates the ties that bind Toyota and its suppliers.

The third category, *sales–distribution keiretsus*, consists of vertically integrated manufacturing and distribution companies. The trading company, the centre of a distribution keiretsu, coordinates a complex manufacturing process that involves thousands of small companies that sell through the keiretsu's distribution network.

The keiretsu controls its own retail system, enabling it to dictate prices, profit margins and exclusive representation through the system. High prices are maintained by establishing customer loyalty and limiting availability of products to keiretsu-owned or -controlled retail stores. Retail loyalty is maintained by giving generous rebates, advertising subsidies and a special 'monopoly' rebate to stores that limit shelf space for competing brands. Matsushita, a distribution keiretsu of consumer electronics, controls 60 wholesalers who sell to 25 000 keiretsu stores. Wholesalers also sell to large consumer electronics stores, department stores, and chain stores, all of whom are encouraged to limit shelf space of competitive brands in order to receive generous rebates and other benefits Matsushita pays for loyalty.

While keiretsus are organized around one of the three core activities, they share many of the same characteristics. Group members typically purchase a small amount of each other's shares and agree not to sell them, a practice called mutual shareholding. Mutual shareholders account for 15 per cent to 20 per cent of member companies' stock. Keiretsu stock is also held by large institutions which pledge, with 'stable shareholding' agreements, not to sell the stock. This means that between 60 per cent and 80 per cent of the stock in keiretsu companies is never traded. This alone gives keiretsu companies the security of knowing that competitors or outsiders will not be able to take over their companies.

Top executives of the group's main bank or trading company characteristically have interlocking directorates and presidents' clubs so that the chief executives of the principal companies can meet. Cross-shareholding is very common among member firms, as is exchange of cooperative directors.

Strong buyer–supplier relationships exist among group members and at least 30 per cent or as much as 50 per cent of the business of member companies is among group members. Members give preferential treatment to one another as customers and vendors. A keiretsu such as Toyota can assemble one of its auto division's cars using parts supplied almost entirely by Toyota-linked suppliers. However, the parent and subsidiary companies both maintain close, cooperative relationships with their major domestic competitors. They buy from and sell to each other, share technology, cooperate on R&D, operate joint ventures, have common banks and shareholders, and coordinate their dealings with foreign competitors. The relationships run very deep. Matsushita is responsible for more than 20 per cent of Japanese VCR production. Matsushita's principal domestic competitor is JVC, a consumer electronics producer whose VCR market share is slightly less than 20 per cent. Yet JVC designs many of Matsushita's products, and Matsushita owns 51 per cent of JVC.[16]

It might appear the keiretsu system would lead to the sluggishness typical of an industry that becomes a monopoly; but keiretsus face strong competition among keiretsu groups within Japan. Each group follows the so-called 'one set principle', that is, they have a company in each major industry—chemicals, electronics, construction trade, mining and so on. Thus, five or six well-backed competitors compete vigorously within the Japanese market.

The stability of member relationships encourages investment in new technologies and allows manufacturers and suppliers to share in the cost of development of new products. Suppliers are brought in at early stages of the design period and are expected to work with the manufacturer to provide continuous design improvement, continual price reductions and technological upgrades. Stability also promotes free flows of information, tightly coordinated production schedules, wide dissemination of technology and long-term planning resulting in better quality and a shorter time between idea and production. Toyota can bring a new car design into production in four years versus the five to eight years needed by US and about five to six years needed by European car manufacturers. More and more European and US car manufacturers are following the Japanese Keiretsu structure. Figure 20.5 illustrates Ford's Keiretsu.

Another important characteristic of the keiretsu system is cooperation among competitors on research and development of new technology. Developing new technology is expensive, and the Japanese do not want to squander resources on too many duplicate efforts, so competitors work together closely on 'precompetitive' research.

Figure 20.5   Ford's Keiretsu

Vehicle Assembly		Financial Services

Vehicle Assembly

Company	Percent Equity
Mazda—Japan	25%
Kia Motors—Korea	10
Aston Martin Lagonda—Britain	75
Autolatina—Brazil Argentina	49
Iveco Ford Truck— Britain	48

Parts Production

Cummins—US Engines	10
Excel Industries—US Windows	40
Decoma International— Canada Body parts, wheels	49

Financial Services

Through seven wholly owned units, Ford extends consumer and commercial credit. It issues car loans, mortgages, and credit cards, does industrial leases, and finances dealer purchases of cars.

Marketing

Owns 49 per cent of Hertz. Hertz and other car rental companies are among Ford's largest customers.

Research and Development

Ford belongs to eight consortiums that do research into environmental issues, better engineering techniques, materials, electric-car batteries, and the Chrysler and General Motors 'precompetitive research' on batteries and materials.

Source: Adapted from 'Learning from Japan', *Business Week*, 27 January 1992, p. 55.

Korean Chaebols

The relation structure of Keiretsu can also be witnessed in other Asian structures. In South Korea, there are industrial conglomerates known as chaebols. One structural difference between the chaebols and Keiretsu in Japan is in ownership and control. Member firms in the keiretsu are said to own minority equity in each other and are headed by the lead bank or the lead firm in the network. In the case of the chaebols, a family and its members own the companies in multiindustries. Furthermore, a circular type of corporate ownership is said to dominate the chaebol structure: company A holds shares or equity in company B which holds equity in company C which holds shares in company A.

The Korean entrepreneurial families have been powerful entities since World War II and during the Park regime (1961–73), it is said that the families fostered close relationships with President Park Chung Hee. The presence of chaebols has been so overwhelming that the government in the 1980s struggled to contain 'the power of the (chaebol) founding families that control much of South Korea's economy'.

A capsule profile of the four largest chaebols in South Korea shows the scope of these industry groups. All four can be characterized as conglomerates since ownership is held by the family and control resides therein. Some have their origin in trading activity resembling the zaibatsu: however, all are now engaged in many key industries including electronics. A relative newcomer is Sunkyong Group' founded in 1953. It has grown into a vertically integrated manufacturer of a broad spectrum of products ranging from petroleum to textiles with annual sales revenue exceeding €18 billion ($20 billion). The backbone of this experiment is said to be Sunkyong Management System and the Super Excellence movement.

Asian Family Business Structures

Business group formation activities in India are comparable to Japanese Keiretsus and Korean Chaebols. In the early part of the twentieth century, the then fledgling entrepreneurial families (such as the Birlas, Mafatlals and Tatas) began to emulate the managing agency system model. In his seminal work, Lokanathan pointed out that the managing agents came to control and manage a large number of similar (industrial) undertakings. Thus, the managing agency system acted as the organizational mechanism that could fill the capital and management needs of the then emerging large-scale industry in India.

Even though the managing agency system was outlawed in 1969, the point to be noted here is that the entrepreneurial families such as the Birlas and the Tatas could expand their business activities and stretch their management acumen and the competence by means of complicated contractual managing agency agreements.

Aditya Birla, in his 52 years of life, had amassed 37 companies into a mammoth €4.5 billion ($5 billion) sales in 16 countries, an empire ranging from textile to cement, iron and aluminum. When he suddenly died in 1995, the mantle passed on to his 29-year old-son.

The case of Voltas, primarily a marketing company within the Tata Group, illustrates how capital allocation to member firms within the Voltas network has been based on relational, rather than cost benefit, considerations. The Tata Group, with its more than €4.5 billion ($5 billion) sales revenue and €230 million ($255 million) operating profits, has a network of autonomous enterprises ranging in business scope from steel and high technology to consumer products and hotels. In its iron and steel sector alone it employs more than 75 000 workers. It is also part of a wide range of international networks and has joint ventures with AT&T, IBM, Mercedes Benz and Silicon Graphics as well as a number of Singapore-based enterprises.

The Tata Group is continuously rearranging its portfolio of networks. Recently it sold its soap division to Unilever, and has withdrawn from a partnership with Pepsico. It should be noted, however, that while there are scores of relatively new entrepreneurial firms in India, some of the single-business firms of the 1950s and 1960s have now emerged as cohesive group companies exhibiting somewhat similar organizational characteristics as those of the Tata or Birla Groups.[17] These family businesses are often run by the family members, who are sent abroad for education to Oxford, Cambridge or Harvard. Most Western MNCs have to accept these management styles as they form partnerships with these family firms while entering India. The management style in these companies is quite different from Western management styles. Western companies planning to do business in these countries need to get an insight into these management systems to efficiently control their operations.

SUMMARY

The extent to which a company can be successful in its international marketing efforts does not just depend upon the nature and suitability of the marketing strategy used. An important factor is the efficient organization of the firm's international activities.

There is no 'right' structure for an international organization. Companies need to find the right balance or 'fit' between the company's objectives, strategies and local environment or customer needs. The structure that allows this 'fit' in an ever-changing international marketing environment is the most suitable.

Important issues to be considered in designing an organization include the choice of centralization versus decentralization of decision making, communication implications of an organizational structure, the position of marketing in an organization, the coordination of the firm's activities and the availability of experienced and skilled personnel.

The development of an effective marketing organization calls for careful recruiting, selecting, training, motivating and compensating of expatriate personnel. It is important that international marketers develop cultural sensitivity and foreign language skills. They have to understand how cultural differences affect management practices and concepts used in the home market, and consequently, whether or not adaptation to the local culture is needed.

QUESTIONS

1. Can a person develop good cultural skills? Discuss.
2. Describe the six attributes of a person with good cultural skills.
3. Interview a local company that has a foreign sales operation. Draw an organization chart for the marketing function and explain why that particular structure was used by that company.
4. Discuss the ideas on which Western management practices are based.
5. Why do companies include an evaluation of an employee's family among selection criteria?
6. Discuss how a family can affect the entire process of selecting personnel for foreign assignment.

7. 'Concerns for career and family are the most frequently mentioned reasons for a manager to refuse a foreign assignment.' Why?
8. If 'the language of international business is English', why is it important for English speaking people to develop a skill in a foreign language? Discuss.
9. The global manager of the year 2010 will have to meet many new challenges. Draw up a sample resume for someone who could be considered for a top-level executive position in a global firm.
10. What are the characteristics of a keiretsu management style?
11. How do chaebols differ from keiretsus?

REFERENCES

1. Colin Gilligant and Martin Hird, *International Marketing: Strategy and Management* (London: Croom Helm, 1986); and Christopher Bartlett and Sumantra Ghoshal, *Transnational Management: Text, Cases and Readings in Cross-Border Management* (Homewood, IL: Irwin, 1992).

2. Simon Majaro, *International Marketing* (London: Unwin Hyman, 1987).

3. H.V. Perlmutter, 'The Tortuous Evolution of the Multinational Corporation', *Columbia Journal of World Business*, January–February 1969, p. 12; and Pervez Ghauri, 'New Structures in MNCs Based in Small Countries', *European Management Journal*, vol. 10, no. 3, 1992, pp. 357–364.

4. This section draws heavily on Colin Gilligant and Martin Hird (1986) and Simon Majaro (1987) refs 1 and 2 above.

5. Minda Zetlin, 'Making Tracks', *The Journal of European Business*, May–June 1994, pp. 40–47.

6. Lori Ioannou, 'Stateless Executives', *International Business*, February 1995, pp. 48–52.

7. Jennifer J. Laabs, 'How Gillette Grooms Global Talent', *Personnel Journal*, August 1993, pp. 65–75.

8. Dennis Stevens and Paul Beamish, 'Forging Alliances in Mexico', *Business Quarterly*, Winter 1993, p. 84.

9. For a discussion of different management styles, see Maud Tixier, 'Management Styles across Western European Cultures', *The International Executive*, July–August 1994, pp. 377–391.

10. Geert Hofstede, *Culture and Organizations: Software of the Mind* (London: McGraw-Hill, 1991).

11. Mariah E. de Forest, 'Insulation from Mexican Cultural Shock', *The Wall Street Journal*, 17 October 1994, p. A-14.

12. Pervez Ghauri and Benjamin Prasad, 'A Network Approach to Probing Asia's Interfirm Linkages', in Benjamin Prasad (ed.), *Advances in International Comparative Management* (Greenwich, NY: JAI Press, 1995), pp. 63–77.

13. John R. Engen, 'Training Chinese Workers', *Training*, September 1994, pp. 79–81.

14. John Child, 'Management in China', in Peter Buckley and Pervez Ghauri (eds), *Multinationals and Emerging Markets* (London: International Thompson Business Press, 1999).

15. Enrich Perotti and Erik Berglof, 'The Governance Structure of the Japanese Financial Firm', *Journal of Financial Economics*, October 1994, pp. 259–265.

16. For a review of changes that may be taken place in Japanese government and keiretsu, see William J. Holstein, 'In Japan, Plus Ça Change . . . ', *Business Week*, 8 August 1994, p. 38–39.

17. Pervez Ghauri and Benjamin Prasad, 'A Network Approach to Probing Asia's Interfirm Linkages', in Benjamin Prasad (ed.), *Advances in International Comparative Management* (Greenwich, NY: JAI Press, 1995), pp. 63–77.

Supplementary Material: Country Notebook and Cases

Part Outline

CN

The Country Notebook—A Guide for Developing a Marketing Plan

A number of books and articles have described strategic marketing planning at corporate or business unit level.[1] Here we are mainly concerned about a marketing plan for a foreign market or a marketing plan for a particular product in one particular market. The guidelines provided here can be used for different markets, however, depending upon the market and the product the emphasis on different parts of the framework may change.[2]

The first stage in the planning process is a preliminary country analysis. The marketer needs basic information to: (1) evaluate a country market's potential, (2) identify problems that would eliminate a country from further consideration, (3) identify aspects of the country's environment that need further study, (4) evaluate the components of the marketing mix for possible adaptation and (5) develop a strategic marketing plan. One further use of the information collected in the preliminary analysis is as a basis for a country notebook.

Many companies, large and small, have a *country notebook* for each country in which they do business. The country notebook contains information a marketer should be aware of when making decisions involving a specific country market. As new information is collected, the country notebook is continually updated by the country or product manager. Whenever a marketing decision is made involving a country, the country notebook is the first database consulted. New product introductions, changes in advertising programmes, and other marketing programme decisions begin with the country notebook. It also serves as a quick introduction for new personnel assuming responsibility for a country market.[3]

This section presents four separate guidelines for collection and analysis of market data and preparation of a country notebook: (1) guideline for cultural analysis; (2) guideline for economic analysis; (3) guideline for market audit and competitive analysis; (4) guideline for preliminary marketing plan. These guidelines suggest the kinds of information a marketer can gather to enhance planning (see Figure CN.1).

The points in each of the guidelines are general. They are designed to provide direction to areas to explore for relevant data. In each guideline, specific points must be adapted to reflect a company's products. The decision as to the appropriateness of specific data and the depth of coverage depends on company objectives, product characteristics, and the country market. Some points in the guidelines are unimportant for some countries and/or some products and should be ignored. Preceding chapters of this book provide specific content suggestions for the topics in each guideline.

CULTURAL ANALYSIS

The data suggested in the cultural analysis include information that helps the marketer make market planning decisions. However, its application extends beyond product/market analysis to an important source of information for someone interested in understanding business customs and other important cultural features of the country.

The information in this analysis must be more than a collection of facts. Whoever is responsible for the preparation of this material should attempt to interpret the meaning of cultural information. That is, how does the information help in understanding the effect on the market? For example, the fact that almost all the populations of Italy and Ireland are Catholic is an interesting statistic but not nearly as useful as understanding the effect of Catholicism on values, beliefs and other aspects of market behaviour. Even though both countries are predominantly Catholic, the influence of their individual and unique interpretation and practise of Catholicism can result in important differences in market behaviour.

Figure CN.1 Country Notebook and Marketing Plan

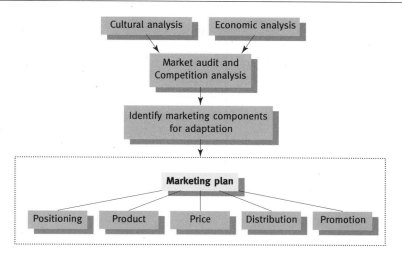

Guidelines

I. Introduction.

Include short profiles of the company, the product to be exported, and the country with which you wish to trade.

II. Brief discussion of the country's relevant history.

III. Geographical setting.
   A. Location.
   B. Climate.
   C. Topography.

IV. Social institutions.
   A. Family
      1. The nuclear family.
      2. The extended family.
      3. Female/male roles (are they changing or static?).
   B. Education.
      1. The role of education in society.
      2. Literacy rates.
   C. Political system.
      1. Political structure.
      2. Stability of government.
      3. Special taxes.
      4. Role of local government.
   D. Legal system.
      1. Organization of the judiciary system.
      2. Code, common, socialist or Islamic-law country?
      3. Participation in patents, trademarks and other conventions.

     E.   Social organizations.
       1. Group behaviour.
       2. Social classes.
       3. Race, ethnicity and subcultures.
     F.   Business customs and practices.
  V. Religion and aesthetics.
     A.   Religion and other belief systems.
       1. Which religions are prominent?
       2. Membership of each religion.
     B.   Aesthetics.
       1. Visual arts (fine arts, plastics, graphics, public colours, etc.).
       2. Importance given to aesthetics.
 VI. Living conditions.
     A.   Diet and nutrition.
       1. Typical meals.
     B.   Housing.
       1. Types of housing available.
       2. Do most people own or rent?
       3. Do most people live in one-family dwellings or with other families?
     C.   Clothing.
       1. National dress.
       2. Types of clothing worn at work.
     D.   Recreation, sports, and other leisure activities.
     E.   Social security.
     F.   Health care.
 VII. Language.
     A.   Official language(s).
     B.   Spoken versus written language(s).
VIII. Executive summary.

     After completing all of the other sections, prepare a *two-page* (maximum length) summary of the major points and place it at the front of the report. The purpose of an executive summary is to give the reader a brief glance at the critical points of your report. Those aspects of the culture a reader should know to do business in the country but would not be expected to know or would find different based on his or her SRC should be included in this summary.

  IX. Sources of information.
   X. Appendixes.

ECONOMIC ANALYSIS

The reader may find the data collected for the economic analysis guideline are more straight-forward than for the cultural analysis guideline. There are two broad categories of information in this guideline: general economic data that serve as a basis for an evaluation of the economic soundness of a country and information on channels of distribution and media availability. As mentioned earlier, the guideline focuses only on broad categories of data and must be adapted to particular company/product needs.

Guidelines

I. Introduction.

II. Population.
    A. Total.
        1. Growth rates.
    B. Distribution of population.
        1. Age.
        2. Sex.
        3. Geographic areas (urban, suburban and rural density and concentration).
        4. Ethnic groups.

III. Economic statistics and activity.
    A. Gross national product (GNP or GDP).
        1. Total.
        2. Rate of growth (real GNP or GDP).
    B. Personal income per capita.
    C. Average family income.
    D. Distribution of wealth.
        1. Income classes.
        2. Proportion of the population in each class.
        3. Is the distribution distorted?
    E. Minerals and resources.
    F. Surface transportation.
        1. Modes.
        2. Availability.
    G. Communication systems.
        1. Types.
        2. Availability.
    H. Working conditions.
        1. Employer–employee relations.
        2. Employee participation.
        3. Salaries and benefits.
    I. Principal industries.
        1. What proportion of the GNP does each industry contribute?
        2. Ratio of private to publicly owned industries.
    J. Foreign investment.
        1. Opportunities?
        2. Which industries?
    K. International trade statistics.
        1. Major exports.
            a. Dollar/euro value.
            b. Trends.
        2. Major imports.
            a. Dollar/euro value.
            b. Trends.
        3. Balance-of-payments situation.
            a. Surplus or deficit?
            b. Recent trends.

      4. Exchange rates.
        a. Single or multiple exchange rates?
        b. Current rate of exchange.
  L. Trade restrictions.
      1. Embargoes.
      2. Quotas.
      3. Import taxes.
      4. Tariffs.
      5. Licensing.
      6. Customs duties.
  M. Extent of economic activity not included in cash income activities.
      1. Countertrades.
        a. Products generally offered for countertrading.
        b. Types of countertrades requested (i.e. barter, counterpurchase, etc.).
      2. Foreign aid received (relevance for the product in question).
  N. Labour force.
      1. Size.
      2. Unemployment rates.
  O. Inflation rates.
IV. Developments in science and technology.
  A. Current technology available (computers, machinery, tools, etc.).
  B. Technological skills of the labour force and general population.
 V. Channels of distribution (macroanalysis).
  This section reports data on all channel middlemen available within the market. Later, you will select a specific channel as part of your distribution strategy relevant to your product.
  A. Middlemen.
      1. Retailers.
        a. Number of retailers.
        b. Typical size of retail outlets.
        c. Customary markup for various classes of goods.
        d. Methods of operation (cash/credit).
        e. Scale of operation (large/small).
        f. Role of chain stores, department stores and specialty shops.
      2. Wholesale middlemen.
        a. Number and size.
        b. Customary markup for various classes of goods.
        c. Method of operation (cash/credit).
      3. Import/export agents.
      4. Warehousing.
      5. Penetration of urban and rural markets.
VI. Media.
  This section reports data on all media available within the country/market. Later, you will select specific media as part of the promotional mix/strategy relevant for your product.
  A. Availability of media.
  B. Costs.
      1. Television.
      2. Radio.

        3. Print.

        4. Other media (cinema, outdoor, etc.).

    C. Agency assistance.

    D. Coverage of various media.

    E. Percentage of population reached by each of the media.

VII. Executive summary.

    After completing the research for this report, prepare a two-page (maximum) summary of the major economic points and place it at the front of the report.

VIII. Sources of information.

IX. Appendixes.

MARKET AUDIT AND COMPETITIVE MARKET ANALYSIS

Of the guidelines presented, this is the most product- or brand-specific. Information in the other guidelines is general in nature, focusing on product categories, whereas data in this one are brand-specific and are used to determine competitive market conditions and market potential.

Two different components of the planning process are reflected in this guideline. Information in Parts I and II, Cultural Analysis and Economic Analysis, serve as the basis for an evaluation of the product/brand in a specific country market. Information in this guideline provides an estimate of market potential and an evaluation of the strengths and weaknesses of competitive marketing efforts. The data generated in this step are used to determine the extent of adaptation of the company's marketing mix necessary for successful market entry and to develop the final step—the action plan.

The detailed information needed to complete this guideline is not necessarily available without conducting a thorough marketing research investigation. Thus, another purpose of this part of the country notebook is to identify the correct questions to ask in a formal market study.

Guidelines

    I. Introduction.

   II. The product.

    A. Evaluate the product as an innovation as it is perceived by the intended market.

        1. Relative advantage.

        2. Compatibility.

        3. Complexity.

    B. Major problems and resistances to product acceptance based on the preceding evaluation. (See Chapter 13 for a discussion of this topic.)

  III. The market.

    A. Describe the market(s) in which the product is to be sold.

        1. Geographical region(s).

        2. Forms of transportation and communication available in that (those) region(s).

        3. Consumer buying habits.

            a. Product-use patterns.

            b. Product feature preferences.

            c. Shopping habits.

        4. Distribution of the product.
          a. Typical retail outlets.
          b. Product sales by other middlemen.
        5. Advertising and promotion.
          a. Advertising media usually used to reach your target market(s).
          b. Sales promotions customarily used (sampling, coupons, etc.).
        6. Pricing strategy.
          a. Customary markups.
          b. Types of discounts available.
    B. Compare and contrast your product and the competition's product(s).
        1. Competitor's product(s).
          a. Brand name.
          b. Features.
          c. Package.
        2. Competitor's prices.
        3. Competitor's promotion and advertising methods.
        4. Competitor's distribution channels.
    C. Market size.
        1. Estimate industry sales for the planning year.
        2. Estimate sales for your company for the planning year.
    D. Government participation in the marketplace.
        1. Agencies that can help you.
        2. Regulations you must follow.
  IV. Executive summary.
    Based on your analysis of the market, briefly summarize (two-page maximum) the major problems and opportunities requiring attention in you marketing mix and place the summary at the front of the report.
  V. Sources of information.
  VI. Appendixes.

PRELIMINARY MARKETING PLAN

Information gathered in Guidelines I through III serves as the basis for developing a marketing plan for your product/brand in a target market. How the problems and opportunities that surfaced in the preceding steps are overcome and/or exploited to produce maximum sales/profits are presented here. The action plan reflects, in your judgement, the most effective means of marketing your product in a country market. Budgets, expected profits and/or losses, and additional resources necessary to implement the proposed plan are also presented.

Guidelines

  I. The marketing plan.
    A. Marketing objectives.
        1. Target market(s) (specific description of the market segment).
        2. Expected sales 20–.
        3. Profit expectations 20–.
        4. Market penetration and coverage.

B. Product adaptation, or modification—using the product component model as your guide, indicate how your product can be adapted for the market (see Chapter 13).
 1. Core component.
 2. Packaging component.
 3. Support services component.
C. Promotion mix.
 1. Advertising.
  a. Objectives.
  b. Media mix.
  c. Message.
 2. Sales promotions.
  a. Objectives.
  b. Coupons.
  c. Premiums.
 3. Personal selling.
 4. Other promotional methods.
D. Distribution: From origin to destination.
 1. Port selection.
  a. Origin port.
  b. Destination port.
 2. Mode selection: Advantages/disadvantages of each mode.
  a. Railroads.
  b. Air carriers.
  c. Ocean carriers.
  d. Motor carriers.
 3. Packing.
  a. Marking and labelling regulations.
  b. Containerization.
 4. Documentation required.
 5. Insurance claims.
 6. Freight forwarder.
  If your company does not have a transportation or traffic management department, then consider using a freight forwarder. There are distinct advantages and disadvantages to hiring one.
E. Channels of distribution (micro analysis).
 This section presents details about the specific types of distribution in your marketing plan.
 1. Retailers.
  a. Type and number of retail stores.
  b. Retail markups for products in each type of retail store.
  c. Methods of operation for each type (cash/credit).
  d. Scale of operation for each type (small/large).
 2. Wholesale middlemen.
  a. Type and number of wholesale middlemen.
  b. Markup for class of products by each type.
  c. Methods of operation for each type (cash/credit).
  d. Scale of operation (small/large).
 3. Import/export agents.

        4. Warehousing.
          a. Type.
          b. Location.
   F. Price determination.
       1. Cost of the shipment of goods.
       2. Transportation costs.
       3. Handling expenses.
       4. Insurance costs.
       5. Customs duties.
       6. Import taxes and value-added tax.
       7. Wholesale and retail markups and discounts.
       8. Company's gross margins.
       9. Retail price.
   G. Terms of sale.
       1. Ex works, fob, fas, c&f, cif.
   H. Methods of payment.
       1. Cash in advance.
       2. Letters of credit.
II. Pro forma financial statements and budgets.
   A. Marketing budget.
       1. Selling expense.
       2. Advertising/promotion expense.
       3. Distribution expense.
       4. Product cost.
       5. Other costs.
   B. Pro forma annual profit and loss statement (first year and fifth year).
III. Resource requirements.
   A. Finances.
   B. Personnel.
   C. Production capacity.
IV. Executive summary.
   After completing the research for this report, prepare a (two-page maximum) summary of the major points of your successful marketing plan and place it at the front of the report.
 V. Sources of information.
VI. Appendixes.
   The intricacies of international operations and the complexity of the environment within which the international marketer must operate create an extraordinary demand for information. When operating in foreign markets, the need for thorough information as a substitute for uninformed opinion is equally as important as it is in domestic marketing. This information should be systematically collected and analysed before it is presented as a base for decision making.[4]

SUMMARY

Market-oriented firms build strategic market plans around company objectives, markets and the competitive environment. Planning for marketing can be complicated even for one country, but when a company is doing business internationally the problems are multiplied. Company objectives may vary from market to market, from product to product and from time to time; the structure of international markets also changes periodically and from country to country, and the competitive, governmental, and economic parameters affecting market planning are in a constant state of flux. These variations require international marketing executives to be specially flexible and creative in their approach to strategic marketing planning.

REFERENCES

1. See e.g. David Aaker, *Strategic Marketing Management*, 4th edn (New York: Wiley, 1995).
2. For going into a new market see, e.g. Franklin Root, *Entry Strategies for International Markets* (Washington DC: Heath and Company, 1994).
3. Tamer S. Cavusgil and Pervez N. Ghauri, *Doing Business in Developing Countries: Entry and Negotiation Strategies* (London: Routledge, 1990).
4. Pervez Ghauri, Kjell Grønhaug and Ivar Kristianslund, *Research Methods in Business Studies: A Practical Guide* (Hemel Hempstead: Prentice-Hall, 1995).

CASES

1

An Overview

CASE 1.1
Selling US Ice Cream in Korea

Effect of Controllable and Uncontrollable Factors

The call from Hong Kong was intriguing: Go to South Korea and be the franchisee of an American premium ice cream to capitalize on the Koreans' new disposable income and their growing appetite for Western fast-food products.

Within six months of my application, the government granted me permission to bring the ice cream, Hobson's, to Seoul with only two nontariff trade conditions: Make my ice cream in Korea after a year of operation and at the same time take on a Korean partner who had at least a 25 per cent stake in the company.

I agreed, and chose Itaewon for my site, figuring that between the Korean bar girls and the US Army up the road it would give me a good cross-section of East and West.

Necessary Ingredient.   Almost a half-year after start-up, I still think it's a timely idea but it certainly hasn't been easy pickings. The Korean bar girls, for instance, think my ice cream is too expensive, and Koreans in general are highly suspicious of new products. Government red tape is horrendous and foreigners are not welcome.

But because internationalization and economic progress are hard to separate, Seoul is coming to accept foreigners and their products as a necessary ingredient for their own growth.

The irony, however, is that Korean intransigence is not the only problem a Yankee entrepreneur faces here: Washington trade-bashing can take its toll as well. The US government has been pressuring this country to raise the value of the won, to make Korean exports more expensive and US imports less. On top of this is Congress's omnibus trade bill, which forces Korea to open its markets or face punitive sanctions on its own exports to the United States. Although these efforts are designed to help American traders like me, I have seen all too often how the best-laid political plans can actually make it more difficult for us to maintain a foothold in these countries.

In fairness it also must be said that some American companies bring this on themselves. Evidence indicates

Adapted from Jay R. Tunney, 'US Ice Cream Fares Poorly in Korea', *The Asian Wall Street Journal Weekly*, 13 February 1989, p. 13; and Henry Shyn, 'Doing Business the Korean Way', *Trade & Culture*, March–April 1995, pp. 28–29.

that American companies are badly outclassed by their failure to take Asian markets seriously and a tendency to follow the laws of least resistance by concentrating on selling within the borders of the United States.

American companies have tried to cheat by getting Congress to force not only Korea, but also Japan, Hong Kong, Singapore and other countries to raise the value of their currency. Those forces are now driving the won to a value of 590 to 600 won for one dollar by this year's end, when just two years ago $1 would buy 890 won. I thus find myself importing more dollars just to stay even with my earlier projections when it was 800 won to the dollar. In other words, it has cost me 16 per cent more dollars just to get started operating, and this was the margin I was hoping I could apply towards profits. Any price increase to recoup losses risks pricing my ice cream out of the Korean market.

Another result of exchange-rate jiggling is inflation. This is a by-product of the won's strengthening against the dollar, reflected in the many outside investment dollars trying to find a home in Korea's currency and stock market.

Consequently, everything comes with a price tag that equals or exceeds what one can buy in the United States. On top of this are import taxes, tariffs and non-tariff barriers on imported capital goods and, in my case, finished ice cream. Duties, for example, range from 20 to 38 per cent additional money.

US trade bullying also fans the flames of anti-Americanism here, and American business pays for that. Even though Washington has some legitimate gripes about closed Korean markets, Koreans feel that they're being pushed around and that the United States doesn't recognize the great strides they have made. For me this resentment has translated into vandalism of my storefront property, such as knocked-down signs, broken patio tables and chairs, plate-glass windows smeared with soda and dirt and even human faeces left on my doorstep. It also manifests itself by Koreans staying away from buying my ice cream.

The Korean bureaucracy seems to share the suspicion of foreigners trying to do business here. When I made arrangements for the arrival of my first ice cream shipment into Pusan a month before the scheduled opening of my store, the authorities informed me that they couldn't care less about my ice cream and that I was illegally in the country. The upshot was my lawyers spent three weeks trying to persuade some second-echelon bureaucrat that I was here under valid reasons, to no avail. Desperate, and a day away from packing my bags and buying a one-way ticket to California, I called the one friend I have in government. By a one-in-a-thousand chance, he knew the second-echelon bureaucrat and was able to clear away his mental block about me.

Figure CS 1.1.1   The International Marketing Task

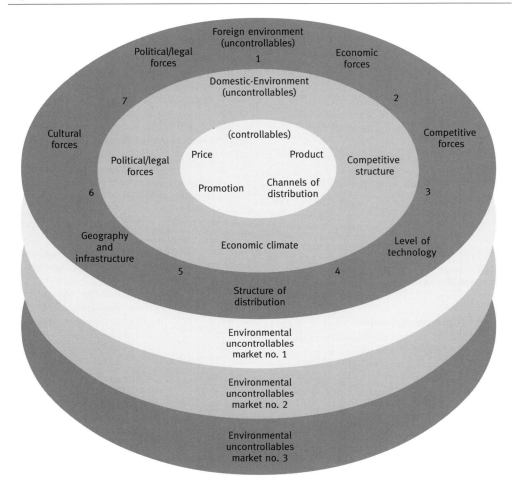

But this was a fluke. I have no doubt that the mental block was the Korean dairy farmers complaining about foreign imports of ice cream, which in turn is part of the bigger picture of pressure that Korean agriculture is receiving from US trade negotiators to open its market.

Nevertheless, there has been some progress. In June 1987, the American Chamber of Commerce here wrote in its annual summary of trade issues that 'access to the Korean market is one of the most frustrating issues faced by American companies in Korea'. A year and a half later, however, the chamber wrote that '1988 has been a good year for the Korean economy and American businesses in Korea. US exports to Korea have increased approximately 40 per cent over 1987. As

1988 progressed, the Korean government took significant steps to open the market providing much broader access for American business.'

The question now is whether American companies can take advantage of the 'much broader access' into the Korean market. This will not be easy, for American business is not what it used to be. Woo Choong Kim, founder of the Daewoo business empire, has said: 'In the old days, Americans worked hard to challenge new frontiers. But as their economy got mature, they became more interested in nice houses, jogging and having a good time than in doing business. How can you compete without dedication? It is not the management system that is not working in American companies, it is the people not working hard.'

Indeed even outgoing Commerce Secretary William Verity recently admitted that although Americans are great at coming up with new inventions, they 'are not good at getting them into products to be sold'.

Establishing a Beachhead. For example, Korean executives were almost throwing machine-tool and welding-machine orders at American companies— with the US concerns dropping the ball almost every time. The reasons given by Koreans were various: inflexibility about the terms of a contract, poor service or just plain not trying hard enough (e.g. not working on Saturdays). The one American company that did measure up was Varian Associates. Its management team projected that the bulk of world manufacturing will be done in Asia in years to come and that right now US companies are missing out on Asia's rush to outfit the factories building more and more of the world's cars, computers and fast-food plants.

Varian installed 18 Korean nationals and several expatriates in a Seoul office to market their equipment and match Japanese service. Unlike other American companies, Varian has accommodated the Korean culture and way of doing business by establishing a beachhead presence in one of the world's fastest-growing markets.

I myself have learned that it is important to be here and to learn their ways. In doing so, we help each other. The Korean company I chose to do business with, for example, will learn from me an ice cream-making technology and formula that enhances its competitiveness in that industry at home and abroad. I, in turn, will learn from my partner how to be competitive in Korea. What neither of us needs is a US Congress trying to make its balance sheets add up nicely by rigging the currency in a way that hurts the very entrepreneurs it is supposed to help, fans the flames of anti-Americanism, and could lead to a trade war where nobody wins.

As a guide use Figure CS 1.1.1 on page 498 and described (as Figure 1.1) in Chapter 1 and do the following:

1. Identify each of the domestic and foreign uncontrollable elements that US ice cream encountered in Korea.
2. Describe how problems encountered with each uncontrollable element may have been avoided or compensated for had the element been recognized in the planning stage.
3. Identify other problems US ice cream may encounter in the future.

CASE 1.2
Nestlé and Unilever—An Analysis

While Unilever and Nestlé have engaged in international marketing their entire corporate existence, they are very different companies in their approaches to international marketing and corporate philosophies. Both companies maintain very extensive Web sites. Your challenge in this case is to visit both Web sites, carefully read the information presented, and write a report comparing the two companies on the points that follow.

1. Philosophies on international marketing.
2. Corporate objectives.
3. Global coverage, that is, number of countries in which they do business.
4. Production facilities.
5. Number of product categories and number of brands within each category.
6. Number of standardized versus global brands for each.
7. Product categories and brands where the two companies compete.
8. Brands that are standardized, that is, what is standardized in each brand and what is localized in each brand.
9. Product research centres.
10. Organization.
11. Environmental concerns.
12. Research and development

After completing your analysis, write a brief statement about the area(s) where Unilever is stronger than Nestlé and vice versa, and where Unilever is weaker than Nestlé and vice versa.

Unilever's Web site is **http://www.unilever.com** and Nestlé's is **http://www.nestle.com**.

CASE 1.3
Nestlé—The Infant Formula Incident*[1]

Nestlé Alimentana of Vevey, Switzerland, one of the world's largest food-processing companies with world-wide sales of over $8 billion, has been the subject of an international boycott. For over 10 years, beginning with a Pan American Health Organization allegation, Nestlé has been directly or indirectly charged with involvement in the death of Third World infants. The charges revolve around the sale of infant feeding formula which allegedly is the cause for mass deaths of babies in the Third World.

In 1974, a British journalist published a report that suggested that powdered-formula manufacturers contributed to the death of Third World infants by hard-selling their products to people incapable of using them properly. The 28-page report accused the industry of encouraging mothers to give up breast feeding and use powdered milk formulas. The report was later published by the Third World Working Group, a lobby in support of less developed countries. The pamphlet was entitled, 'Nestlé Kills Babies,' and accused Nestlé of unethical and immoral behaviour.

Although there are several companies that market infant baby formula internationally, Nestlé received most of the attention. This incident raises several issues important to all multinational companies. Before addressing these issues, let's look more closely at the charges by the Infant Formula Action Coalition (INFACT) and others and the defence by Nestlé.

The Charges. Most of the charges against infant formulas focus on the issue of whether advertising and marketing of such products have discouraged breast feeding among Third World mothers and have led to misuse of the products, thus contributing to infant malnutrition and death. Following are some of the charges made:

- A Peruvian nurse reported that formula had found its way to Amazon tribes deep in the jungles of northern Peru. There, where the only water comes from a highly contaminated river—that also serves as the local laundry and toilet—formula-fed babies came down with recurring attacks of diarrhoea and vomiting.
- Throughout the Third World, many parents dilute the formula to stretch their supply. Some

even believe the bottle itself has nutrient qualities and merely fill it with water. The result is extreme malnutrition.

- One doctor reported that in a rural area, one newborn male weighed 7 pounds. At four months of age, he weighed 5 pounds. His sister, aged 18 months, weighed 12 pounds, what one would expect a 4-month-old baby to weigh. She later weighed only 8 pounds. The children had never been breast-fed, and since birth their diets were basically bottle feeding. For a four-month baby, one tin of formula should have lasted just under three days. The mother said that one tin lasted two weeks to feed both children.
- In rural Mexico, the Philippines, Central America, and the whole of Africa, there has been a dramatic decrease in the incidence of breast feeding. Critics blame the decline largely on the intensive advertising and promotion of infant formula. Clever radio jingles extol the wonders of the 'white man's powder that will make baby grow and glow'. 'Milk nurses' visit nursing mothers in hospitals and their homes and provide samples of formula. These activities encourage mothers to give up breast feeding and resort to bottle feeding because it is 'the fashionable thing to do or because people are putting it to them that this is the thing to do'.

The Defence.   The following points are made in defence of the marketing of baby formula in Third World countries:

- First, Nestlé argues that the company has never advocated bottle feeding instead of breast feeding. All its products carry a statement that breast feeding is best. The company states that it 'believes that breast milk is the best food for infants and encourages breast feeding around the world as it has done for decades'. The company offers as support of this statement one of Nestlé 's oldest educational booklets on 'Infant Feeding and Hygiene', which dates from 1913 and encourages breast feeding.
- However, the company does believe that infant formula has a vital role in proper infant nutrition as (1) a supplement, when the infant needs nutritionally adequate and appropriate foods in addition to breast milk and (2) a substitute for breast milk when a mother cannot or chooses not to breast feed. One doctor reports, 'Economically deprived and thus dietarily deprived mothers who give their children only breast milk are raising infants whose growth rates begin to slow noticeably at

*This case is an update of 'Nestlé in LDCs', a case written by J. Alex Murray, University of Windsor, Ontario, Canada, and Gregory M. Gazda and Mary J. Molenaar, University of San Diego. The case originally appeared in the 5th edition of this text.

about the age of three months. These mothers then turn to supplemental feedings that are often harmful to children. These include herbal teas, and concoctions of rice water or corn water and sweetened, condensed milk. These feedings can also be prepared with contaminated water and are served in unsanitary conditions.'

■ Mothers in developing nations often have dietary deficiencies. In the Philippines, a mother in a poor family who is nursing a child produces about a pint of milk daily. Mothers in the United States usually produce about a quart of milk each day. For both the Philippino and US mothers, the milk produced is equally nutritious. The problem is that there is less of it for the Philippino baby. If the Philippino mother doesn't augment the child's diet, malnutrition develops.

■ Many poor women in the Third World bottle feed because their work schedules in fields or factories will not permit breast feeding. The infant feeding controversy has largely to do with the gradual introduction of weaning foods during the period between three months and two years. The average well-nourished Western woman, weighing 20 to 30 pounds more than most women in less developed countries, cannot feed only breast milk beyond five or six months. The claim that Third World women can breast feed exclusively for one or two years and have healthy, well-developed children is outrageous. Thus, all children beyond the ages of five to six months require supplemental feeding.

■ Weaning foods can be classified as either native cereal gruels of millet or rice, or commercial manufactured milk formula. Traditional native weaning foods are usually made by mixing maize, rice, or millet flours with water and then cooking the mixture. Other weaning foods found in use are crushed crackers, sugar and water, and mashed bananas.

There are two basic dangers to the use of native weaning foods. First, the nutritional quality of the native gruels is low. Second, microbiological contamination of the traditional weaning foods is a certainty in many Third World settings. The millet or the flour is likely to be contaminated, the water used in cooking will most certainly be contaminated, the cooking containers will be contaminated and therefore the native gruel even after it is cooked is frequently contaminated with colon bacilli, staph, and other dangerous bacteria. Moreover, large batches of gruel are often made

and allowed to sit, inviting further contamination.

■ Scientists recently compared the microbiological contamination of a local native gruel with ordinary reconstituted milk formula prepared under primitive conditions. They found both were contaminated to similar dangerous levels.

■ The real nutritional problem in the Third World is not whether to give infants breast milk or formula; it is how to supplement mothers' milk with nutritionally adequate foods when they are needed. Finding adequate locally produced, nutritionally sound supplements to mothers' milk and teaching people how to prepare and use them safely is the issue. Only effective nutrition education along with improved sanitation and good food that people can afford will win the fight against dietary deficiencies in the Third World.

The Resolution. In 1974, Nestlé, aware of changing social patterns in the developing world and the increased access to radio and television there, reviewed its marketing practices on a region-by-region basis. As a result, mass media advertising of infant formula began to be phased out immediately in certain markets and, by 1978, was banned worldwide by the company. Nestlé then undertook to carry out more comprehensive health education programmes to ensure that an understanding of the proper use of their products reached mothers, particularly in rural areas.

'Nestlé fully supports the WHO (World Health Organization) Code. Nestlé will continue to promote breast feeding and ensure that its marketing practices do not discourage breast feeding anywhere. Our company intends to maintain a constructive dialogue with governments and health professionals in all the countries it serves with the sole purpose of servicing mothers and the health of babies'—this quote is from *Nestlé Discusses the Recommended WHO Infant Formula Code.*

In 1977, the Interfaith Center on Corporate Responsibility in New York compiled a case against formula-feeding in developing nations, and the Third World Institute launched a boycott against many Nestlé products. Its aim was to halt promotion of infant formulas in the Third World. The Infant Formula Action Coalition (INFACT, successor to the Third World Institute), along with several other world organizations, successfully lobbied the World Health Organization (WHO) to draft a code to regulate the advertising and marketing of infant formula in the Third World. In 1981, by a vote of 114–1 (three countries abstained and the United States was the only dissenting vote), 118 member nations of WHO endorsed a voluntary code. The eight-page code urged a worldwide ban on promotion and advertising of baby formula and called for a halt to distribution of free product samples and/or gifts to physicians who promoted the use of the formula as a substitute for breast milk.

In May 1981, Nestlé announced it would support the code and waited for individual countries to pass national codes that would then be put into effect. Unfortunately, very few such codes were forthcoming. By the end of 1983, only 25 of the 157 member nations of the WHO had established national codes.

Accordingly, Nestlé management determined it would have to apply the code in the absence of national legislation, and in February 1982 issued instructions to marketing personnel, delineating the company's best understanding of the code and what would have to be done to follow it.

In addition, in May 1982 Nestlé formed the Nestlé Infant Formula Audit Commission (NIFAC), chaired by former Senator Edmund J. Muskie, and asked the commission to review the company's instructions to field personnel to determine if they could be improved to better implement the code. At the same time, Nestlé continued its meetings with WHO and UNICEF (United Nations Children's Fund) to try to obtain the most accurate interpretation of the code.

NIFAC recommended several clarifications for the instructions that it believed would better interpret ambiguous areas of the code; in October 1982, Nestlé accepted those recommendations and issued revised instructions to field personnel.

Other issues within the code, such as the question of a warning statement, were still open to debate. Nestlé consulted extensively with WHO before issuing its label warning statement in October 1983, but there was still not universal agreement with it. Acting on WHO recommendations, Nestlé consulted with firms experienced and expert in developing and field-testing educational materials, so that it could ensure that those materials met the code.

When the International Nestlé Boycott Committee (INBC) listed its four points of difference with Nestlé, it again became a matter of interpretation of the requirements of the code. Here, meetings held by UNICEF proved invaluable, in that UNICEF agreed to define areas of differing interpretation—in some cases providing definitions contrary to both Nestlé's and INBC's interpretations.

It was the meetings with UNICEF in early 1984 that finally led to a joint statement by Nestlé and INBC on 25 January. At that time, INBC announced its suspension of boycott activities, and Nestlé pledged its continued support of the WHO code.

Nestlé Supports WHO Code.   The company has a strong record of progress and support in implementing the WHO Code, including:

- Immediate support for the WHO Code, May 1981; and testimony to this effect before the US Congress, June 1981.
- Issuance of instructions to all employees, agents and distributors in February 1982 to implement the code in all Third World countries where Nestlé markets infant formula.
- Establishment of an audit commission, in accordance with Article 11.3 of the WHO Code, to ensure the company's compliance with the code. The commission, headed by Edmund S. Muskie, was composed of eminent clergy and scientists.
- Willingness to meet with concerned church leaders, international bodies and organization leaders seriously concerned with Nestlé's application of the code.
- Issuance of revised instructions to Nestlé personnel, October 1982, as recommended by the Muskie committee to clarify and give further effect to the code.
- Consultation with WHO, UNICEF and NIFAC on how to interpret the code and how best to implement specific provisions, including clarification by WHO/UNICEF of the definition of children who need to be fed breast milk substitutes, to aid in determining the need for supplies in hospitals.

Nestlé Policies.   In the early 1970s, Nestlé began to review its infant formula marketing practices on a region-by-region basis. By 1978, the company had stopped all consumer advertising and direct sampling to mothers. Instructions to the field issued in February 1982 and clarified in the revised instructions of October 1982 to adopt articles of the WHO Code as Nestlé policy include:

- No advertising to the general public.
- No sampling to mothers.
- No mothercraft workers.
- No use of commission/bonus for sales.
- No use of infant pictures on labels.
- No point-of-sale advertising.
- No financial or material inducements to promote products.
- No samples to physicians except in three specific situations: a new product, a new product formulation, or a new graduate physician; limited to one or two cans of product.

■ Limitation of supplies to those requested in writing and fulfilling genuine needs for breast milk substitutes.

■ A statement of the superiority of breast feeding on all labels/materials.

■ Labels and educational materials clearly stating the hazards involved in incorrect usage of infant formula, developed in consultation with WHO/UNICEF.

Even though Nestlé stopped consumer advertising, it was able to maintain its share of the Third World infant formula market. By 1988, a call to resume the seven-year boycott was called for by a group of consumer activist members of the Action for Corporate Accountability. The group claimed that Nestlé was distributing free formula through maternity wards as a promotional tactic that undermines the practice of breast feeding. The group claims that Nestlé and others have continued to dump formula in hospitals and maternity wards and that, as a result, 'babies are dying as the companies are violating the WHO resolution'.[2] As late as 1997 the Interagency Group on Breastfeeding Monitoring (IGBM) claims Nestlé continues to systematically violate the WHO code. Nestlé's response to these accusations is included on its Web site (see **www.nestlé.com** for details).

The boycott focus is Taster's Choice Instant Coffee, Coffeemate Nondairy Coffee Creamer, Anacin aspirin and Advil.

Representatives of Nestlé and American Home Products rejected the accusations and said they were complying with World Health Organization and individual national codes on the subject.

The New Twist.   A new environmental factor has made the entire case more complex: circa 1998, it was believed that some 3.8 million children around the world have contracted HIV at their mothers' breasts. In affluent countries, mothers can be told to bottle feed their children. However, 90 per cent of the child infections occur in developing countries. There the problems of bottle feeding remain. Further, in even the most infected areas, 70 per cent of the mothers do not carry the virus, and breast feeding is by far the best option. And the vast majority of pregnant women in the developing countries have no idea whether they are infected or not. One concern is that large numbers of healthy women will switch to the bottle just to be safe. Alternatively, if bottle feeding becomes a badge of HIV infection, mothers may continue breast feeding just to avoid being stigmatized. In Thailand, pregnant women are offered testing and, if found HIV positive, are given free milk powder. But in some African countries where women get pregnant at three times the Thai rate and

HIV infection rates are 25 per cent compared to the 2 per cent in Thailand, that solution is much less feasible.

The Issues.   Many issues are raised by this incident. How can a company deal with a worldwide boycott of its products? Why did the United States decide not to support the WHO Code? Who is correct, WHO or Nestlé? A more important issue concerns the responsibility of an MNC marketing in developing nations. Setting aside the issues for a moment, consider the notion that, whether intentional or not, Nestlé's marketing activities have had an impact on the behaviour of many people, that is, Nestlé is a cultural change agent. And, when it or any other company successfully introduces new ideas into a culture, the culture changes and those changes can be functional or dysfunctional to established patterns of behaviour. The key issue is—what responsibility does the MNC have to the culture when, as a result of its marketing activities, it causes change in that culture?

Questions

1. What are the responsibilities of companies in this or similar situations?
2. What could Nestlé have done to have avoided the accusations of 'killing Third World babies' and still market its product?
3. After Nestlé's experience, how do you suggest it, or any other company, can protect itself in the future?
4. Assume you are the one that had to make the final decision on whether or not to promote and market Nestlé's baby formula in Third World countries. Read the section titled 'Ethical and Socially Responsible Decisions' in Chapter 5 as a guide to examine the social responsibility and ethical issues with the marketing approach and the promotion used. Were the decisions socially responsible? Were they ethical?
5. What advice would you give Nestlé now in light of the new problem of HIV infection being spread via mothers' milk?

References

1. The case draws from the following: 'International Code of Marketing of Breastmilk Substitutes', World Health Organization, Geneva, 1981; *INFACT Newsletter*, Minneapolis, MN, February 1979; John A. Sparks, 'The Nestlé Controversy— Anatomy of a Boycott', Grove City, PA, Public Policy Education Funds, Inc.; 'Who Drafts a Marketing Code', *World Business Weekly*, 19 January 1981, p. 8; 'A Boycott over Infant

Formula', *Business Week*, 23 April 1979, p. 137; 'The Battle over Bottle-Feeding', *World Press Review*, January 1980, p. 54; 'Nestlé and the Role of Infant Formula in Developing Countries: The Resolution of a Conflict,' (Nestlé Company, 1985); 'The Dilemma of Third World Nutrition,' (Nestlé SA, 1985), 20 pp.; Thomas V. Greer, 'The Future of the International Code of Marketing of Breastmilk Substitutes: The Socio-Legal Context', *International Marketing Review*, Spring 1984, pp. 33–41; James C. Baker, 'The International Infant Formula Controversy: A Dilemma in Corporate Social Responsibility', *Journal of Business Ethics*, 4 (1985), pp. 181–190; Shawn

Tully, 'Nestlé Shows How to Gobble Markets', *Fortune*, 16 January 1989, p. 75. For a comprehensive and well-balanced review of the infant formula issue, see Thomas V. Greer, 'International Infant Formula Marketing: The Debate Continues', *Advances in International Marketing*, 4 (1990), pp. 207–225. For a discussion of the HIV/breast feeding complication see 'Back to the Bottle?' *The Economist*, 7 February 1998, p. 50.

2. 'Boycotts: Activists' Group Resumes Fight against Nestlé, Adds American Home Products', *Associated Press*, 5 October 1988.

CASES

2

The Cultural Environment of International Marketing

Outline of Cases

CASE 2.1
The Not-so-Wonderful World of Eurodisney*†

Bon Jour, Mickey!

In April 1992, EuroDisney SCA opened its doors to European visitors. Located by the river Marne some 20 miles east of Paris, it was designed to be the biggest and most lavish theme park that Walt Disney Company (Disney) has built to date—bigger than Disneyland in Anaheim, California, Disneyworld in Orlando, Florida and Tokyo Disneyland in Japan. In 1989, 'EuroDisney' was expected to be a surefire moneymaker for its parent Disney, led by Chairman Michael Eisner and President Frank Wells. Since then, sadly Wells was killed in an air accident in the spring of 1994, and EuroDisney lost nearly $1 billion during the 1992–93 fiscal year.

Much to Disney management's surprise, Europeans failed to 'go wacky' over Mickey, unlike their Japanese counterparts. Between 1990 and early 1992, some 14 million people had visited Tokyo Disneyland, with three-quarters being repeat visitors. A family of four staying overnight at a nearby hotel would easily spend $600 on a visit to the park. In contrast, at EuroDisney families were reluctant to spend the $280 a day needed to enjoy the attractions of the park, including *les hamburgers* and *les milkshakes*. Staying overnight was out of the question for many because hotel rooms were so high priced. For example, prices ranged from $110 to $380 a night at the Newport Bay Club, the largest of EuroDisney's six new hotels and one of the biggest in Europe. In comparison, a room in a top hotel in Paris costs between $340 and $380 a night.

In 1994, financial losses were becoming so massive at EuroDisney that Michael Eisner had to step in personally in order to structure a rescue package. EuroDisney was put back on firm ground. A two-year window of financial peace was introduced, but not until after some acrimonious dealings with French banks had been settled and an unexpected investment by a Saudi prince had been accepted. Disney management rapidly introduced a range of strategic and tactical changes in the hope of 'doing it right' this time. Analysts are presently trying to diagnose what went wrong and what the future might hold for EuroDisney.

---

*The name was changed in 1996 to Disneyland Paris.
†This case was prepared by Professor Lyn S. Amine and graduate student Carolyn A. Tochtrop, Saint Louis University, St Louis MO, as a basis for class discussion rather than to illustrate either effective or ineffective handling of a situation.

A Real Estate Dream Come True.
Expansion into Europe was supposed to be Disney's major source of growth in the 1990s, bolstering slowing prospects back home in the United States. 'Europe is our big project for the rest of this century', boasted Robert J. Fitzpatrick, chairman of Euro Disneyland in spring 1990. The Paris location was chosen over 200 other potential sites stretching from Portugal through Spain, France, Italy and into Greece. Spain thought it had the strongest bid based on its year-long, temperate and sunny Mediterranean climate, but insufficient acreage of land was available for development around Barcelona.

In the end, the French government's generous incentives, together with impressive data on regional demographics, swayed Eisner to choose the Paris location. It was calculated that some 310 million people in Europe live within two hours' air travel of EuroDisney, and 17 million could reach the park within two hours by car—better demographics than at any other Disney site. Pessimistic talk about the dismal winter weather of northern France was countered with references to the success of Tokyo Disneyland, where resolute visitors brave cold winds and snow to enjoy their piece of Americana. Furthermore, it was argued, Paris is Europe's most-popular city destination among tourists of all nationalities.

According to the master agreement signed by the French government in March 1987, 51 per cent of EuroDisney would be offered to European investors, with about half of the new shares being sold to the French. At that time, the project was valued at about FFr12 billion ($1.8 billion). Disney's initial equity stake in EuroDisney was acquired for FFr850 million (about $127.5 million). After the public offering, the value of Disney's stake zoomed to $1 billion on the magic of the Disney name.

Inducements by the French government were varied and generous:

- Loans of up to FFr4.8 billion at a lower-than-market fixed rate of interest.
- Tax advantages for writing off construction costs.
- Construction by the French government, free of charge, of rail and road links from Paris out to the park. The TGV (*très grande vitesse*) fast train was scheduled to serve the park by 1994, along with road traffic coming from Britain through the Channel Tunnel or 'Chunnel'.
- Land (4800 acres) sold to Disney at 1971 agricultural prices. Resort and property development going beyond the park itself was projected to bring in about a third of the scheme's total revenues between 1992 and 1995.

Figure CS 2.1.1   Was Opening Day at EuroDisney in France under a Black Cloud?

As one analyst commented, 'EuroDisney could probably make money without Mickey, as a property development alone'. These words would come back to haunt Disney in 1994 as real estate development plans were halted and hotel rooms remained empty, some even being closed during the first winter.

Spills and Thrills.   Disney had projected that the new theme park would attract 11 million visitors and generate over $100 million in operating earnings during the first year of operation. EuroDisney was expected to make a small pretax profit of FFr227 million ($34 million) in 1994, rising to nearly FFr3 billion ($450 million) in 2001. By summer 1994, EuroDisney had lost more than $900 million since opening. Attendance reached only 9.2 million in 1992, and visitors spent 12 per cent less on purchases than the estimated $33 per head. European tour operators were unable to rally sufficient interest among holidaymakers to meet earlier commitments to fill the park's hotels, and demanded that EuroDisney renegotiate their deals. In August 1992, Karen Gee, marketing manager of Airtours PLC, a British travel agency, worried about troubles yet to come: 'On a foggy February day, how appealing will this park be?' Her winter bookings at that time were dismal.

If tourists were not flocking to taste the thrills of the new EuroDisney, where were they going for their summer holidays in 1992? Ironically enough, an unforeseen combination of transatlantic airfare wars and currency movements resulted in a trip to Disneyworld in Orlando being cheaper than a trip to Paris, with guaranteed good weather and beautiful Floridian beaches within easy reach.

EuroDisney management took steps to rectify immediate problems in 1992 by cutting rates at two hotels up to 25 per cent, introducing some cheaper meals at restaurants, and launching a Paris ad blitz that proclaimed 'California is only 20 miles from Paris'.

An American Icon.   One of the most worrying aspects of EuroDisney's first year was that French visitors stayed away. They had been expected to make up 50 per cent of the attendance figures. Two years later, Dennis Speigel, president of the International Theme Park Services consulting firm, based in Cincinnati, framed the problem in these words: '. . . the French see EuroDisney as American imperialism —plastics at its worst'. The well-known, sentimental Japanese attachment to Disney characters contrasted starkly with the unexpected and widespread French scorn for American fairy-tale characters. French culture has its own lovable cartoon characters such as Astérix, the helmeted, pint-sized Gallic warrior who has a theme park located near EuroDisney. Parc Astérix went through a major renovation and expansion in anticipation of competition from EuroDisney.

Hostility among the French people to the whole 'Disney idea' had surfaced early in the planning of the new project. Paris theatre director Ariane Mnouchkine became famous for her description of EuroDisney as 'a cultural Chernobyl'. A 1988 book, *Mickey: the Sting*, by French journalist Gilles Smadja, denounced the $350 million that the government had committed at that time to building park-related infrastructure. In the autumn of 1989, during a visit to Paris, Michael Eisner was pelted with eggs by French Communists. Finally, many farmers took to the streets to protest against the preferential sales price of local land.

Early advertising by EuroDisney seemed to aggravate local French sentiment by emphasizing glitz and size, rather than the variety of rides and attractions. Committed to maintaining Disney's reputation for quality in everything, Chairman Eisner insisted that more and more detail be built into EuroDisney.

For example, the centrepiece castle in the Magic Kingdom had to be bigger and fancier than in the other parks. He ordered the removal of two steel staircases in Discoveryland, at a cost of $200–300 000, because they blocked a view of the Star Tours ride. Expensive trams were built along a lake to take guests from the hotels to the park, but visitors preferred walking. An 18-hole golf course, built to adjoin 600 new holiday homes, was constructed and then enlarged to add another 9 holes. Built before the homes, the course cost $15–20 million and remains under-used. Total park construction costs were estimated at FFr14 billion ($2.37 billion) in 1989 but rose by $340 million to FFr16 billion as a result of all these add-ons. Hotel construction costs rose from an estimated FFr3.4 billion to FFr5.7 billion.

EuroDisney and Disney managers unhappily succeeded in alienating many of their counterparts in the government, the banks, the ad agencies, and other concerned organizations. A barnstorming, kick-the-door-down attitude seemed to reign among the US decision makers. Beatrice Descoffre, a French construction industry official, complained that 'They were always sure it would work because they were Disney'. A top French banker involved in setting up the master agreement felt that Disney executives had tried to steamroller their ideas. 'They had a formidable image and convinced everyone that if we let them do it their way, we would all have a marvellous adventure.'

Disney executives consistently declined to comment on their handling of management decisions during the early days, but point out that many of the same people complaining about Disney's aggressiveness were only too happy to sign on with Disney before conditions deteriorated. One former Disney executive voiced the opinion, 'We were arrogant—it was like "We're building the Taj Mahal and people will come—on our terms."'

Storm Clouds Ahead

Disney and its advisers failed to see signs at the end of the 1980s of the approaching European recession. As one former executive said, 'We were just trying to keep our heads above water. Between the glamour and the pressure of opening and the intensity of the project itself, we didn't realize a major recession was coming.'

Other dramatic events included the Gulf War in 1991, which put a heavy brake on holiday travel for the rest of that year. The fall of Communism in 1989 after the destruction of the Berlin Wall provoked far-reaching effects on the world economy. National defence industries were drastically reduced among Western nations. Foreign aid was requested from the West by newly emerging democracies in Eastern Europe. Other external factors that Disney executives have cited in the past as contributing to their financial difficulties at EuroDisney were high interest rates and the devaluation of several currencies against the franc.

Difficulties were also encountered by EuroDisney with regard to competition. Landmark events took place in Spain in 1992. The World's Fair in Seville and the 1992 Olympics in Barcelona were huge attractions for European tourists. In the future, new theme parks are planned for Spain by Anheuser-Busch with its $300-million Busch Gardens near Barcelona, as well as Six Flags Corporation's Magic Mountain park to be located in Marbella.

Disney management's conviction that it knew best was demonstrated by its much-trumpeted ban on alcohol in the park. This proved insensitive to the local culture because the French are the world's biggest consumers of wine. To them a meal without *un verre de rouge* is unthinkable. Disney relented. It also had to relax its rules on personal grooming of the projected 12 000 cast members, the park employees. Women were allowed to wear redder nail polish than in the US, but the taboo on men's facial hair was maintained. 'We want the clean-shaven, neat and tidy look', commented David Kannally, director of Disney University's Paris branch. The 'university' trains prospective employees in Disney values and culture by means of a one-and-a-half-day seminar. EuroDisney's management did, however, compromise on the question of pets. Special kennels were built to house visitors' animals. The thought of leaving a pet at home during the holiday is considered irrational by many French people.

Plans for further development of EuroDisney after 1992 were ambitious. The initial number of hotel rooms was planned to be 5200, more than in the entire city of Cannes on the Côte d'Azur. This number was supposed to triple in a few years as Disney opened a second theme park to keep visitors at the EuroDisney resort for a longer stay. There would also be a huge amount of office space, 700 000 square metres, just slightly smaller than France's largest office complex, La Défense in Paris. Also planned were shopping malls, apartments, golf courses and holiday homes. EuroDisney would design and build everything itself, with a view to selling at a profit. As a Disney executive commented with hindsight, 'Disney at various points could have had partners to share the risk, or buy the hotels outright. But it didn't want to give up the upside.'

Disney management wanted to avoid two costly mistakes it had learned from the past: letting others build the money-making hotels surrounding a park (as happened at Disneyland in Anaheim); and letting another company own a Disney park (as in Tokyo where Disney just collects royalties). This time, along with 49 per cent ownership of EuroDisney, Disney would receive both a park management fee and royalties on merchandise sales.

The outstanding success record of Chairman Eisner and President Wells in reviving Disney during the 1980s led people to believe that the duo could do nothing wrong. 'From the time they came on, they had never made a single misstep, never a mistake, never a failure', said a former Disney executive. 'There was a tendency to believe that everything they touched would be perfect.' This belief was fostered by the incredible growth record achieved by Eisner and Wells. In the seven years before EuroDisney opened, they took Disney from being a company with $1 billion in revenues to one with $8.5 billion, mainly through internal growth.

Dozens of banks, led by France's Banque Nationale de Paris, Banque Indosuez and Caisse des Depôts & Consignations, eagerly signed on to provide construction loans. One banker who saw the figures for the deal expressed concern. 'The company was over-leveraged. The structure was dangerous.' Other critics charged that the proposed financing was risky because it relied on capital gains from future real estate transactions.

The Disney response to this criticism was that those views reflected the cautious, Old World thinking of Europeans who didn't understand US-style free-market financing. Supporters of Disney point out that for more than two years after the initial public offering of shares, the stock price continued to do well, and that initial loans were at a low rate. It was the later cost over-runs and the necessity for a bail-out at the end of the first year that undermined the initial forecasts.

Optimistic assumptions that the 1980s boom in real estate in Europe would continue through the 1990s and that interest rates and currencies would remain stable led Disney to rely heavily on debt financing. The real estate developments outside Euro-Disney were supposed to draw income to help pay down the $3.4 billion in debt. That in turn was intended to help Disney finance a second park close by—an MGM Studios film tour site—which would draw visitors to help fill existing hotel rooms. None of this happened. As a senior French banker commented later in 1994, EuroDisney is a 'good theme park married to a bankrupt real estate company—and the two can't be divorced'.

Telling and Selling Fairy Tales. Mistaken assumptions by the Disney management team affected construction design, marketing and pricing policies, and park management, as well as initial financing. For example, parking space for buses proved much too small. Restroom facilities for drivers could accommodate 50 people; on peak days there were 200 drivers. With regard to demand for meal service, Disney executives had been erroneously informed that Europeans don't eat breakfast. Restaurant breakfast service was downsized accordingly, and guess what? 'Everybody showed up for breakfast. We were trying to serve 2500 breakfasts in a 350-seat restaurant (at some of the hotels). The queues were horrendous. And they didn't just want croissants and coffee. They wanted bacon and eggs', lamented one Disney executive. Disney reacted quickly, delivering prepackaged breakfasts to rooms and other satellite locations.

In contrast to Disney's American parks where visitors typically stay at least three days, EuroDisney is at most a two-day visit. Energetic visitors need even less time. Jeff Summers, an analyst at debt broker Klesch & Co. in London, claims to have 'done' every EuroDisney ride in just five hours. 'There aren't enough attractions to get people to spend the night', he commented in the summer of 1994. Typically many guests arrive early in the morning, rush to the park, come back to their hotel late at night, then check out the next morning before heading back to the park. The amount of check-in and check-out traffic was vastly underestimated when the park opened; extra computer terminals were installed rapidly in the hotels.

In promoting the new park to visitors, Disney did not stress the entertainment value of a visit to the new theme park. The emphasis on the size of the park 'ruined the magic', said a Paris-based ad agency executive. But in early 1993, ads were changed to feature Zorro—a French favourite, Mary Poppins and Aladdin, star of the huge money-making movie success. A print ad campaign at that time featured Aladdin, Cinderella's castle, and a little girl being invited to enjoy a 'magic holiday'. A promotional package was offered—two days, one night, and one breakfast at an unnamed EuroDisney hotel—for $95 per adult and free for kids. The tagline said, 'The kingdom where all dreams come true'.

Early in 1994, the decision was taken to add six new attractions. In March, the Temple of Peril ride opened, Storybook Land followed in May and the Nautilus attraction was planned for June. Donald Duck's birthday was celebrated on 9 June. A secret new thrill ride was promised in 1995. 'We are positioning Euro-Disney as the No. 1 European destination of short duration, one to three days', said a park spokesperson. Previously no effort had been made to hold visitors for a specific length of stay. Moreover, added the spokesperson, 'One of our primary messages is, after all, that EuroDisney is affordable to everyone'. Although new package deals and special low season rates substantially offset costs to visitors, the overall entrance fee has not been changed and is higher than in the US.

With regard to park management, seasonal disparities in attendance have caused losses in projected revenues. Even on a day-to-day basis, EuroDisney management has had difficulty forecasting numbers of visitors. Early expectations were that Monday would be a light day for visitors and Friday a heavy one. Staff allocations were made accordingly. The opposite was true. EuroDisney management still struggles to find the right level of staffing at a park where high-season attendance can be 10 times the number in the low season. The American tradition of 'hiring and firing' employees at will is difficult, if not impossible, in France where workers' rights are stringently protected by law.

Disney executives had optimistically expected that the arrival of their new theme park would cause French parents to take their children out of school in mid-term for a short break. It did not happen, unless a public holiday occurred over a weekend. Similarly, Disney expected that the American-style short but more frequent family trips would displace the European tradition of a one-month family holiday, usually taken in August. However, French office and factory schedules remain the same, with their emphasis on an August shutdown.

Tomorrowland.   Faced with falling share prices and crisis talk among shareholders, Disney was forced to step forward in late 1993 to rescue the new park. Disney announced that it would fund EuroDisney until a financial restructuring could be worked out with lenders. However, it was made clear by the parent company, Disney, that it 'was not writing a blank cheque'.

In November 1993, it was announced that an allocation of $350 million to deal with EuroDisney's problems had resulted in the first quarterly loss for Disney in nine years. Reporting on fourth-quarter results for 1993, Disney announced its share of Euro-Disney losses as $517 million for fiscal 1993. The overall performance of Disney was not, however, affected. It reported a profit of nearly $300 million for the fiscal year ending 30 September 1993, thanks to strong performance by its US theme parks and movies produced by its entertainment division. This compared to a profit of $817 million for the year before.

The rescue plan developed in the autumn of 1993 was rejected by the French banks. Disney fought back by imposing a deadline for agreement of 31 March

1994, and even hinted at possible closure of Euro-Disney. By mid-March, Disney's commitment to support EuroDisney had risen to $750 million. A new preliminary deal struck with EuroDisney's lead banks required the banks to contribute some $500 million. The aim was to cut the park's high-cost debt in half and make EuroDisney profitable by 1996, a date considered unrealistic by many analysts.

The plan called for a rights offering of FFr6 billion (about $1.02 billion at current rates) to existing shareholders at below-market prices. Disney would spend about $508 million to buy 49 per cent of the offering. Disney also agreed to buy certain EuroDisney park assets for $240 million and lease them back to EuroDisney on favourable terms. Banks agreed to forgive 18 months of interest payments on outstanding debt and would defer all principal payments for three years. Banks would also underwrite the remaining 51 per cent of the rights offering. For its part, Disney agreed to eliminate for five years its lucrative management fees and royalties on the sale of tickets and merchandise. Royalties would gradually be reintroduced at a lower level.

Analysts commented that approval by EuroDisney's 63 creditor banks and its shareholders was not a foregone conclusion. Also, the future was clouded by the need to resume payment of debt interest and royalties after the two-year respite.

Prince Charming Arrives.   In June 1994, EuroDisney received a new lifeline when a member of the Saudi royal family agreed to invest up to $500 million for a 24 per cent stake in the park. Prince Al-Walid bin Talal bin Abdul-Aziz Al-Saud is a well-known figure in the world of high finance. Years ago he expressed the desire to be worth $5 billion by 1998. Western-educated, His Royal Highness Prince Al-Walid holds stock in Citicorp worth $1.6 billion and is its biggest shareholder. The Prince has an established reputation in world markets as a 'bottom-fisher', buying into potentially viable operations during crises when share prices are low. He also holds 11 per cent of Saks Fifth Avenue and owns a chain of hotels and supermarkets, United Saudi Commercial Bank in Riyadh, a Saudi construction company and part of the new Arab Radio and Television Network in the Middle East. The prince plans to build a $100-million convention centre at EuroDisney. One of the few pieces of good news about EuroDisney is that its convention business exceeded expectations from the beginning.

The Prince's investment could reduce Disney's stake in EuroDisney to as little as 36 per cent. The Prince has agreed not to increase the size of his holding for 10 years. He also agreed that if his EuroDisney stake ever exceeds 50 per cent of Disney's, he must liquidate that portion.

The Prince loves Disney culture. He has visited both EuroDisney and Disneyworld. He believes in the EuroDisney management team. Positive factors supporting his investment include the continuing European economic recovery, increased parity between European currencies, the opening of the 'Chunnel', and what is seen as a certain humbling in the attitude of Disney executives. Jeff Summers, analyst for Klesch & Co. in London, commented on the deal, saying that Disney now has a fresh chance 'to show that Europe really needs an amusement park that will have cost $5 billion'.

References

'An American in Paris', *Business Week*, 12 March 1990, pp. 60–61, 64.

'A Charming Prince to the Rescue?' *Newsweek*, 13 June 1994, p. 43.

'EuroDisney Rescue Package Wins Approval', *The Wall Street Journal*, 15 March 1994, pp. A-3, A-13.

'EuroDisney Tries to End Evil Spell', *Advertising Age*, 7 February 1994, p. 39.

'EuroDisney's Prince Charming?' *Business Week*, 13 June 1994, p. 42.

'Disney Posts Loss: Troubles in Europe Blamed', *Los Angeles Times*, 11 November 1993, pp. A-1, A-34.

'How Disney Snared a Princely Sum', *Business Week*, 20 June 1994, pp. 61–62.

'Mickey Goes to the Bank', *The Economist*, 16 September 1989, p. 38.

'The Mouse Isn't Roaring', *Business Week*, 24 August 1992, p. 38.

'Mouse Trap: Fans Like EuroDisney but Its Parent's Goofs Weigh the Park Down', *The Wall Street Journal*, 10 March 1994, p. A-12.

'Saudi to Buy as Much as 24% of EuroDisney', *The Wall Street Journal*, 2 June 1994, p. A-4.

Additional Reading

'Of Mice and Men', *Newsweek*, 5 September 1994, pp. 41–47.

Questions

1. What factors contributed to EuroDisney's poor performance during its first year of operation?

2. To what degree do you consider that these factors were (a) foreseeable and (b) controllable by either EuroDisney or the parent company, Disney?

3. What role does ethnocentrism play in the story of EuroDisney's launch?

4. Do you see a future for (a) EuroDisney, (b) a second Disney park near Paris and (c) other competing theme parks in the region of northern France? Explain and support your answer.

5. How do you assess the cross-cultural marketing skills of Disney?

6. *a.* Do you think success in Tokyo predisposed Disney management to be too optimistic in their expectations of success in France? Discuss.

   b. Do you think the new theme park would have encountered the same problems if a location in Spain had been selected? Discuss.

7. Assume you have been hired by EuroDisney as a consultant to help them 'turn Euro Disneyland around'. Prepare a set of marketing recommendations to present to EuroDisney management. In your recommendations, state the problem you are addressing and the solution you recommend.

CASE 2.2
Cowan Bowman Associates—
International Growth of a Small High
Technology Firm

Background

In December 1990, Cowan Bowman Associates was one of New Zealand's leading commercial software firms, competing in the Australasian accounting software market. The company was founded in 1983 by John Cowan and Don Bowman, and had grown to include four business units, employing approximately 75 people in Australia and New Zealand. In addition, the company managed an extensive dealer network in New Zealand and Australia, and AsiaSoft had recently begun to distribute product in Singapore.

The company was privately owned, and headed by the group managing director, John Cowan. Corporate headquarters were in Auckland, while the head office for Australia was in Melbourne. Branch offices were located in Sydney, Brisbane, Perth, Port Moresby (Australia) and Wellington and Christchurch (New Zealand).

As outlined below, Cowan Bowman had experienced rapid growth since inception, although this growth had begun to taper off. As a result, in late 1990, John Cowan was faced with deciding which growth opportunities should be pursued by his company, in order to maintain or improve market performance.

Company Overview (as of 1990)

The Product Line. Cowan Bowman developed product for the broad accounting/distribution software market for small, medium and large systems in Australasia. All products were based on DataFlex, a leading database and software development tool from the United States.

Business Package was the first product developed in-house, designed to automate accounting functions and produce invoices and statements for medium-sized organizations with senior bookkeeping functions. Trader was then developed as a basic, modular accounting software package targeted at smaller owner-operator firms and educational institutions (for use as a teaching tool). Corporate Series was later designed as a more sophisticated package incorporating foreign

This case was prepared by Dr Nicole Coviello of the University of Calgary, Faculty of Management, Marketing Area, 488 Scurfield Hall, 2500 University Drive NW, Calgary, Alberta T2N IN4, Canada.

currency transactions. It was targeted at larger organizations consisting of groups of companies or subsidiaries that required a full accounting department or treasury.

In addition, Cowan Bowman was the exclusive distributor for DataFlex in Australia and New Zealand (accounting for 10 per cent of DataFlex sales worldwide). Other distributed products included QED2 office productivity software (the leading product of its type in the UK, developed by Quantec) and Q&A, a US market leader for integrated database and word-processing packages, developed by Symantec.

The Market and Competitive Position

Cowan Bowman's buyers were traditionally defined in terms of size (number of employees) and the sophistication of their financial management and accounting requirements. The company competed across product-markets, and its competition included large North American and UK-based multinationals and small niche developers. Thus, the nature of competition varied considerably.

In 1990, Cowan considered his company to be one of the 'bigger organizations' in the Australasian accounting software market. According to the 1988 Compass Hoby Ltd Survey, Cowan Bowman had the third highest name recall over all types of micro-computer software in New Zealand, following Lotus and Microsoft. Cowan believed this was due to the company's breadth of product functionality, its dealer network, its geographic scope in Australasia and ongoing product development. He felt that smaller firms were unable to sustain service levels and growth, and were generally undercapitalized and poorly managed. Conversely, larger firms, although well-resourced with large advertising budgets, competed with a nonlocal, technically weaker product.

Organization and Operating Structure.
Within Cowan Bowman Associates, there were four distinct business units:

- CBA—responsible for software research and development.
- Automation One (A1) New Zealand—responsible for sales and marketing in New Zealand.
- Automation One (A1) Australia—responsible for sales and marketing in Australia.
- Automation One Services—responsible for custom software development.

CBA was the research and development centre for business accounting software in the organization. It was managed directly by John Cowan, and there were two product managers (one responsible for the

Corporate Series, and one responsible for the Trader Series and Business Packages).

The CBA business unit sold its products to both Automation One (A1) operations in an exclusive arrangement. CBA was also responsible for managing operations developed outside of New Zealand and Australia. In total, 12 people were employed in the business unit.

The Automation One (A1) organizations operated as the marketing arms of CBA. Each had branch offices in the major business centres. All branch offices sold CBA products as well as DataFlex, QED2 and Q&A (in New Zealand), and DataFlex and QED2 (in Australia). Sales from the A1 operations were exclusive to their dealer network. There were no direct sales to the end user.

The NZ dealer network consisted of three tiers: a large number of computer retail shops (for Trader), a smaller number of computer companies and chartered accountancy firms (for Business Package) and a small group of carefully selected, technically-skilled computer companies and chartered accountancy firms for Corporate Series. The Australian dealer network was similar to that in New Zealand, although it emphasized Business Package and Corporate Series dealers. The dealer network was being further developed in preparation for Trader's 1991 release in Australia.

Dealers did not receive title to the software; rather, they received 30–45 per cent commission on sales. Dealers and third-party support organizations (often the chartered accountancy firms) provided after-sales support and end-user training services.

Each A1 operation had a general manager responsible for the overall profitable operation and growth of their respective companies. Their responsibilities were focused on sales, marketing, customer service and dealer support. Each was responsible solely for her geographic market and, to a certain extent, buffered John Cowan from day-to-day operations. A1 (New Zealand) employed 14 staff, and A1 (Australia) employed 28.

Finally, A1 Services provided custom solutions for existing and potential users of CBA products. Dealing primarily in New Zealand, 95–98 per cent of sales were to CBA users in the form of product modifications and system add-ons. As of late 1990, seven people were employed in A1 Services, and an A1 Services branch had been established in Melbourne. The A1 Services business unit was identified as having significant growth potential for the organization.

Trend in Sales and Financial Performance.
On 1990, sales were just under $NZ10 million, showing a relative growth rate of 86 per cent since 1987. By country, Australia accounted for slightly less than two-thirds of total sales, with New Zealand making up the remainder.

Of the total 1990 sales, Cowan Bowman's own products accounted for approximately 66 per cent of sales across both markets, with the remainder accounted for by the sale of DataFlex (23 per cent), the growth of A1 Services (9 per cent) and other product sales (2 per cent).

The Evolution of Cowan Bowman Associates

Company Formation.   In the early 1980s, John Cowan, then bureau manager at Universal Data Systems (UDS), recognized that personal computers were an increasing threat to the time-share computer business. This was also recognized by Don Bowman, managing director of a small computer bureau. Both saw an opportunity to develop accounting systems for the growing PC market, and to build a new organization for themselves. In 1983, Cowan and Bowman Associates was formed, with John Cowan and Don Bowman each owning one-third of the new company, and UDS owning the remaining third. The company's focus was on the development of accounting systems. These were intended to run on a variety of operating systems and hardware platforms in New Zealand and, ultimately, overseas.

At the inception of the company, it was Cowan and Bowman's intention to develop products for international markets. Long term, Cowan and Bowman felt that if products were developed solely for the domestic market, there would not be enough business to sustain the type of organization they wanted to grow. The New Zealand accounting software market was seen to be relatively small, while greater opportunities for financial growth and sales volume existed in Australia.

In 1984, Business Package was introduced, a product developed to automate accounting functions and produce invoices and statements. The product met with immediate success, leading to market development activities in both New Zealand and Australia.

Growth in New Zealand.   Based on the initial success of Business Package in New Zealand, A1 New Zealand was formed in 1987. This provided a domestic focus on the marketing and distribution of Business Package and the other products sold by Cowan Bowman, allowing the CBA business unit to focus on the research and development of commercial software. The Trader Series was introduced in July–August 1987, thus extending the CBA line in New Zealand. In 1989, CBA's Corporate Series was introduced, and A1 Services was established to provide added-value to existing and potential users of CBA products.

To serve New Zealand, A1 (New Zealand) used a dealer network reselling to end-users. The original approach of casting the net far and wide to develop the dealer network had evolved to a planned system of approximately 150 Trader dealers, and 70 Business Package dealers (of which 40 were very active). Of the Business Package dealers, 12 chartered accountancy firms and large computer companies had been groomed to market CBA's Corporate Series. Dealers were responsible for selling CBA products as well as DataFlex, QED2 and Q&A. In 1990, A1 (New Zealand) accounted for 38 per cent of total sales. Sales of CBA products accounted for 68 per cent of A1 (New Zealand) sales.

Expansion to Australia. Although Cowan had always anticipated expansion to Australia, the company focused clearly on the New Zealand market for initial product and service development. Concentrating on the domestic market resulted in early success for Business Package and sales of DataFlex. This success resulted in Cowan Bowman being approached by DataFlex's Australian distributor (named Intelligence), with a proposal to sell CBA products in Australia. Cowan had always intended to internationalize his firm's operations to Australia, thus the opportunity was seen to fit the company's long-term strategy. The distributorship was formalized and Cowan Bowman entered the Australian market with Business Package in April 1985.

At that time, no other options for internationalization were considered (e.g. use of a joint venture or a direct salesforce). According to Cowan, his company was too small (eight people) and too busy to give the effort and resources necessary to support anything but a distributorship. The product was a relatively low-cost package item, and Cowan Bowman required volume sales and growth in a short period. As a result, the distributor arrangement provided an immediate opportunity, covering a significant proportion of the set-up costs required to expand to Australia. The distributor provided access to Australian distribution channels, and low risk entry in the attempt to replace the leading competitor in Australia. It offered the potential to maximize economies of scale in terms of people, sales and, ultimately, product development. This was desired in order to enhance Cowan Bowman's competitive position in both New Zealand and Australia, and its market power. The establishment of Australian operations also led to enhanced credibility in New Zealand as the company was seen to be a success story in the export market.

In spite of these benefits, Cowan notes that it was evident from the outset of the agreement that the resources of Intelligence would quickly be stretched, thus requiring financial support. The benefits of entering Australia were seen to outweigh the risks, however, and priority was given to access Australia via Intelligence. Simultaneously, Cowan wanted to improve the stability of Cowan Bowman's management and financial structure in New Zealand, and develop the product line.

By 1986, it was clear that demand for CBA products exceeded the financial and physical resources of Intelligence. Market confidence in Intelligence had dropped, and as the distributor was selling to both dealers and end users, channel conflict developed. Cowan Bowman then made the decision to financially support Intelligence, and on 1 June 1986, a joint venture was formed in the name of Automation One (Australia). Cowan Bowman contributed 50 per cent of the equity base, with an additional 30 per cent from Intelligence, and 20 per cent from an ex-director of Intelligence. The financial situation for Intelligence continued to weaken and, in December 1986, Cowan Bowman bought out the 30 per cent owned by Intelligence. Thus, 20 per cent remained with the ex-director, also managing director of A1 (Australia), and 80 per cent belonged to Cowan Bowman Associates.

Initially, outright acquisition of Intelligence was not considered by Cowan due to the distributor's weak trading position. Although the formation of a joint venture reduced 1986 profitability to Cowan Bowman, the formation of A1 (Australia) allowed the company a greater degree of control in the market.

1990 saw significant changes occur. A1 (Australia) was restructured, involving the resignation of both the Australian managing director and general manager. A1 (Australia) also became a wholly-owned operation of CBA. John Cowan assumed senior management responsibilities for Australia, in addition to his role as group managing director. This continued until a new general manager of A1 (Australia) was appointed in October 1990.

As of December 1990, A1 (Australia) served approximately 150 dealers in a network similar to that of New Zealand. In 1990, Australia accounted for 61 per cent of total company sales, with approximately one-half of those sales generated by Business Package and Corporate Series (the latter was introduced in Australia in 1990). A1 (Australia) also distributed the DataFlex and QED2 products, and the Trader Series was scheduled for a 1991 release.

Expansion to Singapore. In addition to restructuring Australian operations in 1990, John Cowan was involved with negotiating a formal distributorship arrangement for Singapore. The distributor (AsiaSoft) was part of larger group of service and manufacturing companies, and employed approximately 15 people. AsiaSoft distributed other accounting software and off-the-shelf packages, and, while able to programme, the company's marketing expertise was its strength. Further, it was a local distributor with a good understanding of the Singapore market.

According to Cowan, the expansion to Singapore was the result of three issues. Firstly, while the market was estimated to be only one-fifth the size of the New Zealand accounting software market, Cowan saw AsiaSoft as providing good incremental business for CBA, and a stepping stone into Malaysia, Hong Kong and, potentially, China.

Secondly, the expansion to Singapore was also influenced by the development of Corporate Series. Prior to the introduction of this product, moves into Asia or other markets would have been premature as CBA lacked a product appropriate for market needs, in that the market required foreign currency transactions to be incorporated into software packages. Thus, the development and introduction of Corporate Series filled the product gap, enabling consideration of foreign markets. In addition, Cowan noted that although international expansion beyond Australia had been considered since 1987, significant changes in Australia in terms of management structure necessitated consolidation of effort in local markets.

Thirdly, an emergent development also influenced internationalization to Singapore in that a third party (in the A1 Australia dealer network) introduced AsiaSoft to CBA as a potential distributor. Although no other distributor was identified and evaluated prior to signing with AsiaSoft, Cowan believed the key attributes in choosing the distributor were as follows: local knowledge and experience, an established organization in the marketplace, good reputation, access to the market with established distribution channels and financial stability. Further, he required confidence in the distributor's people, in terms of personal rapport, professionalism and technical ability. Given Corporate Series was to be the major product in the Singapore market, it was also important that the distributor had good local and central government connections, providing access to potential purchasers. Further, AsiaSoft was believed appropriate because of its experience in selling and supporting accounting systems.

Overall, Cowan saw the responsibility of AsiaSoft being to establish the Singapore market and represent Cowan Bowman and its product. AsiaSoft was to establish a profile for the product, provide service and support to the dealers, and be responsible for service and support to the end users. The choice of entry mode to Singapore was limited according to Cowan. For example, establishing a direct salesforce would have necessitated developing a sales management structure.

Further, a salesforce would need to overcome significant entry barriers, including the development of local market contacts and establishment of Cowan Bowman and its products in a new market.

Although using a local distributor limited Cowan's control of the AsiaSoft operation, he believed this option to be most appropriate as he did not expect the Singapore market to grow in the same manner as it had in Australia and New Zealand. That is, the market was not expected to hold similar market potential or require an equally high level of management involvement. Therefore, establishment of operations identical to A1 (Australia) and A1 (New Zealand) was felt by Cowan to be inappropriate.

Cowan also recognized that Cowan Bowman's use of an indirect channel could contribute to some loss of marketing flexibility and market control, and squeeze margins. Therefore, the agreement signed in October 1990 was structured to minimize financial risk, and specified that Cowan Bowman would have access to all CBA-related sales information. Client audits could be performed by Cowan Bowman to assess the product and distributor strengths and weaknesses, and examine the performance of support services. Further the key account manager or other CBA personnel planned to travel to Singapore on a regular basis to enhance communication in the relationship, and manage specific user or distributor needs (e.g. installation or training).

Future Growth of CBA?

In December 1990, Cowan noted that the rapid growth of the company had diminished. Further, the domestic accounting software market was flat, and although there was some Australian growth potential due to the introduction of Corporate Series and Trader, that market was perceived by Cowan to be sluggish. This had already resulted in decreased unit sales and margins. Cowan believed market requirements were changing, with an increased need for advanced executive information systems for use as decision support tools.

Cowan Bowman Associates had no formal marketing plan. However, Cowan was clear in his intention to continue to consolidate his company's position in Australia and New Zealand, and pursue development in the area of executive information systems. Cowan wanted to add a complementary product to the line, and extend the company's own role as a distributor (noting that in-house products should account for at least 50 per cent of the business).

In terms of market development, the company had no plans to enter the United States as Cowan believed the market to be too competitive, too big and with too many products. Further, the American market reflected a downward price trend (resulting in big discounts to resellers and decreased profitability), and the market was not seen by Cowan Bowman to be technically astute in terms of accounting software products. Finally, the financial effort required to launch a US product and receive the necessary volume sales was perceived to be prohibitive.

Cowan Bowman was therefore considering opportunities in other markets, given Cowan was concerned that the New Zealand and Australian markets were not large enough to sustain further growth. Therefore, he planned to use Singapore as a learning experience to understand the issues associated with further internationalization. In particular, Cowan was considering moves into the United Kingdom and Malaysia.

Expansion to the United Kingdom and Malaysia?   Cowan believed the United Kingdom held significant potential for all three CBA products, particularly as there was no strong DataFlex-based product in that market. Cowan also noted that CBA had always been interested in the UK market, and had informally monitored it for a number of years. While Cowan had not conducted any formal research on market potential, his interest in the United Kingdom was influenced by an emergent opportunity for market entry when in September of 1990 Cowan Bowman was approached by MSG Business Systems, a small UK software firm interested in balancing its product portfolio with a standardized international product. As the MSG enquiries developed, the UK distributor of DataFlex also expressed stronger interest in distributing CBA products. This organization was quite large, and had access to a strong dealer network and other market contacts. As a result, Cowan was faced with the decision on whether or not to proceed with UK market expansion. If this was deemed feasible, he wondered about the process of distributor selection. No other modes of market entry had been considered.

With regards to Malaysia, Alan Chew, an A1 (New Zealand) dealer, identified an opportunity for Cowan Bowman. Chew was a Malaysian national with business contacts in the foreign market, and introduced the company to UniData, a distributor based in Kuala Lumpur. Cowan Bowman had no previous contact with the Malaysian market, and, based on initial estimates, the market potential was seen to be less financially significant than Singapore. Again, Cowan was faced with the decision of how to proceed, if at all.

Looking even further ahead, Cowan believed that by 1993, Australia would account for 50–60 per cent of sales, New Zealand 20–25 per cent, and overseas markets would account for the remaining 20–25 per cent of sales. He recognized that to achieve this, Cowan

Bowman would require strong management to support its technical product. Further, careful choice of appropriate target markets and improved marketing was believed necessary, and Cowan's priority was to make decisions regarding the UK and Malaysian markets. What should he do?

CASE 2.3
Fujifilm—Kodak Worldwide Competition (A): Government Relations*

The World Trade Organization (WTO) and US's 'Super 301' Clout

In late May 1995, George Fisher, who became in 1993 Kodak's chief executive officer (CEO) from Motorola's CEO, filed with the US Trade Representative Office (USTR) the complaint under a Section 301 petition of the US Trade Act of 1974. Kodak charged that Fujifilm and the Ministry of International Trade and Industry (MITI) of Japan had colluded to prevent Kodak from increasing its 7–10 per cent market share as opposed to Fujifilm's 70 per cent market share in Japan. Kodak reasoned that its 70 per cent market share in the United States would indicate its greater competitiveness in Japan if it were allowed to operate there freely. Fujifilm and MITI denied the charges completely.

Section 301 is dubbed in the international trade parlance as 'Super 301'. The 301 petition escalates immediately United States firms' trade and investment disputes with Japan or any other foreign countries to a politically charged confrontation between the US and foreign government(s). Super 301 empowers the US government unilaterally to institute trade sanctions against the foreign firm and country alleged to be 'unfairly' discriminating against US firms. Facing such 'gun-boat diplomacy' of the US the accused foreign government would often be forced to choose between political 'capitulation' or 'retaliation'. Since January 1994, however, the governments involved have had the option to consent to let the WTO adjudicate the disputes.

Early in December 1997, the three-country judge panel of Switzerland, Brazil and New Zealand of the World Trade Organization unanimously ruled in favour of Fuji Photo Film Co. (Fujifilm) and the Japanese government against Kodak Co. and the US government. The WTO ruling closed the first chapter of the political confrontation between Fujifilm and Kodak, the two worldwide dominant manufacturers of photographic materials. The disappointed Kodak immediately pressured the Clinton Administration to demand a bilateral negotiation with the Japanese government rather than to appeal the ruling with WTO's new judge panel.

*Copyright © Yoshi Tsurumi, 1998, Professor of International Business and Marketing, Baruch College, CUNY. Reproduced with permission. This case is developed on the basis of publicly available documents.

Kodak's Political Offensives. Upon filing the 252 page petition (plus 50 pages of exhibits and appendix) entitled 'Privatizing Protection' Kodak went on well-orchestrated public relations and lobbying campaigns in the United States and Japan. Kodak was counting on the USTR's limited ability to evaluate closely the voluminous report in terms of manpower and time allowed. Kodak was also counting on American mass media's notorious willingness to accept uncritically hyperboles of American firms' executive summary allegations against their foreign competitors. Kodak sent a copy of its petition widely to political and business leaders, editorial page writers of newspapers and magazines, television and radio news and talkshow hosts, and to over 3500 members of the Association of International Business Studies. The AIBS members are mainly drawn from those academics who are teaching international business and marketing courses in the United States and Canada and the rest of the world. Kodak's well-oiled campaigns used the two emotive characterizations of Fujifilm–MITI's alleged anti-competitive measures; 'Privatizing Protection' and 'Liberalization Countermeasures'. The USTR, pro-Kodak members of the US Congress and the American mass media paraded these two phrases as if they were the proofs of Kodak–USTR allegations against Fujifilm–MITI. Kodak's key allegations against Fujifilm and the Japanese government were summarized as follows:

1. After Japan liberalized foreign firms' direct investment in 1971, Fujifilm and MITI had conspired to have Fujifilm and its four key wholesalers 'privately' collude to continue keeping out Kodak products. These key wholesalers led by Asanuma exclusively handle Fujifilm products. Asanuma's 1975 decision to stop carrying Kodak products was a catastrophe for Kodak. The 'Asanuma Incident' was the keystone of Fujifilm's 'liberalization countermeasures'.

2. Japan Fair Trade Commission (JFTC), the anti-trust body, has condoned Fujifilm-wholesalers' exclusion of Kodak products. Besides, to restrict Kodak's sales, the JFTC has permitted Fujifilm to use extremely generous 'progressive rebate schemes' to wholesalers and retailers. The JFTC has refused to enforce its own anti-trust regulations that forbid Fujifilm's exclusionary acts. MITI encouraged the use of progressive volume rebates for Fujifilm to control distributors and retailers. MITI encouraged distributors to align with specific Japanese manufacturers.

3. The JFTC has colluded with Fujifilm to limit

Kodak's 'premium marketing promotions' to the value of the products involved. Accordingly, Kodak has been unable to use such premium promotion schemes as a 'Film Lottery to Win a Trip to Hawaii'.

4. Under Japan's Large Store Law (*Daiten Ho*), MITI has restricted severely the development of large, national merchandiser and grocery chains in order to limit Kodak's sales.

5. As a result, Kodak's market share in Japan has been limited to 7–10 per cent of films and photographic papers. From 1986 to 1988, Kodak spent 5.3 billion yen on advertising in Japan. During the decade of 1985 to 1995, Kodak invested $750 million in Japan. But, because of Fujifilm–MITI collusion to restrict Kodak's sales, Kodak has little to show for such 'enormous' spendings in Japan.

6. Kodak has competed in price in Japan but has not gained market share.

7. Fujifilm's ownership of wholesale photofinishing labs in Japan give it an unfair advantage in the market for photographic paper.

8. Kodak's low market share in Japan when compared to the rest of the world shows the closed nature of the Japanese market.

9. Fujifilm's $10 billion cash surplus demonstrates that it is operating from a protected profit sanctuary.

10. The 'home market advantage', to the extent it exists, cannot explain Fujifilm's dominant position in the Japanese market.

The polemics of 'privatizing protection' and 'liberalization countermeasures' was calculated to fan American public opinion further against Fujifilm and MITI. Ever since the 1989 fall of the Berlin Wall, American public opinion had become increasingly soured against Japan, the only remaining 'threat' to the United States. According to the Gallup Poll in March 1989, 31 per cent of Americans had unfavourable impressions of Japan. By February 1992 long after the collapse of the 'Evil Soviet Empire', 53 per cent of Americans had unfavourable impressions of Japan. According to the Roper Reports, in July 1989 63 per cent of Americans regarded Japan as 'the US Ally'. In November 1991, the same poll showed that only 43 per cent of Americans regarded Japan as the US ally. According to the Harris/Mirror (the *Los Angeles Times*) poll, in March 1990, only 8 per cent of Americans regarded Japan as 'the Greatest Danger to the US'. In February 1992, the same poll showed that 31 per cent of Americans treated Japan as the greatest danger to the United States. Undoubtedly over the years, American

competitors' repeated allegations of Japan's 'unfair trade practices' of cars, semiconductors, financial services, telecommunication equipment, aircargo services and others had taken a toll on American public opinion about Japan.

Kodak and USTR were painting Fujifilm–MITI as one more of 'Japan's unfair practices'. Kodak and USTR were apparently hoping that US political pressure and the 'guilty' verdict in the court of American public opinion would force the Japanese government to set aside an increased market share for Kodak in Japan. Starting in 1985, the Reagan–Bush–Clinton Administrations had acquired from the Japanese government the 'numerically-targeted' market share set aside for American cars, medical equipment and medicines, computers, wood products, semiconductors and telecommunication equipment.

Fujifilm Fights Back

Upon Kodak's Super 301 petition being filed with the USTR, Fujifilm unequivocally denied all Kodak's allegations and declared that it would make public, as soon as it was completed, the detailed refutation of Kodak's 252-page report on Fujifilm–MITI's covert anti-competitive practices. The months of June and July 1995 went by without Fujifilm's further statement on the Kodak–USTR charges. The Japanese government refused to put the Kodak–Fujifilm issue on the agenda of the US–Japan bilateral negotiations. It unequivocally denied the actions and omissions ascribed to MITI or JFTC. It pointed out that the Large Store Law was to protect Japan's small mum-and-dad retailers, not to keep out foreign retail chains. Besides, it added, the Large Store Law was relaxed substantially in 1991 to permit large foreign retail chains like Toys "R" Us to go for a sky-is-the-limit expansion in Japan. The Law was slated to be completely revoked in 1998. JFTC's limit on 'premium promotion marketing' schemes was not to handicap foreign firms like Kodak, but to discourage 'unhealthy gambling frenzy' among children consumers.

Meanwhile, in the United States and Japan, George Fisher, Kodak's chief executive officer (CEO), and his staff and lobbyists were marshalling America's public opinions against Fujifilm and MITI. Exploiting Fujifilm's pregnant silence, Ira Wolf, the USTR officer-turned Kodak's resident chief in Japan, went on the offensive against Fujifilm through Japanese mass media's interviews and TV appearances. The only attempt to counter-balance Kodak's concerted public relations campaigns in the United States and Japan came from one long-time observer of US–Japan political and economic disputes. On 29 June 1995, the CNBC TV News network invited this professor of international business and Alan Wolff (no relationship to Ira Wolf in Japan) who was the USTR-official-turned-attorney-lobbyist for Eastman Kodak to debate the Kodak–Fujifilm dispute. Alan Wolff was with the Dewey Ballantine Law Firm in Washington that had represented Detroit's Big Three, US Steel, Motorola and other American corporate interests concerning their trade disputes with Japan. According to the viewers' responses, this professor successfully exposed the fallacies of Kodak's arguments.

To shore up Kodak's positions, however, on 26 July 1995, Ira Wolf gave a lengthy press conference at the Foreign Press Club of Tokyo and revived the spectre of the Fujifilm–MITI conspiracy by misleading accounts of the issues involved. He even tried to give the impression that Kodak was the innovator of the one-time use camera (a film with lens). In reality, it was Fujifilm that introduced the popular one-time use 35 mm camera in 1987, beating Kodak to the punch by two years in Japan and 18 months in the United States and elsewhere. Ira Wolf added, 'We understand the risks inherent in going ahead with a 301 case, especially given the feelings of the average Japanese consumer about 301. But we decided there was no alternative . . . The Office of the Trade and Investment Ombudsman (Japan) is too weak and Geneva-based WTO does not cover competition policy.'

On 31 July 1995, Minoru Ohnishi, the president and CEO of Fujifilm, broke the silence by making public simultaneously in Tokyo and Washington its 274-page text (plus 270 pages of exhibits and appendix) reply to Kodak. The reply was entitled, 'Rewriting History: Kodak's Revisionist Account of the Japanese Consumer Photographic Market'. Ohnishi chaired Fujifilm's press conference in Tokyo while Osamu 'Sam' Inoue, the president of Fuji Film USA, Inc. of Elmsford, New York, chaired the press conference in Washington after filing the reply with the USTR. The reply was also placed in Fujifilm's worldwide internet Web pages in English and Japanese. The Web pages recorded over 30 000 hits on the first day alone. The voluminous reply was also sent to all the appropriate parties and anyone whom Fujifilm believed might have received a copy of Kodak's 252 page report.

Having been drawn into the Kodak–Fujifilm confrontations by Kodak's extensive public relations campaigns, not only American and Japanese mass media but also other mass media in the world gave rather prominent coverage to Fujifilm's long-awaited response. Fujifilm's employees worldwide voiced that their morale was visibly lifted by their firm's strong reply to Kodak. In the long history of the US–Japan trade disputes of the post-World War II era, Fujifilm's open challenge to a US firm and the US government became a notable first. It was also notable first time that

Japanese chief executives assumed publicly the aggressive roles of spokesmen inside and outside Japan. They visibly laid their credibility and the credibility of their firm on the line. Fujifilm asked the Japanese government to reject outright the Kodak–USTR demand and challenged the US government to take the matter to the WTO for arbitration.

On 21 August 1995 the Foreign Press Club of Tokyo invited Minoru Ohnishi for a lengthy press conference. In his initial statement, Ohnishi called Kodak's nearly 300 pages of allegations 'untrue', 'irresponsible' and 'self-serving'. He stated that Kodak's 'Privatizing Protection' did not rely on facts and attempted to establish Fujifilm's guilt through association, innuendo and mischaracterization of facts. He stated that Fujifilm had wanted to reply to Kodak much earlier, but that he had needed to take time to review carefully almost thirty years of history of the industry and refute Kodak's allegations on nothing but verifiable facts. He implored the USTR to carefully study Fujifilm's documentation and verify its accuracy rather than to simply cooperate with Kodak and accept its irresponsible petition as the truth. He invited the USTR to reject Kodak's Super 301 petition. He continued:

> Kodak has violated all the standards of business ethics. It has shamelessly made false allegations against Fujifilm in a self-serving attempt to use political pressure to accomplish what its own lack of managerial effort and failed marketing strategies have not been able to accomplish. What is most troubling about Kodak's action is not that it attempts to tarnish Fujifilm with false allegations of anti-competitive practices, but that it attempts to exploit growing tensions between the US and Japan on trade issues to the detriment of a crucial bilateral relationship. Fujifilm has no desire or intention to contribute to the deterioration of what many commentators deem the most important bilateral relationship in the world. Kodak's management, however, seems to view the bilateral tensions as an opportunity for Kodak to gain through the political process what it has been unable to gain through the competitive process.

Fujifilm's reply pointed out the following facts concerning Kodak's allegations. Taken together, these revealed facts questioned George Fisher's curious hidden agenda about rolling back Fujifilm's competitive pressures in Japan, the United States, and rest of the world.

1. Over the 25 years covered by Kodak's allegations against Fujifilm, Kodak had never complained to the Japan Fair Trade Commission (JFTC), Japan's anti-trust body,

about Fujifilm's alleged anti-competitive practices.

2. Kodak had never taken its case to the Office of Trade and Investments of the Japanese government, the ombudsman body created to mediate foreign firms' complaints about Japan's market opening measures.

3. Kodak had made no attempt, until May 1995, to place its complaint against Fujifilm onto the successive years of the agenda of the US–Japan bilateral trade negotiations. Until May 1995, the US government had not once cited the photographic material market in Japan as the unfairly closed market in its USTR's annual report on foreign countries' unfair treatment of American goods and services.

4. Kodak's allegation of 'Privatizing Protection' was built on the statement that Fujifilm covertly pressured one leading wholesaler, Asanuma, into handling Fujifilm products exclusively. However, it was well documented that Kodak rejected from 1973 to 1975 Asanuma's repeated requests for handling Kodak products. Asanuma's president made a trip to Kodak's headquarters in Rochester, New York, in 1973, and pleaded for Kodak's business. He was rejected. Kodak's description of the 'Asanuma Incident' was falsified.

5. Just like Kodak's falsification of the Asanuma Incident, Kodak's key allegations against Fujifilm and MITI were based on an unnamed and unidentified 'Consultant' or on rather elementary mistranslations of Japanese documents or uses of such documents out of context. The closer one read Kodak's Super 301 petition, the more dismayed one became at Kodak's rough and loose treatments of 'numbers' and 'facts'.

6. Kodak's allegations were found contradicted by Kodak's own executives before George Fisher became Kodak's CEO late in 1993. Dr Albert Sieg, the previous president of Kodak Japan before Ira Wolf, was repeatedly on the record, saying that Kodak was not saddled with any barriers in Japan and that the import regulations of Japan and the United States were basically wash. In October 1990, Kodak's then CEO, Kay Whitmore, stated publicly that all that was necessary for Kodak's success in Japan was Kodak's own effort.

7. Kodak's and Fujifilm's market shares are mirror images: Kodak has 70 per cent of the US market and approximately 10 per cent of the Japanese market, while Fujifilm has 70 per cent of the Japanese market and roughly 10 per cent of the US market. As to the 'home market advantage', Kodak was singing a completely different tune in its recent Consent Decree of the US Anti-Trust litigation. Kodak argued successfully that Kodak's dominant market position in the United States was due to the 'home player advantage'. Kodak convinced the court that its 36 per cent share of the overall world market does not confer market power (and the consequent ability to control prices and exclude competition), despite its 70 per cent share of the US market. On 2 July 1993, Kodak's reply to the US Justice Department stated that 'vigorous competition now exists in the photographic market worldwide and that market conditions make it virtually impossible for Kodak *or any manufacturer* to exercise market power'.

8. Fujifilm's investment in the United States exceeds Kodak's investment in Japan by hundreds of millions of dollars. And yet, Fujifilm has not been able to increase its market share. Between 1986 and 1988, Kodak spent 5.3 billion yen on advertising in Japan. Over the same period, Konica (14 per cent of market share) spent 8 times as much on advertising and Fujifilm spent 10 times as much.

9. Although Fujifilm's rebates were never more than mildly progressive, even these rebates have been changed. Some rebate programmes have been eliminated at the suggestions of the JFTC. For the one remaining progressive rebate to distributors, the maximum spread between lowest and highest rates is less than 0.6 percentage points. There are currently no progressive rebates to retailers. In fact, Kodak uses far more progressive and exclusionary rebates in the United States to keep out Fujifilm products. From Reagan–Bush to Clinton administrations both Federal Trade Commission and Justice Department of the United States have continued to condone Kodak's egregious anti-trust violations of the 1954 Consent Decree.

10. In fact, the JFTC has enforced vigorously the anti-trust regulations. The JFTC will never permit Kodak's exclusionary rebates to wholesalers and retailers as well as its predatory tactics of its own exclusive

wholesale photofinishing labs in the United States if these were done in Japan.

11. Kodak's marketing failures in Japan include its unwillingness to price its products aggressively. From the fall of 1985 to 1987, the Japanese yen continued to appreciate against the US dollar over 40 per cent to 50 per cent. We braced for Kodak's price-cutting offensive in Japan. But Kodak did not exploit this opportunity to expand its market shares in Japan.

12. The USTR should have rejected Kodak's Super 301 petition as having no merit just as it has rejected a number of similar attempts by US firms. At the minimum, the USTR should have accepted Kodak's petition quietly for verifying Kodak's allegations against Fujifilm and the Japanese government. Instead, the USTR has substituted Kodak's petition for USTR's independent review. The moment Kodak filed the petition, the USTR and Kodak 'separately' went on the one-sided public relations campaigns to bash Fujifilm and the Japanese government.

13. Kodak's charge of Fujifilm's $10 billion profit sanctuary is spurious. The operating profit results of Fujifilm and Kodak have been almost identical over the past 20 years. However, in the last 10 years, Kodak has had $5.5 billion of extraordinary charges against earnings. These are due to its exit from the instant film and camera market, Kodak's settlement with Polaroid, divestiture losses of Sterling Drugs and other restructuring charges. Fujifilm did not cause these extraordinary write-offs of Kodak.

Fujifilm–Kodak Traded Charges

Once in August 1996, Clinton campaigns decided to stop hyping the US trade issues with Japan lest American mass media should scrutinize the real 'results'. The United States continued to negotiate on a low key basis with Japan over the aviation issue. But it put the Kodak issue on the hold sensing that neither the Japanese government nor Fujifilm was likely to budge. Meanwhile, both Kodak and Fujifilm went on public relations campaigns through mass media advertisements in the United States. In September 1996, against Kodak's reluctance, the Clinton Administration suddenly changed its previous stand and appealed the Kodak case to the WTO. The Japanese government and Fujifilm welcomed it.

Fujifilm virtually suspended its public relations campaigns in the United States. However, Kodak had continued with its mass media advertisement campaigns and widespread leafletting to the political, business, mass media and academic circles in the United States.

From summer to autumn of 1997, as the WTO ruling drew to an end, Kodak intensified its lobbying of Congress members and the Clinton Administration. Kodak intensified its direct mail campaigns to opinion leaders of political, business, academic and mass media circles. Its tactics were familiar. Kodak supplied its 'op-ed page summary drafts' and 'talk-point drafts' to its friendly USTR officials, Congressmen and academics who then criticized in the mass media both Fujifilm and the Japanese government. Kodak then circulated such editorials and statements as if they were the independent proof of Kodak's allegations. All these editorials and statements implored the WTO to rule against Fujifilm and the Japanese government. Their common theme was the refrain of 'Don't Permit Japan's Privatizing Protection'.

Study Guide Questions

1. Why do you think George Fisher of Kodak resorted to the Super 301 petition? Was his action ethical? Was there any public interest involved in his action? If successful, what would the American public gain from his action?

2. The Super 301 actions raise diplomatically delicate issues of 'unilateral and extraterritorial application' of US laws and procedures to a sovereign foreign state. Do you agree with the Super 301 clause of the Trade Act? Any better alternative for the United States?

3. Once Kodak decided on the Super 301 petition, has it handled the political and public relations offensive effectively? What else could or should have Kodak done to press its case against Fujifilm and the Japanese government? To improve Kodak's market position in Japan?

4. How well has Fujifilm handled its political and public relations defence against Kodak? What else should or could it have done in Japan and the United States?

5. How do you think Japanese public (consumers) would react to Kodak? How do you think American public (consumers) would react to Fujifilm?

6. Would the economic crisis of Japan and other Asian nations (Asian Contagion) help or hurt Kodak/USTR to press for a bilateral negotiation with Japan?

References

1. See James Bovard, *The Fair Trade Fraud* (New York: St Martin's, 1991), Ch. 8, pp. 227–271.
2. Paul Krugman, *Peddling Prosperity* (New York: Norton, 1994), Ch. 10 and Appendix, pp. 245–292.
3. Simon Evenett, 'As Guilty as the Japanese', *Washington Post*, 8 July 1995, p. A-17.
4. 'Dick Morris helped Kantor get tough on Japan', *Journal of Commerce*, 21 November 1996, pp. 1A and 6A.

CASE 2.4
ELLE goes European!

ELLE, A Long Story

The women's weekly magazine, *ELLE*, was launched in France in 1945, through the impetus of Hélène Gordon Lazareff. Not at all a feminist, she thought that women must seduce then keep hold, that this is the big challenge of their life and that it was necessary to help them to succeed, to teach them how to be beautiful, have smooth skin, sparkling hair, stunning dresses . . . She had defined her target readers: young women, living in medium-sized towns, aged between twenty and thirty-five, who after five years of war wanted to live intensively.

In a ruined France, the consumer society was still far away, but *ELLE* opened the door to a world of disposable things, one season dresses and plastic packaging. Ahead of the times, *ELLE* lost quite a lot of readers after an article headed 'She chose freedom' about a woman who sued for a divorce.

ELLE was the first magazine to have colour advertising and it introduced a new style of presentation: many headlines and blank spaces, and photos and illustrations even in pages of written text. The quality of the colour photographs, the luxuriousness of the presentation, the beauty of the fashion models made it unmatched for some years. Before the other magazines, *ELLE* understood the influence of cinema and television on the evolution of people's looks and tastes; its photos catch movement in action. Parisian *haute couture* sets the fashion and sets *ELLE*'s readers dreaming.

During the 1960s and 1970s, *ELLE* went through a period of decline. It was no longer an *avant-garde* magazine, and was out of step with the great changes affecting the lives of its readers: urbanization, work outside the home, access to higher education. The end of the seventies were the most difficult years. Women readers were losing interest in their own specific press in spite of attempts at readjustments, new launches, even relaunches.

The ideological break following the student movement of 1968, the increasing impact of new media and the fact that women were acquiring a new self-awareness, all explain the divorce between them and their magazines. *ELLE* lost its leadership as it did not manage to remain the mirror of the social changes which transformed its readers.

During the eighties, *ELLE* gave itself a new look by projecting the image of new, liberated women who represented the positive, unaggressive face of feminism.

The woman of the eighties faced contradictory demands—husband, work, children, home—which she turned into a liberating experience. *ELLE* convinced her she could take on all these challenges as long as she obeyed two rules: be efficient and seductive. Homecraft, the art of cooking, useful addresses, cosmetics, readers' letters and stars' secrets are all there, *ELLE* offers the commercialized products of modernity to come to her aid and further her liberation. Articles on independence go hand in hand with an insistence on femininity and feminine values: sensitivity, intuition, imagination, intelligence and creativity without which a society can only lose its dynamism.

In 1989, the circulation of *ELLE* in France averaged about 300 000 copies bought each week for a readership of 2 million women (print run of 500 000 copies). Each edition numbers about 200 pages, more than 80 of which are advertising pages. To this number must be added indirect advertising through articles and all the pages of fashion photos bearing the names of the designers or the distributors of the products.

The original objective has not yet changed. Hélène Gordon Lazareff said: 'Our vocation is to innovate. Giving people appetites is what matters.' *ELLE* is characterized by perpetual innovation, an intuition for doing something new, so many ways of seducing women. It is a magazine that reflects movements and fashions. *ELLE* exemplifies a constant feminine theme: 'Never the same, always the same'

The Internationalization of *ELLE*

In 1983, Hachette, the publisher of the magazine, agreed to grant the *ELLE* label to a French festival organized by the New York department store Bloomingdale's. French fashion parades were organized in ten big American towns and a special issue of *ELLE* with American material was put on sale at Bloomingdale's. The operation was a great success. French advertisers filled 80 pages with advertisements for their products sold in the United States. *ELLE* magazine offered American women an opportunity to identify with French women and the 100 000 copies printed were immediately sold.

The American market offers remarkable opportunities: over 230 million inhabitants, speaking one language and with an almost uniform culture. Considering the excellent results, Hachette decided to publish, for the United States, a monthly *ELLE* magazine in a joint-venture with the Murdoch Group. The 50/50 partnership took the form of cooperation between Hachette which provided the concept; and

News Group Publications of the Murdoch Group, which provided the logistics for launching the magazine in the United States and its mastery of the distribution network.

The magazine is of sumptuous quality with superb photos on glazed paper. The 17 million dollars spent on the launching process were paid off in under three years. In 1988 *ELLE* US made a profit of 16 million dollars. Today, circulation figures are over 800 000, and more than 2100 pages have been sold to advertisers in the course of the year. In the United States it has overtaken *Harper's* and is just behind *Vogue*.

It is considered to be the finest press launch in the United States in recent decades. This success spurred on the Hachette Group which went on to launch new editions of *ELLE* throughout the world at a rapid pace.

In 1985, the publication of an English version of *ELLE* magazine, still in partnership with the Murdoch Group, was also an immediate success. In 1988, circulation figures reached 220 000, 40 per cent higher than the figure for *Vogue* and two-and-a-half times the circulation of *Women's Journal* and *Harper's & Queen*, its prestigious competitors. That year, advertisers bought more than 1300 pages. *ELLE* innovates in a mood of positive rebellion. The magazine reveals new trends, stimulates interests and provokes the English woman.

In 1986, *ELLE* went into partnership in Spain with the group Cambio 16, a subsidiary of Hachette. The magazine is in line with the broadening horizons of its young readers, 75 per cent of whom are under 34. It responds to their desire to progress and to open new frontiers. In October 1987, 121 000 copies were circulated, compared with 90 000 for *Marie-Claire* and 49 000 for *Vogue*. 1200 advertising pages were sold the same year.

In 1987, in joint-venture with RCS Rizzoli, *ELLE* attacked the creative Italian market where many weekly magazines were already in competition. It soon reached a circulation of 120 000 copies. In one year, with 1100 advertising pages sold, the edition trebled its objectives. *ELLE*, even more *avant-garde*, replied to the sophistication of the Italian woman by subtly harmonizing fashion and lifestyle.

One month later, *ELLE* Hong Kong, in a joint venture with Communications and Management Ltd, was published in Chinese. 35 000 copies were circulated in Hong Kong, Singapore and Taiwan. *ELLE* is a shop window of Parisian fashion and reveals the art of the accessory to women used to total look fashion.

At the beginning of 1988, in a joint venture with the Bonnier Group, *ELLE* started up in Sweden. *ELLE* became an unchallenged leader with a circulation of 60 000 copies.

Still in 1988, *ELLE* Brazil was published in a joint-venture with Editoria Abril. Its first number had

210 advertising pages. It reached a circulation figure of 210 000 which later settled at 120 000 copies. The dream of the European woman became a reality thanks to *ELLE*. The potential market is estimated at 13 million women with a big purchasing power.

In August 1988, the launching of *ELLE* China, in a joint venture with Shanghai Publishing House, was a revolutionary event! It was the first Western magazine to be circulated in the People's Republic of China. The main theme of the first number was world fashion, the expression of freedom through clothing. It was sold in more than 4000 sales outlets in different cities. The major fashion and beauty advertisers were associated with this event, although some of their products are still unknown to the Chinese consumers.

An exception in the group, *ELLE* China is designed in Paris with the best photos of the other versions. It has bigger fashion coverage to meet the needs of readers anxious to know the Western lifestyle. However, profitability is uncertain. To respect local traditions, *ELLE* has to offer a copy of each number to the wives of ministers and top civil servants . . . One year after the events of June 1989, the magazine is on sale again in China.

In September 1988, a German version of *ELLE* was published in joint venture with the Burda Group. In West Germany, the market for women's magazines is very competitive, 40 titles are controlled by a small number of powerful groups. Counterattacks of established competitors are fearsome. One week before the launching of *ELLE*, Grüner und Jahr, a subsidiary of Bertelsmann, launched *Viva*, a magazine positioned on exactly the same segment; that of independent, young, intellectual and critical-minded women who as consumers were well informed on upmarket products. Also at stake is a share of the advertising market, valued at DM750 million a year.

The German edition of *ELLE*, masterminded by an exceptional chief editor, produces 90 per cent of its pages of text itself. On the other hand, it gets its photographs from the group photograph pool as the other publications do.

The magazine differentiates itself from its German competitors, which are more practical and functional in approach, bringing with it a dash of fantasy and a new dynamism. 180 000 copies of the first two numbers were sold.

In October 1988, *ELLE* was published in Portugal in a joint venture with the Sojornal Group. The circulation, of 40 000 copies, is limited to the big cities. The magazine shows the way ahead. It is an example of woman's self-assertion and the widening of her horizons.

At the same time, a Greek version of *ELLE* was published in a joint venture with European Publications.

The magazine, circulated mainly in the capital, satisfies the appetite of Greek women for things modern. It reached a circulation of 100 000 copies.

The publication of a new *ELLE* magazine in Canada was launched in August 1989, in a joint venture with Telemedia; then in Holland in September in a joint venture with VDB Magazines (120 000 copies); followed by Australia in February 1990 (130 000 copies) then Turkey was planned for November 1990, in a joint venture with Karacan Publications.

Repositioned Editions

In 1969, a licence for a Japanese edition of *ELLE* was granted to Mag House. This magazine became too different from the initial concept. The contract was cancelled in 1988. It has just been renegotiated in a joint venture with the Time Group.

In 1974, a licence was negotiated with Charkia for an Arabic edition of *ELLE*. A shop window for luxury European products, the magazine had an immediate success with readers with an exceptionally high purchasing power. This licence is being renegotiated. These editions no longer represented the *ELLE* concept.

The Coordination of *ELLE* Europe

The coordination of *ELLE* Europe is based in Paris (France). Its mission is to follow up developments in each country and to learn of successes or failures. It acts as a consultant in order to enable its partners to benefit from its know-how. It tries to establish relationships of confidence and complementarity between teams. The local teams contact the coordination team when they have difficulties.

The coordination of *ELLE* Europe supervises the table of contents of each edition. It transmits it to all the other editorial teams so as to inform them and to enable them to use articles published in it for their own magazines. The pages of text and the fashion pages are also controlled. It is not a matter of standardizing, which would be contrary to the basic idea: to aim at the same group of women, those of the sociocultural advance segment (defined below), knowing that in each country they are at different stages of evolution. It is a question of safe-guarding the coherence of the *ELLE* concept, transmitted by each magazine, while letting collaborators express their creativity at the local level.

However, the news pages are all written locally. In cases of profound disagreement, the team is changed, as happened in Portugal.

The publishing costs of a magazine (writing, buying paper, manufacturing) account for around 60 per cent of the turnover. The group tries to minimize costs by putting articles or photographs in a common pool. The photos are often used again in the same form. The texts are rewritten and adapted to suit the mentality of each country. About 30 per cent of *ELLE* pages are the same in all the editions.

The cover of the magazine is a major element of the marketing-mix. The same design with the *ELLE* logo is what is common to the different editions. The headlines on the cover provide a very strong purchasing motivation. The cover photographs are sometimes the same in different editions, published with a time lag in order to prevent the magazines competing with each other. The French version of *ELLE* is still distributed worldwide and newspaper kiosks in Europe's capitals sell the editions of the different countries of the EEC.

The distribution costs of the magazine represent an average 15 per cent of the turnover. They depend on the complexity of the local distribution in each country. On average, there is one newsagent for 570 households in Europe. For example, there are 96 000 newspaper sales outlets in Germany. A magazine is a perishable product and each new number makes the previous one obsolete. It is important to make an accurate estimate of the numbers of copies to be printed.

Each edition is followed with the help of quantitative indicators: print run, circulation, readership, advertising turnover . . . The editors of the magazines must constantly adapt in order to anticipate the needs of their readers which are always changing. They must also attract a new generation of women who will have a different lifestyle, a different mentality and language.

Before the launching of each new magazine, the local team in charge of editing and marketing it, receives training on the concept and style of *ELLE*. This training period lasts two or three months and takes place in Paris. The team is then autonomous from the organizational point of view and in charge of its own system of production and sales. Under the terms of the contract signed when the joint venture was agreed, the *ELLE* concept has to be respected.

In the first stages of European development, the *ELLE* team had to be imaginative and creative. Negotiations with potential partners were long and mobilized management. The first steps in the Europeanization process were no doubt marked by experimentation, hesitation, intuition and mobilization. Measured both in quantitative and qualitative terms, the cost of the learning process was relatively high and the time spent was rather long.

In the course of the second stage, the effect of the initial learning period contributed in an important way to the intensification of the process. The accumulated know-how made it possible to advance more quickly and at a lower cost in different fields: looking for partners, adapting to local specificities, positioning the product, marketing campaigns, overall designing of the magazine, establishing relations with *ELLE* Europe coordinators in Paris.

A European Women's Readership

Each women's magazine tries to position its product on a specific segment. In order to keep advertisers, it must reach readers with the same consumer habits, an equivalent level of income, and comparable qualifications and interests. However, in the case of *ELLE*, these characteristics are insufficient to define a homogeneous basis of readers throughout Europe.

ELLE referred to a sociological study which shows a similar evolution of lifestyles in European countries. They are all going in the same direction, even if rhythms of evolution and levels of maturity are different.

Two large segments have been defined.

1. The segment of the population that is slow to change. People are attached to national or regional traditions and conventions. This segment has specific characteristics in each European country.
2. The segment of the population that is changing rapidly. People are more homogeneous between different countries and share the same lifestyles if not nationalities. Every year 10 to 15 million people join this segment.

A multidimensional analysis has made it possible to identify three main axes of socio-cultural advance:

1. The first and most important axis, that of **individuality**, contrasts the sociocultural advance (value of autonomy and assertion of one's own individuality) with sociocultural backwardness (the respect of norms, conformity and fear of changes).
2. **Roots and networking** characterize the second axis. It appears as the result of the interaction between social change and social structure. This axis goes from an attachment to roots (a need for familiar groups) to a capacity to be more open and to communicate with new groups.
3. The third axis is that of **reconciliation**. Individuals are increasingly capable of integrating intellectuality and rationality with sensitivity, emotion and intuition.

This study shows that 24 per cent of European women belong to the 'sociocultural advance' group. In France, as in Italy, one-third of women belong to this group whereas only 25 per cent of Spanish women are in it. Less than 17 per cent of German and English

Figure CS 2.4.1

Portrait of the European women
in the **socio-cultural advance segment**

Open:	They enrich themselves by communicating with people and not opposing them.
Comprehensive:	They know how to manage uncertainty and complexity and try to reconcile differences.
Sensitive:	They feel and understand reality with emotion and intuition, not only with intellectuality.
Curious:	Always on the look out, they notice changing trends.
Aesthetic:	Sensitive to design and to the aesthetic quality of products they buy.
Active:	They are dynamic, direct, pragmatic, enterprising.
Demanding:	They want to exploit their vitality potential in order to live life to the full.

women belong to this segment followed, a long way behind, by Portuguese women .

ELLE recruits its European readers out of this population. They are open-minded, refusing traditional or political barriers, and not easily influenced. *ELLE* is a magazine surfing on the crest of the waves, which must reflect the mood of the day and which is written for European women corresponding to the criteria of 'sociocultural advance'.

Its readers are women with a high purchasing power from privileged social categories. Most of them have benefited from higher education. The quality of its very targeted readership makes *ELLE* an effective medium for advertisers.

European Advertisers for *ELLE*

Advertising is the source of more than 60 per cent of the turnover of a women's magazine. The advertising market of the women's press is constantly expanding. This can be explained by, among other factors, the interest of advertisers in the luxury goods sector for media with a large public, which upmarket women's magazines represent. They are mainly international advertisers who are trying to homogenize their communication throughout Europe, and sometimes throughout the world.

European campaigns make it possible not only to ensure a global image for a product but to achieve considerable economies of scale. 30 per cent of the pages of advertising which appear in the different versions of *ELLE* are the same Europewide. The decision to purchase one-third of these is made by a European advertising manager. In 75 big firms, whether they are of European or American origin, there is one single person taking the decisions concerning advertising investments in Europe.

ELLE Europe has one big strength, it sells the same concept to its advertisers in all countries. *ELLE* image is complementary to that of fashion products, perfumes and luxury goods. The success of the American experience gave *ELLE* a reputation and earned true recognition from the European advertisers. This was an incitement for the parent companies of groups in the upmarket product sector to include it in their European campaigns. With 5200 advertising pages in 1988, for the French edition alone, *ELLE* is a champion of advertising pages in magazines.

Interdeco, the company responsible in Paris for advertising sales of *ELLE Europe* and *International*, has a double role:

1. Interdeco carries out direct sales to French advertisers who buy space in the different editions of *ELLE*. The typical example is that of *haute-couture* where sales are carried out in Paris for the American, European or Asian publications.
2. Some advertisers, who have subsidiaries in all countries, buy their advertising spaces locally. The second role of Interdeco is to inform advertisers of the existence of different editions of *ELLE* and of the possibility of negotiating with its local head offices.

Interdeco's subsidiaries are already functioning, in Germany, in England, in Spain, in Italy and in America. A representative in Switzerland, Brussels and Tokyo will soon follow. Offices have been opened in smaller towns. It is a heavy human and financial investment, FFr15 million a year are necessary to equip a subsidiary. But the stakes are high, *ELLE*'s objective is an advertising turnover of FFr500 million in 5 years.

It is an ambitious objective for a market in which planning is difficult. Advertisers have a tendency today to fix relatively short-term strategies, which makes advertising estimates difficult for magazines. This is all the more so as, being published on a weekly or a monthly basis, this type of support offers a great flexibility to the media-planners.

International negotiation makes it possible to circumvent, particularly in France, the increasing power of organizations which centralize the purchasing of advertising space. Committing themselves to purchasing a certain number of pages, the latter use their power to get publishing groups to lower their prices considerably.

Relentless Competition

L'Oréal, the French world's foremost cosmetic group, holds 49 per cent of the monthly magazine, *Marie-Claire*, second in terms of number of copies circulated on the French market of upmarket women's magazines. It recruits its readers on the same segment as *ELLE*.

For almost all the countries shown in Figure CS 2.4.2, the magazine is published by local press groups with the licence of *Marie-Claire*. It was the first to publish a French decoration magazine *Marie-Claire Maison* (190 000 copies sold), followed by *Vogue* with *Vogue Decoration* and *ELLE* with *ELLE Decoration*. *Marie-Claire Maison* has already launched a Spanish version *Casa de Marie-Claire* (62 000 copies—156 000 readers).

The American magazine *Vogue*, leader in Great Britain (180 000 copies sold), has also an edition in each European country. The *Vogue* readers are more traditional, conservative, wealthier and older than *ELLE*'s. Printed on a better quality paper, with a smaller circulation (35 500 copies in France in 1988), the magazine is an advertising leader. For example, in 1986, *Vogue* received more than $40 from advertisers for each copy of the magazine sold in France, whereas *Marie-Claire* only received $6 per copy.

Harper's Bazaar, the prestigious American pioneer in upmarket women's magazines, has an even smaller circulation: 10 000 copies in France and 15 000 in Italy.

In France for example, no less than 57 magazines compete in the women's segment of the market. The leader is *Madame Figaro* (Hersant Group) with 616 000 copies circulated and sold (3000 pages of advertising each year). One page of advertising in this magazine is sold at 1.8 times the price of a page in *ELLE*. *Madame Figaro* was, until now, published only in France. It launched, this year, a Japanese version and a Portuguese one.

What we are witnessing therefore is a match of giants, with the colossal groups of the communications industry competing aggressively and making new moves every day. In February 1990, for example,

Figure CS 2.4.2

Country	Copies	Readers
France	480 000	4 000 000
Japan	300 000	900 000
Italy (leader)	170 000	700 000
Great Britain	160 000	470 000
Germany	120 000	300 000
Spain	93 000	320 000
Latin America	90 000	250 000
The Netherlands	85 000	120 000
Hong Kong	80 000	
Portugal	60 000	210 000
Greece	55 000	100 000
Arabian Gulf	50 000	
Turkey	20 000	35 000
Total	1 700 000	7 400 000

Groupe Express, a subsidiary of Generale Occidentale, celebrated the tenth anniversary of *BIBA* magazine by giving it a new cover design (very *ELLE* like!) and dividing it into three sections: 'business', 'seduction' and 'lifestyles'. The relaunch was supported by a FFr10 million publicity campaign.

In the advertising market, competitors play both the price war and that of quality of customer service. For example, under the name of 'The European force sisters' the German group Bauer grants a reduction of 15–30 per cent to international advertisers who buy advertising space in its four women's magazines simultaneously: *Tina* (Germany), *Bella* (Germany), *Maxi* (France), *Bella* (Great Britain).

With 4 million copies, these titles represent a reading public of 10 million women, which means a purchasing potential of FFr70 million. In order to better inform its customers in advertising, the Bauer group publishes a study on a European country each month.

Problems and Prospects for European Media

A close observation of developments in this industry makes it possible to identify the following trends which will shape the future:

Increasingly Crowded Markets. The Europeanization and the internalization processes are not limited to the segment of women's magazines but affect the whole press sector. Some recent examples stress the intensity of this development: *Penthouse*, after its American, French, English and German editions is trying to conquer the Hungarian market; *Playboy* is following suit; *Esquire* plans to publish Italian, German and Dutch editions very soon; *Fairly* in Germany in the near future; *Fortune* already established in France and in Italy, has its eye on Germany; *Life* is present in Germany and in Italy through a joint venture with local partners.

In short, almost all magazines are discovering the virtues of internationalization. The true pioneer in the industry is the American *Reader's Digest* which, as early as the 1940s, began to market local editions. Today, *Reader's Digest* has 15 European editions in 15 different languages, circulating 28 million copies (6.7 million subscribers).

The saturation of the American market, with very low growth rates, explains, for a large part, the European offensive. What is at stake for the different magazines is to position themselves on the European advertising market which is expanding more rapidly than the US market: for 1990 the experts forecast a growth of 1 to 2 per cent in advertising investments in the United States, 1.8 per cent in Great Britain and 9 per cent in France (15.5 per cent in 1988). The Eastern European new consumer market, which represents 140 million people, must also be taken into account.

An Inevitable Shake-out. But the present boom, according to some observers, may well come to an end in 1993. It has been estimated that there are about 500 general interest magazines on the European market. A shake-out, with unhappy consequences for many magazines, cannot then be excluded. Pessimists assess the survival rate of new magazines in Europe at 10–15 per cent.

A second consequence of this massive arrival of new magazines on the market is the decline of the negotiating power with the advertisers. The practice of reductions of 30–35 per cent for advertisements appearing in several versions of the magazine is common. A secret war to attract advertisers is underway, to the considerable benefit of the latter.

On the advice of their marketing managers, or increasingly of their media-planners, many advertisers have taken refuge outside the media: in direct marketing, sales promotion in stores, fairs and exhibitions, which today represent more than 50 per cent of the total of advertising investments of companies. For the majority of advertisers it is the magazines that will be sacrificed in the case of a serious crisis. Although certain leading titles in the sector have kept their advertising portfolios, the main French news magazines lost from 20–30 per cent of advertising pages between September 1988 and September 1989.

A Tendency for Unity within Diversity. In the coming years, the process of homogenization seems likely to be considerably strengthened with the impact of the accelerated development of European media: cable television, satellites, cinema. This trend is supported both by the incorporation of states into larger units and the transformative effects of global economic and cultural flows. These flows have given rise to 'third cultures' which are transnational and mediate between national cultures; the European monetary system, European law and various European agencies and institutions are examples.

But it is true that a trend towards convergence will not erase the difference in attitude, status and lifestyles across segments. Rather, with the postmodern tendency towards individualism and tribalism, segments are fragmenting into a myriad of 'niches'. As a consequence, the idea of unity through diversity, or unity permitting differences, is becoming more acceptable today.

New Trends in Lifestyles. The 1980s marked the ideological break with the values of progress, of evolution towards a better world, of collective utopias, of the power of science. A French research institute has observed that the strong sociocultural movement towards greater individual autonomy which arose at the end of the 1960s will develop further in the coming decades and no doubt along fresh paths. Being able to control one's destiny, to act freely, to fulfil one's potential, will probably be the values on the increase at the beginning of the 21st century. The values associated with competition which characterized the previous decade are waning at the start of the 1990s and are giving way to more participative, less selfish values. The quest for more autonomy is part of the general movement of greater individual responsibility which goes hand in hand with a feeling of responsibility for the environment: ecology, solidarity, helping one another, establishing networks between people who feel concerned by specific issues.

The aestheticization of everyday life, and thus the aestheticization of consumption, are possibly the strongest characteristics of postmodern European societies. '*Everyday life is an art, as art is part of everyday life*', has become the trademark of the postmodern woman. She is free in her choices to turn each day into a work of art, and she is inspired and nourished by the massive offer of art made available by its reproduction and by the media.

Such an evolution leads to new considerations in product development: it is not the technology but the aesthetics of a product that matters. A product's technical functions should not be embellished as before, rather, its aesthetics are its main function. That the object actually does some 'useful' things—like taking us from A to B or to mash potatoes or keep us warm—is taken for granted. Technological innovation, the

---

Figure CS 2.4.3   Demographic and Lifestyle Trends for the Early Nineties

The Ageing of the Baby Boomers

Most baby boomers will be in their forties soon, not in their thirties as they were during the 1980s. (. . .) There will be fewer young adults in their twenties.

Fewer Traditional Families—More Variety

'Traditional family' has become a rarity; these are the reasons:

- Married women and mothers who work outside the house (this is the most important change in family structure).
- Later marriage age, more unmarried couples living together, big increase in divorce rate, single parent families, 'blended' families.
- More single person (non-family) households: young singles, never married, widows.

Time Pressures

Many people think they work more and have less leisure time. Time pressures are a major concern for many people, especially working women. That last group is the only one that should complain: working women who are more and more likely to be working mothers do have the least amount of free time. However, most others do not work more—still they feel that they have less leisure time.

New research suggests that increased entertainment and other leisure time options create a sense of 'so much to do, and so little time'.

(Horst Stipp, NBC Research)

hallmark of modernism, is being gradually substituted by societal innovation.

The Netherland's media researchers, Marianne de Boer and Sandra Minee, stated in June 1990 that one can no longer make useful distinctions among consumers by means of socioeconomic criteria. Lifestyle segmentation—arranging consumers according to their philosophies, way of life and/or leisure activities—falls short: the same consumer easily enacts a number of lifestyles a day.

They introduced a new measuring instrument for segmenting markets: the individualization scale. This scale has been developed by extensive desk—and qualitative research, and found to be unidimensional in a large survey amongst Dutch women of 18 years and over (details in Figure CS 2.4.4).

Empowering European Marketing of *ELLE* for the 1990s

Without a doubt, *ELLE*'s strategy of Europeanization has met with great success and the management team's satisfaction with these very positive results is all the more justified. In that state of mind, *ELLE*'s managers are entering the 1990s, but what are the prospects in the medium term? The satisfaction mentioned above does not exclude some questions concerning the future. Aestheticization and individualism are now well under way. How can the marketing of *ELLE* cope with these new societal dimensions throughout Europe?

Figure CS 2.4.4   Individualization and Women in the Nineties

In this study, five women-types were distinguished depending on the extent to which they had a positive attitude towards individualization, i.e. the extent to which they experienced independent choices:

- **The Pioneer.** One-quarter of all Dutch women are pioneers. A woman with a lot of opportunities, and many aspirations, but who carries with the freedom to choose also the responsibility to make the right decisions. Her consumer behaviour is: little loyalty to brands and very innovative. She reads most: various daily newspapers, opinion papers and lifestyle magazines.
- **The Supporter.** 11 per cent of Dutch women are supporters. She holds a positive attitude towards individualization, but does not—or no longer—bring her behaviour in line with her ideas. She reads several magazines and daily newspapers.
- **The In-between.** 21 per cent of the women relate strongly to their partner and family as a base from which they undertake outside activities. Very often she will have a part-time job, reads the women's weeklies and special interest magazines. Her consumer behaviour is: average loyalty to brands and average innovation.
- **The Counterpart.** 17 per cent of Dutch women represent the counterpart. She is a conservative woman, who would sooner reject changes than applaud them. She holds a negative attitude towards individualization and thinks in terms of the traditional role pattern. She reads glossy magazines and right-wing oriented papers.
- **The Traditional.** Over a quarter of Dutch women reject individualization. With regard to her consumer behaviour, she does not go in for new products. She reads gossip magazines and likes watching television.

Source: Marianne de Boer and Sandra Minee, *Marketing and Research Today*, June 1990.

CASES

3

Assessing International Market Opportunities

CASE 3.1
AGT, Inc.

AGT, Inc., is a marketing research company. Located in the city of Karachi, Pakistan. Jeff Sons Trading Company (JST) has approached it to look at the potential market for an amusement park in Karachi. As the city is very crowded and real estate costs are very high, it will be difficult to find a large enough piece of land to locate such a facility. Even if there is land available it will be very expensive, and that will have a detrimental effect on the overall costs of the project. JST wants to know the potential of this type of investment. They want the market research to identify if a need for the amusement park exists and, if so, what the public's attitude is towards that type of recreational facility. If a need is found and support is sufficient, then they want to know what type of an amusement park is required by the potential customers. JST will make its investment decision based on the results of this study.

Background

Pakistan qualifies as a less-developed country (LDC). It is a typical developing country of the Third World, faced with the usual problems of rapidly increasing population, sizeable government deficit, and heavy dependence on foreign aid. The economy of Pakistan has grown rapidly in the last decade, with GDP expanding at 6.7 per cent annually, more than twice the population growth. Like any other LDC, it has dualism in its economic system. For example, the cities have all the facilities of modern times, whereas smaller towns have some or none. Such is also true for income distribution patterns. Real per capita GDP is Rupees 10 000, or $400, annually. There is a small wealthy class (1 to 3 per cent), a middle class consisting of another 20 per cent, while the remainder of the population is poor. Half of the population lives below the poverty line. Most of the middle class is an urban working class. Only 24 per cent of the population is literate.

Karachi, the largest city with a very dense population of over six million, has been chosen for the first large-scale amusement park in Pakistan. The recreational facilities in Karachi are very small, including a poorly maintained zoo, and people with families avoid visiting most facilities due to the crowds. There are other small parks, but not enough to cater for such

This case was prepared by Professor William J. Carner, The University of Texas at Austin. Copyright © 1993 by William J. Carner, Ph.D. All rights reserved.

a large population. The main place people go for recreation is the beach. The beaches are not well developed and are regularly polluted by oil slicks from the nearby port. There seems to be a growing need for recreational activity for people to spend their leisure time. It is also true that many of the people in the higher social classes take holidays with their families and spend money on recreational activities abroad. To see that there is a true need for this type of recreational facility, we propose to conduct a marketing research study of its feasibility. Other potential problems facing the project include:

- Communication system is very poor.
- Only a small percentage of the people own their own transportation.
- Public and private systems of transportation are not efficient.
- Law and order is a problem.

Research Objectives

In order to make an investment decision, JST outlined its research objectives necessary to design a marketing strategy that would accomplish the desired return-on-investment goals. These objectives are as follows:

1. Identify the potential demand for this project.
2. Identify the primary target market and what they expect in an amusement area.

Information Needs

To fulfil our objectives, we will need the following information:

Market

1. Is there a need for this project in this market?
2. How large is the potential market?
3. Is this market sufficient to be profitable?

Consumer

1. Are the potential customers satisfied with the existing facilities in the city?
2. Will these potential consumers utilize an amusement park?
3. Which segment of population is most interested in this type of facility?
4. Is the population ready to support this type of project?
5. What media could be used to get the message across successfully to the potential customers?

Location

1. Where should this project be built to attract the most visitors?
2. How will the consumer's existing attitudes on location influence the viability and cost of this project?
3. Will the company have to arrange for transportation to and from the facility if location is outside the city area?
4. Is security a factor in location of the facility?

Recreation Facilities

1. What type of attractions should the company provide at the park to attract customers?
2. Should there be some overnight facility within the park?
3. Should the facility be available only to certain segments of the population or be open to all?

Proposal

With the objectives outlined above in mind, AGT, Inc. presented the following proposal:

The city of Karachi's population has its different economic clusters scattered haphazardly throughout the city. To conduct the marketing research in this type of city and get accurate results will be very difficult. We recommend an extensive study to make sure we have an adequate sampling of the opinion of the target market. Given the parameters above, we recommend that the target market be defined as follows:

Desired Respondent Characteristics

- Upper class—1 per cent (around 60 000).
- Middle class—15 to 20 per cent (around 900 000 to 1 200 000).
- Male and female.
- Age: 15 to 50 years (for survey, market includes all age groups).
- Income level: Rs 25 000 and above per year (Rs 2000 per month).
- Household size—with family will be better for sample.
- Involved in entertainment activities.
- Involved in recreational activities.
- Actively participates in social activities.
- Members of different clubs.
- Involved in outdoor activities.

To obtain accurate information regarding respondent's characteristics, we have to approach the market very carefully because of the prevailing circumstances and existing cultural practices (the country is 97 per cent Muslim). People have little or no knowledge of market surveys. Getting their cooperation, even without the cultural barriers, through a phone or mail survey will be very difficult. In the following paragraphs we will discuss negative and positive points of all types of surveys and select the appropriate form for our study.

The first, and possibly best, method to conduct the survey under these circumstances will be through the mail, which will not only be cheaper but can also cover all the clusters of population easily. We cannot rely totally on a mail survey, as the mail system in Pakistan is unreliable and inefficient. We can go through courier services or registered mail, but it will skyrocket the cost. It will not be wise to conduct a mail survey alone.

The other option is to conduct the survey by telephone. In the city of six million, there are around 200 000 working telephones. Most of the telephones are in businesses or in government offices; there is 1 home telephone per 152 persons. It is not that the people cannot afford a telephone, but that they cannot get one because of short supply. Another problem with a telephone survey is cultural; it is not considered polite to call someone and start asking questions. It is even more of a problem if a male survey member were to reach a female household member. People are not familiar with marketing surveys and would not be willing to volunteer the information we require on the telephone. The positive point in a telephone survey is that most of the upper-class women do not work and can be reached easily. However, we must use a female survey staff. Overall, the chances of cooperation through a telephone survey are very low.

A mall/bazaar intercept could also be used. Again, however, we will face some cultural problems. It's not considered ethical for a male to approach a female in the mall. The only people willing to talk in public are likely to be the males, and we will miss female opinion.

To gather respondent data by survey in a country such as Pakistan, we will have to tailor our existing data collecting methods and make them fit accordingly to the circumstances and cultural practices of the marketplace. As a company based in Pakistan with the experience of living under these cultural practices, we propose the following design for the study and questionnaire.

Design of the Study.   Our study's design will be such that it will have a mixture of three types of surveys. Each survey will focus on a different method. The following are the types of surveys we recommend, tailored to fit in the prevailing circumstances:

1. Mail Survey.   We plan to modify this type of survey to fit into existing circumstances and to be more efficient. The changes made are to counter the inefficient postal system and to generate a better percentage of response. We plan to deliver the surveys to the respondents through the newspapermen. We know that average circulations of the various newspapers are 50 000 to 200 000 per day. The two dailies chosen have the largest circulations in the city.

A questionnaire will be placed in each newspaper and delivered to the respondent. This will assure that the questionnaire has reached its destination. This questionnaire will introduce us to the respondent and ask for his cooperation. The questionnaire will have return postage and the firm's address. This will give the respondents some confidence that they are not volunteering information to someone unknown. A small promotional gift will be promised on returning the completed survey. Since respondents who will claim the gift will give us their address, this will help us maintain a list of respondents for future surveys. Delivery through newspapermen will also allow us to easily focus on specific clusters.

We expect some loss in return mail because there is no acceptable way to get the questionnaires back except through the government postal system. The cost of this survey will be less than it would be if we mailed the questionnaires. As this will be the first exposure for many respondents which allows them to give their views about a nonexisting product, we do not have any return percentage on which to base our survey response expectations. In fact, this may well be the base for future studies.

2. Door-to-Door Interviews.   We will have to tailor the mall/bazaar intercept, as we did in the mail survey, to get the highest possible response percentage. Instead of intercepting at malls, it will be better to send surveyors from door to door. This can generate a better percentage of responses and we can be sure who the respondent is. To conduct this survey, we will solicit the cooperation of the local business schools. By using these young students, we stand a better chance of generating a higher response. Also, we plan to hire some additional personnel, mostly females, and train them to conduct this survey.

3. Additional Mail Survey.   We are planning to conduct this part of the survey to identify different groups of people already involved in similar types of activity. There are 8 to 10 exclusive clubs in the city of Karachi. A few of them focus solely on some outdoor activity such as yachting and boating, golf, etc. Their membership numbers vary from 3000 to 5000. High membership cost and monthly fees have made these clubs restricted to the upper-middle class and the wealthy. We can safely say that the people using these clubs belong to the 90th percentile of income level. We propose to visit these clubs and personally ask for the members' cooperation. We also plan to get the member list and have the questionnaire delivered to them. They will be asked to return the completed questionnaire to the club office or to mail it in the postage-paid reply envelope. We believe that this group will cooperate and give us a quality feedback.

The second delivered survey will be to local schools. With the schools' cooperation, we will ask that this questionnaire be delivered by their pupils to the parents. The cover letter will request that the parents fill out the questionnaire and return it to school. This will provide a good sample of people who want outdoor activities for their children. We hope to generate a substantial response through this method.

Questionnaire Design.   The types of questions asked should help our client make the decision of whether to invest in the project. Through the survey questionnaires, we should answer the question, 'Is the population ready for this project and are they willing to support it?' The questionnaire will be a mixture of both open-ended and closed-ended questions. It will be designed to answer the following questions:

- Is there a market for this type of project?
- Is the market substantial?
- Is the market profitable?
- Will this project fill a real need?
- Will this project be only a momentary fad?
- Is the market evenly distributed in all segments/clusters or is there a high demand in some segments?
- Is the population geared towards and willing to spend money on this type of entertainment facility? If so, how much?
- What is the best location for this project?
- Are people willing to travel some distance to reach this type of facility? Or do they want it within city limits?
- What types of entertainment/rides do people want to see in this amusement park?
- Through what type of media or promotion can the prospective customers best be reached?

Figure CS 3.1.1   Questionnaire

Please tick the appropriate box. Thank you.

1. Are there adequate recreational facilities in the city?

   Yes ☐   No ☐

2. How satisfied are you with the present recreational facilities?
   (Please rate at 0 to 10 degree)

   0—1—2—3—4—5—6—9—8—9—10
   Poor   Excellent

3. How often do you visit the present recreational facilities? (Please tick)

   Weekly ☐
   Fortnightly ☐
   Monthly ☐
   Once in two months ☐
   Yearly ☐
   More (indicate number) ☐
   Not at all ☐

4. Do you visit recreational areas with your family?

   Yes ☐   No ☐

   If no . . . why?

   Security ☐
   Distance ☐
   Expense ☐
   Crowd (not family type) ☐
   Poor service ☐
   Other (please specify) _____
   _____

4. a. Do you stay overnight?

   Yes ☐   No ☐

   If yes, how long? _____
   (Please indicate number of days)

4. b. If no; would you have stayed if provided the right circumstances or facilities?

   Yes ☐   No ☐

5. Have you ever visited an amusement park?
   (Here in Pakistan ☐   Abroad ☐)

   Yes ☐ (Please go to question 5b)
   No ☐ (Please go to question 5a)

5. a. If no . . . why?

   Security ☐
   Distance ☐
   Expense ☐
   Crowd (not family type) ☐
   Poor service ☐
   Other (please specify) _____
   _____

5. b. If yes . . . When did you last visit an amusement park?

   Last month ☐
   Last six months ☐
   Within a year ☐
   Poor service ☐

   Where? _____

6. What did you enjoy most in that park?

   Roller coasters ☐
   Water slides ☐
   Children's play areas ☐
   Shows ☐
   Games ☐
   Simulators ☐
   Other _____

6. a. How much did you spend in that park?
   (approximately)

   Rs. 50 or less ☐
   51 to 100 ☐
   101 to 150 ☐
   151 to 200 ☐
   More than 200 ☐

   Where? _____

6. b. How would you rate the value received?
   (Please rate at 0–10 degree)

   0—1—2—3—4—5—6—7—8—9—10
   Poor   Excellent

7. Would you utilize an amusement park if one was built locally?

   Yes ☐   No ☐

8. What would you like to see in an amusement park? (Please give us your six best choices)

a _____   b _____
c _____   d _____
e _____   f _____

9. Where would you like its location to be?

Within city area   ☐
Beach area   ☐
Suburbs   ☐
Outskirts of city   ☐
Indifferent   ☐

10. How many kilometres will you be willing to travel to the park?

Under 10 km   ☐
11 to 20   ☐
21 to 35   ☐
35 to 55   ☐
55 to 65   ☐
More than 65   ☐

11. How often do you take vacations for recreation purposes?

None   ☐
Once a year   ☐
Twice a year   ☐
More (please specify) _____

Please Tell Us About Yourself:

12. Please indicate your age.

Under 15 years   ☐
16 to 21   ☐
22 to 29   ☐
30 to 49   ☐
50 to 60   ☐
Over 60   ☐

13. Please indicate your gender.

Male   ☐   Female   ☐

14. Are you married?

Yes   ☐   No   ☐

15. How many children do you have?

Please indicate number _____

16 Please indicate your total family income (yearly).

Under 12 000   ☐
Over 12 000 to 15 000   ☐
Over 15 000 to 20 000   ☐
Over 20 000 to 25 000   ☐
Over 25 000 to 40 000   ☐
Over 40 000 to 60 000   ☐
Over 60 000 to 80 000   ☐
Over 80 000   ☐

17. Do you own a transport?

Yes   ☐   No   ☐

18. Any other comments?
(If you need more space, please attach additional sheet)

_____
_____
_____
_____
_____
_____

Thank you, we appreciate your time

Important:
If you **want** us to contact you again in later stages of this project, or will be interested in its results, give us your name and address. We will be glad to keep you informed.

_____
_____
_____

Questions

1. Does the survey satisfy the objectives of the research project?
2. How do the elements of culture affect the research design, collection of data, and analysis? Contrast this with the design, collection of data and analysis of a similar survey project in the United States, Japan or Western Europe.
3. What alternative data collection methods, such as personal interviews at current recreational areas, might be acceptable?

CASE 3.2
Swifter, Higher, Stronger, Dearer*

Television and Sport are Perfect Partners. Each Has Made the other Richer. But Is The Alliance Really So Good for Sport?

Back in 1948, the BBC, Britain's public broadcasting corporation, took a fateful decision. It paid a princely £15 000 (£27 000 in today's money) for the right to telecast the Olympic Games to a domestic audience. It was the first time a television network had paid the International Olympic Committee (IOC, the body that runs the Games) for the privilege.

But not the last. The rights to the Olympics, which opened in Atlanta on 19 July 1996, raised $900 million from broadcasters round the world. And the American television rights to the Olympiads up to and including 2008 have been bought by America's NBC network for an amazing $3.6 billion (see Figure CS 3.2.1).

The Olympics are only one of the sporting properties that have become hugely valuable to broadcasters. Sport takes up a growing share of screen time (as those who are bored by it know all too well). When you consider the popularity of the world's great tournaments, that is hardly surprising. *Sportsfests* generate audiences

beyond the wildest dreams of television companies for anything else. According to Nielsen Media Research, the number of Americans watching the 1996 Super Bowl, the main annual football championship, averaged 94 million. The top eight television programmes in America are all sporting events (see Table CS 3.2.1). A staggering 3½ billion people are likely to watch some part of the 1996 Olympiad—two-thirds of mankind.

Table CS 3.2.1   Sport First

Top 10 TV Programmes in America, September 1995–July 1996, %*

Super Bowl	46.0
Super Bowl Kickoff	35.5
Super Bowl Post	35.0
NFC Championship	33.3
AFC Championship	27.1
NCF Playoff—Sunday	25.4
AFC Championship—Sunday	25.4
NFC Playoff—Saturday	22.2
ER	22.0
Seinfeld	21.2

*% of American households tuning into the average minute of the programme.
Source: Nielsen Media Research.

Figure CS 3.2.1   Chariots for Hire: Olympic Broadcast Rights* ($ billion)

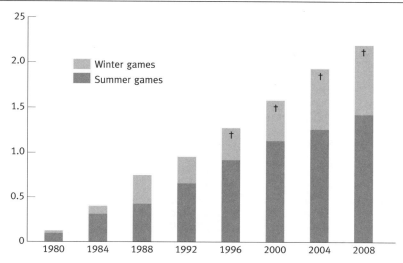

*Rights for 2000–2008 Games negotiated to March 1996.
†Two years earlier.
Source: IOC.

*From *The Economist*, 20 July 1996, pp. 17–19.

The reason television companies love sport is not merely that billions want to tele-gawk at ever-more wonderful sporting feats. Sport also has a special quality that makes it unlike almost any other sort of television programme: immediacy. Miss seeing a particular episode of, say, 'ER' and you can always catch the repeat, and enjoy it just as much. Miss seeing your team beat the hell out of its biggest rival, and the replay will leave you cold. 'A live sporting event loses almost all its value as the final whistle goes', says Steve Barnett, author of a British book on sport. The desire to watch sport when it is happening, not hours afterwards, is universal: a study of South Korea by Spectrum, a British consultancy, finds that live games get 30 per cent of the audience while recording gets less than 5 per cent.

This combination of popularity and immediacy has created a symbiotic relationship between sport and television in which each is changing the other. As Stephen Wenn, of Canada's Wilfrid Laurier University, puts it, television and the money it brings have had an enormous impact on the Olympic Games, including on the timing of events and their location. For instance, an Asian Olympics poses a problem for American networks: viewers learn the results on the morning news.

The money that television has brought into professional basketball has put some of the top players among the world's highest-paid entertainers: a few are getting multiyear contracts worth over $100 million. Rugby has begun to be reorganized to make it more television-friendly; other sports will follow. And, though soccer and American football draw the largest audiences, television has also promoted the popularity of sports which stir more local passions: rugby league in Australia, cricket in India, table tennis in China, snooker in Britain.

What is less often realized is that sport is also changing television. To assuage the hunger for sports, new channels are being launched at a tremendous pace. In America, ESPN, a cable network owned by Capital Cities/ABC, is starting a 24-hour sports news network in the autumn; in Britain, BSkyB, a satellite broadcaster partly owned by Rupert Murdoch, has two sports channels and is about to launch a third. Because people seem more willing to pay to watch sport on television than to pay for any other kind of programming, sport has become an essential part of the business strategy of television empire-builders such as Mr Murdoch. Nobody in the world understands the use of sports as a bait for viewers better than he.

In particular, sport suggests an answer to one of the big problems that will face television companies in the future: how can viewers, comfortable with their old analogue sets, be persuaded to part with the hefty price

Table CS 3.2.2 Big Deals Europe and America			
Event	*Date*	*Buyer*	*$bn*
Olympic Games	1996–2008*	NBC	4.00
World Cup soccer	2002–06	Kirch	2.36
NCA basketball	1995–2002	CBS	1.73
National Football League (NFL)	1995–98[†]	Fox	1.58
Olympic Games	1996–2008	EBU	1.44
English Premier League soccer	1997–2000[†]	BSkyB	0.96
NFL	1995–98[†]	ABC	0.92
NFL	1995–98[†]	NBC	0.87
National Basketball Association	1995–98[†]	NBC	0.75
Dutch Premier League soccer	1996–2004	Sport 7	0.65

*1998 Winter Games bought by CBS.
[†]Season ending.
Sources: *Broadcasting & Cable*; Kagan World Media.

of a new digital set and a subscription to an untried service? The answer is to create an exclusive chance to watch a desirable event, or to use the hundreds of channels that digital television provides to offer more variety of sports coverage than analogue television can offer. This ploy is not new. 'Radio broadcasts of boxing were once used to promote the sale of radios, and baseball to persuade people to buy television sets', points out Richard Burton, a sports marketing specialist at Lundquist College of Business at Oregon University. In the next few years, the main new outlet for sports programmes will be digital television.

Going for Gold

To understand how these multiple effects have come about, go back to those vast sums that television companies are willing to pay. In America, according to Neal Weinstock of Weinstock Media Analysis, total spending on sports rights by television companies is about $2 billion a year. Easily the most valuable rights are for American football. One of the biggest sporting coups in the United States was the purchase by Fox, owned by Mr Murdoch's News Corp, of the rights to four years of National Football League games for $1.6 billion, snatching them from CBS. Rights for baseball, basketball and ice hockey are also substantial (see Table CS 3.2.2.)

Americans are rare in following four main sports rather than one. America is also uncommon in having no publicly owned networks. As a result, bidding wars in other countries, though just as fierce as in America, are different in two ways: they are often fought between public broadcasters and new upstarts, many of them pay channels; and they are usually about soccer.

Nothing better illustrates the change taking place in the market for soccer rights than the vast deal struck in early July by Kirch, a German group owned by a secretive Bavarian media mogul. The group spent $2.2 billion for the world's biggest soccer-broadcasting rights: to show the finals of the World Cup in 2002 and 2006 outside America. That is over six times more than the amount paid for the rights to the World Cups of 1990, 1994 and 1998.

Such vast bids gobble up a huge slice of a television company's budget. In America, reckons London Economics, a British consultancy, sport accounts for around 15 per cent of all television-programme spending. For some television companies, the share is much larger. BSkyB spends £100 million ($155 million) a year on sports, about a third of its programming budget.

This seems to pose a threat to public broadcasting, for, in any bidding war outside America, public broadcasting companies are generally the losers. A consortium of mainly public broadcasters bought the rights to the 1990–98 World Cups for a total of $344 million. This time around, the consortium raised its bid to around $1.8 billion, and still lost. Public broadcasters often do not have the money to compete: in Britain, the BBC spends about 4 per cent of its programme budget on sport in a non-Olympic year, about £15 million a year less than BSkyB.

The problem is that the value of sport to viewers ('consumer surplus', as economists would put it) is much larger than the value of most other sorts of programming. Public broadcasters have no way to benefit from the extra value that a big sporting event offers viewers. But with subscription television and with pay-TV, where viewers are charged for each event, the television company will directly collect the value viewers put on being able to watch.

Because of this, many people (especially in Europe) worry that popular sports will increasingly be available only on subscription television, which could, they fear, erode the popular support upon which public broadcasters depend. In practice, these worries seem excessive. Although far more sport will be shown on subscription television, especially outside America's vast advertising market, the most popular events are likely to remain freely available for many years to come, for two reasons.

First, those who own the rights to sporting events are rarely just profit-maximizers: they also have an interest in keeping the appeal of their sport as broad as possible. They may therefore refuse to sell to the highest bidder. Earlier this year, the IOC turned down a $2 billion bid from Mr Murdoch's News Corp for the European broadcasting rights to the Olympic Games between 2000 and 2008 in favour of a lower bid from a group of public broadcasters. Sometimes, as with the sale of World Cup rights to Kirch, the sellers may stipulate that the games be aired on 'free' television.

Second, the economics of televising sport means that the biggest revenues are not necessarily earned by typing up exclusive rights. Steven Bornstein, the boss of ESPN, argues that exclusive deals to big events are 'not in our long-term commercial interest'. Because showing sport on 'free' television maximizes the audience, some advertisers will be willing to pay a huge premium for the big occasion. So will sponsors who want their names to be seen emblazoned on players' shirts or on billboards around the pitch.

It is not only a matter of audience size. Sport is also the most efficient way to reach one of the world's most desirable audiences from an advertiser's point of view: young men with cash to spend. Although the biggest audiences of young men are watching general television, sporting events draw the highest concentrations. So advertisers of products such as beer, cars and sports shoes can pay mainly for the people they most want to attract.

There are other ways in which sport can be indirectly useful to the networks. A slot in a summer game is a wonderful opportunity to promote a coming autumn show. A popular game wipes out the audience share of the competition. And owning the rights to an event allows a network plenty of scope to entertain corporate grandees who may then become advertisers.

For the moment, though, advertising revenue is the main recompense that television companies get for their huge investments in sport. Overall, according to *Broadcasting & Cable*, a trade magazine, sport generated $3.5 billion, or 10 per cent, of total television advertising revenues in America last year. The biggest purchasers of sports rights by far in America are the national networks. NBC alone holds more big sports rights than any other body has held in the history of television. It can, obviously, recoup some of the bill by selling advertising: for a 30-second slot during the Super Bowl, NBC asked for $1.2 million.

Such deals, however, usually benefit the networks indirectly rather than directly. The Super Bowl is a rarity: it has usually made a profit for the network that airs it. 'Apart from the Super Bowl, the World Series [for baseball] and probably the current Olympics, the big sports don't usually make money for the networks', says Arthur Gruen of Wilkowsky Gruen, a media consultancy. 'But they are a boon for their affiliate stations, which can sell their advertising slots for two or three times as much as other slots'. Although Fox lost money on its NFL purchase, it won the loyalty of affiliate stations (especially important for a new network) and made a splash.

Almost everywhere else, the biggest growth in revenues from showing sports will increasingly come from subscriptions or pay-per-view arrangements. The versatility and huge capacity of digital broadcasting make it possible to give subscribers all sorts of new and lucrative services.

In America, DirectTV and Primestar, two digital satellite broadcasters, have been tempting subscribers with packages of sporting events from distant parts of the country. 'They have been creating season tickets for all the main events, costing $100–150 per season per sport', says John Mansell, a senior analyst with Paul Kagan, a Californian consultancy. In Germany DF1, a satellite company jointly owned by Kirch and BSkyB and due for launch at the end of July, has the rights to show Formula One motor racing. It plans to allow viewers to choose to follow particular teams, so that Ferrari fanatics can follow their drivers, and to select different camera angles.

In Italy, Telepiu, which launched digital satellite television in February, plans to offer viewers a package in September which will allow them to buy a season ticket to live matches played by one or more teams in the top Italian soccer leagues. The system's 'electronic turnstile' is so sophisticated that it can shut off reception for subscribers living in the catchment area for a home game, to assuage clubs' worries that they will lose revenue from supporters at the gate. In fact, top Italian clubs usually have to lock out their fanatical subscribers to avoid overcapacity.

Most skilful of all at using sports rights to generate subscription revenue is BSkyB. It signed an exclusive contract with the English Premier League which has been the foundation of its success. Some of those who know BSkyB well argue that £5 billion of the business's remarkable capital value of £8 billion is attributable to the profitability of its soccer rights.

Winner Take All

Just as the purchase of sporting rights enriches television companies, so their sale has transformed the finances of the sports lucky enough to be popular with viewers. On the whole, the biggest beneficiaries have not been the clubs and bodies that run sports, but the players. In the same way as rising revenues from films are promptly dissipated in vast salaries to stars in Hollywood, in sport the money coming in from television soon flows out in heftier payments to players.

In America, the market for sportsmen is well developed and the cost of players tends to rise with the total revenues of the main sporting organizations (see Figure CS 3.2.2). Elsewhere, the market is newer and so a bigger slice of the revenues tend to stick to the television companies. 'The big difference between sports and movies is the operating margins', says Chris Akers, chairman of Caspian, a British media group, and an old hand at rights negotiations. 'Hollywood majors have per-subscriber deals. No sports federation has yet done such a deal'.

Guided by the likes of Mr Akers, they soon will. Telepiu's latest three-year soccer contract gives the television firm enough revenue to cover its basic costs, guarantees the soccer league a minimum sum and then splits the takings down the middle. In Britain, BSkyB is locked in dispute with the Premier League over the terms of the second half of its rights deal: should the league then be able to opt for half the revenue from each subscriber on top of or instead of a fixed hunk of net profits?

The logical next step would be for some clubs or leagues to set up their own pay-television systems, distributing their games directly by satellite or cable. A few people in British soccer are starting to look with interest at America's local sports networks, such as the successful Madison Square Garden cable network, and to wonder whether Europe might move the same way.

If it does, not all teams will benefit equally. In America, football has an elaborate scheme to spread revenues from national television across teams. But in other sports, including baseball, the wealth and size of a team's local market mean large differences in rights from local television. The New York Yankees make almost $50 million a year from local television rights, says Brian Schechter, a Canadian media analyst. At the other end of the scale, the Kansas City Royals, make $4 million–5 million a year.

Not all players benefit equally, either. Television has brought to sport the 'winner-take-all' phenomenon. It does not cost substantially more to stage a televised championship game than a run-of-the-week, untelevised match. But the size of the audience, and therefore the revenue generated, may be hugely different. As a result, players good enough to be in the top games will earn vastly more than those slightly less good, who play to smaller crowds.

A Referee's Whistle

The lure of money is already altering sport and will change it more. Increasingly, games will be reorganized to turn them into better television. British rugby-union officials are squabbling over the spoils from television rights. Rugby league, whose audiences have been dwindling, won a contract worth £87 million over five years from BSkyB this year in exchange for

Figure CS 3.2.2   To the Winner the Spoils: National Football League ($ billion)

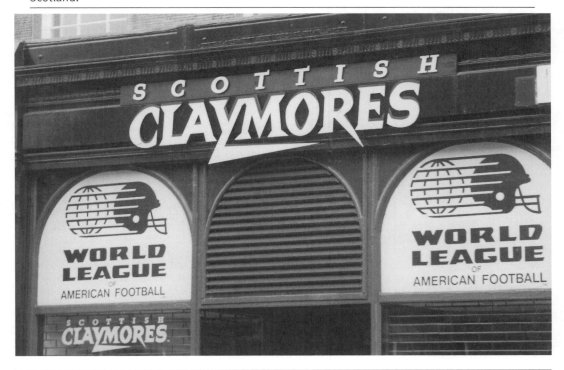

Source: Sports Value.

Figure CS 3.2.3   World Football League Scottish Claymore's Headquarters in Edinburgh, Scotland.

switching its games from winter to summer. Purists were aghast.

Other reorganizations for the benefit of television will surely come. Mr Murdoch wants to build a rugby superleague, allowing the best teams around the world to play each other. A European superleague for soccer is possible. 'At the moment, Manchester United plays AC Milan every 25 years: it's a joke', complains one enthusiast.

Sports traditionalists resist changing their ways for the likes of Mr Murdoch. So far, the big sporting bodies have generally held out against selling exclusive pay-television rights to their crown jewels, and have sometimes deliberately favoured public broadcasters. Regulators have helped them, intervening in some countries to limit exclusive deals with pay-television groups. Britain has just passed a law to stop subscription channels tying up exclusive rights to some big events, such as the Wimbledon tennis championship. In Australia in March, a court threw out News Corp's attempt to build a rugby superleague as the lynchpin of its pay-television strategy.

But the real monopolists are not the media companies, but the teams. Television companies can play off seven or eight Hollywood studios against each other. But most countries have only one national soccer league, and a public that loves soccer above all other sports. In the long run, the players and clubs hold most of the cards. The television companies are more likely to be their servants than their masters.

Questions

1. The following are the prices paid for the American television broadcasting rights of the summer Olympics since 1980:[1] Moscow—NBC agreed to pay $85 million; 1984 in Los Angeles—ABC paid $225 million; 1988 in Seoul—NBC paid $300 million; 1992 in Barcelona—NBC paid $402 million; 1996 to 2008—NBC will pay $3.6 billion. You have been charged with the responsibility of determining the IOC and local Olympic Committee's asking prices for the 2004 television broadcast rights to five different markets: Japan, China, Australia, the European Union and Brazil. Determine a price for each and justify your decisions.

2. Your instructor may assign you to represent either the IOC or any one of the television networks in each of the five countries that have been asked to bid for the broadcast rights for the 2004 Games. Prepare to negotiate prices and other organizational details.

3. The World Football League (WFL), a joint venture between the National Football League (NFL) and Fox Television (owned by Rupert Murdoch's News Corp), has offered you the Edinburgh, Scotland, Claymores franchise. Your Scottish Claymores, should you choose to invest, will be playing against the five WFL teams from London, Barcelona, Amsterdam, Frankfurt and Dusseldorf. What would you be willing to pay for the Claymores? The interested investor will note that a previous incarnation of the WRL with three teams in Europe and seven in the United States folded in its second season in 1992 having lost $50 million.[2]

References

1. See Roy J. Lewicki, Joseph A. Litterer, David M. Saunders, and John W. Minton, *Negotiation: Readings, Exercises and Cases*, 2nd edn (Burr Ridge, IL: Irwin, 1993); and John L. Graham and Yoshihiro Sano, *Smart Bargaining: Doing Business with the Japanese*, 2nd edn (New York: Harper-Collins, 1989), for details regarding the negotiations.

2. Roger Thurow and A. Craig Copetas, 'NFL Goes Long in Its Attempt to Sell World League in Europe', *The Wall Street Journal*, 28 March 1997, p. B-7.

CASE 3.3
Is Europe the Land of Wheat and Honey?

In the early 1990s, two food giants Nestlé and General Mills decided to form a joint venture for the purpose of expanding into the European breakfast cereal market. Initially, each company contributed around $80 million to the partnership. The first markets to be entered were France, Spain and Portugal. In 1992, European sales of breakfast cereals amounted to around $3 billion with almost half of that consumed in the United Kingdom. For example, the average Briton consumes almost 6 kg of cereal per year compared to 44 g in France. The second and third most important markets, both in terms of market size and market growth, are Germany and France. Estimates are that by the year 2000 European breakfast cereal sales would be round $6.5 billion.

The joint venture is called Cereal Partners (CP) and is set to enter France, Spain and Portugal with two General Mills products, namely Golden Grahams and Honey Nut Cheerios. CP decided to go with the Honey Nut version, rather than the plain Cheerios because of the belief that Europeans prefer a sweeter taste and that there is less awareness of health or nutrition. A third product to be offered by CP is a reformulated version of a Nestlé chocolate-flavoured cereal called Chocopic aimed mainly at children. Golden Grahams and Honey Nut Cheerios will be marketed as all-family foods.

Golden Grahams and Honey Nut Cheerios will initially be made by General Mills in the United States and shipped in bulk to Europe for packaging by Nestlé in France. CP wanted to expand quickly in Europe and to retool plants would have been time consuming. France, Spain and Portugal were selected as the first target markets because Nestlé already sells there and has a distribution network in place. Nestlé has a 35 per cent market share in Portugal and a 10 per cent share in France and Spain.

Branding is in line with the single European Market with similar brand names throughout Europe under the Nestlé umbrella label. Only the packaging will printed in the local language. Television advertising is the selected medium to reach consumers. These will not be dubbed-over US commercials, but ads specifically developed for Europe.

By the year 2000, Cereal Partners hopes to reach its goal of $1 billion in sales in Europe.

This case is contributed by Charles Pahud de Mortanges, Maastricht University, Netherlands.

Questions

1. How would you evaluate CP's entry strategy and selection of target markets?
2. Discuss the pros and cons of CP's strategy in terms of products, distribution and promotion.
3. Do you think that CP will reach its goal by the year 2000? Why, or why not?

Further Reading

R. Gibson, 'Is Europe Land of Wheat and Honey?' *The Wall Street Journal Europe*, 17 November 1990, p.6.

R. Lynch, *Cases in European Marketing* (London: Kogan Page, 1993) pp. 60–67.

C. Knowlton, 'Europe Cooks Up a Cereal Brawl', *Fortune*, June 3 1991, p. 61.

CASE 3.4
Hiilipeikko Oy: Market Selection by a Small Firm

In May 1996, Oili Sassi, marketing manager for Hiilipeikko Oy, Finland, was trying to decide how the company should penetrate foreign markets. Hiilipeikko Oy was a small company selling and manufacturing charcoal for barbecues. The company was established in August 1994 and it employed six people; one was mainly responsible for production management, one for marketing and the others worked on different production tasks. During the first accounting period the turnover of Hiilipeikko Oy was approximately FIM500 000.

The product—Peikkohiili—was innovative but expensive compared with its competitors, and, to the company's disadvantage, definitely a seasonal product. The innovativeness of the product was based on the fact that this charcoal ignited without any lighter fluid. The product was packaged in a paper sack—available in two sizes—which acted as the fire lighter. One advantage of Peikkohiili was also its 'greenness'; the package was burnt together with the charcoal leaving no rubbish. Additionally, it was made from pure Finnish hardwood and contained no artificial ingredients. However, manufacturing charcoal is relatively labour intensive and thus the manufacturing costs of the product in Finland were quite high.

In Finland—as well as in Western Europe in general—the barbecue charcoal market was dominated by the large buyers, mainly wholesalers. However, in Finland, because the wholesalers were not yet interested in Peikkohiili, it was mainly sold through retail chains as well as through hardware store chains. Occasionally, the product was also sold directly to some petrol stations and in the summer of 1995 Hiilipeikko started cooperating with Neste-marketing, the latter being responsible for the procurement of goods for a large petrol station chain.

However, Hiilipeikko was not quite able to convince the large Finnish wholesalers of the product's advantages. Price seemed to be the only important factor in their decision-making, although Oili Sassi did try to emphasize other arguments in favour of their product, e.g. it is of high quality, environmentally friendly, easy to use and made in Finland. These arguments, nevertheless, failed to persuade most of the buyers for large wholesalers. The competitors—mainly imported charcoal, half of which came from the former

Soviet Union, the other half mostly from South America, Africa and Far East—could be offered at a significantly lower price.

Because of the lack of interest, the domestic market was not sufficient to sustain Hiilipeikko Oy. However, Oili Sassi thought that with some effort the company could expand into foreign markets. So far efforts to do so had been more or less 'hit or miss', but a more focused strategy was planned for the future, mainly due to limited financial resources. The main sales season for the wholesalers in Finland and in other European countries begins in August. Oili Sassi knew that she had to decide on which markets to focus well before that.

Alternative markets

Sweden.   Sweden was the first market Oili Sassi started with. First, she began with the same approach as in Finland: contacting the buyers for the large wholesalers. On the basis of these contacts, she widened her contact network to other potential customers and professional magazines. The result was the same as in Finland; no particular interest. The price of the product was too high. In the spring 1995, Hiilipeikko participated in a trade fair in Stockholm. A number of new contacts were established, but that was all. Oili Sassi continued looking for new contacts through telephone directories, professional registers, etc. A few of the contacts were also based on a customer survey, which was included in the trade fair participation fee. In spring 1996, Hiilipeikko participated in the trade fair in Stockholm for the second time, this time with more promising results. Oili Sassi came home with the contact addresses of five potential agents and during the following month she received several phone calls, all with the same message: 'You have a very interesting product, which suits the Swedish market very well. We would like to represent you here in Sweden.'

Norway.   In contrast to Sweden, Hiilipeikko Oy had delivered its first export orders to Norway already in the summer of 1995. A Finnish salesman, who was selling other Finnish products in the Stavanger area, agreed to represent the Peikkohiili during the summer season of 1995. Through his contacts, Oili Sassi found an agent who ordered a few thousand packages of Peikkohiili. However, in the spring of 1996, Oili Sassi decided not to offer their product to this agent because of the agent's difficulties in paying for the goods in the previous year.

Denmark.   In the Danish market Hiilipeikko Oy used the services of the commercial secretaries in the Finnish Export Centre in Copenhagen. They did market research on the potential Danish market for Hiilipeikko's product. The results showed that Danish consumers were very alert to environmental issues and very interested in outdoor activities in their leisure time. In Oili Sassi's opinion, the Danish market looked very promising. She also established some contacts, and during a short visit to Copenhagen she met two candidates for agency and one buyer for a wholesaler chain. Both agents were interested in the product and ordered a small amount of it for test marketing during the following summer. However, one candidate seemed to be too small, and its experience in the charcoal business was limited to packaging barbecue charcoal. The other one seemed more suitable for Hiilipeikko's purposes. The buyer for the wholesaler also had a very positive attitude towards the company and its product. His attitude was based both on recommendations of Finnish retailer, Prisma, which also was a Hiilipeikko customer and the marketing efforts of Oili Sassi.

Germany.   In the German market Hiilipeikko Oy marketed itself jointly with Tefal, a Finnish grill manufacturer. In 1995, Tefal marketed its grills in Germany and each grill sold included a package of Peikkohiili and a brochure with more information of the product. Nevertheless, as a result of a rationalization process, Tefal sold its grill manufacturing unit to another company, Opa. Opa was interested in cooperating with Hiilipeikko Oy but mainly in the Finnish market. They were not interested in the German market. Together with other Finnish SMEs interested in German market, Hiilipeikko commissioned a survey on Baumarkt, the largest hardware store chain in Germany. The results of the survey will be available in the near future.

Others.   Based both on articles in several professional journals and an advertisement in the Directory of Finnish Exporters, several unsolicited contacts had been established. Oili Sassi had already met a Finnish businessman living in Switzerland who marketed their product there and a Japanese businessman who was interested in representing their product in Japan. Some enquiries also came from Russian firms, of which the most significant was Habitek, a company importing American grills to Russia. Because of the lack of good charcoal in Russia, Habitek was interested in cooperating with Hiilipeikko. This cooperation would probably be very similar to that with Tefal. However, the Finnish manager of their office in St Petersburg was fired and the new Russian manager did not seem to be as interested in cooperating as his predecessor. Other contacts to which Oili Sassi sent an offer and free samples of the product came from Austria, the United Kingdom, France and Kuwait.

CASE 3.5
Shanghai Volkswagen Corp

'When you see a Santana car running behind you, you had better make way for it, for it is certain to outrun you.' The government news agency quoted this unidentified Shanghai driver's views in early 1985 on the 'Shanghai Santana', which was the admirable product made by the Shanghai Volkswagen Corp. The driver's words did not only point to the car itself, but also predicted that the Shanghai Volkswagen Corp was going to have great success in the potentially huge Chinese car market.

Recently, there have been almost no car makers who have not turned their eyes to the Chinese car market. They are all hoping to get China in gear. They have exerted their efforts. Some of them have found a way while others have got frustrated. Volkswagen AG, Germany's biggest car maker, has finally pulled off the China deal every big motor manufacturer has lusted for. It was the most successful winner among all foreign competitors. In both 1990 and 1991, the Shanghai VW Corp, the joint venture between Volkswagen and China, consecutively stood at no. 1 on the list of Top Ten Joint Ventures in China. The appraisals were jointly sponsored by the *Economic Daily* of China and *China Industrial and Commercial Times,* and the appraisal process included the following indexes: ratio between investment and profit; per-capita profit; labour productivity; accumulative rate of depreciation; per-capita investment; balance of foreign currency; ratio between cost and output value; export rate; and ratio between R&D input and total sales income.[1] Its success story inspired people's interests: Why did this company have such significant success? How is it possible?

Company Background

The Shanghai Volkswagen Corp agreement was signed on 10 October 1984 by the Volkswagen AG and the People's Republic of China in the Great Hall of the People, which is the most noble place in the hearts of the Chinese people, in Beijing. West German Chancellor Helmut Kohl was present for the signing and for the laying of cornerstone on the 50-acre site in a suburb of Shanghai a short time later. The former vice premier Li Peng also appeared at the cornerstone ceremony. It is the first passenger-car manufacturing agreement of its kind with mainland China for foreign

This case was prepared by Hang Li, Theodore F. Smith and C.P. Rao, College of Business & Public Administration, Old Dominion University, Norfolk, VA.

car makers. One Chinese official told the XinHua News Agency that the VW deal represented a '40-year leap forward' for China.

Under the deal, an initial investment of $165 million was spent for the first stages of the ambitious undertaking. The joint company, to be known as Shanghai Volkswagen Automobile Co. Ltd, was established in March 1985, and was initially set to run for 25 years. Volkswagen AG holds a 50 per cent share in the venture. Shanghai Tractor & Automobile Co. has 25 per cent, Shanghai Trust and Consultancy, a subsidiary of the Bank of China, 15 per cent and China National Automobile Industry Corp. the remaining 10 per cent. The company's capital stock was about $67 million.

While the original production target was 20 000 VW Santanas (US Quantum), in the agreement the plant's nominal capacity was 30 000 units annually. Actually, it produced 10 000 cars in 1987 and reached 35 000 units in 1991. The original purchasers were Chinese authorities and taxi companies. Along with increased income for Chinese people, private individuals emerged as new buyers. Domestic consumption had first priority, but the company actually exported some products recently. The daily production of the company increased from 17 cars in 1985 to 100 in 1991. Only 13 per cent of the value of the cars were made in China in 1987, but it included 60 per cent local content in 1991.[2,3]

There is equal Chinese and German representation on the 10-person board of directors, with a Chinese representative as chairman. A four person management committee runs the business activities. They report to the board of directors. China nominates the managing director and head of personnel, and VW supplies the commercial and financial directors for the committee.[4] In 1988, there were 2300 employees in this company. The German technicians are running training schools for the Chinese workers in all aspects of assembly work. The overall cost of labour for Shanghai Volkswagen is far below that paid in Germany or other Volkswagen locations.

The company was established on the site of the former Shanghai Car Factory, which stood in the rice fields 20 miles southwest of Shanghai, China's leading industrial city. The hallways in the office building are clean and bright, in sharp contrast to the ill-lit interiors and clutter of many other Chinese factories. Neat signs are tacked on every office door, identifying the German and Chinese who work inside. There is an air of efficiency and a bustle not usually found in other factories of this country.

For a long time, China depended heavily on imports from Japan. The Chinese government even signed a contract in 1983 with the Japanese to import

250 000 Japanese vehicles. In reality, Japan's exports to China soared from 10 800 in 1983 to nearly 85 000 in 1984. In January and February 1985, Japanese shipments increased by 58 per cent. Since Shanghai Volkswagen was founded, its managers had enthusiasm about the eventual goal to cut China's dependence on Japan, and about Volkswagen's new Asian base, from which it can challenge Japanese car makers in Asia in the coming decade. For Volkswagen, this company is a symbol of the third foothold in three important and—for outsiders—difficult markets. Nissan was putting together up to 60 000 Santanas a year in Japan, and Seat in Spain began assembling four Volkswagen models, reaching 120 000 units a year in 1985.

The company is equipped with internationally advanced technology and facilities. Its engine factory, *painting* workshop and assembly workshop are up to the advanced international standards of the 1980s. Four production lines concentrate on the assembly of Santana CKD parts shipped from Germany.

The Germans offer the most expert technical and financial help for this project, which could cost as much as $1 billion over the 1990s. They dispatch a lot of experts to Shanghai to help the Chinese to modernize and expand the antiquated, existing plant. The latter supply as much cheap labour as needed. The profits of the company are equally shared. Li Jian, the manager of the government-owned Shanghai Automotive Industry Corp, one of Volkswagen's three Chinese partners, was quoted in the Chinese press as predicting a profit of US$154 million in 1991.

Environmental Review

Business people around the world have been well aware of the huge potential market for consumer goods that the 1.2 billion freshly materialistic citizens in China present. But only recently have the world's car makers begun to pay attention to China's appetite for cars. There are too many car plants making too few cars. Although China's own vehicle output has doubled to 300 000 units since 1980, such a rapid growth can't keep up with the surge in demand. The demand for 1985 jumped by nearly 50 per cent, to 500 000 units. Even in 1987, 73 vehicle-making plants produced only 440 000 cars and trucks.[5] This amount of productivity was far from meeting the strong demand. With one car for every 2000 citizens in China (compared with one car for every two citizens in the United States and West Germany, and for every 24 in Hong Kong), and with the country's fast-growing standard of living, the opportunities are obviously there.

Up to the 1980s, owning a car was the symbol of power and high social class in China. Only the government, state-owned enterprises and companies could buy cars. Also, only officials who were at the level of a county magistrate and above had the right to use a car. The car prices were astronomical figures for average people. After Deng's open and reform policy was adopted by the Chinese government in 1978, some regions along the coast became rich, and people in some lines such as entertainment and private businesses became wealthy. They were eager to buy a car in order to show their superiority to the average people. Some film stars and private entrepreneurs shaped the first part of the populus who could afford a car by themselves. With the expansion of economic activities, the demand for cars from state-owned companies and enterprises and the government has increased a lot. If a company wants to buy a car, it must first obtain a quota from the government.

China's domestic industry is unable to serve this market. This has resulted in the creation of black markets for all cars, whether imported outright, made in China or joint-venture factories. Lured by enormous profits, some people in Shandong province and the southern island of Hainan smuggled a large quantity of foreign cars for resale to the mainland. Back-door deals abounded. Many people have to register on a two-year waiting list.[6] However, importation is not a feasible solution, as China is short of hard currency. 'Money should be spent on the edge of the knife', as people say in China. China needs to buy a lot of high production technology and equipment from abroad to replace its present, obsolete machines, some of which were imported from the former Soviet Union 30 years ago. Importing consumer goods is put in the second position by the Chinese leaders. The principal political decision to bolster China's auto industry had been confirmed at the highest level. It would be accomplished through more joint manufacturing ventures and a further cutback in direct imports. In fact, the contracts for bringing in more Japanese vehicles were being allowed to expire after 1985. This can save a large amount of hard currency used for imports on the one hand. On the other hand, through joint ventures, the Chinese car industry can study the advanced world standard technology and make use of foreign currencies from the foreign partners. The quality of the Chinese labour force may also be improved. The government therefore offered many favourable terms to attract foreign investment. Priority regarding land, labour, taxation, transportation, utilities and raw materials is given to joint ventures. To some extent, this even hurt some state-owned enterprises. Although the government encourages the joint ventures to export its products, actually the major portion of the outputs are sold in China due to heavy demands in this country.

Auto Industry in China

There was no auto industry in China when the People's Republic was founded in 1949. With the Soviet Union's help by supplying equipment and expertise, China's first truck rolled off the assembly line in 1956. From that time, China has built about 2400 auto and auto-parts factories, including 119 car and truck assembly plants up to 1985. The industry employed 1.3 million people and produced about 600 000 vehicles in 1991, including superheavy-duty trucks, container vehicles, light trucks for rural use, dump trucks for mining, transport vehicles, limousines, cars and tourist buses.

China is self-sufficient in production of raw materials and components used in making its old models. It can produce more than 95 per cent of the sheet steel, gear steel, spring steel and alloy steel plates needed to make frames, and also has capabilities in producing rubber and plastic fittings, meters and instruments. But these models are too old and out-of-date. They are generally technically backward products based on models from the 1950s, or even the 1940s. These cars are available in only a few models and are too inefficient in terms of fuel consumption and poor performance. The manufacturing plants urgently need to be improved in management, equipment, technology and research. Furthermore, the industry is too decentralized and fragmented, especially in making components. Some inefficient factories should be closed and the scattered components makers should be grouped.

Beginning in 1985, advanced production technology and equipment have been introduced to upgrade China's outdated models in meeting international standards. To rationalize operations, the Chinese government has set up six large motor vehicle companies. According to Mr Liu Xianzeng, a 64-year-old mechanical engineer from the National Automotive Trading Corp of China, China's 'Big Three' plants include: the Shanghai Volkswagen Auto Co., producer of the Santana car; the Changchun Volkswagen Auto Co., producer of Jettas and Golfs; and the Dragon Auto Co., a joint venture between China's Second Auto Works and Citroen, the French manufacturer. The so-called 'Little Three' are Chrysler's joint venture, Beijing Jeep; Guangzhou Peugeot Automotive Co., maker of Peugeot 505 cars and station wagons and 504 pick-up trucks; and a Daihatsu plant in Tianjin, maker of the Charade cars. Trucks and buses are made at the First Auto Works in Changchun and the Second Auto Works in Shi Yan.[7]

In fact, the Changchun Volkswagen Auto Co. has not formed mass production capabilities of making cars, and the Dragon Auto Co. is still under negotiation between China and France. But this is the future skeleton of China's auto industry.

Beijing Jeep Corp started in 1983 as a joint venture between American Motors (purchased by Chrysler in 1987) and Beijing Automotive Works. The Americans have a 38 per cent stake in its partnership with the Chinese. Although this venture had some problems at the beginning, it built on strong returns and in 1990 ranked no. 2 among all foreign joint ventures in terms of revenue.

In 1991, Beijing Jeep raised the output of its US-designed Cherokee by 73 per cent from 1990 to 13 000 units and built 35 000 Chinese four-wheel drive vehicles known as Beijing 212. An official from the company unwilling to be identified acknowledged that in 1991 it had net income of about US$40 million on revenue of US$400 million. It plans to invest RMB1.2 billion (US$225 million) through 1995 to upgrade its plant, bolster annual output of its Cherokee vehicle to 80 000 units and introduce an all-new model based on the Jeep Wrangler to replace the existing BJ2020.

Guangzhou Peugeot is a joint venture between China and France. Peugeot owns a 22 per cent stake in the company, with Guangzhou Automobile Manufacturing holding 46 per cent, Chinese International Trust & Investment Corp 20 per cent, Banque Nationale de Paris 4 per cent and the World Bank's International Finance Corp 8 per cent. After three years of manufacturing about 6000 cars, Guangzhou Peugeot doubled its output in 1991, having RMB233 million in profit with RMB1.5 billion in revenue.[8]

The Chinese government has set goals for dramatically increasing production in its two 5-year plans (1991–2000). The industry produced 78 000 passenger cars in 1991, the government hopes to increase that to 700 000 by the end of the century.[9]

Marketing Mix Strategies

After carefully analysing the particular environment of China, Volkswagen of AG decided to build a joint venture with China, and a number of fundamental operational strategic decisions needed to be made accordingly.

Product. In 27 years, the forerunner of Shanghai VW Corp—Shanghai Car Work—had made 50 000 Shanghai sedans, which were based on the Mercedes 170 model, with an output of 6000 a year. This car is a big four-door one that reminds people, who see it staggering along the streets in Beijing and many big cities, usually carrying government officials, of an American Dodge, vintage 1950s. This car dated from the early 1950s and is definitely out of fashion nowadays.

After the venture was founded, they decided to make the VW Santana model. It was the first model that was especially designed for the local market by foreign manufacturers. They gave it a sound name 'Shanghai Santana', which successfully built a strong brand identification for the car. They painted it with white, red and grey colours which are the popular colours in China. There are no two-door cars in China, because sometimes a car has to take as many persons as possible. Four-door cars are more convenient and have already been accepted by Chinese people. So the plant makes all cars with four doors. In order to meet the technical manufacturing ability of the Chinese industry and people's traditional views that driving is a kind of special technical skill that cannot be easily learned, the factory manufactures manual transmission for the car. Drivers in China are a special social class, which is higher than many people. Partly because they drive for officials, they have more chances to be with officials, the symbol of power in China. Sometimes the drivers can even influence official decisions.

The quality control is based on the standard of Volkswagen in Germany, which is 2.3 (on a five-point scale, with 1 being highest quality). The company has an international quality audit where the car is checked from the customer's point of view. It reached the figure 2.3 in 1988. After that they have a higher quality standard than those produced in Brazil and Mexico. The Shanghai VW started at 3.5.

The company has consistently placed emphasis on increasing the use of Chinese-made parts and components in the manufacture of its cars. In 1991, 83 per cent of domestically made models with 60 per cent of parts made in China reached approved quality levels.[10] Body frames, engines and gear-boxes are all produced in China.

Designing a new model is always in the managers' heads. According to its plan, beginning in 1995, a new car will be produced at its expanded facilities in Shanghai. It is being designed with VW's Brazilian subsidiary and will be based on the current-generation Passat, which is not built in China. The wheelbase will be extended 3.5 inches, and the car will get an all-new body with a larger space inside. 'This is the first step to develop a car by ourselves', said Stefan Messman, Shanghai Volkswagen's deputy managing director in 1992.

Price, Promotion and Distribution. The company has clear knowledge about the Chinese market. It knows that millions of eager buyers are waiting for its cars. Every car is driven off by the customers immediately after it is rolled down from the assembly line. The company really needn't do any promotions at all when the Chinese economy is on the formal road. Just once in a while they advertise on TV or newspapers to increase awareness of 'Shanghai Santana' and upgrade its position in people's eyes. Formally, as China has a central planned economy, there are no private car dealers, at least up to now. All cars are distributed by state-owned companies. Shanghai Volkswagen is not an exception. All Santana cars are distributed by a state-owned company in Shanghai. But because of the strong demand that makes large profits, many people bypass that company and directly buy the cars from the factory through personal relationships. In the market, no other cars such as this are made in the domestic industry. Although Beijing Jeep makes Jeep Cherokee and the Soviet-designed 2020N series, Guangzhou Peugeot makes Peugeot cars, and the Charade cars are made in Tianjin, their production level is too low to fill this market. The imported Japanese cars are sold for over RMB250 000 (US$53 000 at 1990 official exchange rate), and the quantity is decreasing. Concerned with this situation, the Shanghai VW Corp sells its cars, after tax, at RMB178 000 (US$37 800 at 1990 rate)— roughly six times the price the joint venture could charge if it ever exports its cars.[11] The profit margin is so high that in the company's books in the 1988 tax year the profits were handsomely above Volkswagen's worldwide targets. Although the Shanghai Santana ex-works price is unbelievably high compared with that in other countries, the market price that people can buy at from a few automobile trade corporations in some cities is well above RMB210 000, an unbelievable price. And personal relationships in buying a car are still relied on. On the other hand, this shows that China is a huge market, not a potential one, but one that has arrived.

However, to a great extent, China is still a centrally planned economy, and sometimes when problems happen, to the economy, the government has to take some temporary steps to remedy the situation. This definitely influences all industries. When the government adopted an austerity programme in 1989 to curb the inflated economy, the economy went into recession and the market shrank. At this time, in order not to hurt foreign investors' zeal and to show the government's confidence in the open policy, the government bought 1500 Santanas produced in Shanghai, according to a statement by an official in charge of auto venture in the State Planning Commission in the official *China Daily* on 19 November 1989. On the other hand, the company made its efforts, too. As they are very familiar with the importance of the personal relationship in doing business in China, they used it. They even persuaded President Jiang Zeming, who is also China's communist party general secretary and a former mayor of Shanghai, to order the state authorities to buy the factory's unsold backlog of 3000 cars.[12] Generally, this kind of problem has only happened once after the joint venture was established.

Present and Future

After seven years of great effort, Shanghai Volkswagen has formed a manufacturing capacity for 60 000 cars and 100 000 engines a year making itself into the sole car producer with mass production facilities in China.

In order to upgrade features, the company has always adhered to the technical standards of Santanas of the Volkswagen Corp of Germany. The 'Shanghai Santana' has been rated the best vehicle of its kind in an appraisal of manufacture of similar models produced by the Volkswagen Corp subsidiaries in four countries.

By the end of 1991, the company had total production of 106 725 cars and 110 000 engines. Labour productivity reached 9.5 cars per worker, the highest in China and on a close par with the German parent corporation. And in 1992, Volkswagen had sales of 90 000 vehicles with 7.11 billion yuan in the Chinese market. It has become the largest car maker in China.

At present the company is undertaking the second phase of technological renovation. A new model will be introduced in 1995 and the joint venture plans to produce 90 000 of the new cars a year out of a total planned production of 150 000 after 1995.

As time goes by, the Chinese car industry will develop very fast. Other car makers will raise their output greatly and develop as competitors to Shanghai Volkswagen. Although it has a long way to go to meet the demand of this market, which has 1.28 billion people, the Shanghai VW should make a long-term strategic plan to position itself favourably against future competition. The first impending change will be the distribution channel. After the reform reaches a new stage, the company cannot expect the government to distribute all cars and cannot rely on the individual connections to sell large quantities of cars. The company needs to consider building its own distribution channels. Maybe a lot of local automobile trade companies all over the country should receive attention. They will possibly change into tomorrow's car dealers in China. As Volkswagen hopes to use its China operations as a bridgehead for exports to the Asian market, another point to deal with is how to make exports profitable under the present condition where the domestic price is several times higher than that for export.

Anyway, both Chinese and Germans are very optimistic about Shanghai Volkswagen's future.

References

1. Li Rongxia, 'Top Ten Joint Ventures in China', *Beijing Review*, 13 July 1992, pp. 18–25.
2. 'Don't Get Off Yer Bike Yet', *The Economist*, 16 April 1988, pp. 81–82.
3. Yao Jianguo, 'Auto Industry Expands Co-operation', *Beijing Review*, 13 July 1992, pp. 14–16.
4. 'VW, China Sign Auto, Engine Pact', *Automotive News*, 15 October 1984, p. 8.
5. Don't Get Off Yer Bike Yet', *The Economist*, 16 April 1988, pp. 81–82.
6. David Abrahamson, 'Chinese Cars', *Car & Driver*, April 1989, pp. 30–31.
7. Bradford Wernle, 'Chinese Car Industry Tries to Make Inroads', *Craines Detroit Business*, 24 February 1992, p. 9.
8. Jonathan Karp, 'Back on the road', *Far Eastern Economic Review*, 26 March 1992, pp. 49–50.
9. Bradford Wernle, 'Chinese Car Industry Tries to Make Inroads, *Craines Detroit Business*, 24 February 1992, p. 2.
10. Li Rongxia, 'Top Ten Joint Ventures in China', *Beijing Review*, 13 July 1992, pp. 18–25.
11. 'Joint Ventures in China: Inscrutable', *The Economist*, 17 March 1990, pp. 66–68.
12. Joint Ventures in China', *The Economist*, 17 March 1990, pp. 66–68.

Jon Pepper and James V. Higgins, 'Firms Hope To Win Over "Lost" Asian Market', *The Detroit News*, 29 October 1993, p. E-1.

Richard Johnson, 'Beijing Jeep Goes After Its New Competition', *Automotive News*, 5 July 1993, p. 51.

Yao Jianguo, 'Volkswagen Automotive Group to Be Founded', *Beijing Review*, 20 July 1992, p. 36.

Richard Johnson, 'New Models Key to China's Future', *Automotive News*, 6 July 1992, p. 34.

Further Reading

Stephen Vines, 'China Aims for Million Cars', *Automotive News*, 12 December 1988, p. 48.

'Santana heralds China's New Auto Beginnings', *Automotive Industry*, February 1985, p. 24.

H.L. Stevenson, 'Chinese and Germans Team Up To Build VWs', *Automotive News*, 21 October 1985, p. E-2.

Shu Yao, 'What's Happening, What's Ahead in China', *Automotive News*, 21 October 1985, p. E-2.

Dorothy E. Jones, 'European Carmakers Start Honking at the Japanese', *Business Week*, 22 April 1985, p. 50.

'Volkswagen and China: The People's Car', *Automotive News*, 12 December 1988, p. 48.

'China Moves to Aid Joint Ventures in Autos', *New York Times*, 20 November 1989, p. D-10.

'Use of Offshore Funds Reaches Peak', *Beijing Review*, 29 November 1993, p. 29.

'Volkswagen Outlook on China', *Wall Street Journal*, 20 April 1993, p. C-25.

Jim Mann, 'One Company's China Debacle', *Fortune*, 6 November 1989, pp. 145–152.

Developing International Marketing Strategies

CASE 4.1
Global Strategies—What Are They?

Global strategies do not mean huge companies operating in a single world market. They are much more complex. Global competitive strategies are a bit like supernatural creatures: they can be imagined by each individual to suit his or her own reality while evoking a common concern. The best illustrations are the slogans companies use to describe themselves. These range from 'Think Local, Act Global' all the way to the opposite 'Think Global Act Local, with everything in between.'*

Defining Global Strategies

Some 15 years have gone by since the term 'global strategy' entered our vocabulary, enough time to bring some clarity to its definition. We now know what it is and what it is not.

Consider first what it is not. Global strategies are not standard product–market strategies that assume the world to be a single, homogeneous, border-free marketplace. The Uruguay Round of trade and investment liberalization notwithstanding, the world is still a collection of different independent economies, each with its own market characteristics. Each, moreover, has its own societal aspirations that occasionally find expression in protectionist policies of one form or another.

Global strategies are also not about global presence or about large companies. A company can very well operate in all countries of the world; but if what it does in one country has no meaning for what it does in another country, it is no different from the domestic companies it competes with in each location.

To qualify as pursuing a global strategy, a company needs to be able to demonstrate two things: that it can contest any market it chooses to compete in, and that it can bring its entire worldwide resources to bear on any competitive situation it finds itself in, regardless of where that might be.

Selective Contestability.   Just as companies possessing a certain set of technologies and business competencies choose particular market segments to concentrate on, a global company can be selective about the countries in which it operates.

Many small, high-technology companies and luxury good manufacturers do just that. They compete where there is adequate demand to justify the investments needed to access the market; they focus their investments to achieve critical mass only in those markets they are interested in.

The important thing is that they can and are prepared to contest any and all markets should circumstances warrant. They constantly scour the world for market openings, they process information on a global basis and they constitute a 'potential' threat even in places they have not yet entered.

Markets where such contestability exists, as a corollary, start to behave almost as if the company had already entered—provided, of course, the threat of entry is a credible one. This explains why telecom markets the world over are so fiercely competitive from the day they are no longer government or private monopolies. The handful of international players in the equipment business not only are waiting in the wings but have products that conform to international standards and resources they can deploy for market access as soon as opportunity arises

Global Resources for Each Main Street.   The corner shop that carries products by IBM, Philips, Coca-Cola or Du Pont knows from experience that there is something special about these products compared to those supplied by a small local company. In comparison, products from companies such as Nestlé, Unilever or even Procter & Gamble did not seem so special—in the past at least. Their names, formulations and the way they were produced and marketed were not too different from domestic ones.

Just being present in several countries, in other words, does not constitute a global strategy. Globalism is an earned notion rather than being entitlement created by the fact of operating in several countries.

A basic characteristic of a global company is its ability to bring its entire worldwide capabilities to bear on any transaction anywhere regardless of the products it makes. This underlies the importance of organizational integration in global strategies. Transporting capabilities across borders on an as-needed basis requires all local units to be connected and permeable, not isolated from one another.

This is also what allows global strategies to be 'within-border' strategies while, at the same time, being 'cross-border' ones. They are manifest on each Main Street, with local companies sensing they are dealing with a worldwide organization even while the latter employs a local competitive formula.

*Note: The authors do not offer this presentation as the definitive piece on global strategies or global companies but only as a basis for discussion.
Source: Vijay Jolly, 'Global Strategies in the 1990s', *The Financial Post*, 15 February 1997, p. S-6.

Main Attributes of Global Strategy

This dual notion of market contestability and bringing global resources to bear on competition wherever a company is present is really what global strategies are about. Industries where such strategies are prevalent assume a character of their own in which strategies that are geared to one country alone cannot be adopted. What companies do in one country has inevitable consequences for what they do in others.

There is, of course, nothing absolute about global strategies. Being near-cousins of multidomestic strategies, the best way to judge them is in terms of 'degrees of globalness'. At the risk of oversimplification, the more a company scores in each of the following five attributes, the more it can be considered a global competitor based on the definition just given. These include possessing a standard product (or core) that is marketed uniformly across the world; sourcing all assets, not just production, on an optimal basis; and achieving market access in line with the break-even volume of the needed infrastructure.

- *Standard products and marketing mix.* While the advantages of having a standard product and marketing mix are obvious, this attribute involves several trade-offs in practice. Economies of scale in design, production and promotion need to be compared to the greater market acceptance that local adaptation often provides.

If a general conclusion can be drawn, it would be the need at least to aim for a standard 'core' in the product and limiting marketing adaptations to those absolutely necessary. The more integrated countries become economically, the less latitude there is anyway for things such as price discrimination and channel selection. The same applies to situations where buyers themselves are global and expect similar products and terms on a worldwide basis.

- *Sourcing assets, not just products.* Sourcing products and components internationally based on comparative advantage and availability has long been a feature of international business. What is new is the possibility to source assets or capabilities related to any part of the company's value chain. Whether it is capital from Switzerland or national credit agencies, software skills from Silicon Valley or Bangalore or electronic components from Taiwan, global companies now have a wider latitude in accessing resources from wherever they are available or cost-competitive.

The implication of this is that global strategies are as much about asset deployment for market access purposes as they are about asset accumulation abroad. The latter include local capital, technical skills, managerial talent and new product ideas, as well as the host competencies that local partners and institutions can provide. Also, whereas previously assets accumulated locally were mainly to support a local business, it is increasingly possible—and desirable—to separate those needed for local market access from those intended to support the company's business elsewhere.

It is here that we associate partnerships and alliances with global strategy. They can supplement what a company already possesses by way of assets or complement what is missing, thereby speeding up the creation of the needed infrastructure as well as reducing costs and risks.

- *Market access in line with break-even.* For a company to be a credible global competitor it does not need to be among the biggest in its industry. But it has to be big enough to generate the volume of sales the required infrastructure demands and to amortize up-front investments in R&D and promotion.

Today, it is the latter investments that count most. In the pharmaceutical industry, for example, it now costs around US$400 million to come up with a successful new drug. This puts a natural floor on the amount of sales to be generated over the life of the drug. The greater the presence of a company in all of the large markets, and the greater its ability to launch the drug simultaneously in them, the higher the likelihood of profiting from the investment made.

The same argument applies to other investments in intangibles such as brands. If we associate global competitiveness with size, it is chiefly on account of these types of investments. Unlike investments in plants and physical infrastructure, which can result in diminishing returns to scale, intangibles almost always translate into 'big is better'.

- *Contesting assets.* Another distinguishing feature of a global company is its ability to neutralize the assets and competencies of its competitors. If a competitor switches its supply from a high-cost to a low-cost factory it too can do so; if a competitor gains access to a critical technology it can do the same. Similarly, if a competitor is using one market to generate excess cash flow in order to 'invest' in another, it is able to neutralize this advantage by going to the relatively more profitable market itself.

Purely domestic companies and even those that are run on a multidomestic basis, lack such arbitrage possibilities. Just as in sourcing, to exploit these requires a global view of the business and the capacity to manage it in an integrated fashion.

- ■ *All functions have a global orientation.* As much of the foregoing suggests, global competition today is a lot more than simple cross-border competition at the product or service level. It is equally about building and managing a multinational infrastructure. Frequently, the latter means internationalizing all of the competencies and functions of a company: its R&D, procurement, production, logistics and marketing, as well as human resources and finance.

These functions are all geared to providing customers with superior products and services on a worldwide basis. The more they have a global orientation of their own, the greater their contribution to the overall effort. Hence, even if their focus may be primarily national in scope, supporting a local business with no trade, for example, any contribution they can make to other units of the company helps.

These five attributes, taken together, operationalize a global strategy. The degrees of globalness in a strategy are the extent to which each is fulfilled in practice. The fact of not having a standard global product, for example, diminishes the scope of a global strategy but does not entirely destroy it, provided the company scores high on the other attributes. If anything, stressing one attribute to the exclusion of others can even be counterproductive and unfeasible. A good balance between all of them is needed.

Local Adaptation

Another important point to make about these attributes is that they do not assume a single, open global marketplace. Trade and investment liberalization coupled with improvements in transportation and communications are what have made global strategies possible. Trade protection, labour policies, investment incentives and a host of regulations continue to force a country-by-country adaptation of strategies.

It is also these realities, along with the sociocultural differences between countries, that have caused many companies to stress the 'local' dimension in their business. And rightly so. If all companies confront the same set of market conditions, advantage goes to those that adapt their strategies best.

The best way to reconcile these differences with the attributes required of a global strategy is to see them as constraints to global optimization. Localness, in other words, is another variable to incorporate in decision making. Considering it as the basis for the strategy itself, however, is to deny all of the advantages a

global company possesses. This is perhaps the biggest conundrum which companies face today.

While adapting strategies to local conditions offers greater opportunities for revenue generation, it has two main impacts: it causes overinvestment in the infrastructure needed to serve markets, and brings about a lack of consistency in whatever strategy is being pursued.

Neither is intrinsically bad. They can even contribute positively to the end result if approached correctly. All that is needed is to factor them in as variables to be considered, without losing sight of the overall objective of competing effectively both within and across borders.

Consider the issue of overinvestment, especially in capital-intensive businesses such as semiconductors. Companies such as Texas Instruments, NEC and Mitsubishi Electric have consciously located abroad. This not only permits them to benefit from generous investment incentives provided by local governments that want such facilities, but also means they can mobilize local companies as coinvestors to share the capital burden and help with market access.

More contentious is the issue of strategic focus. Should local subsidiaries be allowed to modify products and diversify into businesses that make sense for them only? Or should they be consistent with what the parent company focuses on? The answer to this depends on several things: a company's definition of its business scope and growth vectors; the subsidiary's domain within the overall organization; and the locus of its strategy-making process.

Business scope and growth vectors pertain to a company's attitude to diversification generally. If its products and technologies provide adequate growth opportunities on a worldwide basis, it is probably better off restricting each subsidiary to just those. If, on the other hand, growth is primarily driven through exploring and creating new market opportunities, then local initiatives are usually welcome.

Logitech SA, a world leader in pointing devices for the personal computer industry, for example, permitted and even encouraged its Taiwanese company to develop special software products for the Chinese market because that would be an additional product to fuel its growth, reduce its dependence on the mouse and, incidentally, facilitate access to a new market. A company that comes up with a new cancer treatment, on the other hand, is likely to want to invest all its resources in commercializing that worldwide as quickly as possible.

The more a company's infrastructure and skills become dispersed and the more global responsibilities individual subsidiaries take on, the greater the need to see the initiation of strategies as a global process. What the parent knows and sees may not be the same as subsidiary management. Giving subsidiaries too narrow a mission based on a centralized notion of between-country competition not only constrains their potential for accumulating local resources but diminishes their potential for competing within their country.

Organizational Implications

How companies ought to structure and manage their international operations has been debated as long as the debate on strategy itself. Because organizations need to reflect a wide range of company-specific characteristics—such as size, diversity, age, culture, technology—in addition to their global posture, it has proven hard to be normative. There are, however, certain key design considerations related to global posture that have dominated thinking and practice in recent years.

The most important consideration has to do with the greater need for organizational integration that global strategies require. Hence, when companies first tried to adapt their structures in the 1970s and early 1980s, most of them created elaborate matrix organizations giving equal status to products, geography and functions. While such organizations worked well for some companies, ABB being the leading example, they did not for others. ABB succeeded because of the nature of its business, its superior information system (called Abacus), its investment in developing a number of globally minded managers, and a small but highly effective top management team. What ABB was able to do was to balance finely the need for local autonomy in decision making with the strategic and organizational integration that managing the business on a global basis demanded.

Others that were not able to achieve this balance opted for tilting their matrix in favour of one or the other dimensions. Most often, the dominant dimension became product groups, or strategic business units, the assumption being that integrating each product's business system on a worldwide basis was the best way to optimize strategy and achieve coherence among different local units.

Where these 'product headquarters' were located mattered less and many companies consciously spread them around as a better way to integrate country organizations, give particular local managers a broader domain to look after, and exploit country-specific assets or competencies. Such dispersal had the attendant benefit of also reducing the role (and size) of corporate headquarters.

This fine-tuning of structures continues today. To the extent one can discern a trend for the 1990s it would be one consisting of three things: reverting to a single locus of direction and control, giving greater emphasis to functional strategies instead of business-by-business ones, and creating simple line organizations based on a more decentralized 'network' of local companies.

The move to a single locus is partly on account of the difficulty companies have experienced in managing dispersed product headquarters.

The complex interactions between units they gave rise to, the lack of global reach on the part of some country organizations, and the potential for confusion between corporate roles and business unit functions were apparently not compensated by whatever advantage they offered. But it is equally on account of the recognition of the importance of a coherent set of values, goals, and identity, as well as the need to avoid duplication of functions across the world.

Having functions as the primary dimension to coordinate global strategies also reflects the dual nature of the latter, combining asset deployment for market-access reasons and asset accumulation for sourcing purposes. Another virtue of a functional orientation is that it is usually at this level that global alliances and asset accumulation takes place—the R&D function cooperating with other companies' R&D departments, procurement with suppliers, finance with local finance companies and so on.

While marketing can and should be managed nationally or regionally, R&D, finance and manufacturing lend themselves better to global coordination. Texas Instruments Inc., for example, used to manage its business, including manufacturing, on a regional basis. Four years ago, it introduced the notion of the 'virtual fab', linking all its 17 manufacturing sites around the world into a single organization.

In addition to standardizing equipment and procedures across plants, this allows the company to transfer expertise across units efficiently, allocate production optimally, and interact with development on a global basis. Whereas previously the company had country-by-country salesforces, it now has market-based teams with global responsibility for a product's success. The latter has proved particularly effective in serving the needs of global customers who expect similar conditions worldwide.

Whether to have a single set of global functions or to have them specialized by business unit depends on how diverse the latter are. The lesson companies have learned, however, is to avoid overly complex matrix structures and to allow local units sufficient autonomy at the business level.

The last point refers to the way individual units in a global company need to be treated. Based on the arguments made earlier, what one is seeing is an upgrading of their role, both as a locus for independent entrepreneurial effort and as contributors to the business worldwide.

To perform this expanded role coherently they need greater empowerment coupled with all of the things that a network organization possesses: a commonly shared knowledge base, common values and goals, a common understanding of priorities and precommitments others have made, and a common set of measures to judge performance.

Shared values are known to replace the need for elaborate direction and control. Rather than planning for the synergies and interdependencies that are at the heart of a global strategy, effective networks create them voluntarily and in real time. Global strategies in their present form have proved far too complex and demanding to be implemented in a centralized manner.

Questions

1. Write a critique of each of the major points presented in this case. Based on this critique, write your own definition of a global strategy.
2. What do the authors mean by selective contestability? How practical is this idea for a small international company?
3. The case discusses five attributes that, taken together, operationalize a global strategy. How would you use these attributes to define a global company? A global strategy?
4. Evaluate one of the following companies as to its degree of globalness: Nestlé, Procter & Gamble, Unilever or a company of your choice. Be sure to discuss both why you believe or why you do not believe the company is a global company, has a global product and/or has a global strategy. You may find some information that is helpful at the Web sites for Nestlé: **http://www.nestle.com**; Procter & Gamble: **http://www.pg.com**; and Unilever: **http://www.unilever.com**.

CASE 4.2
Event Marketing in Europe—the Case of Nokia Balalaika Show in Berlin 1994

Introduction

Events in marketing settings can be defined as designed occurrences that communicate messages to target audiences. Event marketing is derived from sponsoring and relates to the specific area of the promotion mix, funding activities, happenings, events and the like, in order to get access to promotional means for displaying, for example, the name, brands and logo of the company. Event marketing complies the *use of unique sponsored activities or events in certain locations and point in time for reaching corporate marketing and communication objectives*. It is one possibility for overcoming the 'noise' and obstacles created by overcommunication in the present international market environment.

The Case Study—Nokia Balalaika Show in Berlin

A case study of the 'Nokia Balalaika Show' in Berlin in 1994 exemplifies an event-marketing situation in practice. The case is followed by a set of questions for students dealing with practical issues as well as event strategies and concepts in marketing.

Background. On 18 June 1994, the 'Nokia Balalaika Show' was performed in Berlin. The show featured a concert by the Leningrad Cowboys, which probably is internationally the most famous Finnish rock band, together with the Russian Red Army Ensemble. The concert was the result of cooperation between the Leningrad Cowboys and the Finnish company Nokia Mobile Phones. As head sponsor for the concert, the company's main aim was to increase the awareness of the name Nokia and to strengthen the Nokia brand in Germany. The reason was obvious because the German market is the company's largest European market. This was also the first time a Finnish company became involved in a project of this magnitude.

Nokia Group. Nokia is a leading global company focused on key growth areas of wire-line and wireless

This case was prepared by Maria Kronvall, Sonera Ltd, PO Box 0405 00051 Sonera, Finland and Jan-Åke Törnroos, Swedish School of Economics and Business Administration, Department of Marketing and Corporate Geography, Helsinki, Finland.

Table CS 4.2.1a   Net Sales by Business Groups of Nokia in 1994 and 1995

Business Groups	1994 MFIM	1995 MFIM
Nokia Telecommunications	6 906	10 341
Nokia Mobile Phones	10 702	16 052
Nokia General Communications Products	11 530	10 837
Others	1 589	458
Nokia Group	30 177	36 810

Table CS 4.2.1b   Net Sales by Business Groups of Nokia in 1996 and 1997

Business Groups	1994 MFIM	1995 MFIM
Nokia Telecommunications	13 333	18 826
Nokia Mobile Phones	21 579	27 643
Other operations	5 197	7 239

Data for 1996 and 1997 are not equivalent due to organizational change
Source: Annual Reports

Table CS 4.2.2   Net Sales by Market Area

Market Areas	1995 FIM36.8 billion (%)	1997 FIM52.6 billion (%)
Finland	9	5
Other European countries	56	51
Americas	13	18
Asia Pacific	19	23
Other countries	3	3

Source: Annual Reports

telecommunications. The firm is a pioneer in developing mobile telecommunication. Nokia is the world's leading developer of digital handsets and wireless data, the world's second largest manufacturer of mobile phones and one of the two leading suppliers of GSM-based cellular networks. Nokia is also a significant supplier of advance transmission systems and access networks, multimedia and equipment, satellite and cable receivers and other telecom-related products.

In 1997, the group employed over 41 000 people, had sales in 130 countries and manufactured in over 10 countries in three continents. The headquarters is situated in Espoo, Finland, and the company's shares are listed on six stock exchanges: New York, London, Helsinki, Paris, Frankfurt and Stockholm. The Nokia Group comprises the following business groups and units: Nokia Telecommunications, Nokia Mobile Phones and Nokia Communications Products, Nokia Ventures Organization and Nokia Research Centre. The most important market areas and net sales in 1995 to 1997 are shown in Tables CS 4.2.1a/b and 4.2.2.

Nokia Mobile Phones.   Growth in the number of cellular phone users lies in the consumer markets and diversification of product lines. Nokia focuses its devel-

opment on future standards and new products for different consumer groups. Strong growth in wireless data communications is anticipated in the years ahead and Nokia is playing a leading role in this development.

The Leningrad Cowboys and the Alexandrov Red Army Ensemble.   The Leningrad Cowboys are a bizarre and extremely enjoyable ten-man show band sporting unicorn hair-do's and half-metre pointed shoes. Their act parodies the clichés of rock stardom, the English language and the Soviet system. 'Other bands ride limousines, we drive tractors.' Despite their quirky humour and light-hearted approach to music, the Cowboys are respected musicians in their homeland, but their popularity is not restricted to Finland. In September 1994, the Leningrad Cowboys appeared at the 11th annual MTV Video Music Awards together with the Alexandrov Red Army Ensemble. MTV invited the two groups to perform jointly between the acts by Aerosmith, the Rolling Stones and Bruce Springsteen. The show was seen by 250 million viewers worldwide.

The highly skilful Alexandrov Red Army Chorus and Dance Ensemble was founded in 1928. Their first visit abroad was to France in 1937, and since then the Ensemble has toured in almost 50 countries all over the world. The present touring company consists of 80 male singers, 40 musicians and 35 dancers.

Total Balalaika Show, Helsinki, Finland, 1993. The background to the Nokia Balalaika Show lies in a similar project in 1993: the Total Balalaika Show in Helsinki. This was the first time the Leningrad Cowboys and the Red Army Ensemble performed together and the show was a success. Seventy thousand people witnessed this event in the main square of Helsinki, on the biggest stage ever built in Finland. For their role as conceivers and producers of this spectacular event, the

Finnish Marketing Federation awarded the Leningrad Cowboys with the Marketing Act of the Year 1993 award. Nokia Mobile Phones participated in this event on a very small scale.

Nokia Balalaika Show and Nokia. The foremost objective for this event was to increase the awareness of the name 'Nokia' in Germany. According to Lauri Kivinen, vice president of communications at Nokia Mobile Phones, the company wanted to give 'contents', to use his words, to both the brand (Nokia) and the product itself (mobile phones). With the Nokia Balalaika Show, Nokia wanted to remove the 'yuppie-label' that mobile phones still carried in 1994. The target audience for the event were people aged 18–35, who at the time were considered to be the most likely buyers of mobile phones within the next five years. The goals were believed to be possible to reach through the Nokia Balalaika Show, which was expected to be the third largest media event in Germany in 1994.

Additionally, the company planned to use the event directly in its product advertising by using the Leningrad Cowboys in TV advertisements and by producing a special Nokia Balalaika Show mobile phone cover. Nokia also intended to invite customers from all around Europe to the event as the Nokia Balalaika Show also happened to coincide with the launching of a new phone, the Nokia 2110 GSM.

Even though the risks were considerable, it was agreed within the company that both a success and a failure would bring the name Nokia onto everybody's lips during that weekend, and that it would therefore be worth while taking the risks. The contract was signed in Stockholm on 14 February 1994 leaving only four months before the event itself.

The Planning Process. Berlin seemed to be the natural choice for the event. Berlin is situated in the heart of the 'New Europe'. It is easily accessible with a developed infrastructure. Berlin is also a city of great historical significance: Berlin was divided into East and West by the cold war, separated by the Berlin Wall. Finally in 1990, as a result of the European reunification, the wall came down and the city was reunited.

The concert was to be held in the former East Berlin to stress the reunification of the city as well as to accentuate the 'East-meets-West' theme presented by the combination of the Leningrad Cowboys and the Red Army Ensemble. Lustgarten was selected to be the perfect spot for the event as it is situated at the Marx-Engel's Platz in East Berlin on the so called 'Museum island'.

The concert was to take place on 18 June 1994 which was a historical date for Berlin and Germany.

This was the date that the allied troops had selected to celebrate their withdrawal from Berlin. The timing of the concert therefore marked the beginning of the integrated 'New Europe' in Germany and considering the time and place, the concert proved to be perfect in view of the company slogan 'Nokia Connecting People'.

The cooperation was made public on 15 February 1994, at the film festival in Berlin the Finnish film-producer Aki Kaurismäki's film *Leningrad Cowboys Meet Moses* had its premiere. The press release was issued in March, when the Leningrad Cowboys were informed that they had been invited to the Film Festival in Cannes where a party was organized to celebrate the release of the Leningrad Cowboys' new single: *Nokia Balalaika Show.*

On 2 June an additional press conference was held in Berlin to which the company had invited around 50 journalists. A Nokia Balalaika Show CD-single was also sent to 100 radio stations in Germany so that it could be played on the air and give the German people a taste of the forthcoming concert.

The last press conference was held together with the Leningrad Cowboys' German record company BMG-Ariola, on 17 June 1, one day before the concert in Lustgarten.

Using the Event for Advertising and Promotion. Nokia Balalaika Show provided a good opportunity for the company to use the event in its promotional activities. The event was used directly in the company's product advertising. A specially designed red Nokia Balalaika Show phone cover was produced in a limited edition and soon after became a collector's item. The phone cover was used in advertisements in the daily newspapers. TV advertisements featured also the Leningrad Cowboys in connection with mobile phones and the slogan 'Nokia Connecting People'. The TV advertisements proved to be most popular with the MTV music channel.

Apart from the CD-single that was released in connection with the film festival in Cannes, Nokia Mobile Phones also made another Nokia Balalaika Show CD which was used, for example, as a business give-away and for other promotional activities.

Posters were made and distributed all around Berlin before the concert together with a limited edition of Nokia Balalaika Show pins.

Nokia Mobile Phones made use of the event by inviting 500 VIP-guests to the Nokia Balalaika Show. Among the guests were journalists from Finland and City Officials from Berlin. In addition, invitation quotas were given to Nokia Mobile Phones Germany and Nokia Mobile Phones Finland who invited their own distributors and other important contacts to the event. The department for European sales held a sales meeting in connection with the event. At the sales meeting a new mobile phone, the Nokia 2110 GSM, was introduced to the market and the participants of the sales meeting were invited to attend at the Nokia Balalaika Show.

The Event—Nokia Balalaika Show 18.6.1994, Berlin

The planning of the concert was not without complications. Before the concert the founder of the Red Army Ensemble, Alexander Alexandrov, unexpectedly died in Moscow. This meant that in the worst case the ensemble had to go back to Moscow to attend his funeral, leaving the Nokia Balalaika Show without one of its main attractions. The concert, however, was perceived to be of more importance than the funeral and the ensemble stayed in Berlin.

The 18 June finally came. Behind the stage you could see the Alte Museum, to the left was the cathedral of Berlin and to the right the river Spree. The concert stage was framed on both sides by two giant Nokia 2110 GSM phone dummies. Each display on the phone made up 4×6 metres of videoscreens, broadcasting the show to people who were standing too far from the stage to be able to see. During the intervals the screen showed Nokia's advertising videos with the slogan 'Nokia Connecting People'. Above the screen there was a banner with the text Nokia Balalaika Show. There were also Nokia ads on the light tower as well as Nokia Balalaika Show posters around Lustgarten.

Just before the concert was to begin, it started to rain heavily and when the warm-up band began playing at 20.00 hours there were only approximately 10 000 people in Lustgarten. Quick thinking was required and someone came up with the brilliant idea to call a few local radio stations. The effect was immediate. Radio Energy encouraged people to get out and get moving to Lustgarten.

The Leningrad Cowboys started to play at 21.00 hours. The concert began with Beethoven's 'Ode an die Freude' and continued with rock classics from the sixties mixed with Russian ballads. At this point there were already 50 000 spectators in Lustgarten and the feeling was said to be 'incredible'. The concert lasted for two hours, after which the Nokia guests were taken by bus to the hotel for the after-show party.

After the Concert

After the concert a video was made of the event and was sent out to the 500 VIP-guests who were invited to the Nokia Balalaika Show. The video has also been used for presentations and for other promotional activities.

Nokia's German PR agency did a survey of the publicity the event received in the media. Quantitative results of this kind are fairly easy to measure but in this case the crucial results are the qualitative results. However, these have not been evaluated by the company. According to Lauri Kivinen, the feedback the company received was only positive which could account for a type of qualitative result. No specific qualitative studies have been carried out. This fact does not imply that the company was oblivious to the importance of measuring results. The main reason was simply the lack of time. The company was undergoing strong growth which means that the company didn't have the necessary time-resources to make thorough follow-up studies of the event.

Questions

1. What are the core characteristics of event marketing and how is it distinguishable from classical promotion or advertising?
2. What are the main strengths and weaknesses of adopting an event-marketing approach to marketing?
3. How can event marketing be used in creating brand awareness in different parts of Europe?
4. When analysing the Nokia Balalaika Show in Berlin, how could the firm benefit imagewise after the concert? How should the event be followed up?
5. Which types of events could be feasible when planning an event-marketing strategy in Europe?

CASE 4.3
Baby Apparel and Dubai Fashions—
Letter of Credit as an Export Payment

Baby Apparel

Baby Apparel was incorporated in December 1981. From a 1500-square-metre factory in Manila employing 35 people with US$181 398 in export sales, the company has grown to two factories employing over 1400 workers with sales of US$8 230 199 (FOB Manila) in 1992.

Baby Apparel, a leading children's wear exporter, specializes in handsmocked children's wear. Handsmocking is a skill that was taught to Filipinos by Spanish nuns during the Spanish regime in the Philippines. To this day, it is said that the Filipinos do better handsmocking than the Spanish. Buyers the world over look to the Philippines for handsmocked dresses because of the quality of the work. Thailand, Malaysia and Indonesia produce handsmocked children's dresses but buyers are said to prefer the quality of Philippine handsmocking. Baby Apparel customers include England's Princess Eugenie and Princess Beatrice.

Baby Apparel's exports to the United States and United Kingdom account for 90 per cent of its production. Its biggest buyer is Norman Marcus Ltd, a UK-based manufacturer and importer. Baby Apparel also sells to JC Penney Company, one of the world's biggest retailers.

Dubai Fashions

1 September 1993, Mr Abdul Alih, managing director of Dubai Fashions, visited Manila to look for a supplier of children's wear with smocking. Dubai Fashions is a garment importer based in the United Arab Emirates; it has shops in Dubai, Sharjah and Alain. Before going to the Philippines, Dubai Fashions had sourced its children's wear from Spain and the United Kingdom. Having heard that the handsmocked children's wear in those countries were imported from the Philippines, Dubai Fashions decided to cut the distribution channel by importing directly from the Philippines. Mr Alih obtained a list of recommended children's wear exporters from the Philippine Commercial Office in Dubai. On top of this list was Baby Apparel.

This case was developed by Professor Luz T. Suplico, De La Salle University, Manila, Philippines. The case is based on a true incident but the persons, figures and data have been disguised.

The Transaction

Although Dubai Fashions liked Baby Apparel's handsmocked dresses instantly, product revisions had to be made to suit the Arab market. Unlike the children's summer dresses sold to JC Penney which had no sleeves and no lining, children's dresses to be sold to Dubai Fashions had to have sleeves and linings. Further, utmost care had to be taken to ensure that designs did not include stars and crosses. A sales contract amounting to US$22 710 covering 2700 pieces, to be delivered no later than 15 December 1993, was signed by Mr Alih and Baby Apparel. On 7 September 1993, the Bank of Oman, the issuing bank, sent an irrevocable Letter of Credit (LC) at sight to the Philippine National Bank, the negotiating bank. The following were some of the LC's terms:

1. Shipment.
   1.1 Port of discharge: Manila.
   1.2 Port of destination: Dubai.
   1.3 Partial shipment: Allowed.
   1.4 Transshipment: Allowed.
   1.5 Shipment expiry date: 15 January 1994.
   1.6 Shipping documents should be presented to the issuing bank within 10 days of issuance but within the validity of the credit.
2. Special Instructions.
   2.1 Invoice should show the manufacturer's name.
   2.2 Bill of Lading should show Bank of Oman as notifying party.
   2.3 Shipment is to be effected by the United Arab Shipping Co. (UASC) line vessel or conference and/or regular line vessel only and a certificate to this effect from the shipping company or its agent must accompany the negotiated documents.
   2.4 A certificate from the owner/master or agent of the vessel or from the manufacturer/exporter is to be presented stating 'To Whom It May Concern' and 'We certify that the vessel is allowed by Arab authorities to call at Arab ports and is not scheduled to call at any Israeli port during its trip to Arab countries.' This certificate is not applicable if shipment was effected on UASC vessel.
   2.5 An inspection certificate is to be issued and signed by the authorized buying agent.

After the receipt of the LC, Baby Apparel produced the reference samples, which were airfreighted to Dubai Fashions. Dubai approved the reference samples without any revision. Thus, Baby Apparel began production as soon as the reference samples were approved. Because of its tight production schedule for its major buyers, Baby Apparel notified Dubai that it was having difficulties in shipping the goods before 15 December 1993.

In the Middle East, all business activities are suspended during Ramadan. Dubai had made an urgent request for shipment no later than 30 December 1993 to assure arrival in UAE before the start of Ramadan, 12 February 1994. Shipment, after 12 January 1994, would mean arrival during Ramadan and Dubai Fashions would be unable to move the merchandise out of the warehouse until Ramadan was over. The order was shipped on 15 January 1994 and was short 4 pieces. The buying agent and Dubai Fashions agreed to waive the short-shipment discrepancy on condition that Baby Apparel send the remaining 4 pieces by courier.

Ocean shipment from Manila to Dubai takes about 30 days on a regular vessel. Since the goods were shipped based on an Irrevocable Letter of Credit at sight, Baby Apparel only had to send the complete set of documents as specified in the LC to the Bank of Oman to be paid. It had expected payment no later than 15 February 1994.

As nonpayment of LCs from the Middle East was a rampant practice, Baby Apparel became increasingly concerned when the Philippine National Bank reported that it could not pay them despite the submission of complete documents. On 20 February, Baby Apparel faxed Dubai Fashions to send proof of shipment to the Philippine National Bank as it was not able to receive payment. Dubai Fashions followed up the payment at the Bank of Oman and the following discrepancies in the documents were reported:

1. The LC had expired.
2. The presentation of shipping documents was late.
3. The invoice did not show the manufacturer's name.
4. The Bill of Lading did not show that Bank of Oman was the notifying party.

Dubai Fashions agreed to waive these discrepancies and the Bank of Oman remitted payment to Baby Apparel through the Philippine National Bank.

Questions

1. Why is it important to follow the terms of the LC? What are the measures which should have been taken by Baby Apparel to prevent the discrepancies found in the LC?
2. If you were the production manager of Baby Apparel, how would you try to prevent a potential short-shipment problem in the next order of Dubai Fashions?
3. What were the special arrangements that Baby Apparel had to make in dealing with Arab importers in terms of the products and shipment?

CASE 4.4
Selling White Dove Shampoo in the Philippines

According to industry sources, shampoo was first introduced in the Philippine market by a multinational company after World War II. Since then the product has grown in popularity and usage largely due to massive advertising and extensive distribution. While specific figures on shampoo production and consumption were unavailable from national or local government agencies, a survey of Filipino family expenditures in 1988 was available from the National Census and Statistics Office (NSCO). It showed that a family spent 3.3 per cent of its annual income for personal care products, which included shampoo. Based on this percentage of expenditures, the value of the personal care products industry would be close to 11 billion pesos. Knowledgeable persons involved in the shampoo business put its value at about 10 per cent of that, or 1.1 billion pesos.

Shampoo is distributed nationwide by several companies, with more than a dozen brands of shampoo in the market. Shampoo is sold in *sari-sari* (*sari-sari* is a Filipino word meaning variety store) stores, drugstores, department stores, supermarkets, superettes or minimarts, beauty specialty shops, salons or beauty parlours and megamalls. Its users, both male and female, young and old, come from all income levels.

In the subcategory of hair care products (from the class of personal care products), a companion item to shampoo was developed which was called hair conditioner or simply conditioner. Celia Torres, production manager of White Dove Philippines Company (WDPC), explained the distinction between the two: 'Shampoo is a chemical preparation for cleaning scalp and hair, while a conditioner is a chemical preparation applied to hair to help restore the strength of, and give body to, hair.'

The Company

The beginning of White Dove Philippines Company can be traced back to 1973. Koji Izumi, president of White Dove Company of Japan, was a visitor to the Philippines looking for a company that could be a distributor of his company's products. While he was having his hair cut in the barbershop of a five-star hotel in Manila, the brand of the barber's chair caught his eye. It was a very familiar brand: Nikko-Montand. He thought then that if the barber's chair could be sold

This case was written by Professor Renato S. Esquerra, De La Salle University, Manila, Philippines.

here, then his White Dove shampoo also would find a good market here. In Japan, White Dove products had been extensively marketed through beauty salons. He sought the barber's help to locate the distributor of the Nikko-Montand barber's chair. The distributor was Leonardo Paras' Commercial Company, a firm engaged in the importation and distribution of barber shop and beauty salon equipment like steamers, hair dryers, shampoo bowls, chairs and other accessories from Japan. Paras was an architect-businessman.

When they met, Izumi explained the purpose of his visit and quickly offered the distributorship of White Dove products in the Philippines to Paras. Izumi believed that, as a distributor of barber shop and beauty salon equipment and accessories, Paras' company would be the right organization to distribute White Dove products in the Philippines. Paras' immediate reaction to Izumi's offer was, 'But I don't know anything about shampoo.'

Izumi assured Paras of all technical assistance, as well as assistance in marketing and research. He invited Paras to Japan.

As an importer of Japanese products, Paras went to Japan every quarter. During one of those trips, he called on Izumi and was given a tour of the White Dove plant. Before leaving for Manila, Paras was given samples of White Dove products. Back home, he distributed the samples to beauty salons. Happily for him, the feedback from the beauty salon's owners and their customers was positive.

Research and Development

It took three years before White Dove Philippines Company (WDPC) became a licensee of White Dove Japan. WDPC was as interested and concerned as its Japanese licenser was in the production of hair care products of high quality and standards. Before the formulations were developed for the products to be marketed in the Philippines, samples of various types of water from many areas in the country were sent to Japan for testing and analysis. Specimens of Filipinos' hair strands were also collected for study. Since White Dove products' formulations were made for Asians, it was not necessary to test for sensitivity of the Filipinos' skin. However, in the matter of essence or scent, it was found that the Filipinos had a preference for stronger scent while the Japanese preferred a milder scent.

Thus, it was 1976 before White Dove Philippines Company officially started. Its first factory was a 60-square-metre back garden space at the Manila residence of Paras. It was there that its initial products—shampoo, rinse and hair treatment—were packed. Packaging was done in plastic bottles made in the Philippines from moulds lent by White Dove Japan.

Table CS 4.4.1   White Dove Philippines Company Print Media Advertising Expenditures*
(in per cent)

Publication	1989	1990	1991	1992[†]
Newspapers:				
Manila Bulletin	40%	35%	40%	40%
Philippine Daily Inquirer	15	20	15	15
The Philippine Star	5	5	5	5
Magazines:				
Mod	10	10	15	15
Woman Today	15	15	10	10
Miscellaneous	10	10	10	10
Women's Quarterly	5	5	5	5
Total	100%	100%	100%	100%

*In selected media only.
[†]Projected.

After four years in Manila, the factory had to move to a suburban town to streamline its operation with modern machinery from Japan. That modernization increased WDPC's production tenfold. The installation of the machinery and the training of manufacturing personnel was supervised by a Japanese technician. To assure that product quality standards set by the licenser were adhered to, White Dove Japan sent a chemist to WDPC every quarter to check on the formulations and the finished products.

Advertising and Promotion

The promotion of White Dove products started with free sampling in beauty salons. This was done in keeping with the system used by White Dove Japan. In Japan, White Dove products were classified as institutional products and sold to and at beauty salons, not directly to the consumer.

Sampling was followed by other promotional activities. A hairstyling show and seminar featuring a foreign hairdresser was held in a five-star hotel in Manila. It was attended by more than 1000 amateur and professional hairdressers. The success of that promotional activity made White Dove Philippines Company a byword among hairdressers and beauty salon patrons.

Eventually, White Dove became a regular sponsor or cosponsor of hairstyling shows and competitions, and national and international beauty contests, and a regular exhibitor in cosmetics and beauty products' fairs. The Hair and Cosmetologists Association of the Philippines (HACAP) had become a regular beneficiary of White Dove's sponsorship of tie-in advertising and promotional shows.

Advertising of WDPC products had been limited to cinema advertising, radio and print media. A larger bulk of its annual advertising budget, roughly four per cent of its national annual sales, went to print media, specifically daily newspapers and weekly and monthly magazines, especially those read by women and young girls. (See Table CS 4.4.1.)

White Dove had used more testimonial advertising than any other type. In its ads, professional hairdressers' photos and the names of shops and their testimonials on White Dove's products were featured. The hairdressers were very happy about these testimonial ads, which they often posted in their shops for their customers to see. The success of White Dove's testimonial advertising eventually induced other shampoo manufacturers to do similar types of advertising.

To tap the retail market, WDPC set up display counters in selected department stores and supermarkets, especially in Metro Manila.

Distribution

The initial promotional sampling of WDPC products in beauty salons, hotels and motels set the pace of the company's distribution. For several years, more than half of WDPC sales were made through these institutions. According to the WDPC marketing department, there were about 10 000 beauty shops in the Philippines in 1991. Twenty-five per cent of them and their customers had been using WDPC products. One of the WDPC products contributed about 60 per cent of the beauty salons' annual income, according to WDPC's research department.

Beauty salons were classified into A, B and Upper C as markets for WDPC products. Class A and B salons

Table CS 4.4.2 White Dove Philippines Company's Other Hair Care Products (1992)

1. Avocado Cream Rinse
2. Lemon Cream Rinse
3. Hair Treatment Liquid
4. Hot Oil Treatment
5. Hair and Scale Rejuvenator Tonic
6. Hair and Scalp Rejuvenator Tonic (with pump spray)
7. Fashionable Gel
8. Hair Styling Gel
9. Hair Spray
10. Styling Mousse

Figure CS 4.4.1 White Dove Philippines Company Mission Statement

White Dove Philippines Company will strive for leadership in the personal care products market by providing the best quality products, with particular emphasis on the products for the care of hair, to Philippine consumers, ensuring that any addition to the product line or mix offering will contribute desirably to the company's volume and market position and, ultimately, its profit standing.

were usually bigger, had more personnel, were air-conditioned, offered more services than just hair trimming and styling and carried inventories of WDPS products. Class A beauty salons carried an inventory of White Dove products worth P30 000 and up; Class B, P10 000 to P30 000; and Upper C, P3000 to P10 000. (See Table CS 4.4.2.)

The average annual sales of White Dove shampoo and conditioner during the period 1989–1992 was P27 000 000. These figures represented about 40 per cent of its national annual sales. (See Table CS 4.4.3.) The remaining 60 per cent represented sales of other WDPC products. According to the sales department of WDPC, its annual sales of shampoo and conditioner were roughly equal to about 5 and 4 per cent, respectively, of the Philippine market.

WDPC distributes its products nationwide through retail outlets which include supermarkets, department stores, drugstores, grocery stores, minimarts, superettes, beauty salons and barber shops. These outlets are serviced by 11 sales representatives and 16 distributors covering the retailers; 7 sales representatives, 6 territorial representatives and 18 subdistributors servicing the salons; and 1 corporate distribution outfit which serves as its marketing arm in the Metro Manila area.

Pricing

The pricing policy of White Dove had been governed by its Mission Statement. Each WDPC product was priced primarily for the A- and B-class market. However, according to Ruben Panlilio, White Dove's marketing director, the prices of WDPC products were set at a competitive level, allowing the company a fairly reasonable return on investment and a margin of profit. (See Table CS 4.4.4.)

New Products for White Dove Philippines Company

In early 1993, Ruben Panlilio, a retired Philippine marketing executive, accepted the invitation of Leonardo Paras, president and general manager of White Dove Philippines Company (WDPC), to be its full-time marketing director.

Eighteen months earlier, WDPC had retained the personal services of Panlilio as marketing consultant on a part-time basis. During that period, Panlilio worked with Paras on the company's marketing operations. The latter had to oversee his company's marketing operations for lack of a senior marketing executive.

During Panlilio's part-time involvement, Paras had asked Panlilio to make a thorough study of the company's operations and submit his recommendations. It was after Paras had read Panlilio's report that he invited Panlilio to assume the post of marketing director.

One of Panlilio's recommendations was for WDPC to introduce new products to increase sales volume and improve its market position and profitability in pursuit of its corporate mission. (See Figure CS 4.4.1.) Two products were recommended by Panlilio. One was a hair cream that would serve as a quick setter and, at the same time, would work as a hair darkener whose effectiveness would be reached after repeated usage. The other was a combination shampoo and conditioner.

Paras and Panlilio both agreed that the two products would be launched in late 1994. Sometime in the middle of 1993, however, a multinational company launched a product described as '2-in-1', which was a combination of shampoo and conditioner. The introduction of the new product was heavily supported by mass-media advertising. Towards the end of the year, about six months after the launch of this new product, Paras called Panlilio to remind him about their meeting to finalize the plans for the two WDPC products' launch.

Table CS 4.4.3   White Dove Philippines Company Annual National Sales, 1989–1992 (in per cent)

Area	1989	1990	1991	1992*
Greater Manila Area	76.5%	76.31%	75.74%	67.58%
North Luzon	8.74	9.47	10.82	12.25
South Luzon	6.20	4.39	5.90	9.31
Visayas	8.63	8.20	5.16	7.03
Mindanao	0.85	1.63	2.38	3.83
Total	100.00%	100.00%	100.00%	100.00%

*The 1992 figures were based on projections by the company.

Table CS 4.4.4   White Dove Philippines Company's Suggested Retail Prices of Shampoo and Conditioner (1992)

	Bottle Size		
Product	100 ml	200 ml	600 ml
Avocado Oil Shampoo	P34.00	P59.50	P165.00
Lemon Shampoo*	31.00	54.00	148.00
Oil Shampoo	31.00	54.00	148.00
Treatment Shampoo	30.00	52.00	†
Treatment Conditioner	30.00	55.00	†
Balance Shampoo	†	52.00	†
All Over Bath Shampoo	(Sold in 175 ml size only for P29.00)		

*Also available in 1000 ml bottle for P195.00.
†Not available in this size bottle.

After receiving the call, Panlilio went over his files of the latest sales figures. The figures showed that the introduction of the 2-in-1 shampoo-conditioner of one of WDPC's competitors had not had any adverse effect on WDPC sales to its institutional customers, beauty salons. At the same time, the shampoo-conditioner's sales at the retail outlets had been increasing, and were, in Panlilio's view, threatening WDPC's sales to beauty salons. To him, it seemed that sales through retail outlets would far exceed sales to beauty salons, thus reversing the trend established over the past many years.

As Panlilio mulled over the market situation revealed by WDPC sales figures, the memory of his conversation with a White Dove Japan chemist, on his quarterly quality inspection trip to the Marikina plant, came to mind. The chemist had said, 'Shampoo is shampoo, Panlilio-san, and conditioner is conditioner. We do not believe they should be mixed.'

Panlilio was a liberal arts graduate of the University of Santo Tomas and had majored in literature. He thought that what the chemist said was something like a line from a poet's words, 'East is East, and West is West, and never the twain shall meet.' He stood up, gathered his files, walked out of the room, closed the door, and went down the passageway towards Paras' office, where they would review the WDPC planned launch of a 2-in-1 shampoo and a 2-in-1 hair cream.

Questions

1. What do you think are the marketing objectives of the company?
2. Were the planned product launches consistent with its marketing objectives?
3. What do you think of its channels of distribution? Should they be changed at all? Why?
4. How would you compare its promotional activities with those that you are familiar with?
5. Why do you think the company was not using television as much as it was using print media?
6. Why was the company pricing its products to the level of the A and B markets? Was it a sound pricing policy? Why?
7. How would you view the company's concern for product quality and the licensor's similar interest in the same?
8. Do you think the company should introduce its own shampoo-conditioner? Should it secure the licenser's approval before doing so?
9. Between the 2-in-1 shampoo with conditioner and the dual-purpose cream, which do you think the company should launch first in the face of its competitor's move?
10. On the whole, how would you evaluate the company's marketing performance?
11. Why do you think it took three years before the Japanese company appointed White Dove Philippines Company its licensee? Why does decision making in a Japanese company take a longer time (compared to American and European companies)?
12. Do you think testing water, hair strands and scent preferences of the Philippine market is a correct research approach? Why?

CASE 4.5
Blair Water Purifiers to India

'A pity I couldn't have stayed for Diwali', thought Rahul Chatterjee. 'But anyway it was great to be back home in Calcutta.' The Diwali holiday and its festivities would begin in early November 1996, some two weeks after Chatterjee had returned to the United States. Chatterjee worked as an international market liaison for Blair Company, Inc. This was his eighth year with Blair Company and easily his favourite. 'Your challenge will be in moving us from just dabbling in less developed countries (LDCs) to our thriving in them', his boss had said when Chatterjee was promoted to the job last January. Chatterjee had agreed and was thrilled when asked to visit Bombay and New Delhi in April. His purpose on that trip was to gather background data on the possibility of Blair Company entering the Indian market for home water purification devices. Initial results were encouraging and prompted the second trip.

Chatterjee had used his second trip primarily to study Indian consumers in Calcutta and Bangalore and to gather information on possible competitors. The two cities represented quite different metropolitan areas in terms of location, size, language and infrastructure—yet both suffered from similar problems in terms of water supplied to their residents. These problems could be found in many LDCs and were favourable to home water purification.

Information gathered on both visits would be used to make a recommendation on market entry and on elements of an entry strategy. Executives at Blair Company would compare Chatterjee's recommendations to those from two other Blair Company liaisons who were focusing their efforts on Argentina, Brazil and Indonesia.

Indian Market for Home Water Filtration and Purification

Like most aspects of India, the market for home water filtration and purification took a good deal of effort

This case was written by Professor James E. Nelson, University of Colorado at Boulder. He thanks students in the Class of 1996 (Batch 31), Indian Institute of Management, Calcutta, for their invaluable help in collecting all data needed to write this case. He also thanks Professor Roger Kerin, Southern Methodist University, for his helpful comments in writing this case. The case is intended for educational purposes rather than to illustrate either effective or ineffective decision making. Some data as well as the identity of the company are disguised. © 1997 by James E. Nelson. Used with permission.

Table CS 4.5.1 Industry Sales Estimates and Forecasts for Water Purifiers in India, 1990–2005 (000 units)

Year	Unit Sales Estimates	Unit Sales Forecast Under . . .		
		Realistic Scenario	Optimistic Scenario	Pessimistic Scenario
1990	60			
1991	90			
1992	150			
1993	200			
1994	220			
1995	240			
1996		250	250	250
1997		320	370	300
1998		430	540	400
1999		570	800	550
2000		800	1200	750
2001		1000	1500	850
2002		1300	1900	900
2003		1500	2100	750
2004		1600	2100	580
2005		1500	1900	420

to understand. Yet despite expending this effort, Chatterjee realized that much remained either unknown or in conflict. For example, the market seemed clearly a mature one, with four or five established Indian competitors fighting for market share. Or was it? Another view portrayed the market as a fragmented one, with no large competitor having a national presence and perhaps 100 small, regional manufacturers, each competing in just one or two of India's 25 states. Indeed, the market could be in its early growth stages, as reflected by the large number of product designs, materials and performances. Perhaps with a next generation product and a world-class marketing effort, Blair Company could consolidate the market and stimulate tremendous growth—much like the situation in the Indian market for cars.

Such uncertainty made it difficult to estimate market potential. However, Chatterjee had collected unit sales estimates for a 10-year period for three similar product categories—vacuum cleaners, sewing machines and colour televisions. In addition, a Delhi-based research firm had provided him with estimates of unit sales for Aquaguard, the largest-selling water purifier in several Indian states. Chatterjee had used the data in two forecasting models available at Blair Company along with three subjective scenarios— realistic, optimistic and pessimistic—to arrive at the estimates and forecasts for water purifiers shown in Table CS 4.5.1. 'If anything,' Chatterjee had explained to his boss, 'my forecasts are conservative because they

describe only first-time sales, not any replacement sales over the 10-year forecast horizon'. He also pointed out that his forecasts applied only to industry sales in larger urban areas, which was the present industry focus.

One thing that seemed certain was that many Indians felt the need for improved water quality. Folklore, newspapers, consumer activists and government officials regularly reinforced this need by describing the poor quality of Indian water. Quality suffered particularly during the monsoons because of highly polluted water entering treatment plants and because of numerous leaks and unauthorized withdrawals from water systems. Such leaks and withdrawals often polluted clean water after it had left the plants. Politicians running for national, state and local government offices also reinforced the need for improved water quality through election campaign promises. Governments at these levels set standards for water quality, took measurements at thousands of locations throughout the nation and advised consumers when water became unsafe.

During periods of poor water quality, many Indian consumers had little choice but to consume the water as they found it. However, better educated, wealthier and more health conscious consumers took steps to safeguard their family's health and often continued these steps year-round. A good estimate of the number of such households, Chatterjee thought, would be around 40 million. These consumers were similar in many respects to consumers in middle- and upper-middle-class households in the United States and the European Union. They valued comfort and product choice. They saw consumption of material goods as a means to a higher quality of life. They liked foreign brands and would pay a higher price for such brands, as long as purchased products outperformed competing Indian products. Chatterjee had identified as his target market these 40 million households plus those in another four million households who had similar values and lifestyles, but as yet took little effort to improve water quality in their homes.

Traditional Method for Home Water Purification. The traditional method of water purification in the target market relied not on any commercially supplied product but instead on boiling. Each day or several times a day, a cook, maid or family member would boil two to five litres of water for 10 minutes, allow it to cool, and then transfer it to containers for storage (often in a refrigerator). Chatterjee estimated that about 50 per cent of the target market used this procedure. Boiling was seen by consumers as inexpensive, effective in terms of eliminating dangerous bacteria, and entrenched in a traditional sense. Many consumers who used this method considered it more effective than any product on the market. However, boiling affected the palatability of water, leaving the purified product somewhat 'flat' to the taste. Boiling also was cumbersome, time-consuming and ineffective in removing physical impurities and unpleasant odours. Consequently, about 10 per cent of the target marked took a second step by filtering their boiled water through 'candle filters' before storage. Many consumers who took this action did so despite knowing that water could become recontaminated during handling and storage.

Mechanical Methods for Home Water Filtration and Purification. About 40 per cent of the target market used a mechanical device to improve their water quality. Half of this group used candle filters, primarily because of their low price and ease of use. The typical candle filter comprised two containers, one resting on top of the other. The upper container held one or more porous ceramic cylinders (candles) which strained the water as gravity drew it into the lower container. Containers were made of plastic, porcelain or stainless steel and typically stored between 15 and 20 litres of filtered water. Purchase costs depended on materials and capacities, ranging from Rs.350 for a small plastic model to Rs.1100 for a large stainless steel model (35 Indian Rupees were equivalent to US$1.00 in 1996). Candle filters were slow, producing 15 litres (one candle) to 45 litres (three candles)

of filtered water each 24 hours. To maintain this productivity, candles regularly needed to be removed, cleaned and boiled for 20 minutes. Most manufacturers recommended that consumers replace candles (Rs.40 each) either once a year or more frequently, depending on sediment levels.

The other half of this group used 'water purifiers', devices that were considerably more sophisticated than candle filters. Water purifiers typically employed three water processing stages. The first removed sediments, the second objectionable odours and colours and the third harmful bacteria and viruses. Engineers at Blair Company were sceptical that most purifiers claiming the latter benefit actually could deliver on their promise. However, all purifiers did a better job here than candle filters. Candle filters were totally ineffective in eliminating bacteria and viruses (and might even increase this type of contamination), despite advertising claims to the contrary. Water purifiers generally used stainless steel containers and sold at prices ranging from Rs.2000 to Rs.7000, depending on manufacturers, features and capacities. Common flow rates were one to two litres of purified water per minute. Simple service activities could be performed on water purifiers by consumers as needed. However, more complicated service required units to be taken to a nearby dealer or an in-home visit from a skilled technician.

The remaining 10 per cent of the target market owned neither a filter nor a purifier and seldom boiled their water. Many consumers in this group were unaware of water problems and thought their water quality acceptable. However, a few consumer in this group refused to pay for products that they believed were mostly ineffective. Overall, Chatterjee believed that only a few consumers in this group could be induced to change their habits and become customers. The most attractive segments consisted of the 90 per cent of households in the target market who boiled, boiled and filtered, only filtered, or purified their water.

All segments in the target market showed a good deal of similarity in terms of what they thought important in the purchase of a water purifier. According to Chatterjee's research, the most important factor was product performance in terms of sediment removal, bacteria and virus removal, capacity (either in the form of storage or flow rate), safety and 'footprint' space. Purchase price also was an important concern among consumers who boiled, boiled and filtered or only filtered their water. The next most important factor was ease of installation and service, with style and appearance rated almost as important. The least important factor was warranty and availability of finance for purchase. Finally, all segments expected a water purifier to be warranted against defective operation for 18 to 24 months and to perform trouble-free for five to ten years.

Foreign Investment in India

India appeared attractive to many foreign investors because of government actions begun in the 1980s during the administration of prime minister Rajiv Gandhi. The broad label applied to these actions was 'liberalization'. Liberalization had opened the Indian economy to foreign investors, stemming from recognition that protectionist policies had not worked very well and that Western economies and technologies—seen against the collapse of the Soviet Union—did. Liberalization had meant major changes in approval requirements for new commercial projects, investment policies, taxation procedures, and, most importantly, attitudes of government officials. These changes had stayed in place through the two national governments that followed Gandhi's assassination in 1991.

If Blair Company entered the Indian market, it would do so in one of three ways: (1) joint working arrangement, (2) joint venture company or (3) acquisition. In a joint working arrangement, Blair Company would supply key purifier components to an Indian company that would manufacture and market the assembled product. Licence fees would be remitted to Blair Company on a per unit basis over the term of the agreement (typically five years, with an option to renew for three more). A joint venture agreement would have Blair Company partnering with an existing Indian company expressly for the purpose of manufacturing and marketing water purifiers. Profits from the joint venture operation would be split between the two parties per the agreement, which usually contained a clause describing buy/sell procedures available to the two parties after a minimum time period. An acquisition entry would have Blair Company purchasing an existing Indian company whose operations then would be expanded to include the water purifier. Profits from the acquisition would belong to Blair Company.

Beyond understanding these basic entry possibilities, Chatterjee acknowledged that he was no expert in legal aspects attending the project. However, two days spent with a Calcutta consulting firm had produced the following information. Blair Company must apply for market entry to the Foreign Investment Promotion Board, Secretariat for Industrial Approvals, Ministry of Industries. The proposal would go before the Board for an assessment of the relevant technology and India's need for the technology. If approved by the Board, the proposal then would go to the Reserve Bank of India, Ministry of Finance, for approvals of any royalties and fees, remittances of dividends and interest (if any), repatriations of profits and invested capital and

repayment of foreign loans. While the process sounded cumbersome and time-consuming, the consultant assured Chatterjee that the government usually would complete its deliberations in less than six months and that his consulting firm could 'virtually guarantee' final approval.

Trademarks and patents were protected by law in India. Trademarks were protected for seven years and would be renewed on payment of a prescribed fee. Patents lasted for 14 years. On balance, Chatterjee had told his boss that Blair Company would have 'no more problem protecting its intellectual property rights in India than in the United States—as long as we stay out of court.' Chatterjee went on to explain that litigation in India was expensive and protracted. Litigation problems were compounded by an appeal process that could extend a case for easily a generation. Consequently, many foreign companies preferred arbitration, as India was a party to the Geneva Convention covering Foreign Arbitral Awards.

Foreign companies were taxed on income arising from Indian operations. They also paid taxes on any interest, dividends and royalties received, and on any capital gains received from a sale of assets. The government offered a wide range of tax concessions to foreign investors, including liberal depreciation allowances and generous deductions. The government offered even more favourable tax treatment if foreign investors would locate in one of India's six Free Trade Zones. Overall, Chatterjee thought that corporate tax rates in India probably were somewhat higher than in the United States. However, so were profits—the average return on assets for all Indian corporations in recent years was almost 18 per cent, compared to about 11 per cent for United States corporations.

Approval by the Reserve Bank of India was needed for repatriation of ordinary profits. However, approval should be obtained easily if Blair Company could show that repatriated profits were being paid out of export earnings of hard currencies. Chatterjee thought that export earnings would not be difficult to realize, given India's extremely low wage rates and its central location to wealthier South Asian countries. 'Profit repatriation was really not much of an issue, anyway', he thought. Three years might pass before profits of any magnitude could be realized; at least five years would pass before substantial profits would be available for repatriation. Approval of repatriation by the Reserve Bank might not be required at this time, given liberalization trends. Finally, if repatriation remained difficult, Blair Company could undertake crosstrading or other actions to unblock profits.

Overall, investment and trade regulations in India in 1996 meant that business could be conducted much easier than ever before. Hundreds of companies from the European Union, Japan, Korea and the United States were entering India in all sectors of the country's economy. In the home appliance market, Chatterjee could identify 11 such firms—Carrier, Electrolux, General Electric, Goldstar, Matsushita, Singer, Samsung, Sanyo, Sharp, Toshiba and Whirlpool. Many of these firms had yet to realize substantial profits but all saw the promise of a huge market developing over the next few years.

Blair Company, Inc.

Blair Company was founded in 1975 by Eugene Blair, after he left his position in research and development at Culligan International Company. Blair Company's first product was a desalinator, used by mobile home parks in Florida to remove salts from brackish well water supplied to residents. The product was a huge success and markets quickly expanded to include nearby municipalities, smaller businesses, hospitals, and bottlers of water for sale to consumers. Geographic markets also expanded, first to other coastal regions near the company's headquarters in Tampa, Florida, and then to desert areas in the southwestern United States. New products were added rapidly as well and, by 1996, the product line included desalinators, particle filters, ozonators, ion exchange resins and purifiers. Industry experts generally regarded the product line as superior in terms of performance and quality, with prices higher than those of many competitors.

Blair Company sales revenues for 1996 would be almost $400 million, with an expected profit close to $50 million. Annual growth in sales revenues averaged 12 per cent for the past five years. Blair Company employed over 4000 people, with 380 having technical backgrounds and responsibilities.

Export sales of desalinators and related products began at Blair Company in 1980. Units were sold first to resorts in Mexico and Belize and later to water bottlers in Germany. Export sales grew rapidly and Blair Company found it necessary to organize its International Division in 1985. Sales in the International Division also grew rapidly and would reach almost $140 million in 1996. About $70 million would come from countries in Latin and South America, $30 million from Europe (including shipments to Africa), and $40 million from South Asia and Australia. The International Division had sales offices, small assembly areas, and distribution facilities in Frankfurt, Germany; Tokyo, Japan; and Singapore.

The Frankfurt office had been the impetus in 1990 for development and marketing of Blair Company's first product targeted exclusively to consumer households—a home water filter. Sales engineers at the Frankfurt office began receiving consumer and distributor requests for a home water filter soon after the fall of the Berlin wall in 1989. By late 1991, two models had been designed in the United States and introduced in Germany (particularly to the eastern regions), Poland, Hungary, Romania, the Czech Republic and Slovakia.

Blair Company executives watched the success of the two water filters with great interest. The market for clean water in LDCs was huge, profitable, and attractive in a socially responsible sense. However, the quality of water in many LDCs was such that a water filter usually would not be satisfactory. Consequently, in late 1994, executives had directed the development of a water purifier that could be added to the product line. Engineers had given the final design in the project the brand name, 'Delight'. For the time being, Chatterjee and the other market analysts had accepted the name, not knowing if it might infringe on any existing brand in India or in the other countries under study.

Delight Purifier

The Delight purifier used a combination of technologies to remove four types of contaminants found in potable water—sediments, organic and inorganic chemicals, microbials or cysts, and objectionable tastes and odours. The technologies were effective as long as contaminants in the water were present at 'reasonable' levels. Engineers at Blair Company had interpreted 'reasonable' as levels described in several World Health Organization (WHO) reports on potable water and had combined the technologies to purify water to a level beyond WHO standards. Engineers had repeatedly assured Chatterjee that Delight's design in terms of technologies should not be a concern. Ten units operating in the company's testing laboratory showed no signs of failure or performance deterioration after some 5000 hours of continuous use. 'Still,' Chatterjee thought, 'we will undertake a good bit of field testing in India before entering. The risks of failure are too large to ignore. And, besides, results of our testing would be useful in convincing consumers and retailers to buy.

Chatterjee and the other market analysts still faced major design issues in configuring technologies into physical products. For example, a 'point of entry' design would place the product immediately after water entry to the home, treating all water before it flowed to all water outlets. In contrast, a 'point of use' design would place the product on a countertop, wall, or at the end of a tap and treat only water arriving at that location. Based on cost estimates, designs of competing products, and his understanding of Indian consumers, Chatterjee would direct engineers to

Figure CS 4.5.1

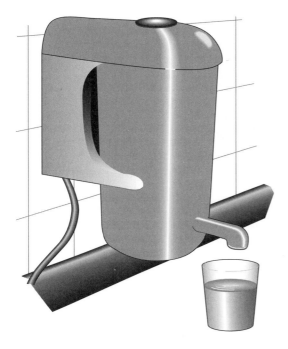

proceed only with 'point of use' designs for the market.

Other technical details were yet to be worked out. For example, Chatterjee had to provide engineers with suggestions for filter flow rates, storage capacities (if any), unit layout, and overall dimensions, plus a number of special features. One such feature was the possibility of a small battery to operate the filter for several hours in case of a power failure (a common occurrence in India and many other LDCs). Another might be one or two 'bells or whistles' to tell cooks, maids, and family members that the unit indeed was working properly. Yet another might be an 'additive' feature, permitting users to add fluoride, vitamins, or even flavourings to their water.

Chatterjee knew that the Indian market would eventually require a number of models. However, at the outset of market entry, he probably could get by with just two—one with a larger capacity for houses and bungalows and the other a smaller capacity model for flats. He thought that model styling and specific appearances should reflect a Western, high technology school of design in order to distinguish the Delight purifier from competitors' products. To that end, he had instructed a graphics artist to develop two ideas that he had used to gauge consumer reactions on his last visit (see Figure CS 4.5.1). Consumers liked both models but preferred the countertop design to the wall-mount design.

Competitors

Upwards of 100 companies competed in the Indian market for home water filters and purifiers. While information on most of these companies was difficult to obtain, Chatterjee and the Indian research agencies were able to develop descriptions of three major competitors and brief profiles of several others.

Eureka Forbes. The most established competitor in the water purifier market was Eureka Forbes, a joint venture company established in 1982 between Electrolux (Sweden) and Forbes Campbell (India). The company marketed a broad line of 'modern, lifestyle products' including water purifiers, vacuum cleaners and mixers/grinders. The brand name used for its water purifiers was 'Aquaguard', a name so well established that many consumers mistakenly used it to refer to other water purifiers or to the entire product category. Aquaguard, with its 10-year market history, was clearly the market leader and came close to being India's only national brand. However, Eureka Forbes had recently introduced a second brand of water purifier called 'PureSip'. The PureSip model was similar to Aquaguard except for its third stage process, which used a polyiodide resin instead of ultraviolet rays to kill bacteria and viruses. This meant that water from a PureSip purifier could be stored safely for later usage. Also in contrast to Aquaguard, the PureSip model needed no electricity for its operation.

However, the biggest difference between the two products was how they were sold. Aquaguard was sold exclusively by a 2500 person salesforce that called directly on households. In contrast, PureSip was sold by independent dealers of smaller home appliances. Unit prices to consumers for Aquaguard and PureSip in 1996 were approximately Rs.5500 and Rs.2000, respectively. Chatterjee believed that unit sales of PureSip were much smaller than unit sales for Aquaguard but growing at a much faster rate.

An Aquaguard unit typically was mounted on a kitchen wall, with plumbing required to bring water to the purifier's inlet. A two-metre long power cord was connected to a 230 volt AC electrical outlet—the Indian standard. If the power supply were to drop to 190 volts or lower, the unit would stop functioning. Other limits of the product included a smallish amount of activated carbon, which could eliminate only weak organic odours. It could not remove strong odours or inorganic solutes like nitrates and iron compounds. The unit's design did not allow for storage of treated water and its flow rate of one litre per minute seemed slow to some consumers.

Aquaguard's promotion strategy emphasized personal selling. Each salesman was assigned to a specific neighbourhood and was monitored by a group leader who, in turn, was monitored by a supervisor. Each salesman was expected to canvass his neighbourhood, select prospective households (e.g. those with annual incomes exceeding Rs.70 000), demonstrate the product, and make an intensive effort to sell the product. Repeated sales calls helped to educate consumers about their water quality and to reassure them that Aquaguard service was readily available. Television commercials and advertisements in magazines and newspapers supported the personal selling efforts. Chatterjee estimated that Eureka Forbes would spend about Rs.120 million on all sales activities in 1996, or roughly 11 per cent of its sales revenues. He estimated that about Rs.100 million of the Rs.120 million would be spent in the form of sales commissions. Chatterjee thought the company's total advertising expenditures for the year would be only about Rs.1 million.

Eureka Forbes was a formidable competitor. The salesforce was huge, highly motivated and well managed. Moreover, Aquaguard was the first product to enter the water purifier market, and the name had tremendous brand equity. The product itself was probably the weakest strategic component—but it would take much to convince consumers of this. And, while the salesforce offered a huge competitive advantage, it represented an enormous fixed cost and essentially limited sales efforts to large urban areas. More than 80 per cent of India's population lived in rural areas, where water quality was even lower.

Ion Exchange. Ion Exchange was the premier water treatment company in India, specializing in treatments of water, processed liquids, and wastewater in industrial markets. The company began operations in 1964 as a wholly-owned subsidiary of British Permutit. Permutit divested its holdings in 1985 and Ion Exchange became a wholly-owned Indian company. The company presently served customers in a diverse group of industries, including nuclear and thermal power stations, fertilizers, petrochemical refineries, textiles, automobiles and home water purifiers. Its home water purifiers carried the family brand name, ZERO-B (Zero-Bacteria).

ZERO-B purifiers used a halogenated resin technology as part of a three-stage purification process. The first stage removed suspended impurities via filter pads, the second eliminated bad odours and taste with activated carbon, and the third killed bacteria using trace quantities of polyiodide (iodine). The latter feature was attractive because it helped prevent iodine deficiency diseases and permitted purified water to be stored up to eight hours without fear of recontamination.

The basic purifier product for the home carried the name 'Puristore'. A Puristore unit typically sat on a kitchen counter near the tap, with no electricity or plumbing hookup needed for its operation. The unit stored 20 litres of purified water. It sold to consumers for Rs.2000. Each year the user must replace the halogenated resin at a cost of Rs.200.

Chatterjee estimated that ZERO-B captured about 7 per cent of the Indian water purifier market. Probably the biggest reason for the small share was a lack of consumer awareness. ZERO-B purifiers had been on the market for less than three years. They were not advertised heavily nor did they enjoy the sales effort intensity of Aquaguard. Distribution, too, was limited. During Chatterjee's visit, he could find only five dealers in Calcutta carrying ZERO-B products and none in Bangalore. Dealers that he contacted were of the opinion that ZERO-B's marketing efforts soon would intensify—two had heard rumours that a door-to-door salesforce was planned and that consumer advertising was about to begin.

Chatterjee had confirmed the latter point with a visit to a Calcutta advertising agency. A modest number of 10-second TV commercials soon would be aired on Zee TV and DD metro channels. The advertisements would focus on educating consumers

Figure CS 4.5.2

with the position, 'It is not a filter'. Instead, ZERO-B is a water purifier and much more effective than a candle filter in preventing health problems. Apart from this advertising effort, the only other form of promotion used was a point-of-sale brochure that dealers could give to prospective customers (see Figure CS 4.5.2).

On balance, Chatterjee thought that Ion Exchange could be a major player in the market. The company had over 30 years' experience in the field of water purification and devoted upwards of Rs.10 million each year to corporate research and development. 'In fact', he thought, 'all Ion Exchange really needs to do is to recognize the market's potential and to make it a priority within the company'. However, this might be difficult to do, given the company's prominent emphasis on industrial markets. Chatterjee estimated that ZERO-B products would account for less than 2 per cent of Ion Exchange's 1996 total sales, estimated at Rs.1000 million. He thought the total marketing expenditures for ZERO-B would be around Rs.3 million.

Singer.   The newest competitor to enter the Indian water purifier market was Singer India Ltd. Originally, Singer India was a subsidiary of The Singer Company, located in the United States, but a minority share (49 per cent) was sold to Indian investors in 1982. The change in ownership had led to construction of manufacturing facilities in India for sewing machines in 1983. The facilities were expanded in 1991 to produce a broad line of home appliances. Sales revenues for 1996 for the entire product line—sewing machines, food processors, irons, mixers, toasters, water heaters, ceiling fans, cooking ranges and colour televisions— would be about Rs.900 million.

During Chatterjee's time in Calcutta, he had visited a Singer Company showroom on Park Street. Initially he had hoped that Singer might be a suitable partner to manufacture and distribute the Delight purifier. However, much to his surprise, he was told that Singer now had its own brand on the market, 'Aquarius'. The product was not yet available in Calcutta but was being sold in Bombay and Delhi.

A marketing research agency in Delhi was able to gather some information on the Singer purifier. The product contained nine stages (!) and sold to consumers for Rs.4000. It removed sediments, heavy metals, bad tastes, odours and colours. It also killed bacteria and viruses, fungi and nematodes. The purifier required water pressure (8 PSI minimum) to operate but needed no electricity. It came in a single counter top model that could be moved from one room to another. Life of the device at a flow rate of 3.8 litres per minute was listed at 40 000 litres—about four to six years of use in the typical Indian household. The product's life could be extended to 70 000 litres at a somewhat slower flow rate. However, at 70 000 litres, the product must be discarded. The agency reported a heavy advertising blitz accompanying the introduction in Delhi—emphasizing TV and newspaper advertising, plus outdoor and transit advertising as support. All 10 Singer showrooms in Delhi offered vivid demonstrations of the product's operation.

Chatterjee had to admit that photos of the Aquarius purifier shown in the Calcutta showroom looked appealing. And, a trade article he found had described the product as 'state of the art' in comparison to the 'primitive' products now on the market. Chatterjee and Blair Company engineers tended to agree—the disinfecting resin used in Aquarius had been developed by the United States government's National Aeronautics and Space Administration (NASA) and was proven to be 100 per cent effective against bacteria and viruses. 'If only I could have brought a unit back with me', he thought. 'We could have some test results and see just how good it is'. The trade article also mentioned that Singer hoped to sell 40 000 units over the next two years.

Chatterjee knew that Singer was a well-known and respected brand name in India. Further, Singer's distribution channels were superior to those of any competitor in the market, including those of Eureka Forbes. Most prominent of Singer's three distribution channels were the 210 company-owned showrooms located in major urban areas around the country. Each sold and serviced the entire line of Singer products. Each was very well kept and staffed by knowledgeable personnel. Singer products also were sold throughout India by over 3000 independent dealers, who received inventory from an estimated 70 Singer-appointed distributors. According to the marketing research agency in Delhi, distributors earned margins of 12 per cent of the retail price for Aquarius while dealers earned margins of 5 per cent. Finally, Singer employed over 400 salesmen who sold sewing machines and food processors door-to-door. Like Eureka Forbes, the direct salesforce sold products primarily in large urban markets.

Other Competitors.   Chatterjee was aware of several other water purifiers on the Indian market. The Delta brand from S&S Industries in Madras seemed a carbon copy of Aquaguard, except for a more eye pleasing, counter top design. According to promotion literature, Delta offered a line of water-related products—purifiers, water softeners, iron removers, desalinators and ozonators. Another competitor was Alfa Water Purifiers, Bombay. The company offered four purifier models at prices from Rs.4300 to Rs.6500, depending on capacity. Symphony's Spectrum brand sold well around Bombay at Rs.4100 each but removed only suspended sediments, not heavy metals or bacteria. The Sam Group in Coimbatore recently had launched its 'Water Doctor' purifier at Rs.5200. The device used a third stage ozonator to kill bacteria and viruses and came in two attractive countertop models, 6- and 12-litre storage. Batliboi was mentioned by the Delhi research agency as yet another competitor, although Chatterjee knew nothing else about the brand. Taken all together, unit sales of all purifiers at these companies plus ZERO-B and Singer probably would account for around 60 000 units in 1996. The remaining 190 000 units would be Aquaguards and PureSips.

At least 100 Indian companies made and marketed

candle filters. The largest of these probably was Bajaj Electrical Division, whose product line also included water heaters, irons, electric lightbulbs, toasters, mixers and grillers. Bajaj's candle filters were sold by a large number of dealers who carried the entire product line. Candle filters produced by other manufacturers were sold mostly through dealers who specialized in small household appliances and general hardware. Probably no single manufacturer of candle filters had more than 5 per cent of any regional market in the country. No manufacturer attempted to satisfy a national market. Still, the candle filters market deserved serious consideration—perhaps Delight's entry strategy would attempt to 'trade-up' users of candle filters to a better, safer product.

Finally, Chatterjee knew that sales of almost all purifiers in 1996 in India came from large urban areas. No manufacturer targeted rural or smaller urban areas and at best, Chatterjee had calculated, existing manufacturers were reaching only 10 to 15 per cent of the entire Indian population. An explosion in sales would come if the right product could be sold outside metropolitan areas.

Recommendations

Chatterjee decided that an Indian market entry for Blair Company was subject to three 'givens' as he called them. First, he thought that a strategic focus on rural or smaller urban areas would not be wise, at least at the start. The lack of adequate distribution and communication infrastructure in rural India meant that any market entry would begin with larger Indian cities, most likely on the west coast.

Second, market entry would require manufacturing units in India. Because the cost of skilled labour in India was around Rs.20 to Rs.25 per hour (compared to $20 to $25 per hour in the United States), importing complete units was out of the question. However, importing a few key components would be necessary at the start of operation.

Third, Blair Company should find an Indian partner. Chatterjee's visits had produced a number of promising partners: Polar Industries, Calcutta; Milton Plastics, Bombay; Videocon Appliances, Aurangabad; BPL Sanyo Utilities and Appliances, Bangalore; Onida Savak, Delhi; Hawkins India, Bombay; and Voltas, Bombay. All companies manufactured and marketed a line of high-quality household appliances, possessed one or more strong brand names, and had established dealer networks (minimum of 10 000 dealers). All were involved to greater or lesser degrees with international partners. All were medium-sized firms—not too large that a partnership with Blair Company would be one-sided, not too small that they would lack managerial

talent and other resources. Finally, all were profitable (15 to 27 per cent return on assets in 1995) and looking to grow. However, Chatterjee had no idea if any company would find the Delight purifier and Blair Company attractive or if they might be persuaded to sell part or all of their operations as an acquisition.

Field Testing and Product Recommendations. The most immediate decision Chatterjee faced was whether or not he should recommend a field test. The test would cost about $25 000, placing 20 units in Indian homes in three cities and monitoring their performance for three to six months. The decision to test really was more than it seemed—Chatterjee's boss had explained that a decision to test was really a decision to enter. It made no sense to spend this kind of time and money if India were not an attractive opportunity. The testing period would also give Blair Company representatives time to identify a suitable Indian company as a licensee, joint venture partner or acquisition.

Fundamental to market entry was product design. Engineers at Blair Company had taken the position that purification technologies planned for Delight could be 'packaged in almost any fashion as long as we have electricity'. Electricity was needed to operate the product's ozonator as well as to indicate to users that the unit was functioning properly (or improperly, as the case might be). Beyond this requirement, anything was possible.

Chatterjee thought that a modular approach would be best. The basic module would be a countertop unit much like that shown in Figure CS 4.5.1. The module would outperform anything now on the market in terms of flow rate, palatability, durability and reliability, and would store two litres of purified water. Two additional modules would remove iron, calcium or other metallic contaminants that were peculiar to particular regions. For example, Calcutta and much of the surrounding area suffered from iron contamination, which no filter or purifier now on the Indian market could remove to a satisfactory level. Water supplies in other areas of the country were known to contain objectionable concentrations of calcium, salt, arsenic, lead or sulphur. Most Indian consumers would need neither of the additional modules, some would need one or the other, but very few would need both.

Market Entry and Marketing Planning Recommendations. Assuming that Chatterjee recommended proceeding with the field test, he would need to make a recommendation concerning mode of market entry. In addition, his recommendation should include an outline of a marketing plan.

Table CS 4.5.2   Investments and Fixed Costs for a Joint Venture Market Entry

| | Operational Scope | | |
	Two Regions	Four Regions	National Market
1998 market potential (units)	55 000	110 000	430 000
Initial investment (Rs. 000)	4 000	8 000	30 000
Annual fixed overhead expenses (Rs. 000)			
Using dealer channels	4 000	7 000	40 000
Using direct salesforce	7 200	14 000	88 000

Licensee Considerations. If market entry were in the form of a joint working arrangement with a licensee, Blair Company financial investment would be minimal. Chatterjee thought that Blair Company might risk as little at $30 000 in capital for production facilities and equipment, plus another $5000 for office facilities and equipment. These investments would be completely offset by the licensee's payment to Blair Company for technology transfer and personnel training. Annual fixed costs to Blair Company should not exceed $40 000 at the outset and would decrease to $15 000 as soon as an Indian national could be hired, trained, and left in charge. Duties of this individual would be to work with Blair Company personnel in the United States and with management at the licensee to see that units were produced per Blair Company's specifications. Apart from this activity, Blair Company would have no control over the licensee's operations. Chatterjee expected that the licensee would pay royalties to Blair Company of about Rs.280 for each unit sold in the domestic market and Rs.450 for each unit that was exported. The average royalty probably would be around Rs.300.

Joint Venture/Acquisition Considerations. If entry were in the form of either a joint venture of an acquisition, financial investment and annual fixed costs would be much higher and depend greatly on the scope of operations. Chatterjee had roughed out some estimates for a joint venture entry, based on three levels of scope (see Table CS 4.5.2). His estimates reflected what he thought were reasonable assumptions for all needed investments plus annual fixed expenses for sales activities, general administrative overheads, research and development, insurance and depreciation. His estimates allowed for the Delight purifier to be sold either through dealers or through a direct, door-to-door salesforce. Chatterjee thought that estimates of annual fixed expenses for market entry via acquisition would be identical to those for a joint venture. However, estimates for the investment (purchase) might be considerably higher, the same or lower. It depended on what was purchased.

Chatterjee's estimates of Delight's unit contribution margins reflected a number of assumptions—expected economies of scale, experience curve effects, costs of Indian labour and raw materials and competitors' pricing strategies. However, the most important assumption was Delight's pricing strategy. If a skimming strategy was used and the product sold through a dealer channel, the basic module would be priced to dealers at Rs.5500 and to consumers at Rs.5900. 'This would give us about a Rs.650 unit contribution, once we got production flowing smoothly', he thought. In contrast, if a penetration strategy was used and the product sold through a dealer channel, the basic module would be priced to dealers at Rs.4100, to consumers at Rs.4400, and yield a unit contribution of Rs.300. For simplicity's sake, Chatterjee assumed that the two additional modules would be priced to dealers at Rs.800, to consumers at Rs.1000 and would yield a unit contribution of Rs.100.

To achieve unit contributions of Rs.650 or Rs.300, the basic modules would employ different designs. The basic module for the skimming strategy would be noticeably superior, with higher performance and quality, a longer warranty period, more features and a more attractive appearance than the basic module for the penetration strategy. Positioning, too, most likely would be different. Chatterjee recognized several positioning possibilities: performance and taste, value for money/low price, safety, health, convenience, attractive styling, avoiding diseases and health related bills, and superior American technology. The only position he considered 'taken' in the market was that occupied by Aquaguard—protect family health and service at your doorstep. While other competitors had claimed certain positions for their products, none had devoted financial resources of a degree that Delight could not dislodge them. Chatterjee believed that considerable advertising and promotion expenditures would be necessary to communicate Delight's positioning. He would need estimates of these expenditures in his recommendation.

If a direct salesforce was employed instead of dealers, Chatterjee thought that prices charged to consumers would not change from those listed above. However, sales commissions would have to be paid in addition to the fixed costs necessary to maintain and manage the salesforce. Under a skimming price strategy, the sales commission would be Rs.550 per unit and the unit contribution would be Rs.500. Under a penetration price strategy, the sales commission would be Rs.400 per unit and the unit contribution would be Rs.200. These financial estimates, he would explain in his report, would apply to 1998 or 1999, the expected first year of operation.

'If we go ahead with Delight, we'll have to move quickly', thought Chatterjee. 'The window of opportunity is open but if Singer's product is as good as they claim, we'll be in for a fight. Still, Aquarius seems vulnerable on the water pressure requirement and on price. We'll need a product category "killer" to win'.

CASE 4.6
Aluminium Containers

Fred Parry is in charge of the Special Applications Unit in the Société des Forges de Modane (SFM) an aluminium alloy producer.

At a meeting with Pietro Torelli, the head of the department, it was decided to carry out a systematic market survey to identify what were the most attractive market segments for the aluminium alloys produced by the 'Special Applications' unit. In the Minutes of the meeting that Torelli sent Parry he stressed: 'We have great difficulties in identifying market opportunities for "special quality" and high purity aluminium alloys. The applications we have tried to develop in the last few months have partly failed. I am convinced that these alloys have potential for clearly defined applications where we can enhance our expertise. I am confirming our interest in luxury cosmetic containers and I would like you to collect as much information as possible so that we can reach a decision.'

La Société des Forges de Modane (SFM)

SFM is a subsidiary within a French group. It is a leader in Europe for processing aluminium. It manufactures aluminium alloy products in strips, sheets, tubes and wire. The use of SFM's products is widespread in that they are found in a number of different industries: cars, construction, engineering, shipbuilding. 40 per cent of sales are exported to Europe, Japan and North America.

SFM is organized around departments, each having a specific production technology and its own production plants. Fred Parry's unit is part of the Laminates Department.

The Laminates Department is composed of three units (three profit centres) corresponding to three distinct leading edge technologies. Each activity is run autonomously by a manager in charge of business development and profitability. Sales are organized through a zone-based salesforce (Europe, North America, South-East Asia and World). The sales organization deals with all the company's day-to-day sales activity, distribution, promotion and technical assistance in all the countries covered. Sales and

This case was written by Robert Salle, Professor of Marketing and Research Director at IRE-Groupe Ecole Supérieure de Commerce de Lyon (France) and Daniel Michel, Professor of Marketing at the Groupe Ecole Supérieure de Commerce de Lyon (France). Copyright © Groupe ESC Lyon, 1997. Reproduction forbidden without prior permission.

marketing strategies are decided by business unit managers, like Fred Parry, and sales managers. Final strategic responsibility lies with the Department and with business unit managers.

The Special Applications Unit of SFM

The activity covers three products:

- *Aluminium offset* is sold in sheet or strip form and is only used for the manufacture of offset sheets. Local competition is stiff and profitability low. This explains management's desire to develop other markets.
- *Special quality aluminium* is sold in sheet, strip or disc form. It includes different aluminium alloys with a very glossy surface. This product also has a guaranteed metallurgical structure that makes it suitable for anodization and electrolytic or chemical glazing.
- *High purity aluminium or titrated aluminium or 'titres'* is sold in sheet, strip or disc form. The products have a standard appearance, but a high level of aluminium (thus an alloy of higher purity). The metallurgical structure is suitable for anodization and chemical or electro-chemical glazing.

The last two techniques are appropriate for luxury cosmetic containers. This market includes bottles and stoppers for perfume, lipstick tubes, powder boxes, liquid sprays, lip pencils and aerosol containers.

This market is called 'cosmetic containers'. These are produced by specialized manufacturers who work for the cosmetics and perfume industry. They use a variety of materials (such as plastic, tin, steel, silver, nickel or aluminium) depending on the costs and presentation required. Glass, which is also widely used by cosmetic manufacturers, is a very different material and is supplied by specialized glass manufacturers, due to the high level of investment required.

Aluminium is the material most widely used by world leaders in perfume (such as Dior, Guerlain, Lancôme, Shisheido, Revlon, L'Oréal, Rochas) for their luxury containers.

Aluminium: Two Techniques for Manufacturing Cosmetic Containers

Complex Technique 'A'.
The manufacturing phases can be described as follows:

- (A1) Stamping in a special press.
- (A2) Polishing the part on an automatic machine with manual feeding of parts. This mechanical process gives the surface a smooth sheen.
- (A3) Chemical or electro-chemical glazing of the polished part. Glazing involves treating the surface chemically or electro-chemically to give it a gloss.
- (A4) Anodization of the glazed component. A chemical or electro-chemical process results in the anodization of the natural protective layer of aluminium called alumina. This layer, several microns thick, is transparent and has many of the characteristics of a glass coating.
- (A5) Colouring of the anodized part.

This technique relies on a very pure quality of aluminium alloy like the one found in the 'titres' category. The chemical glazing provides a degree of surface gloss linked to the degree of aluminium purity.

Simple Technique 'B'.
The manufacturing phases are as follows:

- (B1) Stamping in a special press.
- (B2) Polishing.
- (B3) Coloured or transparent varnishing.

This process requires alloys with less purity than for technique 'A'.

The Particularities of Each Technique.
Technique 'A' gives very high-quality products for the cosmetic containers market. Gloss and surface quality are generally better than with other materials. The material also offers rich possibilities for decoration. All the market leaders in French and European perfumery use this product. The same applies to Japanese and North American competitors present on the European market. Virtually all luxury cosmetic containers found in Europe, manufactured or imported, use technique 'A'. These containers are also the most expensive because of the price of the aluminium used and the complexity of the manufacturing operations. Technique 'A' usually requires high purity aluminium from the 'titres' category. Glossy aluminium from the 'special quality' category is used only when stamping is light.[1]

In technique 'A' the manufacturers can use standard quality aluminium but the resulting quality of the products is not at all the same.

Technique 'B' uses aluminium that is neither titrated quality nor glossy; and thus outside the know-how of the 'Special Applications' unit. Although not downmarket, the product does not give the same quality results as anodized aluminium. The latter is much preferred by container designers, who have also realized that some of the finishings used are not sufficiently resistant to the alcohol found in perfume and some cosmetics. On the other hand costs are lower and quality is sufficient for some applications.

In Europe manufacturers of cosmetic containers use either one technique or the other, rarely both simultaneously.

Trends in the Manufacturing Process of Cosmetic Containers.

A new technique could partly replace the original 'A' technique. This would give a glazed appearance to the surface. As a result the polishing phase (A2) could be eliminated reducing production costs by between 15–20 per cent. The part would be glossed directly and then anodized (A1 + A3 + A4 + A5). This process requires new aluminium alloys different from those used in techniques 'A' and 'B'. This process still presents a number of practical problems, which the Laminates Department has been working on for some time and that it will not perfect for months or even years.

Another trend is identifiable. It results from the developments in the metal plating plastics. Metal layers are deposited on a specially prepared plastic. European and Japanese manufacturers in particular have gained an edge in this technology. However, applications seem limited depending on the shape required and the degree of contrast between matt and gloss finishes. Another disadvantage is that the metal plating tends to come off after continuous hand contact. Containers thus have a shorter life cycle. The advantage is one of cost which is considerably lower than for aluminium based techniques.

SFM's Competitors

For 'special quality' and high purity alloys (titres) SFM's competitor is Germanalu from Germany. Germanalu is the subsidiary of a large internationally orientated group with the same size and level of expertise as SFM. This competitor is well established in Europe and is trying to penetrate the French market. Competition with Germanalu is not based on price.

Other competitors include Italu which is only active in Italy. Two former competitors, the German Daag and the British Balu have stopped 'Special Applications' production.

Americans could be interested in the French market for cosmetic containers, where both volume and profit are high compared to other aluminium products.

The Manufacturers of Cosmetic Containers in Europe (Using Technique 'A')

France.   Spectacular growth in the French perfume and cosmetics industry has had wide repercussions. French firms built a strong position on the world market. As a result technique 'A' has dominated the French market, giving local producers a special expertise in this technique. SFM supplies 75 per cent of the aluminium required by this industry.

French manufacturers of cosmetic containers are enthusiastic about technique 'A'. They export more and more to Europe and to well-known American firms like Max Factor and Revlon. US perfume producers are making efforts to improve the quality of their containers, particularly because they aim at entering the European market.

Most French manufacturers are small and medium enterprises with between 5 and 10 presses for stamping aluminium and, at the most, 100 employees. SFM works with all 18 producers who use 1000 tons a year of 'special quality' and high purity aluminium. The biggest manufacturer uses 300 tons, two others take 200 and the rest is spread between 15 manufacturers. Market growth is about 3 per cent a year, slightly higher than that of Europe as a whole but much less than the annual 5 per cent growth in the United States.

Following a visit to one of these manufacturers Fred Parry made the following remarks:

> The surface treatment is not suited to mass production. The managers of the firm are aware of this but do not have any urgency to remedy the situation. The glazing process (A3) is not monitored closely enough to guarantee a regular high-quality finished product. To obtain the same effect as that of its competitor's products, this firm has to use a purer aluminium alloy, which is more expensive.
>
> Their sloppy working practices (such as bath temperature, level of concentrate, glazing time and choice of electrolytes) result in high wastage and higher production costs. I wonder how long customers will put up with this situation. These firms are faced with the problem of their inability to invest in new machines. They seem unable to listen to their customers. While I recognize their expertise in anodization (A4) and glazing (A3), there is little creation or innovation. They do not understand how to make the most of all the possible applications that aluminium offers in terms of cost reductions and better quality. This expertise is a key success factor for perfume producers who are continually searching for new and original ideas for presenting their products. With the arrival of the Americans, French firms could be in trouble.

Until recently SFM did not know much about either the European market or producers. The latter seem to function in the same way as in France, concentrating on the home market and establishing close links with customers. Possibilities for real innovation are limited and they use much the same equipment as in France. Some have developed a slightly different expertise in the application of aluminium because of the raw material supplied by local aluminium processors. An initial contact by SFM's sales force rapidly led to a number of trial orders from potentially important customers.

Italy.   This is a market of 180 tons a year controlled by two manufacturers that work with Italu. One of them began working with SFM but had difficulty adapting to its grade of aluminium. SFM is looking at how to make a special alloy adapted to its manufacturing process. However, gaining a real position in this market will be difficult due to the presence of Italu.

Spain.   This is a market of 150 tons a year split between four manufacturers that SFM knows well.

Germany.   This is dominated by Germanalu, exclusive supplier of two manufacturers who share the 300 ton market equally. Tests have been started to adapt SFMs alloys to the technology of these German manufacturers.

United Kingdom.   Three manufacturers of cosmetic containers use about 200 tons a year. After the withdrawal of the only British aluminium processor, SFM now supplies a significant part of this market (120 tons a year).

The Perfume Producers

Fred Parry visited several firms that give instructions (e.g. shape and material) to the manufacturers of cosmetic containers. He met different people in purchasing and product design.

Lancôme.   Lancôme does not know much about SFM. SFM is accused of being too expensive for certain qualities of aluminium. In their view, aluminium for perfume containers is a minor activity for SFM which could explain why SFM is perceived as being rigid and resistant to new trends. People even have their own ideas on the strengths and weaknesses of SFM and aluminium processes in general.

Lancôme is well aware of everything that is on offer from its suppliers. It is familiar with the different kinds of alloys, quality of surface and the influence on aluminium processing. It is up to date on the latest technology in glazing and anodization. It is also well informed on the different processes used in Europe and the alternatives in materials and processes that are available.

Lancôme has a lot of information on manufacturers of cosmetic containers throughout the world and closely follows the latest developments of US producers when it meets both in Europe and America. They are abreast of recent trends in packaging which have been pioneered by its American competitors. These trends in packaging are geared towards a more luxurious and appropriate presentation for the European market, and to future changes in the US home market. Lancôme thinks that the move from technique 'B' to technique 'A' is inevitable for part of the market. Lancôme expects stiffer competition among the alloys used for this particular technique.

Lancôme is aware of the weaknesses of its French manufacturers of cosmetic containers. The latter have not invested in the leading edge technology necessary to ensure price and quality competitiveness. Given the cost implications, Lancôme would be ready to support at the most two French producers, thus providing them with a level of activity that could enable them to invest in new technology and processes.

Nina Ricci.   The people Fred Parry met had no particular complaints about the quality of the aluminium delivered, but were understandably unhappy about the price increase of 50 per cent over the last three years. Given that a glazed and anodized aluminium stopper costs about FFr.7 one can understand the impact of such a price rise on the final cost.

Guerlain.   Everyone Fred Parry met considered that French manufacturers offered the best quality in cosmetic containers. Much more important for Guerlain was the lack of creativity on the part of suppliers in finding new and original surface finishes. The Purchasing Department had searched the world over to find the most creative manufacturers. Numerous tests had been conducted with the Japanese on aluminized plastic. Unfortunately, it looks great but deteriorates on contact with perfume and damp hands. Guerlain cannot absorb an annual cost increase of 15 per cent for cosmetic containers, as a result it is looking actively for ways of reducing unit costs.

The Independent Designers

Fred Parry met some of the most well-known independent designers. Several important perfume producers worked with these design consultants. They have an impact on company research decisions for containers and on the materials used. Parry realized that these designers were unfamiliar with all the possibilities that aluminium offers and the various ways it can be processed.

The Manufacturers of Cosmetic Containers in North America (Using Techniques 'A' and 'B')

The US market represents 5000 tons a year of which 90 per cent consists of technique 'B'. The 10 per cent of technique 'A' does not have the same characteristics as its European equivalent. In the United States the 'A' technique aluminium alloys[2] are less sophisticated than in Europe. SFM cannot compete with such low prices. On the other hand, there is increasing interest for special quality alloys sold at $4 per kg and even titrated aluminium alloys at $4.50. For the moment US aluminium producers are unable to offer these alloys to perfume producers.

When the latter need quality containers for export to Europe they work with European cosmetic container producers.

However, the trend on the US home market is towards more luxurious containers. Some perfume producers would like to reposition their products in a higher price bracket where products move faster. As a result they need more original containers that they could use for both domestic and export markets. Suppliers are under pressure to change to the European 'A' technique and to make substantial investments in glazing (A3) and anodization (A4) technology.

The cosmetic containers industry is particularly concentrated with three manufacturers sharing 90 per cent of the market:

Riverside Mfg:	40%
Eyelet Alu:	30%
National Metal Goods:	20%

Riverside Mfg. This firm produces 150 million lipstick tubes a year made of aluminium based on technique 'B', which is its speciality. It has sales of FFr.6 million in France and FFr.7.5 million in the rest of Europe. In the next 2 or 3 years sales in France should reach Ffr.10 million.

This firm is dynamic and well equipped with more than 100 special presses. It also works for firms outside the perfume sector who need its technique 'B' processing.

Riverside Mfg has an anodization and glazing assembly line (US technique 'A') which does not meet the increasing quality demands made by US perfume producers.

At this point in time, Riverside Mfg is investing in European technique 'A' so as to be closer to the European market and to respond to the new demands of US perfume manufacturers.

Eyelet Alu. To increase competitiveness and to respond to the growth in demand this manufacturer has invested in glazing (A3) and anodization (A4) technology (a more sophisticated American version of technique 'A') which gives much better quality than was previously the case.

Eyelet Alu has tried a number of alloys offered by US producers but difficulties remain.

This firm produces a wide range of products which includes lipstick tubes, pencils and mascara containers. Production is well organized with 100 special presses and a sophisticated system for monitoring quality.

National Metal Goods (NMG). NMG has just entered the German market through an agreement with a local firm. The aim of the joint venture is to become the market leader in Europe within five years. NMG hopes to acquire the expertise required to produce cosmetic containers of European quality adapted to the US domestic market.

During a visit to Germany, Fred Parry met senior managers from NMG who expressed considerable interest in a link-up with SFM to develop the US market. NMG has a high quality production unit with 60 special presses.

SFM and the US Market

Fred Parry's conclusion about US manufacturers of cosmetic containers was the following:

> The Americans are strong in production techniques with considerable human and financial resources. They have global ambitions particularly as far as technique 'A' is concerned. The luxury perfume market in the United States is expanding and there is a good chance of US manufacturers of cosmetic containers setting up in Europe. These firms offer good business opportunities for SFM.
>
> These firms are used to much lower prices for aluminium, as they use standard products where the US manufacturers are very competitive. The US market has a number of particularities. Customers buy from wholesalers and not directly from aluminium producers. They purchase in bulk for a given width and thickness. Volume is high and stocks of strip aluminium with different widths and thicknesses are held. Wholesalers hold inventories of a wide variety of aluminium strip in different thicknesses and delivery is rapid. Maintaining the quality of products over time is a key success factor.
>
> Compared to its US competitors SFMs prices are high. However, it seems reasonable to maintain these prices for the special-quality and high-quality aluminium alloys on the condition that service, quality and time of delivery are perfect.

SFM's sales organization in the US reckons that the cosmetic containers market is specific. Orders have to be prepared with great care (e.g. strips cut to the customers required width) and stock maintained. Two wholesalers, Robson and American Alu control the market. They guarantee delivery within 24 hours, hold large inventories and are well equipped to prepare orders.

SFM does not have the resources to become a direct supplier to the cosmetic container market; this would involve a massive investment in buildings, stock and personnel that bears no relation to the kind of market share that SFM can expect. Working with a well-known partner such as American Alu seems more reasonable with the aim of developing and strengthening existing contacts from other departments of SFM.

If SFM can develop good-quality products with a high-quality after-sales service we can try to negotiate an exclusive distribution network with American Alu for this particular segment. However, no such arrangement will be possible without price changes. Profitability will certainly be lower on the US market and SFM will have to adhere to strict delivery and service requirements from US manufacturers.

Challenges and Opportunities for SFM

A meeting took place with Fred Parry, his colleagues and Pietro Torelli to draw some conclusions on the information that Fred had gathered and to identify ways of moving forward. During the discussion two strategic options appeared:

1. The first option aimed at consolidating the position of French and European manufacturers of cosmetic containers confronted with the threat of US manufacturers. The French manufacturers were open to a close cooperation with SFM.

2. The second option recommended a rapid entry onto the US market based on the selection of a wholesaler. According Pietro Torelli: 'If SFM miss the opportunity now, we will have the US aluminium processors over here very soon. Moreover Germanalu is thinking seriously about entering the US market for "cosmetic containers". The agreement between NMG and a German manufacturer of cosmetic containers allows Germanalu to learn about US manufacturers'.

Question

You have the same information as Pietro Torelli and Fred Parry. You have to make a decision and then implement it.

References

1. Aluminium alloy has several different surface treatments, more or less glossy, depending on the type and strength of the laminate used. Stamping can, depending on the depth of the imprint, destroy the surface obtained with the laminate. For deep stampings alloys with a non-glossy surface are used. On the other hand glossy surfaces are used when stamping is shallow and presents no danger to the state of the surface.

2. Present on the US market correspond to standard quality criteria allowing a price of $3.50 per kg.

CASE 4.7
Volvo in a Political Crisis in Iran—
Period Prior to the Political Crisis

After the White Revolution in the early 1960s, the government in Iran instituted agricultural and infrastructure development programmes, and the demand for modern agricultural machines and equipment (tractors and trucks) began to increase. Accordingly, in 1963, negotiations began between Volvo and an Iranian company for a joint-production (JV) factory. Before this period, trucks and tractors had been sold through a joint venture selling agent. This strategy for market expansion (JV for production factory) was selected for two reasons: (1) the Iranian market had become important for Volvo—exports had doubled between 1962 and 1963 from SEK2.2 million to SEK4.5 million and (2) the Iranian partner, Nasir, had earlier been Volvo's agent for trucks and tractors in Iran and was a both rich and prominent person in the Iranian government. Nasir also had a wide network of contacts with politically and financially powerful people.

In 1964, a JV contract was signed for the assembly of trucks, tractors and other agricultural machines. The Swedish subsidiary, Bolinder Munktell (BM), had a leading position in the JV firm through a local firm called Zaymand. Nasir became the general manager of the JV firm, and other managerial functions were undertaken by BM. Additional positions were filled with 250 less qualified Iranian employees. In the first year, the newly established firm produced 600 tractors, 600 trucks and 600 ploughs and harrows. The major parts were to be imported from Volvo, and the less complex components, such as batteries and radiators, were to be produced by local producers. As the level of demand for this equipment continued to increase, and as Nasir had demonstrated how easily all the bureaucratic and financial problems could be solved, the Swedish manager discussed a request from Nasir for more cooperation with headquarters. The managers in Sweden had already observed the increasing sales value in the market, and accordingly, in 1971, they agreed to enter into a new project. They decided to increase the production capacity with a new plant that would be able to manufacture 2000 trucks and tractors. Until this period, Zaymand was also responsible for providing maintenance and service to the buyers. In 1973, the high selling price of oil increased government and private income, and the banks were generous in

This case was prepared by Dr Amjad Hadjikhani, Uppsala University Sweden.

providing loans to farmers and private firms. Demand at all levels for heavy equipment was also increasing, which made the partners in the JV optimistic about the future of the market. Based on his contacts with managers of a firm called Dorman Diesel, Nasir proposed to expand the JV production into other product categories. Volvo agreed to this strategy and in 1974 Volvo started cooperation with Dorman Diesel, which specialized in the production of diesel engines. Dorman Diesel sold 16.5 per cent of its shares to Volvo, and Volvo entered into a licence agreement with Dorman Diesel that made it possible for Volvo to produce turbine-powered engines in Iran. Because of the market expansion, an organizational change became necessary in 1975. Together with two other rich and influential people, Nasir established a new company called Rena Industrial Investment. This company owned 75 per cent of the shases in Zaymand, while the rest of the ownership in Zaymand belonged to Volvo. Zaymand itself owned shares in Dorman Diesel. Production and economic developments were overseen by a small number of Swedish managers from Volvo stationed in Iran, and the other positions were filled by 900 less-qualified Iranians. In addition, since this market was becoming important for Volvo.

Volvo's vice president served on the board of directors. In its 10 years of JV cooperation with Nasir (1964–74), Volvo had changed its marketing strategy from one of exporting to one supplemented by JV and licensing. Although there were several competitors in the market, namely Mercedes, Mack and Leyland, and although Mercedes and Leyland each had already established an assembly line similar to that of Volvo's, by using these strategies, Volvo succeeded in increasing its market share from less than 10 per cent in 1964 to more than 20 per cent in 1974. The Iranian transportation market became very important for Volvo. After truck sales increased to 10 per cent of Volvo's total annual turnover of trucks in 1975, Nasir suggested the possibility of further expansion, and in 1976 a new negotiation phase began, involving the establishment of another assembly production firm, which the Iranian government had decided to permit in response to the high demand for trucks. Volvo's competitors, Mercedes, Mack and Leyland, were also negotiating with the government for the same project. As the planned production capacity for this new plant was more than 20 000 trucks a year and the total production capacity of Volvo during the past year had been about 28 000, this project would allow Volvo to increase its export of components and spare parts to about SEK1 billion. Accordingly, Nasir actively engaged in negotiations with the government and by the end of 1977 the negotiation had progressed well enough for a signed contract between the Iranian government and Volvo to be expected some time early in 1978. The few minor political incidents that occurred at this time were not regarded as a threat to marketing. The partners had no doubt that the minor demonstrations currently taking place would disappear, since they were not caused by the prevailing socioeconomic conditions. Negotiations for the project anticipated a large entry into the market, and all the partners were seriously working towards it.

The First Period of Crisis

Early in 1977, demonstrations against the government intensified. However, these demonstrations seemed disorganized, and it was common knowledge that the demonstrations were in response to inflation and police violence and were not supported by the opposing political groups. Based on concrete information provided by their influential partners, Nasir and the other managers in the local and foreign firms believed that the demonstrations would stop soon as a result of the reforms the government had promised. In any case, Volvo's managers in Iran and Sweden had no plans for withdrawing from this very attractive market.

Even when the political and economic situation became unstable in 1978, Nasir pressed for continued negotiations. The Swedish manager in Iran, however, realized that the level of uncertainty was increasing. He discussed the issue with headquarters and decided to slow down the negotiations. In the early part of 1978, when there were mass demonstrations and assassination attempts against government and American establishments, Volvo succeeded in weathering the disturbances because it was a Swedish company. After a short period, however, the strikes in Teheran became more widespread and began to interfere with production. In these years, the level of uncertainty was relatively low, because Volvo and its partners believed that the Shah's regime would remain in power. Because of his connections to a powerful partner, the manager had access to certain information and by using these connections Nasir and his partners were able to reduce the number of bureaucratic problems they faced. For example, when the turbulence increased, the manager began to import high-quantity technical parts and thus reduced their dependence on customs. The political and economic situation became more unstable in the autumn of 1978. Because it was a Swedish company, Volvo was less vulnerable to this instability, but the political crisis did influence its financial transactions.

At the end of November, the government froze all foreign exchange transactions, and Volvo could not send its export income out of Iran. At the end of 1978, when the situation worsened, Volvo's manager remained in Iran while other foreigners were leaving the country. However, because of the strikes, Volvo's manager could not continue to produce, and the increasing turbulence forced the manager to send Swedish personnel back to Sweden while he stayed to monitor political developments. Even though the halt in production had become costly by the end of 1978 the Swedish headquarters believed the prognosis was favourable for the future production of heavy trucks. They also believed that, even if a new political group took over the government, their plans for the production of the bus chassis, which had been planned before the revolution, would come to fruition. The fundamental question for the manager in Iran was how long these disturbances would continue. The production lines of the competing firms were closed, and their managers had already left Iran. Because of its American origins, Mack had completely withdrawn from the market, despite a heavy capital investment.

The Second Period of Crisis

Early in 1979, the Shah left Iran and the political and economic conditions became worse and even chaotic. When the new leaders proclaimed the nationalization of firms previously owned by the Shah and his family and friends, the level of uncertainty increased for JV firms like Volvo, because it was a foreign firm that had invested in the country and, even worse, because Nasir had been one of its partners. This last issue created complications for Volvo for a long time to come. It was clear that the new leadership did not trust Volvo because of this relationship. The political situation had changed, and the relationship with Nasir, which had helped Volvo before the revolution, was now a liability. By the time the revolution occurred, Nasir and his partner had already transferred all of Volvo's deposit and private money to Europe and the United States and had left the country.

The critical problem for Volvo now was its partnership with people who had very close relationships with the Shah. For this reason, Volvo's ownership in the diesel engine factory seemed less threatened by nationalization. In April 1979, however, Volvo received a message that the truck factory in Iran would in fact be nationalized, which would result in Volvo's 19 per cent share of the factory being taken over by the government. Although the government realized that such a situation would frighten not only Volvo but all other foreign firms as well, they were still suspicious about Nasir and his cooperation with Volvo, and Volvo did not receive any further information about nationalization during 1979.

Volvo's managers in Iran and Sweden discussed how they should react to this state of affairs. There were two simple alternatives: stay or leave. If they left the market, not only their capital investment but their future market operation would be lost, and it would have become easy to connect Volvo with the former regime. After a long discussion, headquarters decided to keep the manager in Iran and to stay in the market, even though staying was more costly than leaving. The manager decided to stay and provide a positive image for Volvo, even though the assembly line had stopped, there was no production, and the company had more than 1400 employees on the payroll.

Accusations directed against Volvo and its partners increased. At the end of 1979, the government finally decided to nationalize only those portions owned by the Iranian partners who were also representing Japanese Nissan in Rena. This meant that Volvo could keep its ownership in all three firms, Rena, Zaymand and Dorman Diesel. With the nationalization of the partners' ownership, a revision group from the government studied all the details in the contract. After several months of investigations, the revision group issued a positive report on Volvo and determined that Volvo could retain its ownership, although there were to be major changes in the boards of directors for Rena and Zaymand, as well as those of the Diesel Company. In 1980, the Ministry of Commerce became responsible for overseeing all three firms. After a short period, this responsibility was transferred to a state organization, the IDRO (Iranian Department of Industrial Organization), which was functioning under the Ministry of Heavy Industry (MHI), and the IDRO soon selected new members for the boards of directors.

The major problem for Volvo at this time was the continuation of political turbulence, which caused a high personnel turnover at the management level and resulted in continual changes in management as well as in management style. This was made even worse by the considerable suspicion among the managers themselves. After 1980, however, the major source of uncertainty for Volvo management was the instability in the political system resulting from the political struggle among different groups and the Iran–Iraq War. In fact, during the investigation by the revision group, Volvo's manager had to stop all deliveries to Iran. In an attempt to build more trust in Volvo, the IDRO made several efforts to convince Volvo's leadership to serve on the boards of directors of the JV firms, because Volvo's manager, unlike those of its competitors, had remained in Iran. Besides that, the IDRO had also come to realize its technological dependency on Volvo. However, the level of uncertainty was still too high for such a commitment, and Volvo's managers consequently selected the strategy of sleeping as this would allow them to stay in the market and continue to monitor the changes. In 1982, the Swedish Export Advisory Council decided to arrange a meeting between representatives of the Swedish industries and the Iranian government. At this meeting, the MHI and the IDRO asked Volvo to discuss the existing cooperation problems and again asked Volvo to take a position on the board of directors. Volvo again refused—Volvo's manager still had difficulty trusting the new partners.

At the end of 1982, a new manager in Volvo became responsible for the Iranian market. Like the earlier manager, this one had to be active while avoiding suspicion. Accordingly, Volvo changed its marketing strategy by establishing a simple kind of supplier–buyer relationship in order to avoid taking new managerial or financial risks. In 1983, Volvo established an office employing two specialists and a few technicians to control local production, despite protests from the IDRO that they themselves could fulfil this mission. At that time, foreign firms were not allowed to have representatives in Iran, so Volvo's stated motivation was to maintain quality control of the products. In reality, however, its main purpose was to watch market conditions. This strategy was not for the sake of the earlier investments in Rena and the respective subsidiaries; Volvo was ready to give up its ownership of these to the local authorities, since the IDRO was discussing new investments. The IDRO requested Volvo again to serve on the board of directors, but the manager refused.

Until 1983, Volvo's manager in Iran found it difficult to establish relationships with local managers in Rena because of the personnel turnover and uncertainty about the future. However, some changes did occur after 1983. For example, more technically qualified personnel stayed longer in their positions. Despite turbulence at the managerial level and the Iran–Iraq War, there was commonly a positive attitude towards Volvo because the Swedish manager had stayed in Iran. This action increased the individual trust towards Volvo's manager and also increased general trust in the brand name. In 1984, the political changes continued, and the Iran–Iraq War intensified. At the beginning of the war, there was a great deal of political instability, and the disparity in their political visions created ambiguity for the firms. After 1984, however, the political situation became more stable, even as economic conditions worsened because of the war. The Swedish manager had several problems to tackle: a never-ending cycle of establishing new relationships, the shortage of foreign exchange currency and, finally, personal safety because Iraq had begun to bomb Teheran. This situation created a complex and difficult bureaucratic hierarchy that became the major problem for both local and Swedish managers. For example, the approval of foreign exchange, necessary for importing components, took at least six months, because the application had to pass through at least four different state departments before any answer was received. As the manager stated: 'The decision to import a component was sent first to the NIIO for checking. From the NIIO, the Appliance Division, it was sent to the Procurement and Distribution Centre (PDC), which deals with price matters. Then the PDC sent it to the Industrial Ministry. Within each department, the decision went through several decision stages. Therefore, some decisions took several years.'

Questions

Assume that you are representing a consulting company and are invited by the headquarters in Volvo to help them. They ask you to analyse the situation and give them suggestions for future marketing. You are going to give a report on the following two main areas. Your first task is to show the managers that you have understood the firm's marketing problem in that critical situation by showing them how and why the firm and the managers reacted in the way they did up until 1984. Your second task is to provide them with solutions in the form of strategies for the firm by giving them appropriate answers to the following questions related to marketing strategies, risk, and personal behaviour.

1. Do you find the way in which Volvo dealt with the market until the 1980s reasonable? How would you describe its former and existing marketing and financial problems?

2. With the help of studies on risk management (traditional ones explaining high risk leads to exit from the market) analyse the situation for the period 1960–80. What does your analysis look like and what is your conclusion?

3. How would you recommend that Volvo's manager handle the problems with personal relationships and trust development?

4. Considering the nature of the crisis, do you think it would be advantageous or disadvantageous to introduce a new person into this situation?

5. Do you think that the decision of the headquarters to reactivate marketing activities was correct?

6. What is your strategic proposal for the future? What is your opinion about leaving the market given that the number of problems are increasing?

CASE 4.8
'What Got Us Here Will Not Take Us Forward'—The Case for Tourism Brand Ireland

Background

Tourism is one of the most important industries and one of the key sources of export income in Ireland with industry earnings exceeding IR£2 billion in 1995. Ireland enjoyed phenomenal and unprecedented success in the decade to 1995 as a tourism destination. Income from, and market share of, the principal tourism generating markets grew very substantially. Income from overseas tourism to the Republic alone in the 1985–95 period was estimated to have grown in real terms by 112 per cent. A much larger proportion of those Britons, Europeans, Americans and Australians travelling abroad included Ireland in their itinerary.

Ireland has long been marketed as a tourist destination internationally, with an annual spend of IR£11 million on advertising in 1995 alone and with an extensive network of sales offices throughout Europe and the United States. A wide variety of creative executions and styles were used, by many different bodies who promoted Ireland as a tourist destination internationally. This material was very rarely coordinated and tended to be developed for individual markets in isolation, and was distinct to that market.

Different strap lines were used in different markets, as illustrated by the examples in Figure CS 4.8.1.

The brand, or set of brands, were not marketed under a single banner, logo or visual identity. Some of the promotional material carried the national tourist authorities' shamrock logos (the shamrock is a symbol associated with Ireland for many years). The majority of trade and tour operator advertising and promotion of Ireland tended not to replicate the positioning portrayed in tourist board or destination advertising.

The Need to Change

> [One] could be forgiven for thinking that this is not the right time to be changing our strategy.
> (Mr Enda Kenny, Irish Minister for Tourism at the launch of the TBI)

While the growth of the industry particularly over the 1980s and 1990s was impressive from both a domestic and an international standpoint, industry strategists

This case was prepared by Dr Joan Buckley, University College, Cork, Ireland.

Table CS 4.8.1

Country	1985 000's	1995 000's
British trips abroad	21 610	41 500
British trips to Ireland	1 123	2 302
Ireland % share	5.2	5.5
Adult European international travel	190 000[1]	214 300
Adult European travel to Ireland	1 000	1 825
Ireland % share	0.5	0.85
US citizens travel to Europe	6 425	8 700
US arrivals in Ireland	393	586
Ireland % share	6.1	6.7
Australians travel to Europe	402	530
Australian arrivals in Ireland	30	75
Ireland % share	7.5	14.2

[1] 1988 data, first year of ETM.
Sources: CSO (UK); CSOP/BFE, European Travel Monitor (ETM); US Dept of Transport; Australian Bureau of Statistics.

Figure CS 4.8.1

Britain	'The Northern Ireland you'll never know: unless you go.'
France	'Vous serez venu pour l'Irlande, vous reviendrez pour les Irlandais.'
	'L'Irlande. Vous l'aimez déja de loin, alors de pres.'
Germany	'Europas Grune Ferieninsel.'
Italy	'L'Amica Verde.'
The Netherlands	'Ireland: A World of Welcome.'
United States	'The Ancient Birthplace of Good Times.'

recognized in 1994–95 that it would be 'naive and complacent in the extreme' to assume that the current pattern of growth would automatically continue in the future.

The factors identified as contributing to the high growth in the 1980s and 1990s were:

- *Product Development Investment.* According to the World Tourism Organization the level of investment in tourism in Ireland, as a percentage of total investment, was one of the highest in the world during 1994.
- *Market Buoyancy/Peace Dividend.* Buoyancy in key markets such as Britain and the United States and an improved image of Ireland as a result of the peace process both contributed to growth.
- *Access/Relative Value.* Increased availability and reduced costs of travel combined with a low inflation rate made Ireland a relatively good

value destination.
- *Fashionability.* Success in music, literature, theatre, sport, film and dance enhanced Ireland's international fashionability.

These factors could not be seen to continue indefinitely due to the vagaries of world economies, the lapse in the Northern Ireland peace process in early 1996 and the reduction in European Union Structural Fund contributions to infrastructural and product development. Additionally continued increases in the volume of tourists visiting Ireland would have a negative effect on the quality and nature of Ireland's tourism product, as has already occurred in areas such as the Costa del Sol in Spain and certain Greek Islands.

In addition to this, increased competition was to be expected with the increased deregulation of international air transport, and increasingly sophisticated international marketing of other destinations. Two final spurs to the strategic repositioning of Ireland as a tourist destination internationally were: (1) the need to extend the benefits of the tourist season beyond the traditional peak season of June to August and (2) to distribute tourism traffic more evenly across the country to avoid the existing emphasis on Dublin and the West Coast of the country to the virtual exclusion of all other areas.

Taking these factors into account Bórd Fáilte (the Irish Tourist Board), in association with the Northern Ireland Tourist Board and industry participants, formulated a strategic redirection of the marketing of Ireland abroad focusing on four key objectives:

- Increase retained revenue.
- Regional distribution impact.
- Extension of the season.
- Increased customer loyalty.

The key outcome of the decision to refocus the marketing of Ireland was the decision to develop a single brand for Ireland, and a coordinated image which would be used in marketing Ireland throughout the world. It was decided to use traditional brand marketing techniques, seeking in time to 'build equity through the efficient deployment of the brand'.[1]

Launch of Tourism Brand Ireland

In November 1996, Bórd Fáilte and the Northern Ireland Tourist Board launched the first ever initiative to actively market the whole island of Ireland as a destination.

> A new all-Ireland project which will promote the island as a single destination for high-spending tourists has been unveiled in Dublin. The £30 million investment also includes a new logo, an interactive Internet site and an international television advertising campaign promoting the island as a clean, green and 'emotional' holiday experience.[2]

Tourism Brand Ireland (TBI) was a significant departure from existing fragmented marketing strategies. It sought to unify the efforts of Bórd Fáilte, the Northern Ireland Tourist Board and tourism industry interests on both sides of the border. In particular, the TBI was intended to optimize investment and ensure consistency in international promotion of Ireland. As Enda Kenny, Irish Minister of Tourism, said at the launch of the TBI:

> The island of Ireland has everything to gain from promoting itself as a collective entity in brand marketing terms around the world.

The new brand was based on extensive consumer research conducted worldwide in July 1995 to establish an appropriate Ireland Brand positioning in a number of key markets. This research yielded a number of consumer preconceptions about Ireland which limited potential tourism to the country. These were: a macho destination, not a family destination, no activities, unsophisticated and a 'Summer only' destination. The research group concluded:

> Existing perceptions among people that have not visited Ireland before are falling significantly short of actual experience. This reality presents us with an opportunity to achieve a dramatic impact by an accurate presentation of the Ireland tourism experience aimed at removing these perceptions.[3]

The TBI development work which built on this research set out to close the perception gap that existed in the international marketplace, moving away from stereotypical images and towards a more realistic image of Ireland. A key desired outcome of the advertising campaign was to develop the following perceptions of Ireland among international consumers: active, authentic, cultural, friendly, personal and memorable.

> The significant point of distinction between Ireland and other destinations lies in the very deep and unique almost emotional experience visitors enjoy on holiday in Ireland.[4]

What Changed in Tourism Brand Ireland?

In association with the international advertising agency DDB Needham, TBI developed a visual identity for Ireland, an all-Ireland visual bank and an advertising approach with a minimum lifespan of three years.

The development of the visual identity sought to incorporate previous strengths and the objectives of the TBI initiative. The previous tourism identities used by the national tourism authorities in Ireland focused on the shamrock symbol. This symbol was strongly identified around the world, but carried with it dated connotations and imagery of Ireland, being related to other images such as leprechauns and crocks of gold. The new tourism identity depicts two people embracing and exchanging a shamrock. The colours make reference to the colours of the Irish landscape, flora and painted houses. This logo continued to use the shamrock insignia, but incorporated it into a much larger logo.

The all-Ireland image bank was filmed to include a variety of different Irish scenes and scenery. This included footage of areas of natural beauty such as the Giants Causeway, musicians, fine dining, castle accommodation, landscape and a variety of images showing people in different contexts.

Development of the Advertising Campaign

Strap lines for advertising were developed which communicated images of Ireland in line with the desired perceptions developed by the strategy team. For example in Germany the strap line used was *Das Leben Neu Erleben*, and in France *Pour une vie différente*.

An initial cultural difficulty occurred in arriving at a strap line to support the new marketing initiative. The strap line to be used in the United Kingdom 'Live a different life' was deemed unsuitable for the US market by market researchers who said it had a sub-conscious resonance to do with gay and lesbian lifestyles. 'Awaken to a different world' was therefore chosen as the tag line for the US promotion campaign.

The chosen strap line in each market was combined with images from the image bank designed to target the desired audience. The combination of images used in promotional copy varied from country to country, and was chosen and sequenced according to the desired copy strategy for each market. Each advertisement used the internationally successful Cranberries song 'Dream' as a backing track.

The advertisements all started with the proposition: 'Before you choose a holiday ask yourself some questions'. Then each advertisement showed the chosen set of images for that market overlaid with questions designed to elicit interest, and to suggest the emotional satisfaction of a visit to Ireland. These questions included 'Do you keep the promises that you make yourself?'; 'Is there magic in the air?'; 'Is Irish rain good for your skin?'; 'Will you feel like a king when you stay in a castle?'; 'Where else can I dance an Irish jig?' As with the combination of images, the questions asked varied according to the target market in order to target the appropriate market segment in each market.

Tailoring Advertisements to Individual Markets

In the advertisements for the German market images of activities including golf, sailing, fishing and swimming, were interspersed in order to target the very active German tourist. Target markets in Germany would also be highly environmentally conscious so many images of high quality, natural food and unspoilt scenery were shown.

In advertisements for the French market the overall emphasis was more sophisticated with more images of women and family groups. The final image differed from that used in other campaigns showing a well-dressed woman on a beach. The final image on advertisements used outside France was a less conventionally dressed woman taking a theatrical bow outside Trinity College, Dublin. Advertisements for the French market

also finished with a Minitel contact point, reflecting the strength of the specifically French reference and booking system. Unlike the campaigns for the United States, Holland, Belgium, Germany and Australia the address for the TBI Internet site (Ireland.travel.ie) was not given. Again this reflected the relative weakness of the Internet as a reference system in France.

The advertising campaign for the United Kingdom market included a further question which was not in any other advertising campaign. This question 'Why do I feel so much at home?', was designed to reduce the perceived risk for some United Kingdom consumers. The consumer research conducted at the outset of the TBI initiative indicated that there was a lack of knowledge about Ireland and that some potential consumers were concerned that there would not be sufficient accommodation, or high-quality food. The addition of the question was also likely to address in part British consumers concerns about overhang from the civil strife in Northern Ireland.

All the advertisements were designed also to counter certain perceptions identified in the initial consumer research. For example the perception that Ireland was not a family destination was addressed by including many images capturing family situations. Some respondents had identified Ireland as a macho destination, largely because of its renowned pub culture which respondents felt was largely male-dominated. In order to counter this perception many images were used in the advertisements which showed a range of age groups of both genders socializing together enjoying pub-related activities. Many of the mainland European advertisements carried images of people enjoying shopping trips to counter the impression among people who had not visited Ireland identified in the preliminary research that Ireland was uninteresting for shopping.

Advertising campaigns were carefully targeted at market segments which would contribute to the overall objectives of the branding initiative, i.e. to maximize revenue and yield, and to counter the effects of seasonality and distribute tourism more evenly throughout the country.

Overall the TBI advertising campaign, supported by development of the visual identity and image bank, was designed as a global advertising campaign that allowed for a consistent image of Ireland to be portrayed internationally. The execution of this global campaign was, however, tailored to ensure appropriate positioning in each target market.

The Outcomes

In the summer of 1997, immediately preceding the launch of Tourism Brand Ireland, there was considerable debate as to the success of this initiative. Industry members felt that national tourism figures had decreased and that TBI was a major contributing factor, in tampering with the highly successful previous formula. However, Bórd Fáilte executives felt that it was too early to determine the effectiveness of TBI and that as a long-term global strategy it should not be evaluated too soon.

Questions

1. Does the perceived drop in international tourist numbers to Ireland indicate that TBI was a failure?
2. Is global branding appropriate for an experiential service product such as tourism to Ireland?
3. How does the international marketing of Ireland as a tourist destination compare with the marketing of your country?

References

1. 'Development of Communications for Ireland as a Tourism Destination Brand', Bórd Fáilte, 1996.
2. *Irish Times*, 12 November 1996.
3. Behaviour and Attitudes Market Research Consultancy.
4. As note 3.

CASE 4.9
AIDS, Condoms and Carnival

Brazil

Half a million Brazilians are infected with the AIDS virus, and millions more are at high risk of contracting the incurable ailment, a federal study reported. The Health Ministry study is Brazil's first official attempt to seek an estimate of HIV-infected residents. Many had doubted the government's prior number of 94 997. The report by the National Programme for Transmissible Diseases/AIDS said 27 million Brazilians are at high risk to contract AIDS, and another 36 million are considered to be at a medium risk. It said Brazil could have 7.5 million AIDS victims in the next decade.

'If we are going to combat this epidemic, we have to do it now', said Pedro Chequer, a health ministry official. Chequer said the Health Ministry would spend $300 million next year, distributing medicine and 250 million condoms and bringing AIDS awareness campaigns to the urban slums, where the disease is most rampant. Last month, Brazil became one of the few countries to offer a promising AIDS drug free to those who need it. The drug can cost as much as $12 000 a year per patient.

AIDS cases in Brazil have risen so dramatically for married women that the state of São Paulo decided that it must attack a basic cultural practice in Latin America: their husbands don't practise safe sex. Last month, the government of Brazil's megalopolis started promoting the newly released female condom.

Many of the new AIDS cases in Brazil are married women who have children, according to a report released last month at the Pan-American Conference on AIDS in Lima, Peru. Worldwide, women constitute the fastest-growing group of those diagnosed with HIV. And of the 30.6 million people who are diagnosed with the HIV virus, 90 per cent live in poor countries.

One Brazilian mother, Rosana Dolores, knows well why women cannot count on male partners to use condoms. She and her late husband never thought of protecting their future children against AIDS. 'We were married. We wanted to have kids', says Mrs Dolores, both of whose children were born with HIV. 'These days, I would advise young people to always use condoms. But married couples . . . who is going to?'

Brazil, with its 155 million people and the largest population in South America, has the second-highest number of reported HIV infections in the Americas, after the United States, according to a report released on 26 November by the United Nations agency, UNAIDS.

Public health officials say one reason why AIDS prevention efforts have failed is many Brazilians just don't like condoms. While use in Brazil has quadrupled in the past six years, it is still the least popular method of birth control—a touchy issue in the predominantly Roman Catholic country. Another reason is that condoms cost about 75 cents each, making them more expensive here than anywhere else in the world, health officials say.

Plus, Latin-style machismo leaves women with little bargaining power. Only 14 per cent of Brazilian heterosexual men used condoms in 1996, according to AIDSCAP, an AIDS-prevention programme funded by the US Agency for International Development. In other studies, many women said they would not ask their partner to use a condom, even if they knew he was sleeping with others.

'Women are afraid of asking their men to have safe sex, afraid of getting beaten, afraid of losing their economic support', says Guido Carlos Levi, a director at the health department at Emilio Ribas Hospital. 'This is not Mexico, but we're quite a machistic society here.'

The frequency with which Latin men stray from monogamous relationships has compounded the problem. In studies conducted in Cuba by the Pan American Health Organization, 49 per cent of men and 14 per cent of women in stable relationships admitted that they had had an affair in the past year.

In light of statistics showing AIDS as the number one killer of women of childbearing age in São Paulo state, public health officials here launched a campaign in December promoting the female condom.

The hope is that it will help women—especially poor women—protect themselves and their children. But the female condom seemed unlikely to spark a latex revolution when it hit city stores 1 January. The price is $2.50 apiece—more than three times the price of most male condoms.

The Family Health Association is asking the government to help subsidize the product and to cut the taxes on condoms that make them out of reach for many poor Brazilians. 'We're looking for a pragmatic solution to prevent the transmission of HIV-AIDS', group president Maria Eugenia Lemos Fernandes said. 'Studies show there is a high acceptance of this method because it's a product under the control of women.'

While 75 per cent of the women and 63 per cent of the men in a pilot study on the female condom said they approved of the device, many women with AIDS say they would have been no more likely to have used a female condom than a conventional one.

Part of the problem is perception: 80 per cent of women and 85 per cent of men in Brazil believe they are not at risk of contracting HIV, according to a study

conducted by the Civil Society for the Well-Being of the Brazilian Family.

Also at risk are married women, 40 per cent of whom undergo sterilization as an affordable way of getting around the Catholic church's condemnation of birth control, health officials noted.

'It's mostly married women who are the victims. You just never think it could be you', says a former hospital administrator who was diagnosed with the virus after her husband had several extramarital affairs. He died two years ago.

'I knew everything there was to know about AIDS—I worked in a hospital—but I never suspected he was going out like that. He always denied it', she says.

While the HIV virus is making inroads in rural areas and among teenagers in Brazil, Fernandes said it doesn't have to reach epidemic proportions as in Uganda or Tanzania. 'There is a very big window of opportunity here.'

Brazil's Health Ministry is adding a new ingredient to the heady mix that makes up the country's annual Carnival—condoms. The ministry will distribute 10 million condoms next month along with free advice on how to prevent the spread of AIDS at places like Rio de Janeiro's sambadrome, where bare-breasted dancing girls attract millions of spectators every year.

'It's considered as a period of increased sexual activity', a spokeswoman at the ministry's AIDS coordination department said on Monday. 'The euphoria provoked by Carnival and the excessive consumption of alcohol make it a moment when people are more likely to forget about prevention', she explained.

Tourists descend on Brazil for Carnival, which is viewed as a time when inhibitions fall away and anything goes.

India

S. Mani's small barber shop in this southern Indian city looks like any other the world over. It's equipped with all the tools of the trade: scissors, combs, razors—and condoms, too.

A blue box full of free prophylactics stands in plain view of his customers as Mr Mani trims hair and dispenses advice on safe sex, a new dimension to his 20-year career. 'I start by talking about the family and children', Mr Mani explains, snipping a client's moustache. 'Slowly, I get to women, AIDS and condoms.'

Many Indian men are too embarrassed to buy condoms at a drugstore or to talk freely about sex with health counsellors and family members. There's one place where they let down their hair: the barber shop. So, the state of Tamil Nadu is training barbers to be frontline soldiers in the fight against AIDS.

Programmes like the barber scheme are what make Tamil Nadu, a relatively poor Indian state that's home to 60 million people, a possible model for innovative and cost-effective methods to contain AIDS in the developing world.

Six years after it was first detected in India, the AIDS virus is quickly spreading in the world's second most-populous nation. Already, up to 5 million of India's 920 million people are infected with HIV—more than in any other country, according to UNAIDS, the United Nations' AIDS agency.

But faced with more immediate and widespread health woes, such as tuberculosis and malaria, officials in many Indian states are reluctant to make AIDS prevention a priority. And in some states, the acquired immune deficiency syndrome is regarded as a Western disease of decadence; officials deny that prostitution and drug use even exist in their midst.

'Some Indian states are still in total denial or ignorance about the AIDS problem', says Salim Habayeb, a World Bank physician who oversees an $84 million loan to India for AIDS prevention activities.

Tamil Nadu, the state with the third-highest incidence of HIV infection, has been open about its problem. Before turning to barbers for help, Tamil Nadu was the first state to introduce AIDS education in high school and the first to set up a statewide information hotline. Its comprehensive AIDS-education programme targets the overall population, rather than only high-risk groups.

In the past two years, awareness of AIDS in Tamil Nadu has jumped to 95 per cent of those polled, from 64 per cent, according to Operations Research Group, an independent survey group. 'Just two years ago, it was very difficult to talk about AIDS and the condom', says P.R. Bindhu Madhavan, director of the Tamil Nadu State AIDS Control Society, the autonomous state agency managing the prevention effort.

The AIDS fighters take maximum advantage of the local culture to get the message across. Tamils are among the most ardent moviegoers in this film-crazed country. In the city of Madras, people line up for morning screenings even during weekdays. Half of the state's 630 theatres are paid to screen an AIDS-awareness short before the main feature. The spots are usually melodramatic musicals laced with warnings.

In the countryside, where cinemas are scarce, a movie mobile does the job. The concept mimics that used by multinationals, such as Colgate-Palmolive Co., for rural advertising. Bright red-and-blue trucks ply the back roads, blaring music from well-known movie soundtracks whose lyrics have been rewritten to address AIDS issues. In villages, hundreds gather for the show, on a screen that pops out of the rear of the truck.

In one six-minute musical, a young husband's infidelity leads to his death from AIDS, the financial ruin of his family and then the death of his wife, also infected. The couple's toddler is left alone in the world. The heart-rending tale is followed by a brief lecture by an AIDS educator—and the offer of a free pack of condoms and an AIDS brochure.

Tamil Nadu's innovations have met with obstacles. It took several months for state officials to persuade Indian government television, Doordarshan, to broadcast an AIDS commercial featuring the Hindu gods of chastity and death. Even then, Mr Madhavan says, Doordarshan 'wouldn't do it as a social ad, so we have to pay a commercial rate'.

Later, the network refused to air a three-minute spot in which a woman urges her husband, a truck driver, to use a condom when he's on the road. Safe infidelity was deemed 'inappropriate for Indian living rooms', says Mr Madhavan. A number of commercial satellite channels have been willing to run the ad.

Tamil Nadu has met little resistance recruiting prostitutes for the cause. For almost a year, 37-year-old prostitute Vasanthi has been distributing condoms to colleagues. With state funding, a nongovernmental agency has trained her to spread the word about AIDS and other sexually transmitted diseases. As an incentive, the state pays participants like Ms Vasanthi, a mother of three, the equivalent of $14 a month, about what she earns from entertaining a client.

Before Ms Vasanthi joined the plan, she didn't know that the condom could help prevent HIV infection. These days, if any client refuses to wear a condom, 'I kick him out, even if it takes using my shoes', she says. 'I'm not flexible about this.' More men are also carrying their own condoms, she says.

Thank barbers such as Mr Mani for that. Especially in blue-collar areas of Madras, men 'trim their hair and beard before frequenting a commercial sex worker', says Mr Madhavan. They can pick up their condom on the way out.

Tamil Nadu launched the barber programme in Madras last March. So far, it has enlisted 5000 barbers, who receive AIDS education at meetings each Tuesday—the barbers' day off. The barbers aren't paid to be AIDS counsellors, but they appear to take pride in their new responsibility.

Over the generations, India's barbers have been respected as traditional healers and trusted advisers. 'If you want to get to the king's ears, you tell his barber', says Mr Madhavan, the state AIDS director. Reinforcing the image of barbers as healers, the local trade group is called the Tamil Nadu Medical Barber Association.

'I first talked about AIDS with my barber', says Thiyagrajan, an electrician in his 40s. 'I don't have multiple partners, so I don't need a condom, but I take them for my friends.'

One recent night, a man in his thirties walked into Aruna Hair Arts, greeted Mr Swami, then headed out the door with a fistful of condoms scooped from the plastic dispenser. 'That's OK', Mr Swami says approvingly. 'He's a regular customer.'

A local nongovernmental organization helps barbers replenish condom stocks by providing each shop with self-addressed order forms. But the central government hasn't always been able to meet supply, for reasons ranging from bureaucracy to price disputes with manufacturers.

Tamil Nadu has started sourcing condoms from elsewhere. But they're too expensive to give away. So the next stage of the barber scheme, just under way, is to charge two rupees (six cents) for a two-condom 'pleasure pack'. The barbers will get a 25 per cent commission. Thus far, the only perk of participating has been a free wall calendar listing AIDS-prevention tips.

Roughly 30 per cent of barbers approached by Tamil Nadu have refused to participate in the AIDS programme, fearing that they would alienate customers. But those who take part insist that carrying the AIDS message hasn't hurt business. 'We give the message about AIDS, but we still gossip about women', says barber N.V. Durairaj at Rolex Salon.

London International Group

London International Group (LIG) is recognized worldwide as a leader in the development of latex and thin film barrier technologies. The Group has built its success on the development of its core businesses: the Durex family of branded condoms, Regent Medical gloves and Marigold household and industrial gloves. These are supported by a range of noncore health and beauty products.

With operational facilities in over 40 countries, 12 manufacturing plants, either wholly or jointly owned, and an advanced research and development facility based in Cambridge, England, LIG is well placed to expand into the new emerging markets of the world.

Durex is the world's number one condom brand in terms of quality, safety and brand awareness. The Durex family of condom brands includes Sheik, Ramses, Hatu, London, Kohinoor, Dua Lima, Androtex and Avanti. Sold in over 130 countries worldwide and leader in more than 40 markets, Durex is the only global condom brand.

The development of innovative and creative marketing strategies is key to communicating successfully with our target audiences. Consumer marketing initiatives remain focused on supporting the globalization of Durex. A series of innovative yet cost-effective

projects have been used to communicate the global positioning 'Feeling Is Everything' to the target young adult market, securing loyalty.

The Durex Global Survey, together with a unique multimillion-pound global advertising and sponsorship contract with MTV have successfully emphasized the exciting and modern profile of Durex and presented significant opportunities for local public relations and event sponsorship, especially in emerging markets like Taiwan.

LIG continues to focus on education, using sponsorship of events such as the XI Annual AIDS Conference held last summer in Vancouver and other educational initiatives to convey the safer sex message to governments, opinion formers and educators worldwide.

Japan

London Okamoto Corporation, the joint venture company between London International Group, plc (LIG) and Okamoto Industries Inc. (Okamoto), recently announced the Japanese launch in spring 1998 of DUREX AVANTI, the world's first polyurethane male condom.

This is the first time an international condom brand will be available in Japan, the world's most valuable condom market, which is estimated to be worth £260 million ($433 million). DUREX AVANTI has already been successfully launched in the United States and Great Britain, and will be launched in Italy and other selected European countries during the next 12 months.

DUREX AVANTI condoms are made from Duron, a unique polyurethane material twice as strong as latex, which enables them to be made much thinner than regular latex condoms thereby increasing sensitivity without compromising safety. In addition, DUREX AVANTI condoms are also able to conduct body heat, creating a more natural feeling, and are the first condoms to be totally odourless, colourless, and suitable for use with oil-based lubricants.

Commenting on the launch, Nick Hodges, chief executive of LIG, said: 'Japan is a very important condom market; with oral contraceptives still not publicly available, per capita usage rates for condoms are among the highest in the world. Our joint venture with Okamoto, Japan's leading condom manufacturer, gives us instant access to this strategically important market.'

The joint venture with Okamoto, which is the market leader in Japan with a 53 per cent share, was established in 1994 with the specific purpose of marketing DUREX AVANTI. Added Mr Takehiko Okamoto, president of Okamoto, 'We are confident that such an innovative and technically advanced product as DUREX AVANTI, coupled with our strong market franchise, will find significant consumer appeal in Japan's sophisticated condom market.'

DUREX AVANTI, which is manufactured at LIG's research and development centre in Cambridge, England, has taken over 10 years to develop, and represents an investment by LIG of approximately £15 million.

Questions

1. Comment on the Brazilian and Indian governments' strategies for the prevention of AIDS via the marketing of condoms.
2. How is the AIDS problem different in the United States compared to Brazil and India?
3. Would the approaches described in Brazil and India work in the United States? Why or why not?
4. Suggest additional ways that London International Group could promote the prevention of AIDS through the use of condoms worldwide.

References

'Half a Million Brazilians Are Infected with the AIDS Virus', *Associated Press*, 21 December 1996.

Andrea McDaniels, 'Brazil Turns to Women to Stop Dramatic Rise in AIDS Cases. São Paulo Pushes Female Condom to Protect Married Women from Husbands. But Costs of Devices Are High', *Christian Science Monitor*, 9 January 1998, p. 7.

'Brazil to Hand Out 10 Million Condoms during Carnival', *Chicago Tribune*, 19 January 1998, p. 2.

Miriam Jordan, 'India Enlists Barbers in the War on AIDS', *The Wall Street Journal*, 24 September 1994, p. A-18.

See for example, **www.lig.com**.

Visit **www.durex.com**.

CASE 4.10
Creating a Global Perspective

Levi Strauss & Co. markets brand-name clothes in more than 60 countries. The company employs a staff of about 1900 people at its San Francisco headquarters, and approximately 37 500 people worldwide. It operates 53 production facilities and 32 customer service centres in more than 50 countries. The company manufactures and markets products under the Levi's, Dockers and Slates brands.

The company is now in the process of changing its advertising from a localized campaign for each country in which it sells its products to a worldwide strategy for all advertising. Levi Strauss & Co. announced global sales of $6.9 billion for the fiscal year ending 30 November 1997. Sales for the year were 4 per cent below the company's record 1996 sales of $7.1 billion.

Sales for the company's North and South American operations (Levi Strauss, the Americas) totalled $4.6 billion for fiscal year 1997. Levi Strauss Europe posted revenues of $1.8 billion for the year. Sales for the company's Asia/Pacific Division were $468 million.

Comparable divisional sales figures for fiscal year 1996 are not available, as this is the first year that Levi Strauss & Co. has reported revenues under its new 'Triad' global organization. The company is a privately held corporation. It does not disclose corporate earnings, quarterly revenues or competitive data on specific business units or brands.

You have been asked to evaluate its present programmes and to make recommendations that will assist management in deciding whether it is better (1) to create advertising campaigns locally or regionally but with a good deal of input and influence from headquarters, as they presently do, (2) to allow campaigns to be created independently by local advertising

Sources: 'Exporting a Legend', *International Advertising*, November–December 1981, pp. 2–3; 'Levi Zipping Up World Image', *Advertising Age,* 14 September 1981, pp. 35–36; David Short, 'Speeding Up the Message by Jumping across Borders', *The European*, 6 June 1996, p. 23; 'Levi's Launches "Dream-Logic" Brand Image Campaign', *Reuters Business Report*, 30 July 1997; Eleftheria Parpis, 'Searching for the Perfect Fit', *ADWEEK Eastern Edition*, 15 September 1997, p. 23; and the following from Levi Strauss & Co.'s Web site: **http://www.levi com**, 'Responsible Commercial Success', 'General Information', 'Levi Strauss & Co., Fact Sheet', 'Levi Strauss & Co.'s Brand Advertising History', and 'Levi Strauss & Co. Announces 1997 Sales Results', 9 February 1998.

companies or (3) to centralize all advertising at national headquarters and develop a consistent worldwide advertising campaign.

You are asked to do the following:

1. Prepare a report listing the pros and cons of each of the three approaches.
2. Make a recommendation about the direction the company should take.
3. Support your recommendation and outline major objectives for whichever approach you recommend.
4. Evaluate all new ads using the SURT test.

The following information should be of assistance in completing this assignment:

Business Vision

Levi Strauss & Co. will strive to achieve responsible commercial success in the eyes of our constituencies, which include stockholders, employees, consumers, customers, suppliers, and communities. Our success will be measured not only by growth in shareholder value, but also by our reputation, the quality of our constituency relationships, and our commitment to social responsibility. As a global company, our businesses in every country will contribute to our overall success. We will leverage our knowledge of local markets to take advantage of the global positioning of our brands, our product and market strengths, our resources, and our cultural diversity. We will balance local market requirements with a global perspective. We will make decisions which will benefit the Company as a whole, rather than any one component. We will strive to be cost effective in everything we do and will manage our resources to meet our constituencies' needs. The strong heritage and values of Levi Strauss & Co. as expressed through our Mission and Aspiration Statements will guide all of our efforts. The quality of our products, services and people is critical to the realization of our business vision.

Products

We will market value-added, branded casual apparel with Levi's branded jeans continuing to be the cornerstone of our business. Our brands will be positioned to ensure consistency of image and values to our customers around the world.

Unlike some competitors, Levi Strauss International does not, in its normal markets, seek targets of opportunity, that is, large one-time shipments to customers it may never serve again. Rather, the goal is to develop sustainable and growing shipment levels to long-term customers.

Business Operations

Levi Strauss & Co. is a global corporation made up of three business units that reflect its 'Triad' global organization:

Levi Strauss, the Americas (LSA) employs approximately 28 000 people throughout the United States, Mexico, Canada, Brazil, Argentina and other countries in Central and South America and the Caribbean. It manufactures and markets products under the Levi's, Dockers, and SLATES™ brands throughout the region and includes five wholly owned-and-operated businesses: Levi Strauss US, Levi Strauss & Co. (Canada) Inc., Levi Strauss Mexico, Levi Strauss do Brasil and Levi Strauss Argentina.

Levi Strauss Europe (LSE) employs approximately 7000 people in a region which is divided into three geographic areas: Europe, Africa and the Middle East. LSE markets and sells its products in the following countries: Austria, Belgium, Croatia, Czech Republic, Denmark, Finland, France, Germany, Greece, Hungary, Ireland, Italy, Luxembourg, The Netherlands, Norway, Poland, Portugal, Russia, South Africa, Spain, Sweden, Switzerland, Tunisia, Turkey and the United Kingdom.

Asia Pacific Division (APD) employs approximately 2400 people and manufactures and markets products for Asia and the Pacific. The division consists of 10 wholly owned-and-operated businesses in Japan, South Korea, Hong Kong, Taiwan, Malaysia, the Philippines, Indonesia, India, Australia and New Zealand; with licensees and distributors in Sapian/Guam, Singapore and Thailand. The Asia/Pacific Division had its beginnings in the 1940s when jeans reached this market through US military exchanges. In 1965, a sales facility was established in Hong Kong.

The Levi's trademark is the most recognized clothing brand and one of the most famous consumer brand names in the world.

Comments

The director of advertising and communications for International shares with you the following thoughts about advertising:

■ The success of Levi Strauss International's advertising derived principally from their judging it consistently against three criteria: (1) Is the proposition meaningful to the consumer? (2) Is the message believable? and (3) Is it exclusive to the brand?
■ A set of core values underlies advertising wherever it is produced and regardless of strategy: honesty/integrity, consistency/reliability; relevance, social responsibility,

credibility, excellence and style. The question remains whether a centralized advertising campaign can be based on this core of values.

- Levi Strauss' marketing plans include 70 countries and recognize the cultural and political differences affecting advertising appeals. Uniform advertising (i.e. standardized) could ignore local customs and unique product uses, while locally prepared advertising risks uneven creative work, is likely to waste time and money on preparation, and might blur the corporate image. Consistency in product image is a priority.

- Levi's is not satisfied with some of the creative work in parts of Latin America. The company wants consistency in Latin American strategy rather than appearing to be a different company in different countries. The company is not satisfied with production costs and casting of commercials, and the fact that local agencies are often resistant to outside suggestions to change. It feels there is a knee-jerk reaction in Latin America that results in the attitude that everything must be developed locally.

- The risks of too closely controlling a campaign result in uninteresting ads compared with decentralizing all marketing, which produces uneven creative quality.

Competition

At the same time that Levi's is looking at more centralized control of its advertising, another jeans maker is going in the opposite direction. Blue Bell International's Wrangler jeans company has just ended a six-month review of its international advertising and decided against coordinating its advertising more closely in Europe.

The concept of one idea that will work effectively in all markets is attractive to Wrangler. Yet the disadvantages are just as clear; the individual needs of each market cannot be met, resistance from local managers could be an obstacle, and the management of a centralized advertising campaign would require an organizational structure different from the present one.

To add to the confusion, a leading European jeans manufacturer, the Spanish textile company Y Confecciones Europeas, makers of Louis jeans, recently centralized its marketing through one single advertising agency. Louis, fourth-largest jeans maker after Levi's Lee Cooper and Wrangler, is intent on developing a worldwide international image for its Louis brand.

Diesel, another major international competitor, has grown from $12 million in US sales in 1995 to $24 million in 1996, with a different vision of Americana,

a mix of '50s kitsch and '90s techno styles. Its 'Successful Living' campaign, created by Paradiset DDB, Stockholm, Sweden, has established the brand worldwide with an edgy, trendsetting consumer. The 'Heritage' ads, which focused on the Western themes often found in jeans ads, won top film honours at the 1997 International Advertising Festival at Cannes.

'Our advertising has always been provocative, different and humorous. One of the things you don't see very much in fashion advertising is humour. We use irony to the point where we make fun of ourselves.'

The company's most recent campaign features the fictitious firm 'Brand O' advertising its ice cream, diet and newspaper products in impoverished North Korea. For example, pictured above a crowd of people waiting in what appears to be a food line is a billboard showing a frolicking couple wearing Diesel Jeans next to a headline that reads, 'Brand O ice cream. For a better tomorrow.'

Diesel's funky retail stores, which feature DJs spinning the latest hip-hop and techno music, only further reinforce the irreverent personality it has built through its image advertising.

Review of Current Ads

A review of a selection of Levi's advertisements from around the world provided the following notes:

- European television commercials for Levi's were supersexy in appeal, projecting, in the minds of some at headquarters, an objectionable personality for the brand. These commercials were the result of allowing complete autonomy to a sales region.

- Levi's commercials prepared in Latin America projected a far different image than those in Europe. Latin American ads addressed a family-oriented, Catholic market. However, the quality of the creative work was far below the standards set by the company.

- Ads for the United Kingdom, emphasizing that Levi's is an American brand, star an all-American hero, the cowboy, in fantasy Wild West settings. In Northern Europe, both Scandinavian and the United Kingdom consumers are buying a slice of America when they buy Levi's.

- In Japan, where an attitude similar to that in the United Kingdom prevails, a problem confronted Levi's. Local jeans companies had already established themselves as very American. To overcome this, Levi's positioned itself against these brands as legendary American jeans with commercials themed 'Heroes Wear Levi's', featuring clips of cult figures such as James Dean. These commercials were very effective and carried Levi's from a 35 per cent to a 95 per cent awareness level in Japan.

- In Brazil, unlike the United Kingdom, consumers are more strongly influenced by fashion trends emanating from the European Continent rather than from America. Thus, the Brazilian-made commercial filmed in Paris featured young people, cool amidst a wild traffic scene—very French. This commercial was intended to project the impression that Levi's is the favoured brand among young, trend-setting Europeans.

- Australian commercials showed that creating brand awareness is important in that market. The lines 'fit looks tight, doesn't feel tight, can feel comfortable all night' and 'a legend doesn't come apart at the seams' highlighted Levi's quality image, and 'since 1850 Levi jeans have handled everything from bucking broncos . . . ' amplified Levi's unique positioning. This campaign resulted in 99 per cent brand awareness among Australians.

Levi's is attempting to refine its image this year (1997) with a bold, new television and print campaign. Scenes from the campaign: a lanky European woman orders a hot dog, a plain hot dog, from a New York City street vendor for a friend's dog because 'he likes it plain'. A young man whose car is filled with carnival toys says goodbye to his friend, a small-town disc jockey dreaming of spinning in the big city. A taxi driver lives out a fantasy of a high-speed car chase. Lenny Kravitz changes his clothes in a gas station. What do any of these scenarios have to do with jeans? Nothing at all—and everything.

The six spots, whose tagline is 'They go on', constitute the first general branding effort undertaken by the 144-year-old company. Backed by an estimated $90 million in media spending, the commercials, directed by Tarsem, teeter between the real and surreal and eschew traditional storytelling structure. Instead, a shared scene connects the ads, and each spot includes circuitous glimpses of the lives of the perennially hip Levi's wearer. The fabric that holds the characters together is the Levi's label and the spirit the red tag represents.

Here was an opportunity to market the brand over-all, focusing on the originality and the youthfulness inherent in the overall brand values.

Levi's, says the director of advertising, 'is always going to be the real deal. We won't want to be a flashy, hyped brand. We have a quiet strength in a way. We have to balance that authenticity and stay current.'

Levi's 'Launderette' commercial, featuring Marvin Gaye's classic song 'Grapevine', aired in Europe and boosted sales there by 800 per cent. This spot—now a classic—was satirized twice the following year in advertising and comedy programming and the song became popular again. Levi's Europe 'Drugstore' TV spot won advertising awards in Berlin, London, Cannes and Milan. European consumers rated 'Drugstore' the second best commercial from Levi's this decade. They rank Levi's 'Taxi' TV spot, featuring a sexy cross-dresser, the best of the decade.

'Clayman', an animated tale of a winsome hero clad in Levi's 501 jeans who rescues a beauty trapped in a burning building, is the company's first global commercial. It runs in countries on all five continents. These commercials celebrate the Levi's brand and its core values of originality and youthfulness. According to Derek Bowden, chief executive officer of Saatchi Europe, all ads have to meet what is called the 'SURT' test; the commercials have to be 'Simple, Universally Recognized and Truthful'.

Name Index

Name Index

Subject Index